TAX-EXEMPT DERIVATIVES

A GUIDE TO LEGAL CONSIDERATIONS FOR LAWYERS, FINANCE PROFESSIONALS, AND MUNICIPAL ISSUERS

STEVEN D. CONLON

VINCENT M. AQUILINO

PRINCIPAL AUTHORS AND CO-EDITORS

SECTION OF URBAN, STATE AND LOCAL GOVERNMENT LAW

ABA AMERICAN BAR ASSOCIATION

Printed in the United States of America.

Library of Congress Catalog Card Number 93-73878
ISBN 0-89707-931-0

99 98 97 96 95 5 4 3 2 1

SUMMARY OF CONTENTS

CONTENTS

HOW TO USE THIS BOOK

This book is intended to assist the reader in understanding the legal issues relating to tax-exempt derivative financial products and to serve as a desk reference for the reader who deals with these matters on a recurring basis. Accordingly, its eight chapters of text include both a general discussion of these products and extensive discussions of the related federal income tax, securities, bankruptcy, and municipal law. A detailed table of contents is included to assist the reader in referring to specific sections of the chapters.

The book also includes additional resource material that we hope will be useful. The proposed model statute authorizing governmental entities to enter into swap transactions developed by the International Swaps and Derivatives Association, Inc. (ISDA, formerly the International Swap Dealers Association), is included as an appendix to Chapter 7. The form of ISDA master agreement and the U.S. municipal counterparty schedule that is typically used for interest rate swaps entered into with U.S. municipalities are included as an appendix to Chapter 8. Additional tax, securities, bankruptcy law, and swap source materials (current as of November 1993) are included for reference in the section of the book titled Primary Sources.

In order to keep the book to a manageable size, we have not generally included cases since we have assumed that the reader can readily obtain the cases referenced herein. A table of cases follows the Primary Sources section of the book. We have, however, included in the Primary Sources section the complete text of *Hazell v. Hammersmith and Fulham London Borough Council and others*, the 1991 English House of Lords decision holding that English municipalities did not have the power to enter into interest rate swaps.

Finally, at the very back of the book we have included a glossary that defines various terms used in the book. Another important aspect of the glossary is that it includes the names of various derivative products currently in the market (as of November 1993).

To obtain maximum satisfaction from this book, it must be read under proper conditions. So find a comfortable chair with good lighting, put on some relaxing background music (classical, jazz, rap, or heavy metal, depending upon your tastes), get a big bowl of popcorn and your favorite beverage, and enjoy!

Steven D. Conlon
Vincent M. Aquilino
November 6, 1993

ACKNOWLEDGMENTS

The idea for this book developed out of our discussions with Matthew Lewin of our office, past chair of the Public Finance Committee of the Urban, State, and Local Government Law Section of the American Bar Association. Starting in 1988 we had been involved in the development of different types of tax-exempt derivatives and shortly thereafter began to evaluate a wide variety of these products for investors. That work has significantly expanded since that time, and we have had the privilege of watching this market change and the different types of products grow at a rapid pace. Given this history, we were excited that a book addressing the legal issues relating to tax-exempt derivatives would serve as a useful tool for municipal finance lawyers, issuers, and investors and agreed to the project before fully comprehending how much work would be involved.

Writing and editing a book is a significant undertaking. Although the time we have spent on this project has left its mark on us, our efforts were assisted in many direct and indirect ways by a number of people. We would like to thank them all, and any omission is inadvertent.

We would like to extend special thanks to Suzanne Russell, Tim Mohan, and Scott Jardine of our firm, who have worked with us extensively in structuring and evaluating tax-exempt derivatives over the past several years and with whom we consulted in our drafting and editing of many portions of the book. Dale S. Collinson, chair of the tax department of the New York office of Willkie, Farr & Gallagher, co-authored with us our earlier article on tax issues relating to secondary market tax-exempt derivative products, the genesis for Chapter 5 of the book, and we would like to fully acknowledge his contribution in that regard and our indebtedness to him. We also would like to thank Bob Lockner, a partner in our firm's banking department, who reviewed drafts of significant portions of the book and provided invaluable comments and suggestions. The initial manuscript was reviewed by Thomas R. Melloni of Burak & Anderson in Burlington, Vermont, and we would like to thank him for his review and for his valuable advice.

The other chapter authors also spent a significant amount of time and effort on this project. Bob Aicher and Dan Johnson are widely respected in their fields and we are extremely indebted to them that they took the time to participate in this project. We would also like to acknowledge Bill Libit, Elizabeth Swanson, and all of the Chapman and Cutler lawyers who assisted the authors in their efforts.

Jeff Berry, David Cholst, and Steve Frost, the other partners in the firm's tax department, have provided us with invaluable insights on tax issues on an ongoing basis regarding these products. We would also like to thank Ann Acker, Walt Begley, Steve Clark, Rick Cosgrove, Pat Curtner, Lynda Given, Darrell "Buzz" Larsen, Jim Richardson, Hal Sutter, and John Trofa, partners in our firm with whom we have worked on tax-exempt derivative issues, along with all the members of the firm and attorneys at Chapman and Cutler.

We would like to thank the following individuals and their respective firms for their input on the glossary and for permitting us to include the names of their products: Ed Curland, Merrill Lynch; Jean Diaz, Citibank; Gary Gray, Lehman Brothers; Aaron Gurwitz, Goldman Sachs; Tracy Keays and Liam Stokes, J.P. Morgan: Mike Kolodner, Bear Stearns; Josh Siegel, First Boston; and Chuck Stafford, Donaldson, Lufkin & Jenrette.

Suzanne Russell, Colleen Gartland, and Alan Kennard of our office assisted us in a number of important ways as we put the book into final form, along with Elizabeth Knoll, who handled word processing and related matters. Noel Suarez, one of our resident computer experts, provided invaluable assistance on development of the tables and diagrams in the book. Research assistance was provided by Robert Luberda, assistant librarian, and William Tiderman, library clerk. Finally, we would like to thank the following proofreaders: Daniel Brennan, Carolyn Day, Helena Echols, Diana Gallardao, Mark Kolodny, Bruce Lespinasse, Leah Mayes, and Brian Rabinowitz.

This project took over a year to complete and involved the type of late-night and week-end drafting and review sessions that you might expect. Significant portions of the manuscript were originally written on a Macintosh PowerBook, and much of our drafting and review work took place on both coasts, in airplanes, hotels, and in other interesting locations around the country. Those exploits, however, to the extent publishable, are best left for some other publication.

Steven D. Conlon
Vincent M. Aquilino
CHAPMAN AND CUTLER
Chicago, Illinois

ABOUT THE AUTHORS

Steven D. Conlon is an associate in the Chicago office of the law firm of Chapman and Cutler. He advises mutual funds and investment banks on the development and evaluation of new financial products. He is vice chair of the Financial Transactions Committee of the Section of Taxation of the American Bar Association (the "Section") and was previously co-chair of its Asset Securitization Subcommittee. He chaired the Bond Attorneys' Workshop 1992 Derivatives Panels and 1993 Advanced Derivatives Panels. He is also chair of the Complex Financial Products Task Force of the Section's Regulated Investment Companies Committee and served as principal author of its report on mutual fund tax issues regarding investments in synthetic tax-exempt securities. Mr. Conlon and Vincent Aquilino have co-authored a chapter for the *Handbook of Derivatives and Synthetics* scheduled to be published by Probus Publishing in the spring of 1994. Mr. Conlon has also co-authored a number of articles on the taxation of financial products in publications such as the *Journal of Taxation, TAXES Magazine, Tax Law Review,* and *Tax Notes.* He is an adjunct professor at Illinois Institute of Technology Chicago Kent College of Law and teaches Taxation of Financial Service Entities in the Financial Services Law L.L.M. program. Mr. Conlon received his B.B.A. summa cum laude from Loyola University of Chicago and his J.D. cum laude from its School of Law.

Vincent M. Aquilino is a partner in the Chicago office of Chapman and Cutler. He is chair of the firm's derivative products group and a senior partner in its tax department. He has chaired recent seminars on tax-exempt derivatives and has served as a panelist or a speaker at a number of seminars dealing with the legal issues relating to a variety of financial products. Mr. Aquilino and Steven Conlon have co-authored a chapter for the *Handbook of Derivatives and Synthetics* scheduled to be published by Probus Publishing in the spring of 1994. He has submitted written comments and testified on a number of recent Internal Revenue Service regulation projects. In addition to overseeing all tax opinions rendered by the firm relating to derivative products, Mr. Aquilino is responsible for tax opinions rendered by the firm relating to asset securitization transactions, REMICs, investment trusts, and investment companies. He has worked extensively in the leveraged lease and corporate finance areas, including international financing transactions such as off-shore financing projects and cross-border leasing. In the tax-exempt area, Mr. Aquilino's experience includes tax-exempt industrial development bond financings, health care, municipal, and other Section 103-related financings. His professional activities have also included teaching law school federal income tax courses. Mr. Aquilino received his B.A. summa cum laude and M.B.A. from DePaul University of Chicago and his J.D. from Northwestern University School of Law.

Suzanne M. Russell is an associate in the Chicago office of the law firm of Chapman and Cutler. She is involved in various federal and state tax issues relating to financial products and investment structures. Ms. Russell co-authored "Tax Considerations for Mutual Funds Investing in Asset-Backed and Derivative Securities," published in the January 1993 issue of *TAXES Magazine,* and the Report on Federal Income Tax Issues Under Subchapter M of the Internal Revenue Code Relating to the Qualification of Tax-Exempt Synthetic Debt Held by Money Market Mutual Funds, which was submitted by the American Bar Association Section of Taxation to the Internal Revenue Service in 1992. She is a member of the Complex Financial Products and Current Developments Task Forces of the Regulated Investment Companies Committee of the Section of Taxation. She received her B.A. from the College of the Holy Cross and her M.B.A. with high honors and J.D. from the University of Notre Dame.

W. Scott Jardine is a partner in the Chicago office of Chapman and Cutler. Mr. Jardine concentrates his practice on securities law matters with an emphasis on tax-exempt derivative securities and on investment company representation, including the representation of unit investment trusts and open-end and closed-end management investment companies. Mr. Jardine has been a panelist/lecturer on securities law issues relating to tax-exempt derivatives and co-authored the chapter on tax-exempt derivatives in the workbook for the 1992 and 1993 Bond Attorneys' Workshops in Chicago. Mr. Jardine's experience also includes private and public offerings of equity and debt securities and broker-dealer and investment adviser regulation. He received his B.S.A. from the University of Illinois and his J.D. from the University of Illinois College of Law.

Daniel L. Johnson is a partner in the Chicago office of Chapman and Cutler and has concentrated his practice in municipal finance law. He has served as bond counsel for a wide variety of municipal transactions involving numerous types of municipal issuers and has extensive experience in elementary and secondary education system financings. Mr. Johnson's areas of particular municipal finance expertise include legislative drafting, tax and state aid anticipation obligations, special service areas and special assessments, installment purchase contracts, municipal leases, advance refundings, and student loan obligations. He has been a frequent panelist and lecturer at seminars and conferences on municipal finance topics and has also authored articles on municipal finance. Mr. Johnson received his B.A. summa cum laude from Cornell College and his J.D. with honors from the University of Illinois College of Law.

William M. Libit is a partner in the Chicago office of Chapman and Cutler and has concentrated in the fields of public finance and securities laws. He has acted as bond counsel and underwriter's counsel in publicly offered, traditional municipal financings and as bond counsel, underwriter's counsel, and special tax counsel for private activity bond issues, including airport financings, hospital financings, port facility bonds, solid-waste disposal facilities bonds, resource recovery bonds, and exempt small issues. He has also acted as special counsel to various municipal issuers in connection with interest rate swap transactions and other municipal derivative securities. Mr. Libit has extensive experience with the use of letters of credit to secure municipal obligations and has served as counsel for investment banking firms acting as remarketing agents for variable-rate demand bond programs. In addition, Mr. Libit represents underwriters and issuers in connection with public offerings of registered securities and in other aspects of their business involving the federal securities laws. Mr. Libit received his B.A. magna cum laude from Emory University and his J.D. from Northwestern University School of Law.

Elizabeth D. Swanson is an associate in the Chicago office of Chapman and Cutler and is a member of the firm's municipal department. She serves as bond counsel on a wide variety of municipal financings, including general obligation and revenue financings for various municipalities, school districts, and other special districts. She also serves as counsel to investment banking firms in connection with the underwriting or remarketing of municipal securities. Ms. Swanson received her B.A. magna cum laude from Drake University and her J.D. from Northwestern University School of Law.

Robert D. Aicher is a partner in the Chicago office of Chapman and Cutler and has concentrated in banking and bankruptcy law for the past sixteen years. He has extensive experience in structuring transactions as counsel to banks providing credit and liquidity support for publicly offered debt in municipal, asset-backed securitization and project financings. Mr. Aicher is the partner with responsibility for rendering preference and other bankruptcy-related opinions in connection with rated transactions. He is on retainer for one of the major rating agencies. Mr. Aicher's traditional banking practice includes drafting of domestic and Eurodollar revolving and term loan agreements; structuring and drafting secured financings, including both personal property and real estate; Arab-Israeli boycott statutes and regulations; and non-bankruptcy workouts of all forms including negotiated compositions and assignments for the benefit of creditors. As a member of the Banking Law Committee Section of Business Law panel on "The Outer Limits of *Deprizio*" at the 1990 Annual Meeting of the American Bar Association, Mr. Aicher presented "Impact of *Deprizio* on Credit Enhanced Securities and Preference Opinions." He is a co-author of "Characterization of a Transfer of Receivables as a Sale or a Secured Loan upon Bankruptcy of the Transferor," published in the Winter 1991 issue of the *American Bankruptcy Law Journal*, and "Avoidance Powers Available to the FDIC in a Bank Insolvency," published in the inaugural issue (November/December 1991) of the *Journal of Bankruptcy Law and Practice*. Mr. Aicher received his B.A. magna cum laude from the University of Michigan and his J.D. magna cum laude from the University of Michigan Law School.

CHAPTER 1

An Introduction to Tax-Exempt Derivatives

Steven D. Conlon
Vincent M. Aquilino

What Is a Tax-Exempt Derivative?

The word *derivative* is defined as "not original; secondary."[1] In the municipal finance markets, the term "tax-exempt derivative" has a related but broader meaning (or meanings), identifying a range of both primary and secondary market products (other than traditional fixed or floating interest rate bonds) structured to provide tax-exempt income[2] to investors. In this context, the term refers to state-of-the-art tax-exempt investments.

Tax-exempt derivatives in the form of so-called synthetic floating-rate tax-exempt bonds currently enjoy high profiles in a market environment that is highly sensitive to change in product, structure, and features. These bonds rely on sophisticated interest rate mechanisms such as "inverse floaters," stripped tax-exempt bonds, and tax-exempt asset-backed securities, including interests in trusts holding tax-exempt lease receivables.

In the taxable market, the term "derivative product" is often used to describe interest rate, foreign currency, equity, bond, and commodity indexed contracts known as "swaps," "caps," "floors," and "collars"[3] and other products that replicate the economic effects of certain investments in those markets without actually requiring participation in the underlying bond, foreign currency, stock, or commodity markets.

The "taxable"[4] interest rate swap and related derivative products market, which began its real development in the early 1980s, is now a multi-trillion-dollar market.[5] A driving force in its growth has been the use of derivative products to manage asset and liability interest rate exposure without requiring the redeployment of assets or the renegotiation of liabilities.[6] Derivative products thus often provide treasurers and other money managers with financial management flexibility and transaction cost savings.

State and local governmental units and tax-exempt borrowers in conduit financings have begun to enter into these contracts because they have come to appreciate the potential benefits that interest rate swaps and related derivative products offer. The sophistication of governmental unit or conduit borrowers and their advisers has generally reached a level at which the evaluation of interest rate swaps or similar contracts in connection with new or outstanding tax-exempt financings is in many cases straightforward. Interest rate swaps and similar types of derivative products used by municipal issuers and other tax-exempt bond market participants and the tax-exempt financings linked to these contracts are referred to as "tax-exempt derivatives."

The term "tax-exempt derivative" thus encompasses a myriad of investments sold in the municipal finance markets, including investor-targeted products with innovative features structured to deliver tax-exempt interest; interest rate swaps, caps, and floors entered into by state and local governmental units and conduit borrowers; and tax-exempt bonds hedged with interest rate swaps or similar derivative products. These are summarized in Exhibit 1-1.

Why Are Tax-Exempt Derivatives Popular?

Like many financial products, tax-exempt derivatives have been developed to meet investor needs not being fully satisfied by existing tax-exempt products. Although there are a variety of types of tax-exempt derivatives that satisfy a number of different objectives, the recent popularity of tax-exempt derivatives has been sparked by two different gaps in the market—one in the short-term tax-exempt market, where investor demand currently exceeds supply, and another arising from investor demand for specialized tax-exempt securities that hedge interest rate risks.

There is significant investor demand for short-term, floating-rate tax-exempt debt. Much of this demand is from the tax-exempt money market fund industry, which has grown to a $100 billion market since its emergence in the late 1970s. Unfortunately for investors, the recent history of comparatively low long-term tax-exempt interest rates combined with the preference of many municipal issuers for fixed-rate debt has resulted in the issuance of significant amounts of long-term, fixed-rate tax-exempt debt. As a result, the supply of short-term, floating-rate tax-exempt debt and, in particular, high-quality money market eligible tax-exempt debt, has not kept pace with demand. Certain types of tax-exempt derivatives attempt to satisfy this excess demand by creating floating-rate tax-exempt securities for investors while providing long-term, fixed-rate financing to municipal issuers.

Persistent low long-term tax-exempt rates are also responsible for the other market demand that has triggered much of the growth of this market. Sophisticated investors and sophisticated money managers such as portfolio managers for tax-exempt bond funds are constantly pursuing increased yield, particularly in a low interest rate environment. Certain types of tax-exempt derivatives, such as inverse floaters, are designed to provide above-market current returns in exchange for additional interest rate risk.

Another reason for the emergence of this market is rooted in the use of tax-exempt derivatives as portfolio hedges. Federal securities laws require mutual funds to establish "investment policies" that can be changed only

EXHIBIT 1-1

Tax-Exempt Derivatives

- Investments with innovative features sold in municipal finance markets
- Interest rate swaps, caps, and floors
- Tax-exempt bonds hedged with swaps or similar derivative products

through the cumbersome process of obtaining shareholder approval. As a result, many mutual funds are not able to participate directly in the interest rate derivatives market. Moreover, interest rate derivatives such as interest rate swaps, caps, and floors generate taxable income, which tax-exempt mutual funds try to avoid or minimize. Certain types of tax-exempt derivatives are structured as bonds with an interest rate having hedge-like characteristics. Thus, these derivatives are intended to qualify as investments that are permissible under the existing investment policies of many mutual funds. They generate tax-exempt interest rather than taxable swap payments. As is the case with any hedging product, the specific types of tax-exempt derivatives that provide these characteristics can differ significantly. Some hedge upward or downward rate movements, while others provide a hedge that works in either direction. The nature of the hedge, its magnitude, and the absolute limit on the hedge provided by the derivative can differ significantly.

Included in Exhibit 1-2 are two examples that illustrate the basic reasons, benefits, and risks associated with two common forms of tax-exempt derivative transactions.

Benefits and Risks of Tax-Exempt Derivatives to Issuers

Tax-exempt derivatives are structured to deliver varying benefits to different market segments and participants. These products satisfy certain basic investor objectives, addressing market supply and demand imbalances, with resultant yield benefits to issuers or investors.

While the discussion will illustrate certain investor and issuer concerns, it does not purport to provide a comprehensive discussion of the benefits and burdens of investing in or issuing derivatives, or of the legal issues associated with these products. Moreover, regardless of the potential benefits associated with the products, issuers and investors must carefully evaluate the risks, both legal and economic.

Certain derivative products are structured to provide benefits to the issuers and underlying obligors of tax-exempt bonds. (These parties will be referred to throughout as governmental issuers and conduit borrowers and

EXHIBIT 1-2

EXAMPLE 1: CREATION OF A "PRIMARY" DERIVATIVE

Issuer wishes to enter into a fixed-rate obligation. It could issue fixed-rate bonds. Alternatively, it can issue floating-rate bonds *and* enter into a swap agreement with swap counterparty in which:

- The notional principal amount on the swap equals the principal amount of the bonds.
- Issuer makes payments to swap counterparty based on the fixed rate, and
- Swap counterparty makes payments to issuer based on the variable rate.

Potential Benefits:

- Net fixed-rate cost of borrowing may be less than if fixed-rate bonds were issued.

Potential Risks:

- Swap counterparty will fail to perform, and issuer will be subject to floating interest rate risk.
- Issuer may not be able to take into account net fixed interest rate cost for arbitrage yield restriction and rebate purposes.

EXAMPLE 2: CREATION OF A "SECONDARY" DERIVATIVE

Holder wants to sell its fixed-rate bonds but also wants to retain an interest in the spread between the long-term fixed rate and a particular short-term variable rate. Holder creates a secondary derivative by selling the bonds at par and providing liquidity support in return for a fee measured by the difference between the fixed and variable rate.

Potential Benefits:

- Realizing cash on sale of the bonds.
- Receipt of fee measured by the spread between the fixed long-term rate and the variable short-term rate.

Potential Risks:

- Risk of providing credit support may be greater than spread received, depending upon market conditions.
- Sponsor could end up repurchasing the bonds as a result of providing liquidity support.

will be described in more detail in Chapter 2.) For example, a governmenttal issuer or conduit borrower can use an interest rate swap to convert its variable-rate obligation on a floating-rate bond to a fixed payment obligation. This type of transaction may provide it with net lower fixed borrowing costs than if it issued fixed-rate bonds. It also gives the governmental issuer or conduit borrower the flexibility to make the rate conversion *after* the bonds are issued at transaction costs that are lower than if refunding bonds had been issued. Issuing floater/inverse floater combinations may also provide the governmental issuer or conduit borrower with lower net borrowing costs than those for fixed-rate bonds.

Financial intermediaries such as investment banks and credit enhancers provide their products and services as components in the structuring of derivatives and thus may also benefit from the use of these products. Also, the holder of seller-financed tax-exempt obligations (such as lease receivables) could sell interests in the receivables at a favorable price in the form of pooled tax-exempt derivative securities. Proceeds from the sale could be used to generate cash to finance new originations.

Although the benefits of tax-exempt derivatives to issuers may appear attractive, issuers should carefully consider the potential risks. For example, consider a governmental issuer that issues floating-rate bonds and enters into an interest rate swap to effectively convert its variable-payment obligation to a fixed obligation. Assume that the net fixed rate to the issuer (taking into account the swap) is 6½ percent. If interest rates decline after the bonds are issued, the floating rate on the bonds will likewise decline. However, because of the swap, the issuer will nevertheless effectively be obligated to continue to make payments at 6½ percent. The governmental issuer could terminate the swap, but the swap agreement will typically provide for the payment of a swap termination fee that will take into account the change in interest rates. In short, the decline in market interest rates will afford little, if any, economic opportunity for the governmental issuer.

Similarly, an investor will find that an inverse floating-rate bond is an attractive investment in a falling interest rate environment. However, in an environment of rising interest rates, the value of the bond will decrease at an accelerated rate relative to the decrease in value of a fixed interest rate bond.

Benefits and Risks of Tax-Exempt Derivatives to Investors

As discussed above, derivative products are often structured to provide investors with important benefits. For example, tender option certificates are structured to satisfy investors' requirements, such as money market funds that have an acute need for short-term tax-exempt investments. Inverse floating-rate bonds provide investors with enhanced returns in a falling interest rate environment, while embedded cap bonds provide enhanced returns in a rising rate environment.

Tax-exempt derivatives may provide tax-exempt interest in a form of investment that may appear economically identical to a direct investment in a tax-exempt bond. However, many of the primary market products, and all of the secondary market products described in the following chapters, raise additional issues that are not present in the evaluation of a direct investment in a typical tax-exempt bond.

In addition to benefits, however, tax-exempt derivatives present risks to investors that they should carefully consider before purchasing these products. These risks fall into two basic categories, investment risks and special legal risks.

Investment Risks

INVESTMENT VOLATILITY. Investors should consider the impact of changes in interest rates on these products, particularly investments such as inverse interest rate bonds, derivative rate bonds, and stripped tax-exempt bonds. Typically a product that provides an investor with economic benefits in one rate environment may saddle the investor with losses in the opposite environment.

LIMITATIONS ON LIQUIDITY. Investors should consider the limitations on the liquidity of these products. In the case of tender option certificates, for example, the investor's primary liquidity right, the tender option feature, may not be available if certain events occur. As a result, the investor bears the economic risk associated with the underlying tax-exempt bond, which is usually the opposite of the risks the investor anticipated in acquiring the derivative.

CHANGES IN TENDER DATES AND INTEREST RATE RESETTING DATES. Certain types of tax-exempt derivatives are "multimodal"; that is, the period between tender dates or rate reset dates can be changed at the discretion of the remarketing agent. An investor should consider potential mode changes and their impact on the desirability or eligibility of a particular tax-exempt derivative as a portfolio investment.

Special Legal Risks

TAXABLE INCOME RISKS. The tax disclosure and opinion language for most tax-exempt derivatives is quite different from the disclosure language typically found in "plain vanilla" tax-exempt bond issues. In deciding whether to purchase a particular derivative, investors must focus on differences in disclosure language and the strength of the legal opinions dealing with the delivery of tax-exempt interest.

STATE TAX TREATMENT. In many cases the state income tax treatment of a derivative product is not addressed. Certain tax-exempt bonds are also exempt from state income taxes. Does the derivative product generate similar state tax benefits given that the bond is not directly held by the investor? Also to be considered is whether the custodial account or trust holding the bond creates a taxable entity for state tax purposes.

SECURITIES LAWS CONSIDERATIONS. Mutual fund purchasers of tax-exempt derivatives must comply with the Investment Company Act of 1940, and sponsors that structure derivative products must consider whether the products are subject to federal securities registration under either the Securities Act of 1933 or the Investment Company Act of 1940.

Overview of Legal Issues

A wide variety of legal issues must be considered in connection with tax-exempt derivatives. The issues fall into several categories:

- *Federal and state income tax issues.* To what extent is the income from these products tax-exempt, and what collateral consequences apply to municipal issuers (such as arbitrage rebate) and investors (such as compliance with special rules applicable to mutual funds)?
- *Federal securities and state "blue sky" laws issues.* Are the products subject to registration under the Securities Act of 1933 or the Investment Company Act of 1940?
- *Municipal law issues.* Does a municipal issuer have the power to enter into interest rate swaps and similar types of agreements, and are these contracts enforceable?
- *Federal bankruptcy law issues.* How does the bankruptcy of a participant affect payments on an interest rate swap or cap?

The legal issues relating to tax-exempt derivatives are summarized in Chapter 4. Chapters 5 through 8 address the tax, securities, municipal, and federal bankruptcy law issues in detail.

What Topics Does This Book Cover?

This book is intended to provide municipal finance attorneys and other municipal finance professionals with guidance in dealing with the overriding federal income tax, federal securities, federal bankruptcy, and state law considerations that should be taken into account by state and local governmental units, conduit borrowers, and other municipal market participants structuring, evaluating, marketing, or purchasing tax-exempt derivatives. The principal purpose of the book is to address the key legal issues relating to tax-exempt derivatives. However, to provide the necessary framework for a discussion of the legal issues, the first three chapters of this book discuss in general terms what tax-exempt derivative products are, their benefits and risks, and how they are structured and used. This discussion is intended as background and is not the principal focus of the book. Accordingly, the book does not purport to provide a comprehensive discussion of the types of products or their financial analysis.

While issues that may be of particular relevance to specific types of investors, credit enhancement providers, or other market participants may not be fully addressed in the chapters to follow, specific issues as they relate to a variety of market participants are discussed. Practical limitations have prevented us from providing a complete discussion of state-by-state law considerations (including state tax, "blue sky" securities, and municipal laws concerns). Finally, because tax-exempt derivatives are a relatively recent phenomenon, there can be little doubt that the law relating to these products will change as courts and administrative bodies address the legal issues that tax-exempt derivatives raise. Recently, given the continued growth of the derivatives market, both market regulators and participants have begun to focus on whether additional regulation is needed. For the most part, these concerns have related to bank participation in the taxable swap market and potential risk exposure to banks as a result of these activities.[7] With respect to tax-exempt derivatives, market participants have proposed tax legislation that would create "tax-exempt municipal investment conduits" (TEMICs).[8] The TEMIC proposal is intended to provide increased certainty regarding the tax treatment of tax-exempt derivatives. We hope this book will be helpful to you in understanding a growing segment of the municipal finance market.

Notes

1. THE RANDOM HOUSE DICTIONARY OF THE ENGLISH LANGUAGE 536 (2d ed. 1987).

2. By "tax-exempt" we mean income that is excludable from gross income for federal income tax purposes (although such income may be taken into account for purposes of the alternative minimum tax, the environmental tax, the branch profits tax, the taxation of social security and railroad retirement benefits, and the taxation of passive income earned by certain S corporations). "Bond" refers to any obligation (including notes or interests in leases that constitute financing leases) that constitutes an "evidence of indebtedness" for federal income tax purposes.

3. *See* Chapter 2, *infra,* for definitions of swaps, caps, and floors.

4. "Taxable" is used in this context to refer to swaps that are not structured for municipal market participants. As discussed later, all interest rate swaps, including interest rate swaps targeted to municipalities, generate taxable income.

5. William Glasgall & Bill Javetski, *Swap Fever: Big Money, Big Risks,* BUS. WK., June 1, 1992, at 102 ($5 trillion outstanding in swap contracts worldwide); Steven Lipin & William Power, *"Derivatives" Draw Warnings from Regulators,* WALL ST. J., Mar. 25, 1992, at C1 (derivatives market may be as large as $10 trillion); Pat Widder, *Trillions at Stake in the Swaps Market,* CHI. TRIB., June 22, 1992, section 4, at 1.

6. *See, e.g.,* Glasgall & Javetski, *supra* note 5. The products can also be used as investments rather than as hedging devices.

7. In 1993, a number of participants in this market, referred to as the "Group of Thirty," released its report on this issue. *See* Steven Lipin, *Banks Try to Avoid Rules on Derivatives,* WALL ST. J., July 22, 1993, at C1. Also, the Office of the Comptroller of the Currency released Banking Circular 277 on "Risk Management of Financial Derivatives" (Oct. 27, 1993). The House Banking Committee held hearings on derivative product risks to banks in October 1993. *See generally* Kenneth H. Bacon, *Lawmakers Question Agencies' Ability to Regulate the Derivatives Market,* WALL ST. J., Oct. 29, 1993, at A7. In addition to concerns relating to the participation of banks in this market, the Securities and Exchange Commission is examining the appropriateness of providing additional regulation in this market. *See generally* Kenneth H. Bacon, *U.S. Announces Some Guidelines for Derivatives,* WALL ST. J., Sept. 28, 1993, at A5.

8. *See* Lynn Stevens Hume, *Bond Industry Officials Send Temic Proposal to Treasury, Congress,* THE BOND BUYER, Sept. 14, 1993, at 1.

CHAPTER 2

Understanding Tax-Exempt Derivatives

Steven D. Conlon
Vincent M. Aquilino

This chapter generally describes tax-exempt derivatives, their features and their structure. The chapter begins with a section that defines important terms that will be used throughout this book. The later sections of the chapter provide a more detailed description of each of the basic types of tax-exempt derivative products. The following chapter addresses how tax-exempt derivatives are used by different market participants and provides insights into the legal and market forces that have resulted in the development of these products.

Definitions and Terms

In the definitions set out below we have attempted to avoid trademarked terms that are used in connection with products specific to a particular underwriter or investment house, even though many market participants may be familiar with those proper terms and acronyms. A glossary in which certain product names are listed as of the date of publication and can be cross-referenced is included for the reader's convenience at the back of the book.

A *primary* tax-exempt derivative (or "primary product") refers to a tax-exempt bond issued directly by a state or local governmental unit or an entity that qualifies as an "on behalf of issuer" for federal income tax purposes.[1] State and local governmental units and entities that qualify as "on behalf of issuers" are referred to as *governmental issuers.* Underlying borrowers in tax-exempt bond conduit financings ("conduit bond issues," such as industrial development bonds and qualifying private activity bonds issued for the benefit of private businesses and not-for-profit hospitals, health care organizations, and educational institutions) are referred to as *conduit borrowers.* Examples of primary tax-exempt derivatives include inverse floaters and derivative rate bonds, some of which are sometimes referred to as embedded swap bonds and embedded cap bonds (these products are discussed below).

A *secondary* tax-exempt derivative (or "secondary product") refers to a custodial receipt, trust certificate, or other security that is not directly issued by a governmental issuer. Because the receipt, certificate, or other security is not a tax-exempt bond issued directly by a governmental issuer, a secondary product must derive its tax exemption from a tax-exempt bond that must be included as part of the tax-exempt derivative (the "related tax-exempt bond"). Examples of secondary products include so-called tender option bonds, trust certificates with interest rate swaps, stripped tax-exempt bonds, and certificates representing an interest in a pool of tax-exempt obligations (discussed below).

An *interest rate swap* is a type of contract under which two parties agree to make payments to each other. One party typically makes payments that are determined by reference to a *fixed* interest rate on a stated principal amount (the "fixed-rate payor"). The other party (typically referred to as the "counterparty") makes payments determined by reference to a *floating* interest rate that is periodically reset on a stated principal amount (the "floating-rate payor"). In the usual case, the payment obligations of the parties are "netted" against each other, and only the party owing the greater amount makes a net payment to the other party. A key aspect of this basic form of interest rate swap is that neither party actually lends or pays the stated principal amount used to calculate each party's payment obligations. For this reason the principal amount for these contracts is referred to as "notional," used merely as a means of measuring each party's payment obligations under the contract. In certain cases, one of the parties to an interest rate swap will require the payment of an up-front premium (an "adjustment fee" or "off-market swap premium") when the swap is "off-market" (i.e., when the rates on the swap do not reflect then current market rates). The fixed rate is a function of prevailing market interest rates of the same tenor.

Under an *interest rate cap,* a party *pays* an up-front premium (the "cap premium") (alternatively, the cap premium may be paid in installments) in exchange for the counterparty's promise to pay the amount by which a floating interest rate on a notional principal amount exceeds an agreed fixed interest rate (the "cap rate," commonly referred to as the "strike rate") on the same notional principal amount at specified times during the term of the cap. An interest rate cap can be used to protect the purchaser against the cost of floating interest rates exceeding the cap rate.

Under an *interest rate floor,* a person *receives* an up-front premium (the "floor premium") in exchange for the obligation to pay the counterparty the amount by which an agreed fixed interest rate (the "floor rate," commonly referred to as the "strike rate") on a notional principal amount exceeds a floating interest rate on the same notional principal amount at specified times during the term of the floor. Interest rate floors can be sold to realize proceeds today in exchange for the obligation to make payments if floating interest rates drop below the floor rate.

An interest rate *collar* is a single agreement that combines a cap and a floor, with one party paying if the floating rate exceeds the cap rate and the other party paying if the floating rate drops below the floor rate. A conventional interest rate swap could be viewed as a collar with the same strike rate for both the cap rate and the floor rate (i.e., an agreement under which in return for receiving a cap rate the fixed-rate payor is willing to provide the same rate as a floor rate to the other party).

A variety of related products are being used in the municipal bond markets, including "forward swaps" (an agreement to begin a swap at a future date) and "swaptions" (an agreement that gives a party the option of requiring the counterparty to enter into a swap at a future date). Interest rate swaps, caps, floors, collars, forward swaps, swaptions, and similar types of contracts can be generically described as "notional principal contracts" (NPCs) because the obligations of the parties under such contracts are all determined by reference to a notional principal amount specified in the contract.

The International Swaps and Derivatives Association, Inc. (ISDA, formerly the International Swap Dealers Association), has developed standard terminology and contract forms for various types of notional principal contracts such as swaps, caps, and floors.[2] Many dealers in interest rate swaps and similar contracts are ISDA members. Almost all dealers, whether or not members of ISDA, use the ISDA document forms or contracts based on these forms. In 1992 ISDA introduced a standard form of schedule to its standard basic swap contract for swaps entered into with governmental units, the ISDA Municipal Swap Form Contract. This contract, along with the municipal law issues raised by interest rate swaps, caps, floors, and similar contracts, is discussed in Chapter 7 on municipal law issues.

Exhibit 2-1 is an alphabetical listing of the terms introduced and defined in this chapter.

Primary Derivative Products

Inverse Floaters

The inverse floater, a new type of tax-exempt bond, has made its appearance during the past several years. Interest payable on an inverse floater is based on a relatively complex formula tied to a floating rate, base rate, and multiplier. For example, consider the interest rate formula on an inverse floater that provides for the payment of interest at 14 percent (the "ceiling rate") minus the current interest rate on a specified floating-rate index or floating-rate bond (the "referenced floating rate") (but only to the extent that the referenced floating rate does not exceed the ceiling rate). The term "inverse floater" describes the interest rate formula that causes the interest rate to rise when the referenced floating rate declines, and vice versa (compare illustrations 1 and 2 in Exhibit 2-2).

Inverse floaters have been issued in tandem with tax-exempt bonds called floaters or floating-rate bonds that provide for payments of interest based on a current market interest rate formula. In this text, the issuance of

EXHIBIT 2-1

List of Key Terms

- adjustment fee
- cap premium
- cap rate
- collars
- conduit bond issuer
- conduit borrower
- certificates representing an interest in a pool of tax-exempt obligations
- counterparty
- derivative rate bond
- embedded cap bond
- embedded swap bond
- fixed-rate payor
- floating-rate payor
- floor premium
- floor rate
- forward swaps
- governmental issuer
- interest rate cap
- interest rate floor
- interest rate swap
- inverse floater
- notional principal amount
- notional principal contract (NPC)
- off-market swap premium
- primary product
- related tax-exempt bond
- secondary product
- strike rate
- stripped tax-exempt bond
- swaptions
- tender option bond
- trust certificates with interest rate swaps

inverse floaters and floaters in tandem is referred to as a "floater/inverse floater combination." As a conceptual matter, there is a great deal of flexibility in the floating interest rate formula that could be used by a floater issued as part of a floater/inverse floater combination. Typically, however, such floating-rate bonds have either been "dutch auction rate bonds" or "indexed-rate bonds."

EXHIBIT 2-2

Inverse Floater Rate =

Ceiling Rate – Referenced Floating Rate

ILLUSTRATION 1:

If the **ceiling rate** is 14% and the **referenced floating rate** is 5.5%, then the **inverse floater rate** is 8.5%.

ILLUSTRATION 2:

If the **ceiling rate** is 14% and the **referenced floating rate** is 3.5%, then the **inverse floater rate** is 10.5%.

- The *higher* the **referenced floating rate,** the *lower* the **inverse floater rate.**

Dutch Auction Rate Bonds

The floating interest rate on a dutch auction rate bond is determined through a "dutch auction" procedure, which takes place on a periodic basis (typically, every 28 days).[3] An auction agent appointed at the time the bonds are issued receives orders submitted by bondholders on whether they wish to continue to hold their bond regardless of the rate established by the auction (a "hold request"), sell their bond regardless of the rate established by the auction (a "sell request"), or sell their bond unless the interest rate established by the auction is at least equal to a rate designated by the bondholder (a "specified rate sale request"). The auction agent also solicits requests from potential purchasers of the bonds regarding whether they want to purchase bonds regardless of the rate established by the auction (a "purchase request") or purchase bonds provided that the interest rate established by the auction is at least equal to a rate designated by the bondholder (a "specified rate purchase request").

On the auction date, it is the auction agent's job to match the sell requests and specified rate sale requests with the purchase requests and specified rate purchase requests until, by reference to the specified rate purchase requests, a minimum interest rate is established for the bonds. The matching of sale requests to establish the uniform interest rate for the bonds is called "clearing the auction." The interest rate *for all of the dutch auction rate bonds* for the period ending on the next auction date is set to equal the *minimum* interest rate necessary to match all of the sell requests (this rate will be based on the highest specified rate purchase request that was matched with a specified rate sale request in the auction). This process is illustrated in Exhibit 2-3.

If on any auction date the auction agent is unable to match all of the sell requests, the auction is described as having "failed." One important consequence of a so-called failed auction is that the existing bondholders that have submitted sell requests are unable to sell their bonds through the auction process as of the failed auction date. In addition, dutch auction rate bonds typically provide for payments of interest for the next interest rate

EXHIBIT 2-3

Clearing the Auction

	MATCHED WITH	
Sell Requests	⇒	Purchase Requests
Specified Rate Sale Requests	⇒	Specified Rate Purchase Requests

Interest rate established by the auction process is the *minimum* interest rate necessary to match all sale requests.

Failed Auction

	NOT MATCHED WITH	
Sell Requests	⃠	Purchase Requests
Specified Rate Sale Requests	⃠	Specified Rate Purchase Requests

Interest rate is based on a pre-established *backup* rate.

period based on an index-based floating rate (the "backup rate") when a failed auction occurs since the dutch auction process was unable to successfully establish an applicable interest rate. The backup rate is often structured as a higher than normal interest rate (sometimes referred to as a penalty rate) to compensate existing bondholders for the lack of the liquidity they expected the dutch auction process would ordinarily provide and to encourage the governmental issuer or conduit borrower and the auction agent to take appropriate steps to facilitate successfully clearing the auction on future auction dates.[4]

There have been several failed auctions involving dutch auction rate tax-exempt bonds.[5] Floating-rate bonds that are issued as part of the floater/inverse floater structure need not be dutch auction rate bonds. As we have noted earlier, the interest rate on a floater can also be determined by more conventional means, either by reference to an index or through a remarketing agent.

Floater/Inverse Floater Combinations

In many instances, governmental issuers have issued bond issues comprised of both floater bonds and inverse floater bonds. Typically the inverse floaters issued as part of the bond issue rely on a referenced floating rate, which is the identical rate used to compute interest payable on the related floating-rate bonds (Exhibit 2-4 describes the principal features). Under these circumstances, changes in the amount of interest payable on the floating-rate bonds are effectively offset, as an economic matter, by opposite changes in the interest payable on the inverse floaters, resulting in an effective net fixed-rate payment by the governmental issuer or conduit borrower for the combined floater/inverse floater bond issue (see Exhibits 2-5 and 2-6).

Thus, floater/inverse floater combinations provide governmental issuers and conduit borrowers with a net fixed interest rate payment obligation. However, it is not necessary, as an economic matter, for the issuer of an inverse floater to use a floater/inverse floater combination to achieve a net fixed-rate payment obligation. Instead, an issuer could enter into an interest rate swap to achieve the same basic economic result (although this ignores swap counterparty credit risk, and there may be a number of significant federal income tax and municipal law differences between these two approaches).

Derivative Rate Bonds

Recently, tax-exempt bonds have been issued that provide for interest payments based on formulas directly tied to interest rate indices such as J. J. Kenny or the PSA Municipal Swap Index.[6] Interest payments on these bonds are based on a formula (the "derivative rate formula") that includes a fixed-rate component as well as a supplemental component economically resembling an interest rate swap or cap.[7] Bonds bearing interest rates tied to these formulas are generically referred to as "derivative rate bonds." (See Exhibit 2-7 for a listing of the common characteristics of derivative rate bonds.)

EXHIBIT 2-4

Floater/Inverse Floater Combinations

PRINCIPAL FEATURES

- Two different types of bonds — equal principal amounts:
  - Floater bonds
  - Inverse floater bonds
- Floater and inverse floater bond interest formulas are symmetrical, resulting in fixed net payment obligations of the issuer.
- Floating rate is set by a dutch auction process, by a remarketing agent, or by reference to an index.
- Inverse floater typically has a "linkage" right permitting the holder to purchase on demand an equal amount of floater bonds, effectively transforming the investor's return from an inverse floating rate to a fixed rate.

In addition to the basic interest rate formula of derivative rate bonds, other features common to derivative rate bonds are generally driven by the interest rate risk associated with the derivative rate formula. While on the one hand governmental issuers and conduit borrowers typically focus on the interest rate payment risk associated with an obligation to pay interest based on the derivative rate formula, on the other hand prospective investors often focus on the potential rate of return risk associated with reduced yields on a derivative rate bond in certain interest rate environments. In addition, because derivative rate bonds are of relatively recent vintage, investors may be concerned about the liquidity of these products.

Reasons for Certain Derivative Rate Bond Characteristics

While governmental issuers and conduit borrowers may hedge the interest rate risk associated with derivative rate bonds, the potential mismatch between the typical maturity of a municipal bond and the term of an interest rate swap, cap, or similar type of hedge raises concern because it may be difficult for the issuer to obtain an efficiently priced hedge that covers the interest rate risk for the entire term of the bond.

Municipal bonds often have final or weighted average maturities in excess of ten, fifteen, or even twenty years.[8] However, debt instruments issued in the domestic taxable debt markets (with the notable exception of the U.S. Treasury market) typically have comparatively shorter maturities.[9]

EXHIBIT 2-5

Floater/Inverse Floater Combinations

INTEREST RATE FORMULA

The essential ingredient of a floater/inverse floater combination is the offsetting amount of interest payable on the related floating-rate bonds, which effectively results in a fixed-rate payment obligation of the issuer.

	Principal Amount	Rate Formula	Example
Inverse Floater	$ 50 Million	16% – Auction or Index Rate	16% – 4% = 12% ($ 6m)
Floater	$ 50 Million	Auction or Index Rate Capped at 16%	4% ($ 2m)
Total	$ 100 Million	Issuer's Obligation Is Fixed at 8% of $ 100 Million	8% ($ 8m)

Interest rate swaps, caps, and similar types of derivative products likewise have terms that are typically less than ten years (five to seven years).[10] This is because commercial and investment banks, which are the principal providers of interest rate swaps, are reluctant to extend credit beyond ten years. The typical maturity of swaps and caps has not impeded the development of the taxable interest rate swap and taxable derivatives market, perhaps because of the shorter duration of taxable debt instruments (often ten years or less).[11]

Derivative rate bonds sometimes address the significant mismatch between the duration of many interest rate swaps, caps, and similar derivative products and the term to maturity for many tax-exempt bonds by providing for a scheduled rate conversion prior to maturity. For example, a derivative rate bond with a twenty-year maturity may provide for interest payments based on the derivative rate formula for the first five to eight years the bonds are outstanding. At the end of this period, the derivative rate bond would provide for a conversion from the payment of interest based on the derivative rate formula to a specified fixed rate. As a result, after this initial period expires, future interest payments would be at a fixed rate. (See Exhibit 2-8.) Because such a bond would provide for interest payments based on the derivative rate formula for only five to eight years, the governmental issuer or conduit borrower could hedge the interest rate risk associated with the derivative rate formula by acquiring a hedge of equal duration.

EXHIBIT 2-6

Floater/Inverse Floater Combinations

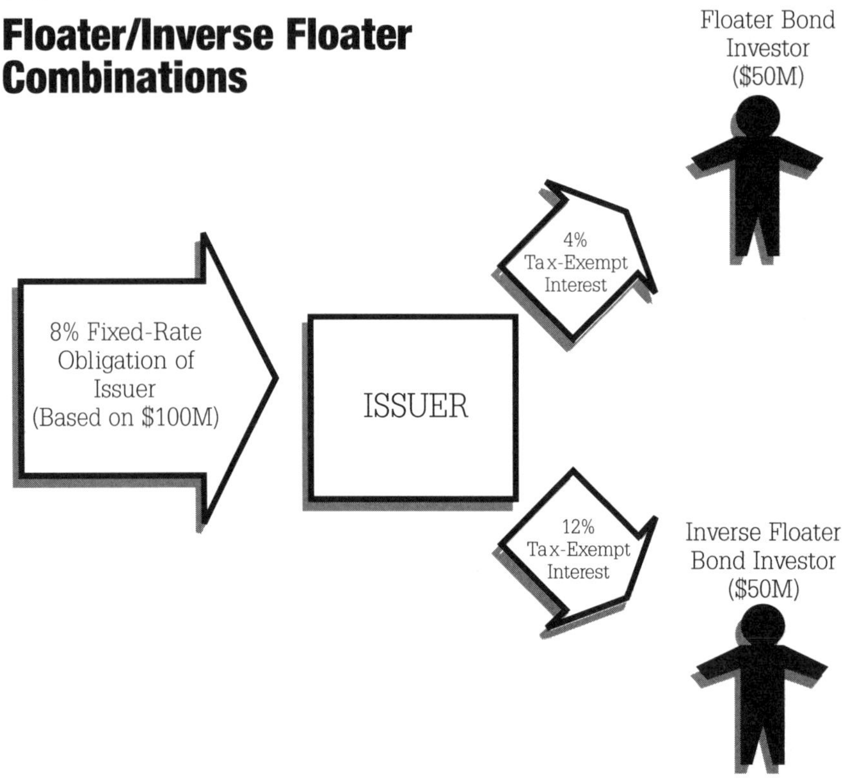

In addition to governmental issuer concerns regarding interest rate risk, investors may be concerned about the interest rate risks associated with owning a derivative rate bond before it converts to a fixed interest rate mode (i.e., while the interest payments are based on a derivative rate formula). This concern may be addressed by giving the investor the right to request that the governmental issuer (or some other party) terminate the derivative rate formula interest rate mode before the scheduled conversion date and convert the interest rate on the bonds to a fixed rate. If the early conversion election is exercised, the appropriate fixed interest rate for the bonds must be determined.

Embedded Swap Bonds

The term "embedded swap bond" identifies a derivative rate bond that provides a derivative rate formula with a fixed interest rate and a supplemental component economically resembling an interest rate swap. Exhibit 2-9 describes the interest rate formula on an embedded swap bond. The

EXHIBIT 2-7

Derivative Rate Bonds

- Derivative rate formula (may include "turbos")
- Scheduled rate conversion
- Early conversion election
- Types of derivative rate bonds
  - Embedded swap bonds
  - Embedded cap bonds
  - Stand-alone inverse floaters (i.e., inverse floater not issued as part of a floater/inverse floater combination could be described as a derivative rate bond)

exhibit shows the three basic reference rates included in the derivative rate formula for an embedded swap bond—the fixed rate (FR), which is included in the fixed-rate component of the formula, the swap variable rate (SVR), and the swap fixed rate (SFR). (The SVR and SFR are both included in the supplemental component of the rate formula.) The supplemental rate component may also include a "turbo" (multiplier) adjustment (turbos and their impact are discussed separately below).

Derivative rate bonds with a derivative rate formula based upon swaps are often called embedded swap bonds. The interest rate payable on these instruments is economically similar to the return received by an investor holding a fixed interest rate bond with the same interest rate as the FR and an interest rate swap with the same referenced interest rate terms as the SVR and SFR set forth in the derivative bond rate formula.

The derivative rate formula affects the bondholder's return in the same manner as a swap because if the variable-rate formula moves in one direction, the amount of interest payable on the bonds rises. If the referenced variable rate moves in the opposite direction, the amount of interest payable on the bonds declines. The formula includes an interest rate swap-like component because the bondholder may ultimately receive less than the fixed interest rate included in the derivative rate formula. This is economically equivalent to making payments to a counterparty on a swap when the bondholder has purchased a fixed-rate bond and entered into a separate interest rate swap with terms comparable to those for the derivative rate bond. However, the amount of interest payable on a derivative

EXHIBIT 2-8

Derivative Rate Bonds

- Scheduled rate conversion after year 8
- 20-year bond

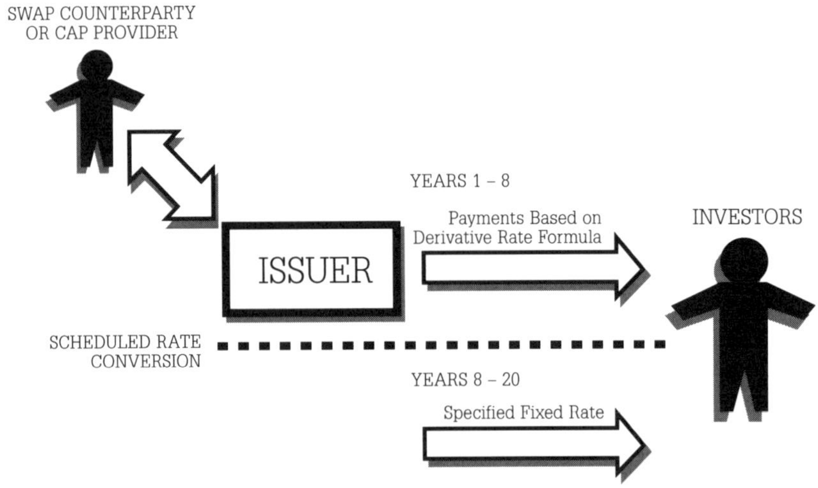

rate bond pursuant to a derivative rate formula will not truly resemble the acquisition of a fixed-rate bond and a separate interest rate swap because the amount of interest payable on a derivative rate bond to an investor will likely be subject to various state or local law limits on the maximum permissible rate (such as usury limits) and may provide for a minimum rate. Conversely, the holder of a derivative rate bond would typically never make ongoing payments to the issuer of the bond. (This risk could arise if instead of purchasing a derivative rate bond, the investor purchased a separate fixed-rate debt instrument and entered into a swap. Under certain scenarios, such as upon early swap termination, the investor could end up making payments on the swap in excess of the fixed rate on the fixed-rate bond.) These differences are summarized in Exhibit 2-10.

An embedded swap bond can be structured so that payments to the investor increase if the swap variable rate exceeds the swap fixed rate. An investor concerned about rising interest rates might purchase an embedded swap bond with this characteristic, while an investor expecting current interest rates to fall might purchase an embedded swap bond providing for payments that increase if the swap fixed rate exceeds the swap variable rate (i.e., if interest rates fall).

EXHIBIT 2-9

Embedded Swap Bonds

INTEREST RATE FORMULA

The essential ingredient of an embedded swap bond is the interest rate formula that effectively replicates a fixed rate plus a swap.

The key components of such a rate formula are:

- Interest paid = FR + [turbo (FLR - BR)]
- FR = long-term fixed interest rate on the bonds
- Turbo = multiplier
- FLR = floating rate that investor is trying to hedge
- BR = base rate

Embedded Cap Bonds

The term "embedded cap bond" could be used to describe a derivative rate bond that provides for a derivative rate formula with a fixed interest rate component and a supplemental component economically resembling an interest rate cap. Exhibit 2-11 generically describes the interest rate formula on an embedded cap bond.

As is the case with the embedded swap bond, there are three basic reference rates included in the derivative rate formula for an embedded cap bond—the fixed rate (FR), which is included in the fixed-rate component of the formula, the cap variable rate (CVR), and the cap fixed rate or "strike rate" (SR). The CVR and SR are both included in the supplemental component of the rate formula. The supplemental rate component of an embedded cap bond may also include a turbo adjustment. Turbos and their impact from both an economic and a tax standpoint are discussed below.

Derivative rate bonds with this type of derivative rate formula are often called embedded cap bonds because the interest rate on the bond is economically equivalent to the return an investor would receive if it purchased a fixed interest rate bond and an interest rate cap with the same rate terms as the CVR and SR in the derivative rate formula.

The derivative rate formula affects the bondholder's return in the same manner as a cap because if the referenced variable rate in the formula moves above the strike rate, the amount of interest payable on the bonds increases. The formula includes an interest rate cap-like component because the bondholder can ultimately receive more than the fixed interest

EXHIBIT 2-10

Differences Between Embedded Swap Bond and Acquisition of Swap

- Interest rate on embedded swap bond is subject to limits on maximum rate
- Holder of embedded swap bond does not make ongoing payments to issuer
- Rate formula of embedded swap bond may provide for a minimum rate

rate included in the derivative rate formula, which is the economic equivalent of receiving payments from the provider of a cap (if the bondholder had purchased a fixed-rate bond and a separate interest rate cap with terms comparable to those for the derivative rate bond). However, as with the embedded swap bond, the amount of interest payable on an embedded cap bond will not truly resemble a fixed-rate bond and a separate interest rate cap because the maximum amount of interest payable will likely be subject to various state or local law limits.

Turbo Rate Formulas

The interest rates payable on the primary products just discussed are affected by changes in interest rates (determined by reference to the particular variable rate referenced in the interest rate formula for the bond). Recently, derivative rate bonds have included turbo or multiplier adjustments in the supplemental component of the derivative rate formula.[12] The turbo is typically 2 or 3, and the amount of interest determined under the supplemental component of the rate formula is multiplied by this factor. The inclusion of a turbo factor in the rate formula may significantly increase the volatility of interest rate changes produced by relatively minor changes in the variable interest rate referenced in the bond's interest rate formula. Exhibit 2-12 illustrates the impact of changes in interest rates on an embedded cap bond that includes a turbo factor.

The potentially dramatic effect that turbo factors have on derivative rate bond interest rates raises some fundamental concerns. The issuer's ability to meet its obligations to pay interest may be affected because the potential amount of interest payable on a bond with a turbo may be significantly higher than projected at the time of bond issuance. The turbo factor obviously exaggerates the effect of changes in the interest rate climate on

EXHIBIT 2-11

Embedded Cap Bonds

INTEREST RATE FORMULA

The essential ingredient of an embedded cap bond is the interest rate formula that effectively replicates a fixed rate plus a cap.

The key components of such a rate formula are:

- Interest paid = FR + [turbo (FLR - BR)]
- FR = long-term fixed interest rate on the bonds
- Turbo = multiplier
- FLR = floating rate that investor is trying to hedge
- BR = base rate

payments of interest on a derivative rate bond. Also, because of the potential magnitude of interest payments, the turbo factor may raise concerns whether amounts designated as interest as a matter of state law qualify as tax-exempt interest for federal income tax purposes. State or local law ceilings on permissible interest rates may also pose concerns, some of which are discussed in Chapter 5.

Detachable Call Bonds

Detachable call bonds are another type of tax-exempt bond structure that is considered a primary market tax-exempt derivative. Over two billion dollars of these securities were issued as a part of larger tax-exempt bond issues in 1992.[13]

During the first part of 1993, significant media attention was focused on whether and under what circumstances the detachable call right might potentially affect the tax-exempt status of the related bonds.[14] The tax issues relating to these securities are discussed in Chapter 5.

Tax-exempt bonds (including many plain vanilla tax-exempt bonds) often provide the governmental issuer or conduit borrower with the right to call the bonds after a specified number of years, often a minimum of ten years from the date of issue, at a price equal to their par amount, plus accrued interest and a gradually decreasing premium. The issuer's call rights permit it to retire bonds that have been outstanding ten years or

EXHIBIT 2-12

Turbo Factors

FORMULA:

Interest Rate =
Base Rate + [Turbo (Floating Rate – Fixed Rate)]

ASSUMPTIONS:

Floating Rate = 9.2%

Base Rate = 8%

Fixed Rate = 8%

SCENARIO 1 – TURBO = 0

Interest Rate = Base Rate = 8%

SCENARIO 2 – TURBO = 2

Interest Rate = 8% + [2 x (9.2% – 8%)] = 10.4%

SCENARIO 3 – TURBO = 3

Interest Rate = 8% + [3 x (9.2% – 8%)] = 11.6%

SCENARIO 4 – TURBO = 4

Interest Rate = 8% + [4 x (9.2% – 8%)] = 12.8%

more (or whenever the call rights permit). This right is obviously advantageous to the issuer in a falling interest rate environment. In 1992 and 1993, for example, many tax-exempt bonds issued in the early 1980s at relatively high interest rates were called[15] as issuers refinanced their debt at 1992's and 1993's lower rates.[16]

An issuer's typical call rights have had noticeable consequences for both issuers and investors. From an issuer's perspective, because the market generally required that an issuer's call rights could not be exercised until ten years after the bonds were issued, an issuer's ability to obtain interest rate savings due to any decreases in market interest rates after the bonds were issued but before the ten-year call date were constrained.

Basically, an issuer could obtain interest rate savings only by "advance refunding" the bonds (i.e., issuing bonds to fund an escrow account that was invested and then used to retire the refunded bonds on a future call date). Certain restrictions on advance refundings exist. First, private activity bonds issued for the benefit of conduit borrowers (except 501(c)(3) bonds) generally cannot be advance refunded.[17] This restriction on advance refundings prevents many conduit borrowers from accessing market rate savings before the call date. Second, tax-exempt bonds that can be advance refunded (such as governmental bonds and 501(c)(3) bonds) can only be advance refunded once.[18] Thus, a governmental issuer must determine, as of a particular point in time, that the then-available interest rate savings justify the issuance of advance refunding bonds. Later increases in potential interest rate savings due to further reductions in current market interest rates are lost since the bonds have already been advance refunded. Finally, in order for a governmental issuer to obtain rate savings through an advance refunding, it must incur the issuance costs of the advance refunding issue. These costs deter some transactions.[19]

In addition to issuer constraints on accessing interest rate savings occurring before the call date, the creation of detachable call bonds was motivated by investor concerns about the impact of an early call on their investment portfolio yield. These concerns were exacerbated by the redemption in 1992 and 1993 of a significant number of tax-exempt bonds.[20] In light of the potential effects of call rights on issuers and investors, it was believed that market makers and market risk takers desired to acquire the issuer's call rights for later sale at a profit.

A detachable call bond, in its simplest form, permits the early redemption or "call" of a tax-exempt bond once it has been outstanding for a set period (typically ten years), similar to that of a typical municipal bond except that the decision to exercise the call right can be transferred ("detached") by the governmental issuer to a third party. Whoever holds the detachable call right controls whether the bond will be called (i.e., the governmental issuer does not retain the right to independently exercise the call). Whether a particular governmental issuer has the power to issue detachable call rights under applicable municipal law must be considered.

There are three basic ways in which detachable call rights could be sold. First, an issuer of outstanding tax-exempt bonds could, after obtaining the necessary consents and amendments, convert its call right on an outstanding issue of tax-exempt bonds into a detachable call right. This type of transaction, which involves changes to the original terms of a bond issue already outstanding, raises tax-exempt bond "reissuance" concerns.

Second, newly issued tax-exempt bonds could be structured with terms that permit the issuer to transfer its call rights to a third party at a later date. An issuer's right to detach its call rights is generally subject to the receipt of an opinion of bond counsel at the time that the transfer of the call rights is permitted under municipal law and the transfer will not adversely affect the tax-exempt status of the bonds. Presumably, the issuer's power to issue detachable call rights under applicable municipal law would have been taken into consideration at the time the bonds were originally issued.

Third, newly issued tax-exempt bonds could be structured to provide for detachable call rights relating to the bonds that are freely transferable to third parties and, in fact, are sold to third parties at the time the bonds are issued.

Secondary Derivative Products

The term "secondary derivative products" refers to custodial receipts, trust certificates, or other securities that are not directly issued by a governmental issuer and must therefore derive their tax-exempt status from one or more tax-exempt bonds (which we will refer to as "related tax-exempt bonds") that must be included as an integral component of the derivatives. All secondary products require some type of device such as a custodial account or trust to hold the related tax-exempt bonds and to issue the custodial receipts or trust certificates to investors as evidence of their beneficial ownership.

Before we describe these products, a word of caution is in order: the various types of secondary products are often easily confused because their names and features are similar. Moreover, sponsors of various secondary products generally describe them by reference to features that almost all (if not all) secondary products share. In addition, some sponsors of secondary products refer to certain of their products as a type of bond, when in fact they represent an indirect interest in the related bond(s). Thus, without reviewing the specifics of a particular product, one might assume that certain products that are really secondary derivative products are plain vanilla tax-exempt bonds or primary products.

The general discussion of secondary products that follows focuses on certain key product characteristics. Whenever one considers a particular tax-exempt derivative, it is important to understand these characteristics.

Tender Option Certificates

The key characteristic of a tender option certificate (sometimes referred to as a tender option bond) is that the holder of such a certificate has the right to "tender" or "put" its certificate at a predetermined price (typically par plus accrued interest at an agreed rate) on various dates, provided that certain procedural notice requirements are met. This type of secondary product involves a related tax-exempt bond that is held pursuant to either a custodial arrangement or a trust. An investor holds a certificate or custodial receipt evidencing its ownership interest in the related bond. The investor also holds the associated tender right or put option, either as an integral part of the trust certificate or custodial receipt or pursuant to a separate agreement. The investor is entitled to receive its share of distributions of principal and interest on the related bonds, after taking into account any fees associated with the trust or custodial account (and any fees associated

EXHIBIT 2-13

Tender Option Certificates/Synthetic Floating-Rate Securities

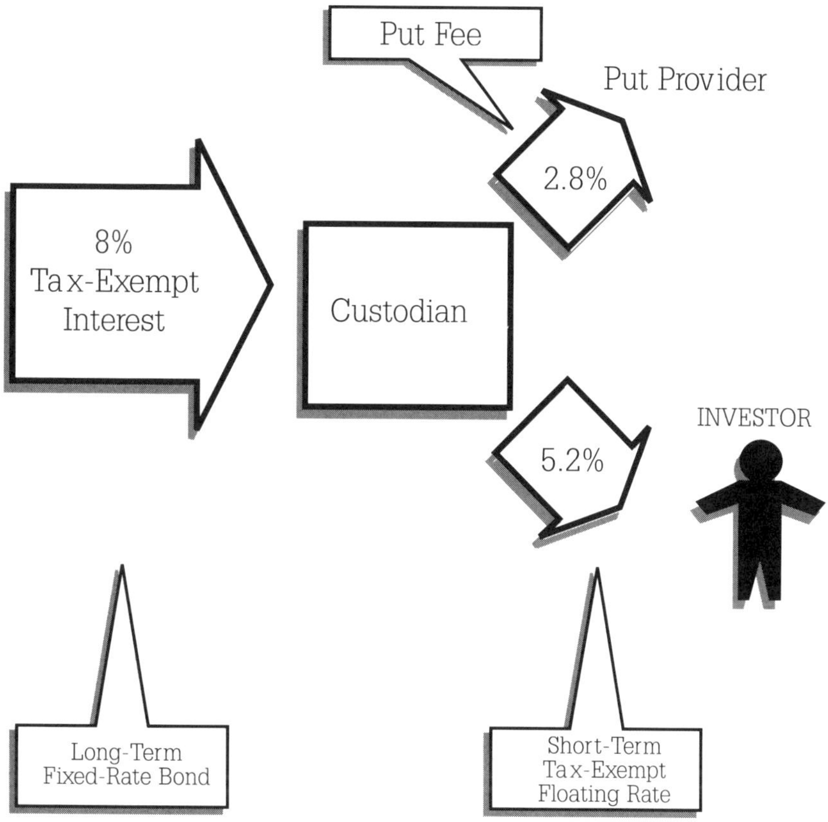

with the tender right). Exhibit 2-13 illustrates the basic characteristics of tender option certificates.

The investor's tender right (which could also be viewed as a put option) is described as *conditional* because it cannot be exercised on or after the occurrence of certain specified events. These events, which vary from product to product, are sometimes referred to as "put fall-aways" because the investor's ability to exercise its tender right automatically terminates (falls away) upon their occurrence. Examples of fall-aways include a determination of taxability of the related bonds, the failure of the issuer of the related bond (or, in the case of credit-enhanced bonds, the failure of a bond insurer or other type of credit enhancer) to pay principal or interest on time, and the bankruptcy or insolvency of the issuer of the related bond (or the bond insurer or other type of credit enhancer in the case of credit enhanced bonds). The conditional nature of the tender right and the nature of the put fall-aways are a result of federal income tax concerns raised by put options (discussed in a later chapter), as well as business-related credit concerns of the parties.

Because of the conditional nature of the tender right (and the nature of certain of the put fall-aways), its principal purpose is to provide investors with liquidity, rather than to protect them against default risk associated with the related tax-exempt bond. Accordingly, this type of tender right is referred to as a "liquidity put."

Even though the put is conditional, it has two important effects. First, it can be used to effectively convert a long-term tax-exempt bond with a remaining maturity of more than 397 days into a money market fund eligible security. Second, because of the liquidity put, investors are willing to accept a short-term, current market floating tax-exempt rate tied to the length of the period before the tender right can be exercised (i.e., daily, weekly, monthly, semiannually, etc.). The difference between the rate of interest paid on the related bond and the short-term floating tax-exempt rate that an investor will accept with respect to a tender option derivative may be used to pay fees (including fees to the provider of the liquidity put) or can be distributed to others. In the case of a trust certificate with an interest rate swap (which is a separate derivative product type), the rate differential is paid to a swap counterparty.

Even though the investor holds either a trust certificate or custodial receipt evidencing its ownership interest in the related bond, certain types of tender option derivatives are structured to qualify as partnerships for federal income tax purposes.

Tender Option Swap Derivatives

One type of tender option derivative is structured with the use of interest rate swaps. Like a common tender option derivative, this type of secondary product also involves a related tax-exempt bond that is held pursuant to either a custodial arrangement or a trust. An investor holds a certificate or custodial receipt evidencing its ownership interest in the related bond. The investor also holds the associated tender right or put option, either pursuant to a separate agreement or as an integral part of the trust certificate or custodial receipt. The investor is entitled to receive its share of distributions of principal and interest on the related bonds after taking into account any fees associated with the trust or custodial account (and any fees associated with the tender right).

The distinguishing feature of a tender option swap derivative is that the trustee or custodian enters into an interest rate swap agreement on behalf of the trust or custodial account at the time the trust or custodial account is created. A market maker in interest rate swaps (typically a bank or investment bank) will act as the swap counterparty. The trust or custodial account will be the fixed-rate payor on the swap; the counterparty will be the floating-rate payor. The fixed rate on the swap will equal the interest rate on the related tax-exempt bonds. The referenced floating rate in the swap agreement will equal or approximate the short-term floating rate the investors expect to receive in light of the liquidity put, subject to an adjustment that takes into account the expenses of the trust or custodial account.

Accordingly, in a tender option swap derivative the rate differential, net of expenses, will be paid to the swap counterparty. The rate differential will ordinarily result in payments from the trust or custodial account to the swap counterparty unless the referenced floating rate exceeds the interest rate on the related tax-exempt bonds, in which case payments will be made from the swap counterparty to the trust or custodial account. As discussed in Chapter 5 on federal income tax considerations, payments received by the trust or custodial account from the swap counterparty will not constitute tax-exempt income.

Moreover, because the referenced fixed rate is typically higher than the market fixed rate, the terms of the interest rate swap in a tender option swap derivative will ordinarily result in the receipt of an "adjustment fee" or "off-market swap premium" by the trust or custodial account from the swap counterparty. This fee or premium is used in conjunction with funds received from investors to fund the acquisition of the related bonds by the trust or custodial account. The adjustment fee or off-market swap premium raises taxable income and amortization concerns that are discussed in Chapter 5.

Except for the receipt of any adjustment fee by the trust or custodial account and the ongoing distribution or receipt of payments under the swap agreement, the structure economically resembles the basic tender option derivative. This is illustrated by the diagram set forth in Exhibit 2-14 (which for ease of illustration ignores the up-front fee).

Stripped Tax-Exempt Bonds and Coupons

A stripped bond or coupon represents an interest in a particular payment of interest or principal on a debt instrument. It does not represent a right to receive a proportionate interest in all of the then-remaining payments of principal and interest (and any other payments such as call premiums or contingent payments) on the debt instrument.[21] This definition has its historical roots in a time when bearer bonds were issued with interest payment coupons attached. Investors could simply "clip" and sell one or more of these interest coupons while the bond itself could either be sold or retained. Exhibit 2-15 illustrates this basic model.

However, many stripped bonds and coupons vary significantly from this simplistic, prototypical strip. One type, the single payment strip, represents the right to receive a single payment (resembling a zero coupon bond). Another, the multiple payment strip, represents the right to receive a number of payments. Depending on how a multiple payment strip is structured, it may be acquired at a discount or it may resemble a current interest-bearing debt instrument ("synthetic current pay strip")

EXHIBIT 2-14

Products with Swaps

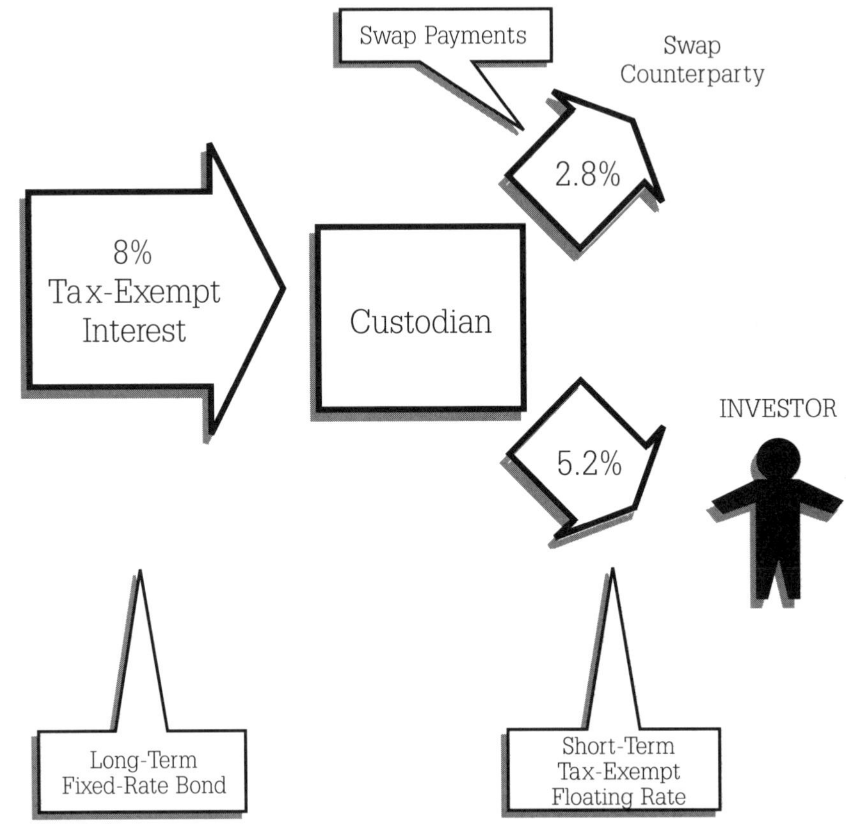

Many debt instruments provide for interest payments at a floating interest rate. The floating rate may be subject to a minimum rate or floor as well as a maximum rate or ceiling. Some debt instruments provide for contingent payments in certain cases. For example, a commercial mortgage loan may provide for an additional interest payment (or payments) based on a percentage of gross revenues or proceeds received from the sale of the real estate securing the mortgage loan. In addition, many debt instruments (both fixed- and floating-rate debt) are subject to early retirement ("call risk") under various circumstances. If a debt instrument is retired early, the issuer would not be obligated to make interest payments arising after the date the bond is called ("post-call coupons"), and a call premium may be paid in connection with the early retirement.

Floating interest rates, contingent payments, and the impact of call risk on an investor's receipt of post-call coupons and call premiums create

EXHIBIT 2-15

Stripped Bonds

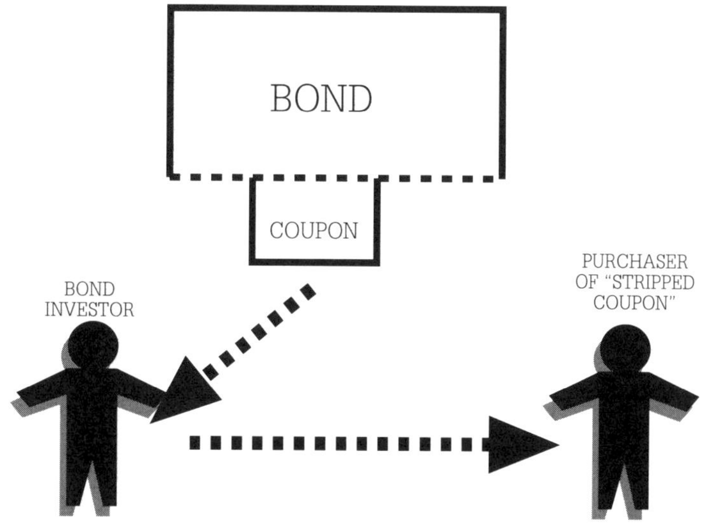

potential variations in the amount and timing of receipts of cash on a debt instrument. These variations create issues in the structuring of stripped bonds and coupons. Which investor holding an interest in a stripped bond or coupon will bear the risk if less interest is received on the underlying debt instrument, and who will benefit if additional interest, contingent payments, or premiums are received? As a result of these potential issues, unless a debt instrument is a fixed interest rate, noncallable or pre-called security, the structuring of stripped bonds and coupons should carefully account for all potential payment variations on the underlying debt instrument.

In addition, without regard to the payment characteristics and risks of the underlying debt instrument, a potential purchaser of a stripped bond or coupon may desire certain features. For example, an investor may desire a synthetic current pay strip that provides for current payments based on a floating interest rate or index, even if the underlying debt instrument is a fixed interest rate security. Conversely, an investor may desire a synthetic current pay strip that provides for current payments based on a fixed interest rate, even if the underlying debt instrument is a floating interest rate security. Both of these strips may be properly described as "variable strips," since the amount payable does not bear a constant, fixed relationship to the payment characteristics of the underlying debt instrument. Certain types of variable strips can be described as "squeezable strips" if the amount payable thereon *ordinarily* bears a constant, fixed relationship with the payment characteristics of the underlying debt instrument but the amount payable can be reduced by changes in certain variables (for example, if the floating interest rate on a debt instrument approaches a rate ceiling or if certain expenses are incurred).

Moreover, the right to receive payments of interest or principal on a debt instrument may not necessarily be labeled as a stripped bond or coupon. Federal income tax law may treat something as a strip even if it is described as something else. For example, servicing fees paid in various trust structures may be treated as stripped coupons to the extent that they exceed a reasonable fee for services rendered. This issue is discussed in more detail in Chapter 5.

Exhibit 2-16 lists the types of stripped bonds and coupons described above.

In addition to the evolution in the types of stripped bonds and coupons, the manner in which stripped bonds and coupons are created has changed. Today, the underlying bond is typically transferred to a trust or custodial account, and certificates are issued that represent the different types of stripped bond and coupon interests created with respect to the underlying debt instrument held by the trust or custodial account.

Pools of Tax-Exempt Obligations

Although many secondary products are based on a single tax-exempt bond (or bonds of the same maturity from the same issue of bonds), some secondary products are pooled products representing an interest in a pool of a number of tax-exempt bonds of diverse issuers. This type of product is created by transferring a number of tax-exempt bonds to a trust or custodial account and issuing certificates representing a beneficial interest in the pool. Various types of tax-exempt derivatives can be structured as pooled products. For example, a tender option derivative can be based on a pool of bonds rather than a single bond. Stripped bonds and coupons can be structured from a pool of bonds. Another type of secondary product is known as a "straight pass-through" certificate. In this type of product, diagrammed in Exhibit 2-17, an investor's certificate represents an interest in a pool of bonds. Payments of interest and principal on the bonds are passed through to the investor after receipt by the trust that has issued the certificate. Unlike tender option derivatives and stripped bonds and coupons, the basic economic characteristics of the underlying bonds held in the pool are simply aggregated and reflected in the terms of the investor's certificate.

A number of mechanical issues arise in structuring a pooled product because of the differing terms and risks associated with each of the bonds in the pool. For example, if a bond having an average maturity longer than the weighted average maturity of the bonds in the pool is prepaid at an earlier than anticipated date, this will affect the pool's remaining weighted average maturity. Similarly, if a bond with a higher-than-average interest rate is prepaid at an earlier than anticipated date, this will obviously affect the weighted average pass-through interest rate from the pool that can be paid to investors. These examples illustrate only a few of the complexities

EXHIBIT 2-16

Types of Strips

- Single payment strips
- Multiple payment strips
- Synthetic current pay strips
- Variable strips
- Squeezable strips
- Excess servicing strips

EXHIBIT 2-17

Straight Pass-Through Pooled Product

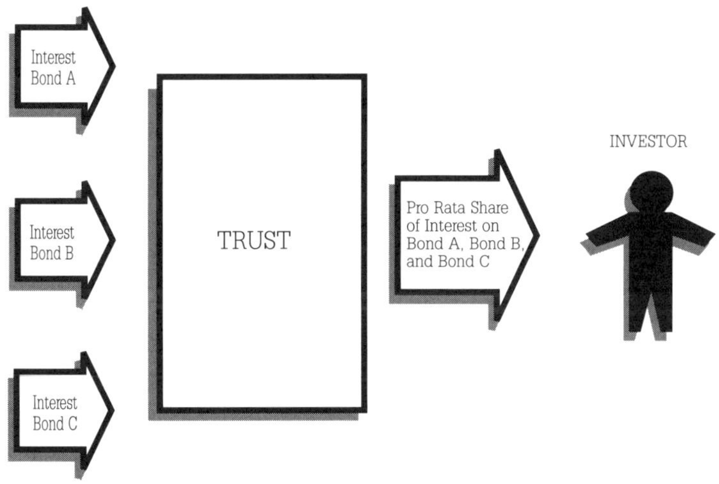

that arise when a number of tax-exempt bonds are structured and sold as part of a single pool.

The pooling of tax-exempt bonds permits an investor to achieve diversification of credit risk because an investor's certificate in a pooled product will, in general, take into account the varying credit risks of all the bonds in the pool. The blending of bond credit risk that a pooled product presents is an important aspect of this type of product. Moreover, if the pool is properly structured, letters of credit, bond insurance, and other credit enhancement techniques can be used to further enhance the credit quality of the product.

Other Types of Custodial Receipts

The types of secondary products described above demonstrate how characteristics of a tax-exempt bond can be indirectly modified. Trusts and custodial accounts and the certificates and receipts evidencing ownership interests therein can be used for many purposes. For example, a bond and a letter of credit or bond insurance policy could be deposited into a trust as a means of enhancing the credit of the bond, which may create marketing advantages for the bond seller. As indicated at the outset, almost all secondary products rely on a trust or custodial account to accomplish their objectives. Given this common feature, it is important to carefully review and understand the operation and objectives of a particular secondary product, rather than simply to focus on its name or product label.

Notes

1. Under Section 148(f)(4)(D)(ii)(I) of the Code, there is aggregation of the issuer and an entity that issues bonds on behalf of the issuer under the small-issuer exception to the arbitrage rebate rules.

2. ISDA was formed in 1984 and its office is located in New York City.

3. While the rate-setting process typically occurs every 28 days, interest on bonds is typically payable semiannually.

4. This is the intent of the penalty rate rather than its legal obligation or effect.

5. *See, e.g.*, Steven Dickson, *Tucson Electric Converts Variable Rates to Fixed, Ending Dismal Auctions,* THE BOND BUYER, Dec. 13, 1991, at 4; Steven Dickson, *Tucson Electric Enjoys Second Auction Success but Hopes to Eliminate Process in December,* THE BOND BUYER, Nov. 14, 1991, at 1; Steven Dickson, *Tucson Dutch Auction Finally Succeeds, Driving Dow Rate, Following 16 Failures,* THE BOND BUYER, Oct. 11, 1991, at 2; Steven Dickson, *Triple-A Rating and 12.6% Yield Still Cannot Lure Tucson Investors,* THE BOND BUYER, Sept. 12, 1991, at 1.

6. The J. J. Kenny Index is calculated weekly by J. J. Kenny Co., Inc., based on the yield of tax-exempt securities that are repriced every seven days. The PSA Municipal Swap Index was introduced by the Public Securities Association and is a seven-day index based on actual weekly resets, composed of tax-exempt variable-rate issues of $10 million or more.

7. *E.g.*, indexed INFLOS, Cap RITES, Short RITES.

8. *See, e.g.*, Kathie O'Donnell, *$2 Billion Ontario Offering Is on Deck After Last Week's New-Issue Stampede,* THE BOND BUYER, Jan. 11, 1993, at 3 (in one week, 28% of the new issuance came in the 30-year and longer maturities).

9. *Id.* (10 years is typically the favored maturity for recent corporate issuances).

10. *See* William Chew, *Interest Rate Swaps for Municipal Issuers,* STANDARD & POOR'S CREDITWEEK, Dec. 1990, at 1, 3 (swaps do not generally run more than 8 to 10 years); Steven Dickson, *Swaps and Inverse Floaters Offer Insurers Easy Niche in Growing Derivatives Market,* THE BOND BUYER, Mar. 30, 1992, at 2A (noting that although traditional swaps extend only about 5 to 7 years into the life of the underlying bond deal, several deals have been executed with longer maturities to cover the entire life of the issue, but

that swap insurance is generally required for maturities of over ten years).

11. *See supra* note 9.

12. Inverse floating-rate bonds could also be structured with turbo factors.

13. *See* Aaron Pressman, *Tax Law Could Be Menace to Tax Exemption of Detachable Calls, Treasury Official Says,* THE BOND BUYER, Jan. 27, 1993, at 1.

14. *See, e.g., id;* Lynn Stevens Hume, *Rules on Arbitrage, Reissuance May Be Altered to Address Call Option Bonds,* THE BOND BUYER, Feb. 9, 1993, at 1; Constance Mitchell, *Latest Muni Derivative Gets U.S. Scrutiny,* WALL ST. J., Feb. 11, 1993, at C1; Aaron Pressman, *Detachable Call Options Become Focus of Treasury Meeting, Marketing Concerns,* THE BOND BUYER, Feb. 4, 1993, at 1.

15. *See, e.g.,* Tom Herman, *Coping with January's Barrage of Bond Calls,* WALL ST. J., Dec. 24, 1992, at A13.

16. Assuming that the called bonds were not advance refunded, in which case the old bonds were refinanced at the rate of the advance refunding bonds, based upon when the advance refunding bonds were issued.

17. IRC § 149(d)(2).

18. IRC § 149(d)(3)(A).

19. *See generally* Jonathan Fuerbringer, *Municipal Bond Issuers Are Learning to "Detach,"* N.Y. TIMES, Dec. 21, 1992, at C5; Dennis Walters, *Detachable Call Options Provide Issuers with a New Twist on Bond Refinancing,* THE BOND BUYER, Dec. 14, 1992, at 2A.

20. *See supra* note 16.

21. In the case of a loan participation, an investor acquires a pro rata interest in all of the principal and interest due on the loan. In contrast, in the case of a strip, the ownership of the right to receive principal is separated from the ownership of the right to receive payments of interest (the coupon).

CHAPTER 3

How Tax-Exempt Derivatives Are Used

Steven D. Conlon
Vincent M. Aquilino

This chapter describes how tax-exempt derivative products are used and discusses some of their advantages and disadvantages. The first section discusses the uses and benefits of interest rate swaps, caps, floors, and similar contracts. The latter part of this chapter discusses the uses and benefits of specific tax-exempt derivatives.

The Uses and Benefits of Swaps, Caps, Floors, and Forwards

Interest rate swaps and related derivative products currently make up a multitrillion-dollar market whose development is perhaps most directly attributable to the use of derivative products as hedging devices in the management of interest rate risks. As substitutes for direct portfolio and liability transactions, derivatives may be less expensive and more responsive asset and liability management tools.

Interest rate swaps, caps, floors, and related products may be used in hedging strategies in the management of an entity's liabilities or investments. For example, an organization that finds it beneficial to issue floating-rate debt can purchase a cap to manage its exposure to rising interest rates. Similarly, if the entity holds floating interest rate investments but needs assurance that its investment portfolio will generate a specified cash flow, it can purchase a floor to ensure that downward interest rate movements do not adversely impact its ability to generate cash. In hedging its assets or liabilities, an organization may enter into a swap, cap, or floor that provides for payments tied to a floating-rate index (for example, LIBOR, commonly used as the floating-rate index in the swap market) that differs from the floating rate the organization is attempting to hedge (for example, the Kenny rate for tax-exempt securities). The interest rate risk measured by the exposure to the difference between the swap, cap, or floor variable-rate index and the floating-rate index the organization is attempting to hedge is referred to as "basis risk." Basis risk also exists if the indexed rate (such as the applicable Kenny rate) does not accurately track the party's rate on its floating-rate asset or liability (such as the rate on a particular floating-rate tax-exempt bond).

Alternatively, in exchange for an up-front fee, an organization can take a more active "trader"-type role (versus hedging) and obligate itself to make payments on caps and floors. The moneys generated from fees earned in providing such products can then be invested.

Many organizations actively use swaps, caps, and floors as part of an investment program in conjunction with the strategies employed to control the risks associated with asset and liability positions. They enter into swaps, caps, and floors and other transactions from time to time to change or re-establish positions previously dismantled through prior liquidations of their swaps, caps, and other derivative contracts.

An ever-present risk in using derivatives as hedging vehicles or as part of a trading strategy is the risk that the counterparty will fail to fulfill its payment obligations. Counterparty credit risk, which is inherent in derivative products, is not present in plain vanilla tax-exempt bond issuances. Thus, consider the investor presented with the option of either issuing a fixed-rate bond at an interest rate of 7 percent or entering into a two-part transaction comprised of issuing a floating-rate bond bearing an interest rate based on the PSA Municipal Swap Index and entering into a floating to fixed interest rate swap that effectively converts the issuer's floating-rate liability to a fixed interest rate obligation of 6.9 percent. (See Exhibit 3-1.) In this example, if the counterparty to the swap fails to perform, the governmental issuer remains obligated to pay interest at the floating PSA Municipal Swap Index rate. If rates have risen, the issuer could be obligated to pay a rate significantly in excess of 7 percent.

In structuring a derivative product, counterparty credit risk is addressed by evaluating the credit quality of the counterparty before entering into the swap or cap. Recently, a number of Wall Street investment banking firms have created highly capitalized subsidiaries in order to obtain high credit ratings, thereby avoiding firm credit risk that could constrain their swap-writing business.[1] Similarly, bond insurers have recently begun to insure counterparty credit risk in municipal swap transactions.

Another advantage of interest rate swaps and similar types of derivative products is that generally speaking they can be terminated—either directly, subject to a termination payment (which, depending upon interest rates at termination, may either be paid or received by the terminating party), or indirectly, by entering into an offsetting contract. This flexibility permits management of potential future losses under a swap or cap and also generally permits a person to immediately realize any embedded gain in its swap or cap position, rather than deferring realization. Many tax-exempt bonds cannot be redeemed until ten years after the date they are issued. The ability to terminate or enter into offsetting swaps, caps, floors, and other derivatives generally provides greater flexibility to the issuer than the ten-year call rights prohibition typically found in a tax-exempt bond.

EXHIBIT 3-1

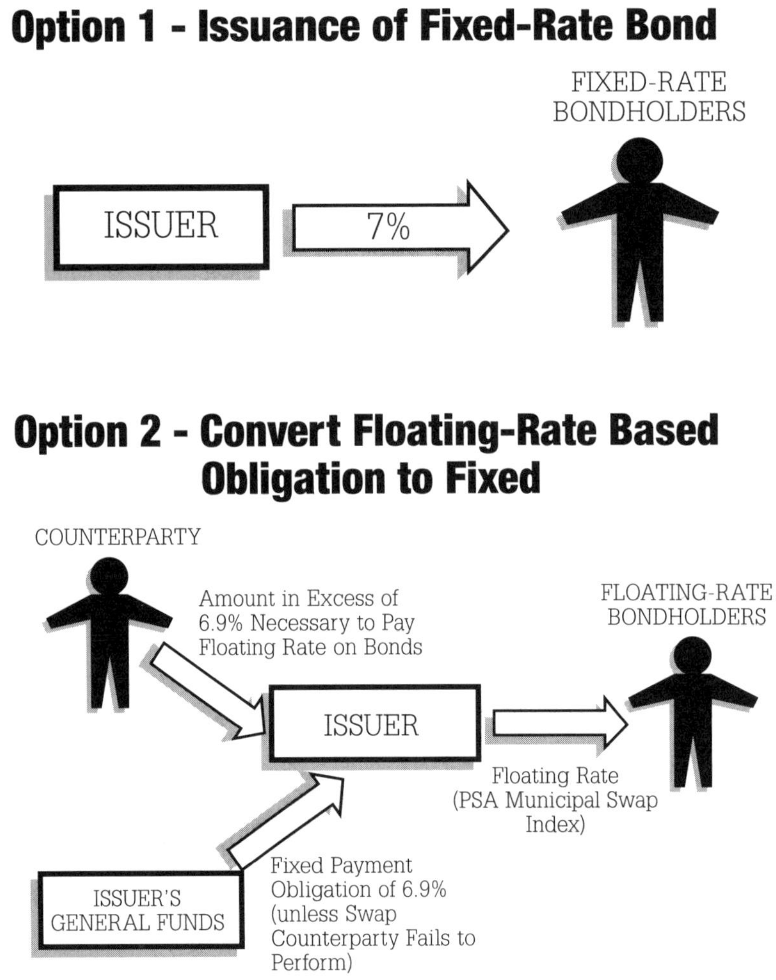

Interest Rate Swaps

Interest rate swaps can be used to convert a governmental issuer's or conduit borrower's floating- or fixed-rate liability on a bond issue. The costs of entering into an interest rate swap to effectively make this conversion may be less than the cost of refunding the obligation. In the example discussed above and illustrated in Exhibit 3-1, the issuer has essentially converted a PSA Municipal Swap Index-based floating-rate obligation to a fixed-rate obligation. Depending upon the interrelationships of the derivative products and bond markets, a governmental issuer or conduit borrower may find that it can obtain a net lower fixed interest rate through issuing a floating-rate obligation and swapping to a fixed rate than through issuing fixed-rate debt. Conversely, a governmental issuer or conduit borrower that has issued fixed-rate debt but desires to convert its obligation to a floating rate in the belief that the floating rates will be lower can enter into a fixed to floating swap to achieve similar debt service savings. (See Exhibit 3-2.)

Interest Rate Caps

A governmental issuer or conduit borrower can purchase an interest rate cap to hedge its risks in connection with the issuance of floating-rate bonds. For example, assume that an issuer has issued floating-rate bonds based on the Kenny municipal bond index and has also purchased an interest rate cap with a strike rate of 6 percent. The governmental issuer would purchase a cap in order to eliminate the risk that the floating rate will rise above the interest rate cap strike rate. If the Kenny index-based floating-rate bonds rise above 6 percent, the issuer would receive payments under the cap. Thus, the interest rate cap protects the issuer from market rate risks should the Kenny index exceed 6 percent. (See Exhibit 3-3.)

Unlike the purchaser of an interest rate swap, the purchaser of a cap is not typically obligated to make ongoing payments. The issuer benefits from downward movements in its payment obligation on the bonds and is pro-

EXHIBIT 3-2

Conversion of Fixed to Floating

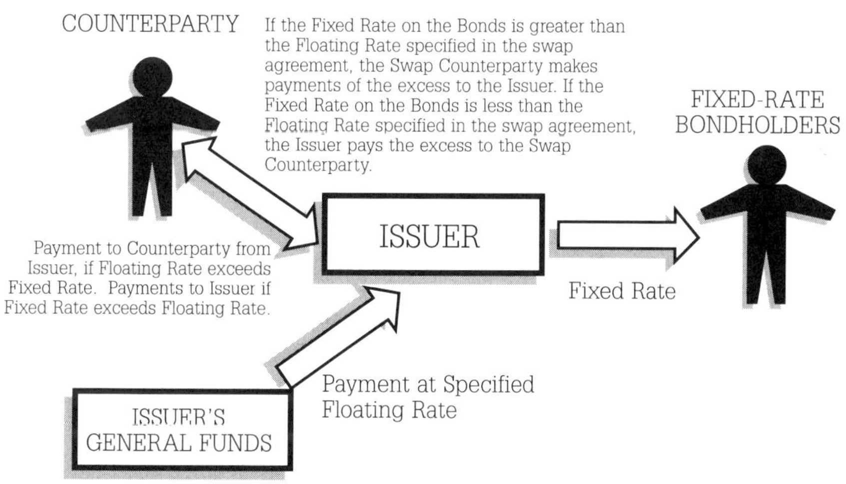

EXHIBIT 3-3

Interest Rate Caps

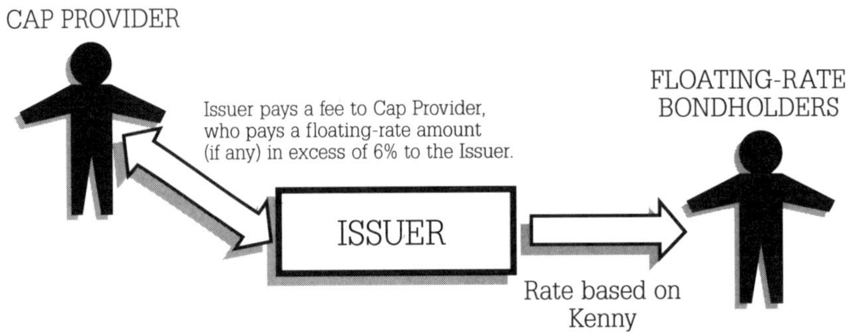

tected by the cap from upward movements in interest rates once market rates exceed the strike rate. Similarly, the cap provider is obligated to make payments only if the indexed rate exceeds the strike rate. However, a governmental issuer must typically pay a premium to the cap provider at the time the contract is executed.

A governmental issuer or conduit borrower can also "write" an interest rate cap agreeing to make payments if the indexed rate exceeds the strike rate. An issuer may be willing to take the rate risk inherent in agreeing to make payments on an interest rate cap because it will receive the up-front fee for assuming this risk. Ignoring arbitrage concerns discussed in Chapter 5, the up-front fee could be invested and, depending upon the movements in the indexed rate relative to the strike rate and the yield the issuer earns on investing the up-front fee, writing an interest rate cap may prove to be either profitable or costly. As previously indicated, it must be concluded that the governmental issuer has the power under applicable municipal law to write an interest rate cap contract.

Interest Rate Floors

In an interest rate floor, if the indexed rate falls *below* the strike rate, the purchaser of the interest rate floor *receives* payments equal to the difference between the strike rate and the current indexed rate. An interest rate floor ensures the purchaser that its return will not decline below the strike rate.

Consider an issuer that has acquired floating-rate investments. Assume that the issuer uses earnings from these funds to pay certain specified expenses and operating costs and that it has determined that it must earn 5 percent on its investments in order to meet these obligations. If current rates on the floating-rate investments fall below 5 percent, the issuer will be unable to satisfy its costs and expenses from investment earnings. By purchasing an interest rate floor with a strike rate of 5 percent, the issuer is assured that it will meet its goal, since earnings below 5 percent on the floating-rate investments will be supplemented by payments from the counterparty to the issuer under the floor contract. (See Exhibit 3-4.)

A governmental issuer or conduit borrower can also write an interest rate floor for an up-front lump-sum fee for undertaking the inherent interest rate risk. One key difference between writing an interest rate floor and writing an interest rate cap is that the writer's absolute risk on a floor is limited to the strike rate, since the most the writer would ever pay would occur if the indexed rate used in the floor contract approached zero. As with interest rate caps, a governmental issuer's power to enter into a floor contract under municipal law must be considered.

Interest Rate Collars

An interest rate collar is a combination of a cap and a floor. A purchaser of a collar *receives* amounts if the indexed rate rises above the strike rate on the cap and *makes* payments if the indexed rate falls below the strike rate on the floor. Because the purchaser is obligated to make payments if the strike rate falls below the floor, it has effectively written the floor component of the interest rate collar. Typically, instead of receiving an up-front

EXHIBIT 3-4

Interest Rate Floors

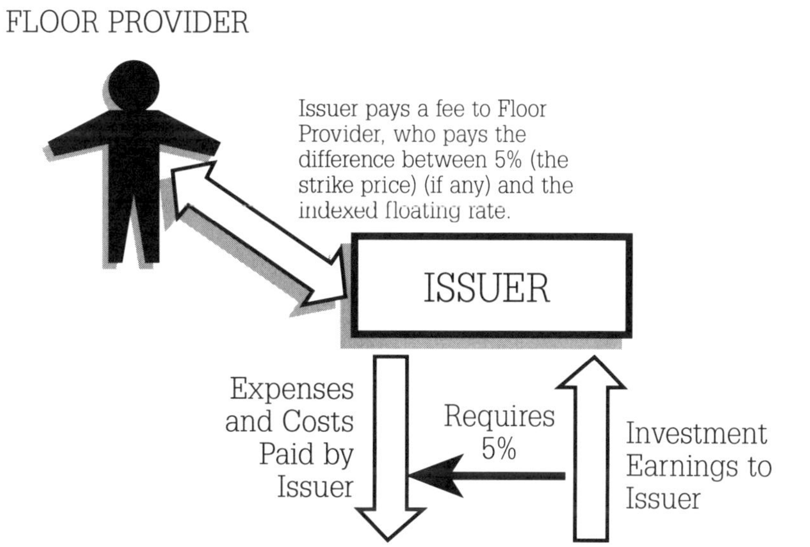

fee, the risk borne by the purchaser on the floor component of the contract is effectively used to offset a portion of the cost of the cap component of the collar.

For example, assume that an issuer has floating-rate debt outstanding and is concerned about its potential payment obligation on the debt if the indexed rate exceeds 9 percent. The issuer purchases an interest rate collar with a strike rate on the cap of 9 percent and a strike rate on the floor of 6 percent. This cap and floor purchase will protect the issuer from movements in the indexed rate above 9 percent because if current market rates exceed 9 percent it will receive payments under the collar contract that it can use to offset its higher liability on its floating-rate debt; if the indexed rate falls below 6 percent, it will be required to make payments under the collar contract. Accordingly, if the indexed rate falls below 6 percent, it will effectively continue to pay 6 percent on its liabilities because, although its payment obligation on its floating-rate debt will be less than 6 percent, its payment obligation on the interest rate collar, when added to its obligation on the debt, will equal 6 percent. (See Exhibit 3-5.)

Although the issuer does not receive the benefit of lower financing costs when the indexed rate falls below the floor rate of the collar, an issuer may prefer a collar because the up-front fee (if any) that might be paid to the counterparty on the collar contract will be less than the fee payable on an interest rate cap with a comparable strike rate, and the issuer may not be troubled by the potential minimum payment obligation triggered by the floor component of the collar.

Swaptions and Forward Swaps

An issuer may wish to enter into "swaptions" or "forward swaps." A swaption provides the purchaser with the *option* (but not the obligation) to enter into a swap at a future date. A forward swap *requires* that the parties enter into a swap at a future date (alternatively, it could be viewed as a swap where payments begin at a future date). These types of contracts may be beneficial to the person wishing to lock in (either the right or the obligation to enter into) an interest rate hedge for some future period. These contracts may be used to achieve interest rate savings for bonds that cannot currently be advance refunded.

Commodity Forwards

A commodity forward contract that protects the purchaser from changes in the price of the commodity is a contract under which the purchaser promises to purchase a specified quantity of some commodity, such as diesel fuel, on a specified date at an agreed price (typically, the contract will provide for a cash payment made based on the difference in price rather than physical delivery of the commodity). A governmental issuer or conduit borrower may find commodity forward contracts advantageous if, for example, it is concerned about rising diesel fuel prices for its transportation system.

EXHIBIT 3-5

Interest Rate Collars

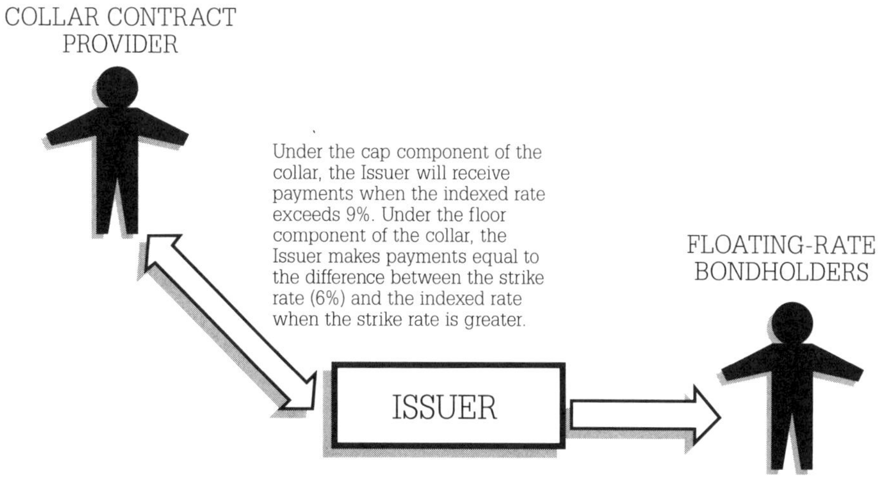

If indexed rate is 12%, the Issuer will receive 3%.
If indexed rate is 4%, the Issuer will pay 2%.

The Uses and Benefits of Specific Primary Tax-Exempt Derivatives

Floater/Inverse Floater Combinations

Inverse floating-rate bonds, with their high yield potential in a falling interest rate environment, provide investors with highly desirable investment features.[2] A governmental issuer or conduit borrower issuing bonds that include a floater/inverse floater combination may obtain financing costs lower than those for fixed-rate bonds.

Dutch Auction Rate Bonds

Dutch auction rate bonds use a specified auction process on a recurring basis to set the interest rate on the bonds. The auction process, which is highly mechanical, could be viewed as more objective than the process by which a remarketing agent determines the appropriate interest rate for a bond, since the remarketing agent's determination is based on its judgment of the market. For this reason governmental issuers and conduit borrowers may believe that the auction process is likely to establish a lower interest rate than one determined by a remarketing agent.

In addition, the auction process serves as a substitute for the tender right associated with many variable-rate demand bonds. However, because the holder of an auction rate bond is not provided with an unconditional tender right, the issuer does not have to pay the costs typically associated with obtaining a liquidity facility, such as a letter of credit, to support an obligation to purchase the bonds.

There are potential detriments associated with the auction process that should be considered. First, because the auction process is mechanical in nature, there is the possibility that the auction will "fail," leaving an issuer with the obligation to pay an above-market penalty rate until a successful remarketing takes place. Second, the auction process does not provide a holder with the unconditional right to tender its bonds for purchase. If the auction fails, the holder may be unable to dispose of the bond. As a result, an auction rate bond may be less liquid than a typical variable-rate demand bond. It is also possible that a failed auction will increase investor concerns about liquidity, thus adversely affecting the ongoing interest rate payable on the bonds (compared with that for a similar variable-rate demand bond).

Since the holder of an auction rate bond does not have the unconditional right to tender its bond, an auction rate bond will not typically constitute an "eligible investment" for a money market fund under Rule 2a-7 of the Investment Company Act of 1940.

Derivative Rate Bonds

Derivative rate bonds provide for interest payments based on formulas tied to interest rate indices such as Kenny or the PSA Municipal Swap Index that include a fixed-rate and supplemental-rate component economically resembling an interest rate swap or cap. Derivative rate bonds benefit investors principally because the interest payments on the instrument include a swap or cap component that the investor can use to hedge other investments.

An investor could obtain the basic economic benefits offered by a derivative rate bond by directly investing in a conventional fixed-rate or floating-rate bond and entering into an interest rate swap or cap. However, this option may not be available to certain investors, such as those who may be subject to investment restrictions that prohibit them from entering into such contracts. A derivative rate bond may provide a means for avoiding such restrictions.

In addition, if an investor entered into an interest rate swap or cap contract directly, income recognized under the contract would be taxable, not tax-exempt. However, payments on a properly structured derivative rate bond would be *interest* and could, therefore, qualify as tax-exempt for federal income tax purposes.

The potential benefits to investors inherent in a derivative rate bond may also afford issuers a lower financing rate. The debt service on a derivative rate bond issue (taking into account any hedge that an issuer may enter into in connection with a derivative rate bond) may be less than the debt service that the issuer would have incurred on a comparable fixed interest rate bond issue.

If the formula-based floating interest rate for the bond moves adversely to the issuer, this could result in unacceptable interest payments. Moreover, investor concerns regarding the rate formula used in a derivative rate bond could make it difficult for an existing holder to sell the bond at an acceptable price, raising concerns about liquidity. As indicated in the preceding chapter, some derivative rate bonds permit the holder to request an early conversion to address these concerns. Such an election will prevent future changes in interest rates from having an adverse effect on an investor, but will not necessarily fully protect the investor from adverse economic consequences. For example, the fixed rate established under the terms of the bond as a result of the early conversion may be less than the comparable market fixed rate.

Embedded Swap Bonds

An embedded swap bond offers investors and issuers many of the benefits described above. An embedded swap bond includes an interest rate component resembling an interest rate swap. This component can reduce the interest payable to an investor below the fixed rate (FR) specified in the rate formula for the bond. Because the investor is subject to the risk of reduced interest rates in certain interest rate environments, the investor may demand a higher floating interest rate than would otherwise be payable on a comparable embedded cap bond.

Embedded Cap Bonds

As described in the general discussion on derivative rate bonds, embedded cap bonds offer benefits to investors and issuers. Unlike the interest rate payable on an embedded swap bond, the interest rate payable on an embedded cap bond will not fall below the fixed rate specified in the bond's rate formula. The interest rate payable on the bond will in all likelihood take into account the "cost" of the embedded cap to the investor.

Turbo Rate Formulas

Some derivative rate bonds use a rate formula that includes a so-called turbo adjustment as a supplemental component. Derivative rate bonds with this feature provide that the supplemental component of the rate formula is multiplied by a factor called the turbo. The inclusion of a turbo factor in the rate formula for a bond increases the magnitude or volatility of changes in the interest rate payable on the bond that are produced by changes in the variable rate referenced in the bond's rate formula.

This rate volatility permits the embedded swap or cap component of the interest rate formula to have an effect equivalent to that of an interest rate swap or cap based on a notional principal amount greater than the principal amount of the bond. For example, consider an embedded swap bond with a

EXHIBIT 3-6

"Turbo" Rate Formulas

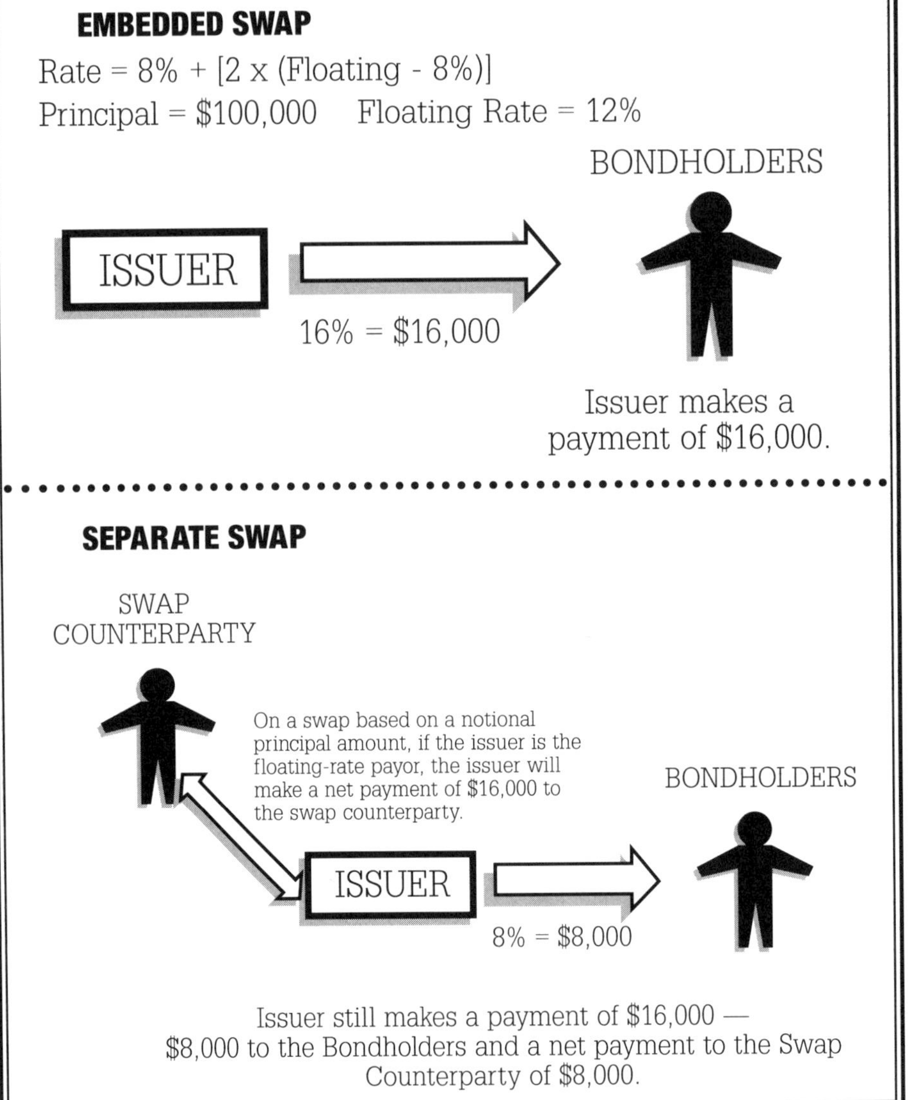

stated principal amount of $100,000 and a turbo factor of 2. The portion of the interest rate component of this bond that resembles an interest rate swap will be equivalent to an interest rate swap based on a notional principal amount of $200,000. This is illustrated in Exhibit 3-6.

An investor considering the purchase of a derivative rate bond as a hedging vehicle might find a turbo factor desirable because it enhances the hedging effect of the bond, making a large bond principal purchase unnecessary. Consider an investor desiring to hedge a $200,000 portfolio with either a non-turbo derivative rate bond or a derivative rate bond with a turbo factor of 2. If the investor acquires the derivative rate bond without a turbo factor, it will need to purchase $200,000 of the derivative rate bond to hedge its $200,000 portfolio, but if the investor acquires the derivative rate bond with a turbo factor of 2, a bond with a $100,000 principal amount will achieve the equivalent hedge.

Of course, the turbo factor also increases the volatility of the investment as interest rates change. The issuer would be subject to similar risks on its obligation on the bonds, although it may enter into hedging transactions to minimize or eliminate interest rate risk.

Detachable Call Bonds

Detachable call bonds enable the issuer to sell or "detach" the call rights associated with a particular tax-exempt bond. The issuer may sell the call rights either at the time the bond is issued or at a later date. Either way, detachable call rights give an issuer a means of obtaining immediate economic gain from the call rights—a critical benefit, of course, to a municipality that needs to raise cash. Detachable call rights may provide an issuer with a means of obtaining the financial benefits associated with reductions in market interest rates that have occurred since its bonds were issued but before the date the bonds can be called. The later sale of detachable call rights by an issuer may prove less costly than an advance refunding of the outstanding bonds.

In addition to the federal income tax concerns discussed in Chapter 5, an issuer should consider that the sale of its call rights locks in the value it will receive for favorable changes in interest rates. Once the call rights have been sold, an issuer may be required to keep outstanding tax-exempt bonds for a significantly longer period than it otherwise would, given changes in market interest rates.

For example, consider an issuer that issues a fixed-rate bond subject to a call on any date beginning after the bond has been outstanding for at least ten years. Assume that the bond documents fully permit the issuer's call right to be detached and sold to a third party. Four years after the bonds are issued, current market rates for fixed-rate bonds comparable to the issuer's detachable call bond are lower than the rate on the detachable call bond. As a result, assume that the call right has a value of $2 million and the issuer sells the call at that time. A year later, assuming that current rates have fallen even more, so that the issuer's call right is worth $2.5 million, the $500,000 increase in value is realized by the current holder of the call, not the issuer, since the issuer has already sold its call right.

A governmental issuer must consider whether it has the power under applicable municipal law to sell its call right (i.e., whether the purchaser of the call rights has rights that are valid and enforceable).

The Uses and Benefits of Specific Secondary Market Tax-Exempt Derivatives

Tender Option Certificates

Tender option certificates resemble short-term tax-exempt debt and provide investors with an additional source of supply for short-term tax-exempt paper. This may be important as a result of several basic market considerations, including, perhaps most importantly, the fact that the demand side of the short-term tax-exempt market has increased over the past fifteen years. This phenomenon is primarily due to the dramatic increase over that period in the number of institutional investors such as tax-exempt money market funds in need of short-term investments because of securities laws requirements.

During the same period, federal tax law changes have restricted the issuance of certain types of tax-exempt bonds, commonly referred to as "industrial development bonds" (IDBs) or "private activity bonds," that are issued for the benefit of conduit borrowers such as large corporations. These tax law changes have restricted market entry by those types of conduit borrowers most likely to issue variable-rate demand obligations. Although the development of the municipal swap market may ultimately alter this environment, many of the more traditional municipal bond market participants (such as governmental issuers) have typically preferred to issue fixed-rate bonds.

In addition, because long-term tax-exempt interest rates have trended downward during the recent past, many governmental issuers and conduit borrowers in the tax-exempt market have opted to issue fixed-rate debt in order to take advantage of these historically favorable rates, further reducing the supply of short-term tax-exempt obligations.

It is fair to say that these factors have contributed significantly to the low supply and high demand for the short-term tax-exempt paper market. Tender option certificates have helped fulfill investors' appetite for these instruments. The certificates offer investors a means of dealing with the supply shortfall of more traditional short-term tax-exempt paper, such as tax anticipation notes and variable-rate demand bonds.

Tender option certificates permit an investor to obtain a "synthetic" product that is a substitute for the scarce "natural" short-term tax-exempt bonds and serve to assist the investor in addressing credit quality concerns. Credit enhancement that addresses default risk can be embedded in the tender option structure to obtain a higher credit rating of the "long" bond characteristics of the derivative product. Some tender option structures employ two types of enhancement devices. One device, the default risk enhancement, will provide coverage if the issuer of the underlying bond fails to timely pay principal or interest on the bonds. The other device, the liquidity enhancement, will provide the investor with certainty that the tender option provider's conditional put-right obligation will be satisfied.

Since default risk enhancement can be embedded in a tender option derivative structure, long-term fixed-rate bonds that might not otherwise satisfy the investor's credit quality standards can be converted into eligible investments. This general statement, of course, ignores the potential costs or availability of credit enhancement.

Although tender option certificates can serve as a useful alternative source of supply for investors seeking high-quality, short-term tax-exempt securities, there are inherent risks to be considered, the most critical of which is the conditional nature of an investor's right to tender these securities. Chapter 5 provides a detailed discussion of the federal income tax rules that effectively prevent secondary market products from including unconditional tender rights. Accordingly, the tender right associated with a secondary market tender option certificate is *conditional* and subject to immediate termination, *without the right of exercise,* if certain specified events occur.

For example, many tender option certificates provide that the associated tender right is subject to immediate termination if the underlying bond fails to qualify as tax-exempt or if the governmental issuer or conduit borrower (or, in the case of a structure employing default risk enhancement, the credit enhancer covering such risk) fails to timely pay principal or interest on the underlying bond. Likewise, if the governmental issuer or conduit borrower (or default risk credit enhancer, if applicable) files for bankruptcy or is declared bankrupt, or the credit rating on the underlying bond (taking into account any default risk enhancement, if applicable) is lowered to below investment grade, the associated tender right will terminate.

Obviously, because an investor's right to tender is lost if any of the specified events occurs, an investor must consider the possible risk of loss and its ability to continually assess and monitor the likelihood that these events could occur. In particular, money market funds, because of special securities laws rules, must take special care that they have appropriately assessed these risks. Recently, a fund adviser and one of its portfolio managers were subjected to Securities and Exchange Commission sanctions for failing to properly account for the conditional nature of the tender rights granted in connection with secondary market tender option certificates.[3]

The federal income tax law and SEC concerns of mutual funds that invest in conditional tender right derivative products have special importance for investors considering the acquisition of tender option certificates.

Tender Option Swap Derivatives

While tender option swap derivatives have the same basic benefits and risks as tender option certificates, because they employ interest rate swaps, additional factors need to be considered. Interest rate swaps raise both swap counterparty credit risk and taxable income risk. Payments to an investor under an interest rate swap (including indirect payments that an investor is deemed to have received through a secondary market derivative) produce taxable income. Moreover, any adjustment fee or premium received by the trust must be amortized and, depending upon the amount of other payments made on the swap, may also result in taxable income to an investor. These concerns are addressed in more detail in Chapter 5.

Stripped Tax-Exempt Bonds and Coupons

Stripped tax-exempt bonds and coupons may also serve as substitutes for certain types of tax-exempt bonds. For example, the right to a specified interest coupon, payable at a specified date, is the economic equivalent of a zero coupon bond. Stripping a tax-exempt bond permits the transformation of a current interest-bearing obligation into a series of zero coupon bonds. This ability to create the economic equivalent of zero coupon tax-exempt bonds is particularly beneficial in those states that do not permit the issuance of zero coupon debt.

In addition, setting aside securities laws constraints, various specified portions of stripped principal and interest payments can be spliced together to create synthetic current interest-bearing securities. Stripped tax-exempt bonds could be assembled so that the synthetic securities created from the bond may more effectively satisfy market demand for securities with particular characteristics.

Both securities laws and federal income tax laws place limits on the flexibility of structuring stripped bonds and coupons. For example, unless the stripped bond or coupon resembles the denomination and amount of the underlying bond in a prescribed manner, the stripped security may be treated as a separate security, distinct from the underlying bond for securities laws purposes. As a result, the stripped security may not be eligible for the same securities laws registration exemption as the underlying tax-exempt bond.

Similarly, federal income tax law requires that stripped bonds and coupons represent specified portions of the payments on the underlying tax-exempt bond that are determined and fixed as of the time the stripped security is created. Tax practitioners often describe stripping arrangements that do not satisfy this fixed obligation requirement as "variable strips." A structure that resulted in the creation of variable strips, unless structured to qualify as a partnership for federal income tax purposes, raises concerns that it would not be classified as a "pass-through entity." Such a structure could jeopardize the treatment of amounts paid to investors holding the variable stripped interests as tax-exempt income.

Pools of Tax-Exempt Obligations

Some secondary market custodial receipts or trust certificates represent interests in tax-exempt pools of obligations including tax-exempt leases and industrial development bonds.

Structures that involve pools of tax-exempt lease receivables are similar to asset securitization transactions involving receivables that generate taxable income, such as auto loan receivables trusts and equipment lease receivables trusts. These types of transactions benefit the originator or receivables seller principally by providing an efficient mechanism for obtaining long-term receivables financing.

Many tax-exempt leases are entered into in connection with the financing of relatively small-ticket items with a lease-by-lease cost of not more than $100,000 to $200,000. The securitization of small leases through pooling and issuing certificates of participation enables investors to make economically viable tax-exempt lease investments while focusing on the overall integrity of the pool rather than individual leases.

An institutional investor owning a portfolio of tax-exempt bonds might sell them as a pool to avoid "cherrypicking" by potential purchasers of the higher credit quality bonds, leaving those of lower quality to the seller. As a result of tax law changes affecting the tax benefits of owning tax-exempt bonds (i.e., changes to the alternative minimum tax in 1986 and restrictions on interest expense deductions triggered by the acquisition of tax-exempt bonds), many banks have disposed of their tax-exempt bond portfolios through pooled tax-exempt derivative structures. The disposition of tax-exempt leases or bonds through pooled structures permits the seller to reposition its portfolio, including the investment in or origination of additional tax-exempt obligations.

An inherent benefit of the pooling of tax-exempt leases or bonds is the diversification of credit risk. Depending upon the diversity of the pooled leases or bonds, the pool structure may serve to minimize the potential risk that a payment default will occur with respect to *all* of the bonds or leases in the pool. Although a portion of the payments generated by the pool of leases or bonds will be affected if *any* of the tax-exempt obligations in the pool defaults, this risk may be manageable as a percentage of the overall pool. This risk can either be assumed by the investor or credit enhancement can be acquired to insulate the investor's portfolio risk. Credit enhancement may be economically feasible because the pool's credit risk (on an aggregate basis) can be quantified.

Other Types of Custodial Receipts

Investors must undertake a careful economic and legal analysis of the structure of the trust or custodial arrangement to which the custodial receipt relates with particular emphasis on the potential risks and benefits associated with particular products.

One type of custodial receipt structure involves the attachment of bond insurance or other credit enhancement in which the custodian or trustee holds the underlying bond and insurance policy, letter of credit, or other form of credit enhancement. The custodial receipt evidences the rights associated with both the bond and the credit enhancement device and permits the custodian or trustee to intercept payments received on the underlying bond to pay credit enhancement fees. This product provides a credit enhancer with assurance that ongoing credit enhancement fees will be fully satisfied.

Notes

1. *See* Yvette D. Kantrow, *Continental, Citi Scrap Plans to Form Swaps Units; Citibank, Continental Got Cool Response from OCC,* AM. BANKER, Dec. 17, 1992, at 1; Aaron Pressman, *Salomon Brothers Inc. Creates Derivatives Unit; Merrill Plans Upgrade,* THE BOND BUYER, Feb. 10, 1993, at 1; Michael Siconolfi, *GE Keeps Kidder from Forming Derivatives Unit,* WALL ST. J., Feb. 12, 1993, at C1.

2. Inverse floaters offer investors comparatively higher yields, although with greater risks associated with rising short-term interest rates. *See* Thomas T. Vogel, Jr., & Robert McGough, *Muni Funds Sink or Swim with "Inverse Floaters,"* WALL ST. J., Mar. 16, 1993, at C1.

3. Investment Management Co. and Harrop, Investment Company Act of 1940 Release No. 19,224 (Jan. 22, 1993). *See infra* Chapter 6 for a discussion of securities law considerations.

CHAPTER 4

An Overview of the Legal Issues Relating to Tax-Exempt Derivatives

Steven D. Conlon
Vincent M. Aquilino

This chapter presents an overview of legal issues and practical matters that should be considered in connection with tax-exempt derivatives. It is intended to put the important issues in perspective rather than to resolve them. Later chapters address key federal income tax and federal securities laws issues and certain municipal law and federal bankruptcy law considerations relevant to tax-exempt derivatives.

Given the different and continually changing types of tax-exempt derivative products in the marketplace, it is not the goal of this chapter to provide an exhaustive analysis of all of the legal considerations that may be relevant. Some of the issues discussed here are relevant only to certain derivative products. Because most tax-exempt derivatives are of recent vintage, the governing law is likely to change. Our goal is to provide a starting point for the reader's own review and evaluation of the legal issues regarding these products.

Structural Considerations

Validity and Enforceability

Tax-exempt derivatives are structured to achieve investor and issuer objectives. Fundamentally, tax-exempt derivatives are *investments* of one form or another, or are other types of *financial contracts* that may not be classified as investments (swaps, caps, floors, etc.). Regardless, it is important to determine that the terms of the investment arrangement or financial contract are *valid and enforceable* under applicable state and federal laws.

In the case of secondary market derivatives, this will often be a relatively straightforward matter of analyzing applicable contract law and, possibly, special regulatory laws applicable to banks and others that act as intermediaries. It would not be uncommon for an opinion of counsel to address the enforceability of the trust agreement, custodial account, tender agreement, or related documents that comprise any derivative product, whether primary or secondary.

In the case of primary market derivatives, applicable state and local laws that vary significantly from state to state must be considered as part of this analysis. Typically, the municipal finance markets demand the receipt of a legal opinion by a law firm designated as *bond counsel* that addresses state or local municipal finance law concerns in determining whether a tax-exempt bond is valid and enforceable. This long-standing practice has its roots in the reaction of the financial markets to the repudiation by certain governmental issuers of their obligations on bonds issued during the late 1800s, which freed the issuing municipalities from the obligation to pay investors in accordance with the terms of the bonds as issued.[1]

In light of this market practice, bond counsel will typically be expected to deliver the same type of validity opinion for derivative rate bonds, inverse floaters, dutch auction rate bonds, and other primary products that is routinely rendered in more common municipal financing transactions where governmental issuers directly participate. Whether the distinguishing features of primary market derivative products raise special validity and enforceability concerns will depend upon the product specifics and applicable state and local law.

Interest rate swaps, caps, floors, and other types of notional principal contracts that are used in the municipal markets involve a governmental issuer or conduit borrower and a swap counterparty, which is typically a bank. These contracts are new, are not "bonds," and do not directly involve the municipal finance markets. Accordingly, the municipal markets have not developed standard practices to address the validity and enforceability issues raised by these contracts.

Chapter 7 discusses the municipal law issues raised by swaps, floors, caps, and similar notional principal contracts when governmental issuers participate in these contracts. A number of concerns discussed therein are raised under municipal law, including potential concerns regarding the validity of these contracts in light of the 1991 decision by the House of Lords in the *Hammersmith* case, which held that swaps entered into by several boroughs of London were unenforceable because the municipalities did not have the power to enter into such contracts under municipal law.[2] The International Swaps and Derivatives Association (ISDA, formerly the International Swap Dealers Association), on behalf of various market participants, has developed model legislation giving governmental issuers the power to enter into notional principal contracts in order to protect banks and other swap dealers that enter into these contracts.[3]

Conduit borrowers should not typically be subject to the special municipal law considerations applicable to governmental issuers. Accordingly, the determination of whether a conduit borrower's obligations under a notional principal contract are valid and enforceable against it should be a relatively straightforward process involving the analysis of corporate or other laws governing the applicable conduit borrower, as well as its organizational documents and proceedings conducted in connection with its participation in the contract.

Regardless of whether a governmental issuer or conduit borrower enters into a swap, cap, floor, or similar type of notional principal contract as part of a tax-exempt financing, it may be prudent to obtain separate legal opinions that the contract is valid and enforceable with respect to *both* the governmental issuer or conduit borrower and the bank or swap dealer acting as counterparty on the contract.

Timing of Payments

Secondary market tax-exempt derivatives, because they involve both an underlying tax-exempt bond and a custodial arrangement or trust (and possibly credit enhancement of one form or another), raise issues regarding the timing of payments. The practical or mechanical issue is one of analyzing when payments will be received by the trust or custodian on the related bonds and when payments are expected to be made to investors. This issue arises so frequently that it merits attention particularly if any delays between the receipt of funds and payments to the investor are present. There are potential economic consequences of failing to invest such funds, as well as potential taxable income issues that arise if such funds are invested in a manner that generates taxable income.

Issues also arise with respect to primary derivative products. Since cash flow timing issues are an inherent aspect of any tax-exempt financing, however, it is assumed that the parties will place at least the same level of emphasis on these concerns in the case of primary derivative products as they generally do with a tax-exempt financing.

Notional principal contracts permit a great deal of "customization" by the parties regarding the timing of payments. The parties should consider the extent to which the timing of swap, cap, floor, or similar notional principal contract payments satisfies the needs of the participating governmental issuer or conduit borrower. If the swap or similar contract is used in connection with a tax-exempt financing, this issue may merit special attention.

Book Entry or Physical Certificates

Many securities are sold in so-called book entry form, under which ownership of a particular security is determined by a notation made in a master ownership record rather than through the delivery of a certificate in physical form to the investor. In structuring a derivative product, it should be considered whether the features of the particular derivative can be properly accounted for under the ownership record system that the parties intend to use.

Credit Enhancement, Liquidity Mechanisms, and Credit Ratings

Credit Enhancement

As is often the case with financial products, parties may be concerned about the credit risk associated with a governmental issuer's or conduit borrower's payment obligations on a primary market tax-exempt derivative product or, in connection with a secondary market product, the related tax-exempt bond. This credit analysis will take into account the nature of the financing and the source and extent of revenues and security for the bonds and will differ depending upon whether, for example, the bonds are limited source obligations issued to finance a particular project or are general obligation bonds of the governmental issuer. Credit risk of this nature, because it may affect the marketability or viability of the derivative product, is often addressed through credit enhancement devices of one sort or another (a bank-issued letter of credit, a third-party payment guarantee, or a bond insurance policy, for example).

The use of credit enhancement devices in connection with a tax-exempt derivative, whether it is a primary market product, a swap or other form of notional principal contract, or a secondary market product, raises additional legal issues that should be considered.

Credit enhancement devices must be evaluated with regard to whether such arrangements (1) are generally valid and enforceable, (2) provide for payments in amounts and at times that are consistent with the investor's expectations, (3) adequately insulate the investor from relevant credit risks associated with the governmental issuer or conduit borrower, and (4) may be adversely affected by federal bankruptcy laws or other special federal regulatory laws. Because credit enhancement devices are regularly used in a variety of financings, the relevant legal issues should have generally been addressed in other contexts.[4]

Liquidity Devices

As discussed in earlier chapters, certain secondary market tax-exempt derivative products employ liquidity devices to address investor concerns, including federal securities regulatory concerns of money market funds that invest in tax-exempt securities and their ability to timely dispose of a particular investment. In addition to their associated credit risks, liquidity devices raise three basic types of legal issues:

1. Do they "work" as intended?
2. Do they cause the tax-exempt derivative to qualify as a money market fund eligible investment under applicable federal securities laws?
3. Do they create risks that distributions on the derivative will constitute taxable rather than tax-exempt income to the investor?

With regard to whether liquidity devices work as intended, most of the same issues regarding credit enhancement should be considered. The impact of liquidity devices on whether a tax-exempt derivative is an eligible investment for a money market fund under applicable federal securities regulations is discussed in Chapter 6. Taxable income risks associated with liquidity devices are addressed in Chapter 5.

Credit Ratings

Many financial products obtain a credit rating provided by one or more national rating organizations. In connection with the delivery of a credit rating that takes into account a credit enhancement device, a rating agency will consider various credit-related and legal risks associated with the particular credit enhancement device. Regardless of the scope of the rating agency's review of various risks and its rating criteria, parties should carefully consider the limited function of credit ratings and the various express and implied limitations associated with the credit rating on a particular financial product.

In providing credit ratings for various types of tax-exempt derivative products, the rating agencies have developed specific criteria and limitations on their ratings for these products.[5] These guidelines may be important to the parties in the development and evaluation of a particular tax-exempt derivative product.

Tax Considerations

Overview

The important tax issues relating to tax-exempt derivatives vary significantly with the type of tax-exempt derivative. The key tax issues for primary market tax-exempt derivatives are very different from those for secondary market products. In addition, certain issues arise only in the case of specific types of tax-exempt derivatives (such as secondary market products that employ liquidity devices) and certain types of investors (such as banks or mutual funds that are subject to their own special tax rules). The relevant tax issues for various types of tax-exempt derivative products are discussed in detail in Chapter 5.

However, there are certain basic issues that should be considered regardless of the type of tax-exempt derivative—even though some of the issues may be easier to resolve for some types than for others.

Tax-Exempt "Interest" Paid on a "Bond"

Only *interest* paid on *indebtedness* issued by a *governmental issuer* qualifies as tax-exempt for federal income tax purposes, and only if a number of special federal income tax rules applicable to tax-exempt bonds are satisfied. Because secondary market products are structured by market intermediaries rather than governmental issuers, a related tax-exempt bond issued by a governmental issuer must be part of the product structure in order for the product to deliver tax-exempt interest. This issue is discussed in more detail in the section of Chapter 5 on secondary market tax-exempt derivatives.

In addition, because the governmental issuer's obligation must constitute *debt* for federal income tax purposes, payments by a governmental issuer on a swap or other notional principal contract do not qualify as tax-exempt even though they may economically resemble interest payments. This issue is discussed in more detail in the section of Chapter 5 dealing with primary market derivative products.

Finally, because only payments of interest can qualify as tax-exempt, the interest rate formulas of derivative rate bonds, embedded swap and cap bonds, and inverse floaters must be analyzed to determine whether amounts paid pursuant to such formulas qualify as interest for federal income tax purposes. This issue is discussed in more detail in the section of Chapter 5 dealing with primary market derivative products.

Arbitrage and Arbitrage Rebate Compliance Issues

One of the important sets of special federal income tax rules that must be satisfied in order for an obligation to qualify as a tax-exempt bond is the arbitrage and arbitrage rebate rules. In many cases these rules prohibit a governmental issuer or conduit borrower from investing bond proceeds and certain other investments related to tax-exempt bonds at an investment yield in excess of the yield (or interest cost) that the governmental issuer or conduit borrower effectively pays on the bonds ("bond yield") or require the governmental issuer or conduit borrower to *rebate* to the U.S. Treasury any earnings on such investments in excess of bond yield. The governmental issuer or conduit borrower typically promises to comply with these requirements in connection with the issuance of the bonds.

Primary market products such as derivative rate bonds, inverse floating-rate bonds, dutch auction rate bonds, and other variable-rate debt instruments require special consideration in determining the bond yield for arbitrage and arbitrage rebate purposes of the bond issue of which such bonds are a part. It must be determined whether and to what extent interest rate swaps, caps, floors, and similar types of notional principal contracts that are part of a tax-exempt financing must be taken into account in determining whether the related tax-exempt bonds satisfy applicable arbitrage and arbitrage rebate requirements. The arbitrage and arbitrage rebate issues relating to derivative rate bonds, inverse floating-rate bonds, dutch auction rate bonds, and detachable call bonds and the impact of interest rate swaps and similar types of notional principal contracts are discussed in more detail in the section of Chapter 5 dealing with primary market derivative products.

Reissuance

When the terms of a bond are materially changed, for federal income tax purposes the bond is treated as if it were retired and replaced by a newly issued bond (or "reissued"). If a bond is reissued, the determination of whether it qualifies as tax-exempt will be based on applicable federal income tax law as of the date it is reissued. If governing federal income tax law has changed since the original issuance date of the bond and the bond does not satisfy the provisions of law that apply as of the date it is reissued, interest payments on the bond subsequent to the date of reissuance will not qualify as tax-exempt.

It must be considered whether various types of changes in interest rates and other terms that occur with respect to primary market derivative products cause a reissuance that would require a determination that the bond remains tax-exempt.

Secondary market derivative products may involve features that are distinguishable from the terms of the underlying tax-exempt bonds that are part of such products. Reissuance concerns are discussed in Chapter 5.

"Double Taxation"

Corporate earnings are often described as subject to "double taxation" because both the corporation and its shareholders (when such earnings are distributed to them as dividends) are subject to federal income tax.

Business and investment arrangements, including trusts in certain cases, may be taxable as corporations for federal income tax purposes, regardless of whether such business or investment activities are conducted by corporations. If such arrangements were taxable as corporations, they could be subject to double taxation under federal income tax law. The imposition of a corporate *layer* of tax could adversely affect investor returns and make the arrangement unattractive to investors.

Derivative products and the arrangements associated with such products may raise concerns regarding whether double taxation could be imposed. This issue is discussed in the section of Chapter 5 on secondary market derivative products.

State Tax Concerns

Interest on some bonds may be exempt from both federal and state (or local) income taxation. Exemption from state taxation is based on applicable state law. It should be considered whether state tax exemptions apply to tax-exempt derivatives and whether double taxation could be imposed on derivative products by states or localities.

Securities Laws Considerations

Securities Registration

Federal securities laws require the registration of publicly offered securities unless an exemption applies. Securities issued by governmental issuers are generally exempt from registration. However, because secondary market derivative products are typically issued by financial market intermediaries rather than by governmental issuers, it must be determined whether such derivatives are subject to federal securities laws registration. This issue is discussed in Chapter 6.

Investment Company Registration

Federal securities laws require investment companies to register under separate rules and subject investment companies and parties affiliated with such companies to compliance with special rules. Secondary market derivative products and the arrangements associated with such products may raise issues regarding whether an investment company exists that is subject to registration. This issue is also discussed in Chapter 6.

Special Rules on Investments by Mutual Funds

Because mutual funds are investment companies, they are subject to federal securities laws rules that impose certain restrictions on their investment activities. Money market funds are subject to additional securities law restrictions on their investments. These restrictions, which may affect a mutual fund's (or a money market fund's) ability to invest in a tax-exempt derivative, are discussed in Chapter 6.

Bankruptcy and Insolvency Considerations

Overview

In evaluating the credit risks associated with any investment, the investor and, to the extent the investment obtains a credit rating, the rating agency must consider the potential economic and legal consequences of the bankruptcy or insolvency of the governmental issuer, conduit borrower, and any persons that provide credit enhancement or stand behind any liquidity facility. The relevant legal issues and their resolution will in part be affected by the structure of the investment arrangement and the particular facts and the legal relationships of the parties. Applicable law may vary because some types of entities are eligible for relief under federal bankruptcy law while other types of entities are not. For example, banks and insurance companies, which often act as credit enhancers or liquidity providers, are not covered by federal bankruptcy law. Thus, the relevant issues are highly dependent upon a number of factors. Moreover, the determination of the material legal issues and their resolution are likely to be governed by broader doctrines applicable in the bankruptcy and insolvency area. Accordingly, this book does not attempt to generally address these considerations although we recognize their significance.

Special Concerns Regarding Trusts

Secondary market tax-exempt derivative products often employ custodial arrangements or trusts as an integral component. Accordingly, in addition to the more typical bankruptcy and insolvency issues that arise with many forms of investments, secondary market tax-exempt derivative products raise additional concerns. Chapter 8 discusses some of these concerns, including whether trusts employed as a part of a secondary market tax-exempt derivative product can be subject to bankruptcy proceedings that could adversely affect the parties' expectations regarding the timing and amount of payments distributed from such trusts to investors.

Special Concerns Regarding Swaps

As previously discussed, governmental issuers are using interest rate swaps, caps, floors, and similar contracts in managing interest rate risk associated with their investments and their liabilities, including their debt service obligations on tax-exempt bonds. These types of contracts are used to hedge interest rate risk in connection with both primary market and secondary market tax-exempt derivative products. The bankruptcy law considerations relating to swaps and similar contracts are also discussed in Chapter 8.

Notes

1. *See generally* Sylvan G. Feldstein, *Municipal Bond Defaults and Remedies: An Historical Overview,* 4 MUN. FIN. J., 8, 11–12 (Winter 1983).

2. Hazell v. Hammersmith and Fulham London Borough Council and others, [1991] 1 All E.R. 545 (H.L. 1991).

3. Lynn Stevens Hume, *Swap Dealers Group's Model Legislation Would Give Issuers Authority for Swaps,* THE BOND BUYER, Oct. 23, 1991, at 1.

4. *See, e.g.,* Timothy P. Mohan, William J. Fellerhoff & Carol McAlpine, *Injunctions Against Letters of Credit in Chapter 11 Proceedings,* Vol. 24, No. 4, URB. LAW. 1013 (Fall 1992); William J. Fellerhoff & Robert D. Aicher, *Avoidance Powers Available to the FDIC in a Bank Insolvency,* J. BANKR. L. PROC. Nov./Dec. 1991; Robert D. Aicher, *Impact of* Deprizio *on Credit Enhanced Securities and Preference Opinions,* presented at the American Bar Association 1990 Annual Meeting as panelist on The Banking Law Committee Section of Business Law panel on "The Outer Limits of *Deprizio,*" Aug. 7, 1990.

5. *See generally Understanding Custodial Receipts: Inverse Floaters,* MOODY'S PUB. FIN. PERSPECTIVE ON STRUCTURED FIN. (Dec. 1, 1992); *Moody's Rating Criteria for Custodial Receipts,* MOODY'S PUB. FIN. PERSPECTIVE ON STRUCTURED FIN. (Apr. 15, 1991); *Rating Tender Option Bonds,* STANDARD & POOR'S CREDITWEEK 41 (Mar. 30, 1992).

CHAPTER 5

Federal Income Tax Considerations for Tax-Exempt Derivatives

Steven D. Conlon
Vincent M. Aquilino
Suzanne M. Russell

As a fundamental matter, the principal goal of tax-exempt derivatives is the delivery of tax-exempt income to investors.[1] The federal income tax considerations relating to derivative products are therefore of critical importance.

The tax issues relating to derivative products differ for a primary product (i.e., a tax-exempt bond with certain derivative characteristics directly issued by a governmental issuer) and a secondary product (i.e., a custodial receipt or tender option certificate evidencing an interest in an underlying tax-exempt bond). Inherently these products present a number of tax consequences that need to be evaluated. Collateral tax consequences will vary depending upon circumstances, such as the nature and tax position of the investors acquiring the derivative, the nature and tax position of the governmental issuer of or conduit borrower on the tax-exempt bond, the type of tax-exempt derivative, and, in the case of a secondary product, whether the derivative is issued on or near the date the underlying bond is issued.

The first section of this chapter addresses the key issues relating to primary market tax-exempt derivatives; the second discusses the fundamental issues relating to secondary market tax-exempt derivatives; and the third discusses certain collateral issues. The federal income tax treatment of swaps, caps, floors, and similar contracts is discussed in conjunction with the related investor-targeted derivative—i.e., the tax issues relating to swaps used in conjunction with primary derivatives are discussed in the section on primary market tax-exempt derivatives, and the tax issues relating to swaps used in conjunction with secondary derivatives are discussed in the section on secondary market tax-exempt derivatives.

Set forth at the end of this chapter as Exhibit 5-3 is a grid listing various types of tax-exempt derivative structures and identifying the tax issues to consider in analyzing each.

Primary Market Products

Key tax questions to consider in connection with a primary market tax-exempt derivative include the following:

1. Are the payments on the bond tax-exempt interest?
2. What are the arbitrage yield and rebate implications associated with primary market tax-exempt derivatives?
3. What is the treatment of amounts paid or received for bond proceeds expenditure purposes?
4. Do rate mode changes or other events trigger a "reissuance"?

The Definition of "Interest" for Tax Purposes

Only *interest* on a tax-exempt bond is tax-exempt to an investor.[2] So the question of critical import is, what exactly is interest? In its simplest terms, interest is defined for federal income tax purposes as compensation paid for the use or forbearance of money.[3] The interest rate formula can vary from the straightforward fixed rate to the sophisticated complex rate formula based upon varied indices. Complex floating-rate mechanisms are of relatively recent vintage and have received little judicial attention. They must, therefore, be carefully examined to make certain that the formula itself does not cause a recharacterization of the payment as other than interest.[4]

Most of the guidance issued by the Internal Revenue Service (IRS) having any application to the issue of what interest is can be found in the 1986 Proposed Original Issue Discount (OID) Regulations, first issued in 1986 and amended in 1991.[5] Revised Proposed OID Regulations issued in late 1992 replaced much of the 1986 Proposed OID Regulations.[6]

The 1986 Proposed OID Regulations narrowly defined variable-rate interest mechanisms as those based upon an objective interest index. Payments made on a debt instrument that were not based on either a fixed interest rate or an objective interest index were generally treated as "contingent payments."[7]

The 1992 Proposed OID Regulations significantly expanded the definition of variable-rate mechanisms, replacing the objective interest index concept with a broader range of permissible rate modes. As was the case under the 1986 Proposed OID Regulations, payments on a debt instrument that do not fall within these expanded definitions are treated as contingent interest. The potential consequences of classifying interest payments as contingent payments are discussed below.

Under the 1992 Proposed OID Regulations, interest on a variable-rate debt instrument may be based on a "qualified floating rate" or an "objective rate."[8] A qualified floating rate is defined as a rate with respect to which variations can reasonably be expected to measure contemporaneous changes in the cost of newly borrowed funds, such as a rate based on the commercial paper rate or an inflation index.[9] Although certain restrictions (such as an interest rate ceiling or floor) will not preclude a rate from being considered a qualified floating rate, a rate subject to a ceiling or a similar restriction that is very likely to cause the interest rate in at least one accrual period to be less than the overall expected return is not a qualified floating rate.[10] A rate subject to a floor or a similar restriction that is very likely to cause the interest rate in at least one accrual period to be significantly more than the overall expected return on the debt instrument will also not be a qualified floating rate.[11]

An objective rate is defined as a rate (other than a qualified floating rate) based on the price of property that is actively traded, or based on an index of prices of such property, such as a rate based on changes in the price of a commodity index.[12] A rate that is not itself a qualified floating rate but is based on one or more qualified floating rates (such as a multiple of a qualified floating rate) is also an objective rate.[13] However, an objective rate must be determined using a single formula that is fixed throughout the debt instrument's term.[14] As an exception to the definition of an objective rate, the 1992 Proposed OID Regulations provide that an interest rate pertaining to tax-exempt debt does not qualify as an objective rate if the issuer, contemporaneously with the issuance of the debt, enters into one or more financial contracts (other than another debt instrument it has issued, as would be the case if a floater/inverse floater combination were issued) that substantially offset the variations of the stated interest.[15] This exception is discussed later in the section on the 1992 Proposed OID Regulations. Other exceptions include rates subject to caps and floors as described above with respect to qualified floating rates,[16] and rates based on the price of nonfunctional currency of the taxpayer or a qualified business unit.[17]

Dutch Auction Rate Bonds

As described in Chapter 2, dutch auction rate bonds take their name from the mechanism used to establish the interest rate thereon. The IRS issued two notices in 1988 (Notice 88-27, 1988-1 C.B. 496, and Notice 88-90, 1988-2 C.B. 414) holding that payments of interest determined pursuant to a dutch auction procedure or by an independent remarketing agent are not contingent payments.[18] Practitioners viewed these notices as essentially eliminating the concern that payments of interest on a debt instrument based on an auction rate procedure may not qualify as tax-exempt interest.

Inverse Floaters

An inverse floating-rate bond bears an interest rate that moves inversely to a specified floating interest rate. When the specified floating rate declines, the inverse floating rate increases. The interest rate on an inverse floater is capped at a rate that is typically well in excess of prevailing market rates (as of the date the bond is issued). Accordingly, the interest rate on an inverse floater is commonly expressed as the cap rate minus the specified floating rate. Tax-exempt inverse floaters are often issued in tandem with tax-exempt floating-rate bonds, such as dutch auction bonds in floater/inverse floater combinations. Accordingly, the interest rate on such a tax-exempt inverse floater would be expressed as the cap rate minus the current dutch auction rate on the related dutch auction rate bonds.

A key tax issue is whether the amount paid on an inverse floating rate instrument constitutes interest for federal income tax purposes. Since 1987, inverse floating interest rate bonds (floating inversely to LIBOR, the London Interbank Offered Rate) have been issued in large dollar amounts as part of the mortgage-backed securities market. Since then practitioners have had little practical concern regarding the character of the payments on these types of inverse floaters as interest to the extent the inverse floaters are based upon floating-rate indices that qualify as an objective interest index under the 1986 Proposed OID Regulations or as a dutch auction or remarketing agent based index covered by the IRS notices discussed above.[19]

Moreover, an inverse interest rate formula is a permissible variable-rate formula under the 1992 Proposed OID Regulations.[20] These Proposed Regulations describe a rate of 10 percent compounded monthly, minus the value of one-month LIBOR. As discussed above, a debt instrument qualifies as a variable-rate debt instrument under the 1992 Proposed OID Regulations if, among other things, interest is based on either a qualified floating rate or an objective rate. Since the rate is not reasonably expected to measure contemporaneous variations in the cost of newly borrowed funds, it is not a qualified floating rate. Since it is based on a qualified floating rate, however, it qualifies as an objective rate.

Foreign Currency Denominated Bonds

An innovative way for municipalities to issue debt and sell it in another country is to denominate the bonds in the currency of the targeted country.[21] Such bonds could also be marketed in the United States to U.S. taxpayers interested in foreign currency denominated instruments. Such bonds may also be accompanied by the use of currency swaps and interest rate swaps to protect or hedge the municipality against adverse movements in the relative value of the dollar against the foreign currency.

Certain tax issues potentially limit the benefits of issuing foreign currency denominated bonds. Treasury Regulation Section 1.988-3(c)(2) prevents a U.S. taxpayer who has invested in these types of bonds from deducting exchange rate losses.[22] Under Section 988, foreign currency gains on foreign currency denominated tax-exempt bonds would not be treated as tax-exempt interest but would generate taxable income to a U.S. investor. As a result of these potential disadvantages (taxable foreign currency income and disallowed foreign currency losses), it may be prudent to issue *taxable* foreign currency denominated bonds (rather than tax-exempt bonds) in order to avoid various restrictions applicable to tax-exempt bonds and market the bonds to non-U.S. investors (although the sale of taxable bonds to foreign investors raises potential U.S. withholding tax considerations).[23]

"Bifurcation" Concerns

The 1986 Proposed OID Regulations were amended in February of 1991 to include a rule that under certain circumstances a debt instrument providing for contingent payments is divisible for tax purposes into a fixed-rate debt instrument and a separate property right.[24] This so-called bifurcation rule applied to interest rate formulas tied to the value of stock, commodities, or other publicly traded property. The bifurcation rule was not revised by the 1992 Proposed OID Regulations. However, the preamble to the 1992 Proposed OID Regulations indicated that the rules for contingent debt would be revised by future regulations.

The bifurcation rule of the 1986 Proposed OID Regulations provided that interest payments based on such formulas would not be treated as interest. Accordingly, if the bifurcation rule applied, the payments made under such formulas could not qualify as tax-exempt.[25] However, this rule did not apply to formulas tied to interest rate indices and accordingly does not affect derivative rate bonds.

In January of 1993, the IRS issued new proposed contingent payment regulations, but because of the change in administration, they were not immediately made effective. It is expected, however, that these regulations will be officially released after they have been reviewed by President Clinton's administration.

The 1993 Contingent Payment Regulations replace the contingent payment rules of the 1986 Proposed OID Regulations. In general, the 1993 Contingent Payment Regulations no longer apply the bifurcation rule of the 1986 Proposed OID Regulations. Instead, they focus on whether the payments provided for under the terms of the debt instrument are "market-based contingent payments," which include a payment based on the price or yield of personal property that is actively traded or on an index of the prices or yields of such property.[26] Market-based contingent payments also include payments based on one or more qualified floating interest rates, the variations of which can be substantially hedged through the use of property that is actively traded.[27] The definition of market-based contingent payments would include amounts paid pursuant to various interest rate indices. The new rule is broad in application, including many contingent debt instruments that would not be subject to the bifurcation rule of the 1986 Proposed OID Regulations.

The 1993 Contingent Payment Regulations generally treat debt instruments with market-based contingent payments on a "unified" rather than a bifurcated basis, and require that the computation of interest income and interest expense relating to a market-based contingent debt instrument for any tax year be determined under one of several alternative methods.[28] Debt instruments providing for contingent payments that do not qualify as market-based would be bifurcated under the 1993 Contingent Payment Regulations in a manner slightly different than under the prior rule, taking into account the discounted value of the noncontingent payments (computed at the applicable federal rate).[29]

However, the 1993 Contingent Payment Regulations do not include rules for tax-exempt debt instruments that provide for contingent payments and specifically "reserve" on the treatment of such tax-exempt debt.[30] Moreover, the IRS has requested comments on the proper treatment of such tax-exempt debt instruments, including whether any portion of the contingent payments would be more appropriately treated as taxable income on an option or forward contract than as tax-exempt interest.[31] The rules of these proposed regulations also do not apply to "hedged" contingent payment debt instruments (whether tax-exempt or not) where issuers or holders hedge the variations attributable to the contingent payments on the debt instrument, since the IRS is continuing to assess the treatment of such debt.[32]

In addition to making it clear that derivative rate bonds are not covered by the rules of the 1993 Contingent Payment Regulations, the preamble to the proposed regulations indicates that the IRS is considering the appropriate treatment of these debt instruments and that new rules could impact their tax treatment. Presumably, given the nature of the discussion in the preamble, any new IRS rules would be prospective, although it is possible that they could be applied retroactively.

The 1992 Proposed Original Issue Discount Regulations

In the preamble to the 1992 Proposed OID Regulations the Treasury Department indicated that it is considering the appropriate treatment of tax-exempt bonds with "embedded" options, forwards, and swaps. Since these types of bonds are not specifically described in the 1992 Proposed OID Regulations, it is not clear what types of derivative rate bonds will be addressed in the future guidance. We have noted that the rules of the 1992 Proposed OID Regulations relating to variable-rate debt instruments essentially provide that a tax-exempt bond that constitutes an inverse floater or includes a turbo factor in its interest rate formula will not qualify as a variable-rate debt instrument if the issuer, contemporaneously with the issuance of the bond, enters into one or more financial contracts (other than a debt instrument of the issuer) that substantially offset the variations in the stated interest rate on the bond. This rule would appear to apply to many derivative rate bonds since the issuer (or underlying obligor) will typically enter into an offsetting hedge to achieve a net fixed-rate payment obligation on the bond. The impact of this rule, however, is less clear, because under the 1993 Contingent Payment Regulations, the IRS has reserved on the issuance of guidance regarding tax-exempt bonds with contingent payments.

Given the lack of IRS guidance, the failure of derivative rate bonds to qualify as variable-rate obligations does not appear to affect whether payments on the bonds would constitute tax-exempt interest. Moreover, it is important to note that both the 1992 Proposed OID Regulations and the 1993 Contingent Payment Regulations have prospective effective dates.[33]

Accordingly, in light of the prospective effective dates of both the 1992 Proposed OID Regulations and the 1993 Contingent Payment Regulations and the fact that the IRS has reserved on issuing guidance on this issue, the tax-exempt character of payments on derivative rate bonds does not appear to have been directly affected by either the 1992 Proposed OID Regulations or the 1993 Contingent Payment Regulations. However, the statement in the preamble to the regulations that the Treasury Department and the IRS are studying this area and the language in the text of both sets of proposed regulations suggest that further changes will be forthcoming.

Linking the Issuer's Obligation to Swaps and Caps

A governmental issuer of a derivative rate bond or the related conduit borrower may enter into an interest rate swap or cap to insulate itself from the floating interest rate risk associated with a derivative rate bond. Purchasers of the derivative rate bond, credit enhancers, rating agencies, and the governmental issuer or conduit borrower will consider the risk that the swap counterparty or cap provider will fail to make payments to the issuer. If the swap counterparty or cap provider fails to perform, must or should the governmental issuer or conduit borrower be fully at risk for any shortfall on the debt service on the derivative rate bond attributable to this failure? If the governmental issuer or conduit borrower is liable for any such shortfall, prospective investors, rating agencies, and credit enhancers would thus need to consider the credit risk associated with the ability of the governmental issuer or the conduit borrower to make payments from other sources of funds at the floating rate provided for in the derivative rate bond. Credit risk of this nature on the part of the governmental issuer or conduit borrower may be unattractive.

Alternatively, it could be suggested that the source of payments on the derivative rate bonds that are intended to be derived from the cap or swap could be limited source obligations payable solely from amounts received from the swap or cap provider. Although this approach addresses credit risks, there is a concern about whether this approach creates tax risks. The limited nature of the governmental issuer's obligation on the bond raises the following concern. If the floating-rate portion of the interest rate formula sourced from the swap or cap is properly treated as a component of interest payable on the bond, it will qualify as tax-exempt interest. However, if the derivative rate bond is viewed as the acquisition by the investor of a fixed-rate bond from a municipal issuer and a separate swap directly between the investor and either the municipal issuer or a third party, payments on the swap or cap would be taxable since the source of payment is the swap counterparty, not interest on a municipal bond.

A prudent approach to avoid this concern would require that the governmental issuer or conduit borrower be fully obligated on the derivative rate bond regardless of the swap counterparty's or cap provider's performance on its obligation.

State Law Treatment of the Payments

Derivative rate bond issuers must consider any state law restrictions that may prevent the issuance of a bond with the desired interest rate formulation. If a municipality issued a security providing for payments that did not qualify as interest as a matter of state law or treated such amounts as distinct from the debt obligation issued by the municipality, it would be necessary to consider whether such amounts could nevertheless be treated as interest on a municipal obligation (and, therefore, tax-exempt interest) for federal income tax purposes. It should be noted that payments of interest on a tax-exempt lease (i.e., a so-called financing lease rather than a true lease) are properly treated as payments of interest on indebtedness for federal income tax purposes, regardless of their state law character.[34] This is the case even though the lease is not treated as indebtedness and the payments are not treated as payments of principal or interest as a matter of applicable state law.[35]

Arbitrage Yield and Rebate: "Integration" of Swaps, Caps, and Other Interest Rate Derivatives

Governmental issuers and conduit borrowers are limited by federal income tax law as to the amount of arbitrage profit they may earn by favorably investing the proceeds of a tax-exempt bond. In many cases the law requires that the issuer "rebate" any positive arbitrage to the government.[36] These arbitrage yield and rebate restrictions are exceedingly complex.[37] Failure to comply with these restrictions will cause interest on the bonds to be treated as taxable on a retroactive basis. It is thus critical to consider the extent to which municipal interest rate swaps must be taken into account by governmental issuers and conduit borrowers in determining compliance with arbitrage yield and rebate restrictions.

A municipal interest rate swap can impact the determination of whether a tax-exempt bond satisfies arbitrage yield and rebate restrictions. If the governmental issuer or conduit borrower uses the swap to hedge *its liability* on its tax-exempt bonds, must the swap be taken into account in determining the yield on the bonds for purposes of determining whether it has earned a positive arbitrage on the investment of bond proceeds? Exhibit 5-1 illustrates the concern with the issue of whether a swap or other type of interest rate hedge must be "integrated" in determining bond yield.

The recently released final arbitrage regulations, generally effective July 1, 1993, provide a special rule under which bond yield may take into account certain payments made or received on hedging transactions such as swaps or caps.[38] In the case of bonds issued before the effective date of the 1993 Final Arbitrage Regulations, whether a swap or cap could be taken into account for bond yield purposes may have been based upon either the proposed form of the 1993 Final Arbitrage Regulations (the 1992 Proposed Arbitrage Regulations)[39] or Private Letter Ruling 9046065, dated May 23, 1990. There are a number of differences between the qualified hedge rule

EXHIBIT 5-1

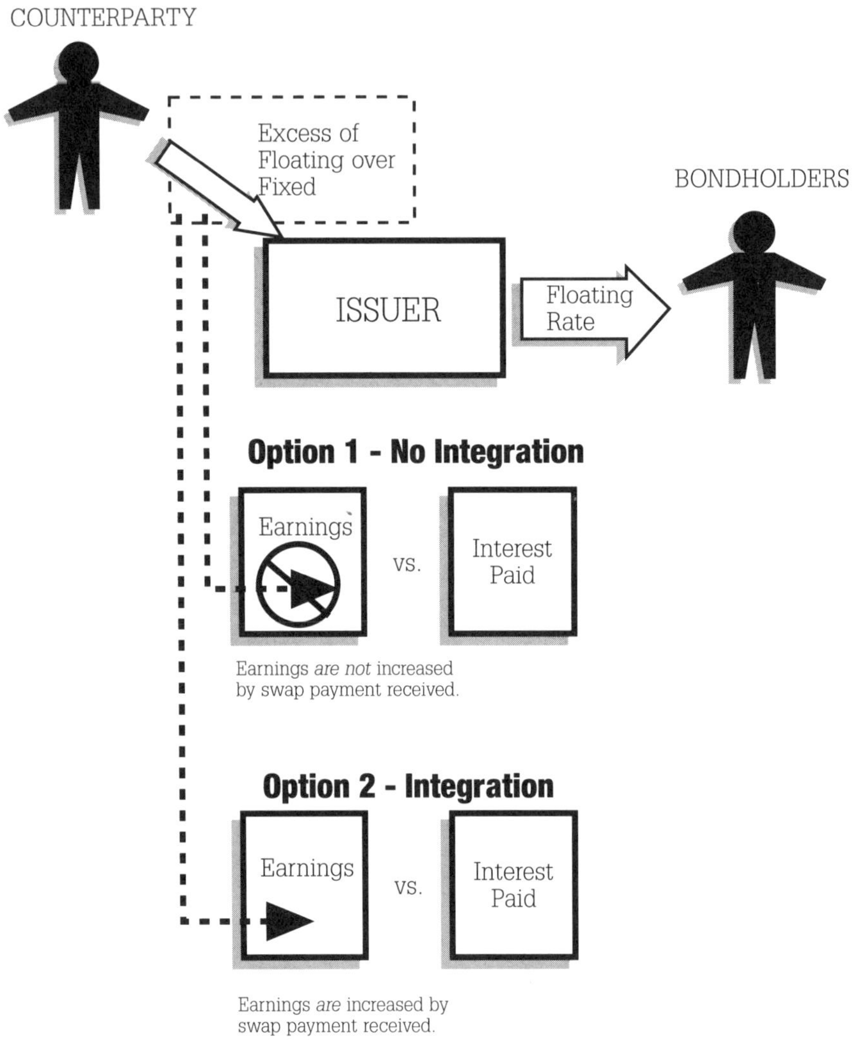

contained in the 1993 Final Arbitrage Regulations and the 1992 Proposed Arbitrage Regulations.[40] A discussion of these differences is beyond the scope of this text.

As indicated above, prior to the effective date of the Final Arbitrage Regulations, Private Letter Ruling 9046065, dated May 23, 1990, may have been relevant. This private letter ruling permitted a municipality to "integrate" a financial guarantee policy resembling an interest rate swap with its stated obligation on an issue of bonds in determining bond yield for arbitrage purposes. This ruling requires that the bond be almost perfectly hedged by the swap. In making this determination, the ruling outlined three critical factors: (1) the swap must be entered into at the same time that the bonds are issued; (2) it must run for the entire particular interest rate mode or term of the bonds; and (3) it must use the same variable rate as the bonds—there must be no basis risk on the swap. Thus, under the reasoning and requirements of this ruling, swaps were rarely eligible for integration in computing bond yield.

A governmental issuer or conduit borrower may also use an interest rate swap to hedge its return on *its investment* of bond proceeds. Thus, in considering whether bond proceeds have been invested at a positive arbitrage over bond yield, it must be determined whether interest rate swaps will be integrated on the investment side. Of course, a governmental issuer's or conduit borrower's desire to seek or avoid integration will depend upon the ultimate success of the swap. There is no specific authority on this issue, although it appears appropriate to consider the extent to which a particular swap matches up with a specific investment of bond proceeds. Again, it would appear more likely that an interest rate swap would not be integrated (unless it was closely tied to a particular investment) for this purpose.

Moreover, it must be considered whether a swap may also be a *direct* investment of bond proceeds in investment-type property subject to arbitrage yield restriction or arbitrage rebate analysis if bond proceeds (including sinking fund proceeds or pledged proceeds) are used to pay a yield adjustment fee or premium, otherwise fund the swap, cap, or floor (including the payment of ongoing payments), or are directly pledged to support the municipality's payment obligation on the swap or hedge. This issue is addressed below under "Initial Premiums Received or Paid and Bond Proceeds Expenditures." The 1993 Final Arbitrage Regulations do not address the extent to which a swap or similar type of hedge will be treated as investment property, although they do indicate that hedging contracts do not qualify under the qualified hedge rule if the contract contains a "significant investment element."[41] However, the definition of "investment-type property"[42] may be helpful on this point.

The 1993 Final Arbitrage Regulations

The 1993 Final Arbitrage Regulations provide specific guidance relating to the impact of swaps and caps for purposes of the arbitrage yield restriction and rebate rules. As indicated earlier, the regulations are generally effective for obligations issued after June 30, 1993 (although due to a transition rule, for obligations issued after June 30, 1993, and before August 15, 1993, in essence an issuer can elect to apply the rules in effect on June 30, 1993).

The Qualified Hedge Rule

In order for a governmental issuer or conduit borrower to determine whether it has complied with both the arbitrage yield restriction and rebate requirements, it must compare the yield on its tax-exempt bond issue to the yield on investments made with the bond proceeds. The 1993 Final Arbitrage Regulations contain a regulatory provision (the qualified hedge rule) allowing certain hedging transactions, such as swaps and caps, to be incorporated into the computation of bond yield for arbitrage rebate and yield restriction purposes.[43]

If a governmental issuer or conduit borrower enters into a qualified hedge (as defined in the regulations), payments made or received by the issuer are taken into account in determining bond yield. Unless a special "floating to fixed" hedge rule applies (to be discussed later), the bond issue to which the qualified hedge relates is treated as a variable-yield issue for arbitrage yield restriction and rebate purposes.[44] Different rules apply under the regulations depending on whether a bond issue is treated as a variable-yield issue or as a fixed-yield issue. Special rules apply when a hedge is terminated or when the hedged bonds are redeemed.

Definition of a Qualified Hedge

In order to constitute a qualified hedge, the following requirements must be met:

1. the contract must be a *hedge* entered into primarily to reduce the governmental issuer's or conduit borrower's risk of interest rate changes with respect to a borrowing and must not have a significant investment element;[45]
2. the contract must be entered into between the governmental issuer or conduit borrower (or the political subdivision on behalf of which the governmental issuer issues the bonds) and an unrelated party;[46]
3. the hedge must cover *all* of one or more groups of substantially identical bonds in the issue (i.e., all of the bonds having the same interest rate, maturity, and terms) or the same specific identifiable interest payments on each of the substantially identical bonds of the issue;[47]
4. the changes in the value of the contract must be primarily interest rate based;[48]
5. the contract must not hedge an amount larger than the governmental issuer's or conduit borrower's risk with respect to interest rate changes on the hedged bonds;[49]
6. the payments to the governmental issuer or conduit borrower under the contract must closely correspond, in both time and amount, to the specific interest payments being hedged on the bonds;[50]
7. payments on the contract must not accrue earlier than the sale date of the hedged bonds and must not accrue longer than the hedged interest payments on the hedged bonds;[51]
8. payments to the hedge provider from the governmental issuer or conduit borrower (if any) must be reasonably expected to be made from the same source of funds that, absent the hedge, would be reasonably expected to be used to pay principal and interest on the hedged bonds;[52] and

9. the hedge must be identified by the actual issuer on its books and records maintained for the hedged bonds on or before the later of the date on which the parties enter into the contract or the issue date of the hedged bonds.[53]

These hedge rule requirements are summarized in Exhibit 5-2.

EXHIBIT 5-2

Qualified Hedge Rule Requirements

The terms of the hedge must correspond to the terms of the bond issue by satisfying the following requirements:

- Contract must be a hedge, must be entered into to reduce interest rate risk, and must not have a significant investment element.
- Contract must be entered into with an unrelated party.
- Hedge must cover all of one or more groups of substantially identical bonds of the issue.
- Changes in value of contract must be primarily interest rate based.
- Amount hedged must not exceed interest rate risk.
- Payments received under the contract must correspond closely to hedged interest payments.
- Payments must not accrue earlier than sale date and longer than interest payments on hedged bonds.
- Payments must be reasonably expected to be made from same source of funds as for interest and principal.
- Hedge must be identified on books and records for bonds on or before later of date contract is entered into or bonds are issued.

Definition of a Hedge

A contract constitutes a hedge if it is entered into primarily to reduce the governmental issuer's or conduit borrower's risk of interest rate changes relating to a borrowing. The regulations include an interest rate swap, an interest rate cap, a futures contract, a forward contract, and an option as examples.[54] A commodity swap or option does not qualify.[55]

The regulations provide that a contract does not qualify as a hedge if *it contains a significant investment element* (i.e., an expected return).[56] The regulations focus on whether the payments under the contract do not correspond closely in time and amount to the interest payments on the bond being hedged.

The regulations provide that an interest rate swap generally contains a significant investment element if it requires *any* payments other than "periodic payments" defined under regulations generally applicable to interest rate swaps (such as an up-front fee for an off-market swap).[57] The regulations provide that an interest rate cap generally contains a significant investment element if the cap rate under the contract is less than the "on-market" swap rate on the date the cap is entered into.[58] The on-market swap rate is based on the fixed rate for which the rate or index under the cap contract could be swapped in an on-market interest rate swap with no payments other than periodic payments and a term equal to the term of the cap.

The Identification Requirement

As indicated above, in order to constitute a qualified hedge, a hedge must be identified by the actual issuer on its books and records maintained for the hedged bonds before the later of the date on which the parties enter into the contract or the issue date of the hedged bonds. The regulations require that the identification contain sufficient detail to establish that the requirements of the qualified hedge rule (and, if applicable, the floating to fixed hedge rule) have been satisfied.[59] Moreover, the regulations require that the hedge must be noted on all forms filed with the Internal Revenue Service for the bond issue after the date the hedge is entered into.

Accounting for Qualified Hedges

In general, payments made or received by a governmental issuer or conduit borrower on a qualified hedge are treated as payments made or received, as appropriate, on the hedged bonds that are taken into account in determining the yield on the hedged bonds, and the payments are reasonably allocated in the periods to which the payments relate (payments made by a governmental issuer or conduit borrower are allocated based upon general federal income tax principles, including the regulations applicable to swaps and other notional principal contracts).[60] Payments received by the governmental issuer or conduit borrower are taken into account in the period that the interest payment on the bond to which the hedge relates is required to be made.[61]

Payments on the contract that are allocable to the reduction of risk of interest rate changes and to the hedge provider's overhead are taken into account under the rules just discussed.[62] Payments for services or other items under the contract that are not expressly treated as payments relating to the reduction of risk of interest rate changes and to the hedge provider's overhead are not taken into account for bond yield purposes.[63]

Termination Payments

A termination of a qualified hedge includes any sale, assignment or other disposition of the hedge by the governmental issuer or conduit borrower, or the acquisition by the governmental issuer or conduit borrower of an offsetting hedge.[64] A "deemed" termination of the hedge occurs when the hedged bonds are redeemed.[65] A hedge is not treated as terminated merely because the counterparty assigns its interest in the hedge.[66]

What if the governmental issuer or conduit borrower immediately enters into an identical replacement hedge upon the termination of an existing hedge? Payments made or received upon termination of a qualified hedge are treated as payments made or received on the hedged bonds.[67] The payments are reasonably allocated to the remaining periods originally covered by the terminated hedge in a manner that reflects the economic substance of the hedge.[68]

Upon a deemed termination of a hedge, the fair market value of the contract on the bond redemption date is treated as a termination payment made or received.[69] Any deemed termination payment received by the issuer reduces, but not below zero, the amount of interest on the hedged bonds for the computation period ending on the termination date. The excess amount of the deemed termination payment, if any, is reasonably allocated over the bond years in prior periods to the extent necessary to eliminate any excess.[70]

If the hedged bonds are redeemed using the proceeds of a refunding issue, the termination payment on the hedge is treated as a payment on the refunding issue, rather than on the *refunded issue*.[71] If hedged bonds are advance refunded and the refunding bonds (rather than the hedged bonds themselves) are redeemed, the redemption of the refunding bonds triggers the deemed termination of the hedge, and the deemed payment, determined as described above, is treated as a payment on the redeemed refunding bonds for bond yield purposes.

The Special Floating to Fixed Hedge Rule

As previously indicated, in general a bond issue for which there is a qualified hedge is treated as a variable-yield issue. However, if the requirements of a special floating to fixed hedge rule are satisfied, the issue will be treated as a fixed-yield issue.[72]

In addition to the requirements applicable to qualified hedges discussed above, the following requirements must be satisfied in order to qualify for the fixed hedge rule:

1. the contract must be an interest rate swap;[73]
2. the date on which payments begin to accrue on the swap is not later than fifteen days after the issue date of the hedged bonds;[74]
3. the term of the swap is equal to the term of the hedged bonds or the entire period during which the hedged bonds bear interest at variable interest rates;[75]
4. payments to be made or received under the swap are reasonably expected to correspond closely, in time (generally, within fifteen days) and amount, to payments on the hedged bonds (i.e., no nonperiodic payments under the contract);[76]
5. the notional principal amount used to compute both fixed and variable payments on the swap equals the principal amount of *all* of the variable-yield bonds in the issue;[77] and
6. under the swap, the issuer of the bonds makes level payments based on a fixed interest rate and receives payments based on a variable interest rate that is substantially the same as the interest rate on the hedged bonds ("substantially the same" would permit a governmental issuer or conduit borrower to swap from an indexed thirty-day tax-exempt rate, for example, even though the variable rate on the hedged bonds is based on the *specific* thirty-day tax-exempt rate for the bonds, determined by a remarketing agent).[78]

If the special floating to fixed hedge rule applies, the fixed-rate payments made by the governmental issuer or conduit borrower on the interest rate swap (without reducing or "netting" the issuer's fixed-rate payment obligation with the swap counterparty's variable-rate payment obligation on the swap) are substituted for the actual interest payments on the hedged bonds for bond yield computation purposes.[79]

If the qualified hedge is terminated "early" (i.e., before the bonds are redeemed), the bond issue is treated as if it has been retired and is "reissued" as of the date of such termination for arbitrage yield computation purposes.[80] The redemption price of the bond issue as of the deemed redemption date and the issue price of the deemed reissued bonds are based on the aggregate values of all the bonds of the issue on the hedge termination date. If a termination payment is made or received in connection with the termination of the swap, the rules discussed above regarding termination payments apply. Finally, the regulations provide that if the swap is terminated within five years after the issue date of the bonds, the special floating to fixed hedge rule does not apply and, for purposes of determining yield on the bonds for rebate purposes (the yield of the bonds for arbitrage yield restriction purposes is unaffected), the bonds are treated as variable-yield bonds, rather than fixed-yield bonds. Presumably, this rule applies only to early terminations, as the paragraph heading states.[81]

Internal Revenue Service Discretion

Even if a contract otherwise constitutes a qualified hedge, the IRS can determine, based on all the facts and circumstances, that the contract should not be treated as a qualified hedge if it would provide a material potential for arbitrage, or if a principal purpose for entering into the contract was arbitrage potential.[82] The regulations provide, as an example, that a contract requiring a substantial nonperiodic payment may constitute, in whole or in part, an embedded loan, investment-type property, or other investment. The regulations also permit the IRS to issue a revenue ruling or revenue procedure specifying that contracts that do not otherwise meet the requirements set forth in the regulations could constitute qualified hedges.[83]

Finally, if an issuer enters into a hedge that is not properly identified or otherwise fails to meet the requirements of a qualified hedge, the IRS may recompute the yield on the associated bond issue, taking into account the hedge, if the failure to take the hedge into account distorts the yield or otherwise fails to clearly reflect the economic substance of the transaction.[84]

Analysis of the Qualified Hedge Rule

In general, whether a governmental issuer or conduit borrower will be able to take a swap, cap, or floor into account for purposes of determining bond yield is a matter of planning (to make certain that the requirements set forth above can be satisfied). The restrictions on "significant investment elements" contained in the 1993 Final Arbitrage Regulations may impede the ability to qualify certain transactions under the qualified hedge rule. As the derivatives market evolves, it is likely that additional concerns will arise. Hopefully, the IRS will issue appropriate guidance to facilitate the use of hedging devices that do not result in arbitrage abuses.[85]

Initial Premiums Received or Paid and Bond Proceeds Expenditures

Many hedging contracts involve the receipt or payment of an initial amount, along with the mandatory (in the case of an interest rate swap) or optional (in the case of an interest rate cap, floor, or collar) ongoing payments under the contract. What are the consequences of the receipt and payment of these types of initial amounts by a governmental issuer or conduit borrower? What are the consequences if the governmental issuer or conduit borrower pays these initial amounts from bond proceeds?

In general it would appear appropriate to treat initial amounts paid by the governmental issuer or conduit borrower as interest in computing bond yield, based on the reference to the hedge provider's overhead included in Treasury Regulation Section 1.148-4(h)(3)(i), unless such amounts were for services or other items[86] or were "substantial" nonperiodic payments.[87]

If a governmental issuer or conduit borrower uses bond proceeds to *pay* an initial swap or cap premium and the swap or cap constitutes a qualified hedge, it would appear appropriate to treat such expenditures as analogous to credit enhancement expenditures, since credit enhancement (as is the case with qualifying hedges) can be taken into account in computing bond yield if it constitutes a "qualified guarantee." Although regulations have not yet been issued addressing the qualification of expenditures of bond proceeds for either credit enhancement or hedges, it is important to note that the relevant legislative history indicates that credit enhancement expenditures relating to qualified guarantees are generally treated as "bad money" subject to the 5 percent expenditure limit for private activity and 501(c)(3) bonds, but are not generally treated as "issuance costs" subject to the "2 percent limit" of Section 147(g) of the Code.[88]

If a governmental issuer or conduit borrower receives amounts in connection with a hedge, it must be considered whether such receipts are "proceeds" subject to qualifying expenditure analysis.

Reissuance Concerns

The Proposed 1001 Regulation

On December 1, 1992, the Treasury released Proposed Regulation Section 1.1001-3, which applies in a broad range of contexts (to both taxable and tax-exempt debt) and addresses the question whether a direct or indirect modification of a debt instrument triggers a "realization event" for federal income tax purposes under Section 1001 of the Internal Revenue Code. In the context of tax-exempt bonds and tax-exempt derivatives, the Proposed 1001 Regulation could affect the determination of whether a tax-exempt bond has been "reissued" (i.e., deemed retired and replaced by a newly issued bond) for federal income tax purposes.[89]

This determination is important because if the bond is deemed reissued, it will be necessary to determine that the "reissued" bond (which is, for federal income tax purposes, considered to be a newly issued debt obligation) complies with all of the then current requirements that a bond must satisfy (determined as of the date the bond is treated as reissued) in order to qualify as tax-exempt. Due to changes in law, however, it may be impossible for certain tax-exempt bonds, if reissued, to qualify as tax-exempt.[90]

Under the Proposed 1001 Regulation, a realization event (and therefore a reissuance) is triggered if a "modification" of the debt instrument by the issuer or the holder takes place and the modification is "significant."[91] The Proposed 1001 Regulation treats the following types of modifications as significant:

1. changes in interest rate or yield;
2. changes in the timing and/or amount of payments;
3. changes in obligor or security, including changes in credit enhancement (different rules apply depending upon whether the obligation is recourse or nonrecourse); and
4. changes in the nature of the debt instrument (including changes that convert a fixed-rate debt instrument to a floating-rate or contingent payment debt instrument, or vice versa).[92]

The Proposed 1001 Regulation defines a modification as "any alteration in any legal right or obligation (including the addition or deletion of a right or obligation) of the issuer or a holder of a debt instrument, whether the alteration is evidenced by amendment of the instrument, conduct of the parties, or otherwise."[93] Fortunately, the Proposed 1001 Regulation includes the so-called Automatic Rule and the Unilateral Exercise Rule, which provide two important exceptions from this otherwise extremely broad definition.

Under the Automatic Rule, the Proposed 1001 Regulation provides that "an alteration of a legal right or obligation is not a modification if it occurs by operation of the original terms of the instrument."[94] Consider the application of the Automatic Rule in the context of a debt instrument with a fifteen-year term whose original terms provide that it shall bear interest at a floating rate for five years and then will automatically convert to a predetermined fixed interest rate for an additional ten years. A change in the terms that converts it from a floating-rate debt instrument to a fixed-rate debt instrument would constitute a significant modification, thereby triggering a reissuance. Here, however, because the Automatic Rule applies, the change in interest rate modes is not treated as a modification. Accordingly, it cannot be regarded as a significant modification and a reissuance is not triggered upon conversion.

The second important exception to the definition of a modification, under the Unilateral Exercise Rule, provides that "[a]n alteration that occurs through one party's exercise or waiver of a right under the instrument is by operation of the original terms provided that the exercise or waiver is unilateral."[95] However, the Proposed 1001 Regulation further provides that the exercise of a right is not unilateral (and therefore not eligible for this exception) if it:

1. creates a right in the other party to alter or terminate the instrument, or to put the instrument to a third party;
2. requires consent of the other party, unless that consent may not be unreasonably withheld; or
3. requires consideration, unless the amount of consideration is fixed on the issue date.[96]

As with the Automatic Rule, the Unilateral Exercise Rule permits an issuer to avoid triggering a reissuance. For example, consider a debt instrument with a fifteen-year term that provides, pursuant to its original terms, that interest will be paid at a floating rate, although the issuer has the right to convert the rate on the bond to a predetermined fixed rate at any time. The issuer's exercise of its conversion right will convert the bond from a floating-rate debt instrument to a fixed-rate debt instrument. Because the conversion is a result of the exercise of the issuer's unilateral right to convert that was contained in the original terms of the bond, however, it will qualify under the Unilateral Exercise Rule and, therefore, the bond will not be deemed to have been reissued.

The terms of many tax-exempt bonds are exceedingly complex. While the exercise of rights inherent in these instruments may appear unilateral, they may not qualify for the Unilateral Exercise Rule. Many other modifications may occur with respect to tax-exempt bonds that may require analysis under the Proposed 1001 Regulation.

Notice 88-130

Reissuance guidance for tax-exempt issues is embodied in IRS Notice 88-130, 1988-2 C.B. 543, issued prior to the Proposed 1001 Regulations. Notice 88-130 is not as broad in application as the Proposed 1001 Regulation, and simply provides special rules for determining whether various rights and changes result in a tax-exempt bond being treated as reissued. Although Notice 88-130 includes two sets of rules—one applicable to tax-exempt bonds and a second applicable to so-called qualified tender bonds—its principal focus is on the special rules applicable to tender bonds and the general impact of tender rights on any tax-exempt bond.[97]

Tender bonds are floating-rate bonds that provide holders with the right to tender their bonds for repurchase under certain circumstances. A tender bond often permits the manner in which interest payments on the bond are made to be changed. Notice 88-130 addresses the impact of tender rights and whether interest rate mode changes on tender bonds trigger a reissuance.

Under the general rules of Notice 88-130 applicable to all bonds other than qualified tender bonds, a bond is considered retired if a material term of the bond is changed (a sale or exchange event). The general rules also treat a bond as retired if it is purchased by the issuer (or someone acting on behalf of the issuer). In addition, under the general rules, any bond subject to a tender right *is deemed to have been purchased by the issuer on each tender date* (regardless of whether the tender right is exercised). Accordingly, an important aspect of the general rules is that any bond subject to a tender right that is governed by the general rules would be deemed retired and therefore reissued on every tender date (regardless of whether the bond is in fact tendered for repurchase).

Notice 88-130 also provides special rules for "qualified tender bonds," the real focus of the notice. A qualified tender bond is any tender bond whose final stated maturity date is no later than the earlier of (1) 35 years after the date of issue, or (2) the latest day reasonably expected (as of the date of issue) to be required to carry out the governmental purpose of the issue of which the bond is a part. A bond will be deemed to meet the second requirement if the average maturity of the issue of which the bond is a part does not exceed 120 percent of the average reasonably expected economic life of the facilities being financed with the proceeds of the issue.

In contrast to bonds that do not meet the criteria for being considered qualified tender bonds, a qualified tender bond eligible for the special rule applicable to tender bonds is not considered retired on every tender date merely because of the existence of a tender right. In addition, the special rule makes it clear that various interest rate mode changes (and certain other changes) do not result in the retirement and reissuance of a qualified tender bond.[98]

Application to Primary Market Tax-Exempt Derivatives

Many of the operating rules of Notice 88-130 that relate to tender bonds fall outside the scope of this book. While this discussion is not intended to cover the subject of reissuance or the particular issues that may arise under the Proposed 1001 Regulation or Notice 88-130 with respect to tax-exempt bonds, it is focused on particular provisions of primary market tax-exempt derivatives and whether they raise reissuance concerns.

The interest rate of dutch auction rate bonds is periodically reset through the dutch auction process. This rate-changing mechanism is not the type of redetermination of the interest rate that would constitute a significant modification or a reissuance under the Proposed 1001 Regulation or Notice 88-130. Because the holder of a dutch auction rate bond does not typically have the right to tender its bond for purchase, a dutch auction rate bond should not raise concerns that could trigger a reissuance under the special rules of Notice 88-130.

In certain floater/inverse floater combinations, the holder of one of the inverse floating-rate bonds has the right, known as a linkage right, to acquire one of the related floating-rate bonds from its existing holder at a specified price, resulting in a "linkage" of the floater with the inverse floater. An investor who holds both an inverse floating-rate bond and a corresponding floating-rate bond has essentially established a fixed-rate investment because changes in the rate on the inverse floating-rate bond will be offset by equal changes in the rate on the floating-rate bond. The bond documents may give an investor holding a linked pair of floating and inverse floating-rate bonds the right to exchange them for a fixed-rate bond (the "linked certificate") that essentially corresponds to the combined terms of the linked securities except that the investor is no longer liable for its share of dutch auction expenses (because its linked investment makes the auction irrelevant to the investor). The investor has the discretion to exchange the linked certificate for the separate floating-rate and inverse floating-rate securities in order to be able to separately sell the floating and inverse floating-rate bonds.

A key issue to be resolved when examining the linkage right is whether its exercise or the exchange of the floating-rate and inverse floating-rate bonds for a linked security triggers a reissuance. First, the linkage right does not give the holder of the floating-rate bond a right to put its auction rate bond. It functions as a call right rather than a put right. Accordingly, the linkage right should not be considered a tender right within the meaning of Notice 88-130 and should not trigger a reissuance under the rules of the notice. Second, the acquisition of the floating-rate security by an inverse floating-rate security holder pursuant to a linkage right does not appear to affect the terms of either debt instrument except with respect to the right to obtain the linked security and the fact that the rate payable on the linked security will not take into account the costs of the auction process. Changes in the interest rate pursuant to the receipt of a linked security should generally qualify under the Unilateral Exercise Rule of the Proposed 1001 Regulation. Accordingly, the receipt of a linked security (or exchange of a linked security for separate floating-rate and inverse floating-rate bonds) should not be treated as modifications for purposes of the Proposed 1001 Regulation. As a result, they could not be treated as significant modifications and could not trigger reissuance events under the Proposed 1001 Regulation.

Derivative Rate Bonds

Derivative rate bonds do not typically provide holders with tender rights and should not trigger reissuance concerns under Notice 88-130. However, since derivative rate bonds provide for changes in interest rate modes, it must be determined whether mode changes may cause an unintended reissuance.

In Chapter 2 we discussed the fact that derivative rate bonds often provide for a scheduled rate conversion after a specified number of years. Upon the occurrence of such a conversion, the interest rate on the derivative rate bond changes from the rate based on the derivative rate formula to a fixed interest rate. If under the bond's terms the conversion is automatic, it should qualify under the Automatic Rule and not constitute a reissuance under the Proposed 1001 Regulation.

Derivative rate bonds also often permit an early conversion election by which the investor can request the issuer (remarketing agent or underlying conduit borrower) to terminate the derivative rate formula based interest rate mode on a derivative rate bond before the scheduled conversion date. The relevant issue is whether a change in interest rate mode pursuant to an early conversion election is eligible for the Unilateral Exercise Rule. The answer depends upon several considerations, which at this time have not been fully resolved.

Special Considerations for Detachable Call Bonds

The federal income tax issues relating to detachable call bonds have created considerable controversy in the municipal bond industry.[99] The tax issues raised by detachable call bonds fall into three basic categories.

Reissuance Concerns

First, detachable call bonds raise reissuance concerns. If the bond to which the detachable call relates is treated as reissued, it would be necessary to determine that it qualifies as tax-exempt, based upon the law as of the date the bond is reissued.

Detachable call bonds can raise reissuance concerns in several different ways. For example, if the terms of an existing tax-exempt bond are amended to permit the issuer to detach its call right and sell it to a third party, it must be considered whether this type of amendment results in a reissuance. Under the Proposed 1001 Regulation, an amendment of this type would be treated as a modification because it was not contemplated in the original bond documents. The Proposed 1001 Regulation includes a special rule regarding puts and calls that results in a "significant modification" (and therefore a reissuance) "if the put or call right has significant value at the time of its addition or deletion."[100] The Proposed 1001 Regulation further provides that "[t]he alteration of an existing put or call right is a significant modification if the alteration significantly affects its value."[101] Presumably the issuer and the holder would not incur the costs of amending the terms of the bonds to permit the detachment of the call right by the issuer if it did not have significant value. Accordingly, under the Proposed 1001 Regulation the amendment of an existing bond issue to permit the detachment of the issuer's call right is likely to trigger a reissuance.[102]

If the terms of the bonds as issued permitted the detachment of the issuer's call rights, it is possible that the sale of the call rights may qualify for the Unilateral Exercise Rule, since it is assumed that the issuer's decision to sell the call rights would not require bondholder consent at the time of sale. If the Unilateral Exercise Rule applies, the sale of the call rights would not be treated as a modification of the bonds and therefore the special "significant modification" rule for puts and calls would not apply. Under this analysis, a later sale of call rights pursuant to the original terms of a bond issue should not trigger a reissuance under the Proposed 1001 Regulation. This same conclusion would be reached, for essentially the same reason, if the call right were detached and sold to a third party at the time the bonds were issued.

It is important to note that Treasury and IRS officials have indicated that detachable call rights structured as part of the original terms of a tax-exempt bond issue are not explicitly addressed by the Proposed 1001 Regulation.[103] It is possible that the Proposed 1001 Regulation could be revised or other future IRS guidance could be issued that may result in a reissuance under a detachable call bond structure if the issuer's call rights are detached, although hopefully any such guidance would be applicable on a prospective basis.

Arbitrage Concerns—Bond Yield

Detachable call bonds raise arbitrage and rebate questions—in particular, whether the call sale proceeds affect the bond yield. A governmental issuer or conduit borrower cannot generally invest bond proceeds at a yield that is materially higher than the yield on the bonds[104] and must generally rebate any excess.[105] Therefore, the determination that the sale of call rights reduces bond yield could cause the governmental issuer or conduit borrower to fail to comply with the yield restriction requirements for the bond proceeds and simultaneously increase its rebate liability. Failure to comply with the yield restriction requirement or to pay the appropriate rebate liability under the arbitrage rebate rule could cause the bond to become taxable, possibly on a retroactive basis.[106]

Bond yield is determined by taking into account the amount of the issue price of the bonds, as determined under the original issue discount rules of the Internal Revenue Code,[107] and the amount the issuer will pay on the bonds, subject to certain adjustments (for qualifying guarantees and qualified hedges).[108] If the governmental issuer or conduit borrower sells its call rights in connection with the original issuance of the bonds, it would appear appropriate to take the proceeds into account for arbitrage purposes.

What if the call rights are sold later? The 1993 Final Arbitrage Regulations include a yield recomputation rule applicable to fixed-yield issues that is triggered as of the date of any transfer, waiver, modification, or similar transaction with respect to any right that is part of the terms of a bond or is otherwise associated with a bond (e.g., a redemption right).[109] Because the 1993 Final Arbitrage Regulations explicitly provide that this special recomputation rule applies for purposes of Treasury Regulation Section 1.148-3, which governs arbitrage rebate, it appears clear that this special rule does not apply for arbitrage yield restriction purposes in the case of fixed-yield issues. The preamble to the 1993 Final Arbitrage Regulations provides that no implication is intended regarding whether the sale of a detachable call is a reissuance of the associated bond under Section 1001 of the Code, and there is no specific rule in the Final Arbitrage Regulations addressing the sale of call rights in the context of variable-yield issues.

Thus, in the case of bonds subject to the 1993 Final Arbitrage Regulations, the subsequent sale of detachable call rights will have an arbitrage rebate effect on the associated bond issue.

The tenor of most of the articles that have discussed IRS and Treasury concerns regarding detachable call rights prior to the release of the 1993 Final Arbitrage Regulations was that Treasury and the IRS have been concerned that the later sale of call rights could retroactively affect the yield on the issuer's bonds.[110] Although the 1993 Final Arbitrage Regulations include a rule that affects the rebate computation (but not the yield restriction analysis) of fixed-yield bonds subject to the final regulations, concerns raised regarding the "retroactivity" of yield determination triggered as a result of subsequently selling a call right for bonds that are not subject to the 1993 Final Arbitrage Regulations do not appear consistent with the general rule that the issue price of a bond is determined as of the date of its issuance, not at a later date, regardless of events that may occur later.

Arbitrage Investment and Qualifying Expenditure Concerns

In addition to considering the effect that the sale of the issuer's call rights could have on the determination of bond yield, it must also be considered whether the amount the issuer receives from selling its call rights constitutes sale proceeds or investment proceeds. Bond proceeds and investment proceeds are subject to yield restriction and rebate.[111] If the moneys constitute sale or investment proceeds, the issuer's investment of the call rights sale proceeds at a yield in excess of the yield on the bonds or failure to rebate any earnings from the investment in excess of bond yield could cause the bonds to be taxable on a retroactive basis.

In addition, if the sale proceeds from the call rights are treated as bond proceeds, various expenditure tests may apply. For example, 95 percent of the proceeds of a 501(c)(3) bond issue must be allocated to qualifying expenditures for the bonds to qualify as tax-exempt. It is necessary to consider the potential application of these requirements to call rights sale proceeds received by an issuer, regardless of whether such proceeds are received at the time the bonds were originally issued or later.

Future Developments

At this writing, although the 1993 Final Arbitrage Regulations include the rule just discussed that would require a rebate recomputation as a result of a subsequent sale of a call right, the preamble to the final regulations also makes it clear that Treasury and the IRS are still considering whether they believe there are additional tax implications of detachable call bonds and that they have not yet fully determined (presumably on a prospective basis) the appropriate tax treatment.[112] Treasury and IRS officials have indicated their concern that the sale of the call rights results in tax-exempt bonds being outstanding longer than market conditions would dictate.[113] Issuers nonetheless have issued these bonds because detachable calls provide them with flexibility and cost savings unavailable through conventional advance refunding transactions. Hopefully, future IRS guidance in this area will take into account the economic benefits that detachable call bonds offer to governmental issuers.

Secondary Market Products

Evaluating a secondary market tax-exempt derivative involves consideration of the following fundamental tax issues:

1. Where and what are the risks associated with the tax-exempt bond around which the derivative is structured?
2. What steps must be taken to ensure that the investor will be the tax owner of the bond (or the owner of an instrument that will flow through tax-exempt interest to the investor)?
3. Does the derivative include other components that result in either taxable income to the investor or other adverse tax consequences?

The basic rule is that to qualify as a tax-exempt bond generating tax-exempt interest, the instrument must be the obligation of a state or local governmental unit. Applying this basic rule to secondary market tax-exempt derivatives involves a two-step analysis:

1. identifying and evaluating the "tax-exempt bond" component of the derivative; and
2. ensuring that the investor will be considered the owner of the tax-exempt bond (or an instrument that will flow through tax-exempt interest to the investor).

Structuring secondary market tax-exempt derivatives rests on two issues of critical concern:

1. whether the payments on the related bond constitute interest for federal income tax purposes;[114] and
2. whether the operation of the secondary market derivative results in the reissuance of the underlying tax-exempt bond.[115]

Certain secondary market tax-exempt derivatives are structured with trusts or custodial accounts to hold the underlying tax-exempt bond.[116] The trust or custodial account may issue more than one class of certificates representing differing interests, and it must be determined whether the tax-exempt interest paid on the bond "passes through," retaining its tax-exempt character when distributed to investors. Accordingly, trusts and custodial accounts are structured to be classified as either trusts, which requires compliance with the "Sears Regulations,"[117] or as partnerships, which requires compliance with the "four-factor test" of partnership classification[118] and restrictions on publicly traded partnerships.[119]

Certain secondary market tax-exempt derivatives permit the investor to "put" the security to the sponsor or a third party on a recurring basis (daily, weekly, monthly, etc.). The put obligation may be backed by a liquidity facility pursuant to a bank letter of credit. Although the rights associated with these types of secondary market tax-exempt derivatives closely resemble those of variable-rate demand bonds, these rights are not part of the underlying tax-exempt bond (i.e., integral to the underlying bond). Put rights and similar arrangements must be analyzed to determine whether they adversely impact the treatment of the investor as the owner of the associated tax-exempt bond, for if the investor is not treated as the tax owner of the bond, distributions received by the investor will not be tax-exempt. Unfortunately, since 1983 the IRS has indicated that it will not generally issue rulings on the ownership issue. Furthermore, the guidance issued by the IRS[120] and the courts prior to that time focuses on the investor's control over and benefits and burdens relating to the underlying bond—essentially establishing a facts-and-circumstances test that does not include a clear safe harbor.

Certain tax-exempt derivatives raise issues under the stripped bond rules. The federal income tax rules applicable to stripped tax-exempt bonds may result in taxable income to investors whenever there is a separation of any portion of an interest payment that has not yet been paid from the principal payments of the bond. Stripped tax-exempt bonds and certain other secondary market tax-exempt derivatives contemplate the separation of all or a portion of various cash flows associated with a particular tax-exempt bond between different investors. In addition, a recent IRS revenue ruling[121] recharacterized "excess" mortgage servicing fees retained in the securitization of residential mortgage loans as stripped interests in the associated mortgage loans. By analogy, this ruling suggests that fees structured into a secondary market tax-exempt derivative that are excessive or unreasonable may trigger application of the bond-stripping rules.

Certain secondary market tax-exempt derivatives make use of interest rate swaps. The federal income tax consequences of interest rate swaps, caps, and floors, and related types of notional principal contracts[122] are still somewhat uncertain. In October of 1993, the IRS issued final regulations dealing with limited interest rate swap and other notional principal contract issues.[123] Although the Final Swap Regulations answer certain issues relating to the tax consequences of interest rate swaps,[124] it must be considered whether the swaps include "embedded loans" or swap premiums that may result in taxable income to an investor and whether the swaps are governed by the regulations.[125]

Secondary market tax-exempt derivatives that provide for differing payment dates on the underlying tax-exempt bond from the date payments are made to the investor should be reviewed to determine if the temporary investment of money between those dates results in taxable income to the investor.

Determining Whether the Underlying Bond Is Tax-Exempt

In order to qualify as a tax-exempt bond for federal income tax purposes, the underlying bond must represent the obligation of a "state or political subdivision thereof"[126] and comply with technical rules set forth in the Internal Revenue Code (private activity bond test, private loan test, arbitrage and arbitrage rebate requirements, registration, restrictions on U.S. government guarantees, Form 8038 filing requirements, hedge bond restrictions, etc.).[127]

If the tax-exempt bonds are issued to benefit a private business ("private activity bonds"), additional requirements must be met (restrictions on the use of bond proceeds, volume cap, restrictions on the weighted maturity of the bonds based upon the expected life of the project, restrictions on financing land or used property, public approval, and restrictions on the financing of issuance costs) in order for the interest to qualify as tax-exempt.[128]

Compliance with these additional requirements may prove difficult in certain cases, thus increasing the risk that the underlying bond will either not qualify or will lose its tax-exempt status. For example, in the case of bonds issued to finance low-income multifamily rental housing, ongoing requirements regarding the rental of specified percentages of housing units to low-income persons must be satisfied over a substantial period of time.[129]

Tax counsel to the sponsor of the secondary market tax-exempt derivative *does not typically address whether the underlying tax-exempt bond qualifies as tax-exempt for a number of reasons, including the fact that:*

1. the determination of whether a bond qualifies as tax-exempt is complex, and tax counsel to the sponsor may not have access to all the facts that must be evaluated in making this determination (particularly if the bonds were issued some time ago);
2. tax counsel may not have the expertise to determine under the particular state law whether the bonds were validly issued; and
3. the cost of tax and enforceability opinions may be prohibitive.

As a result, the bond underlying a secondary product should be reviewed to determine the basis on which it is tax-exempt, the type of underlying bond, and whether the legal opinion relating to its tax-exempt status has been rendered by nationally recognized bond counsel. Quite often, different series of the same secondary market tax-exempt derivative will comprise different issues of underlying tax-exempt bonds. Accordingly, a review of the underlying bond of each series should be considered even when a new series of the same secondary market tax-exempt derivative is structured or evaluated.

In certain types of secondary market tax-exempt derivatives such as tax-exempt asset-backed securities, small denomination obligations (for example, financing leases) may be pooled. It may be particularly difficult, or impossible, to evaluate the tax-exempt status of each of the underlying tax-exempt obligations. In certain cases the underlying obligations may not have been accompanied by legal opinions of bond counsel regarding their tax-exempt status because of their small dollar amount. Investors may require that the sponsor of the security representing an interest in the underlying obligations provide indemnification to the investor against the risk that the underlying obligations are taxable, rather than tax-exempt. Thus, these transactions may require a more sophisticated level of review.

Considering Whether the Structure Triggers the Deemed Exchange of the Underlying Tax-Exempt Bond

A secondary market tax-exempt derivative may obtain its economic value from several financial elements—credit enhancement and pooling of credit risk, reallocation of cash flows, and yield curve benefits due to differing perceived maturities between the underlying bond and the tax-exempt derivative structure. The enhancement of the economic value of the derivative through these devices may raise the issue of whether there has been a deemed exchange of the underlying bond. Tax counsel to the sponsor of the derivative should address the question of whether there is any adverse impact on the tax exemption of the underlying bond as a result of reissuance.[130]

First, the terms of the underlying bond may be modified to make it more appropriate for the tax-exempt derivative structure. Second, the tax-exempt derivative structure, taken together with the terms of the bond, could be viewed as having effected a material change in the terms of the bond. Because a change in interest rate of more than 25 basis points (one-fourth of 1 percent) will result in a deemed exchange of a debt instrument under the Proposed 1001 Regulation,[131] tax-exempt derivatives should be carefully considered to ascertain that this threshold is not crossed with respect to the underlying bond. Changes in maturity must also be considered, since an extension of a bond's final maturity date that exceeds five years or 50 percent of the original term of the bond, whichever is less, will result in a deemed exchange under the Proposed 1001 Regulation.[132] Moreover, whether the addition of credit enhancement triggers a deemed exchange depends on whether the bond is considered a recourse or a nonrecourse instrument (although these terms are not defined) in the Proposed 1001 Regulation and whether a "modification" arises between the issuer of the underlying bond and its holder.[133]

Because almost all secondary market tax-exempt derivatives involve the payment of fees to various service providers such as custodians and trustees, put providers, and letter of credit banks, and these fees are typically paid out of interest payments received on the underlying bond, it could be argued that this structural feature causes a change in the interest rate on the underlying bond. The amount paid to service providers that represents reasonable fees for services performed should not under any circumstance trigger the reissuance of the underlying tax-exempt bond.[134] Moreover, the bond-stripping rules of Section 1286 of the Code clearly support the conclusion that diversion of portions of interest payments to different investors does not trigger the reissuance of a stripped bond.[135] This rule would also apply if fees in excess of reasonable compensation for services rendered constituted a stripped interest in the related bond. Thus, one must inquire under what circumstances a derivative structure could be deemed to trigger the reissuance of the related tax-exempt bond as a result of an effective change in the interest rate on the underlying bond. It would seem that this might arguably be the case only in the instance in which the person receiving interest payments or fees in excess of reasonable compensation was the issuer or underlying obligor of the bond and the arrangement was entered into in order to effect a change in the interest rate paid by the governmental issuer or conduit borrower.

Determining Whether the Trust or Custodial Account Is a "Pass-Through" Entity

Trust or Partnership?

Except in the case of qualifying mutual funds,[136] dividends received by shareholders, even if paid out of interest payments received on tax-exempt bonds, are generally taxable as ordinary income.[137] The *character* of the interest paid on the tax-exempt bonds does not *pass through* to the shareholders of a corporation. Thus, it is critical to avoid classifying the trust, custodial device, or other arrangement employed in the tax-exempt derivative as a "corporation" or "association taxable as a corporation."

In the 1940s the courts developed a strict rule for avoiding corporate classification for passive investment trusts.[138] Revenue rulings issued by the IRS since that time have continued to construe this rule narrowly.[139] It could be argued that many trust or custodial arrangements should be ignored, and not be subject to entity classification analysis. However, on the basis of comments of Treasury officials and others, it would appear that the IRS has rejected this approach.[140] Only in the most limited cases—for example, the establishment of an indenture trust or similar device relating directly to a bond—has the IRS ignored the existence of the trust.[141]

Therefore, in light of the draconian results if a trust, custodial account, or other arrangement employed in connection with a tax-exempt derivative is classified as an association taxable as a corporation, this issue must be thoroughly considered by tax counsel. Because trusts and partnerships qualify as pass-through entities,[142] secondary market tax-exempt derivatives are typically structured to make certain that the trust, custodial account, or other arrangement employed therewith would be classified as either a trust or a partnership for federal income tax purposes. Typically, tax counsel will specifically opine that the trust qualifies as a grantor trust or a partnership for federal income tax purposes.

Trust Classification—The Sears Regulations

The Sears Regulations restrict the trustee's or custodian's power to vary the investments of the trust or custodial account and generally require that there be only one class of beneficial interests. These rules substantially restrict:

1. the deposit of additional assets or property into the trust or account after the date of its creation;
2. the disposition of the assets held by the trustee or custodian to take advantage of market conditions;
3. the reinvestment of cash received by the trust or account;
4. the creation of reserve funds; and
5. the creation of multiple classes of beneficial interests.[143]

RESTRICTIONS ON MULTIPLE CLASS TRUSTS. Under the Sears Regulations, a trust that has more than one class of beneficial interests will not be classified as a trust for federal income tax purposes unless the multiple classes have been created merely to facilitate direct investment in the assets of the trust. If a trust does not qualify as a trust for federal income tax purposes, it will be deemed either a partnership or an association taxable as a corporation, depending upon the application of other tax law principles. If the trust is classified as an association, the investors holding interests in the trust could be considered "shareholders" and the distributions of trust income would be characterized as taxable "dividends."

The Sears Regulations include four examples to provide guidance on whether a multiple class trust merely facilitates the direct investment in the underlying assets of the trust.[144]

Example (1) describes a multiple class trust holding a pool of prepayable residential mortgage loans where one class of certificate holders receives prepayments on the mortgage loans at a rate faster than the other class of certificate holders (a "fast-pay/slow-pay" feature). Because direct ownership of the underlying mortgage loans would not permit the investor to allocate prepayment risk, the example concludes that this type of fast-pay/slow-pay trust would *not* qualify as a trust for tax purposes. The holding of this example substantially restricts flexibility in structuring multiple class trusts holding prepayable bonds such as mortgage revenue bonds.

Example (2) describes a multiple class trust holding a pool of prepayable residential mortgage loans involving two classes of certificate holders where the rights of both classes are identical except that the right to receive payments on one of the classes of certificates is subordinate, on an ongoing basis (rather than on a cumulative basis), to the payment to the other class of certificate holders in the event of payment default on the underlying mortgage loans (a "senior/subordinated" feature). Because the senior/subordinated feature merely functions as a limited recourse guarantee from the subordinated class of certificate holders to the senior class and an investor obtaining a direct ownership interest in the mortgage loans could obtain a similar limited recourse guaranty, the example concludes that the trust qualifies as a trust for federal income tax purposes. In 1992, the IRS issued guidance that explicitly permits investors to hold subordinated interests in grantor trusts.[145] This ruling indicates a reversal of an earlier adverse private letter ruling adopting the position that the ownership of subordinated interests by investors caused a trust to be classified as an association.[146]

Because of example (1)'s restriction on fast-pay/slow-pay trusts and the restrictions on the accumulation and investment of money by trusts under the Sears Regulations, a "cumulative" subordination feature, where all payments to the subordinated class of certificate holders are deferred until after the senior certificate holders are fully paid, does not appear permissible.

Example (3) of the Sears Regulations involves a trust holding shares of stock that issues two classes of certificates—one class entitling the holders thereof to payments of dividends on the stock and one class entitling the holders thereof to any capital appreciation in the shares (a "dividend-appreciation" stripping feature).[147] Because direct ownership of the underlying stock would not permit the investor to allocate the right to dividends and appreciation inherent in the stock, the example concludes that this type of dividend-appreciation stripping trust would *not* qualify as a trust for tax purposes. The holding of this example is important because, in connection with example (4) discussed below, it suggests that income-stripping arrangements should be carefully scrutinized to avoid recharacterization risk.

Example (4) of the Sears Regulations provides that a trust with multiple classes of beneficial interests where each class represents the right to a *specific payment* on the underlying bond held by the trust qualifies as a trust for federal income tax purposes, even though it has more than one class of beneficial interests, because the existence of multiple classes merely facilitates the direct investment in the assets of the trust. Example (4) specifically refers to the stripped bond rules of Section 1286 of the Code in determining that the multiple class trust merely facilitates direct investment in the assets of the trust.

Based upon example (4), the issuance of multiple classes of beneficial interests in a trust or custody account where each class represents the right to specific stripped bonds or coupons should not adversely affect the classification of the trust or custody account as a trust for federal income tax purposes. However, given the narrow exceptions to the general prohibition against multiple class trusts under the Sears Regulations, the reference to "particular payments" in example (4), and guidance regarding the scope of other examples under the Sears Regulations, tax advisers are concerned that a trust that facilitates a "variable strip" would not be classified as a trust.

A so-called variable strip represents an interest in a stripped bond or coupon that is determined by reference to variables such as an interest rate index (e.g., the right to all or a portion of an interest coupon on a fixed-rate bond where the amount is determined by reference to a bank's prime rate) or bond prepayment speed.[148] Whether the stripped bond rules have any application to a variable strip is unclear.[149] To the extent the stripped bond rules are intended to apply, the valuation of a variable strip appears difficult at best. There is concern regarding whether a trust or custodial arrangement that facilitates a variable strip falls within the safety net of example (4).

PASS-THROUGH STATUS UNDER THE GRANTOR TRUST RULES. While all entities classified as trusts for federal income tax purposes are "pass-through entities," the rules applicable to simple and complex trusts under Subchapter J of the Code are rather complicated, involving, among other things, the allowance of a deduction to the trust for distributions and rules for characterizing the type of income (e.g., capital gains or ordinary income) taxable to the trust's beneficiaries. The rules governing "grantor trusts" are much simpler. Based on a long line of published revenue rulings involving mortgage pass-through trusts and unit investment trusts, a trust or custody account that is classified as a trust under the investment trust rules of Treasury Regulation Section 301.7701-4 should qualify as a grantor trust for federal income tax purposes.[150] Investors in grantor trusts are treated as directly owning a fractional interest in each of the assets held by the trustee or custodian.[151]

Because the grantor trust rules treat investors as direct owners of a fractional interest in each of the trust assets, the investor must take into account the allocable purchase price of the fractional interest in any bond held by the trust in determining whether the bond premium amortization rules apply and whether gain is recognized upon the receipt of payments on the bonds by the trust or the disposition of trust assets.[152]

Partnership Classification

It is not necessary or determinative that an entity be structured as a partnership under state business law to be classified as a partnership for federal income tax purposes. The IRS has recently issued private letter rulings classifying trusts used in so-called hub and spoke investment arrangements as partnerships for federal income tax purposes.[153] Under Treasury Regulation Section 301.7701-2, the Partnership Classification Regulations, an investment entity that does not qualify as a trust will be classified as a partnership, rather than an association taxable as a corporation, if it lacks at least two of the following four factors:

1. continuity of life;
2. centralized management;
3. limited liability; and
4. free transferability of ownership interests.[154]

It should be noted that in analyzing the issue of whether the factors of limited liability and free transferability are lacking, it must be determined that trust provisions intended to make a partner subject to unlimited liability for trust or custodial account expenses are fully enforceable under applicable state law and that provisions intended to restrict the transferability of ownership interests therein are likewise enforceable.[155] Because these factors may be the basis for concluding that a trust or custodial account is a partnership for tax purposes, a state law enforceability opinion clearly addressing these issues is important.

CONTINUITY OF LIFE. The Partnership Classification Regulations provide that an organization intended to qualify as a limited partnership lacks continuity of life if upon the bankruptcy of any general partner the partnership will be dissolved, unless the remaining general partners (if any) agree to continue the partnership or unless at least a majority of the remaining limited partners agree to continue the partnership.[156] Many secondary market tax-exempt derivatives intended to qualify as partnerships for federal income tax purposes are structured to lack continuity of life.

CENTRALIZED MANAGEMENT. The Partnership Classification Regulations provide that centralized management is the concentration of authority to make business decisions on behalf of the entity that do not require ratification by the members of the organization.[157] Although it is somewhat unclear whether the actions normally permitted to be taken by a trustee, custodian, or agent with respect to passive trusts or custodial accounts that merely hold tax-exempt bonds and certain other assets rise to the level of centralized management, typically there is no ongoing requirement for investor ratification of actions. Moreover, requiring investor ratification would severely restrict these structures. Accordingly, generally it should be assumed that a trust, custodial account, or other arrangement possesses centralized management.[158]

LIMITED LIABILITY. The Partnership Classification Regulations provide that an organization possesses limited liability if under local law there is no member who is personally liable for the debts of or claims against the organization.[159] Moreover, the regulations provide that any person who is personally liable for partnership liabilities cannot merely be a "dummy" but must instead be a party possessing substantial assets.[160] For the entity to be treated as not possessing limited liability, a corporate general partner must have a net worth equal to at least 10 percent of the total contributions to the entity and must be expected to continue to have a sufficient net worth throughout the entity's life.[161] This ruling position addresses the potential for circumvention of the net worth rule by the use of a thinly capitalized corporate general partner.

The IRS does not apply a percentage of contributions net worth test to individuals who act as general partners, presumably because any personal liability is substantial to individuals who have some substantial net worth. Many practitioners put their focus on this real risk to the general partner and are, therefore, willing to render opinions that entities qualify as partnerships for tax purposes even when the general partner's net worth, as a percentage of the total contributions of the investors, is less than 10 percent.[162]

In addition, IRS guidelines for obtaining private letter rulings on the status of an entity as a partnership require that the general partners maintain a substantial stake in the partnership.[163] Under the guidelines, the general partners must continually maintain an interest of at least 1 percent in all material items of partnership income, gain, loss, deduction, or credit.[164] The guidelines also generally require that the general partners maintain throughout the life of the partnership minimum capital account balances in the partnership equal to the lesser of 1 percent of the aggregate positive capital account balances of the members of the partnership or $500,000.[165]

FREE TRANSFERABILITY OF INTEREST. The Partnership Classification Regulations provide that an entity has free transferability of interests if its members have the power, without the consent of other members, to transfer all of the attributes of their interests.[166] In order to avoid having free transferability, entities are often structured so that the transfer of an investor's interest is subject to the sole and discretionary consent of the general partner. In addition, recent guidance by the IRS in Revenue Procedure 92-33 provides that a partnership will generally lack free transferability of interests if, throughout the life of the partnership, the transferability of interests representing more than 20 percent of the interests in partnership capital, income, gain, loss, deduction, and credit is restricted.[167] In evaluating free transferability, state law should be analyzed to determine whether a restriction on transfer is enforceable. In many cases, since free transferability without the consent of the general partner may be essential to the marketing of the derivative, it may not be possible to satisfy the requirements of the revenue procedure. In those cases, attempting to limit free transferability obviously may not be an acceptable option.

SECTIONS 7704 AND 7701(I)—RESTRICTIONS ON PUBLICLY TRADED PARTNERSHIPS AND TAXABLE MORTGAGE POOLS. It is important to make certain that an entity intending to qualify as a partnership is not reclassified as a corporation as a result of the publicly traded partnership rules enacted under the Revenue Act of 1987 (Section 7704 of the Code) or the taxable mortgage pool rules of Section 7701(i) of the Code. In Notice 88-75, the IRS established guidelines for determining whether a partnership will be considered a publicly traded partnership (a PTP).[168] Concluding that secondary market tax-exempt derivatives structured as partnerships do not constitute PTPs often relies on the so-called private placement safe harbor. This safe harbor is met if (1) the derivative has been issued in a transaction that was not registered under the Securities Act of 1933; and (2) either (a) the derivative does not have more than 500 investors or (b) the initial price of each investment in the derivative is at least $20,000 and the partnership agreement provides that no interest in the derivative can be subdivided into units smaller than the $20,000 minimum denomination.[169] The 500-investor prong of the safe harbor is often not relied on because each indirect owner of any interest in the derivative (through a grantor trust, partnership, or S corporation) must be counted in determining the number of investors.

Application of the taxable mortgage pool rules requires determining whether a partnership with multiple classes of equity interests could be considered equivalent to debt pursuant to Section 7701(i)(2)(D) and whether such equity classes would be viewed as having more than one "maturity." The taxable mortgage pool rules require taxpayers to securitize taxable mortgage-backed securities under the real estate mortgage investment conduit (REMIC) rules of the Code. However, tax-exempt derivatives cannot be sold as REMICs because income accruing on REMIC regular interests is not tax-exempt (they are treated as debt of the REMIC, rather than of a state or local governmental entity). Thus, the applicability of the rules to tax-exempt derivatives appears inappropriate. However, it is important to note that there is at present no IRS guidance directly addressing whether the taxable mortgage pool rules apply to secondary market tax-exempt derivatives backed by mortgage-backed debt.

CONSEQUENCES OF PARTNERSHIP CLASSIFICATION.[170] Partnerships have flexibility in allocating their income among investors if the allocations have substantial economic effect.[171] The partnership allocation rules are far more flexible than the exception permitted for multiple class trusts under example (4) of the Sears Regulations, and there has been considerably more guidance than under the bond-stripping rules of Section 1286 of the Internal Revenue Code.

However, although tax-exempt income flows through a partnership as a result of the special allocation rules of the Code, a partner is treated as owning only one asset—the partnership interest, not a fractional interest in each asset held by the partnership.[172] The partnership will have its own tax basis in the bonds. Unless a special election is made (which triggers complex tax reporting obligations),[173] the partnership's basis in its assets will not reflect changes in market value that are taken into account by investors when they purchase or sell their partnership interests in the secondary market.[174]

In order to ensure that tax-exempt income will flow through a partnership to the investors, it must be ascertained that the investor's interest is properly classified as equity rather than debt. Very little federal income tax authority exists pertaining to whether an interest in a partnership that is purportedly equity should be reclassified as debt.[175] More typically, the cases have addressed whether partnership debt should be reclassified as equity.[176]

Unless an election is made by the partnership under Section 761(a) of the Code not to be taxed as a partnership,[177] investors in a secondary market tax-exempt derivative structured as a partnership will receive IRS Form K-1, setting forth tax return information.

Determining Whether the Investor Owns the Underlying Bond

There is a substantial body of law dealing with the issue of whether a put right provided by a third party to the putative owner of a tax-exempt bond jeopardizes the investor's status as owner of the bond. The transaction could be classified as a repurchase agreement or "repo"—i.e., a loan by the investor to the put provider with the put provider treated as the true owner of the bond for federal income tax purposes.[178] If a transaction is a repo, distributions received by the investor would be treated as having come from the put provider (who is probably not a state or local issuer) and would be viewed as taxable interest on the repo loan to the put provider.

In a 1982 ruling, the IRS held that a mutual fund that had acquired puts from a dealer to cover a percentage of its municipal bond portfolio to ensure sufficient liquidity of the portfolio for shareholder redemption purposes remained the tax owner of the bonds.[179] The fund invested in a portfolio of short-term tax-exempt bonds with a remaining maturity of one year or less. The bonds were acquired at fair market value from a municipal bond dealer. The puts were nonassignable and terminated if the mutual fund disposed of the related bonds. The price paid for the puts was determined on an arm's-length basis and was in addition to the fair market value price paid for the bonds. There were no restrictions on the sale or disposition of the bonds by the mutual fund. In addition, there were no call agreements, either formal or informal, expressed or implied, between the mutual fund and the dealer. After discussing the judicial precedent, the IRS reduced the tax ownership analysis to a basic two-pronged test:

1. Which party to the transaction had the right to dispose of the property? and
2. Which party bore the risk of loss or retained the opportunity for profit with respect to the property?

Answering these two questions, the ruling held that the mutual fund had control over the bonds because the fund was holding the bonds for its benefit and was free to dispose of them at any time. The ruling also held that the mutual fund held a greater share of the benefits of ownership on the bonds than the seller because (1) "the [fund] was entitled to the full benefit of any appreciation in the value of the obligations"; (2) the separate price paid for the puts, which was based upon risk assessment by the dealer, established that the puts were independent of the bonds; (3) the primary purpose of the puts was to increase the liquidity of the mutual fund's portfolio rather than to shift the risk of loss; and (4) the puts were for a period substantially less than the term of the bonds. Based on this analysis, the IRS concluded in the ruling that the mutual fund was the owner of the bonds, notwithstanding the fact that puts were simultaneously acquired from the dealer.

In 1983, the IRS issued Revenue Procedure 83-55, which stated that the IRS would not ordinarily issue rulings regarding the "[d]etermination as to who is the true owner of property in cases involving the sale of securities, or participation interests therein, . . . to be purchased by either the seller or a third party."[180] It is believed that Revenue Procedure 83-55 was issued to have a chilling effect on various put programs involving tax-exempt bonds that were being structured by banks in 1982 and 1983—and it did.

Analyzing the Investor's Control over the Underlying Bond

The first prong of the ownership test set forth above focuses on the investor's control over the bond (i.e., the right to dispose of the bond). Secondary market tax-exempt derivatives that provide the investor with put rights typically permit the investor to retain some control over the underlying bond. This is often done by permitting the investor to opt out of the put right and the obligation to pay the ongoing put fee, subject to a nonprohibitive termination fee intended to compensate the put provider for unwinding any hedge associated with providing the put. Depending on the specifics of the derivative, the investor may be permitted to opt out at any time or during "windows" occurring either when the derivative is created or over time. Other secondary market derivative products permit the investors to vote to force the sale of the underlying bond.

In the case of partnership-structured derivatives that permit the partners to put their partnership interests, the relevant analysis should be focused on the investors' right to dispose of their partnership interests, rather than on their right to force the disposition of the underlying bonds held by the partnership, because the tax law does not treat partners as directly holding fractional interests in the underlying assets of the partnership.[181]

Analyzing the Burdens and Benefits Relating to the Underlying Bond That Are Retained by the Investor

The second prong of the ownership test focuses on whether the investor has retained the benefits and burdens of owning the underlying bond. Secondary market tax-exempt derivatives that provide the investor with put rights typically are structured to make certain the investor has the right to obtain all or a portion of the potential profit associated with the underlying bond.[182]

At the same time, secondary market derivatives that include put rights are also typically structured to make certain the investor remains subject to certain risks of loss. For example, it is typical that the investor cannot exercise the put right if the underlying bonds are subject to an event of taxability, if the underlying bonds are significantly downgraded by a rating agency, or if there is a default in the payment of principal or interest.[183]

The Stripped Bond Rules

When Do the Stripped Bond Rules Apply?

A bond is considered stripped if ownership of the right to receive principal on the bond is separated from the ownership of any coupon that has not yet become payable.[184] A "coupon" includes any right to receive interest on a bond.[185] Since there is essentially no difference between the two, the term "stripped tax-exempt bond" will be used to generically describe both the right to receive principal payments and the right to receive interest payments.

The stripped tax-exempt bond rules were originally enacted to curb perceived abusive transactions. Holders of bonds were stripping the interest coupons from bond principal, selling stripped bonds (i.e., the principal portion) at discounts, and recognizing tax losses because the holders' tax basis in the underlying bond was allocated entirely to the principal portion of the bond. This perceived abuse is illustrated by the following example:

> An investor acquired at par a bond on its issue date. The bond's terms included (1) a principal amount of $100 due entirely at maturity, (2) a ten-year term, and (3) interest at a stated rate of 10 percent, payable semiannually. The investor's tax basis in the bond was $100. The investor stripped all of the interest coupons from the bond and sold the principal portion (i.e., the stripped bond) to a third party for $38. Under prior law, the investor would claim a $62 loss on the sale for federal income tax purposes ($38 sales proceeds received less $100 tax basis).

The principal focus of the stripped bond rules as originally enacted was the allocation of tax basis among the various components of the underlying bond. Section 1286 of the Internal Revenue Code requires an allocation of tax basis based on the relative fair market values of the cash flows (i.e., the interest coupons and principal payments comprising a bond) that the underlying bond represents.

Stripped tax-exempt bonds are clearly covered by the stripped bond rules of the Internal Revenue Code. In addition, many other types of tax-exempt derivatives may be subject to these rules if either (1) they explicitly provide for an allocation of rights to receive interest and principal payments on a bond that is not constant and uniform for all payments on the bond or (2) fees received by a service provider relating to the derivative are in excess of reasonable compensation for services rendered.[186] As discussed above, if it is believed that the tax-exempt derivative results in the stripping of the underlying bond, it should be considered whether the manner in which payments on the bond are allocated constitutes a so-called variable strip, which raises Sears Regulations concerns. Sears Regulations concerns may be particularly relevant when bonds subject to prepayment risk (especially prepayable premium rate bonds) are stripped.[187]

Basic Principles of the Stripped Bond Rules

Section 1286(b) of the Internal Revenue Code requires an allocation of tax basis when a bond is stripped based upon the relative fair market values of the stripped components of the bond.[188] Section 1286(a) of the Code requires the seller and any investor purchasing a stripped bond or coupon to treat the stripped bond or coupon as a bond issued with an original issue discount equal to the difference between its purchase price (in the case of the seller, its allocable tax basis) and the stated redemption price at maturity in the case of a stripped bond or the amount payable in the case of a stripped coupon. The holder of a stripped taxable bond generally includes the original issue discount in taxable income on a daily basis as it accrues by reference to the original issue discount rules of Section 1272 of the Code.

If a stripped bond or coupon is later sold, the new purchaser must treat the entire difference between its purchase price and the amount payable as original issue discount.

Long before the original enactment of the stripped bond rules in 1982, the IRS ruled that an investor was entitled to treat the receipt of payment on a municipal bond interest coupon as tax-exempt only if the investor also owned the principal portion of the bond.[189] In addition, the stripped bond rules as originally enacted did not include special rules for tax-exempt bonds. In 1986, the stripped bond rules were amended to provide that all or a portion of the original issue discount on a stripped tax-exempt bond would be treated as tax-exempt original issue discount.[190]

Potential Taxable Income Concerns Under the Stripped Bond Rules

The special provisions of the stripped bond rules relating to stripped tax-exempt bonds treat the investor's original issue discount as tax-exempt only if the investor's yield, determined as of the date of purchase, does not exceed the "coupon rate" on the underlying tax-exempt bond (or the original yield if the investor so elects and can adequately establish the original yield on the underlying bond, if higher).[191] If the investor's yield exceeds the coupon rate, the excess yield is treated as taxable original issue discount that is included in the investor's taxable income as it accrues.[192]

An investor purchasing a stripped tax-exempt bond (or other tax-exempt derivative subject to stripped bond rules) should carefully consider whether the yield on the investment (determined as of the date of purchase) exceeds the coupon rate on the underlying tax-exempt bond. Typically this rule does not pose problems in today's market because many bonds being stripped and securitized were originated in higher interest rate environments. However, investors should note that the stripped bond rules require that this determination be made *whenever* a stripped tax-exempt bond is purchased. Accordingly, secondary market transactions involving stripped tax-exempts and other tax-exempt derivatives subject to these rules in a relatively high interest rate market environment could result in the receipt of taxable original issue discount to purchasers. This could adversely impact their after-tax yield and could accordingly impact the amount realized by purchasers in today's market that dispose of their interests in a future high interest rate market.

The IRS has recently issued final regulations relating to the tax treatment of stripped bonds.[193] These regulations contain a formula for determining when original issue discount on a stripped bond will be considered *de minimis* and treats the original issue discount on a stripped bond as zero if the amount of original issue discount, determined as of the date the stripped bond is purchased, is less than one-fourth of 1 percent for each full year the stripped bond is outstanding. The *de minimis* rule was intended to permit investors to avoid the onerous stripped bond rules as they relate to taxable bonds. The final regulations clarify an ambiguity contained in the prior temporary regulation[194] by explicitly stating that the *de minimis* rule does not apply to the tax-exempt portion of original issue discount on stripped tax-exempt bonds. Otherwise, the *de minimis* rule would prevent investors from relying on the stripped tax-exempt bond rules to increase their tax basis in the stripped bond to the extent of any *de minimis* original issue discount. Thus, but for this clarification, because the investor's basis would not increase, the receipt of payments on the stripped bond would trigger the recognition of capital gain in an amount equal to the amount of income that would have been treated as tax-exempt original issue discount had the stripped bond rules applied.[195]

Concerns Relating to Interest Rate Swaps

Payments on Swap Received by the Investor Are Taxable

Because payments on an interest rate swap are not interest on a bond for federal income tax purposes,[196] net payments received on an interest rate swap will, in general, be taxable income to the recipient, regardless of whether they are paid by a corporation, an individual, a partnership, or a state or local governmental unit.[197] Investors in a tax-exempt derivative that includes an interest rate swap should evaluate the likelihood that they will receive net payments on the swap during any tax year.

Taxable Income Considerations Relating to Swap Premiums

In many cases, an initial premium must be paid, or is received, at the time an interest rate swap is entered into. Swap premiums are paid when a swap is "off-market" (i.e., when the terms of the swap are inconsistent with dealer quotes for swaps with similar payment and maturity characteristics). In structuring an "at-market" interest rate swap, the parties reach agreement regarding the appropriate fixed rate, given the agreed floating-rate index, and, typically, neither party will make an up-front payment. Typically, municipal market participants specify the fixed interest rate that they want the swap to bear.[198] Accordingly, the swap premium takes into account the difference between the fixed rate on the interest rate swap that the parties desire and the fixed rate the swap would have borne had it been structured at the prevailing market fixed rate.

Swap premiums received by an investor may result in taxable income in one of two ways:

1. If the investor receives the premium and it is not treated as an embedded loan (as discussed below), the amount of the premium amortized during any tax year of the investor may exceed the net ongoing swap payments accrued by the investor during the tax year. The excess would be taxable income recognized during the tax year.
2. If the investor pays the premium and it is treated as an embedded loan, the investor may be deemed to have received taxable interest income on its deemed loan to the swap counterparty.

AMORTIZING SWAP PREMIUMS RECEIVED. The ability of the investor to offset the taxable income generated by the swap premium with future payments made on the swap is critical. The Final Swap Regulations and prior IRS guidance make it clear that the IRS takes the position that an investor receiving an interest rate swap premium must take the premium into account in computing taxable income under a reasonable method of amortization.[199] Under the Final Swap Regulations, reasonable methods of amortization are generally limited to a method that takes into account the values of a series of cash-settled forward contracts that replicate the swap—a so-called level payment constant yield method. The Final Swap Regulations do not permit the use of a straight-line method or any other methods.[200]

The Final Swap Regulations provide that the amount of a swap premium amortized by an investor for a particular tax year must then be netted with any ongoing swap payments or receipts that accrue to the investor for the tax year.[201] Thus, an investor will recognize taxable income on an ongoing basis as a result of the receipt of a swap premium only if the amount of swap premium amortized by the investor for a particular year exceeds the investor's net ongoing payments accrued on the swap for the tax year. Understanding in advance how much of the swap premium will be amortized each tax year enables the investor to address this type of taxable income risk by identifying market rate thresholds at which ongoing swap payments will be insufficient to fully offset the amount of swap premium amortized for any particular tax year.

EMBEDDED LOANS—CONSIDERING THE IMPACT OF SWAP PREMIUMS PAID. The Final Swap Regulations introduced the concept of the "embedded loan" where the swap premium is "significant." Unfortunately, the regulations do not provide any safe harbor or bright-line test on the issue of what constitutes a significant swap premium.[202] Instead, they merely include two examples—an example that treats the swap premium as an embedded loan involving a premium equal to 66.7 percent of the net present value of the fixed payments on the swap and an example that does not treat the swap premium as an embedded loan involving a premium equal to 9.1 percent of the present value of the fixed payments on the swap. If the swap premium is significant, it is recharacterized as a loan by the party paying the premium to the party receiving it, and a portion of the ongoing payments made on the swap is recharacterized as payment on the loan.[203] The regulations treat the embedded loan as including an interest component.[204] As previously discussed, it is likely that interest earned by the payor of the swap premium on the embedded loan will be taxable interest income.[205]

Thus, investors should consider whether the swap premiums they pay are subject to recharacterization under the Final Swap Regulations as embedded loans. Although there is a broad gap between the relative levels of the swap premiums in the examples set forth in the regulations, investors should consider whether any swap premium they pay significantly exceeds the 9.1 percent amount included in the favorable example contained in the regulations.

Taxable Income Considerations Relating to Dispositions of Swap-Type Derivatives or the Unwinding of the Associated Swap

The early termination of an interest rate swap or the disposition of a swap-type derivative raises additional taxable income concerns. First, any unamortized swap premium received by an investor should be recognized as income at the time of termination or disposition of the swap-type derivative, taking into account any additional payments due or payable upon disposition, including swap termination payments.[206] Second, the investor may recognize an offsetting gain or loss upon the disposition of the underlying tax-exempt bond relating to the tax-exempt derivative. Thus, it must be considered whether any net income or gain recognized on the disposition or termination of the swap can be offset by any gain or loss recognized upon the disposition of the bond. Gain or loss on the disposition of the bond will generally qualify as capital gain or loss.[207] The key issue is whether gain or loss recognized upon the termination or disposition of the swap is also characterized as capital in nature.

Prior to the release of the Final Swap Regulations, it was believed that the income recognized as a result of the termination of a swap (as opposed to the sale of an interest in a swap accomplished through the sale of a swap-type derivative) would be characterized as ordinary income because the termination would not constitute a "sale or disposition" for tax purposes, a prerequisite for capital gain or loss treatment.[208] However, the Final Swap Regulations treat interest rate swaps as actively traded property for purposes of the straddle rules of Section 1092 of the Code (the straddle rules impact the timing and character of losses recognized on certain hedged transactions).[209] Characterization of an interest rate swap as part of the straddle does result in the characterization of gain recognized on termination of the swap as capital gain, permitting the gain to be offset with any loss recognized on the disposition of the related bond.[210]

Timing Differences and Taxable Income Concerns

Tax-exempt derivatives may be structured with a timing lag between the date payments on the underlying tax-exempt bond are received by the trust or custodial account and the date payments are made to investors. The trust or custodial account may provide for the investment of amounts held prior to distribution to investors. The temporary investment of these amounts by the trust or custodial account raises taxable income concerns. The direct payment of any temporary earnings received on taxable temporary investments would clearly constitute taxable income to the investor because the earnings would not be part of the issuer's obligations on the underlying tax-exempt bond.[211] Unfortunately, although the income on the investments, if attributable to the investor, is taxable, the offsetting expense may not be deductible; Section 265 of the Code restricts deductions for investors other than corporations that relate to the receipt of tax-exempt income.[212] Accordingly, as a tax matter it may be prudent for any temporary investments made by the trust or custodial account to be in tax-exempt instruments.

Ordinary Income Concerns

The Revenue Reconciliation Act of 1993[213] enacted in August 1993 contained two provisions that potentially raise ordinary income concerns for investors in tax-exempt derivatives.

First, the 1993 Act amended Section 1278 of the Code, such that tax-exempt bonds purchased after April 30, 1993, are subject to the market discount rules of the Code. Market discount is defined, in general, as the amount (if any) by which the stated redemption price at maturity exceeds an investor's purchase price unless the total amount of market discount is not in excess of a *de minimis* amount.[214] As a result of the 1993 Act, the accretion of market discount on a tax-exempt bond that, under prior law, was treated as capital gain is taxable as ordinary income.

Second, the 1993 Act adds to the Code a new Section 1258, which characterizes capital gains as ordinary income in the case of certain financial transactions that are "conversion transactions," effective for transactions entered into after April 30, 1993. Conversion transactions include, among other things, certain straddles and certain transactions marketed or sold as producing capital gains where substantially all of the taxpayer's expected return is attributable to the time value of the net investment.

Collateral Tax Considerations

State Tax Treatment

The state tax consequences of issuing and investing in tax-exempt derivatives should be considered. For example, in some cases the distributions on a secondary market derivative may not be exempt for state income tax purposes, even if distributions on the underlying tax-exempt bond would be tax-exempt if received directly by the investor. Similarly, although the direct ownership of a tax-exempt bond may be exempt from state intangibles taxes, the state may impose an intangibles tax on the indirect ownership of the same bond through a derivative structure.

Allocation of Basis—Computation of Gain or Loss

Many secondary market tax-exempt derivatives are comprised of several different components, such as a tax-exempt bond (or several), a put right, and possibly an interest rate swap. The investor may be required to allocate his or her basis in the derivative among the different components based on their relative fair market values as of the date the derivative is acquired. Gain or loss realized on the sale or other disposition of the derivative or one of its components may similarly be subject to allocation among the components of the tax-exempt derivative.

Additional Concerns for Mutual Funds Investing in Derivatives

In order to qualify as regulated investment companies (RICs) and avoid entity level taxation, mutual funds must satisfy specific requirements relating to the character of their income, the diversity of their investments, and the timely income distribution to their investors.[215]

Because many secondary market tax-exempt derivatives are structured from a number of distinct components, counsel and tax advisers to mutual funds are faced with a myriad of technical issues that must be considered in evaluating the derivative. For example, a synthetic floater may be comprised of an underlying bond that bears an interest rate of 8 percent. After the payment of a put fee, however, the net payment to the investing mutual fund is only 5 percent (8 percent reduced by an assumed put fee of 3 percent). To comply with the income distribution requirements applicable to RICs, is the RIC required to take into account the entire 8 percent earned on the underlying tax-exempt bond, or is it permitted to take into account the net amount received, reduced by the 3 percent put fee?[216] Similarly, is the put right a separate security that must be evaluated under the diversification test applicable to RICs?[217]

Concerns Associated with Hedging Transactions

The Supreme Court's 1988 decision in *Arkansas Best Corp. v. Commissioner*[218] raised considerable controversy about the tax character of gains and losses from hedging transactions.[219] *Arkansas Best* involved a holding company that bought stock in a bank. When the stock was sold at a loss, the holding company treated the loss as ordinary, arguing that it bought the stock to acquire the bank as part of its business operations and therefore its treatment of the loss as ordinary was allowable under the long-standing doctrine of *Corn Products Refining Co. v. Commissioner*,[220] which had been interpreted as standing for the principle that gains and losses arising from everyday business operations are ordinary rather than capital in nature. In *Corn Products*, the Supreme Court held that hedging gains relating to hedging transactions

EXHIBIT 5-3

Tax Issues Relevant for Particular Tax-Exempt Derivatives

Type of Derivative	Are Payments Interest?	Reissuance?	Arbitrage Yield or Rebate?	Trust or Partnership?	Ownership of Bond?	Strip Rules?	Swap Issues?	Timing Issues?
Primary Products								
Dutch Auction Bonds	X	X	X	N/A	N/A	N/A	N/A	N/A
Inverse Floaters	X	X	X	N/A	N/A	N/A	N/A	N/A
Foreign Currency Denominated Bonds	X	X	X	N/A	N/A	N/A	N/A	N/A
Detachable Call Bonds	X	X	X	N/A	N/A	N/A	N/A	N/A
Secondary Products								
Stripped Tax-Exempts	N/A	X	N/A	X	N/A	X	N/A	X
Synthetic Floaters	N/A	X	N/A	X	X	X	X	X
Custodial Receipts	N/A	X	N/A	X	X	X	X	X
Tax-Exempt Asset-Backed Securities	N/A	X	N/A	X	N/A	X	N/A	X
Muni Preferred Shares	N/A	N/A	N/A	N/A	N/A	N/A	N/A	N/A

Note that this table assumes that the underlying bond component of the derivative product qualifies as a tax-exempt bond and does not address other collateral issues, issues of special significance to certain types of investors, or state tax issues.

that were realized by a corn processor with respect to hedging its corn inventory risk were ordinary. In rejecting the holding company's arguments and distinguishing *Corn Products,* the Supreme Court in *Arkansas Best* concluded that the *Corn Products* decision had been based on a reading of the exception to capital asset treatment for inventory contained in Section 1221 of the Code, a reading that was inappropriate with respect to the *Arkansas Best* facts since the bank stock did not constitute "inventory" of the holding company. Moreover, the Supreme Court stated that in order to qualify for ordinary loss treatment, property must be specifically included in Section 1221 of the Code, which does not generally encompass hedges.

The Tax Court recently held in *Federal National Mortgage Ass'n v. Commissioner*[221] that various transactions entered into by the Federal National Mortgage Association (FNMA) as part of a hedging program resulted in ordinary gain or loss. During the 1980s, FNMA implemented hedging transactions against anticipated issuances of debentures, commitments to purchase notes of the Alaska Housing Finance Corporation, and convertible commitments. The IRS had asserted that the gains and losses arising from these transactions were capital, although they had been reported by FNMA as ordinary. However, the Tax Court refused to establish a "business hedging" exception from the rule of *Arkansas Best,* and instead, held that ordinary income or loss treatment was available if any of the exceptions from the definition of a capital asset under Section 1221 applied. The court, through a liberal reading of Section 1221(4), which provides that accounts or notes receivable acquired in the ordinary course of trade or business for services rendered or from the sale of 1221(1) property are not capital assets, found that both the hedging transactions relating to FNMA's acquisition of mortgages and the hedging transactions related to its mortgage acquisition financing program were sufficiently connected to Section 1221(4) to be excluded from the definition of "capital asset." Based on this broad interpretation of 1221(4)-related hedging, the Tax Court held that the transactions entered into by FNMA to reduce its interest rate risk in connection with the issuance of debentures and mortgage commitments were hedges and, as such, qualified as ordinary gain or loss, an interpretation consistent with the Supreme Court's analysis in *Arkansas Best.* Unfortunately, there were concerns that it could be difficult for many other taxpayers to establish that their hedging transactions were connected with Section 1221(4)-type matters and therefore to establish that they were entitled to ordinary gain or loss treatment on the transactions.

The inability to claim ordinary losses with respect to hedging transactions is clearly a critical concern for those who engage in such transactions for risk management purposes. Because of the significance of this issue as a matter of tax policy and the fact that it is being litigated by the IRS in a number of cases, the IRS issued temporary and proposed regulations addressing this issue in October of 1993.[222]

Notes

Chapter sections headed "Secondary Market Products" and "Collateral Tax Considerations" are essentially a revision of an article by Steven D. Conlon, Vincent M. Aquilino, and Dale S. Collinson, *Tax Law Fundamentals of Tax-Exempt Derivatives*, published in 1992 (55 TAX NOTES 381, Apr. 20, 1992).

1. As discussed later, payments on an interest rate swap, cap, or floor do not constitute "interest" for federal income tax purposes and therefore cannot qualify as tax-exempt.

2. I.R.C. § 103.

3. *See, e.g.*, Old Colony R.R. v. Commissioner, 284 U.S. 552 (1932); Deputy v. du Pont, 308 U.S. 488 (1940); Fall River Elec. Light Co. v. Commissioner, 23 B.T.A. 168 (1931); Rev. Rul. 69-188, 1969-1 C.B. 54.

4. However, the IRS has issued some guidance. *See, e.g.*, Rev. Rul. 85-119, 1985-2 C.B. 60; IRS Notice 88-27, 1988-1 C.B. 496; IRS Notice 88-90, 1988-2 C.B. 414; IRS Notice 88-130, 1988-2 C.B. 543 (the Notices do not directly address the status of the payments as interest or whether the ongoing resetting of interest rates thereunder results in reissuance).

5. 51 Fed. Reg. 12,022 (Apr. 8, 1986); 56 Fed. Reg. 8308 (Feb. 28, 1991). Note, however, that Prop. Treas. Reg. Section 1.1275-4(a) provides that the regulations were not intended to influence whether an instrument constitutes debt or equity for tax purposes. Although the OID rules of the Code do not directly apply to tax-exempt bonds (Section 1272(a)(2)(A) of the Code), the rules indirectly apply pursuant to Section 1288 of the Code.

6. Upon the release of the 1992 Proposed OID Regulations the 1986 Proposed OID Regulations were withdrawn. The 1992 Proposed OID Regulations are proposed to be effective for debt instruments issued on or after 60 days after the date final OID regulations are published. 57 Fed. Reg. 60,754 (Dec. 22, 1992). Accordingly, a "guidance gap" arises with respect to debt instruments issued after Dec. 21, 1992, but before the effective date of final regulations.

7. *See generally* Steven D. Conlon, Peter J. Connors & Mary Sue Butch, *Contingent Debt Instruments Are "Divided and Conquered" Under the New OID Proposed Regs.*, 75 J. TAX'N 46, 48–49 (July 1991).

8. Prop. Treas. Reg. Section 1.1275-5(a)(3).

9. Prop. Treas. Reg. Section 1.1275-5(b)(1), -5(d), Examples 3 and 4. A multiple of a qualified floating rate is generally not considered a qualified floating rate.

10. Prop. Treas. Reg. Section 1.1275-5(b)(2).

11. *Id.*

12. Prop. Treas. Reg. Section 1.1275-5(c), -5(d), Example 5.

13. Prop. Treas. Reg. Section 1.1275-5(c).

14. *Id.*

15. Prop. Treas. Reg. Section 1.1275-5(c)(2)(ii).

16. Prop. Treas. Reg. Section 1.1275-5(c)(2)(i).

17. Prop. Treas. Reg. Section 1.1275-5(c)(2)(iii).

18. However, the Notices do not treat such rate mechanisms as "objective interest indices" under Prop. Treas. Reg. Section 1.1275-5(b). IRS Notice 88-130, 1988-2 C.B. 543 (relating to whether the modification of interest rates and other terms of a tax-exempt bond will constitute a reissuance of a bond for Section 103 purposes), also arguably supports the treatment of a remarketing agent based rate as a permissible rate, although it does not directly address this issue.

19. Although, as discussed below, the 1992 Proposed OID Regulations explicitly reserve on the tax treatment of tax-exempt debt instruments with embedded options, forwards, and swaps.

20. *See* Prop. Treas. Reg. Section 1.1275-5(d), Example 8.

21. *See* Jonathan Fuerbringer, *Yen Bonds to Be Offered by New York,* N.Y. TIMES, Mar. 9, 1993, at C1 (recent New York issue of yen denominated bonds ("Samurai bonds") targeted for sale in Japan).

22. The advent of this provision had a chilling effect on foreign currency denominated bond issues in 1987; *see* Glen Craney, *Foreign Debt Market Proves Less Tempting to Muni Issuers Than Analysts Predicted,* THE BOND BUYER, July 7, 1987, at 1; *see also* IRS Announcement 87-57, 1987-26 I.R.B. 52.

23. A more thorough discussion of foreign currency denominated debt is omitted.

24. Prop. Treas. Reg. Section 1.1275-4(g).

25. Note that the authority of the IRS to apply the Proposed OID Regulations to reach this result is questionable because the legislative grant of rulemaking authority relating to the OID rules under Section 1275(d) relates to the *timing* of income recognition—not the character of income (taxable v. tax-exempt). Even if the bifurcation rule of Prop. Treas. Reg. Section 1.1275-4(g) does not apply, the application of other provisions of the contingent payment rules that require payments to be taken into account by issuers and investors at the time they become "fixed" raises potential timing issues for certain types of bonds.

26. Prop. Treas. Reg. Section 1.1275-4(a)(7)(i)(A).

27. Prop. Treas. Reg. Section 1.1275-4(a)(7)(i)(B), (C).

28. Prop. Treas. Reg. Section 1.1275-4(b)(2)(ii).

29. Prop. Treas. Reg. Section 1.1275-4(d).

30. Prop. Treas. Reg. Section 1.1275-4(g).

31. Prop. Treas. Reg. Section 1.1275-4 (Section B of the preamble).

32. *Id.; see also* Prop. Treas. Reg. Section 1.1275-4(b)(11).

33. *See supra* note 6 for a description of the effective date relating to the 1992 Proposed OID Regulations. Likewise, the effective date for the 1993 Contingent Payment Regulations is 60 days after the date the regulations are finalized.

34. *See* Rev. Rul. 55-540, 1955-2 C.B. 39.

35. *See* Priv. Ltr. Rul. 7821068 (Feb. 24, 1978).

36. I.R.C. § 148(f).

37. *See generally* FREDERIC L. BALLARD, JR., ABCS OF ARBITRAGE (1992); Jeffrey D. Berry and Anthony R. Rosso, *Tax Exempt Bond Arbitrage Proposals Are Complex, but Still Simplify Existing Rules,* J. TAX'N 228 (Apr. 1993).

38. Treas. Reg. Section 1.148-4(h). The 1993 Final Arbitrage Regulations are contained in 58 Fed. Reg. 33,510 (June 18, 1993).

39. 57 Fed. Reg. 53,046 (Nov. 6, 1992).

40. *Compare* Treas. Reg. Section 1.148-4(h) with Prop. Treas. Reg. Section 1.148-4(h).

41. *See* Treas. Reg. Section 1.148-4(h)(2)(i)(B) and the reference in Treas. Reg. Section 1.148-4(h)(5)(i) to the potential characterization of certain hedging contracts as an embedded loan, investment-type property, or other property.

42. Treas. Reg. Section 1.148-1(b).

43. Treas. Reg. Section 1.148-4(h).

44. Treas. Reg. Section 1.148-4(h)(1).

45. Treas. Reg. Section 1.148-4(h)(2)(i)(A).

46. Treas. Reg. Section 1.148-4(h)(2)(ii).

47. Treas. Reg. Section 1.148-4(h)(2)(iii).

48. Treas. Reg. Section 1.148-4(h)(2)(iv).
49. Treas. Reg. Section 1.148-4(h)(2)(v).
50. Treas. Reg. Section 1.148-4(h)(2)(vi).
51. Treas. Reg. Section 1.148-4(h)(2)(vii).
52. Treas. Reg. Section 1.148-4(h)(2)(viii)) (Does this mean that the swap payments cannot be paid out of bond proceeds or is it sufficient that this portion of the bonds is paid from the same revenue source? See Treas. Reg. Section 1.148-6(d)(3)(ii)(2)).
53. Treas. Reg. Section 1.148-4(h)(2)(ix).
54. Treas. Reg. Section 1.148-4(h)(2)(i)(A).
55. Treas. Reg. Section 1.148-4(h)(2)(iv).
56. Treas. Reg. Section 1.148-4(h)(2)(i)(B).
57. *Id.*
58. *Id.*
59. Treas. Reg. Section 1.148-4(h)(2)(ix).
60. Treas. Reg. Section 1.148-4(h)(3)(i).
61. Treas. Reg. Section 1.148-4(h)(3)(iii).
62. Treas. Reg. Section 1.148-4(h)(3)(i).
63. Treas. Reg. Section 1.148-4(h)(3)(ii).
64. Treas. Reg. Section 1.148-4(h)(3)(iv)(A).
65. *Id.*
66. Note that the definition of "termination" set forth in Treas. Reg. Section 1.148-4(h)(3)(iv)(A) only references the sale, assignment, or other disposition of the hedge *by the issuer,* not the counterparty.
67. Treas. Reg. Section 1.148-4(h)(3)(iv)(B).
68. *Id.*
69. Treas. Reg. Section 1.148-4(h)(3)(iv)(C).
70. *Id.*
71. Treas. Reg. Section 1.148-4(h)(3)(iv)(D).
72. Treas. Reg. Section 1.148-4(h)(4)(i).
73. *Id.*
74. Treas. Reg. Section 1.148-4(h)(4)(i)(A).
75. Treas. Reg. Section 1.148-4(h)(4)(i)(B).
76. Treas. Reg. Section 1.148-4(h)(4)(i)(C).
77. Treas. Reg. Section 1.148-4(h)(4)(i)(D).
78. Treas. Reg. Section 1.148-4(h)(4)(i)(E).
79. Treas. Reg. Section 1.148-4(h)(4)(ii)(A).
80. Treas. Reg. Section 1.148-4(h)(4)(ii)(B).
81. Treas. Reg. Section 1.148-4(h)(4)(ii)(C).
82. Treas. Reg. Section 1.148-4(h)(5)(i).
83. Treas. Reg. Section 1.148-4(h)(5)(ii).
84. Treas. Reg. Section 1.148-4(h)(5)(iii).
85. *See generally* Juliann Avakian-Martin, *IRS Considering Extending Arbitrage Bond Qualified Hedge Rules,* HIGHLIGHTS & DOCUMENTS, Aug. 3, 1993, at 1386; Lynn Stevens Hume, *Arbitrage Rules a Hit: Single Set of Standards Wins Industry Praise for Simplicity, Ease,* THE BOND BUYER, July 8, 1993, at 1.
86. *See* Treas. Reg. Section 1.148-4(h)(3)(ii).
87. *See* Treas. Reg. Sections 1.148-4(h)(2)(i)(B) and (h)(5)(i).
88. *See* GENERAL EXPLANATION OF THE TAX REFORM ACT OF 1986, 100th Cong., 1st Sess. 1202-03 (1987) (hereinafter 1986 BLUEBOOK); H.R. Conf. Rep. No. 841, 99th Cong., 2d Sess. II-746 (1986).

89. The Proposed 1001 Regulation was issued, in part, in response to controversy generated by the Supreme Court's decision in Cottage Savings Ass'n v. Commissioner, 111 S. Ct. 1503 (1991). *See generally* Richard L. Bacon & Harold L. Adrion, *Taxable Events: The Aftermath of Cottage Savings,* 59 TAX NOTES 1227 (May 31, 1993)(Part I), 59 TAX NOTES 1385 (June 7, 1993) (Part II).

90. A number of restrictions, principally with respect to "industrial development bonds" (IDBs), were enacted over the past thirteen years, principally in 1984 and 1986, and prevent the use of tax-exempt bond proceeds for certain expenditures permitted under prior law. Some of these restrictions do not have "grandfathering provisions."

91. Prop. Treas. Reg. Section 1.1001-3(a).

92. Prop. Treas. Reg. Section 1.1001-3(e).

93. Prop. Treas. Reg. Section 1.1001-3(c)(1).

94. Prop. Treas. Reg. Section 1.1001-3(c)(2)(i). Note that the Automatic Rule does not apply if the change pursuant to the original terms of the instrument results in an instrument or property right that is not debt for federal income tax purposes. Prop. Treas. Reg. Section 1.1001-3(c)(3).

95. Prop. Treas. Reg. Section 1.1001-3(c)(2)(i).

96. Prop. Treas. Reg. Section 1.1001-3(c)(2)(i)(A).

97. *See generally* Margaret C. Henry, Reissuance Revisited, 42 TAX NOTES 91 (Jan. 2, 1989).

98. An exception to the special rule applicable to qualified tender bonds arises when there is an interest rate mode change that increases the rate period from a period of one year or less to a period exceeding one year or decreases the rate period from a period of more than one year to a period of one year or less (a "Short/Long Qualified Tender Change"). If a Short/Long Qualified Tender Change occurs in addition to another change to the bonds, retirement of a qualified tender bond will result. *See* IRS Notice 88-130, 1988-2 C.B. 543 (Section 2.2).

99. Lynn Stevens Hume, *Rules on Arbitrage, Reissuance May Be Altered to Address Call Option Bonds,* THE BOND BUYER, Feb. 9, 1993, at 1; Constance Mitchell, *Latest Muni Derivative Gets U.S. Scrutiny,* WALL ST. J., Feb. 11, 1993, at C1.; Aaron Pressman, *Detachable Call Options Become Focus of Treasury Meeting, Market Concerns,* THE BOND BUYER, Feb. 4, 1993, at 1; Aaron Pressman, *Tax Law Could Be Menace to Tax Exemption of Detachable Calls, Treasury Official Says,* THE BOND BUYER, Jan. 27, 1993, at 1; Lee A. Sheppard, *Call Me: Lower Interest Costs Without Advance Refunding,* 58 TAX NOTES 1012 (Feb. 22, 1993).

100. Prop. Treas. Reg. Section 1.1001-3(e)(2)(iv).

101. *Id.*

102. Note that prior to the issuance of this special rule for puts and calls in the Proposed 1001 Regulation, there were no specific authorities addressing the effect of amending a bond's terms to permit the detachment of the issuer's call rights. Because the sale of the call rights affected the bond's actual maturity, existing authorities such as Rev. Rul. 73-160, 1973-1 C.B. 365, would appear to have supported the conclusion that the sale of the call rights did not trigger a reissuance.

103. See Lynn Stevens Hume, *Rules on Arbitrage, Reissuance May Be Altered to Address Call Option Bonds,* THE BOND BUYER, Feb. 9, 1993, at 1; Aaron Pressman, *Detachable Call Options Become Focus of Treasury Meeting, Market Concerns,* THE BOND BUYER, Feb. 4, 1993, at 1.

104. I.R.C. § 148(a)(1).

105. § 148(f).

106. *See* § 148; 1986 BLUEBOOK, *supra* note 88, at 1201.

107. § 148(h).

108. *See* Prop. Treas. Reg. Sections 1.148-4(f), (h); 1986 BLUEBOOK, *supra* note 88, at 1202-03.

109. Treas. Reg. Section 1.148-4(b)(4).

110. *See supra* note 103.

111. I.R.C. § 148.

112. *See* Lynn Stevens Hume, *Arbitrage Rebate Requirements Won't Go Away, Officials Caution,* THE BOND BUYER, January 28, 1993, at 1.

113. This concern, in its simplest terms, would appear consistent with legislative changes to the advance refunding rules of the Code that require that advance refunded bonds be called at the earliest possible call date. *See* I.R.C. § 149(d)(3)(A)(iii); 1986 BLUEBOOK, *supra* note 88, at 1213–14.

114. Payments that do not constitute interest may result in taxable income to the investor.

115. If a bond is considered "reissued" for federal income tax purposes, it is treated like a newly issued bond on the date of reissuance. It would qualify as tax-exempt only if it complies with all of the requirements of the Code (taking into account available transition rules) applicable to bonds issued on the date of reissuance.

116. Note that a trust that merely serves as a security arrangement for bondholders (e.g., an indenture trust) is generally not considered a trust for these purposes. *See* Rev. Rul. 76-265, 1976-2 C.B. 448.

117. Treas. Reg. Section 301.7701-4(c). These regulations are commonly referred to as the Sears Regulations because they were issued in response to a multiple-class investment trust structured by Dean Witter, a Sears affiliate.

118. Treas. Reg. Sections 301.7701-2, -3.

119. I.R.C. § 7704.

120. Rev. Rul. 82-144, 1982-2 C.B. 34.

121. Rev. Rul. 91-46, 1991-2 C.B. 358. *See generally* Steven D. Conlon, Mary Sue Butch & Robert C. MacDonald, *IRS' New Position on Excess Mortgage Servicing Affects Both Lenders and Investors,* 76 J. TAX'N 38 (January 1992).

122. Treas. Reg. Section 1.446-3(c)(3) defines a "notional principal amount" as "any specified amount of money or property that, when multiplied by a specified index, measures a party's rights and obligations under the contract, but is not borrowed or loaned between the parties as part of the contract."

123. Treas. Reg. Section 1.446-3; Treas. Reg. Section 1.1092(d)-1; 58 Fed. Reg. 53,125 (Oct. 14, 1993) (the "Final Swap Regulations"). Note that the Final Swap Regulations merely address the *timing of income and expense recognition* and the applicability of the straddle rules and do not directly address other issues such as the character of swap income, U.S. withholding tax issues, or arbitrage and arbitrage rebate related issues. Private Letter Ruling 9046065, dated May 23, 1990, addresses the arbitrage implications of a "financial guaranty policy" that essentially acts as an interest rate swap. A Treasury official subsequently expressed concerns regarding the impact of interest rate swaps on arbitrage and arbitrage rebate computations. Lynn Stevens Hume, *Treasury Attorney Asks Bond Industry to Provide Input on Rate Swaps,* THE BOND BUYER, Oct. 3, 1990, at 1. In addition, the Final Swap Regulations do not include rules regarding embedded loan characterization in the case of caps and floors. Instead, these rules have currently been retained in proposed form. For commentary relating to the proposed form of swap regulations (56 Fed. Reg. 31,350 (July 10, 1991)), *see, e.g.,* comment letters to the IRS from Joanne Ames of the American Bankers Association, dated Sept. 23, 1991 (available as Document 91-8246, 91 TNT 203-34 from Tax Analysts); Vincent M. Aquilino & Steven D. Conlon of

Chapman and Cutler, dated Sept. 20, 1991 (available as Document 91-8187, 91 TNT 203-35 from Tax Analysts); Vincent M. Aquilino & Steven D. Conlon of Chapman and Cutler, dated Sept. 10, 1991 (available as Document 91-7801, 91 TNT 195-32 from Tax Analysts); Stephen L. Gordon on behalf of the International Swap Dealers Association, dated Sept. 27, 1991 (available as Document 91-8426, 91 TNT 210-50 from Tax Analysts).

124. Although it should be noted that except for Treas. Reg. Section 1.1092(d)-1 relating to the treatment of interest rate swaps and other notional principal contracts for purposes of the straddle rules, the Final Swap Regulations include a prospective effective date for notional principal contracts entered into on or after Dec. 13, 1993.

125. *See* Comment letter to the IRS from Aquilino & Conlon, dated Sept. 20, 1991, *supra* note 123. *See generally* Michael A. Clark, *Lost in the Hedge Row: Searching for Ordinary Results on Transactions to Minimize Business Risks,* 69 TAXES 834, 845–48 (Dec. 1991).

126. I.R.C. § 103(a). Pursuant to Section 103(c)(2) of the Code, 48 U.S.C. Section 745, 48 U.S.C. Section 1423a, and 48 U.S.C. Section 1403, bonds issued by Puerto Rico, Guam, and the U.S. Virgin Islands may also qualify as tax-exempt, provided that they comply with the requirements applicable to domestic issues. I.R.C. § 149(c)(2)(B).

127. I.R.C. § 103(b)(3), § 149(a) (registration); I.R.C. § 141(a) (private activity bond test); I.R.C. § 141(c) (private loan financing test); I.R.C. § 148 (arbitrage and arbitrage rebate); I.R.C. § 149(b) (restrictions on U.S. government guarantees); I.R.C. § 149(e) (Form 8038 filing requirements); I.R.C. § 149(f) (restrictions on certain pooled financing bonds); I.R.C. § 149(g) (restrictions on hedge bonds).

128. I.R.C. §§ 142–145, § 147 (restrictions on the use of bond proceeds); I.R.C. § 146 (volume cap); I.R.C. § 147(b) (restrictions on the weighted maturity of the bonds); I.R.C. § 147(c) (restrictions on the financing of land or used property); I.R.C. § 147(f) (public approval); I.R.C. § 147(g) (restrictions on the financing of issuance costs).

129. Section 142(d)(1) of the Code requires that the tests must be satisfied through the applicable "qualified project period."

130. If a bond is reissued, the IRS believes that approval of the material modifications by the governmental entity issuing the bond must be obtained. See Rev. Rul. 81-281, 1981-2 C.B. 18.

131. Prop. Treas. Reg. Section 1.1001-3(e)(1).

132. Prop. Treas. Reg. Section 1.1001-3(e)(2)(ii).

133. Prop. Treas. Reg. Section 1.1001-3(e)(3)(iii).

134. This conclusion is consistent with the focus of the Proposed 1001 Regulation which is on modifications "between a holder and an issuer." Prop. Treas. Reg. Section 1.1001-3(b).

135. The stripped bond rules would not be necessary if bonds were reissued every time interest or principal payments were divided up among different investors.

136. Mutual funds that elect and qualify as "regulated investment companies" (RICs) under the Code can designate their dividends as "exempt-interest dividends" under the rules of Section 852(b)(5) of the Code provided that certain requirements set forth therein are satisfied. Shareholders receiving properly designated exempt-interest dividends are permitted to treat such dividends as tax-exempt interest for federal income tax purposes.

137. This assumes that the corporation has adequate current or accumulated earnings and profits to result in such distributions being classified as dividends under the Code and ignores the impact of the dividends-received deduction available to corporate shareholders under certain circumstances.

138. The referenced rule is that the trust must not grant the trustee any power to vary the investment of the trust. *See, e.g.,* Commissioner v. North Am. Bond Trust, 122

F.2d 545 (2d Cir. 1941), *cert. denied,* 314 U.S. 701 (1942); Pennsylvania Co. for Insurances v. United States, 146 F.2d 392 (3d Cir. 1944); Commissioner v. City Nat'l Bank & Trust Co., 142 F.2d 771 (10th Cir.), *cert. denied,* 323 U.S. 764 (1944); Pennsylvania Co. for Insurances v. United States, 138 F.2d 869 (3d Cir. 1943), *cert. denied,* 321 U.S. 788 (1944); Commissioner v. Buckley, 128 F.2d 124 (9th Cir. 1942); Commissioner v. Chase Nat'l Bank of City of N.Y., 122 F.2d 540 (2d Cir. 1941); Hamilton Depositors Corp. v. Nicholas, 111 F.2d 385 (10th Cir. 1940); Brooklyn Trust Co. v. Commissioner, 80 F.2d 865 (2d Cir.) *cert. denied,* 298 U.S. 659 (1936).

139. *See, e.g.,* Rev. Rul. 89-124, 1989-2 C.B. 262; Rev. Rul. 86-92, 1986-2 C.B. 214; Rev. Rul. 78-149, 1978-1 C.B. 448; Rev. Rul. 75-192, 1975-1 C.B. 384; Rev. Rul. 73-460, 1973-2 C.B. 424; Rev. Rul. 61-175, 1961-2 C.B. 128.

140. The IRS has issued a number of published and private letter rulings relating to the classification of mortgage pass-through trusts (relating to GNMA-insured mortgage pass-through certificates) as "grantor trusts" under the Code. *See, e.g.,* Rev. Rul. 84-10, 1984-1 C.B. 155 (FNMA pass-through certificates); Rev. Rul. 77-349, 1977-2 C.B. 20 (privately insured pass-through certificates); Rev. Rul. 74-169, 1974-1 C.B. 147 (GNMA pass-through certificates); Rev. Rul. 71-399, 1971-2 C.B. 433 (FHLMC pass-through certificates); Rev. Rul. 70-545, 1970-2 C.B. 7 (GNMA pass-through certificates); Rev. Rul. 70-544, 1970-2 C.B. 6 (GNMA pass-through certificates). It is the authors' understanding that the IRS was originally asked to rule that the mortgage pass-through trusts simply were not "entities" for tax purposes (they clearly rejected this approach in adopting the grantor trust holding set forth in the referenced rulings).

141. *See* Rev. Rul. 76-265, 1976-2 C.B. 448.

142. However, the pass-through mechanics and rules for partnerships and trusts are very different.

143. *See, e.g.,* Rev. Rul. 89-124, 1989-2 C.B. 262 (deposit of "substantially similar securities" during a 90-day initial period); Rev. Rul. 78-149, 1978-1 C.B. 448; and Rev. Rul. 75-192, 1975-1 C.B. 384. Published rulings do not directly address the disposition of assets to take advantage of the market or the creation of reserve funds, although representations required by the IRS in certain private letter ruling requests regarding restrictions on the reinvestment of trust assets support the existence of such restrictions.

144. Treas. Reg. Section 301.7701-4(c)(2).

145. Rev. Rul. 92-32, 1992-1 C.B. 434.

146. Priv. Ltr. Rul. 8929030 (April 21, 1989). This ruling had been sharply criticized by commentators; *see generally* Mary Sue Butch & Steven D. Conlon, *Should Transfers of Subordinated Interests in Investment Trusts Be Restricted?,* 50 TAX NOTES 1009 (Mar. 4, 1991). It should be noted that prior to the issuance of Rev. Rul. 92-32, the IRS issued Private Letter Ruling 9132027, dated May 8, 1991 (permitting the transfer of the subordinated interest in certain loan pools by a state-appointed conservator), and Private Letter Ruling 9202011, dated October 8, 1991 (permitting the transfer of subordinated interest to related entities or by a receiver to a third party and "outside reserve fund" and related guarantee transfers).

147. The financial product on which the example was based was the Americus "Prime"/"Score" Trusts, which sold two separate interests of the type described in the example in the stock of large, publicly held corporations. The Americus Trusts avoided the holding of the example because they were "grandfathered." Priv. Ltr. Rul. 8009040070E (Sept. 4, 1980) and Priv. Ltr. Rul. 8505035 (Apr. 27, 1984).

148. Similar concerns arise with respect to "squeezable strips." A squeezable strip represents a right to receive payments that is capped and subject to reduction (possibly to zero) as a result of changes in some other variable (or variables). Hence, the strip may be "squeezed" by changes in the other variable.

149. Section 1286(f) of the Code grants the IRS authority to issue regulations under the stripped bond rules regarding their application in the case of "varying rates of interest."

150. *Supra* note 140.

151. Because the investors are treated as directly owning the assets held by the trust, distributions from the trust are essentially ignored for federal income tax purposes.

152. The bond premium amortization rules of Section 171 of the Code are *mandatory* in the case of tax-exempt bonds. It may be difficult for many investors to fully account for an investment in a tax-exempt derivative by separately analyzing their fractional interest in each asset held in the related trust or custodial account, although this may have limited practical significance. *See* Conlon, Butch & MacDonald, *supra* note 121, for a discussion of fractional ownership concerns in the context of mortgage pass-through certificates.

153. An investment trust structured to qualify as a partnership for tax purposes is the "hub" and various entities that invest therein are the "spokes." *See* Priv. Ltr. Rul. 9116006 (May 4, 1990); Priv. Ltr. Rul. 9117012 (May 7, 1990); Priv. Ltr. Rul. 9117008 (May 7, 1990); Priv. Ltr. Rul. 9233046 (May 21, 1992); Priv. Ltr. Rul. 9233047 (May 21, 1992); Priv. Ltr. Rul. 9233048 (May 21, 1992); Priv. Ltr. Rul. 9233049 (May 21, 1992); Priv. Ltr. Rul. 9233050 (May 21, 1992).

154. Treas. Reg. Section 301.7701-2(a)(1), (2) and (3).

155. Rev. Proc. 92-88, 1992-42 I.R.B. 39, sets forth guidelines pertaining to the classification of limited partnerships formed under a state statute that corresponds to the Uniform Limited Partnership Act. Under Rev. Proc. 92-88, a limited partnership that satisfies its stated requirements pertaining to (1) minimum interest of general partners in partnership items (which must generally be at least 1 percent); (2) minimum capital account balance of general partners (which must generally be at least 1 percent of the total positive capital balances or $500,000 whichever is less); (3) continuity of life (which will be satisfied if a partnership is formed under a state limited partnership act that corresponds to the Uniform Limited Partnership Act as determined in a revenue ruling); and (4) limited liability (which generally requires the general partner (or partners collectively) to have a net worth equal to at least 10 percent of the total contributions to the partnership (not including any interest in the partnership)) will be treated as a partnership for federal income tax purposes without obtaining a ruling.

156. Treas. Reg. Section 301.7701-2(b)(1) provides generally that an organization has continuity of life if the death, insanity, bankruptcy, retirement, resignation, or expulsion of any member will not cause the dissolution of the organization. It includes a special rule for limited partnerships such that continuity of life does not exist if the retirement, death, or insanity of a general partner causes a dissolution of the partnership unless the remaining general partners agree to continue the partnership, or unless all remaining members agree to continue the partnership. This special rule has been clarified by Rev. Proc. 92-35, 1992-1 C.B. 790, and a proposed amendment to Treas. Reg. Section 301.7701-2(b)(1) to provide that if the bankruptcy or removal of a general partner of a limited partnership causes a dissolution of the partnership unless the remaining general partners or at least a majority in interest of all remaining partners agree to continue the partnership, continuity of life does not exist.

157. Treas. Reg. Section 301.7701-2(c)(3).

158. This is particularly true in light of the focus of the regulations on the number of members of the partnership in determining whether an entity possesses centralized management and the provision in the IRS guidelines relating to partnership ruling requests that provides that the IRS will not rule on centralized management if more than

80 percent of the total interests in the entity are limited partnership interests. Treas. Reg. Section 301.7701-2(c)(1); Rev. Proc. 89-12, 1989-1 C.B. 798 (Section 4.06).

159. Treas. Reg. Section 301.7701-2(d)(1).

160. Treas. Reg. Section 301.7701-2(d)(2). This rule only applies to limited partnerships.

161. Rev. Proc. 89-12, 1989-1 C.B. 798 (Section 4.07).

162. This observation is based simply upon the personal observations of the authors and is not intended to simplistically ignore the analysis of the general partner's net worth and business that was made by counsel.

163. Rev. Proc. 89-12, *supra* note 161.

164. Section 4.01 of Rev. Proc. 89-12, *supra* note 161.

165. Section 4.03 of Rev. Proc. 89-12, *supra* note 161.

166. Treas. Reg. Section 301.7701-2(e)(1).

167. Rev. Proc. 92-33, 1992-1 C.B. 782.

168. IRS Notice 88-75, 1988-2 C.B. 386.

169. Section II.A. of IRS Notice 88-75, *supra* note 168.

170. It must be ascertained that the investors hold a true partnership (i.e., equity) interest in the structure rather than a demand note (i.e., debt) interest in order to conclude that tax-exempt income will flow through to the investors.

171. *See* I.R.C. § 704(b) and the related Treasury Regulations issued thereunder.

172. *See, e.g.,* I.R.C. § 721.

173. A so-called Section 754 election, which triggers the application of inside basis step-up rules under Section 743 of the Code.

174. See generally I.R.C. § 723 and § 743.

175. There are, however, a few cases. *See, e.g.,* Hunt v. Commissioner, 59 T.C.M. 635 (1990) (a guaranteed return of capital plus a return on investment did not adversely impact partnership status); Investors Ins. Agency, Inc. v. Commissioner, 72 T.C. 1027 (1979), *aff'd,* 677 F.2d 1328 (9th Cir. 1982) (when a guarantor became obligated to make ongoing payments under a legally enforceable and unconditional, rather than contingent, obligation, a "debt" arose).

176. *See, e.g.,* Hartman v. Commissioner, 17 T.C.M. 1020 (1958); Hambuechen v. Commissioner, 43 T.C. 90 (1964); *see also* Rev. Rul. 72-350, 1972-2 C.B. 394.

177. Under Section 761(a)(1) of the Code and Treas. Reg. Section 1.761-2(a)(2), certain "investment partnerships" may elect to be excluded from the provisions of Subchapter K (dealing with partnership taxation) of the Code. Specifically, under Treas. Reg. Section 1.761-2(a)(2), the participants of an electing partnership must (i) own the investment property as co-owners; (ii) reserve the right separately to take or dispose of their shares of any property acquired or retained; and (iii) must not actively conduct business or irrevocably authorize some person or persons acting in a representative capacity to purchase, sell, or exchange such investment property (although an individual participant may delegate authority to purchase, sell, or exchange his share of any such investment property for his account for a period of up to one year). *See, e.g.,* Priv. Ltr. Rul. 7951006 (Aug. 21, 1979); Gen. Couns. Mem. 38025 (July 20, 1979); Gen. Couns. Mem. 37016 (Feb. 25, 1977). Also, partnership classification would trigger special unified audit and litigation procedures that would apply to all of the investors with respect to their interests in the partnership if it was ever audited by the IRS. Subchapter C of Chapter 63 of Subtitle F of the Code (Sections 6221 through 6233) applies to the tax treatment of partnerships and partners in administrative and litigation matters.

178. First Nat'l Bank in Wichita v. Commissioner, 19 B.T.A. 744 (1930), *aff'd,* 57 F.2d 7 (10th Cir. 1932); Bank of Cal. v. Commissioner, 30 B.T.A. 556 (1934), *aff'd,* 80 F.2d 389 (9th Cir. 1935); American Nat'l Bank of Austin v. United States, 421 F.2d 442 (5th Cir.

1970), *rev'g* 296 F. Supp. 512 (W.D. Tex. 1968); Union Planters Nat'l Bank of Memphis v. United States, 426 F.2d 115 (6th Cir. 1970), *rev'g* 295 F. Supp. 1151 (W.D. Tenn. 1968); Third Nat'l Bank in Nashville v. United States, 71-1 U.S.T.C. para. 9248 (M.D. Tenn. 1971), *aff'd,* 454 F.2d 689 (6th Cir. 1972); First Am. Nat'l Bank of Nashville v. United States, 467 F.2d 1098 (6th Cir. 1972), *aff'g* 327 F. Supp. 675 (M.D. Tenn. 1971); Citizens Nat'l Bank of Waco v. United States, 551 F.2d 832 (Ct. Cl. 1977); American Nat'l Bank of Austin v. United States, 573 F.2d 1201 (Ct. Cl. 1978); Rev. Rul. 74-27, 1974-1 C.B. 24; Rev. Rul. 73-27, 1973-1 C.B. 46; Rev. Rul. 82-144, 1982-2 C.B. 34.

179. Rev. Rul. 82-144, *supra* note 178.

180. 1983-2 C.B. 572. This "no ruling" position is currently set forth in Section 4.01(2) of Rev. Proc. 93-3, 1993-1 I.R.B 77.

181. Although it should be considered whether the investor's putative partnership interest qualifies as such, after taking into account the totality of the transaction, including any related put right.

182. It is generally agreed that the right to obtain any upside associated with the underlying tax-exempt bond is the key right in analyzing the potential benefits and burdens retained by the investor. For example, there seems little doubt that one would be treated as the "owner" of a residence for tax purposes even if the house were fully insured against every risk imaginable and the owner purchased a put permitting the sale of the house at cost but retaining full rights to any appreciation in its value. Counsel to the sponsor that provides a legal opinion relating to the tax ownership of the bond carefully evaluates the investor's profit potential, typically relying on representations of fact provided by persons such as the sponsors of such programs.

183. In the case of secondary market derivative products where the underlying bond has been insured or a letter of credit provides credit enhancement against the risk of issuer default, the put right typically falls away if the credit enhancer goes bankrupt, defaults in its obligation to pay on the bonds, or the rating on the underlying bonds is significantly downgraded.

184. I.R.C. § 1286(e)(2). Can the stripped bond rules apply if a bond is owned by a partnership and there are different classes of partnership interests? The answer would clearly appear to be no, since partnerships are separate entities for tax purposes and a partnership interest is clearly equity *in the partnership itself* rather than a direct interest in each of underlying assets of the partnership. However, at least one IRS attorney has suggested that the stripped bond rules should be applied. *See* Lee A. Sheppard, *Financial Products: The Switchboard Approach,* 60 TAX NOTES 942 (Aug. 16, 1993).

185. § 1286(e)(5).

186. *See generally* Conlon, Butch & MacDonald, *supra* note 121. Note that the sale of a typical "participation" in a bond (i.e., where an investor acquires a pro rata interest in all of the principal and interest due on a bond) is not considered a strip because the investor and the seller hold rights to receive both principal and interest in the underlying bond and such rights are proportionate with regard to each payment of principal and interest due on the bond. Focusing on the policy behind the stripped bond rules—the proper allocation of tax basis upon the sale of a portion of a bond—it does not appear necessary to apply such rules. If a person sells a percentage of all of the payments due on a bond, including principal, it appears clear that the seller would allocate its tax basis in the bond by the same percentage in calculating the amount of gain or loss upon the sale of the participation. Note that a participation where one investor receives a higher interest rate than another does not result in an identical percentage interest in all bond interest and principal payments, and application of the stripped bond rules may be appropriate to fairly allocate the basis in the bond of the person creating the participation to the participation interest sold.

187. This is because prepayment risk substantially diminishes the value of future interest payments because prepayments on the bond may essentially wipe those payments out. Attempts to allocate prepayment risk raise fast pay/slow pay concerns under example (1) of the Sears Regulations and concerns regarding whether the structure falls within the friendly confines of the "specific payments" requirement of example (4) of the regulations.

188. Section 1286(b) of the Code also requires the seller to immediately recognize as taxable income any accrued but unpaid interest and accrued market discount on the bond that has not previously been included in taxable income. Amounts included in taxable income by a seller under this rule increase its allocable tax basis in the bond.

189. Rev. Rul. 58-536, 1958-2 C.B. 21.

190. Section 1879(s) of the Tax Reform Act of 1986, Pub. L. No. 99-514 (1986).

191. I.R.C. § 1286(d).

192. § 1286(d)(1)(A)(ii).

193. Treas. Reg. Section 1.1286-1, 57 Fed. Reg. 61, 811 (Dec. 29, 1992).

194. Temp. Reg. Section 1.1286-1T, 56 Fed. Reg. 38, 339 (Aug. 13, 1991).

195. The final stripped bond rules also adopt an "aggregation" approach that was advocated by commentators. *See* Conlon, Butch & MacDonald, *supra* note 121, at 44.

196. Except to the extent a portion of the swap is recharacterized as an "embedded loan" under the Final Swap Regulations, as discussed in the text below. Although payments on an interest rate swap resemble interest, as discussed above, interest is defined for federal income tax purposes as amounts paid for the use or forbearance of money. *Supra* text accompanying note 3. Because the parties to an interest rate swap do not borrow or lend the principal amount, the tax law definitional requirements would not be met. *See generally* Clark, *supra* note 125, at 846.

197. The concept of "net" payments is discussed below. Also, as a technical matter the Final Swap Regulations focus on the accrual of amounts under a swap, rather than the receipt of payments on the swap. *See* Treas. Reg. Section 1.446-3(e)(2)(i).

198. This is often true in the case of both states or local governmental units that use swaps as hedging devices relating to specific rate obligations or synthesizing fixed-rate payment obligations and interest rate swaps used in the synthetic tax-exempt floaters and similar types of derivatives.

199. Treas. Reg. Section 1.446-3(f); IRS Notice 89-21, 1989-1 C.B. 651.

200. This aspect of the regulations has been criticized by the commentators. *See, e.g.*, Comment letter to the IRS from Ames, *supra* note 123.

201. Treas. Reg. Section 1.446-3(d).

202. The Final Swap Regulations have been criticized in this regard. *See* Aquilino & Conlon, *supra* note 123.

203. Treas. Reg. Section 1.446-3(g)(4).

204. *Id.*

205. It should be noted that because the Final Swap Regulations provide that interest on an embedded loan be so treated for all purposes of the Code, it is possible that a swap premium received by a state or local governmental unit that is recharacterized as an embedded loan could be structured to qualify as a tax-exempt bond (assuming that such a loan is treated as an exercise of the governmental unit's borrowing function).

206. Treas. Reg. Section 1.446-3(h)(2). In many cases, the early termination of an interest rate swap may require the payment by a party of a termination payment to compensate for its early termination. Early termination payments are not always triggered and would not typically be triggered if an investor simply transfers his interest in a swap-type derivative to a new investor.

207. This assumes that the investor holds the tax-exempt derivative as a "capital asset" for federal income tax purposes. Note that disposition of a bond at par through the sale of a swap-type derivative could generate a capital loss on the disposition of the bond that may offset income realized on the disposition of the investor's interest in the swap if the bond was deemed to have been purchased by the investor with bond premium and such premium had not been fully amortized under Section 171 of the Code.

208. *See, e.g.*, Peter J. Connors & Henry S. Lovejoy, American Bar Association, Section of Taxation, Committee on Sales and Financial Transactions, *Comments on the Treatment of Interest Rate Swap Payments* (1988)(available as Document 88-6463, 88 TNT 155-37, from Tax Analysts).

209. Treas. Reg. Section 1.1092(d)-1(c). Note that this rule is effective for interest rate swaps and other notional principal contracts entered into on or after July 8, 1991. Treas. Reg. Section 1.1092(d)-1(d).

210. I.R.C. § 1234A. Note that certain interest rate swaps tied to bond-specific floating interest rates may not technically qualify as interest rate swaps under the Swap Regulations. As a result, they may not clearly be treated as part of a straddle eligible for capital gain treatment.

211. Under the terms of the bond, the issuer's obligation ended on the date payments were made to the trust or custodial account holding the bond.

212. Section 265 of the Code *does* limit interest expense deductions relating to the purchase and carrying of tax-exempt bonds by all taxpayers, including corporations. The deductibility of expenses otherwise deductible under Section 212 of the Code may be limited by the "2 percent rule" of Section 67, which prevents an individual from deducting certain amounts except to the extent that such amounts, when taken together with other expenses for the tax year, exceed 2 percent of the taxpayer's adjusted gross income.

213. Pub. L. No. 103-66 (1993).

214. I.R.C. § 1278(A)(2). If a debt instrument was issued at an original issue discount, the debt instrument's "revised issue price" is used as its stated redemption price at maturity for purposes of measuring market discount. I.R.C. § 1278(a)(2)(B).

215. *See* I.R.C. §§ 851(b)(2), (b)(3), (b)(4), 852(a), and 4982. For more detailed discussions of mutual fund issues relating to derivatives, *see* Steven D. Conlon & Suzanne M. Russell, *Tax Considerations for Mutual Funds Investing in Asset-Backed and Derivative Securities*, 71 TAXES 12 (Jan. 1993); Steven D. Conlon, Cameron N. Cosby, Steven J. Gee, David J. Mangefrida, Suzanne M. Russell, & Jeffrey S. Sion, American Bar Association, Section of Taxation, Regulated Investment Companies Committee, *Report on Federal Income Tax Issues Under Subchapter M of the Internal Revenue Code Relating to the Qualification of Tax-Exempt Synthetic Debt Held by Money Market Mutual Funds* (1992) (available as Document 92-10781, 92 TNT 241-23, from Tax Analysts and summarized at 58 TAX NOTES 227 (Jan. 11, 1993)). Mutual funds may seek to invest in partnerships that have made a Section 761 election. *See supra* note 177. This may permit the investing fund to avoid the potential application of the basic partnership income timing principles of Section 706 of the Code. However, it could be argued that the ordinary partnership income timing rules are inappropriate and should not apply for purposes of determining whether an investing fund has complied with the 90 percent income distribution requirement of Section 852(a) and the 98 percent excise tax distribution requirement. *See, e.g.*, Priv. Ltr. Rul. 9235023 (May 29, 1992).

216. Ordinarily put fees are treated as capitalizable, not deductible. *See, e.g.*, Rev. Rul. 78-182, 1978-1 C.B. 265.

217. Section 851(b)(4) of the Code requires a fund to diversify certain of its investments by restricting a fund from generally holding more than 5 percent of its assets in the securities of a single issuer. For purposes of this test, it seems appropriate to treat the issuer of the underlying bond as the issuer of the put. *See* S. Rep. No. 1236, 94th Cong., 2d Sess. 544 (1976); Rev. Rul. 83-69, 1983-1 C.B. 126; Priv. Ltr. Rul. 8823067 (Mar. 11, 1988); Priv. Ltr. Rul. 8810023 (Dec. 7, 1987); Priv. Ltr. Rul. 8809053 (Dec. 7, 1987); Gen. Couns. Mem. 39700 (Nov. 16, 1987).

218. 485 U.S. 212 (1988).

219. William B. Crawford, Jr., *IRS Rule Change Putting Futures Hedging at Risk,* CHI. TRIB., Feb. 21, 1993, sec. 7, at 1; Jerome B. Libin & G. Garner Prillaman, *The FNMA Case—The Fate of Interest Rate Hedging After* Arkansas Best, 57 TAX NOTES 1071 (Nov. 16, 1992); Gregory J. Millman, *The Tale of* Arkansas Best: *When Markets Move Faster Than Laws,* BARRON'S, Nov. 9, 1992, at 10.

220. 350 U.S. 46 (1955).

221. 100 T.C. No. 36 (June 17, 1993).

222. *See* Temp. Reg. Section 1.1221-2T; 58 Fed. Reg. 54,037 (Oct. 20, 1993); Prop. Treas. Reg. Section 1.1221-2, and Prop. Treas. Reg. Section 1.446-4, 58 Fed. Reg. 54,075 (Oct. 20, 1993). Given the limited scope of the definition of a hedging transaction under Temp. Reg. Section 1.1221-2T(b), which excludes hedges relating to capital gain generating assets, it is unclear whether a legislative solution will continue to be sought. For a discussion of concerns expressed prior to the release of the temporary and final regulations, *see, e.g., Business Coalition Continues to Push for Legislative Solution to* Arkansas Best, DAILY TAX REP. (BNA), Aug. 25, 1993, at G-4; Letter to Treasury from Edward D. Kleinbard of Cleary, Gottlieb, Steen & Hamilton, dated May 26, 1993, reprinted in HIGHLIGHTS & DOCUMENTS, June 11, 1993, at 3350; Letter to Edward D. Kleinbard from Michael Schler of Cravath, Swaine & Moore, dated June 14, 1993, reprinted in HIGHLIGHTS & DOCUMENTS, July 2, 1993, at 161.

CHAPTER 6

Securities Law Considerations for Tax-Exempt Derivatives

W. Scott Jardine

Primary market tax-exempt derivative securities generally involve the issuance of securities by governmental issuers. Governmental issuers are excluded from the provisions of the Investment Company Act of 1940, as amended,[1] pursuant to Section 2(b) thereof,[2] and securities they issue are exempted from the Securities Act of 1933, as amended,[3] pursuant to Section 3(a)(2) thereof.[4] While novel issues may arise in connection with the issuance of any particular primary market tax-exempt derivative security, the securities law issues typically involved in the issuance of securities by governmental issuers have been dealt with on numerous occasions.[5]

It is important to distinguish primary market securities, which directly involve a governmental issuer, from secondary market tax-exempt derivative security structures that consist of trusts, partnerships, and custodial and other arrangements containing securities previously issued by governmental issuers but deposited into the derivative structure without any involvement of the governmental issuer or issuers.[6] The same securities law issues that apply to primary market derivative products may or may not apply to a particular secondary market tax-exempt derivative security. This chapter will focus on the issues that must be considered when structuring *secondary* market tax-exempt derivative securities, including the fundamental issues of whether the securities, their issuers, or the instruments under which they are issued must be registered or qualified under various securities laws. The chapter will then discuss certain issues that arise under the federal securities laws for one of the principal types of purchasers of secondary market tax-exempt derivative securities, tax-exempt mutual funds.

The Securities Act

The purpose of the Securities Act is to provide full and fair disclosure of the character of securities sold in interstate commerce and to prevent fraud in the sale thereof.[7] To effectuate this purpose, Section 5 of the Securities

Act provides that no security may be offered for sale unless a registration statement has been filed with the Securities and Exchange Commission (the "Commission") as to such security, and no security may be sold unless a registration statement is in effect as to such security.[8] Notwithstanding the provisions of Section 5, however, certain securities are exempted from the registration requirements of the Securities Act pursuant to Section 3 thereof.[9] In addition, certain transactions in securities are exempted from such registration requirements pursuant to Section 4.[10] Because of the significant amount of time and expense involved in the registration process and the ongoing reporting requirements triggered by the registration of a security,[11] it is frequently desirable to avoid the registration of tax-exempt derivative securities under the Securities Act. Consequently, it is necessary to determine whether a tax-exempt derivative security is exempted pursuant to the provisions of Section 3 or whether the transactions in which such security will be offered and sold are exempted pursuant to the provisions of Section 4.

The **Merrill Lynch** *Analysis—No New Security*

Section 3(a)(2) of the Securities Act exempts securities issued by, among others, any state or territory of the United States, or any political subdivision of a state or territory, or by any public instrumentality of one or more states or territories.[12] Most municipal securities underlying tax-exempt derivative securities are exempted from registration under the Securities Act by virtue of Section 3(a)(2). However, the tax-exempt derivative securities that are created by a secondary market derivative security structure are not necessarily themselves exempted under Section 3(a)(2). The creation of a tax-exempt derivative security may involve the creation of a new security because the issuer may be deemed to be the trust, partnership, or other entity through which the derivative security is created rather than a governmental issuer the securities of which are eligible for the Section 3(a)(2) exemption. Such a security must be analyzed separately from the underlying municipal security to determine whether a separate exemption from the registration requirements of the Securities Act is available for the newly created security. If a new security is created, it is unlikely that the new security is exempted pursuant to Section 3(a)(2).

In a series of no-action letters, the staff of the Commission's Division of Corporation Finance (the "Staff") has indicated the circumstances in which it will not deem a new security to be created.[13] The most recent of these no-action letters in the context of tax-exempt derivative securities is *Merrill Lynch, Pierce, Fenner & Smith Incorporated* (hereinafter, *Merrill Lynch*).[14] *Merrill Lynch* involved a program pursuant to which Merrill Lynch, Pierce, Fenner & Smith Incorporated offered custodial receipts representing principal and interest components of municipal bonds (stripped tax-exempt bonds). The Staff's view that the custodial receipts were exempt from registration under Section 3(a)(2) was based upon representations that:

1. the owners of the stripped securities would have all the rights and privileges of owners of the underlying municipal securities;
2. each receipt holder, as a real party in interest, would have the right, upon default of the underlying municipal securities, to proceed directly and individually against the issuer of those securities; and
3. a receipt holder would not be required to act in concert with other receipt holders or the custodian bank.

The Staff's position was further conditioned on the program sponsor's obtaining an opinion of counsel with respect to such representations, as well as the following factors:

1. each receipt represented the entire interest in a discrete, identified interest payment or principal payment on the underlying municipal security;
2. the custodian bank performed only clerical or ministerial services on behalf of the receipt holders;
3. neither the sponsor nor the custodian bank additionally would guarantee or otherwise enhance the creditworthiness of the underlying municipal security or the stripped security;
4. the custodian bank undertook to notify receipt holders in the event of a default, and to forward to receipt holders copies of all communications from the issuer of the underlying municipal security to the holders of such securities;
5. an opinion of counsel was provided indicating that the underlying municipal securities would not be considered assets of either the sponsor or the custodian bank; and
6. other factors were not present, such as remarketing agreements, that would require the investors in the stripped coupon securities to rely upon the sponsor to obtain the benefit of their investment.

The theory underlying the Staff's position apparently is that if the securities underlying an arrangement (e.g., municipal bonds) are exempted from the provisions of the Securities Act, interests therein (e.g., custodial receipts) are exempted from such provisions if there are no significant changes in the rights of the holders of such interests vis-à-vis the issuer of the underlying security. The nine elements of the *Merrill Lynch* analysis are in part intended to ensure that no such change in the rights of the receipt holders is present. It is essential that the security underlying an arrangement that relies on the *Merrill Lynch* analysis is itself an exempted security under the Securities Act. Most municipal securities underlying tax-exempt derivative securities are exempted securities under Section 3(a)(2). Nonetheless, the exempted security status of the underlying municipal security should be confirmed when structuring or analyzing any tax-exempt derivative securities arrangement. A tax-exempt derivative structure that satisfies all of the elements of the *Merrill Lynch* analysis (illustrated in Exhibit 6-1) and contains an underlying tax-exempt bond that is itself exempt under Section3(a)(2) is exempt on the basis of the underlying bond's ex-

EXHIBIT 6-1

No New Security Analysis – Section 3(a)(2) "Merrill Lynch" Requirements

- Holders have all the rights and privileges of owners of the underlying municipal securities.
- Holders have the right to proceed directly and individually against the issuer.
- Holders are not required to act in concert.
- Each receipt represents a discrete, identified interest payment or principal payment.
- Custodian performs only clerical or ministerial services.
- Neither the sponsor nor the custodian guarantees or otherwise enhances creditworthiness.
- Custodian undertakes to notify receipt holders in the event of a default and to forward to receipt holders copies of all communications from the issuer.
- Opinion of counsel is given that the underlying municipal securities are not assets of either the sponsor or the custodian bank.
- No other factors are present that require the investors to rely upon the sponsor to obtain the benefit of their investment.

emption. Thus, the interests issued pursuant to such a structure may be publicly offered and sold without registration under the Securities Act.

Certain aspects of the *Merrill Lynch* analysis should be noted when structuring any derivative security in reliance thereon. The requirement that each receipt or each derivative security must represent the entire interest in a discrete, identified interest or principal payment on the underlying security precludes the subdividing or reinvestment of cash flows on the underlying security, although it is permissible to combine entire discrete cash flows for sale in units.[15] It is also permissible for a holder who receives an entire payment on a security to pay a portion of that payment to a service provider as a reasonable fee for the services provided. In addition, counsel should carefully scrutinize the activities being undertaken by the sponsor of a derivative security and the custodian or trustee, to ensure that such activities are within the parameters of the *Merrill Lynch* analysis.

The *Merrill Lynch* analysis does not necessarily prohibit the addition of credit enhancement or a liquidity facility to the underlying municipal security if such credit enhancement or liquidity facility is not provided by the sponsor of the derivative security or the custodian. However, because many forms of credit enhancement are themselves considered to be separate securities under the Securities Act, it is essential that any credit enhancement or liquidity facility is itself an exempted security under the Securities Act.[16] The exemptions applicable to such instruments include Section 3(a)(2) for securities issued by a bank and Section 3(a)(8)[17] for insurance policies. Finally, it should be noted that, notwithstanding the fact that a tax-exempt derivative security is an exempted security under the *Merrill Lynch* analysis and is therefore exempt from the registration requirements of Section 5, the offer and sale of such security is nonetheless subject to the antifraud provisions of Rule 10b-5[18] promulgated under the Securities Exchange Act of 1934, as amended (the "Exchange Act").[19]

Private Placements

Many secondary market tax-exempt derivative securities that do not satisfy the criteria set forth in *Merrill Lynch* or otherwise qualify as exempted securities are offered and sold in transactions exempt from the registration requirements of the Securities Act by virtue of Section 4(2) of the Securities Act.[20] Section 4(2) exempts transactions by an issuer not involving any public offering (i.e., a "private offering"). The analysis as to whether the private offering exemption provided by Section 4(2) is available for a particular transaction depends on all the facts and circumstances surrounding the offering. According to the United States Supreme Court in *Securities and Exchange Commission v. Ralston Purina Co.*, the availability of the private offering exemption "should turn on whether the particular class of persons affected need the protection of the [Securities] Act."[21] However, the fact that a security is sold to a limited number of institutional investors does not, by itself, establish the availability of the exemption provided by Section 4(2).

In 1962, the Commission issued a release ("Release No. 4552") setting forth certain of the Commission's views regarding the availability of the private offering exemption.[22] According to the Commission, whether a transaction is one that does not involve any public offering is "essentially a question of fact and necessitates a consideration of all surrounding circumstances, including such factors as the relationship between the offerees and the issuer, the nature, scope, size, type and manner of the offering."[23] While an exhaustive analysis of the release and the private offering exemption is beyond the scope of this chapter, several items are worth noting:

Number of offerees. The Commission emphasized that the number of persons to whom the offering is extended is relevant only to the question of whether such persons have the requisite association with and knowledge of the issuer to make the exemption available, although, as a matter of practice, many securities are offered pursuant to Section 4(2) to a large number of offerees.

Identity of offerees. Consideration must be given to the identity of the actual purchasers and to the identity of the offerees. Negotiations or conversations with or general solicitations of an unrestricted or unrelated group of prospective purchasers for the purpose of ascertaining who would be willing to accept an offer of securities are inconsistent with a claim that the transaction does not involve a public offering, even though ultimately there may only be a few knowledgeable purchasers.

Size of offering. The size of an offering may also raise questions as to whether the offering can be completed within the "strict confines" of the exemption, although, as a matter of practice, many securities are offered and sold pursuant to Section 4(2) in large offerings.

Facilities used in public offering. When the services of a facility through which public distributions are normally effected are used to place the securities, special care must be taken to avoid a public offering. In addition, public advertising prior to sale is inconsistent with a claim of private offering.

Acquisition for investment. An important factor is whether the securities offered have come to rest in the hands of the initial purchasers or whether such purchasers are merely conduits for a wider distribution. If the purchasers acquire the securities with a view to public distribution, the seller assumes the risk of a possible violation of the registration requirements of the Securities Act.

Integration of offerings. Finally, a determination as to whether an offering is public or private should also include a consideration of whether it should be regarded as a part of a larger offering. The following factors were specified in Release No. 4552 as relevant to such questions of integration: whether (1) the different offerings are part of a single plan of financing, (2) the offerings involve the issuance of the same class of security, (3) the offerings are made at or about the same time, (4) the same type of consideration is to be received, and (5) the offerings are made for the same general purpose. A related series of offerings may be considered to be a single offering even if made by ostensibly separate issuers. Since most issuers of secondary market tax-exempt derivative securities that rely on Section 4(2) also rely on Section 3(c)(1) of the Investment Company Act[24] as the basis for their exclusion from the provisions of the Investment Company Act, and because certain recent no-action letters analyzing integration under both Section 3(c)(1) and Section 4(2) have applied factors for analyzing integration under Section 3(c)(1) other than the five factors specified in Release No. 4552, the question of integration of offerings of related issuers relying on Section 3(c)(1) is discussed more fully below.

In 1982, the Commission adopted Regulation D under the Securities Act, which provides exemptions from the registration requirements of the Securities Act for certain offerings.[25] In particular, Rule 506 of Regulation D (illustrated in Exhibit 6-2) provides a nonexclusive "safe harbor" exemption within the private offering exemption of Section 4(2).[26] To qualify for an exemption under Rule 506, an offering must meet the following requirements:

1. The issuer must reasonably believe that there are no more than 35 purchasers from the issuer other than "accredited investors" as defined in Rule 501(a) of Regulation D.[27]
2. The issuer must furnish certain specified information to any purchaser that is not an accredited investor.
3. Each purchaser that is not an accredited investor must have such knowledge and experience in financial and business matters as to be capable of evaluating the merits and risks of the prospective investment or the issuer must reasonably believe that the purchaser has such knowledge and experience.
4. No general solicitation or general advertising may be used to offer the securities.
5. A Notice of Sale on Form D must be filed with the Commission no later than 15 days after the first sale of securities.
6. It should be noted that Rule 506 places no limitation on the number of offerees or the size of the offering.

Rule 504[28] and Rule 505[29] of Regulation D also provide exemptions from the registration requirements of the Securities Act. However, such rules are not safe harbors under the private offering exemption but rather

EXHIBIT 6-2

Rule 506

- Fewer than 35 purchasers (not including accredited investors)
- Specific information required sent to non-accredited investors
- No general solicitation or general advertising
- Notice of sale filed with Commission
- Securities sold are "restricted securities"

are exemptions adopted pursuant to Section 3(b) of the Securities Act, which enables the Commission to adopt rules and regulations that exempt securities from the Securities Act by reason of the small amount involved or the limited character of the public offering.[30]

Certain other items should be considered in connection with the sale of tax-exempt derivative securities in reliance upon Section 4(2) or Rule 506. Purchasers of such securities are customarily required to sign investment representation letters, which form part of the basis for the issuer's reliance upon Section 4(2) or Rule 506. Such letters typically include representations as to the nature of the purchaser and its knowledge and experience, a representation that the purchaser is purchasing the security for investment purposes, an acknowledgment that certain information was provided to the purchaser, and an acknowledgment that the securities are not being registered and the purchaser is bound by any applicable restrictions on the transfer of the securities. Securities sold pursuant to Section 4(2) or Rule 506 are "restricted securities" that cannot be resold absent the registration thereof under the Securities Act or an applicable exemption therefrom. In addition, the documents pursuant to which the security is issued and the security itself typically contain legends or language describing any applicable restrictions on transfer.

Resales of Privately Placed Securities

Securities offered and sold pursuant to Section 4(2) or Rule 506 are "restricted securities" under the Securities Act.[31] Any purchaser that resells a restricted security must make sure not to be deemed to be an "underwriter" under Section 2(11) of the Securities Act in order to preserve an exemption from the registration requirements for such resale.[32] If the purchaser is not an underwriter, the resale may be exempt from the registration requirements of the Securities Act pursuant to Section 4(1), which exempts transactions by "any person other than an issuer, underwriter, or dealer."[33]

A common method by which a purchaser may resell restricted securities without being deemed to be an underwriter is a sale or sales pursuant to Rule 144 under the Securities Act.[34] However, because of the requirements of Rule 144 with respect to the public availability of information about the issuer, the required holding period of the security, the limitation on the amount of securities that can be sold in a particular time period, and the required manner of sale, Rule 144 is not a particularly effective or efficient means of reselling restricted securities within three years from the purchase thereof. In addition, in certain circumstances a purchaser of restricted securities may resell them in private resales pursuant to the so-called Section 4½ exemption without being deemed to be an underwriter. However, owing to the lack of authority explaining the dimensions and conditions of such exemption, purchasers of restricted securities may decline to rely on the Section 4½ exemption in making such resales.

In 1990, the Commission adopted Rule 144A, which provides that a person who offers or sells securities in compliance with its provisions shall not be deemed to be an underwriter of such securities within the meaning of Sections 2(11) and 4(1) of the Securities Act.[35] In order to qualify under Rule 144A, an offer or sale must meet the following conditions:

1. The securities must be offered or sold only to a "qualified institutional buyer," as defined in Rule 144A, or to an offeree or purchaser that the seller and any person acting on behalf of the seller reasonably believe is a qualified institutional buyer.[36]
2. The seller and any person acting on its behalf must take reasonable steps to ensure that the purchaser is aware that the seller may rely on Rule 144A.
3. The securities offered or sold must not have been, when issued, of the same class as securities listed on a national securities exchange or quoted in an automated interdealer quotation system, and must not be securities of an open-end investment company, unit investment trust, or face-amount certificate company that is or is required to be registered under the Investment Company Act.
4. Upon request, the purchaser and the seller must have the right to receive certain information regarding the issuer.

Many tax-exempt derivative securities that are initially offered and sold in reliance on Section 4(2) or Rule 506 are structured to be eligible for resale under Rule 144A. The documents pursuant to which such securities are issued often contain a provision that requires the issuer or the sponsor to deliver the information required by Rule 144A upon the request of the purchaser or the seller. In some cases, transfers may not be made pursuant to Rule 144A unless the prospective purchaser has delivered sufficient evidence that it is a qualified institutional buyer and an acknowledgment that the seller may be relying upon Rule 144A. It is important to note that Rule 144A is available to exempt only resales of securities, as opposed to Section 4(2) and Regulation D, which exempt initial sales by the issuer of securities.

Other Securities Act Exemptions; Bank Guarantees

To the extent that a letter of credit or other security issued by a bank guarantees all payments to be made on a tax-exempt derivative security, the tax-exempt derivative security may be an exempted security pursuant to the provision of Section 3(a)(2) of the Securities Act, which exempts any security guaranteed by a bank. The relevant no-action letters issued by the Staff indicate that, in order to rely on this exemption, counsel should ensure that the guarantee covers all payments to be made on the security for the full term of the security.[37] In addition, the guarantee should cover payments on the derivative security itself, not payments on the municipal security underlying the security.[38] Any reliance upon a bank guarantee to provide an exemption for an underlying tax-exempt derivative security under Section 3(a)(2) should be based on a careful analysis of the relevant no-action letters.

Registration Under the Securities Act

An issuer or sponsor of derivative securities that are not exempted from registration under the Securities Act by Section 3(a)(2) may determine that it is desirable to offer the derivative securities publicly. Since the exemption provided by Section 4(2) would not be available for a public offering of such securities, the securities would have to be registered under the Securities Act. On October 28, 1992, the Commission adopted amendments to the eligibility requirements for use of Form S-3 for registration of securities under the Securities Act.[39] Form S-3 is a "short-form" registration statement that generally allows issuers to rely on the Commission's system of integrated disclosure by incorporating prior public information from filings under the Exchange Act.[40] As a result of the amendments, asset-backed securities may be registered on Form S-3 without regard to the reporting history, if any, of the issuer of such securities, provided that the securities being registered are investment grade. For purposes of Form S-3, an asset-backed security is a security that is serviced primarily by the cash flows of a discrete pool of receivables or other financial assets. The amendments to Form S-3 should simplify the registration process and disclosure requirements for issuers or sponsors of tax-exempt derivative securities who desire to register and publicly offer their securities.[41] The amendments will also allow tax-exempt derivative securities registered on Form S-3 to be offered on a continuous basis pursuant to the "shelf" registration provisions of Rule 415 under the Securities Act.[42]

The Investment Company Act

The Investment Company Act was enacted to regulate the activities of investment pools, which, prior to 1940, were subject to various abuses at the hands of their managers and their affiliates.[43] Under Section 7(a) of the Investment Company Act,[44] no investment company may offer or sell any security or engage in interstate commerce unless the investment company is registered pursuant to Section 8 thereof.[45] Under Sections 3(a)(1) and 3(a)(3),[46] respectively, an investment company is defined as any issuer that "is or holds itself out as being engaged primarily, or proposes to engage primarily, in the business of investing, reinvesting, or trading in securities" or that "is engaged or proposes to engage in the business of investing, reinvesting, owning, holding, or trading in securities, and owns or proposes to acquire investment securities having a value exceeding 40 per centum of the value of such issuer's total assets (exclusive of Government securities and cash items) on an unconsolidated basis."[47] These definitions are broad enough to encompass many trusts, partnerships, and custodial and other arrangements that issue derivative securities. Any issuer that meets either definition is an investment company for purposes of the Investment Company Act unless it is excepted from the definition of investment company or otherwise exempted from the Investment Company Act.

Owing to the burdensome nature of substantive regulation imposed on registered investment companies by the various provisions of the Investment Company Act, many trusts, partnerships, and custodial or other arrangements that issue tax-exempt derivative securities are not able to comply with certain of its provisions. For example, Section 17(a) of the Investment Company Act prohibits an affiliated person of a registered investment company from selling property to or purchasing property from such investment company as principal.[48] In addition, Section 18 imposes limitations on the nature and amount of "senior securities" that a registered management investment company can issue.[49] Most issuers of tax-exempt derivative securities would find these requirements prohibitive.[50] In addition, the Investment Company Act imposes certain reporting requirements on registered investment companies that derivative security issuers could find to be prohibitively expensive and burdensome.[51] Consequently, it is necessary to determine whether the creation of a trust, partnership, or custodial or other arrangement that issues tax-exempt derivative securities results in the creation of an issuer falling within the definition of investment company under Section 3(a), and, if so, whether such issuer is excepted from the definition of investment company or is otherwise exempted from the provisions of the Investment Company Act.

The Merrill Lynch *Analysis—No New Issuer*

If the creation of a trust, partnership, or custodial or other arrangement that issues tax-exempt derivative securities does not result in the creation of an issuer for purposes of the Securities Act, such trust, partnership, or custodial or other arrangement also may not be treated as an investment company subject to registration under and compliance with the Investment Company Act. The staff of the Division of Investment Management (the "Investment Management Staff") of the Commission has, through a series of no-action letters, set forth the circumstances in which it will not deem a new issuer and therefore an investment company to have been created for purposes of the Investment Company Act. The most recent of these letters in the context of tax-exempt derivative securities is *Merrill Lynch*.[52] The Investment Management Staff's view in *Merrill Lynch* that no investment company was created was based on the same representations and conditions as the response of the Staff of the Division of Corporation Finance. Thus, if the creation of a tax-exempt derivative security does not result in the creation of a security for purposes of the Securities Act under the *Merrill Lynch* analysis, it should not result in the creation of an investment company for purposes of the Investment Company Act.

Private Investment Companies—Section 3(c)(1)

If the creation of a tax-exempt derivative security does result in the creation of an investment company because the criteria set forth in *Merrill Lynch* are not satisfied, the trust, partnership, or custodial or other arrangement through which such security is created should be analyzed to determine whether it may be excepted from the definition of investment company by one of the provisions of Section 3(c) of the Investment Company Act or by any rule under the Investment Company Act. An exception commonly used for issuers whose securities are privately placed under Section 4(2) of the Securities Act or Regulation D thereunder is Section 3(c)(1), which excepts any issuer that is not making and does not at present propose to make a public offering of its securities and whose outstanding securities (other than short-term paper) are beneficially owned by not more than 100 persons.[53]

No Public Offering

The "no public offering" prong of Section 3(c)(1) is interpreted consistently with the requirements of Section 4(2) of the Securities Act.[54] Because Rule 506 of Regulation D is a safe harbor under Section 4(2), offerings that qualify for the safe harbor of Rule 506 will satisfy the no public offering requirement.[55] However, since the exemptions provided by Rule 504 and Rule 505 of Regulation D are promulgated pursuant to Section 3(b) of the Securities Act and are not safe harbors under the private offering exemption of Section 4(2), offerings made pursuant to Rule 504 or Rule 505 will not necessarily satisfy the no public offering requirement of Section 3(c)(1).[56]

100 Beneficial Owners

The second prong of Section 3(c)(1) requires that the outstanding securities of an issuer must be beneficially owned by not more than 100 persons. Beneficial owners of the issuer's short-term paper do not need to be counted in meeting this requirement. While certain tax-exempt derivative securities have features, such as liquidity puts, that may be used to shorten the maturity of such securities for other purposes (such as for purposes of Rule 2a-7 as discussed below), it is not clear whether such securities constitute "short-term paper" for purposes of Section 3(c)(1).[57]

In determining the number of beneficial owners of an issuer's securities, beneficial ownership of a security by a company (including a corporation, partnership, association, joint-stock company, trust, fund, or any organized group of persons) is generally deemed to be beneficial ownership by one person. However, if such company owns 10 percent or more of the issuer's outstanding *voting securities*, beneficial ownership by such company is deemed to be beneficial ownership by the holders of such company's outstanding securities, other than short-term paper (the "10% Rule").[58] There is an exception to the 10% Rule if, as of the date of the most recent acquisition by such company of securities of that issuer, the value of all securities owned by such company of all issuers that are or would, but for the 10% Rule, be excluded from the definition of investment company pursuant to Section 3(c)(1) does not exceed 10 percent of the value of such company's assets (the "10% Exception").[59] Thus, the Section 3(c)(1) exception may be preserved with respect to an issuer, notwithstanding the ownership of more than 10 percent of such issuer's outstanding voting securities by certain companies, if the composition of each of such companies' assets satisfies the 10% Exception.

Notwithstanding the availability of the exception provided by Section 3(c)(1) in reliance on the 10% Exception, an issuer that relies on the 10% Exception is deemed to be an investment company for purposes of Section 12(d)(1) of the Investment Company Act, which restricts the amount of securities of any investment company (including an issuer relying on the 10% Exception) that a registered investment company may acquire and the amount of securities of any registered investment company that an investment company (including an issuer relying on the 10% Exception) may acquire.[60] As discussed below, this is a key consideration when structuring tax-exempt derivative securities that are intended to be excepted from the definition of investment company pursuant to Section 3(c)(1) and to be sold to registered investment companies.

Voting Securities

The 10% Rule (and the related restrictions on investment company purchases pursuant to Section 12(d)(1) of the Investment Company Act) applies only if a company owns 10 percent of the outstanding *voting securities* of the Section 3(c)(1) issuer. The term "voting security" is defined in Section 2(a)(42) of the Investment Company Act as ". . . any security presently entitling the owner or holder thereof to vote for the election of directors of a company. . . ."[61] Trusts, partnerships, custodial arrangements, and other entities, which are the issuers of most tax-exempt derivative securities relying on the Section 3(c)(1) definition, generally do not have boards of directors. However, the Investment Management Staff has indicated, through numerous no-action letters, that certain rights possessed by holders of securities issued by those types of issuers are rights that are analogous to the power to vote for the election of directors and, as a result, the interests owned by such holders will be deemed to be voting securities. These rights include, among others, the right of limited partners to remove a general partner or to elect a new general partner where the existing general partner becomes bankrupt, or dissolves or withdraws from the partnership;[62] the right of holders of interests in a trust to remove or replace the trustee;[63] and the right to exercise a controlling economic influence over the issuer.[64]

In determining whether a tax-exempt derivative structure is eligible for the exception provided by Section 3(c)(1), it is important to remember that if the trust, partnership, or custodial or other arrangement is not treated as having issued voting securities, the 10% Rule does not apply, the 10% Exception is not necessary, and an examination of purchasing companies' assets is not required. In certain no-action letters, the Investment Management Staff, in reaching a determination as to whether an interest was a voting security, relied upon representations that no investor formed for purposes of investing in the issuer of such interests or itself relying on the exception from the definition of investment company contained in Section 3(c)(1) will acquire 10 percent or more of such interests.[65] A security may be less likely to be deemed a voting security where it represents an interest in an entity that is a passive investment vehicle as opposed to an actively managed investment vehicle.[66] These factors should be considered when reaching any determination as to whether a particular interest is a voting security.

Integration

An issue that should be considered by sponsors of tax-exempt derivative securities programs structured in reliance on Section 3(c)(1) is that of integration under the Investment Company Act. The integration concept generally allows the Commission to look behind ostensibly separate issues, issuers, or transactions to see if, in economic reality, they are really a single issue, issuer, or transaction.[67] The concepts of integration under the Securities Act and integration under Section 3(c)(1) of the Investment Company Act differ. The former involves the combination of ostensibly separate offerings to determine whether the combined offering qualifies for an exemption under the Securities Act; the latter involves the combination of ostensibly separate issuers to determine the number of beneficial owners of the combined issuer's outstanding securities under Section 3(c)(1) of the Investment Company Act (i.e., whether the 100-holder limit has been exceeded).[68] While the Staff has traditionally analyzed issues of integration under the Securities Act under the five-factor test enunciated in Release No. 4552, a recent no-action letter, which involved questions of integration under both the Securities Act and Section 3(c)(1) of the Investment Company Act, determined the resolution of such issues based on the integration test and standards applicable under Section 3(c)(1).[69]

Integration under Section 3(c)(1) has been applied to entities with common investment advisers, promoters, sponsors, and general partners.[70] The test to be used in determining whether integration is required under Section 3(c)(1) is whether an interest in one issuer, as compared to an interest in a second issuer, would be considered materially different by a reasonable investor qualified to purchase both.[71] In making such determination, the issuers should be analyzed to determine if they have (1) the same investment objectives, (2) the same types of portfolio securities, and, particularly, (3) similar portfolio risk/return characteristics.[72] A key factor in making this determination is whether the issuers are designed for distinct groups of investors. However, the creation of separate derivative security issuers for arbitrary investor classifications is not sufficient to avoid integration under the Investment Company Act.[73] The question of integration under Section 3(c)(1) should be carefully considered in any derivative securities program that involves multiple issuers relying on Section 3(c)(1).[74]

Asset-Based Exemptions—Section 3(c)(5) and Rule 3a-7

Two provisions of the Investment Company Act except issuers from the definition of investment company based, at least in part, on the composition of the issuer's assets and the nature of the securities issued by the issuer. One exception, Section 3(c)(5),[75] has been relied upon for many years to exempt a number of different structures. The other exception, Rule 3a-7,[76] was recently enacted in response to certain recommendations of the Commission's Division of Investment Management in its 1992 report, *Protecting Investors: A Half Century of Investment Company Regulation* (the "Investment Company Act Report").[77]

Section 3(c)(5)

Section 3(c)(5) of the Investment Company Act excepts from the definition of investment company any person who is not engaged in the business of issuing redeemable securities, face-amount certificates of the installment type, or periodic payment plan certificates, and who is primarily engaged in one or more of certain specified businesses. While the prohibition against an entity's issuing face-amount certificates of the installment type and periodic payment plan certificates is generally not relevant to issuers of tax-exempt derivative securities, the prohibition against issuing redeemable securities may result in the ineligibility of certain tax-exempt derivative structures for the Section 3(c)(5) exception. The issues involved in determining whether a security is a redeemable security are discussed below in connection with Rule 3a-7, but are identical to the issues involved in making such determination under Section 3(c)(5).

The specified businesses in which an issuer relying on Section 3(c)(5) must be primarily engaged are:

(A) Purchasing or otherwise acquiring notes, drafts, acceptances, open accounts receivable, and other obligations representing part or all of the sales price of merchandise, insurance, and services;

(B) Making loans to manufacturers, wholesalers, and retailers of, and to prospective purchasers of, specified merchandise, insurance, and services; and

(C) Purchasing or otherwise acquiring mortgages and other liens on and interests in real estate.

An issuer may rely on Section 3(c)(5) only if it is *primarily* engaged in one or more of the businesses set forth above.

A tax-exempt derivative security issuer whose assets are composed primarily of a pool of tax-exempt leases may be able to rely on Section 3(c)(5). However, the leases should be analyzed to determine whether they are in fact equipment financing leases and, therefore, represent "all or a part of the sales price of merchandise" under subparagraph (A).[78] A tax-exempt derivative security issuer whose assets are composed primarily of tax-exempt mortgage bonds also may be able to rely on Section 3(c)(5). Through a series of no-action letters, however, the Investment Management Staff has placed certain limitations on the availability of Section 3(c)(5) to issuers holding mortgage bonds.[79] Essentially, the Investment Management Staff's position with respect to mortgage bonds is intended to ensure that investors in the Section 3(c)(5) entity would be in the same position they would be in if the entity owned the mortgages underlying the bonds.[80] Accordingly, the derivative issuer should hold the entire issue of bonds and the bond trustee should assign its right to foreclose the mortgage to the derivative security issuer.[81] In addition, the Investment Management Staff has interpreted the "primarily engaged" requirement of Section 3(c)(5) to require that at least 55 percent of the issuer's assets be in mortgages and other liens on and interests in real estate and an additional 25 percent in real estate related assets, with no restriction on the remaining 20 percent.[82]

Rule 3a-7

In May 1992, the Division of Investment Management published the Investment Company Act Report, which made certain legislative and regulatory recommendations aimed at maintaining and improving the level of investor protection under the Investment Company Act, facilitating competition and capital formation by removing barriers under the Investment Company Act, and encouraging innovation.[83] As part of the Investment Company Act Report, the Division of Investment Management analyzed the treatment of structured financing under the Investment Company Act.[84]

After reviewing the structured finance market and the applicability of the Investment Company Act to such market, the Division of Investment Management recommended that the Commission adopt a rule exempting structured financings from the Investment Company Act, subject to requirements that would address the potential investor protection concerns presented by structured financings.[85] In response to the Division of Investment Management's recommendation, the Commission adopted Rule 3a-7 in November 1992. Rule 3a-7 exempts from the definition of investment company any issuer who is engaged in the business of purchasing, or otherwise acquiring, and holding eligible assets (and in activities related or incidental thereto) and who does not issue redeemable securities, provided that such issuer satisfies the four specific requirements discussed below.[86]

Redeemable Securities

An issuer relying on Section 3(c)(5) or Rule 3a-7 may not issue redeemable securities. A "redeemable security" is defined in Section 2(a)(32) of the Investment Company Act as "any security, other than short-term paper, under the terms of which the holder, upon its presentation to the issuer or to a person designated by the issuer, is entitled (whether absolutely or only out of surplus) to receive approximately his proportionate share of the issuer's current net assets, or the cash equivalent thereof. . . ."[87] Tax-exempt derivative securities issued by entities relying on Section 3(c)(5) or Rule 3a-7 and, in particular, securities subject to liquidity puts must be analyzed to determine whether they are redeemable securities under Section 2(a)(32). In a series of no-action letters under Section 3(c)(5), the Investment Management Staff has determined that liquidity puts may be structured so as not to create redeemable securities.[88] However, it is not clear whether the Investment Management Staff would reach such a determination in the context of a liquidity put exercisable upon a very short notice period (e.g., fourteen days or less), apparently because of a concern that investors would confuse securities subject to such a put with those issued by open-end management investment companies.[89] In fact, as finally adopted, Rule 3a-7 prohibits the issuance of redeemable securities; however, as initially proposed by the Commission, Rule 3a-7 would have also prohibited the issuance of debt securities that entitle holders to receive principal and accrued interest within a short period of time after demand (i.e., within fourteen days).[90] The Commission release that adopted Rule 3a-7 (the "Adopting Release") did not clarify whether securities subject to such short-term liquidity puts would be deemed to be redeemable securities.[91] The Adopting Release simply cautioned that counsel concerned about whether a security would be a redeemable security under Rule 3a-7 should examine the no-action letters under Section 3(c)(5) for guidance.[92] Accordingly, securities subject to short-term liquidity puts, as well as certain other securities that allow holders thereof access to underlying assets (e.g., inverse floaters that may be "linked" with floaters to obtain an underlying bond), should be carefully analyzed in light of the relevant no-action letters, the Commission's statements in the Adopting Release, and the release that initially proposed Rule 3a-7 for adoption (the "Proposing Release")[93] to ascertain whether they are redeemable securities for purposes of Rule 3a-7.

An issuer relying on Rule 3a-7 (illustrated in Exhibit 6-3) must be engaged in the business of purchasing, or otherwise acquiring and holding eligible assets and in activities related or incidental thereto. "Eligible assets" is defined in Rule 3a-7 as "financial assets, either fixed or revolving, that by their terms convert into cash within a definite time period plus any rights or other assets designed to assure the servicing or timely distribution of proceeds to security holders."[94] While this definition does not specifically identify particular classifications of assets, the Commission stated in the Adopting Release that it is intended to include all the assets provided as examples in the Rule as originally proposed, including notes, bonds, debentures, evidences of indebtedness, certificates of deposit, leases, installment contracts, interest rate swaps, repurchase agreements, guaranteed investment contracts, accounts receivables, chattel paper, cumulative preferred stock, guarantees, annuities, and participations or beneficial interests in any of the foregoing and any other assets that serve solely to support the credit of the issuer's securities, such as letters of credit, guarantees, and cash collateral accounts.[95] The definition also includes liquidity arrangements that support the payment of the securities and the underlying assets.[96]

The four remaining requirements of Rule 3a-7 are, generally, as follows:

1. The issuer must issue fixed-income securities or other securities entitling holders thereof to receive payments that depend primarily on the cash flow from eligible assets. "Fixed-income securities" generally include securities entitling the holder thereof to a stated principal amount; interest on a principal amount calculated by reference to a fixed rate, or to a standard or formula unrelated to market value changes; interest on a principal amount calculated by refer-

EXHIBIT 6-3

Elements of Rule 3a-7 Exception

- No "redeemable securities" may be issued
- Issuer must be engaged in the business of purchasing, acquiring, and holding eligible assets
- Issuer must issue "fixed income securities"
- Limitations on types of securities sold to other than certain accredited investors or qualified institutional investors
- Acquisition or disposition of assets only under predetermined conditions
- Independent trustee may be required

ence to auctions or remarketings; an amount equal to specified fixed or variable portions of the interest received by the issuer; and any combination of such amounts.[97]

2. Securities sold to persons other than certain accredited investors or qualified institutional buyers must be fixed income securities rated in one of the four highest long-term debt rating categories or an equivalent short-term category. Unrated fixed income securities may be sold to certain specified accredited investors as defined in Regulation D. Any securities may be sold to qualified institutional buyers and to persons involved in the organization or operation of the issuer and their affiliates.
3. The issuer may acquire additional eligible assets or dispose of eligible assets only if: the assets are acquired or disposed of only in accordance with the terms and conditions set forth in the instruments pursuant to which the issuer's securities are issued; such acquisition or disposition does not result in a downgrading in the rating of the issuer's outstanding fixed-income securities; and such acquisition or disposition is not for the primary purpose of recognizing gains or decreasing losses resulting from market value changes.
4. If the issuer issues securities other than securities that are exempted from the Securities Act by Section 3(a)(3)[98] thereof, Rule 3a-7 requires the issuer to appoint an independent trustee, to take reasonable steps to ensure that such trustee has a perfected security interest in the eligible assets, and to take actions necessary to deposit certain cash flows in a segregated account.

Because Rule 3a-7 was only recently adopted, there are no publicly available no-action letters interpreting its requirements. Accordingly, any issuer of tax-exempt derivative securities that is structured to comply with Rule 3a-7 should be carefully analyzed in light of the Investment Company Act Report, the Adopting Release, and the Proposing Release to ensure that reliance upon Rule 3a-7 is justified.

It is important to note that Section 3(c)(5) and Rule 3a-7 are exceptions only under the Investment Company Act. They are unlike Section 3(c)(1), which, of necessity, has an accompanying exemption under Section 4(2) of the Securities Act. Consequently, an independent exemption under the Securities Act must be established for each offer and sale of securities issued by a derivative securities issuer excepted by Rule 3a-7 or Section 3(c)(5). Alternatively, such securities must be registered under the Securities Act.

Other Investment Company Act Exceptions

In April 1992, legislation was introduced in both houses of the 102d Congress to amend Section 3(c)(1) and adopt a new exception to the definition of investment company.[99] Identical legislation was introduced in the Senate in February of 1993.[100] The proposed amendments to Section 3(c)(1) would have three effects:

1. The 10% Exception would be eliminated;
2. Any issuer relying on the amended Section 3(c)(1) would be an investment company only for purposes of the provisions of Section 12(d)(1) that apply to the purchase by such issuer of securities issued by registered investment companies; and
3. The 10% Rule would apply only to companies that are investment companies or would have been investment companies but for the exception contained in Section 3(c)(1) or Section 3(c)(7) (discussed below).

With the deletion of the 10% Exception it would be essential under the amended Section 3(c)(1) that any tax-exempt derivative issuer relying on the amended Section 3(c)(1) not issue any voting securities 10 percent or more of which could be purchased by certain companies with numerous beneficial owners.

Proposed Section 3(c)(7) would except from the definition of investment company any issuer whose outstanding securities are owned exclusively by persons who, at the time of the acquisition of such securities, were "qualified purchasers." Qualified purchasers would be defined in a rule adopted by the Commission based on a determination that such persons do not need the protection of the Investment Company Act. Such determination would be based on such factors as financial sophistication, net worth, knowledge and experience in financial matters, amount of assets owed or under management, and relationship with the issuer. In the Investment Company Act Report, the Division of Investment Management stated its view that an accredited investor standard would be too low and that, at least initially, the definition of qualified institutional buyer in Rule 144A would represent an appropriate level of sophistication for institutions.[101] Any issuer relying on Section 3(c)(7) would be an investment company only for purposes of the provisions of Section 12(d)(1) that apply to the purchase by such issuer of securities issued by registered investment companies. While the amendments to Section 3(c)(1) and Section 3(c)(7) have not yet been enacted, it is possible that such amendments will be enacted in the present or future sessions of Congress.

Other Securities Laws

In addition to the issues discussed above, the offer and sale of tax-exempt derivative securities also involves certain issues under the Trust Indenture Act of 1939, as amended,[102] and the securities or "blue sky" laws of the various states.

The Trust Indenture Act

The Trust Indenture Act generally requires that debt securities may not be sold to the public unless they are issued pursuant to a trust indenture that conforms to specified standards. The registration statement relating to securities registered under the Securities Act must contain certain information and documents, and the indenture relating to such securities must be qualified under the Trust Indenture Act.[103] Certain securities are exempted from the requirements of the Trust Indenture Act. For example, any certificate of interest or participation in two or more securities having substantially different rights and privileges is exempted under Section 304(a)(2).[104] Any security exempted from the provisions of the Securities Act by Section 3(a)(2) (e.g., many tax-exempt bonds) or Section 3(a)(8) thereof is exempted under Section 304(a)(4).[105] Any guarantee of any of the foregoing exempted securities is exempted under Section 304(a)(7).[106] In addition, the indenture qualification[107] does not apply to any transaction exempted from the provisions of Section 5 of the Securities Act by Section 4(2) thereof (i.e., private placements). Most tax-exempt derivative securities fall within one or more of these exemptions. However, prior to the offer and sale of any tax-exempt derivative security, an exemption from the provisions of the Trust Indenture Act should be confirmed. This may be particularly relevant in light of the adoption of Rule 3a-7, since a tax-exempt derivative security excepted under Rule 3a-7 may be registered under the Securities Act (and therefore may be subject to the qualification requirements of the Trust Indenture Act).

"Blue Sky" Requirements

Most state securities or "blue sky" laws do not require the registration or qualification of investment companies or trust indentures. However, virtually every state securities law contains a provision requiring the registration or qualification of securities prior to their offer or sale to any person in such state, absent an applicable exemption.[108] Most state blue sky laws provide an exemption for securities issued by states, political subdivisions of states, and agencies, authorities, or instrumentalities of the foregoing.[109] Many blue sky laws also exempt offers and sales to specified institutions.[110] In addition, many jurisdictions contain a "limited offering" exemption.[111] Notwithstanding the applicability of any particular exemption to any offer or sale of a security, a notice filing or perfection of an exemption is often required.[112] While a detailed analysis of the applicability of such exemptions is beyond the scope of this chapter, the laws of each jurisdiction in which a tax-exempt derivative security is offered or sold should be examined, prior to such offer or sale, to determine whether an applicable exemption exists.

Considerations for Purchasers That Are Investment Companies Registered Under the Investment Company Act

One of the largest single groups of purchasers of tax-exempt derivative securities is investment companies registered under the Investment Company Act ("registered funds"). Certain requirements of the Investment Company Act may impact the amount of tax-exempt derivative securities that registered funds may purchase or the nature of tax-exempt derivative securities that registered funds may acquire. In addition, many registered funds are "money market" mutual funds, which are required to comply with the stringent requirements of Rule 2a-7 under the Investment Company Act, a rule that imposes specific standards as to the nature, quality, and maturity of the securities such funds may purchase.[113]

The Fund of Funds Provisions

Section 12(d)(1) of the Investment Company Act imposes limitations on the purchase by registered funds of securities issued by other investment companies. Under Section 12(d)(1)(A), it is impermissible for a registered fund to acquire any security issued by any other investment company if, immediately after such acquisition, the registered fund owns (1) more than 3 percent of the total outstanding voting stock[114] of the acquired company, (2) securities issued by the acquired company having a value exceeding 5 percent of the value of the total assets of the registered fund, or (3) securities issued by the acquired company and all other investment companies having a value exceeding 10 percent of the value of the total assets of the registered fund.[115] As discussed above, tax-exempt derivative issuers are typically structured to be excepted from the definition of investment company. However, an issuer excepted from such definition pursuant to Section 3(c)(1) that issues voting securities, so that the Section 3(c)(1) exception is available only after application of the 10% Exception to the 10% Rule (a "12(d)(1) Issuer"), is nonetheless deemed to be an investment company for purposes of Section 12(d)(1).[116] Thus, the purchase by a registered fund of securities issued by a 12(d)(1) Issuer raises Section 12(d)(1) issues.

The following four examples are illustrative of issues that may arise. First, a registered fund could purchase 10 percent or more of a 12(d)(1) Issuer's outstanding voting securities. This would clearly be in violation of the first prong of Section 12(d)(1)(A), since the registered fund would own, as a result of such purchase, over 3 percent of the total outstanding voting stock of the 12(d)(1) Issuer.

Second, a registered fund could purchase less than 10 percent but more than 3 percent of the 12(d)(1) Issuer's outstanding voting securities. If, prior to or concurrently with such purchase, any other company purchased in excess of 10 percent of the 12(d)(1) Issuer's outstanding voting securities, and the ownership by such entity necessitated reliance by the 12(d)(1) Issuer on the 10% Exception, the 12(d)(1) Issuer would be an investment company for purposes of Section 12(d)(1). Consequently, the registered fund's purchase of over 3 percent of the 12(d)(1) Issuer's outstanding voting stock would violate the first prong of Section 12(d)(1)(A).

Third, a registered fund could purchase less than 3 percent of the 12(d)(1) Issuer's outstanding voting securities. If the 12(d)(1) Issuer's reliance on the 10% Exception was necessitated by a prior or concurrent purchase of the 12(d)(1) Issuer's outstanding voting securities, as in the second example, the 12(d)(1) Issuer would be an investment company for purposes of Section 12(d)(1). Consequently, the securities issued by the 12(d)(1) Issuer would be included in the registered fund's calculations under the second and third prongs of Section 12(d)(1)(A). If, for example, as a result of such purchase, the registered fund had invested over 10 percent of its total assets in securities issued by investment companies, including the 12(d)(1) Issuer, the registered fund would be in violation of the third prong of Section 12(d)(1)(A).

Finally, a registered fund could purchase securities issued by the 12(d)(1) Issuer that were not voting securities. If the 12(d)(1) Issuer issued another class of securities that were voting securities, and the 12(d)(1) Issuer was required to rely on the 10% Exception, it would be an investment company for purposes of Section 12(d)(1). Consequently, the nonvoting securities issued by the 12(d)(1) Issuer would be included in the registered fund's calculations under the second and third prongs of Section 12(d)(1)(A).

As the foregoing discussion illustrates, prior to the purchase by a registered fund of any security issued by an issuer relying on Section 3(c)(1), it is essential to determine whether the security being purchased is a voting security and whether the issuer is relying on the 10% Exception.

Investment Objectives and Policies

Section 8(b) of the Investment Company Act,[117] Items 4 and 13 of Form N-1A,[118] and Items 8 and 17 of Form N-2[119] require registered open-end investment companies ("open-end funds")[120] and closed-end investment companies ("closed-end funds"),[121] respectively, to disclose their investment objectives and policies in their registration statements. Investment companies that seek to distribute exempt-interest dividends to their shareholders generally have investment policies limiting their permissible investments primarily to investments that generate tax-exempt interest.

However, funds have a variety of ways of articulating such policies. For example, certain funds restrict their permissible investment to securities issued by specified municipal entities. Other funds have recently adopted amendments to their investment policies in order to provide the flexibility to invest in specified tax-exempt derivative securities.[122] Still other funds have policies that restrict their investment to municipal securities but apply only to the investment of 80 percent of the funds' assets. Prior to any purchase of a tax-exempt derivative security by a registered fund, the security should be analyzed to determine whether the purchase thereof falls within the purchasing fund's articulated investment policies.

Rule 2a-7

Many purchasers of tax-exempt derivative securities are money market funds that are subject to the requirements of Rule 2a-7 under the Investment Company Act.[123] Under Rule 2a-7, a fund that complies with certain requirements as to the quality and maturity of portfolio instruments may use the amortized cost method of valuing its portfolio securities or the penny-rounding method of computing price per share. The use of such methods enables a fund to maintain a constant price per share, typically $1.00.

Under Rule 2a-7, a money market fund generally may not purchase a security with a remaining maturity of greater than 397 calendar days or maintain a dollar-weighted average portfolio maturity that exceeds 90 days.[124] The maturity of a security is generally deemed to be the period remaining until the date noted on the face of the instrument as the date on which the principal amount must be paid.[125] However, a variable-rate instrument that is subject to a demand feature is deemed to have a maturity equal to the longer of the period remaining until the next readjustment of the interest rate or the period until the principal amount can be recovered through demand.[126] Under the rule, a "variable-rate instrument" means a security whose terms provide for the adjustment of its interest rate on set dates and, upon such adjustment, can reasonably be expected to have a market value that approximates its par value.[127] A "demand feature" is a right to sell a security for its principal amount that may be exercised at any time on no more than 30 days' notice or at specified intervals not exceeding 397 calendar days upon not more than 30 days' notice.[128] A tax-exempt derivative security being considered for purchase by a money market fund should be analyzed to determine whether either its principal amount is due within 397 days, it constitutes a "variable-rate instrument" subject to a "demand feature," or it is otherwise eligible for the maturity-shortening provisions of Rule 2a-7.

Money market funds must also limit their portfolio investments to instruments that are determined to present minimal credit risk and are at the time of purchase "eligible securities."[129] Eligible securities generally include securities with remaining maturities of 397 days or less that are rated in one of the two highest rating categories for short-term debt obligations and unrated securities that are determined to be of comparable quality.[130] If a demand instrument (e.g., a variable-rate instrument subject to a demand feature) has an unconditional demand feature, it may be determined to be an eligible security based solely on whether the demand feature is an eligible security.[131] A demand instrument that does not have an unconditional demand feature is not an eligible security unless it meets the requirements for being an eligible security (i.e., has the requisite short-term ratings) and the demand instrument has been rated in one of the two highest rating categories for long-term debt obligations or is determined to be of comparable quality.[132] Most tax-exempt derivative securities, for tax reasons, have demand features that are conditional (i.e., they are not exercisable upon a default in the payment of principal or interest on the underlying security). In addition, derivative securities may have put features that are backed by *lines* of credit that may not be drawn on if specified bankruptcy or default events occur. Any money market fund contemplating the purchase of a tax-exempt security with a conditional demand feature should ensure that the security has the requisite short-term and long-term ratings or is determined to be of comparable quality.

Rule 2a-7 also provides that immediately after the acquisition of any put by a tax-exempt money market fund, with respect to 75 percent of such fund's total assets, no more than 5 percent of the fund's total assets may be invested in securities issued by or subject to puts from the same institution.[133] A "put" is defined in Rule 2a-7 as a right to sell a security within a specified period of time at a specified exercise price that may be sold, transferred, or assigned only with the underlying security.[134] This definition includes demand features that may be used to shorten the maturity of variable-rate instruments. Accordingly, a tax-exempt money market fund is limited in the amount of securities it can purchase that are part of a derivative securities program containing demand features provided by a single institution.

The Investment Management Staff has imposed certain additional restrictions on money market fund purchases of derivative securities. For example, money market funds are not permitted to purchase "inverse floaters."[135] Letters of intent and auction mechanisms do not constitute demand features that may be used to shorten maturities under Rule 2a-7.[136] Also, money market funds should purchase tax-exempt derivative securities subject to conditional demand features only if, at the time of purchase and at the time of each tender opportunity, the fund reasonably expects, based on its analysis of market interest rate trends, that prevailing short-term tax-exempt rates will not exceed the maximum rate on such securities at the time of the next interest rate adjustment and that the circumstances that would result in termination of the demand feature will not occur prior to the next opportunity to tender the security. The fund must exercise the demand feature or otherwise dispose of the securities prior to the time the demand feature is scheduled to expire.[137]

Restrictions on Ownership of Illiquid Securities

Open-end funds must limit their investments in "illiquid" securities to 15 percent of their assets.[138] This limitation is 10 percent with respect to money market funds.[139] An illiquid security is a security that may not be sold or disposed of in the ordinary course of business within seven days at approximately the value at which the fund has valued the investment on its books.[140] The Commission has historically taken the position that restricted securities are illiquid securities for purposes of such limitations.[141] However, the Commission indicated in the release adopting Rule 144A that the determination of the liquidity of Rule 144A eligible securities is a question of fact for the board of directors of a fund to determine, based on the trading market for the specific security.[142] Accordingly, an analysis of the trading market for any restricted tax-exempt derivative security, particularly a security with a short-term liquidity put, may lead to the conclusion that such security is not illiquid for purposes of the limitation on illiquid securities.

Conclusion

The structuring and distribution of any tax-exempt derivative security necessarily involve a number of issues under the federal and state securities laws. It is essential that counsel carefully consider such issues in order to ensure that the offer and sale of such security are in compliance with the law and that the security is an appropriate investment for the target investor audience.

Notes

The author gratefully acknowledges the helpful comments of Steven L. Clark and the assistance of Alice G. Owings.

1. 15 U.S.C.A. §§ 80a-1 to 64 (1981, Supp. 1993).
2. 15 U.S.C.A. § 80a-2(b).
3. 15 U.S.C.A. §§ 77a–77aa (1981, Supp. 1993).
4. 15 U.S.C.A. § 77c(a)(2).
5. For a discussion of securities law considerations in the area of tax-exempt municipal bonds, *see* DAVID G. ORMSBY, THE APPLICATIONS OF THE FEDERAL SECURITIES LAWS TO THE ISSUANCE AND SALE OF MUNICIPAL SECURITIES (PLI, 1990). For a discussion of securities law considerations in the taxable municipal bond arena, *see* Steven L. Clark, *Taxable Municipal Bonds: A Working Guide to Federal Securities Law Considerations,* 7 MUN. FIN. J. 183 (1986).
6. *See* Kelling & Co. Inc., SEC No-Action Letter, pub. avail. Oct. 22, 1984, for an example of primary tax-exempt derivative securities (lease certificates of participation) that directly involve governmental units.
7. 15 U.S.C.A. § 77a.
8. 15 U.S.C.A. § 77e.
9. 15 U.S.C.A. § 77c.
10. 15 U.S.C.A. § 77d.
11. Section 15(d) of the Securities Exchange Act of 1934, as amended, requires each issuer who has filed a registration statement that has become effective under the Securi-

ties Act to file certain periodic information, documents, and reports. 15 U.S.C.A. § 78o(d).

12. 15 U.S.C.A. § 77c(a)(2).

13. A no-action letter is a letter from the staff of a particular division or divisions of the Commission that sets forth either the staff's interpretation of a particular statute, rule, or regulation, or the enforcement position of the staff with respect to a proposed transaction. No-action letters are typically limited to and based upon the specific facts set forth in the requesting letter. While no-action letters do not have precedential value and are binding on the Commission only with respect to its enforcement position based on the specific facts set forth in the requesting letters, they are relied upon by practitioners as statements of the staff's views concerning application of the federal securities laws to particular transactions.

14. Merrill Lynch, Pierce, Fenner & Smith Inc., SEC No-Action Letter, pub. avail. Sept. 26, 1990.

15. *See* CRT Government Securities, Ltd., SEC No-Action Letter, pub. avail. Aug. 4, 1992.

16. The theory underlying the exemption of a derivative security with liquidity or credit enhancement under the *Merrill Lynch* analysis is that the offer and sale of the derivative security is simply the offer and sale of an interest in a municipal security that is itself exempt and the offer and sale of an interest in the credit enhancement or liquidity instrument, which itself is also an exempted security. Accordingly, the use of a credit enhancement or liquidity instrument that is not itself an exempted security does not fit within the *Merrill Lynch* analysis.

17. 15 U.S.C.A. § 77c(a)(8).

18. 17 C.F.R. § 240.10b-5 (1992).

19. 15 U.S.C.A. §§ 78a–78ll (1981, Supp. 1993).

20. 15 U.S.C.A. § 77d(2).

21. SEC v. Ralston Purina Co., 346 U.S. 119, 125 (1953).

22. Non-Public Offering Exemption, Securities Act Release No. 4552 (Nov. 6, 1962).

23. *Id.*

24. 15 U.S.C.A. § 80a-3(c)(1).

25. 17 C.F.R. §§ 230.501–508 (1992).

26. 17 C.F.R. § 230.506.

27. "Accredited investor" is defined in Rule 501(a) under the Securities Act as:

> any person who comes within any of the following categories, or who the issuer reasonably believes comes within any of the following categories, at the time of the sale of the securities to that person:
>
> (1) Any bank as defined in section 3(a)(2) of the Act, or any savings and loan association or other institution as defined in section 3(a)(5)(A) of the Act whether acting in its individual or fiduciary capacity; any broker or dealer registered pursuant to section 15 of the Securities Exchange Act of 1934; any insurance company as defined in section 2(13) of the Act; any investment company registered under the Investment Company Act of 1940 or a business development company as defined in section 2(a)(48) of that Act; any Small Business Investment Company licensed by the U.S. Small Business Administration under section 301(c) or (d) of the Small Business Investment Act of 1958; any plan established and maintained by a state, its political subdivisions, or any agency or instrumentality of a state or its political subdivisions for the benefit of its employees, if such plan has total assets in excess of $5,000,000; any employee benefit plan within the meaning of the Employee Retirement Income Security Act of 1974 if the investment decision is made by a plan fiduciary, as defined in section

3(21) of such Act, which is either a bank, savings and loan association, insurance company, or registered investment adviser, or if the employee benefit plan has total assets in excess of $5,000,000 or, if a self-directed plan, with investment decisions made solely by persons that are accredited investors;

(2) Any private business development company as defined in Section 202(a)(22) of the Investment Advisers Act of 1940;

(3) Any organization described in Section 501(c)(3) of the Internal Revenue Code, corporation, Massachusetts or similar business trust, or partnership, not formed for the specific purpose of acquiring the securities offered, with total assets in excess of $5,000,000;

(4) Any director, executive officer, or general partner of the issuer of the securities being offered or sold, or any director, executive officer, or general partner of a general partner of that issuer;

(5) Any natural person whose individual net worth, or joint net worth with that person's spouse, at the time of his purchase exceeds $1,000,000;

(6) Any natural person who had an individual income in excess of $200,000 in each of the two most recent years or joint income with that person's spouse in excess of $300,000 in each of those years and has a reasonable expectation of reaching the same income level in the current year;

(7) Any trust, with total assets in excess of $5,000,000, not formed for the specific purpose of acquiring the securities offered, whose purchase is directed by a sophisticated person as described in § 230.506(b)(2)(ii); and

(8) Any entity in which all of the equity owners are accredited investors.

17 C.F.R. § 230.501(a).

28. 17 C.F.R. § 230.504.
29. 17 C.F.R. § 230.505.
30. 15 U.S.C.A. § 77c(b).
31. *See* 17 C.F.R. § 230.502(d); 17 C.F.R. § 230.144(a)(3).
32. Section 2(11) of the Securities Act defines "underwriter" as:

    any person who has purchased from an issuer with a view to, or offers or sells for an issuer in connection with, the distribution of any security, or participates or has a direct or indirect participation in any such undertaking, or participates or has a participation in the direct or indirect underwriting of any such undertaking; but such term shall not include a person whose interest is limited to a commission from an underwriter or dealer not in excess of the usual and customary distributors' or sellers' commission. As used in this paragraph the term "issuer" shall include, in addition to an issuer, any person directly or indirectly controlling or controlled by the issuer, or any person under direct or indirect common control with the issuer. 15 U.S.C.A. § 77b(11).
33. 15 U.S.C.A. § 77d(1).
34. 17 C.F.R. § 230.144 (1992).
35. 17 C.F.R. § 230.144A (1992).
36. "Qualified institutional buyer" is defined in Rule 144A(a) as:

    (i) Any of the following entities, acting for its own account or the accounts of other qualified institutional buyers, that in the aggregate owns and invests on a discretionary basis at least $100 million in securities of issuers that are not affiliated with the entity:

(A) Any *insurance company* as defined in section 2(13) of the Act;

(B) Any *investment company* registered under the Investment Company Act or any business development company as defined in section 2(a)(48) of that Act;

(C) Any *Small Business Investment Company* licensed by the U.S. Small Business Administration under section 301(c) or (d) of the Small Business Investment Act of 1958;

(D) Any *plan* established and maintained by a state, its political subdivisions or any agency or instrumentality of a state or its political subdivisions, for the benefit of its employees;

(E) Any *employee benefit plan* within the meaning of Title I of the Employee Retirement Income Security Act of 1974;

(F) Any *trust fund* whose trustee is a bank or trust company and whose participants are exclusively plans of the types identified in paragraph (a)(1)(i)(D) or (E) of this section, except trust funds that include as participants individual retirement accounts or H.R. 10 plans;

(G) Any *business development company* as defined in section 202(a)(22) of the Investment Advisers Act of 1940;

(H) Any organization described in section 501(c)(3) of the Internal Revenue Code, corporation (other than a bank as defined in section 3(a)(2) of the Act or a savings and loan association or other institution referenced in section 3(a)(5)(A) of the Act or a foreign bank or savings and loan association or equivalent institution), partnership, or Massachusetts or similar business trust; and

(I) Any *investment adviser* registered under the Investment Advisers Act.

(ii) Any *dealer* registered pursuant to section 15 of the Exchange Act, acting for its own account or the accounts of other qualified institutional buyers, that in the aggregate owns and invests on a discretionary basis at least $10 million of securities of issuers that are not affiliated with the dealer, *provided that* securities constituting the whole or a part of an unsold allotment to or subscription by a dealer as a participant in a public offering shall not be deemed to be owned by such dealer;

(iii) Any *dealer* registered pursuant to section 15 of the Exchange Act acting in a riskless principal transaction on behalf of a qualified institutional buyer;

(iv) Any investment company registered under the Investment Company Act, acting for its own account or for the accounts of other qualified institutional buyers, that is part of a family of investment companies which own in the aggregate at least $100 million in securities of issuers, other than issuers that are affiliated with the investment company or are part of such family of investment companies. Family of investment companies means any two or more investment companies registered under the Investment Company Act, except for a unit investment trust whose assets consist solely of shares of one or more registered investment companies, that have the same investment adviser (or, in the case of unit investment trusts, the same depositor), Provided That, for purposes of this section:

(A) Each series of a series company (as defined in Rule 18f-2 under the Investment Company Act) shall be deemed to be a separate investment company; and

> (B) Investment companies shall be deemed to have the same adviser (or depositor) if their advisers (or depositors) are majority-owned subsidiaries of the same parent, or if one investment company's adviser (or depositor) is a majority-owned subsidiary of the other investment company's adviser (or depositor);
>
> (v) Any entity, all of the equity owners of which are qualified institutional buyers, acting for its own account or the accounts of other qualified institutional buyers; and
>
> (vi) Any *bank* as defined in section 3(a)(2) of the Act, any savings and loan association or other institution as referenced in section 3(a)(5)(A) of the Act, or any foreign bank or savings and loan association or equivalent institution, acting for its own account or the accounts of other qualified institutional buyers, that in the aggregate owns and invests on a discretionary basis at least $100 million in securities of issuers that are not affiliated with it and that has an audited net worth of at least $25 million as demonstrated in its latest annual financial statements, as of a date not more than 16 months preceding the date of sale under the Rule in the case of a U.S. bank or savings and loan association, and not more than 18 months preceding such date of sale for a foreign bank or savings and loan association or equivalent institution.

17 C.F.R. § 230.144A (1992).

37. *See* E.F. Hutton & Company, Inc., SEC No-Action Letter, pub. avail. Sept. 27, 1985, for an example of the factors that must be considered in determining whether a guarantee provides sufficient coverage to provide an exemption for the underlying security under Section 3(a)(2) of the Securities Act. *See also* International Venture Finance, Ltd., SEC No-Action Letter, pub. avail. July 1, 1983. Because of federal income tax concerns regarding tax ownership and the "benefits and burdens" analysis discussed in Chapter 5, it may not be possible to structure a secondary market derivative so that the bank unconditionally guarantees all payments (effectively providing both default and liquidity protection) on the derivative security.

38. *See* Imperial Bank, SEC No-Action Letter, pub. avail. Dec. 15, 1982.

39. 57 Fed. Reg. 48,970 (Oct. 29, 1992).

40. Fed. Sec. Law Rep. (CCH) ¶ 7,152.

41. For examples of tax-exempt derivative securities registered on Form S-3, *see* ML Municipal Asset Backed Corporation (file No. 33-56252); Lehman Structured Assets Inc. (file No. 33-59368); and Dean Witter Asset Corporation (file No. 33-56598).

42. 17 C.F.R. § 230.415 (1992).

43. H.R. Rep. No. 2639, 76th Cong., 3d Sess. 10 (1940).

44. 15 U.S.C.A. § 80a-7(a).

45. 15 U.S.C.A. § 80a-8.

46. 15 U.S.C.A. § 80a-3(a)(1), (3).

47. Under Section 3(a)(2) of the Investment Company Act, the definition of investment company also includes "any issuer which is engaged or proposes to engage in the business of issuing face-amount certificates of the installment type, or has been engaged in such business and has any such certificate outstanding." 15 U.S.C.A. § 80a-3(a)(2). "Face-amount certificate" is defined in Section 2(a)(15) of the Investment Company Act as:

> any certificate, investment contract, or other security which represents an obligation on the part of its issuer to pay a stated or determinable sum or sums at a fixed or determinable date or dates more than twenty-four months after the date of issuance, in consideration of the payment of periodic installments of a stated

> or determinable amount (which security shall be known as a face-amount certificate of the "installment type"); or any security which represents a similar obligation on the part of a face-amount certificate company, the consideration for which is the payment of a single lump sum (which security shall be known as a "fully paid" face-amount certificate). 15 U.S.C.A. § 80a-2(a)(15).

Issuers of tax-exempt derivative securities generally do not fall within the definition contained in Section 3(a)(2).

48. 15 U.S.C.A. § 80a-17(a).

49. 15 U.S.C.A. § 80a-18.

50. For example, Section 17(a) of the Investment Company Act would prohibit the initial deposit of securities into most derivative securities structures and would also prohibit any substitution of assets by sponsors. Section 18 of the Investment Company Act would prohibit the capital structure of many tax-exempt derivative securities structures including, for example, most floaters/inverse floaters structures.

51. Rule 30b1-1 under the Investment Company Act requires registered management investment companies to file semiannual reports on Form N-SAR. 17 C.F.R. § 270.30b1-1. A similar requirement applies to registered unit investment trusts. *See* 17 C.F.R § 270.30a-1. Rule 30d-1 requires registered management investment companies to send semiannual reports to shareholders. 17 C.F.R. § 270.30d-1.

52. Merrill Lynch, *supra* note 14.

53. 15 U.S.C.A. § 80a-3(c)(1).

54. *See* Arthur E. Fox, SEC No-Action Letter, pub. avail. Dec. 12, 1974.

55. *See* Stars & Stripes GNMA Funding Corp., SEC No-Action Letter, pub. avail. Apr. 17, 1986.

56. *See* Continental Bank, SEC No-Action Letter, pub. avail. Sept. 2, 1982; San Jose Capital Corp., SEC No-Action Letter, pub. avail. Feb. 14, 1983.

57. *See* Meuse, Rinker, Chapman, Endres & Brooks, SEC No-Action Letter, pub. avail. May 1, 1989, which involved a trust that issued certificates with periodic tender rights. No-action relief was granted on the basis that the certificates were not voting securities, not on the basis that the certificates were short-term paper for purposes of Section 3(c)(1) of the Investment Company Act.

58. 15 U.S.C.A. § 80a-3(c)(1)(A).

59. *Id.*

60. *Id.*

61. 15 U.S.C.A. § 80a-2(a)(42).

62. *See* Horsley Keogh Venture Fund, SEC No-Action Letter, pub. avail. Apr. 27, 1988.

63. *See* Meuse, Rinker, Chapman, Endres & Brooks, *supra* note 57.

64. *See id.; see also* Clemente Global Growth Fund v. Pickens, 705 F. Supp. 958 (S.D.N.Y. 1989).

65. *See* Meuse, Rinker, Chapman, Endres & Brooks, *supra* note 57.

66. *Id.*

67. *See* Joseph H. Moss, SEC No-Action Letter, pub. avail. Feb. 27, 1984.

68. As a result of integration under the Securities Act, two or more offerings, each of which satisfies the requirements for an exemption, could be integrated into one offering that does not satisfy the requirements for any exemption. Similarly, as a result of integration under Section 3(c)(1) of the Investment Company Act, two or more issuers, each of which has fewer than 100 beneficial owners of its outstanding securities, could be integrated into one issuer that has more than 100 beneficial owners of its outstanding securities.

69. *See* Madison Park Investment Management, Inc., SEC No-Action Letter, pub. avail. Apr. 4, 1986. The response of the Division of Corporation Finance also noted that the securities in which each would invest had not been specified in advance of purchase, thereby creating an implication that a fixed, specified investment portfolio could be a factor in determining whether integration was required.

70. *See* Monument Capital Management, Inc., SEC No-Action Letter, pub. avail. July 12, 1990.

71. Prescott, Ball & Turben (PBT) Covered Option Fund, SEC No-Action Letter, pub. avail. Feb. 17, 1979.

72. *Id.*

73. Oppenheimer Arbitrage Partners, SEC No-Action Letter, pub. avail. Dec. 26, 1985.

74. It is unclear whether an issuer relying on Section 3(c)(1) of the Investment Company Act could be integrated with an issuer relying on a different exception or exemption from the Investment Company Act. In a no-action letter, Resolution Trust Corporation, the Investment Management Staff did not require integration of an issuer exempted under Section 2(b) of the Investment Company Act with issuers excepted under Section 3(c)(1) of the Investment Company Act. However, it is not clear whether this position could extend to issuers that are excepted or exempted by provisions other than Section 2(b) of the Investment Company Act. *See* Resolution Trust Corporation, SEC No-Action Letter, pub. avail. July 18, 1991.

75. 15 U.S.C.A. § 80a-3(c)(5).

76. 17 C.F.R. § 270.3a-7.

77. PROTECTING INVESTORS: A HALF CENTURY OF INVESTMENT COMPANY REGULATION, (SEC Division of Investment Management Report) (May 1992) [hereinafter INVESTMENT COMPANY ACT REPORT].

78. *See, e.g.,* B.C. Ziegler and Company, SEC No-Action Letter, pub. avail. Sept. 11, 1991; U.S. Municipal Lease Acceptance Corporation, SEC No-Action Letter, pub. avail. Apr. 11, 1983.

79. *See, e.g.,* Merrill Lynch, Pierce, Fenner & Smith Incorporated, SEC No-Action Letter, pub. avail. Nov. 4, 1981; Hereth, Orr & Jones, Inc., SEC No-Action Letter, pub. avail. Oct. 25, 1982; Marian Bass Securities, Inc., SEC No-Action Letter, pub. avail. July 9, 1984; Shearson Lehman/American Express, Inc., SEC No-Action Letter, pub. avail. Mar. 20, 1985; Salomon Brothers Inc., SEC No-Action Letter, pub. avail. June 17, 1985.

80. *Id.*

81. *Id.*

82. *See* Greenwich Capital Acceptance, Inc., SEC No-Action Letter, pub. avail. Aug. 8, 1991.

83. *See* INVESTMENT COMPANY ACT REPORT, *supra* note 77, at xxi–xxii.

84. *See* INVESTMENT COMPANY ACT REPORT, *supra* note 77, at 1–101.

85. *See* INVESTMENT COMPANY ACT REPORT, *supra* note 77, at xxiii.

86. 17 C.F.R. § 270.3a-7.

87. 15 U.S.C.A. § 80a-2(a)(32).

88. *See* La Quinta Motor Inns, Inc., SEC No-Action Letter, pub. avail. Jan. 4, 1989; McDonald & Company Securities, SEC No-Action Letter, pub. avail. Dec. 14, 1983.

89. *See* Shearson Lehman/American Express Inc., SEC No-Action Letter, pub. avail. Mar. 20, 1985, in which the Investment Management Staff granted no-action relief under Section 3(c)(5) of the Investment Company Act in the context of liquidity puts requiring seven days' notice. However, the Investment Management Staff simultaneously issued another letter cautioning that its response as it pertained to the issue of whether the securities in question were "redeemable securities" should not be relied upon by third parties as a staff interpretive or enforcement position.

90. 57 Fed. Reg. 23,980 (June 5, 1992).
91. 57 Fed. Reg. 56,248 (Nov. 27, 1992).
92. *Id. See* n.24 of the Adopting Release.
93. *See* Proposing Release, *supra* note 90.
94. 17 C.F.R. § 270.3a-7(b)(1).
95. 57 Fed. Reg. 56,248; *see* text accompanying n.21 of the Adopting Release.
96. *Id.*
97. 17 C.F.R. § 270.3a-7(b)(2).
98. 15 U.S.C.A. § 77c(a)(3).
99. H.R. 4938, S. 2518, 102d Cong., 2d Sess. (1992).
100. S. 2209-02, 103d Cong. 1st Sess. (1993).
101. *See* INVESTMENT COMPANY ACT REPORT, *supra* note 77 at 100.
102. 15 U.S.C.A. § 77aaa to 77bbbb (1991, Supp. 1993).
103. 15 U.S.C.A. § 77eee.
104. 15 U.S.C.A. § 77ddd(a)(2).
105. 15 U.S.C.A. § 77ddd(a)(4).
106. 15 U.S.C.A. § 77ddd(a)(7).
107. 15 U.S.C.A. § 77ddd(b)(1).
108. *See, e.g.,* The Illinois Securities Law of 1953, Section 5, Blue Sky L. Rep. (CCH) ¶ 22,124.
109. *See, e.g.,* The Missouri Uniform Securities Act, Section 409.402(a), Blue Sky L. Rep. (CCH) ¶ 35,114.
110. *See, e.g.,* The California Corporate Securities Law of 1968, Section 25102(i), Blue Sky L. Rep. (CCH) ¶ 11,133. *But see* The California Corporate Securities Law of 1968, Section 25403, Blue Sky L. Rep. (CCH) ¶ 11,274, which may affect the offer or sale in California of a tax-exempt derivative security that includes a municipal obligation of a California issuer absent the prior written consent of that issuer.
111. *See, e.g.,* The Texas Securities Act of 1957, Section 109.13, Blue Sky L. Rep. (CCH) ¶ 55,563.
112. *See, e.g.,* The Iowa Uniform Securities Act, Section 502.202(1), Blue Sky L. Rep. (CCH) ¶ 25,112.
113. 17 C.F.R. § 270.2a-7.
114. While the term "voting stock" is not defined in the Investment Company Act, it is generally interpreted consistently with the term "voting security." *See* Meuse, Rinker, Chapman, Endres & Brooks, *supra* note 57.
115. 15 U.S.C.A. § 80a-12(d)(1)(A).
116. 15 U.S.C.A. § 80a-3(c)(1)(A). *See supra* text accompanying note 59.
117. 15 U.S.C.A. § 80a-8(b).
118. Fed. Sec. Law Rep. (CCH) ¶ 51,208.
119. Fed. Sec. Law Rep. (CCH) ¶ 51,223.
120. An open-end investment company is any investment company that is not a face-amount certificate company or a unit investment trust and that is offering for sale or has outstanding any redeemable security of which it is the issuer. Open-end investment companies are typically referred to as mutual funds. 15 U.S.C.A. § 80a-5(a)(1).
121. A closed-end investment company is any investment company that is not a face-amount certificate company, unit investment trust, or open-end investment company. 15 U.S.C.A. § 80a-5(a)(2).
122. *See, e.g.,* the Supplement dated Feb. 2, 1993, to the Prospectus dated Nov. 16, 1992, of Dreyfus Municipal Bond Fund, Inc., which provides, in part:

> The Fund may purchase custodial receipts representing the right to receive certain future principal and interest payments on Municipal Obligations which un-

derlie the custodial receipts. A number of different arrangements are possible. In a typical custodial receipt arrangement, an issuer or a third party owner of Municipal Obligations deposits such obligations with a custodian in exchange for two classes of custodial receipts. The two classes have different characteristics, but, in each case, payments on the two classes are based on payments received on the underlying Municipal Obligations. One class has the characteristics of a typical auction mechanism. This class's interest rate generally is expected to be below the coupon rate of the underlying Municipal Obligations and generally is at a level comparable to that of a Municipal Obligation of similar quality and having a maturity equal to the period between interest rate adjustments. The second class bears interest at a rate that exceeds the interest rate typically borne by a security of comparable quality and maturity; this rate also is adjusted, but in this case inversely to changes in the rate of interest of the first class. If the interest rate on the first class exceeds the coupon rate of the underlying Municipal Obligations, its interest rate will exceed the rate paid on the second class. In no event will the aggregate interest paid with respect to the two classes exceed the interest paid by the underlying Municipal Obligations. The value of the second class and similar securities should be expected to fluctuate more than the value of a Municipal Obligation of comparable quality and maturity and their purchase by the Fund should increase the volatility of its net asset value and, thus, its price per share.

123. 17 C.F.R. § 270.2a-7.
124. 17 C.F.R. § 270.2a-7(c)(2).
125. 17 C.F.R. § 270.2a-7(d).
126. 17 C.F.R. § 270.2a-7(d)(3).
127. 17 C.F.R. § 270.2a-7(a)(21).
128. 17 C.F.R. § 270.2a-7(a)(4).
129. 17 C.F.R. § 270.2a-7(c)(3).
130. 17 C.F.R. § 270.2a-7(a)(5).
131. 17 C.F.R. § 270.2a-7(c)(3)(i).
132. 17 C.F.R. § 270.2a-7(c)(3)(ii).
133. 17 C.F.R. § 270.2a-7(c)(4)(ii).
134. 17 C.F.R. § 270.2a-7(a)(12).

135. *See* Letter dated Dec. 6, 1991, from Marianne K. Smythe, Director of the Division of Investment Management, to Matthew P. Fink, President of the Investment Company Institute.

136. *See* Letter dated June 5, 1986, from Kathryn B. McGrath, Director of the Division of Investment Management, to Paul B. O'Kelly, Assistant Regional Administrator of the Securities and Exchange Commission; *see also* Goldman, Sachs & Co., SEC No-Action Letter, pub. avail. Sept. 7, 1988.

137. *See* Nuveen Advisory Corp., SEC No-Action Letter, pub. avail. Sept. 4, 1990.

138. *See* Guide 4 to Form N-1A, 4 at 17 C.F.R. § 274.11A.

139. *See* Letter dated Dec. 9, 1992, from Marianne K. Smythe, Director of the Division of Investment Management, to Matthew P. Fink, President of the Investment Company Institute.

140. *See* Guide 4 to Form N-1A, *supra* note 138.

141. *See* Securities Act Release No. 6862, Fed. Sec. L. Rep. (CCH) ¶ 84,523 (Apr. 23, 1990).

142. *See id.;* the Commission did not require any particular factors to be considered by the board of directors in making this determination. The Commission also stated that

the following factors, although not necessarily determinative, would be reasonable for a board of directors to consider with respect to a Rule 144A eligible security: (1) the frequency of trades and quotes for the security; (2) the number of dealers willing to purchase or sell the security and the number of other potential purchasers; (3) dealer undertakings to make a market in the security; and (4) the nature of the security and the nature of the marketplace (e.g., the time needed to dispose of the security, the method of soliciting offers, and the mechanics of transfer).

CHAPTER 7

Municipal Law Considerations for Municipal Interest Rate Swaps: A Growing Trend in the Municipal Marketplace

Daniel L. Johnson
William M. Libit
Elizabeth D. Swanson

Several years ago, interest rate swaps were virtually nonexistent in the municipal[1] marketplace; today they represent a $15-billion-per-year industry,[2] and their popularity is growing. An increasing number of issuers of municipal obligations are discovering that financial devices such as interest rate swaps give them an opportunity to enhance their investor base, offset exposure to floating-rate debt, pay lower interest rates, and ultimately generate meaningful cost savings.[3] As the swap industry increases its focus on municipalities, however, municipalities and swap providers need to understand the unique issues that municipalities bring to such transactions. Currently one of the major concerns confronting swap market participants is whether swap transactions involving certain municipalities could be held to be unenforceable against such municipalities on the basis that those municipalities are not empowered to enter into such transactions.

Characteristics of Municipal Interest Rate Swaps; General Issues

The interest rate swap structure most commonly employed by municipalities is the exchange of floating-rate debt for fixed-rate debt.[4] Typically, a municipality will agree to make payments determined by reference to a fixed interest rate on a stated principal amount, referred to as the "notional" amount,[5] while the swap provider will agree to make payments determined by reference to a floating interest rate on that notional amount. Because of the high demand for fixed-rate payors in the swap market, municipalities ordinarily pay at a rate below the prevailing interest rate on comparable fixed-rate bonds.[6] It is estimated that such a structure can save a municipality approximately 10 to 20 basis points on its cost of funds, compared to a conventional municipal fixed-rate structure.[7] This, however, is not the only structure used by municipalities. In recent years, as interest rates have fallen, some municipalities have chosen to exchange fixed rates for variable rates.[8] With the widespread belief that interest rates may have bottomed out, however, most municipalities are now attempting to lock themselves into low rates to avoid the risk of market volatility.[9] Municipalities have also entered into interest rate caps and floors, forward swaps, and swaptions, and some have considered entering into currency swaps. These transactions are generally described in Chapter 2.

Detachable call options are very different from the financial products described above, but the attraction to municipalities is the same—protection from rising borrowing costs. A call is a municipality's option to buy back its bonds in the future at a set price.[10] It enables a municipality to purchase its high interest rate bonds from bondholders should interest rates decline.[11] In the case of a detachable call, a municipality would sell this option to someone else, leaving the municipality without the right to call its bonds.[12] Deals can be structured so that detachable calls can be sold at the time the bonds are issued or at some point in the future.[13] If the detachable calls are sold at the time the bonds are issued, the proceeds of the sale may enable a municipality to reduce the size of its borrowing.[14] It is thought that detachable calls sold sometime after the issuance of the bonds can offer municipalities the same sort of savings they may now be able to achieve with what is referred to as an "advance refunding."[15]

Because interest rate swaps are the primary product seen thus far in the municipal marketplace and because they are likely to have the widest application in the future, this chapter will focus on the interest rate swap. However, it should be noted that most of the issues applying to interest rate swap transactions apply to caps, floors, collars, and similar products referenced above as well. In addition, these other products may raise issues not raised by interest rate swaps.[16]

Differences Between Municipal Swaps and Corporate Swaps

Interest rate swap transactions involving municipalities differ from typical corporate swaps in several ways. One of these ways is the index chosen to determine the variable interest rate. The index most commonly used in corporate swaps is LIBOR. However, use of LIBOR exposes municipalities to "basis risk," as discussed below, since the interest rate on most, if not all, variable-rate municipal debt obligations is based on indices other than LIBOR. As a result, most municipal swaps are tied to indices such as Kenny's thirty-day High Grade Note Index[17] and the new Public Securities Association Swap Index,[18] although LIBOR is used in some cases.

Another difference between the corporate market and the municipal market is that corporate swaps have historically had relatively short terms—five to seven years. This is changing, and swaps with terms of ten to twenty years have become more common. This change is important to the growth of the municipal swap market since the term of most bond deals exceeds ten years[19] and municipalities are generally concerned with "tail risk" (i.e., interest-rate risk on the municipality's obligations on the bond after the swap expires).[20]

The Municipal Swap Market Is at an Earlier Stage

The municipal swap market is not yet as sophisticated as the corporate swap market, which has reached a level of maturity that allows for competitive bidding of corporate swap transactions.[21] Reaching that level could take the municipal market many years. At this point in the development of the municipal market, transactions still require the sort of care and attention only possible in a negotiated deal.[22] Part of the reason for this may be the lack of financial sophistication of officials of some smaller municipalities; it is believed that such municipalities are not ready to simply go out into the marketplace and solicit bids.[23]

Counterparty Credit Concerns

Another concern facing municipalities is their ability to accurately judge the creditworthiness of a swap provider in a potential swap transaction. This is particularly important in instances where the municipality is considering entering into a ten- to twenty-year relationship with the swap provider. As new swap dealers enter the municipal swap market, municipalities will have to find a way to measure the creditworthiness of such swap dealers and make this determination a part of their decision process. Some states have attempted to deal with this issue statutorily.[24] Swap insurance may help alleviate some of the concern regarding swap provider creditworthiness. The market for such insurance is not yet well developed, however, so it is difficult to predict how easily obtainable and how costly such insurance would be for a particular transaction.

Municipal Law Concerns

The use of interest rate swaps by municipalities presents a number of unique municipal law concerns as well. These include whether a particular municipality is authorized by state law to enter into a swap transaction and whether statutory and constitutional debt limitations apply to a municipality's indebtedness under a swap transaction. In addition, issues involving statutory interest rate limitations, the source of payments made by municipalities in connection with swap agreements, public bidding requirements, and state gambling laws should also be of concern to municipalities and swap providers.

Authority

A key impediment to the development of the municipal swap market has been concerns regarding the authority of municipalities to enter into swap transactions. In the late 1980s, several English municipalities challenged the validity of interest rate swaps that they had entered into with banks after interest rates took a turn for the worse and the swaps became money-losing propositions for them. The swap industry carefully followed the litigation because of its chilling effect on the willingness of market participants to enter into swap transactions with municipalities.

On January 24, 1991, the English House of Lords issued its decision in *Hazell v. Hammersmith and Fulham London Borough Council and others.*[25] The government auditor, appealing the decision of a lower court, challenged the legality of the borough council's swaps on the ground that they amounted to speculative trading for profit.[26] He asserted that since the council did not have the authority to enter into swap transactions, the swaps it had entered into were unenforceable against it.[27] The auditor's claims, if accepted by the court, would have resulted in significant losses for the banks that had provided the swaps.

The banks conceded that local authorities such as the council lacked express authority to enter into swaps but argued that such local authorities had sufficient implied power to enter into certain nonspeculative swap transactions.[28] They asserted that local authorities had an implied power, based on their express borrowing powers or, in the alternative, their alleged power of debt management, to enter into "replacement" swaps and "reprofiling" swaps.[29] In addition, the banks argued that after a certain date the council was entitled to enter into swap transactions in order to mitigate the effects of previous unlawful swaps.[30]

The court first looked at the basic powers of a local authority, explaining, "[a] local authority, although democratically elected and representative of the area, is not a sovereign body and can only do such things as are expressly or impliedly authorized by Parliament."[31] The court examined the swap transactions entered into by the council and found them to be speculative in nature.[32] Describing the difference between speculative swaps and nonspeculative swaps, the court stated:

> The transactions in the swap market which are now impugned were not carried out in order to enable the council to borrow or to enable the council to choose to borrow at a fixed rate rather than at a variable rate or vice versa. The transactions were undertaken in the hope that the burden of interest payable in respect of borrowings by the council would be mitigated by profits from swap contracts whereby the council successfully forecast movements in interest rates.[33]

It concluded that the swaps characterized by the banks as replacement swaps and reprofiling swaps were just as speculative as the other swaps entered into by the council.[34]

The court then examined the express borrowing powers of local authorities and the powers it found to be implied thereby and incidental thereto.[35] It stated:

> [A] local authority can do anything which is calculated to facilitate or is conducive or incidental to the local authority's function of borrowing. . . . Swap transactions could be said to "facilitate" borrowing if the prospect of being able to reduce the burden of interest by swaps encouraged the local authority to enter into a borrowing which it would otherwise decide against. But this approach is impermissible. A local

> authority when considering expenditure must carefully consider the amount required to be borrowed and the resources available for payment of interest and capital. A local authority which borrowed in reliance on future successful swap operations would be failing in its duty to act prudently in the interests of the ratepayers. Similarly, swap operations cannot be said to be "conducive to" borrowing because local authorities should not be encouraged to borrow by the prospect of swap transactions. It was submitted that swap transactions are "incidental to" borrowing. The . . . difficulty is that a swap transaction is a separate collateral contract which may be undertaken long after a borrowing has been effected.[36]

The court further observed that a "power is not incidental merely because it is convenient or desirable or profitable"[37] and pointed out that local authorities do not necessarily have the same powers regarding borrowing and speculation as private corporations have but rather are limited to the powers given them by the statutes that govern them.[38]

The court then went on to find that debt management is not a power of a local authority but rather "a phrase which describes prudent and lawful activities on the part of the local authority."[39] It stated that if swap transactions were lawful, local authorities would be under a duty to consider entering into them as part of their duty of debt management, but "if a swap transaction is not lawful then it cannot be lawful for a local authority to carry out a swap transaction under the guise of debt management."[40] The court also dismissed the banks' argument that the council had the power to enter into swaps to mitigate the effects of previous unlawful swaps, stating that it had already concluded that a local authority had no power to enter into swaps, so it followed that other swap transactions, even those entered into for mitigation purposes, were unlawful as well.[41]

In the end, the court held that the swaps entered into by the council were invalid because the council did not have the authority—express, implied, or incidental to an express power—to enter into them.[42] It is important to note that while it found the swaps involved in *Hammersmith* to be speculative, the court did not limit its holding to speculative swaps. Although the case involved English municipalities and was decided under English law, there is concern that it could influence a state court reviewing a like matter in the United States, due to the similarities in the scope of powers of American and English municipalities.

Thus, in the United States it is also necessary for municipalities and swap providers to determine whether the municipalities have the requisite authority under applicable state law to enter into swap transactions. The authority of municipalities to engage in financial transactions (including entering into agreements such as interest rate swaps) is not as broad as the authority of private corporations or individuals. A principle developed in the nineteenth century known as Dillon's rule holds that powers of a municipality should be narrowly construed:

> A municipal corporation possesses and can exercise the following powers and no others: (1) Those granted in express words; (2) Those necessarily or fairly implied in or incident to the powers expressly granted; and (3) Those essential to the declared objects and purposes of the corporation—not simply convenient, but indispensable.[43]

Under Dillon's rule, doubts concerning the authority of a municipality to exercise a particular power are resolved against the grant of power. For the most part, this rule is currently applied in a more reasonable fashion.[44] In addition, home rule powers are generally considered an exception to Dillon's rule.[45] Home rule municipalities may need only to ascertain whether any constitutional or statutory limitations have been placed on their power to enter into swap transactions.[46] However, the rule retains its vitality in a number of states (although it is important to note that the rule is not followed in all states)[47] and for non-home rule municipalities within some states,[48] and thus illustrates the importance of determining whether a particular municipality has the authority under applicable state law to enter into a swap. The court in *Hammersmith* effectively applied Dillon's rule when it concluded that a local authority had only the powers granted to it by Parliament.[49] Dillon's rule and other limitations on municipal authority provide a court with a basis for invalidating a municipality's participation in an interest rate swap in much the same way as the House of Lords did in *Hammersmith.* Even in states in which municipalities are not strictly bound by Dillon's rule, it is not necessarily clear that municipalities have the authority to enter into swap transactions.[50]

Authority to enter into swap transactions may be found in a state's constitution, in municipalities' charters, in statutory provisions, or in case law interpreting such laws.[51] Some states, such as Illinois and California, have enacted legislation that expressly permits municipalities to enter into swaps. In addition, home rule units of local government in many states have authority under their state constitutions to enter into interest rate swap transactions.[52] The scope of the statutory schemes of states that have expressly authorized municipal swap transactions varies widely. In Illinois, for example, non-home rule municipalities with an aggregate principal amount of outstanding bonds equaling $10 million or more, the state, and certain state agencies have the express authority to enter into swap transactions.[53] California's swap provisions are even broader than Illinois' statutory grants. In California, the state and any political subdivision thereof may enter into all types of interest rate swaps and currency swaps.[54] Some statutes require that the swap be directly tied to a particular issue of debt.[55] Others mandate that the swap transaction be entered into at the same time the debt is being issued, thus requiring a municipality to structure its swap transaction at the same time it is structuring its financing.[56] Swap statutes may also specify what may be pledged by the municipality as security for the swap.[57]

Not all municipalities have express authority to enter into swaps. A municipality's authority to enter into swap transactions could be derived from its general power to enter into contracts.[58] Most municipalities have the authority to execute contracts and are permitted to do so in furtherance of their other powers and duties.[59] Thus, where a municipality has the power to borrow and invest, it may be argued that it has sufficient authority to enter into swap transactions in furtherance of those powers.[60] Municipalities relying on such an argument need to proceed with caution, however, because to date the argument has not been validated by any court. Moreover, the consequences to a municipality and/or swap provider of discovering that a municipality that has entered into a swap agreement lacked requisite authority to do so can be very great, as demonstrated in *Hammersmith.*

In some states, municipalities simply do not have the authority to enter into swap transactions.[61] In others, it is unclear whether or not authority exists. This uncertainty will make it very difficult for such municipalities to enter the swap market.

In the fall of 1991, ISDA, then called the International Swap Dealers Association, released proposed model legislation for adoption by state legislatures that would grant virtually all municipalities within a state adopting such legislation the power to enter into interest rate swaps and related types of notional principal contracts. The model legislation appears in Appendix 7A at the end of this chapter. Section (B)(i) of the model legislation provides that all municipalities may enter into, modify, amend, and terminate swap agreements.[62] Section (B)(ii) limits the power of municipalities to enter into swaps and similar contracts by providing that such contracts may only be entered into to manage interest rate or similar risks.[63] Section (E) provides that a swap participant may rely on representations by the municipality that it has the authority to enter into a swap transaction.[64] Adoption of legislation such as the ISDA model, which clarifies the authority of municipalities to enter into swap transactions, should have the effect of increasing the number of potential swap providers desiring to enter into swaps with municipalities and, as a consequence thereof, increasing competition and producing lower-cost swap transactions for municipalities. Moreover, to the extent uncertainty regarding municipal authority is currently factored into pricing decisions, reducing such uncertainty may also reduce costs to municipalities.

Even where a municipality has the constitutional or statutory authority to enter into swap transactions, it must follow proper state law procedures in adopting the ordinance or resolution authorizing a particular swap transaction. Interest rate swaps are typically entered into under a master agreement that authorizes multiple swaps, all subject to the terms of the master agreement. The governing body of the municipality often authorizes the execution and delivery of the master agreement and names one or more corporate officers to actually enter into individual swaps. In order to avoid improper delegation of authority of the governing body, however, certain criteria or parameters should be enumerated in the authorizing ordinance or resolution. These include the maximum monetary size of any swap, the maximum term of years of any swap, and, if required by statute, the maximum interest rate. If the swap is required by applicable law to be tied to a specified series of bonds, the authorized officer should also be delegated the power to identify the particular municipal bonds to which each swap is tied. Notwithstanding the foregoing, there is a concern that a delegation of power authorizing swaps using the criteria described above would still be considered by a court to be too broad. For example, assume that a municipality authorized a swap with a term of ten years. Although it is clear that a swap with a ten-year term could be executed by the authorized officer promptly after authorization by the governing body, there is some question whether, nine years later, the authorized officer could execute a one-year swap.

Both the municipality and the swap provider may desire maximum flexibility to enter into additional swaps or other transactions contemplated by the master agreement or to take advantage of new opportunities that may arise in the future in the swap market. This desire for flexibility must be balanced with concerns regarding improper delegation of power. Consequently, municipalities and swap providers should consult with counsel regarding the ability of the municipality to enter into other transactions under the master swap agreement after the initial swap. Municipalities should also ensure that other procedural requirements, such as publication requirements and the provision of open meetings statutes, are met in adopting any ordinance or resolution authorizing swap transactions.

Debt Limitations

Another legal issue presented by municipal interest rate swaps is whether a swap will be treated as debt for purposes of statutory or state constitutional debt limitations. Such statutory and constitutional restraints on the issuance of debt by municipalities typically apply to general obligation debt and are typically understood to exclude debt, such as revenue bonds, that is not backed by the full faith and credit of the municipality and by the power to levy an unlimited ad valorem tax to pay such debt. However, the issue of whether swaps will be considered debt under state law is generally not clear from the statutory language.[65]

Under an interest rate swap transaction, a municipality would be subject to certain potential monetary obligations to the swap counterparty over a term of years. This appears to be the case even though the actual amount of the municipality's monetary obligations on the swap would be dependent on the effect of market interest rate movements on the amounts payable on the swap. Such an obligation may be subject to the same debt limitations as any other long-term contractual obligation. In some states, this result can be avoided if the swap transaction is payable solely from special funds or current general governmental revenues.[66] The latter result may be difficult to achieve, since most swap agreements have terms of several years. However, some courts have recognized the "conditional obligation doctrine," which states that if payments made under long-term contracts are conditioned upon the receipt of a service in the year payment is due, the municipality's obligation will be treated as incurred in each year of the contract when the service is actually performed.[67] If swap contracts are treated as debt, not only must municipalities include such contracts in their debt limit calculations when they desire to enter into a swap transaction or to issue subsequent debt, but in some cases voter approval may be necessary before a municipality would be permitted to enter into a swap transaction.

Some states have by statute determined whether indebtedness under swap transactions is considered debt for the purposes of debt limitations.[68] To date, this issue has not been examined by any courts, leaving participants in certain municipal swap transactions with no guidance on how indebtedness under a swap transaction will be treated.

Other Issues

In addition to issues involving municipal authority and debt limitations, other issues that may affect a municipality's ability or desire to enter into a swap transaction include statutory interest rate limitations, the source of payments made by municipalities in connection with swap transactions, public bidding requirements, and gambling laws.

Statutory Interest Rate Limits

One significant issue that municipalities must consider relates to statutory interest rate limitations. Most states impose restrictions on the rates of interest permitted on municipal debt. If such restrictions are found to apply to indebtedness under swaps, caps on the payments made under swap transactions may be necessary. In Illinois, for example, payments under a swap are treated as interest on the underlying bonds,[69] and thus the payments must not cause such interest to exceed the applicable statutory interest rate limit. This would suggest the utilization of low interest rate bonds in order to maximize the permitted amount of swap payments.

Prior to entering into a swap transaction, municipalities and swap providers should also consider the source of whatever payments the municipality may be required to make under the swap. For example, the fact that a municipality may enter into a swap agreement with respect to an issue of its general obligation (full faith and credit) bonds or its revenue bonds does not mean that the municipality's obligations under the swap agreement are payable from the same source as the swapped bonds, i.e., property tax revenues or pledged fund revenues. Typically, payments made by a municipality are payable only out of funds lawfully available and annually appropriated. A municipality may be able to appropriate only as much as it can demonstrate that it will need for the succeeding period. However, the request for such appropriation may have to be made considerably before the time that the amount of the payments on the municipality's swap transaction will have been calculated. A municipality may be put in the situation of being obligated to pay the swap provider under a swap agreement without having funds lawfully available for such purpose. Swap providers may request a pledge of the full faith and credit taxing powers of the municipality; however, some municipalities are required by statute to put the question to referendum before they can agree to such a pledge and some simply do not have statutory authorization to grant their full faith and credit taxing powers for such a purpose.

Public Bidding Requirements

Public bidding requirements may present an issue for municipalities that are required by law to conduct a public bidding process before awarding contracts in connection with the issuance of debt or the acquisition of supplies and services. It is possible that some of these statutes could be interpreted to require a municipality to elicit bids from the public before it can enter into a swap.[70]

Additional Concerns

Some concern has also been expressed that the speculative nature of an interest rate swap transaction could give rise to grounds for invalidating a swap contract or even imposing criminal liability under some states' gambling laws. Parties to a swap may be found to be speculating, rather than practicing, proper risk management, or making illegal wagers on the fluctuations in the floating interest rate.[71] Some state statutes, such as New York's, proscribe courts from enforcing gambling contracts.[72] It has been argued that if parties can demonstrate they have an investment or some stake in the outcome of the swap, it is less likely that participation in the swap transaction will be called a wager.[73] It may be argued that where the notional amount reflects actual obligations, parties have a "stake" in the swap.[74] In addition, a municipality entering into swap transactions is well advised to document its risk management motivations in the swap contract and in its authorizing ordinance or resolution.

Conclusion

Interest rate swaps can provide municipalities with many valuable benefits, the most significant of these being a means to manage their financial risks against fluctuations in interest rates. As the municipal swap industry grows and becomes more sophisticated, more municipalities will be encouraged to make swap transactions a part of their debt and investment management strategies. Understanding and contending with the municipal law issues involved in such transactions is crucial for such municipalities and potential swap providers. In addition, the resolution of these issues will help the municipal swap industry become as lucrative for its participants as the corporate swap industry currently is for its participants.

For states that have not already done so, enactment of legislation giving municipalities express authority to enter into swap transactions and determining whether indebtedness under swaps constitutes debt for the purposes of debt limitations will clear up many of the current concerns regarding municipal swaps. The municipal swap industry will develop fully when no ambiguities concerning these issues remain. ISDA's model statute is a good place for state legislatures to start their consideration.

Today, most municipal interest rate swaps involve municipalities large enough to be able to reconcile the risks involved and absorb any increased payments above debt service on their bonds that might result from their swap transactions. Most smaller municipalities lack the requisite sophistication to contend with such risks. In addition, smaller municipalities are more likely to need to know what their payment obligations are going to be at any given time and will have more difficulty absorbing big increases in their payment obligations. As the municipal swap market continues to develop, the industry will have to find a way to resolve the concerns of all municipalities—large and small—wishing to take advantage of the many potential benefits of swap transactions.

Notes

1. This chapter will use terms such as "municipal" and "municipality" to refer not only to municipal corporations but to the states and all political subdivisions thereof and all departments, agencies, boards, commissions, or authorities of a state or political subdivision thereof.

2. *Municipal Swap Transactions Backed by Private Placements,* PRIVATE PLACEMENT REP., Nov. 9, 1992, at 6.

3. *Id.*

4. *Swaps Popularity Increasing in the Municipal Market,* GLOBAL GUARANTY, Sept. 14, 1992, at 7.

5. The notional amount is used merely as a means of measuring each party's payment obligation under a swap agreement and may or may not have a relation to actual indebtedness of one of the swap participants.

6. Robert K. Sharp. *Financial Products in the Municipal Market,* TAX-EXEMPT FINANCING, 1992, 325 PLI/Tax 313, 317 (Feb. 1992).

7. *Swaps Popularity Increasing in the Municipal Market, supra* note 4, at 7.

8. William Tucker, *Don't Like Your Interest Rate? How About a Swap?,* PUB. FIN./WASH. WATCH, Oct. 26, 1992, at 4.

9. *Id.*

10. Jonathan Fuerbringer, *Municipal Bond Issuers Are Learning to "Detach,"* N.Y. TIMES, Dec. 21, 1992, at 7, col. 1.

11. *Id.*

12. *Id.*

13. *Id.*

14. Dennis Walters, *Detachable Call Options Provide Issuers with a New Twist on Bond Refinancing,* THE BOND BUYER, Dec. 14, 1992, at 2A.

15. Jonathan Fuerbringer, *supra* note 10, at 7. In an advance refunding, to effect borrowing cost savings, a municipality issues bonds at a lower interest rate in order to raise money to pay off existing higher interest rate bonds. The existing bonds are paid off by setting up an escrow and buying government securities, which are used to redeem the bonds when they become callable. *Id.* With detachable calls, rather than

locking in lower rates, a municipality would instead extract savings by selling the detachable calls to interested investors. Dennis Walters, *supra* note 14, at 2A. An additional benefit of detachable calls is that municipalities that are prohibited from doing advance refundings would not be prohibited from selling detachable calls. Jonathan Fuerbringer, *supra* note 10, at 7.

16. Note, however, that municipalities may not find some of these products as useful as others. For example, municipalities generally do not have foreign currency exposure, so they may have no use for currency swaps.

17. J.J. Kenny Co.'s 30-day High-Grade Note Index has been the most widely used index in the municipal swap market. Lynn Stevens Hume & Steven Dickson, *Details Emerging on PSA's Index for Swap Contracts; Debut Set for April,* THE BOND BUYER, Mar. 5, 1992, at 1, 4. It is an index of short-term tax-exempt municipal securities prepared by Kenny Information Systems.

18. The Public Securities Association made its swap index available in 1992. It is a seven-day variable-rate index and was specifically designed for the municipal swap market. *Id.*

19. Steven Dickson, *Municipals Under Construction: Derivatives Make Their Mark,* THE BOND BUYER, Oct. 22, 1991, at 1A, 7A.

20. For example, upon expiration of the swap prior to the maturity of the related bonds, the cost of a new swap may be much more expensive for the municipality than the cost of the original deal, and the market at the time the swap expires is such that the municipality could have problems meeting debt service requirements without a swap in place. Steven Dickson, *supra* note 19, at 7A.

21. Ted Hampton, *Can the Municipal Market Handle Bidding for Swaps? Some Have Their Doubts,* THE BOND BUYER, Oct. 22, 1991, at 4A.

22. *Id.*

23. *Id.* at A6.

24. For example, in New Mexico, municipalities are permitted to enter into swap agreements only if the long-term obligations of the swap provider are highly rated or the obligations of the swap provider are either guaranteed or collateralized. N.M. STAT. ANN. § 6-18-8.1 (Michie Supp. 1992).

25. [1991] 1 All E.R. 545 (H.L. 1991).

26. *Id.* at 545.

27. *Id.* at 549.

28. *Id.* at 553. The banks were in effect conceding that many of the swaps entered into by the council were speculative in nature.

29. *Id.* at 553–54. The court explained that under a "replacement" swap, the notional amount does not exceed the principal sum borrowed. *Id.* at 552. In addition, the effect of the contract and any subsequent swap transaction entered into for the same purpose is said to convert indirectly a fixed interest obligation into a variable interest obligation or vice versa. *Id.* Under a "reprofiling" swap, a party is said to be simply increasing the proportion that its variable interest rate obligations bear to its fixed interest rate obligations. *Id.* at 553.

30. *Id.* at 553.

31. *Id.* at 548.

32. *Id.* at 550.

33. *Id.*

34. *Id.* at 552–53.

35. *Id.* at 548, 554.

36. *Id.* at 554.

37. *Id.* at 556.
38. *Id.*
39. *Id.* at 558.
40. *Id.*
41. *Id.* at 561.
42. *Id.* at 561, 566.
43. 1 J. DILLON, LAW OF MUNICIPAL CORPORATIONS 448–49 (5th ed. 1911).
44. *See* 2 EUGENE MCQUILLAN, MUNICIPAL CORPORATIONS § 10.18a (3d ed. rev. 1988).
45. *Id.* at § 10.25.
46. Thomas A. McGavin, Jr., *Interest Rate Swaps in the Municipal Market,* 10 MUN. FIN. J. 217, 223 (1989).
47. *See, e.g.,* Livingston Parish Police Jury v. Lee, 598 So. 2d 1086 (La. Ct. App. 1991); Ticonderoga Farms, Inc. v. County of Loudoun, 409 S.E.2d 446 (1991); *In re* Ball Mountain Dam Hydroelectric Project, 576 A.2d 124 (1990).
48. *See, e.g.,* Patrick Media Group, Inc. v. Ad-Ex, Inc., 608 N.E.2d 427 (Il. App. Ct. 1992); City and County of Denver v. State, 788 P.2d 764 (Colo. 1990); Osborne v. State, 439 N.E.2d 677 (Ind. Ct. App. 1982).
49. *See* 1 All E.R. 545 at 548.
50. A court could reasonably determine that absent an express grant, a municipality's general power to contract may not be sufficient authority since the court may view the situation as one in which the municipality is incurring debt without specific authority such as that found in bond statutes. *But see* McGavin, *supra* note 46, at 221.
51. McGavin, *supra* note 46, at 220–21.
52. *See, e.g.,* ILL. CONST. art. VII, § 6.
53. 30 ILL. COMP. STAT. 305/7 (Smith-Hurd Supp. 1993); 30 ILL. COMP. STAT. 425/6 (1992) (State of Illinois); 30 ILL. COMP. STAT. 360/2-8 (1992) (Rural Bond Bank); 20 ILL. COMP. STAT. 3505/7.53 (1992) (Illinois Development Finance Authority); 20 ILL. COMP. STAT. 3805/2 (1992) (Illinois Housing Development Authority); 70 ILL. COMP. STAT. 210/10 (1992) (Metropolitan Pier and Exposition Authority); and 70 ILL. COMP. STAT. 3615/4.14 (1992) (Regional Transportation Authority).
54. CAL. GOV'T CODE §5922 (West Supp. 1993).
55. *See, e.g.,* ARK. CODE. ANN. § 19-9-707(4) (Michie Supp. 1991); FLA. STAT. ANN. § 159.825 (West 1990); 30 ILL. COMP. STAT. 305/7 (Smith-Hurd Supp. 1993); N.M. STAT. ANN. § 6-18-8.1 (Supp. 1992); OHIO REV. CODE ANN. § 133.22 (Baldwin 1991); N.C. GEN. STAT. § 63A-9 (1992); and TEX. REV. CIV. STAT. ANN. art. 4413(501) (Vernon Supp. 1993).
56. *See, e.g.,* CONN. GEN. STAT. ANN. § 7-130g (West 1989).
57. *See, e.g.,* ALA. CODE §§ 41-1-42(2)(b), 41-1-43 (Supp. 1992); ARK. CODE. ANN. § 19-9-707(5) (Michie Supp. 1991); CAL. GOV'T CODE § 5922 (West Supp. 1993); FLA. STAT. ANN. § 159.825(7) (West 1990); and N.M. STAT. ANN. § 6-18-8.1 (Supp. 1992).
58. McGavin, *supra* note 46, at 221.
59. *Id.* at 221.
60. *Id.* at 221.
61. Maryland, South Carolina, South Dakota, Tennessee, Utah, West Virginia, and Wyoming, for example, neither give express authority to enter into swap transactions nor grant home rule powers that could include the power to enter into swap transactions to the municipalities therein.
62. International Swap Dealers Association, MODEL SWAP LEGISLATION § (B)(i).
63. MODEL SWAP LEGISLATION § (B)(ii).

64. MODEL SWAP LEGISLATION § (E).

65. In Illinois, however, it is clear that swaps are not treated as debt. The statute provides in pertinent part: "Any [swap] agreement or contract shall not be taken into account with respect to any debt limit applicable to the [municipality]." 30 ILL. COMP. STAT. 305/7 (Smith-Hurd Supp. 1993).

66. Thomas A. McGavin, Jr., *Interest Rate Swaps in the Municipal Markets,* SWAPS AND OTHER DERIVATIVES IN 1992, 778 PLI/Corp. 267, 277–79 (1992).

67. *Id.* at 279.

68. *See, e.g.,* 30 ILL. COMP. STAT. 305/7 (Smith-Hurd Supp. 1993); LA. REV. STAT. ANN. § 1429 (West 1989 & Supp. 1992); MICH. COMP. LAWS ANN. § 133.15 (West 1992); and N.M. STAT. ANN. § 6-18-8.1 (Supp. 1992); *see also supra* note 65.

69. 30 ILL. COMP. STAT. 305/7 (Smith-Hurd Supp. 1993).

70. McGavin, *supra* note 66, at 280.

71. Ronald L. Cheng, Note, *Legal Doctrines Restricting the Secondary Market in Interest Rate Swaps,* 26 COLUM. J. TRANSNAT'L L. 313, 325 (1988).

72. *Id.* at 326.

73. *Id.*

74. *Id.* at 327.

APPENDIX 7A

International Swap Dealers Association Proposed Model Statute Authorizing Governmental Entities to Enter into Swap Transactions

The Legislature finds and declares that the incurring or carrying of obligations and making and managing of investments by this government, subdivisions hereof and related governmental entities involves a variety of interest rate, payment, exchange and other risks and that a number of financial instruments are available to offset, hedge, or reduce, and improve net costs and we therefore desire to clearly establish that this government, subdivisions hereof and related governmental entities have express statutory authority to take advantage of those instruments. Notwithstanding any other provision of law applying to this government, subdivisions hereof and related governmental entities, all of the following may apply:

(A) Definitions

As used in this Statute, the following definitions apply, unless the context otherwise indicates:

(i) "Obligations" mean bonds, notes, bond anticipation notes, commercial paper, or other evidences of indebtedness, or lease, installment purchase, or other agreements or other purchasing programs or certificates of participation therein.

(ii) "Governmental Entity" means the state (or the equivalent thereof) or any political subdivision thereof, or any department, agency, board, commission, or authority of the state or any such political subdivision, or any public corporation, authority, agency, board, commission, or other public entity controlled by the state or any such political subdivision.

(iii) "Swap Agreement" means (a) an agreement (including terms and conditions incorporated by reference therein) which is a rate swap agreement, basis swap, forward rate agreement, commodity swap, interest rate

---

Model Statute Authorizing Governmental Entities to Enter into Swap Transactions Proposed by the International Swap Dealers Association, THE BOND BUYER, Oct. 23, 1992, at 25.

option, forward foreign exchange agreement, rate cap agreement, rate floor agreement, rate collar agreement, currency swap agreement, cross-currency rate swap agreement, currency option, any other similar agreement (including any option to enter into any of the foregoing), (b) any combination of the foregoing or (c) a master agreement for any of the foregoing together with all supplements.

(B) Swap Agreements

(i) Subject to clause (ii) below, any Governmental Entity may from time to time enter into (and modify, amend and terminate) one or more Swap Agreements that it determines to be necessary or desirable in connection with, or incidental to, the conduct of its activities, whether commercial or governmental in nature, including in connection with the issuance, carrying or securing of Obligations or the acquisition or carrying of investments. Swap Agreements entered into by a Governmental Entity shall contain such provisions, including payment, term, security, default and remedy provisions, and shall be with such parties, as the Governmental Entity shall determine to be necessary or desirable after due consideration to the creditworthiness of such parties.

(ii) No Governmental Entity shall enter into any Swap Agreement pursuant to this subdivision other than for the purpose of managing an interest rate, currency, commodity price, investment or similar risk, that arises in connection with, or incidental to, the activities of the Governmental Entity, and no Governmental Entity shall carry on a business of acting as a dealer in Swap Agreements.

(C) Foreign Currency

Obligations issued by a Governmental Entity may be payable in accordance with their terms, in whole or in part, in currency other than lawful money of the United States of America, provided that the Governmental Entity enters into a Swap Agreement or similar agreement for payments in lawful money of the United States of America, which covers the entire amount of the debt service payment obligation of the Governmental Entity with respect to the Obligations payable in other currency, and provided further that if the term of that agreement is less than the term of the Obligations, the Governmental Entity shall covenant to enter into additional agreements as may be necessary to cover the entire amount of the debt service payment obligation.

(D) Credit Enhancement

In connection with entering into any Swap Agreement the Governmental Entity may enter into credit enhancement or liquidity agreements with such payment, security, default, remedy and other terms and conditions as the Governmental Entity determines.

(E) Enforceability

Absent bad faith or actual knowledge to the contrary, a counterparty that enters into any Swap Agreement with a Governmental Entity may rely on a representation by that Governmental Entity that it is authorized or empowered to enter into such Swap Agreement, and notwithstanding the failure by that Governmental Entity to comply with the provisions in this Statute, that counterparty may enforce such Swap Agreement against the Governmental Entity.

(F) Preemption

To the extent that this Statute is inconsistent with any other general statute or parts thereof, now or hereafter enacted, this Statute is controlling.

(G) Construction

It is the intent of the Legislature that this Statute be liberally construed.

CHAPTER 8

Bankruptcy Concerns Relating to Tax-Exempt Derivatives

Robert D. Aicher

Bankruptcy Issues Relating to Trusts, Related Parties to Trusts, and Transfers of Assets to Trusts

As discussed in previous chapters, in many transactions the structuring of a secondary market tax-exempt derivative product involves the formation of a trust or similar arrangement. Tax-exempt bonds are transferred to a trust, which in turn issues certificates evidencing undivided ownership interests in the tax-exempt bonds to investors. These investors normally understand that they are purchasing the credit risk of the obligated party on the bonds deposited in the trust. If, for example, the assets in a trust are New York City bonds, and New York City files a Chapter 9 municipal bankruptcy proceeding, the purchasers of the trust certificate know or should know that the recovery of their investment will be subject to the inevitable problems associated with such bankruptcy proceeding. However, these certificate holders do not expect the trust formed to hold the tax-exempt bonds to become a debtor in a bankruptcy proceeding. If New York City is solvent and paying its bonds as they become due, certificate holders would be shocked to find that the trust, which does no more in their minds than act as a stakeholder, could file or be placed involuntarily into bankruptcy. Likewise, the certificate holder would not be pleased[1] to find that the bankruptcy of the sponsor of the trust or another certificate holder had an adverse impact upon the proposed payments to be received on the trust assets. While in most circumstances it is unlikely that the economics of a derivative product would create a situation in which the bankruptcy of the trust would be desirable to any of the parties connected with the transaction, this sanguine assumption is not true of all derivative products. Accordingly, a threshold question in structuring a secondary market derivative product is determining whether and when the trust or the assets held in the trust may become subject to the jurisdiction of a bankruptcy court and the concomitant inevitable delays and costs.[2]

Eligibility of Trusts for Bankruptcy Relief

Generally a trust is not eligible to become a debtor in a bankruptcy proceeding.[3] As a consequence, the investment community takes a great deal of comfort from the fact that many secondary market derivative products use trusts to own the assets that form the principal credit associated with the transaction. Should the trust be eligible for bankruptcy and in fact become the subject of a bankruptcy proceeding, numerous problems could occur that would interfere with the expected flow of cash from the assets in the trust to the holder of the security. These problems include not only the imposition of the automatic stay[4] and the potential recovery as preferences of payments that have previously been made to the holders of the certificates,[5] but also the possibility that the certificates or other securities issued by the trust might be treated as individual liabilities of the trust rather than simply a pass-through of the assets held by the trust. In this circumstance the trust could attempt to "reorganize" the obligations it "owes" on its certificates, thereby potentially materially altering the expected returns and benefits to the holders of the certificates. To the extent that a trust has certificate holders whose interests are not identical, the potential for the trust's bankruptcy ineligibility to be questioned becomes much greater. It may be in the best interest of one group of certificate holders to attempt to file an involuntary proceeding against the trust to prevent another group of certificate holders from receiving expected benefits from the trust if the receipt of these benefits inures to the detriment of the first group. Accordingly, a determination that the trust is ineligible for relief under the Bankruptcy Code is a critical aspect of structuring many secondary market derivative products.

Notwithstanding the general rule discussed above, bankruptcy courts have held in certain situations that trusts are debtors eligible for relief under the Bankruptcy Code. The provisions of Section 109 of the Bankruptcy Code specify who may become a debtor in a bankruptcy case.[6] Only a "person" or a "municipality" may become a debtor under Section 109, and the Bankruptcy Code defines the term "person" to include individuals, partnerships, and corporations.[7] A "corporation" is in turn defined to include a "business trust"[8] and, accordingly, all other types of trusts have been deemed by courts to be ineligible for bankruptcy relief.[9]

The term "business trust," however, is not defined in the Bankruptcy Code, and it has been left to the courts to determine whether a trust is a business trust and therefore eligible for bankruptcy relief.[10] To date, courts have not taken a unified approach to this issue, and the result has been considerable confusion as to whether and when a trust may be a debtor under the Bankruptcy Code.

Although not always applied in a consistent manner from case to case, three basic analytical approaches appear to have been adopted by the courts in determining whether a trust is a business trust. One approach focuses on whether the trust is a business trust under applicable state law. A second approach analyzes the elements that define a business trust for purposes of the Internal Revenue Code. A third approach analyzes the purposes, organization, and activities of the trust to determine whether it is a business trust.

State Law Approach

Some courts have looked to the status of the trust under state law to determine whether the trust should be considered a business trust under the Bankruptcy Code.[11] As one court stated, "[s]ince the Bankruptcy Code does not define what constitutes a business trust, and since the decisions are, if not hopelessly divided, at least certainly divergent, this Court must look to state law for guidance."[12] Courts adopting this approach have focused on whether the trust has met the requirements for classification as a business trust under applicable state law.[13] A trust that fails to meet the requirements of a business trust under state law is held not to qualify as a debtor under the Bankruptcy Code.[14]

Although reliance on the status of a trust under state law may seem reasonable in light of the lack of specific guidance in the Bankruptcy Code, some courts have criticized this method of defining a business trust.[15] These courts argue that reliance on a state law definition of business trust violates congressional intent to create uniform bankruptcy rules,[16] since the use of this method by necessity creates inconsistencies in the application of the Bankruptcy Code.[17]

Internal Revenue Code Approach

Some courts have incorporated the elements defining a business trust for purposes of the Internal Revenue Code in determining whether the trust is also a trust for Bankruptcy Code purposes.[18] These courts have adopted the test enunciated by the United States Supreme Court in *Morrissey v. Commissioner* for establishing a business trust under federal tax law.[19] Specifically, the Court in *Morrissey* provided that a business trust for tax purposes has the following characteristics: (1) business purposes and functions, (2) title to property held by the trustee, (3) transferable certificates of beneficial interest, (4) centralized management, (5) continuity of life, and (6) limited liability. Courts have analyzed the presence or absence of these criteria on a case-by-case basis to determine whether a business trust exists.[20] As with reliance on applicable state law, this method has been criticized by some courts that "do not agree that [Internal Revenue Code] cases are particularly relevant for Bankruptcy Code purposes."[21] The logic of this approach could be troubling for those derivative products that create a trust for state law purposes but rely for tax law purposes upon a contrary characterization of the trust, for example, as a partnership, which clearly is eligible for Bankruptcy Code relief.[22]

Business Purpose Approach

A third, less formulistic approach, which has been adopted by a majority of courts, analyzes the purpose, organization, and activities of the trust. Unfortunately, when analyzing these aspects of a trust, the courts have failed to reach a consensus on what factors are critical in determining whether a trust is a business trust under the provisions of the Bankruptcy Code. *In re Treasure Island Land Trust,*[23] one of the earliest and most frequently cited cases defining a business trust for bankruptcy law purposes, stated that

> business trusts are created for the purpose of carrying on some kind of business or commercial activity for profit; the object of a nonbusiness trust is to protect and preserve the trust res. The powers granted in a traditional trust are incidental to the principal purpose of holding and conserving particular property, whereas the powers within a business trust are central to its purpose. It is the business trust's similarity to a corporation that permits it to be a debtor in bankruptcy.[24]

A later court summarized the view of the *Treasure Island* court by stating that:

> [t]he primary consideration in most cases has been the overt purpose of the trust. If its purpose is to protect the trust res, the trust is found to be ineligible for bankruptcy protection. If the purpose is profit oriented, the trust is found to be an eligible business trust.[25]

Although the primary focus of courts adopting this method has clearly been on the purpose of the trust, recent cases suggest that the analysis should be a broader three-part test. This approach requires that, for a trust to be a business trust for Bankruptcy Code purposes, it must (1) be engaged in business activities, (2) have "at least some of the attributes of a corporation," and (3) "be formed for a business or commercial purpose."[26]

To determine the existence or nonexistence of the three requirements set forth above, courts have found a number of factors to be instructive. To determine whether a trust is actively engaged in business activities, courts have focused on the actual operations of the trust. Factors considered include the types of assets held by the trust,[27] the types of activities in which the trust is engaged,[28] and whether the activities have turned a profit.[29]

In determining whether a trust has any of the attributes of a corporation, courts have looked at the structure of the trust.[30] The primary emphasis has been on the presence of transferable ownership interests, which are likened to equity interests in a traditional corporation.[31] Courts have also looked at whether any outside investors have made contributions of capital to the trust.[32] In addition, some courts have found the existence of a fixed termination date for the trust to be indicative of nonbusiness status.[33]

The most thoroughly analyzed of the three requirements has been the presence or absence of a business purpose. In making this determination, courts have reviewed the agreements creating the trust to determine the express purposes of the trust,[34] the powers granted to the trustee,[35] and the identity of the beneficiaries to determine their relationship to the trust.[36]

Mixing of Methods

Since it is unclear which method should be used in determining whether a trust is a business trust for Bankruptcy Code purposes, a number of courts have combined the three methods described above in an apparent effort to avoid reversal on appeal resulting from the application of the wrong standard.[37] In general, in pursuing this issue, many courts appear to have taken a result-oriented approach, first determining whether as a policy matter the trust should be eligible for bankruptcy relief and then citing factors that support their conclusions. As one court observed, an "examination of the case law indicates that the decisions all go off on their own particular facts and do not stand for any general proposition. . . ."[38] A more cynical court claimed that "[t]he decisions are sharply, and perhaps hopelessly, divided on the meaning of 'business trust.'"[39]

Property of Trust Subject to Bankruptcy of Beneficiary

Even if the trust is not eligible for bankruptcy relief, there is at least a theoretical possibility that the property in the trust could be affected by the bankruptcy of a beneficiary. While this is not a serious problem for derivative products having a large number of potential owners, in the case of a trust where most of the certificates will be owned by a single purchaser, particular care must be given to avoid the application of the bankruptcy case law that has grown up surrounding Illinois land trusts. If this case law were applied to a derivative product, the bankruptcy of a large holder of the certificates of the trust could cause that holder's bankruptcy problems to impact the trust assets, thereby potentially disrupting cash flow for the other holders.

An Illinois land trust is a trust created by the execution of a deed of trust transferring all legal *and equitable* title to real property to a trustee. A separate trust agreement between the trustee and the beneficiary recites that all legal and equitable title is retained by the trustee and an assignable personal property interest is granted the beneficiary. Under the trust agreement, all money advanced by the trustee must be paid by the beneficiary, and the trustee is not required to pay any taxes or assessments. The trustee may not act with respect to the real property except on written authorization of the beneficiary, and the beneficiary may order the land sold at any time.[40] Several cases have held that although Illinois-type land trusts are not themselves eligible for bankruptcy relief, the trust assets will nevertheless be treated as part of the estate of a *bankrupt beneficiary.*[41] These cases have then proceeded, *upon the bankruptcy of the beneficiary,* to impose the automatic stay and otherwise limited access to the trust assets by *creditors of the trust.* These courts have relied on the powers of the bankruptcy court as a court of equity and looked through the form to what they view as the substance of the transaction.[42]

Several factors have been important in the decision by courts to look through the form of the trust. Most important of these has been the singularity of ownership and control of the assets by the beneficiary in connection with these types of trusts.[43] As one court has noted, the "beneficiary is certainly the owner of the land in the economic sense."[44] It is not without some ironic fascination with the case law in this area that the author notes that these factors, which have led courts to include trust assets in the estate of beneficiaries, are many of the same factors that have led courts to conclude that trusts are not business trusts for purposes of Section 109 of the Bankruptcy Code.[45]

Substantive Consolidation

Even if a trust is itself ineligible for bankruptcy relief, it is possible that the assets and liabilities of the trust could be aggregated with those of a related entity that is a debtor under the Bankruptcy Code under the doctrine of substantive consolidation.[46] Care must be taken in structuring a trust to ensure that there exists no relationship between the trust and a third party so significant that the substantive consolidation doctrine could be triggered. This is of particular concern with regard to the sponsor of the trust. While substantive consolidation has arisen principally in the context of parent and subsidiary corporations, the basic concepts are equally applicable to other entities, including trusts and their sponsors. A simple observance of formalities relating to the trust to make clear to the world that the trust exists as a separate entity distinct from its sponsor with no commingling of assets or other attributes referred to below in the parent/subsidiary context should provide significant comfort with respect to this concern.

Substantive consolidation is not expressly authorized under the Bankruptcy Code. Instead, it has been developed by bankruptcy courts through the exercise of their powers under Section 105(a) of the Bankruptcy Code, which permits bankruptcy courts to take equitable action in furtherance of their specific Bankruptcy Code powers.[47] If used, the doctrine of substantive consolidation may result in the pooling of assets of, and claims against, separate entities, the satisfaction of liabilities from the resulting common asset pool, and the combination of creditors of the otherwise separate entities for purposes of voting on reorganization plans.[48]

Because there are no statutorily prescribed standards for substantive consolidation, courts examine the facts of each case to determine whether consolidation is warranted. As a result of this case-by-case approach, it is never entirely clear whether substantive consolidation will be granted or denied.

Historically, owing to the perceived unfairness of ordering involuntary combination of the assets of entities with different ratios of assets to liabilities, courts were sparing in their use of the power to consolidate.[49] Absent fraud or wrongdoing, substantive consolidation was allowed only when the relationships of the entities involved were so intertwined that the time and expense necessary to separate them would threaten the ability of creditors to realize upon any assets of the bankruptcy debtor.[50] Some recent courts have shown more willingness to consolidate entities,[51] shifting their focus from an analysis of whether one entity proposed to be consolidated with another is the instrumentality of such other entity to an evaluation of the overall equitable effect of the substantive consolidation.

Instrumentality Test

Early courts used the "instrumentality test" to determine whether consolidation was appropriate. This test requires courts to determine whether elements similar to the factors for determining whether to "pierce the corporate veil" in the corporate law context are present. In *Fish v. East*,[52] the Tenth Circuit set forth the following factors for determining whether a subsidiary is a "mere instrumentality" of the parent such that the two entities should be treated as one:

1. The parent corporation owns all or a majority of the stock of the subsidiary.
2. The parent and subsidiary corporations have common directors or officers.
3. The parent corporation finances the subsidiary.
4. The parent corporation subscribes to all of the capital stock of the subsidiary or otherwise causes its incorporation.
5. The subsidiary has grossly inadequate capital.
6. The parent corporation pays the salaries or expenses or losses of the subsidiary.
7. The subsidiary has substantially no business except with the parent corporation or no assets except those conveyed to it by the parent corporation.
8. In the papers of the parent corporation, and in the statements of its officers, "the subsidiary" is referred to as such or as a department or division.
9. The directors or executives of the subsidiary do not act independently in the interest of the subsidiary but take direction from the parent corporation.
10. The formal legal requirements of the subsidiary as a separate and independent vehicle are not observed.[53]

If an analysis of these factors showed the subsidiary to be an instrumentality of the parent, corporate separateness would be disregarded "where not to do so [would] defeat public convenience, justify wrong or protect fraud."[54]

A second set of elements was introduced in *In re Vecco Construction Industries, Inc.*[55] According to the *Vecco* court, the following criteria should be considered by courts in determining whether it is proper to allow substantive consolidation:

1. The degree of difficulty in segregating and ascertaining individual assets and liability.
2. The presence or absence of consolidated financial statements.
3. The profitability of consolidation at a single physical location.
4. The commingling of assets and business functions.
5. The unity of interests and ownership between the various corporate entities.
6. The existence of parent and inter-corporate guaranties on loans.
7. The transfer of assets without formal observance of corporate formalities.[56]

Although the factors enunciated in *Fish* and *Vecco* have frequently been used by courts in analyzing whether substantive consolidation is appropriate,[57] courts have gradually shifted away from a mechanical application of these factors to an overall balance of the equities of consolidation.[58] One of the earliest opinions articulating the premise that the equity of consolidation must be taken into account came from Judge Friendly in *Chemical Bank New York Trust Co. v. Kheel.*[59] In his concurring opinion, Judge Friendly stated that "[e]quality among creditors who have lawfully bargained for different treatment is not equity but its opposite."[60] The need to protect the interests of creditors was also underscored in the Second Circuit's decision in *In re Flora Mir Candy Corp.*[61] In *Flora Mir,* the court refused to order consolidation because of accounting difficulties when the claims of debenture holders stood to be extinguished or diluted as a result of the consolidation. The court cautioned that consolidation is a measure vitally affecting substantive rights "which should be used sparingly because of the possibility of unfair treatment of creditors."[62]

Balancing Test

In response to these decisions, the court in *In re Snider Brothers, Inc.*[63] established a test that focused on the interests of creditors. The court held that "the only real criterion is . . . the economic prejudice of continued debtor separateness versus the economic prejudice of consolidation" and stated that no one set of factors or elements could mandate consolidation in every instance.[64] Further, the fact that corporate formalities may have been ignored does not per se lead to the conclusion that it would be equitable to consolidate separate estates.[65]

The *Snider Brothers* court provided two distinct standards of proof for each consolidation issue.[66] First, the "applicant must show that there is a necessity for consolidation, or a harm to be avoided by use of . . . consolidation."[67] The evidence in support of such an application must show more than a mere unity of interest or commingling of funds. Instead, it must show harm that has resulted from the manner in which the entities are operated or a prejudice that would result if the relevant entities are not consolidated.[68] Second, once the applicant has established the need for consolidation, "there is still the matter of the defense that the benefits of consolidation do not outweigh the harm to be caused to the objector."[69]

Thus, a creditor that is certain to suffer harm may be entitled to the denial of a consolidation request.

Although most recent courts have followed the *Snider Brothers* balancing test, the instrumentality test has not been completely abandoned. Rather, proponents of consolidation have been required to demonstrate the existence of the consolidation elements required under the instrumentality test and then submit proof of the harm resulting from the existence of such elements.[70] Some elements have tended to have a stronger impact on consolidation decisions than others. For example, the intermingling of corporate accounts and records has proven to be an important factor in favor of consolidation.[71] Stock ownership, common officers and directors, interaffiliate transfers, and consolidated financial statements and tax returns, on the other hand, have been afforded little weight because they are typical of most affiliated corporations.[72]

In addition, certain fact patterns have been more persuasive than others in convincing courts to consolidate. Where creditors have shown that they justifiably relied on the assets of a group of entities or the credit of a parent, courts have been more likely to consolidate the applicable entities.[73] In contrast, courts have hesitated to grant consolidation where the creditor has looked solely to the creditworthiness of a single debtor and has not relied on the credit of related entities.[74]

The recent substantive consolidation case most frequently cited by courts and commentators is the Second Circuit decision in *In re Augie/Restivo Baking Co.*[75] The *Augie/Restivo* court refused to grant the debtors' motion to substantively consolidate two baking companies.[76] The court analyzed the considerations discussed by previous courts in determining whether substantive consolidation was warranted and found them all to be "merely variants" of the following two factors:

1. whether creditors dealt with the entity as a single economic unit and "did not rely on their separate identity in extending credit," or
2. whether the affairs of the debtors are so entangled that consolidation will benefit all creditors.[77]

In analyzing the first factor, the court focused on the expectations of the lenders. Here the court found that loans had been made by all relevant creditors on the basis of the financial strength of the separate debtors alone.[78] In analyzing the second factor, the court indicated that the consolidation of separate debtors where assets and business functions have been commingled should not be "Pavlovian."[79] Instead, it should only be used after a determination that "all creditors will benefit because untangling is either impossible or so costly as to consume the assets."[80]

True Sale v. Secured Loan Issues

Another possible risk is that the transfer of the related tax-exempt bond to the trust might be recharacterized from a sale to a secured loan transaction. That is, rather than a sale from the sponsor to the trust, after which the trust owns the securities, the trust could be considered to simply have lent money to the sponsor with the sponsor continuing to own the securities and having merely pledged the securities to the trust to secure its borrowing. The result of such loan treatment would inject the credit risk of the sponsor into the derivative product. If the sponsor, rather than the trust, owns the securities, upon the sponsor's bankruptcy the automatic stay will prevent the trust from continuing to pay the collections from the securities to the holder of the certificates.[81] If the lien upon the securities was not properly perfected, the only asset of the trust may be an unsecured loan to the sponsor.[82] In addition, if the pledge was not perfected, the payments previously made by the trust to the holder could be recoverable as a preference.[83] Even if the pledge was properly perfected, the related tax-exempt bond in the trust would be "property of the estate" of the sponsor in bankruptcy and subject to use, sale, or lease by a bankruptcy trustee acting on behalf of the sponsor.[84]

Accordingly, it is critical to the integrity of many derivative products that the relationship between the sponsor and the trust be characterized as a sale of the related tax-exempt bond to the trust, not a disguised loan. The question of whether a transaction is a sale or a loan in this context is largely a matter of state law.[85] Courts have looked at a number of factors in deciding this issue, including the following:

1. Recourse to the seller of the assets.[86]
2. Retention of servicing of the assets by the seller and the commingling of proceeds.[87]
3. The accounting, regulatory, and tax treatments of the transaction.[88]
4. Failure by the purchaser to investigate the credit of the debtor on the underlying assets.[89]
5. The presence of a right in favor of the seller to excess collections on the assets.[90]
6. Retention by the seller of an option to purchase the assets.[91]
7. The presence of a right in favor of the seller to unilaterally alter pricing terms or to alter or compromise the other terms of the assets.[92]
8. The language of the documents and the intent and conduct of the parties.[93]

No one factor has been found conclusive in determining whether a transaction is a sale or a loan, although extensive recourse to the seller has sometimes been an exception. A bright-line test for determining what types of transactions are sales and what types are loans has yet to emerge from the courts.

Recourse to the Seller

The most important factor looked at by courts in determining whether a purported sale of assets is in fact a secured loan is the presence of recourse to the seller. This recourse can take the form of a repurchase obligation, a guaranty of collectibility by the seller, a failure to extinguish or reduce independent obligations of the seller after the ostensible sale has been made, or a holdback of sale proceeds from the seller as reserves that are released only as the assets are paid. Although the presence of recourse to the seller has been deemed by courts to be an important factor indicating a loan,[94] there is authority to the effect that recourse alone, without the presence of other factors suggesting a loan, does not preclude true sale treatment.[95] Moreover, some courts have held transfers to be sales even when partial or full recourse existed in conjunction with other factors that were also indicative of a secured loan.[96]

The recourse provisions considered in most decisions to date that have held sale transactions to be disguised secured loans have generally been very broad in scope. The transaction documentation involved in these decisions permitted recourse to the seller for nonpayment of the assets for any reason. In most instances it also required the seller to repurchase assets that did not comply with the seller's representations and warranties regarding such matters as the legality and validity of the sale transaction and the absence of disputes and setoff rights relating to the assets. Because of the breadth of these recourse provisions, few courts have expressly addressed the question whether recourse for the breach of a representation or warranty that is not related to the creditworthiness of the debtor on the underlying assets is less suggestive of a secured loan than recourse for assets in the event that the debtor on the underlying assets is unable to pay.

In *In re Federated Department Stores, Inc.*,[97] the Bankruptcy Court for the Southern District of Ohio recognized the distinction discussed above. It approved a purchase arrangement for the debtor to obtain post-petition financing of receivables on favorable terms. Among the reasons cited by the court for the approval of the transaction was that the right of recourse to the seller in the transaction was "not related to any defaults in payment under the [assets]" by the obligors thereon.[98]

In the context of derivative products, special attention should be directed to liquidity protection given the holders of the certificates that is provided by the sponsor of a trust who "sold" the related tax-exempt bonds to the trust. Although liquidity is usually directly provided by a letter of credit, the sponsor frequently has an obligation to reimburse the letter of credit bank for any liquidity draws. Improperly structured liquidity could constitute recourse that may cause the initial deposit of the related tax-exempt bonds to be recharacterized as a secured loan to the sponsor rather than a sale to the trust.

Retention of Servicing by Seller

A number of courts have noted that the seller's continued servicing of the transferred assets is indicative of a loan rather than a sale.[99] Such arrangements have been found to be particularly problematic where the seller/servicer commingles asset proceeds with its own general operating funds.[100] On the other hand, other courts have found a true sale of assets to exist despite a retention of the servicing, in particular where proceeds of collection have been deposited in lock-box or other accounts in control of the purchaser.[101]

Accounting, Regulatory, and Tax Treatments

The treatment of the transaction for accounting, regulatory, and tax purposes may be persuasive evidence of the intent of the parties.[102] The proper accounting treatment for the seller for identical transactions may be substantially different depending upon the seller's identity. The accounting profession, in FASB 77, has chosen to emphasize whether the benefits of ownership of the assets have been transferred, and has taken a somewhat lenient view of the issue of retention of recourse.[103] FASB 77 requires for sale treatment that the transferor surrender control of future economic benefits in the assets.[104] It does not, however, impose absolute limits on obligations of the seller to repurchase assets or provide other recourse. Rather, it merely requires that the amount of recourse be subject to reasonable estimation.[105]

The principal bank regulators have taken a contrary, and much more restrictive, approach in formulating regulatory accounting principles.[106] The general rule for purposes of these principles is that a transfer of assets is to be reported as a sale only if the transferring financial institution

1. retains no risk of loss from the assets transferred resulting from any cause and
2. has no obligation to any party for the payment of principal or interest on the assets transferred resulting from:
   a. default on principal or interest by the obligor of the underlying instrument or from any other deficiencies in the obligor's performance,
   b. changes in the market value of the assets after they have been transferred,
   c. any contractual relationship between the seller and purchaser incident to the transfer that, by its terms, could continue even after final payment, default, or other termination of the assets transferred, or
   d. any other cause.[107]

Other Factors

Courts have also analyzed the other factors listed above in determining whether a transaction is a true sale or a loan. In particular, courts will often discuss the language that the parties used in the documents governing the transaction. Courts have focused on such terms as "security" or "collateral" where other relevant factors indicate a loan, and on terms such as "sale" or "absolutely convey" where other factors support (or do not preclude) sale treatment.[108] In one case, the language in an agreement and conduct of the parties were sufficient to persuade a court that a transaction was a sale, despite the presence of full recourse provisions.[109] Most courts, however, have de-emphasized the language used in the documents and have focused instead on intent and actual conduct.[110]

The above discussion indicates that the most important factor in obtaining sale treatment in a bankruptcy case is the ability to demonstrate that most or all of the economic risks and benefits of the assets (including control over the assets and the relation with the debtor thereunder) have been transferred. All attributes of the transaction should be documented as a sale. The parties should strive to establish a documented record at the time of the transfer that clearly expresses the intent of both to achieve a true sale.

Servicing of assets may be left in the hands of the seller without necessarily precluding sale treatment. However, such servicing should be treated as a separate contractual relationship based on agency principles, with an appropriate arm's-length servicing fee. Contracting with an independent agent to service on behalf of the purchaser will provide more support to later arguments that the transaction is a sale. Any recourse may exceed a reasonable prediction of losses and costs associated with the assets, based on historical experience, but the extent of such excess should be minimized. To the extent that it can be demonstrated that recourse to the seller has been bargained for as part of the determination of an overall sale price, the right of recourse should be less suggestive of a secured loan. The right of direct recourse to the seller for breaches of representation and warranty as to the legal validity, proper documentation, and existence of the assets as represented should not preclude sale treatment, provided that most other attributes of the transaction conform to a true sale.

Finally, it should be noted that obtaining a true sale structure will not necessarily insulate the cash flow on the assets from all bankruptcy risk. The automatic stay in bankruptcy applies to property of the estate, which is broadly defined to include "all legal or equitable interests of the debtor in property as of the commencement of the case." If the seller retains any interest in the assets and proceeds, including a mere possessory interest as a servicer and collector, an attempt to take control of that property without court approval would violate the stay. If the transaction is a true sale, the automatic stay should not affect the substantive rights of the purchaser. Nevertheless, if the seller has retained an interest in the assets, the purchaser will be delayed by having to seek relief from the stay through the bankruptcy court before taking control of the assets and proceeds.

A ruling of the United States Court of Appeals for the Tenth Circuit (which, unfortunately, was rendered after this chapter was submitted for publication and accordingly cannot be discussed in detail) casts doubt as to whether any derivative structure involving the sale of accounts receivable or tax-exempt municipal leases of personal property with sufficient connections to the jurisdiction of such court can be structured as a "true sale." The case, *Octagon Gas Systems, Inc. v. Rimmer*, No. 92-6065 (10th Cir. May 27, 1993), concluded that because a sale of "accounts" is governed by Article 9 of the Uniform Commercial Code (UCC), the purchaser of accounts is in fact a secured lender and not an owner of the accounts for bankruptcy purposes. Thus, accounts sold are to be included in the bankruptcy estate of the ostensible seller. While the *Octagon* ruling relates to "accounts," sale of "chattel paper" is also governed by Article 9 of the UCC. Chattel paper, for purposes of the UCC, includes leases of "specific goods," and therefore the logic of the *Octagon* ruling extends to municipal leases of personalty. While the case is wrongly decided, it is, nevertheless, the law of the Tenth Circuit at present and, until some applicable change in law occurs, must be respected as such in transactions with connections to that jurisdiction.

Bankruptcy and Insolvency Issues Associated with Swaps

Many tax-exempt derivative products (both primary and secondary market products) use interest rate swaps to provide for the payment of a variable rate of interest to the security holder. For example, in certain secondary market products, the trust or other vehicle pursuant to which synthetic floating-rate securities are issued holds a tax-exempt security that pays interest at a fixed rate. The trust enters into an agreement with a third party to pay that fixed rate of interest in exchange for a variable rate of interest approximating a rate that would be payable on conventional tax-exempt variable-rate securities. In an embedded swap structure, the issuer of or other obligor under the tax-exempt bonds enters into the interest rate swap agreement with the third party. The credit risk of the party agreeing to pay the variable rate may be introduced into the transaction through the swap arrangement. The following describes how swap agreements operate generally and how such agreements are treated under applicable law in the event of the insolvency of one of the parties to the arrangement.

Characteristics of Swap Agreements

As discussed in prior chapters, an interest rate swap agreement is a contract between two parties (sometimes called "counterparties") to make periodic interest payments to each other with respect to some "notional" principal amount of money. One counterparty has typically borrowed money with interest payable at a fixed rate, and wishes instead to pay a variable rate. That party will enter into a swap agreement with another counterparty who has incurred variable-rate debt but is willing to "swap" those interest payments in order to pay a fixed rate. Depending upon the projected spread between fixed and variable rates over the life of the arrangement at the time the swap is executed, one counterparty may pay a premium (usually at the outset of the transaction) sufficient to induce the other counterparty to swap its existing interest rate obligations. When corresponding interest payments come due under the swap, the parties typically will "net" or offset their payment obligations, leaving the party with the greater payment obligation to pay the "net" amount. If movements in the variable rate occur from one payment period to the next, the amount owed on an upcoming payment date by the party paying the variable rate will change, and hence the net amount payable under the interest rate swap will change as well.

The description above is of one individual swap transaction. Most parties engaging in swap transactions, however, will enter into a number of individual transactions with the same counterparty over time. These transactions typically are governed by a "master agreement" between these parties. Also, in addition to individual interest rate swap transactions as described above, counterparties may enter into other types of hedging transactions, such as caps, floors, collars, and currency exchange agreements. Rather than attempting to describe each of these types of transactions, it is sufficient for purposes of this discussion to point out that all these transactions may be entered into, and governed under, a single master agreement, and that all of these hedging devices involve payment obligations from one counterparty to another, or in some instances (as is the case with the basic swap transaction described above) concurrent payment obligations from both counterparties to each other.

The master agreement typically used in these transactions provides that when one or more specified "events of default" occur with respect to an individual transaction, the other party may "cross-default" and accelerate all individual agreements executed under the master agreement. The master agreement will usually provide for a netting of all offsetting payment obligations between the two parties and include a formula for the calculation of damages payable to the nondefaulting party. If the defaulting party's obligations are secured, the related security agreement typically will provide for the liquidation of collateral upon default to the extent necessary to satisfy unpaid obligations. A party's commencement of insolvency proceedings is invariably included as an event of default in a master agreement.

Thus, credit risk and insolvency risk are inherent in any individual swap. But, because individual swaps are seldom entered into in isolation, counterparties have tended to view their credit exposure on a "net" basis, expecting to be able to quickly liquidate their positions on this basis if an insolvency occurs, in accordance with provisions of their master agreements.

Master Swap Agreements

In structuring and reviewing derivative products using swaps, particular attention should be paid to the swap documentation to determine whether modifications are necessary to preserve the payment expectations of the solvent party upon the insolvency of its counterparty. Many interest rate swaps relating to tax-exempt derivative products are documented using the ISDA master agreement reproduced at the end of this chapter as Appendix 8A and referred to in the following discussion, or a similar master swap agreement. If multiple transactions are documented under the same master agreement, the operation of the netting provisions of such agreement could result in the fixed-rate payor's receiving less than the full value of the payment obligation due under the applicable swap from the variable-rate payor upon the variable-rate payor's insolvency.

For illustrative purposes only, assume a very simple example. (For a variety of reasons, including the options the parties could have selected under the master agreement, the liquidated damages provisions, and the timing of payment dates and periods over which interest accrues, the real world would seldom work so neatly.) First assume that New York City issues two derivative products involving embedded swaps and enters into two swaps with Last National Bank under a master agreement. Assume that swap one is for the benefit of Bonds Series A and swaps a fixed rate of 7 percent for a floating rate. Assume that swap two is for the benefit of Bonds Series B and swaps a fixed rate of 5 percent for a floating rate. Assume that the floating-rate indices are the same. Assume also that the Series A Bonds and the Series B Bonds are in identical principal amounts. Assume Last National Bank fails and the floating-rate index is at 6 percent. Under the master agreement netting provisions, Last National Bank could owe nothing. The payment obligation of Last National Bank to New York City for the benefit of the Series A Bonds will in all likelihood be netted against the payment obligation of New York City to First Bank from the Series B Bonds.

It should be emphasized that the netting concern may not be of practical importance if the fixed-rate payor is a trust or other single-purpose entity created solely for purposes of the individual derivative product transaction and therefore will not enter into additional swaps with the same counterparty. In addition, if the obligor on the assets relating to the derivative product, rather than the counterparty, is directly obligated to pay the variable rate to the investor and is merely hedging its interest rate risk by entering into the interest rate swap, the netting of multiple swap positions is of less importance.[111]

Since 1986 ISDA has published several form master swap agreements. The most recent forms are the two ISDA master agreements published in 1992. This section focuses primarily on the relevant provisions of the 1992 ISDA master agreement (Local Currency—Single Jurisdiction).[112] This master agreement, consisting of a form agreement with an attached form of schedule, contains various optional provisions that the parties may elect to apply to their agreement. The master agreement (including the schedule and all swap transactions entered into between the two parties) is intended to form a single agreement and not a series of separate contracts.

Three provisions of the master agreement deal with netting. First, Section 2(c) provides that amounts owed on the same date, in the same currency, and for the same swap transaction will be netted so that the party with the larger payment obligation will pay the net amount.[113] Second, by deleting subsection 2(c)(ii), the parties to the master agreement can provide that payments due on the same day in the same currency will be netted regardless of whether such amounts are payable on the same swap transaction.[114] The third type of netting provided for is the netting of the value of multiple swap transactions upon termination of the master agreement.[115]

Termination of the master agreement could result from the insolvency of one of the parties. Section 6(a)[116] provides that if an event of default (including the bankruptcy default contained in Section 5(a)(vii)[117] occurs, the nondefaulting party may terminate all outstanding swap transactions by giving not more than twenty days' notice to the defaulting party. The parties to the agreement may, however, opt to have "automatic early termination" apply to the master agreement.[118] If they choose this option, all swap transactions under the master agreement will automatically terminate upon the occurrence of certain insolvency events[119] and immediately preceding the institution of other insolvency events.[120]

Treatment of Swap Agreements in Insolvency Proceedings

Perhaps the single most important question for any user of swaps and similar hedging devices is whether the parties may rely on the liquidation and netting provisions of their master agreements in determining their true credit exposure to a potentially insolvent counterparty. Congress has answered this question "yes" with respect to counterparties whose insolvencies are administered under provisions of federal law. These counterparties include domestic federally insured financial institutions, whose insolvencies are administered pursuant to the Federal Deposit Insurance Act (FDIA),[121] as amended by the Financial Institutions Reform, Recovery and Enforcement Act of 1989 (FIRREA);[122] and nonbank domestic corporations and similar business entities, whose insolvencies are administered pursuant to the Bankruptcy Code.[123] Presented below is an analysis of the treatment of swap transactions under each of these bodies of law, with the discussion focusing particularly on special provisions addressing the important question posed above.

One type of counterparty not mentioned above is the domestic insurance company. Insurance company insolvencies are administered not under federal law but under the laws of the company's chartering state. A treatment of insurance company insolvencies is beyond the scope of this chapter. One could expect, however, that the same general issues discussed below, and addressed by specific provisions of the Bankruptcy Code and the FDIA, might arise under state laws addressing insurance company insolvencies. In addition, this discussion does not address insolvencies involving foreign counterparties, such as branches or agencies of foreign banks, or foreign nonbank corporations.

Swaps Under the Bankruptcy Code

Status of Swaps Prior to 1990 Amendments

Prior to the 1990 amendments to the Bankruptcy Code, it was not clear that a party to a swap agreement could exercise liquidation and netting rights in the event of the bankruptcy of a counterparty. The Bankruptcy Code appeared to prevent the solvent party to a swap from terminating the swap in accordance with the swap agreement and also appeared to give a bankruptcy trustee (or debtor in possession in a reorganization) discretion to determine whether to assume or reject the swap.

Upon the bankruptcy of a counterparty to a swap agreement, the first obstacle to the solvent party was the Bankruptcy Code's automatic stay provision.[124] The stay generally prevents any creditor from recovering pre-petition claims against a debtor, enforcing a lien against the property of the debtor securing pre-petition debt, and setting off any pre-petition obligation owing to the debtor against any claim of the debtor.[125] In the context of swaps, this broad coverage effectively would prevent a solvent party from immediately declaring its swap agreement in default, calculating its net liquidated damages, and, in the case of master agreements secured by collateral, liquidating such collateral.

In addition to the automatic stay, Section 365 of the Bankruptcy Code also potentially restricted a solvent party's exercise of its rights under a master agreement.[126] Section 365(a) provides for the bankruptcy trustee's assumption or, in the alternative, rejection of executory contracts of the bankrupt.[127] An executory contract generally is defined as an agreement on which performance remains due from both parties.[128] Because swaps require both parties to make future interest payments, a swap agreement "almost certainly constitutes an 'executory' contract[.]"[129]

In order to preserve rights under executory contracts while the trustee determines whether or not to assume the contract, Section 365(e) prohibited executory contracts from being modified or terminated solely because of the insolvency or bankruptcy of the debtor.[130] Assumption under Section 365(a), coupled with the prohibition on termination contained in Section 365(e), would clearly defeat the expectation of a solvent counterparty for a quick netting and liquidation of positions under its master agreement.

Under Section 365, if the trustee decided to assume the swap agreement, the solvent party would remain bound by its terms. Section 365 would also permit the bankruptcy trustee to reject unfavorable swaps (leaving the solvent counterparty with a claim against the bankrupt's estate for amounts due on such swaps). In addition, because the trustee under Section 365 was not required to immediately decide whether to assume or reject, a savvy trustee might attempt to time its decisions so as to take full advantage of any prevailing movements in variable interest rates.

If the trustee decided to reject, instead of assume, an individual swap, the swap would be deemed breached as of the date immediately before the filing of the bankruptcy petition.[131] This breach would allow the solvent party to terminate the agreement and to file a claim against the bankruptcy estate for damages.[132] Again, it was not entirely clear under the pre-1990 version of the Bankruptcy Code how the termination and damages provisions would operate with respect to rejected swaps, particularly if a trustee attempted to assume some individual swaps, and reject others, governed by the same master agreement.

Another problematic issue raised by the pre-1990 version of the Bankruptcy Code was whether obligations owed under swap agreements and liens granted thereunder were subject to the avoidance powers granted to the bankruptcy trustee under the provisions of the Bankruptcy Code. For example, it was unclear whether obligations payable under swap arrangements were indebtedness of the debtor/counterparty and thus whether payments made under the swap arrangement could be subject to recovery as preferences under Section 547 of the Bankruptcy Code.

Treatment of Swaps After 1990 Amendments

With the enactment of a series of amendments to the Bankruptcy Code in June of 1990 (collectively, the "Amendments"),[133] solvent counterparties to swap agreements are now afforded more favorable treatment in the event that the other counterparty to the swap agreement becomes a debtor in a bankruptcy proceeding. In general, solvent swap counterparties may now exercise their rights under swap agreements to net their positions under these agreements and to liquidate the swap arrangement. The bankruptcy trustee is now also prohibited from selectively terminating individual swaps under a master agreement. The Amendments have also made it clear that the major avoidance powers available to bankruptcy trustees do not apply in connection with swap arrangements. According to the legislative history relating to the passage of the Amendments, the purpose of the Amendments was "to ensure that the swap . . . financial [market is] not destabilized by uncertainties regarding the treatment of [its] financial instruments under the Bankruptcy Code."[134] The legislative history notes that U.S. bankruptcy law has "long accorded special treatment to transactions involving financial markets, to minimize volatility."[135]

The Amendments added several new provisions to the Bankruptcy Code and amended various other provisions. First, it added definitions of "swap agreement" and "swap participant" to the Bankruptcy Code. A "swap agreement" is broadly defined as

> an agreement (including terms and conditions incorporated by reference therein) which is a rate swap agreement, basis swap, forward rate agreement, commodity swap, interest rate option, forward foreign exchange agreement, rate cap agreement, rate floor agreement, rate collar agreement, currency swap agreement, cross-currency swap agreement, currency option, any similar agreement (including any option to enter in to any of the foregoing); . . . any combination of the foregoing; or . . . a master agreement for any of the foregoing together with all supplements.[136]

A "swap participant" is defined as "an entity that, at any time before the filing of the petition, has an outstanding swap agreement with the debtor."[137]

Second, Congress amended Section 362(b) of the Bankruptcy Code, which provides for exceptions to the application of the automatic stay. This amendment adds a new exception to the automatic stay for

> the setoff by a swap participant, of any mutual debt and claim under or in connection with any swap agreement that constitutes the setoff of a claim against the debtor for any payment due from the debtor under or in connection with any swap agreement against any payment due to

> the debtor from the swap participant under or in connection with any swap agreement or against cash, securities, or other property of the debtor held by or due from such swap participant to guarantee, secure or settle any swap agreement.[138]

The purpose of this provision is to permit the swap participant to make a final accounting of the net amount due from or owed to the bankruptcy debtor under any swap agreement.[139] The provision "does not authorize any setoff which would otherwise be unlawful under any provision of law other than the provisions of the Bankruptcy Code."[140]

Third, a new subsection (g) was added to Section 546 of the Bankruptcy Code. Section 546 places certain limitations on the bankruptcy trustee's avoiding powers.[141] The new provision states that "[n]otwithstanding sections 544, 545, 547, 548(a)(2) and 548(b) of this title, the trustee may not avoid a transfer under a swap agreement, made by or to a swap participant, in connection with a swap agreement and that is made before the commencement of the case, except under section 548(a)(1) of this title."[142] Subsection (g) prohibits the avoidance of most pre-petition transfers made under swap agreements to a swap participant. It also protects normal transfers of collateral made in connection with a swap agreement.

Fourth, Section 548(d)(2) of the Bankruptcy Code was amended to add a new subparagraph (D).[143] Section 548 authorizes the bankruptcy trustee to avoid fraudulent transfers.[144] The new provision states that "a swap participant that receives a transfer in connection with a swap agreement takes for value to the extent of such transfer."[145] The purpose of this new provision is to exempt swap agreement setoffs from scrutiny by the bankruptcy trustee and the bankruptcy court as to whether the setoff was actually fair value for the amount owed.

Fifth, Section 553 of the Bankruptcy Code was amended to make reference to Section 362(b)(14) of the Bankruptcy Code in order to prevent a bankruptcy trustee from recovering setoffs permitted under that section.[146] Section 553(b)(1) sets out the circumstances under which a bankruptcy trustee may recover certain pre-petition setoffs.[147] According to the legislative history, Section 553(b)(1) is

> designed for instances in which a financial institution or other creditor has taken advantage of an opportunity to excessively improve its financial position with respect to the debtor in the days immediately prior to the debtor's filing a bankruptcy petition. Because of the routine nature of swap agreement setoffs, [the amendment] exempts them from the section 553(b)(1) safeguard, as previously enacted legislation has exempted setoffs involving securities contracts, commodities contracts, forward contracts, and repurchase agreements.[148]

Thus the amendment provides that the "improvement in position test" articulated in Section 553(b)(1) does not apply to setoffs permitted under new Section 362(b)(14).[149]

Finally, a new Section 560 was added to the Bankruptcy Code. It provides:

> The exercise of any contractual right of any swap participant to cause the termination of a swap agreement because of a condition of the kind specified in section 365(e)(1) of this title or to offset or net out any termination values or payment amounts arising under or in connection with any swap agreement shall not be stayed, avoided, or otherwise limited by operation of any provision of this title or by order of a court or administrative agency in any proceeding under this title. As used in this section, the term "contractual right" includes a right, whether or not evidenced in writing, arising under common law, under law merchant, or by reason of normal business practice.[150]

Section 560 preserves "a swap participant's contractual right to terminate a swap agreement and offset any amounts owed under it in the event that one of the parties to the agreement files a bankruptcy petition or becomes insolvent, or in the event that a trustee or custodian is appointed for the party."[151] The intent of the new provision is to "permit either the non-debtor swap participant or the trustee to terminate a swap agreement, so that a swap agreement may continue after the bankruptcy petition is filed only by mutual consent of both the non-debtor swap participant and the trustee."[152] It is not intended to preempt the statute of frauds or any other provision of law other than the provision of the Bankruptcy Code.[153]

The Amendments did not put to rest every issue concerning the treatment of swap agreements under the Bankruptcy Code. For example, the Amendments do not specifically address the consequences of the bankruptcy of a guarantor of the obligations of a swap participant. While the language in some sections may be broad enough to cover guarantors, other sections are not as broadly worded. For example, payments made on behalf of a swap participant by a guarantor do not appear to be protected by Section 546(g) of the Bankruptcy Code,[154] and accordingly may be subject to recovery as preferences in the event of the bankruptcy of the guarantor.

In addition, it should be noted that Section 901 of the Bankruptcy Code, which enumerates the provisions of the Bankruptcy Code that apply to cases brought under Chapter 9,[155] includes all of the sections created or amended by the Amendments except Section 560. Thus, Section 560 does not apply in the event of the bankruptcy of a municipality.

Swaps Under FDIA and FIRREA

As mentioned above, domestic financial institutions insured by the FDIC are not subject to the Bankruptcy Code.[156] Rather, when such an institution becomes insolvent, its insolvency is administered pursuant to a separate body of federal law, principally codified in the FDIA, as amended by FIRREA.[157] Problems similar to those arising under the pre-1990 Bankruptcy Code, however, appear to have been largely addressed by special provisions of FIRREA addressing swaps and similar financial instruments. The discussion below first addresses generally the procedures involved in administration of a bank insolvency and outlines the provisions of FIRREA that, absent special provisions for swaps, would raise problems for swap parties similar to those possible in pre-1990 Bankruptcy Code proceedings. This section then describes how Congress has addressed those problems in the "qualified financial contract" provisions of FIRREA. In addition, the discussion raises other issues involving swaps in bank insolvencies that are unique to insolvencies administered by the FDIC. For convenience, references below are to the insolvency of FDIC-insured commercial banks; swaps involving insolvent FDIC-insured savings and loans would be treated virtually identically under the same provisions of law.

The Insolvency Process and the FDIC's General Power to Transfer Contracts

When a bank that is party to a swap agreement becomes insolvent, its primary regulator will appoint a conservator or receiver to administer the insolvency proceedings.[158] In the case of a national bank, the primary regulator is the Comptroller of the Currency; in the case of a state-chartered bank, it is typically the state banking commissioner or similar regulator at the state level. If a national bank becomes insolvent, or otherwise meets the statutory regulatory conditions authorizing appointment of a conservator or receiver, the Comptroller may appoint the FDIC as conservator, and must appoint the FDIC as receiver.[159] In the case of a state bank, the state regulator may choose to appoint the FDIC as conservator or receiver, or the appropriate federal bank regulator may, in certain circumstances and in consultation with the state regulator, appoint the FDIC as conservator or receiver. (In addition, the FDIC, in certain instances where it believes depositors' interests are not being protected, may appoint itself conservator or receiver of a state-chartered bank.)[160]

When the FDIC is appointed conservator or receiver for an insolvent bank, one of its first tasks is to ascertain the value of assets held by the bank, together with the amount of claims against the bank. In undertaking this evaluation, which must be done very quickly, the FDIC will consider a number of options as to how to administer the bank's insolvency.[161] If the FDIC determines that no solvent institution would be interested in purchasing any of the bank's assets, and assuming any of its deposits or other liabilities, then the FDIC may immediately place the bank into receivership, pay insured deposits directly from the insurance funds, and liquidate the assets of the institution, paying to creditors a pro rata share of claims that are proven in the receivership proceedings. If, however, the insolvent bank has desirable depositor and other customer relationships that would be attractive to a solvent institution wishing to expand its business, the FDIC may use the insurance funds to render assistance in a different form. The FDIA, as amended by FIRREA, authorizes the FDIC to use the insurance funds to infuse cash (by direct payment, purchase of undesirable assets, loans secured by such assets, etc.) sufficient to induce a solvent institution to purchase some or all of the assets of, and assume the deposits and (sometimes) other liabilities of, the insolvent bank.[162] These assets and liabilities include the bank's rights under, and obligations with respect to, existing contracts. In order to assure the FDIC the opportunity to transfer such contract rights and obligations, Congress has generally prohibited the nondefaulting party to an existing contract from exercising any rights it may have to terminate and accelerate its contract with the bank arising solely because of the insolvency of the bank.[163]

The FDIC can accomplish the above-described "purchase and assumption" transaction (P&A) either immediately upon taking over the institution (if it has located and received satisfactory bids from prospective purchasers at that time) or later, after it has had a chance to market the assets and liabilities of the insolvent institution and solicit bids from interested purchasers. In the latter scenario, the FDIC usually chooses to form an interim institution, known as a "bridge bank," to assist in ultimately accomplishing a P&A.[164] A bridge bank is a new corporate entity, chartered in the form of a national bank, that the FDIC will direct to purchase from the insolvent bank certain desirable loans and other assets, while assuming all deposit liabilities (and sometimes some other liabilities) of the insolvent institution.[165] The FDIC will infuse sufficient cash into the bridge bank to enable it to operate as a new, solvent bank, which the FDIC will then attempt to sell in a P&A transaction with an outside, solvent institution. The assets and liabilities that the FDIC has not transferred in a P&A, or to an interim bridge bank, remain with the insolvent institution, which is placed into receivership.

Special Provisions Limiting Transferability of Swaps

Any individual interest rate swap transaction may represent either an asset of, or a liability against, the insolvent bank. Whether a swap is an asset or a liability depends upon whether the "netting" of corresponding payments under the swap entitles the bank to receive payment, or instead obligates the bank to pay. This, in turn, may depend on movements in variable interest rates occurring since the execution of the swap. If swap agreements were treated like other contractual claims against, or assets of, the insolvent bank, the FDIC could prohibit any termination or acceleration and, in its discretion, choose either to transfer an individual contract in a P&A (or to a bridge bank) or not transfer the contract, which would then remain as part of the receivership estate. If so permitted, the FDIC might attempt to maximize the attractiveness of a P&A by transferring only those contracts that constituted assets. This treatment would defeat the intent of the contracting parties in entering into a master agreement governing all individual swap transactions; the parties would not be able to net individual transactions and determine a fixed claim for damages with respect to the termination and acceleration of all individual swap and other hedging agreements governed by the master agreement.

Congress recognized that treating swap transactions like other contract claims against the insolvent bank would lead to great uncertainty and turmoil in the financial markets. As a result, similar to its decision in the context of the Bankruptcy Code as affected in the 1990 Amendments, Congress has adopted within FIRREA some limitations on FIRREA's general prohibition on contract termination and acceleration on insolvency, as well as on the FDIC's unfettered rights to enforce and transfer such contracts to another institution.

These limitations appear within the provisions of FIRREA concerning qualified financial contracts (QFCs).[166] They apply only when the FDIC is acting as receiver for the insolvent bank. A QFC is any "securities contract, commodity contract, forward contract, repurchase agreement, swap agreement, and any similar agreement that the [FDIC] determines by regulation" to be a QFC.[167] A swap agreement, for purposes of the QFC provisions, is any "rate swap agreement, basis swap, commodity swap, forward rate agreement, interest rate future, interest rate option purchased, forward foreign exchange agreement, rate cap agreement, rate floor agreement, rate collar agreement, currency swap agreement, cross-currency rate swap agreement, currency future, or currency option purchased or any other similar agreement," and includes any combination of such agreements and any option to enter into such agreements. FIRREA also provides that if individual swap transactions listed above are executed under a master agreement, those transactions, together with the master agreement, are to be treated as a single swap agreement for purposes of the QFC provisions.[168]

While FIRREA provides that swap agreements and other QFCs are to be treated differently than other contracts with respect to the FDIC receiver's ability to enforce and transfer such contracts, the statute merely limits the FDIC's power in this regard—it does not eliminate these powers. FIRREA, as interpreted by the FDIC in a policy statement, permits the FDIC receiver to transfer a swap agreement notwithstanding termination and acceleration rights arising upon insolvency so long as the FDIC notifies the affected counterparty prior to the close of business on the business day following the FDIC's appointment.[169] Also, the FDIC receiver must transfer *all* QFCs between the insolvent bank and the counterparty (including its affiliates) to a single solvent institution; if it does not transfer all, it may not transfer any. Thus, the FDIC receiver is prohibited not only from picking and choosing among favorable versus unfavorable swaps governed by a single master agreement but also from picking and choosing among *any* favorable or unfavorable QFCs, whether or not governed under the same master agreement.[170]

If the FDIC receiver fails to make such transfer of all QFCs and give timely notice thereof, the affected party is entitled to exercise its acceleration and liquidation rights, notwithstanding FIRREA's general prohibition applicable to other, non-QFC contracts.[171] The exercise of these rights is, however, subject to requirements and limitations otherwise applicable to efforts to enforce contracts against the receivership.[172] That is, the counterparty must file a claim with the receiver with respect to its accelerated master agreement, in accordance with the claims process under FIRREA. This is required even with respect to a fully secured claim.[173] The FDIC receiver, if it has not timely transferred the swap agreement and the other QFCs involving the affected party, will most likely repudiate the swap agreement and other QFCs and relegate the affected party to a claim for damages against the receivership estate.[174] These damages, with respect to swap agreements and other QFCs, are determined as of the date of repudiation and may include reasonable costs of cover and similar liquidated damages customary in the industry with respect to such contracts.[175] If the claim under the swap agreement is secured, the affected counterparty may exercise any nonjudicial self-help remedies that are otherwise available.[176] But if realizing upon the collateral requires attachment or execution upon property through a judicial proceeding, FIRREA prohibits that attachment or execution against property in the FDIC's possession as receiver.[177] Also, although no automatic stay applies in a bank insolvency proceeding, the FDIC in its discretion may stay any judicial action to enforce claims against assets of the insolvent bank.[178]

If the claim under the swap agreement is not secured, recovery will be limited to a pro rata share of available assets remaining in the receivership, just as with any other unsecured claim arising under a non-QFC. In cases where a receiver or conservator has been appointed on or prior to August 10, 1993, whether any assets are available to satisfy these claims may depend, in large measure, upon whether the bank is subject to "depositor preference" laws granting priority to depositors over other general creditors of the bank. For federally insured institutions placed into insolvency proceedings after that date, a new federal statute mandates that all depositors be preferred over other general unsecured creditors, regardless of contrary state law.[179] This also means that depositors in national banks will receive preferred status in insolvency proceedings commenced after that date. In a national bank insolvency, depositors are not preferred and share pro rata with other creditors.[180] But in slightly less than one-half of the states, depositors in state-chartered banks are preferred—and the FDIC accedes to the depositors' preferred position when it pays the depositors or otherwise infuses cash sufficient to cause a solvent institution to assume their deposits.[181]

As noted above, the time limitation that FIRREA imposes on the FDIC's ability to transfer a swap agreement does not apply if the FDIC is acting as conservator for the insolvent bank.[182] In a conservatorship, the general rule under FIRREA applies even with respect to swap agreements and other QFCs—that is, the contracts may not be terminated or accelerated solely because of the insolvency of the bank, and the FDIC may continue to enforce the contracts against counterparties and transfer the contracts without restriction. Like the FDIC receiver, however, the FDIC conservator must abide by the "all or none" rule with respect to transfers of QFCs. If the FDIC conservator chooses not to transfer, it may repudiate the swap agreement within a "reasonable" time and relegate the counterparty to a claim for damages against the conservatorship.

The FDIC has not recently used conservatorship in administering bank insolvencies. Instead, as discussed above, when it desires to operate the insolvent bank as a going concern for a period of time prior to arranging a P&A with an outside entity, the FDIC will form a bridge bank and transfer certain assets and deposit liabilities to that bridge bank, concurrently placing the insolvent bank into receivership. Nonetheless, conservatorship remains an option available to the FDIC and the FDIC could, in consultation with the insolvent bank's primary regulator, seek to have that regulator appoint the FDIC as conservator rather than as receiver.

Finally, while FIRREA's provisions permit the FDIC to enforce swap agreements notwithstanding insolvency, these provisions would not prohibit a counterparty from exercising its termination and acceleration rights under a master agreement in the event some other default (such as payment default) occurred.[183] Thus, the FDIC, in order to retain its rights to enforce and transfer such contracts in a P&A or to a bridge bank, must continue to perform its obligations with respect to such swap agreements.

The practical value to a counterparty of the time limits imposed upon the FDIC receiver in accomplishing the transfer of a swap agreement appears small. If the FDIC wishes to transfer the swap agreement but cannot accomplish the transfer prior to the deadline imposed by FIRREA, it remains in the interest of a swap counterparty to wait until the transfer is accomplished rather than exercising its termination rights. If the counterparty is owed money on a "net" basis under the master agreement, and that party waits until the FDIC accomplishes a transfer of all its swap agreements and other QFCs, the counterparty will have a claim against a solvent entity. A counterparty would generally prefer this to a claim against the receivership of an insolvent bank. If the party instead owes money under the master agreement, then that counterparty should be indifferent whether the swap agreement is transferred—it will owe money either to the receivership or to an acquiring bank in a P&A (or a bridge bank). Only a counterparty who is owed money under the master agreement, whose claim under the agreement is fully secured, and who is in a position to exercise nonjudicial self-help remedies obtains any real benefit from these QFC provisions.[184] That counterparty, if the FDIC does not timely transfer its swap agreement and other QFCs, may accelerate and liquidate its collateral to satisfy its secured claim, and will merely need to file a "protective" proof of claim with the FDIC receiver in order to comply with the claims process under FIRREA. The party need not wait for the FDIC to repudiate or otherwise determine the claim.[185]

Transfer Avoidance Safeguards

In addition to providing special treatment with respect to insolvency termination rights under swap agreements, FIRREA provides some additional protections to swap counterparties. These protections are not afforded parties to other, non-QFC contracts.

As noted above, FIRREA permits the FDIC as conservator or receiver to repudiate contracts that it deems, in its discretion, "burdensome" to the insolvent bank. FIRREA provides that the FDIC may not, however, use its repudiation powers to avoid any otherwise valid security interest in assets of the insolvent bank, unless that interest was "taken" in contemplation of insolvency or with the intent to hinder, delay, or defraud the bank or its creditors.[186] The meaning of this exception to the repudiation power is unclear. This exception (contained in Section 11(e)(11) of the FDIA, as amended by FIRREA), it has been suggested, could be interpreted as granting to the FDIC the affirmative power to avoid security interests "taken" by a secured party in contemplation of insolvency or with intent to hinder, delay, or defraud.[187] Under this interpretation, Section 11(e) arguably creates for the FDIC a new preference and fraudulent transfer avoidance power, applicable to transfers of security interests, which power is in addition to the preference avoidance powers already available to the FDIC under Section 91 of the National Bank Act and any additional avoidance powers that may be available under state law with respect to insolvent state-chartered banks.

In order to make clear that transfers with respect to swap agreements and other QFCs could not be avoided, Congress has provided an additional exception in FIRREA that appears, by its terms, to safeguard nearly all QFC transfers from attack as preferences or fraudulent conveyances. That provision, which is Section 11(e)(8)(C)(i) of the FDIA, states:

> Notwithstanding paragraph (11) [of Section 11(e)], the [FDIC], whether acting . . . as conservator or receiver . . . may not avoid any transfer of money or other property in connection with any qualified financial contract with an insured depository institution.[188]

The meaning of the language "[n]otwithstanding paragraph (11)" is unclear. The language appears intended to provide comfort that the Section 11(e)(11) provisions (discussed in the preceding paragraph), to the extent that they create any new avoidance power with respect to security interests, do not apply to transfers of money or other property made in connection with security interests related to QFCs. This language, however, does not appear to otherwise limit the broad scope of the provision at Section 11(e)(8)(C)(i)—that the FDIC may not avoid any transfer of money or other property in connection with any QFC.

Section 11(e)(8)(C)(i), as written, would preclude the FDIC from attacking any transfers with respect to QFCs under any available theories, whether preference, fraudulent conveyance, derived from federal law, or from state law. FIRREA provides for one exception, however, to this broad safeguard for QFC transfers. The FDIC may avoid QFC transfers if it determines that the recipient of the transfer had the actual intent to hinder, delay, or defraud the institution or its creditors.[189] This apparently requires the FDIC to demonstrate that the recipient had actual fraudulent intent—a difficult burden of proof. Mere evidence of a "constructive" fraudulent conveyance, such as inadequate consideration, is not enough to show actual intent. In the context of transfers under swap agreements and other QFCs, it appears unlikely that many transfers will ever be received with actual fraudulent intent. Accordingly, the FIRREA safeguards for QFC transfers appear to effectively shield such transfers from nearly all the FDIC's avoidance powers.

Written Agreement Requirements

FIRREA contains one other provision that could affect the rights of a counterparty under a swap agreement. As discussed above, the FDIC must act quickly to determine the value of assets and amount of claims against an insolvent bank, in order to determine as quickly as possible whether a P&A or bridge bank transaction would be beneficial or feasible. The most accessible evidence as to the value of assets, and the existence and amount of claims, is contained in the books and records of the insolvent bank. Accordingly, Congress has, in a somewhat inartfully drafted provision of FIRREA, mandated that the FDIC need only recognize claims against the bank that it had the opportunity to discover in examining the bank's books and records.[190]

Section 11(d)(9) of the FDIA[191] requires that agreements that do not meet certain requirements "shall not form the basis of, or substantially comprise, a claim against the receiver or the Corporation [i.e., the FDIC]." The requirements referred to in Section 11(d)(9) are incorporated by reference from another section of the FDIA, Section 13(e), which reads as follows:

> No agreement which tends to diminish or defeat the interest of the Corporation in any asset acquired by it . . . either as security for a loan or by purchase or as receiver of any insured depository institution, shall be valid against the Corporation unless such agreement—(1) is in writing, (2) was executed by the depository institution and any person claiming an adverse interest thereunder, including the obligor, contemporaneously with the acquisition of the asset by the depository institution, (3) was approved by the board of directors of the depository institution or its loan committee,which approval shall be reflected in the minutes of said board or committee, and (4) has been, continuously, from the time of its execution, an official record of the depository institution.[192]

These requirements are sometimes said to represent a codification of the federal common law doctrine announced by the United States Supreme Court in *D'Oench, Duhme & Co. v. FDIC.*[193] This doctrine provides that the FDIC is immune from defenses to, or offsetting counterclaims with respect to, the enforcement of assets that it acquires in rendering assistance to the bank, when those defenses or counterclaims are based upon agreements not contained in the books and records of the insolvent institution, and which agreements are part of a scheme designed or tending to mislead the FDIC concerning the value of assets or claims against the institution.[194] The *D'Oench* doctrine has been applied by some courts to defeat affirmative claims made against a bank receivership where such claims did not appear evident upon the books and records of the institution.[195]

In fact, the statutory requirements of Section 11(d)(9) and 13(e) of the FDIA are more strict than the *D'Oench* requirements, since an agreement could appear in the records of the bank, not tend to mislead the FDIC, and yet not strictly comply with all of the requirements of Section 13(e). Of more significance, a strict application of Section 11(d)(9) and Section 13(e) with respect to swap agreements and other QFCs would require banks and their counterparties to change long-standing practices with regard to documentation and authorization of such contracts. For example, most swap transactions are not approved individually by directors or loan committees. Also, a counterparty to a swap agreement can have no sure way of knowing whether the agreement is "continuously, from the time of its execution," a part of the "official records" of the bank.

Because these provisions caused such concern in the financial markets, the FDIC attempted to address these concerns in a policy statement. The FDIC has stated that, notwithstanding the language of Section 13(e), it will recognize QFC claims against a conservatorship or receivership where (1) the QFC is evidenced by a writing (signed, if this would otherwise be required under state law) sent to the bank "reasonably contemporaneously" with the parties' actual agreement; (2) the bank, by corporate action (demonstrable by a party's good faith reliance on a resolution or the written representation of a vice president or higher officer at the bank), is authorized to enter the transaction under applicable law; and (3) the writing is maintained in the bank's books and records, or the counterparty making a claim otherwise establishes "by appropriate evidence (including the production of copies)" the existence of the writing and the evidence of the bank's authority.[196]

The approach described in the policy statement appears intended to strike a compromise between the interests of QFC claimants and the interest of the FDIC in not being misled as to the value of a bank's assets. A counterparty to a swap agreement with a bank, if concerned about the possible deterioration of the bank's credit, should take all feasible steps to assure that the bank complies with the requirements outlined in the FDIC policy statement.

Notes

The author wishes to thank the following individuals for their invaluable assistance in writing this chapter: Rafael L. Cook, Timothy P. Mohan, William J. Fellerhoff, Ronald J. Hacker, Elizabeth D. Swanson, and Ger P. O'Donnell. The author also wishes to thank the following individuals for their research assistance: Grace L. Shaff, Lisa M. Engel, and Mary M. Marcoccia.

1. Saying "not be pleased" is, of course, an understatement. In fact, certificate holders who find themselves in this situation have a tendency to sue people, an unpleasant result for all involved.

2. This section of the chapter does not address bankruptcy issues relating to tax-exempt derivative products that are structured under custody arrangements that are not properly classified as trusts under applicable state law. In addition, this section of

the chapter addresses insolvency issues only under the Bankruptcy Code. Different laws and principles apply to insolvency proceedings relating to entities, such as financial institutions and insurance companies, that are not eligible for relief under the Bankruptcy Code. A discussion of these laws and principles is beyond the scope of this section.

3. *In re* Old Second Nat'l Bank of Aurora, 7 B.R. 37 (Bankr. N.D. Ill. 1980); *accord In re* Cahill, 15 B.R. 639 (Bankr. E.D. Pa. 1981); *In re* Armstead and Margaret Wayson Trust, 29 B.R. 58, 59 (Bankr. D. Md. 1982).

4. 11 U.S.C. § 362(a). Section 362(a) of the Bankruptcy Code provides that the filing of a bankruptcy petition:

> operates as a stay, applicable to all entities, of—
>
> (1) the commencement or continuation, including the issuance or employment of process, of a judicial, administrative, or other action or proceeding against the debtor that was or could have been commenced before the commencement of the case under this title, or to recover a claim against the debtor that arose before the commencement of the case under this title;
>
> (2) the enforcement, against the debtor or against property of the estate, of a judgment obtained before the commencement of the case under this title;
>
> (3) any act to obtain possession of property of the estate or of property from the estate or to exercise control over property of the estate;
>
> (4) any act to create, perfect, or enforce any lien against property of the estate;
>
> (5) any act to create, perfect, or enforce against property of the debtor any lien to the extent that such lien secures a claim that arose before the commencement of the case under this title;
>
> (6) any act to collect, assess, or recover a claim against the debtor that arose before the commencement of the case under this title;
>
> (7) the setoff of any debt owing to the debtor that arose before the commencement of the case under this title against any claim against the debtor; and
>
> (8) the commencement or continuation of a proceeding before the United States Tax Court concerning the debtor.

5. 11 U.S.C. § 547(b). Section 547(b) of the Bankruptcy Code provides:

> (b) Except as provided in subsection (c) of this section, the trustee may avoid any transfer of an interest of the debtor in property—
>
> (1) to or for the benefit of a creditor;
>
> (2) for or on account of an antecedent debt owed by the debtor before such transfer was made;
>
> (3) made while the debtor was insolvent;
>
> (4) made—
>
> (A) on or within 90 days before the date of the filing of the petition; or
>
> (B) between ninety days and one year before the date of the filing of the petition, if such creditor at the time of such transfer was an insider; and
>
> (5) that enables such creditor to receive more than such creditor would receive if—

(A) the case were a case under chapter 7 of this title;

(B) the transfer had not been made; and

(C) such creditor received payment of such debt to the extent provided by the provisions of this title.

6. 11 U.S.C. § 109(a) (providing that "only a person that resides or has a domicile, a place of business, or property in the United States, or a municipality, may be a debtor under this title").

7. 11 U.S.C. § 101(41) (providing that the term " 'person' includes individual, partnership, and corporation, but does not include governmental unit, *Provided, however,* that any governmental unit that acquires an asset from a person as a result of operation of a loan guarantee agreement, or as receiver or liquidating agent of a person, will be considered a person for purposes of section 1102 of this title").

8. 11 U.S.C. § 101(9) (providing that the term " 'corporation' (A) includes (i) association having a power or privilege that a private corporation, but not an individual or a partnership, possesses; (ii) partnership association organized under a law that makes only the capital subscribed responsible for the debts of such association; (iii) joint-stock company; (iv) unincorporated company or association; or (v) business trust; but (B) does not include limited partnership").

9. *See, e.g., In re* Old Second Nat'l Bank of Aurora, 7 B.R. at 38; *In re* Cahill, 15 B.R. at 640; *In re* Armstead and Margaret Wayson Trust, 29 B.R. at 59.

10. *In re* Parade Realty, Inc., Employees Retirement Pension Trust, 134 B.R. 7, 9 (Bankr. D. Haw. 1991) ("there is no definition or explanation of the term business trust, nor are there any legislative comments giving guidance to the interpretation of that term").

11. *See, e.g., In re* SCR Trust, 20 B.R. 17, 18 (Bankr. M.D. La. 1982) (stating that "[s]ince th[e] Trust can only be a personal trust under the [state] law which allowed its creation, the engagement in numerous business activities cannot serve to convert it into a business trust . . ."); *In re* Mohan Kutty Trust, 134 B.R. 987 (Bankr. M.D. Fla. 1991) (holding that real estate trust was not a business trust under the Code); *In re* Heritage North Dunlap Trust, 120 B.R. 252 (Bankr. D. Mass. 1990) (holding that fourteen trusts each holding a single piece of real estate were not business trusts under the Code); *In re* Village Green Realty Trust, 113 B.R. 105 (Bankr. D. Mass. 1990) (holding that nominee trust was not a business trust under the Code); *In re* Constitutional Trust No. 2-562, 114 B.R. 627 (Bankr. D. Minn. 1990) (holding that trust with home as asset was not a business trust under the Code). Obviously, this method can only be applied where the particular state has a means of defining the trust. *See In re* Heritage North Dunlap Trust, 120 B.R. at 254–255 (dismissing bankruptcy actions by certain Massachusetts trusts because they did not meet Massachusetts statutory requirements of a business trust while dismissing bankruptcy actions by certain New Hampshire trusts because they were not business trusts as the term was defined by New Hampshire case law).

12. *In re* Village Green Realty Trust, 113 B.R. at 113; *accord In re* Heritage North Dunlap Trust, 120 B.R. at 254 (stating that since "the Code does not define what constitutes a business trust, [the court will] look to state law").

13. *See, e.g., In re* Mohan Kutty Trust, 134 B.R. at 989; *In re* Constitutional Trust No. 2-562, 114 B.R. at 631–32.

14. *See, e.g., id; but cf. In re* St. Augustine Trust, 109 B.R. 494, 496 (Bankr. M.D. Fla. 1990) (stating that while noncompliance with statutory requirements is "not dispositive of whether a trust is eligible for relief under [the Code], it is a factor to be considered

when analyzing the nature of a trust"); *In re* Treasure Island Land Trust, 2 B.R. 332, 335 (Bankr. M.D. Fla. 1980) (stating that "by virtue of the Supremacy Clause of the United States Constitution, Article VI, [a] failure to register [as a business trust as required under state law] cannot affect its eligibility for relief under the [Code; h]owever, it does give a reading of the Trust's intent").

15. *See, e.g., In re* Woodsville Realty Trust, 120 B.R. 2, 4 n.2 (Bankr. D.N.H. 1990) (disagreeing with the conclusion "in *In re Village Green Realty Trust, supra,* that the federal definition is controlled by state law"); *In re* Arehart, 52 B.R. 308, 310 (Bankr. M.D. Fla. 1985) (stating that "[w]hether an entity is eligible for relief under [the] Code is purely a matter of federal law").

16. *See In re* Arehart, 52 B.R. at 310–11 (stating that "this [method] is not what Congress intended when it enacted the bankruptcy laws in this country in conformity with the mandate of Article I, §8, Cl. 4 of the Constitution, which provides that 'Congress shall have the power . . . to establish . . . uniform laws on the subject of bankruptcies'"); *In re* Woodsville Realty Trust, 120 B.R. at 4 n.2 (stating that "in the absence of [any] explicit contrary Congressional intent, the Bankruptcy Code definition of qualified trust debtors was to be developed on a uniform national basis by case-by-case adjudication").

17. *See In re* Arehart, 52 B.R. at 310 (stating that application of this method "would result in different results in different states and an entity would be eligible for relief in one state but not in another").

18. *See, e.g., In re* Mosby, 61 B.R. 636 (E.D. Mo. 1985) (holding that family trust was not a business trust under the Code), *aff'd per curiam,* 791 F.2d 628 (8th Cir. 1986); *In re* St. Augustine Trust, 109 B.R. at 494 (same); *In re* Vivian A. Skaife Irrevocable Trust Agreement No. 1, 90 B.R. 325 (Bankr. E.D. Tenn. 1988) (same); *In re* Betty L. Hays Trust, 65 B.R. 665 (Bankr. D. Neb. 1986) (same); *In re* Margaret E. DeHoff Trust I, 114 B.R. 189 (Bankr. W.D. Mo. 1990) (same); *In re* L & V Realty Trust, 61 B.R. 423 (Bankr. D. Mass. 1986) (holding that trust with only one asset, a piece of real estate, was not a business trust under the Code).

19. 296 U.S. 344, 359 (1935).

20. *See, e.g., In re* Mosby, 61 B.R. at 636; *In re* St. Augustine Trust, 109 B.R. at 494; *In re* Vivian A. Skaife Irrevocable Trust Agreement No. 1, 90 B.R. at 325; *In re* Betty L. Hays Trust, 65 B.R. at 665; *In re* Margaret E. DeHoff Trust I, 114 B.R. at 189; *In re* L & V Realty Trust, 61 B.R. at 423.

21. *In re* Woodsville Realty Trust, 120 B.R. at 5 n.3.

22. For example, in *In re* Medallion Realty Trust, 103 B.R. 8 (Bankr. D. Mass. 1989), *aff'd,* 120 B.R. 245 (D. Mass. 1990), the court reclassified a real estate trust as a partnership in light of state law and federal tax decisions. Despite the fact that the relationship between the "partners" was established via a trust instrument, the court concluded that the trust vehicle was a "mere conduit" for their income. *Id.* at 12. The court concluded that the degree of control exercised by the beneficiaries over the trust and the profit-seeking nature of the trust's activities were sufficient to warrant the trust's reclassification as a partnership eligible for relief under the Bankruptcy Code. *Id.* at 14.

23. 2 B.R. 332 (Bankr. M.D. Fla. 1980) (holding that a land trust was not a business trust under the Code); *accord In re* Dolton Lodge Trust No. 35188, 22 B.R. 918 (Bankr. N.D. Ill. 1982) (same); *In re* Jay M. Weisman Irrevocable Children's Trust of 1981, 62 B.R. 286 (Bankr. M.D. Fla. 1986) (holding that irrevocable children's trust was not a business trust under the Code); *but see In re* Medallion Realty Trust, 103 B.R. at 11–12 (holding that a nominee trust meets the requirements of a business trust under the Code (but was actually a partnership) and stating that the "distinction between the conduct of a

business and the preservation of trust principal through investment, moreover, seems too fine for practical application. . . . I conclude, therefore, that Congress intended to permit bankruptcy relief for all trusts which are created for the purpose of transacting business and whose beneficiaries make a contribution in money or money's worth to the enterprise, without regard to whether the trust has characteristics of a corporation such as separate certificates of ownership").

24. 2 B.R. at 334.

25. *In re* Universal Clearing House Co., 60 B.R. 985, 991 (D. Utah 1986) (holding that a "clearinghouse" with outside investors and a business purpose was a business trust under the Code).

26. *In re* BKC Realty Trust, 125 B.R. 65, 66 (Bankr. D.N.H. 1991) (holding that family trust was not a business trust under the Code); *accord In re* Parade Realty, Inc., Employees Retirement Pension Trust, 134 B.R. at 11 (holding that pension plan trust was not a business trust under the Code after summarizing "the requirements of a business trust, namely 1) the trust must be actively engaged in and doing business, 2) the trust must have some of the significant attributes of a corporation, primarily the transferability of interests in the trust, and 3) the trust must have been formed primarily for a business purpose"); *but see In re* Medallion Realty Trust, 103 B.R. at 8.

27. *See, e.g., In re* Jay M. Weisman Irrevocable Children's Trust of 1981, 62 B.R. at 288; *In re* North Shore Nat'l Bank of Chicago, Land Trust No. 362, 17 B.R. 867, 869 (Bankr. N.D. Ill. 1982) (holding that Illinois land trust was not a business trust under the Code); *In re* Old Second Nat'l Bank of Aurora, 7 B.R. at 38.

28. *See, e.g., In re* Jay M. Weisman Irrevocable Children's Trust of 1981, 62 B.R. at 288; *In re* Universal Clearing House Co., 60 B.R. at 992; *In re* Captran Creditors Trust, 53 B.R. 741, 744 (Bankr. M.D. Fla. 1985); *In re* Treasure Island Land Trust, 2 B.R. at 335; *In re* Arehart, 52 B.R. at 310; *In re* Dreske Greenway Trust, 14 B.R. 618, 622 (Bankr. E.D. Wis. 1981); *In re* Old Second Nat'l Bank of Aurora, 7 B.R. at 38, *In re* Westchester County Civil Service Employees Ass'n, Inc., Benefit Fund, 111 B.R. 451, 456 (Bankr. S.D.N.Y. 1990) (holding that collective bargaining agreement nonprofit trust fund was not a business trust under the Code).

29. *See, e.g., In re* Arehart, 52 B.R. at 310; *In re* Westchester County Civil Service Employees Ass'n, Inc., Benefit Fund, 111 B.R. at 456. The trust need not have actually had a profit where it was clearly designed for that purpose. *See, e.g., In re* Universal Clearing House Co., 60 B.R. at 992. Several cases have modified this requirement, holding that the trust need only be "created to transact business for the benefit of investors." *In re* Medallion Realty Trust, 103 B.R. 8, 11 (Bankr. D. Mass. 1989); *accord In re* Affiliated Food Stores, Inc. Group Ben. Trust, 134 B.R. 215 (Bankr. N.D. Tex. 1991) (holding that trust formed to provide low-cost insurance was a business trust under the Code); *In re* Captran Creditors Trust, 53 B.R. at 744 (holding that liquidation trust is a business trust under the Code since the "Trust was in actuality performing the final business of its predecessor corporation . . . while the Trust was not created for the purpose of generating a profit in the normal sense, the fact that the trustees were managing the assets in order to maximize the payoff to the creditors is sufficient to warrant the conclusion that the Trust in this case is a business trust"); *In re* Tru Block Concrete Products, Inc., 27 B.R. 486, 491 (Bankr. S.D. Cal. 1983) (same); *contra In re* Hemex Liquidation Trust, 129 B.R. 91, 97 (Bankr. W.D. La. 1991) (holding that liquidation trust was not a business trust under the Code since "its creation is owed to an intention to go out of, rather than continue in, business. . . . [I]t was formed solely to change the nomenclature of its predecessor, suspend its operations, qualify for fa-

vored tax treatment regarding the transfer, and provide a vehicle for carrying out the contract of sale").

30. "The business trust is a voluntary pooling of capital by a number of people who are the holders of freely transferable certificates evidencing beneficial interests in the trust estate." *In re* Armstead and Margaret Wayson Trust, 29 B.R. 58, 59 (Bankr. D. Md. 1982) (holding that testamentary trust was not a business trust under the Code).

31. *See, e.g., In re* Parade Realty, Inc., Employees Retirement Pension Trust, 134 B.R. at 11; *In re* Walker, 79 B.R. 59, 62 (Bankr. M.D. Fla. 1987) (holding that testamentary trust was not a business under the Code); *In re* Johnson, 82 B.R. 618, 619 (Bankr. S.D. Fla. 1988); *In re* Woodsville Realty Trust, 120 B.R. at 5. "The importance of the transferability of the interests of a business trust cannot be overemphasized." *In re* Parade Realty, Inc., Employees Retirement Pension Trust, 134 B.R. at 11 (stating that "[w]hile transferability need not be evidenced by actual certificates, the beneficial interests in any purported business trust must be transferable").

32. *See, e.g., In re* Parade Realty, Inc., Employees Retirement Pension Trust, 134 B.R. at 11; *In re* BKC Realty Trust, 125 B.R. at 67; *In re* Medallion Realty Trust, 103 B.R. at 11; *In re* Walker, 79 B.R. at 62; *In re* Arehart, 52 B.R. at 309; *In re* Woodsville Realty Trust, 120 B.R. at 5.

33. *See, e.g., In re* Johnson, 82 B.R. at 619; *In re* Woodsville Realty Trust, 120 B.R. at 5. One court also found the "casual method of handling the receipts and disbursements pertaining to the [trust] is more typical of a nonbusiness trust than of a business trust." *In re* Ophir Trust, 112 B.R. 956, 959 (Bankr. E.D. Wis. 1990) (holding that trust with home as sole asset was not a business trust under the Code).

34. "[I]n examining the debtor as an entity the focus should not be on what the debtor is *called* but rather on what the debtor actually is and the purpose it has been created to carry out." *In re* Dolton Lodge Trust No. 35188, 22 B.R. at 925.

35. *See, e.g., In re* Universal Clearing House Co., 60 B.R. at 992; *In re* BKC Realty Trust, 125 B.R. at 67; *In re* Hemex Liquidation Trust, 129 B.R. at 97; *In re* Treasure Island Land Trust, 2 B.R. at 334; *In re* Vivian A. Skaife Irrevocable Trust Agreement No. 1, 90 B.R. at 328; *In re* St. Augustine Trust, 109 B.R. at 496; *In re* Arehart, 52 B.R. at 310 (holding that land development trust to which beneficiaries contributed money was a business trust under the Code); *In re* Dreske Greenway Trust, 14 B.R. 618, 623 (Bankr. E.D. Wis. 1981) (holding that trust which acquired and leased property "by virtue of its own business activities" was a business trust under the Code); *In re* Citizens Bank & Trust Co. of Park Ridge, 8 B.R. 812, 815 (Bankr. N.D. Ill. 1981) (holding that land trust was not a business trust under the Code). However, the "mere fact that the settlor intended to enhance the assets through commercial activity does not equate [the trust] with a corporation and, therefore, bring it within the scope of § 101([9])." *In re* Milani Family Irrevocable Trust, 62 B.R. 6, 7 (Bankr. S.D. Fla. 1986).

36. *See, e.g., In re* Universal Clearing House Co., 60 B.R. at 992; *In re* Captran Creditors Trust, 53 B.R. 741, 744 (Bankr. M.D. Fla. 1985) (holding that liquidation trust is a business trust under the Code); *In re* Village Green Realty Trust, 113 B.R. at 114; *In re* Vivian A. Skaife Irrevocable Trust Agreement No. 1, 90 B.R. at 328; *In re* St. Augustine Trust, 109 B.R. at 496; *In re* Arehart, 52 B.R. at 310; *In re* Dreske Greenway Trust, 14 B.R. at 622; *In re* Johnson, 82 B.R. 618, 619 (Bankr. S.D. Fla. 1988) (holding that a family trust was not a business trust under the Code); *In re* Old Second Nat'l Bank of Aurora, 7 B.R. 37, 38 (Bankr. N.D. Ill. 1980) (holding that Illinois land trust was not a business trust under the Code); *In re* Ralph Faber Trust, 113 B.R. 599, 601 (Bankr. D.N.D. 1990) (holding that trust with principal asset family farm was not a business trust under the Code); *In re* Woodsville Realty Trust, 120 B.R. 2, 5 (Bankr. D.N.H. 1990) (holding that trust which owned real estate was not a business trust under the Code).

37. *See, e.g., In re* Tru Block Concrete Products, Inc., 27 B.R. at 486; *In re* Hemex Liquidation Trust, 129 B.R. at 91; *In re* Mohan Kutty Trust, 134 B.R. at 987; *In re* St. Augustine Trust, 109 B.R. at 494.

38. *In re* Gonic Realty Trust, 50 B.R. 710, 712 (Bankr. D.N.H. 1985).

39. *In re* Medallion Realty Trust, 103 B.R. at 10.

40. *In re* Gladstone Glen, 628 F.2d 1015, 1017 (7th Cir. 1980) (quoting People v. Chicago Title & Trust Co., 389 N.E.2d 540, 542 (Ill. 1979)). The court also noted that

> it is apparent that true ownership lies with the beneficiaries though title lies with the trustee. The trustee derives all of his power from the beneficiary and acts solely on the beneficiary's behalf. The beneficiary may withdraw or modify the trustee's authority at any time. Indeed, there is not a single attribute of ownership, except title, which does not rest in the beneficiary. The rights of creation, modification, management, income and termination all belong to the beneficiary. In reality the transfer to the trustee is a formality involving a shifting of legal documents. The land trust is, in fact, a fiction which has become entrenched in the law of this State and accepted as a useful instrument in the handling of real estate transactions. Outside of relationships based on legal title, the trustee's title has little significance.

In re Gladstone Glen, 628 F.2d at 1018 (quoting Chicago Title & Trust Co., 389 N.E.2d at 545) (citations omitted).

41. *See, e.g., In re* Gladstone Glen, 628 F.2d at 1019 (holding that the debtor-beneficiary of an Illinois land trust is the equitable owner of the real property held in the trust under the Bankruptcy Act); *In re* Ameriswiss Associates, 148 B.R. 349 (Bankr. S.D. Fla. 1992) (holding that rents from property held in an Illinois-type land trust established pursuant to Florida law were property of the estate of the debtor-beneficiary); *In re* Langley, 30 B.R. 595, 600 (Bankr. N.D. Ind. 1983) (holding that property held in an Illinois-type land trust established pursuant to Indiana law was property of the estate of the debtor-beneficiary). "While *Gladstone Glen, supra,* was decided under the former Bankruptcy Act, the reasoning and result remain applicable under the Bankruptcy Code." *In re* Langley, 30 B.R. at 599.

42. *See, e.g., In re* Gladstone Glen, 628 F.2d at 1019.

43. *Id.* at 1018.

44. *Id.*

45. *See supra* discussion of Business Purpose Approach.

46. Substantive consolidation is the process by which the assets and liabilities of different entities are aggregated in order to effect more equitable distribution of property among creditors. Eastgroup Properties v. Southern Motel Ass'n, Ltd., 935 F.2d 245, 248 (11th Cir. 1991).

47. 11 U.S.C. § 105(a). Section 105(a) of the Bankruptcy Code provides:

> (a) The court may issue any order, process, or judgment that is necessary or appropriate to carry out the provisions of this title. No provision of this title providing for the raising of an issue by a party in interest shall be construed to preclude the court from, sua sponte, taking any action or making any determination necessary or appropriate to enforce or implement court orders or rules, or to prevent an abuse of process.

48. *In re* Augie/Restivo Baking Co., 860 F.2d 515, 518 (2d Cir. 1988).

49. *In re* Snider Bros., Inc., 18 B.R. 230, 234 (Bankr. D. Mass. 1982) (substantive consolidation almost always threatens to prejudice the rights of creditors because separate debtors will almost always have different asset to liability ratios. Creditors of a debtor

whose ratio is higher than that of its affiliate will recover a lower percentage of their claim to the extent that the ratio of the merged estates is lower).

50. Chemical Bank New York Trust Co. v. Kheel, 369 F.2d 845, 847 (2d Cir. 1966). *See, e.g., In re* Flora Mir Candy Corp., 432 F.2d 1060, 1063 (2d Cir. 1970) (accounting difficulties did not justify consolidation, particularly when claims of debenture holders would be extinguished or diluted).

51. *See In re* Vecco Constr. Indus., Inc., 4 B.R. 407, 409 (Bankr. E.D. Va. 1980) (liberal trend in allowing consolidation arises from result of increased judicial recognition of widespread use of interrelated corporate structures by subsidiary corporations operating under parent entity's corporate umbrella for tax and business planning purposes).

52. 114 F.2d 177, 191 (10th Cir. 1940).

53. *Id.*

54. *Id.*

55. 4 B.R. 407 (Bankr. E.D. Va. 1980).

56. *Id.* at 410.

57. *See, e.g., In re* Drexel Burnham Lambert Group, Inc., 138 B.R. 723, 764 (Bankr. S.D.N.Y. 1992).

58. *See, e.g., In re* Snider Brothers, Inc., 18 B.R. 230 (Bankr. D. Mass. 1982).

59. 369 F.2d 845 (2d Cir. 1966).

60. *Id.* at 848.

61. 432 F.2d 1060 (2d Cir. 1970).

62. *Id.* at 1062–63. *See also In re* Continental Vending Mach. Corp., 517 F.2d 997, 1001 (2d Cir. 1975) (since consolidation in bankruptcy vitally affects substantive rights, inequities must be heavily outweighed by practical considerations such as accounting difficulties and expenses that may occur where interrelationships of groups are highly complex or untraceable).

63. 18 B.R. 230 (Bankr. D. Mass. 1982).

64. *Id.* at 234.

65. *Id.*

66. *Id.* at 238.

67. *Id.*

68. *Id.*

69. *Id.* The approach taken by courts with respect to the prejudice to an objecting creditor's interests is uncertain. Some courts apply an objective standard that examines the adverse economic impact of consolidation. *See In re* Steury, 94 B.R. 553 (Bankr. N.D. Ind. 1988). Other courts have applied a subjective standard that examines the creditor's subjective expectations at the time the credit was extended (*i.e.*, that the creditor looked solely to the credit of a single debtor). *See In re* Donut Queen, Ltd., 41 B.R. 706, 711 (Bankr. E.D.N.Y. 1984).

70. *See, e.g., In re* Donut Queen, Ltd., 41 B.R. at 709–711 (factors evaluated within larger context of balancing prejudice resulting from consolidation with prejudice creditor alleges from debtor separateness); *In re* Luth, 28 B.R. 564 (Bankr. D. Idaho 1983) (seven *Vecco* factors used to weigh prejudice of consolidation and prejudice of separation).

71. *See, e.g.,* Holywell Corp. v. Bank of New York, 59 B.R. 340, 347 (S.D. Fla. 1986); *In re* Baker & Getty Fin. Servs., Inc., 78 B.R. 139, 142 (Bankr. N.D. Ohio 1987) (substantive consolidation ordered in light of "extensive and unrestricted commingling of corporate and personal assets").

72. *See, e.g.,* Flora Mir Candy Corp., 432 F.2d 1060, 1062–63 (2d Cir. 1970) (consolidation of corporate debtors denied by court despite affiliate relationship).

73. *See, e.g., In re* Munford, Inc., 115 B.R. 390, 398 (Bankr. N.D. Ga. 1990).

74. *See, e.g., In re* Donut Queen, Ltd., 41 B.R. 706 (Bankr. E.D.N.Y. 1984).

75. 860 F.2d 515 (2d Cir. 1988).

76. *Id.* at 521.
77. *Id.* at 518.
78. *Id.* at 519.
79. *Id.*
80. *Id.*
81. 11 U.S.C. § 362(c). *See supra* note 4.
82. Pursuant to the provisions of Section 544(a) of the Bankruptcy Code, the trustee in bankruptcy is given the power to avoid liens that are not properly perfected under applicable state law. 11 U.S.C. § 544(a). Section 544(a) of the Bankruptcy Code provides in full as follows:

> (a) The trustee shall have, as of the commencement of the case, and without regard to any knowledge of the trustee or of any creditor, the rights and powers of, or may avoid any transfer of property of the debtor or any obligation incurred by the debtor that is voidable by—
>
> (1) a creditor that extends credit to the debtor at the time of the commencement of the case, and that obtains, at such time and with respect to such credit, a judicial lien on all property on which a creditor on a simple contract could have obtained such a judicial lien, whether or not such a creditor exists;
>
> (2) a creditor that extends credit to the debtor at the time of the commencement of the case, and obtains, at such time and with respect to such credit, an execution against the debtor that is returned unsatisfied at such time, whether or not such a creditor exists; or
>
> (3) a bona fide purchaser of real property, other than fixtures, from the debtor, against whom applicable law permits such transfer to be perfected, that obtains the status of a bona fide purchaser and has perfected such transfer at the time of the commencement of the case, whether or not such a purchaser exists.

83. 11 U.S.C. § 547(b). *See supra* note 5.
84. 11 U.S.C. § 363.
85. A more thorough discussion of these issues in the context of receivables is contained in Robert D. Aicher and William J. Fellerhoff, *Characterization of a Transfer of Receivables as a Sale or a Secured Loan upon Bankruptcy of the Transferor,* 65 AM. BANKR. L.J. 181 (1991). *See also* Steven L. Schwartz, *The Parts Are Greater Than the Whole: How Securitization of Divisible Interests Can Revolutionize Structured Finance and Open the Capital Markets to Middle-Market Companies,* COLUM. BUS. L. REV. 139 (1993), and Jason H. P. Kravitt, ed., SECURITIZATION OF FINANCIAL ASSETS, ch. 5, § 5.93 (Prentice Hall Law & Business 1991, 1993-1 Supp.).
86. *See infra* notes 94–98 and accompanying text.
87. *See infra* notes 99–101 and accompanying text.
88. *See infra* notes 102–107 and accompanying text.
89. *See, e.g.,* Mid-Atlantic Supply, Inc. v. Three Rivers Aluminum Co. (*In re* Mid Atlantic Supply Co.), 790 F.2d 1121, 1123 (4th Cir. 1986) (failure to investigate credit of account debtor indicative of loan); Bear v. Coben (*In re* Golden Plan of Calif., Inc.), 829 F.2d 705, 710 n. 6 (9th Cir. 1986) (failure of mortgage participation investors to conduct independent credit investigation concerning underlying purchased loans suggestive of a loan).
90. Several decisions have held that overcollateralization, with a right in the seller of the assets to retain collections above a predetermined amount, is evidence of a loan rather than a sale. *See, e.g.,* Dewhirst v. Citibank (Arizona) (*In re* Contractors Equip. Supply Co.), 861 F.2d 241, 245 (9th Cir. 1988); Levin v. City Trust Co. (*In re* Joseph Kanner Hat Co.), 482 F.2d 937, 940 (2d Cir. 1973); Hasset v. Sprague Elec. Co. (*In re* O.P.M. Leasing Servs., Inc.), 30 B.R. 642, 646–48 (Bankr. S.D.N.Y. 1983); *In re* Evergreen Valley

Resort, Inc., 23 B.R. 659, 661 (Bankr. D. Me. 1982); First Nat'l Bank v. Hurricane Elkhorn Coal Corp. II (*In re* Hurricane Elkhorn Coal Corp. II), 19 B.R. 609, 617 (Bankr. W.D. Ky. 1982); Gold Coast Leasing Co. v. California Carrots, Inc., 93 Cal. App. 3d 274, 278, 155 Cal. Rptr. 511, 514 (1979); England v. Indus. Comm'n (*In re* Visiting Home Servs., Inc.), 643 F.2d 1356, 1359 (9th Cir. 1981).

91. Several decisions have found the presence of an option to repurchase assets in favor of the seller as indicative of a loan. *See, e.g.,* Levin v. City Trust Co. (*In re* Joseph Kanner Hat Co.), 482 F.2d at 940; *see* Malone v. Celeron Oil & Gas Co. (*In re* Currie), 57 B.R. 224, 225 (Bankr. M.D. La. 1986); *In re* Evergreen Valley Resort, Inc., 23 B.R. at 661.

92. *See, e.g.,* Major's Furniture Mart, Inc. v. Castle Credit Corp., 602 F.2d 538, 546 (3d Cir. 1979) (seller's ability to unilaterally alter pricing terms indicative of a loan).

93. *See* infra notes 108–110 and accompanying text.

94. *See Major's Furniture Mart, Inc.,* 602 F.2d at 544–46 (repurchase obligation of seller upon default on underlying mortgages). *See also* Dewhirst v. Citibank (Arizona) (*In re* Contractors Equip. Supply Co.), 861 F.2d 241, 245 (9th Cir. 1988) (failure by buyer to extinguish existing obligation of seller in connection with sale of receivables indicative of loan); Fireman's Fund Insurance Cos. v. Grover (*In re* Woodson Co.), 813 F.2d 266, 271 (9th Cir. 1987) (seller's purchase of insurance policy to insure purchasers of assets against loss evidence of loan); Castle Rock Indus. Bank v. S.O.A.W. Enters. (*In re* S.O.A.W. Enters.), 32 B.R. 279, 282–83 (Bankr. W.D. Tex. 1983) (guarantee of "sale" of participation by seller indicative of a loan).

95. *See Major's Furniture Mart, Inc.,* 602 F.2d at 545; People v. Serv. Inst. Inc., 101 Misc. 2d 549, 421 N.Y.S.2d 325, 327 (Sup. Ct. 1979); U.C.C. § 9-502 comment 4 (1990). *But see* GRANT GILMORE, 2 SECURITY INTERESTS IN PERSONAL PROPERTY § 44.4, at 1230 (1965) ("If there is a right to charge back uncollectible accounts . . . or a right to claim a deficiency, then the transaction should be held to be for security [rather than a sale]").

96. *See, e.g.,* Bear v. Coben, 829 F.2d at 710.

97. 1990 Bankr. LEXIS 2453 (Bankr. S.D. Ohio Nov. 21, 1990).

98. *Id.* at *5.

99. *See, e.g.,* Southern Rock, Inc. v. B&B Auto Supply, 711 F.2d 683, 685 (5th Cir. 1983); Petron Trading Co. v. Hydrocarbon Trading & Transport Co., 663 F. Supp. 1153, 1159 (E.D. Pa. 1986).

100. *See, e.g.,* Petron Trading Co., 663 F. Supp. at 1153. *See also* Ables v. Major Funding Corp. (*In re* Major Funding Corp.), 82 B.R. 443, 448 (Bankr. S.D. Tex. 1987).

101. *See* Bear v. Coben, 829 F.2d at 707, 709.

102. The tax treatment of these transactions is the subject of extensive discussion in Chapter 5 of this book and is not repeated here.

103. REPORTING BY TRANSFERORS FOR TRANSFERS OF RECEIVABLES WITH RECOURSE, Statement of Financial Accounting Standards No. 77 (Fin. Accounting Standards Bd. 1983).

104. *Id.* § 5. Section 5 of FASB 77 provides in full as follows:

> A transfer of receivables with recourse shall be recognized as a sale if all of the following conditions are met:
>
> (a) *The transferor surrenders control of the future economic benefits embodied in the receivables.* Control has not been surrendered if the transferor has an option to repurchase the receivables at a later date.
>
> (b) *The transferor's obligation under the recourse provisions can be reasonably estimated.* Lack of experience with receivables with characteristics similar to those being transferred or other factors that affect a determination at the transfer date of the collectability of the receivables may impair the ability to make a

reasonable estimate of the probable bad debt losses and related costs of collections and repossessions. A transfer of receivables shall not be recognized as a sale if collectability of the receivables and related costs of collection and repossession are not subject to reasonable estimation.

(c) *The transferee cannot require the transferor to repurchase the receivables except pursuant to the recourse provisions.*

105. *Id.*

106. *See* REPORTS OF CONDITION AND INCOME REVISION OF THE INSTRUCTION FOR THE TREATMENT OF SALES OF ASSETS (Federal Financial Institutions Examination Council Oct. 28, 1985).

107. *Id.*, Insert to Glossary, at A-32.

108. *See* Bear v. Coben (*In re* Golden Plan of Calif., Inc.), 829 F.2d 705, 709, 710 n.3 (9th Cir. 1986) (provision in assignment agreement *"without recourse"* suggests sale where other countervailing factors are not present); Goldstein v. Madison Nat'l Bank, 89 B.R. 274, 277 (D.D.C. 1988) ("orders, assigns, transfers and sets over" language supported sale treatment); *In re* First City Mortgage Co., 69 B.R. 765, 767–68 (Bankr. N.D. Tex. 1987) (language in document coupled with preexisting debtor-creditor relationship indicated loan); Lyon v. Ty-Wood Corp., 212 Pa. Super. 69, 239 A.2d 819, 821 (1968) (absolute conveyance language was dispositive).

109. Hatoff v. Lemons & Assocs. (*In re* Lemons & Assocs.), 67 B.R. 198, 209–10 (Bankr. D. Nev. 1986).

110. *See* Major's Furniture Mart, Inc. v. Castle Credit Corp., 602 F.2d 538, 545 (3d Cir. 1979) ("it is more important what parties actually do than what they say they do"); First Nat'l Bank v. Hurricane Elkhorn Coal Corp. II (*In re* Hurricane Elkhorn Coal Corp. II), 19 B.R. 609, 616 (Bankr. W.D. Ky. 1982); Annotation, *When Transfer of Accounts or Other Choses in Action Is Deemed a Sale Rather Than a Pledge as Security for a Loan, and Vice Versa,* 95 A.L.R. 1197 (1935) ("[t]he courts will generally determine the intention of the parties, and the nature of the transaction, by reference not to what they called it, but to what they in fact meant to and did effect").

111. A municipal counterparty may, however, be relying on the cash flow from the swap and may therefore establish its annual appropriations in reliance thereon. Accordingly, any disruption in the payments it receives under the swap may potentially disrupt its fiscal planning.

112. The ISDA master agreement with the attached form of U.S. Municipal Counterparty Schedule is reproduced at the end of this chapter as Appendix 8A.

113. *See* master agreement at 2.

114. *See* master agreement at 2.

115. *See* Sections 6(e)(i) and (ii) of the master agreement on pages 7 and 8 of the master agreement.

116. *See* master agreement at 6.

117. *See* master agreement at 4.

118. *See* Section 6(a) of the master agreement on page 6 of the master agreement.

119. The insolvency events that trigger automatic termination upon the occurrence thereof are those specified in Sections 5(a)(vii)(1), (3), (5), (6) and, to the extent analogous thereto, (8).

120. The insolvency events that trigger automatic termination effective immediately preceding such relevant proceeding or the presentation of the relevant petition are those specified in Section 5(a)(vii)(4) and, to the extent analogous thereto, (8).

121. 12 U.S.C. § 1811 *et seq.*

122. Financial Institutions Reform, Recovery and Enforcement Act of 1989, Pub. L. No. 101-73, 103 Stat. 183. FIRREA is codified in various sections of Title 12 of the U.S. Code. For purposes of this chapter, provisions of FIRREA will be cited to the applicable sections of Title 12.

123. These entities would appear to include for all relevant purposes broker dealers subject to the jurisdiction of the Securities Investor Protection Corporation (SIPC) under the Securities Investor Protection Act of 1970 (SIPA). 15 U.S.C. §78aaa *et seq.* SIPC membership is mandatory for all persons registered as brokers and dealers under Section 15(b) of the Securities Exchange Act of 1934. 15 U.S.C. §78ccc(a)(2)(A). If SIPC determines that one of its members is in danger of failing to meet its obligations to customers, it may file an application for a protective decree, which the court must grant if it finds that the broker or dealer is insolvent, is the subject of bankruptcy or similar proceedings, or is unable to meet certain requirements of federal securities laws. 15 U.S.C. §78eee.

After the court issues a protective decree, a court-appointed trustee begins liquidation of the debtor broker or dealer. The SIPA liquidation proceeding is conducted in accordance with the rules established under the Bankruptcy Code, except where such rules are inconsistent with SIPA. 15 U.S.C. §78fff(b). Because SIPA is concerned with the protection of the debtor's customers, its provisions primarily deal with customers' claims, while other claims are handled under the Bankruptcy Code. Any property remaining after distribution pursuant to SIPA becomes a part of the general estate of the debtor and is distributed pursuant to the Bankruptcy Code. 15 U.S.C. §78fff-2(c). In addition, transactions and property not covered by SIPA are governed by the provisions of the Bankruptcy Code.

It does not appear that SIPA's liquidation procedures apply to interest rate swaps in which the debtor was a participant. SIPA covers only transactions between the debtor and its customers or transactions between the debtor and other brokers or dealers involving the purchase or sale of securities. A customer is any person "who has a claim on account of securities received, acquired, or held by the debtor in the ordinary course of its business as a broker or dealer from or for the securities accounts of such person for safekeeping, with a view to sale, to cover consummated sales, pursuant to purchases, as collateral security, or for purposes of effecting transfer." 15 U.S.C. §78lll(2). The debtor, as holder of an interest rate swap, is not holding the interest rate swap on behalf of the other party to the swap for any of these purposes listed in the statute.

Furthermore, an interest rate swap must be characterized by SIPA as a security for the act to apply; SIPA's definition of a security does not specifically include an interest rate swap, and excludes unregistered "investment contracts." 15 U.S.C. §78lll(14). Although the issue has not been litigated to date, because an interest rate swap does not appear to be considered a security under SIPA, and because the relationship between the parties to a swap does not appear to be a customer relationship as defined by SIPA, interest rate swap transactions appear to fall outside the scope of SIPA and should be covered under the Bankruptcy Code. Nevertheless, the wording of the standard SIPC protective order is quite broad and could arguably be read to stay actions that would otherwise be taken by swap counterparties to enforce their rights against brokers and dealers subject to the jurisdiction of SIPC. Because of the lack of case law and the broadness of the protective order, caution is recommended in these situations.

124. 11 U.S.C. §362(a). *See supra* note 4 and accompanying text.

125. *Id.*

126. 11 U.S.C. §365.

127. 11 U.S.C. §365(a). Section 365(a) of the Bankruptcy Code provides:

> (a) Except as provided in sections 765 and 766 of this title and in subsections (b),

(c), and (d) of this section, the trustee, subject to the court's approval, may assume or reject any executory contract or unexpired lease of the debtor.

128. The Bankruptcy Code does not define the term "executory contract." The test that is applied by most courts is that articulated by Professor Vern Countryman in *Executory Contracts in Bankruptcy; Part I,* 57 MINN. L. REV. 439, 460 (1973), which provides that an executory contract is:

> a contract under which the obligations of both the bankrupt and the other party are so far unperformed that the failure of either to complete performance would constitute a material breach excusing the performance of the other.

129. Schuyler K. Henderson, *Termination of Swaps Under U.S. Insolvency Laws,* INT'L FIN. L. REV. 17, 19 (Dec. 1984).

In order for a contract to be assumed or rejected in the discretion of the trustee, the bankruptcy court had to determine that it was not "a contract to make a loan, or extend other debt financing or financial accommodations, to or for the benefit of the debtor." 11 U.S.C. § 365(c)(2). If a court found a swap agreement to be a loan or financial accommodation, the debtor would have been prohibited from assuming the swap under Section 365(c)(2). It is uncertain whether a swap would have been found to be a loan or financial accommodation with the meaning of Section 365. The legislative history of the Code suggests that the drafters intended to include only "normal financing transactions and not other commercial arrangements that provide for payments to be made over time." *Cunningham and Rogers,* 689 PLI/Corp at 565. Further, because a standard swap involves only an exchange of payments on a notional principal amount, it could be argued that a swap did not qualify as a loan or financial accommodation because financing was not being extended to any party. *Id.* However, given the fact that a similar financial instrument—a repurchase agreement (a "repo")—has been determined to be a loan, it could also be argued that a swap agreement qualified as a loan. In the 1982 bench decision of the Southern District of New York in *In re* Lombard-Wall, Inc., No. 82-B-11556 (Bankr. S.D.N.Y. Sept. 14, 1982), a purchaser bought debt securities from a seller who agreed to repurchase the securities at a later date. Although the parties to the repos attempted to structure them as separate purchases and sales, the court ruled that a repo was a secured loan for bankruptcy purposes. Despite the similarities between repos and swaps, however, it should be noted that the repo's characterization as a loan may have been based on the fact that the repo purchaser in Lombard-Wall was not entitled to possession of the underlying securities and had no right to deal with them during the term of the agreement. *See In re* Bevill, Bresler & Schuman Asset Management Corp., 67 B.R. 557, 584 (D.N.J. 1986). Because there was not much case law that was helpful in determining whether a swap constituted a loan or a financial accommodation, the characterization of a swap would have been left to the discretion of the bankruptcy court. It has been suggested that a court probably would have determined that a swap did not constitute a loan or financial accommodation, as such a finding would result in the automatic termination of the swap. *See* Henderson, at 19. By allowing the trustee to assume swaps valuable to the debtor and to reject those that were disadvantageous, the court could enhance the debtor's equity.

If a swap agreement would have been determined to be a loan or financial obligation, the swap would not have been capable of assumption, entitling the solvent party to seek relief from the automatic stay in order to terminate the swap agreement. 11 U.S.C. § 365(c)(2). If, however, the swap was not characterized as a loan or financial obligation, the trustee would have had the right to decide whether to assume or reject the agreement. 11 U.S.C. § 365(d).

130. 11 U.S.C. § 365(e).

131. 11 U.S.C. § 365.

132. *Id.*

133. Act of June 25, 1990, Pub. L. No. 101-311, 104 Stat. 267 ("An Act to Amend Title 11 of the United States Code Regarding Swap Agreements and Forward Contracts"). The Amendments became effective on June 25, 1990.

134. H.R. REP. NO. 484, 101st Cong., 2d. Sess. 1 (1990).

135. *Id.* at 2.

136. 11 U.S.C. § 101(55)

137. 11 U.S.C. § 101(56).

138. 11 U.S.C. § 362(b)(14).

139. H.R. REP. NO. 484, *supra* note 134, at 5.

140. *Id.*

141. 11 U.S.C. § 546(g).

142. *Id.*

143. 11 U.S.C. § 548(d)(2).

144. 11 U.S.C. § 548.

145. 11 U.S.C. § 548(d)(2).

146. 11 U.S.C. § 553. *See supra* note 138 and accompanying text.

147. 11 U.S.C. § 553(b)(1).

148. H.R. REP. NO. 484, *supra* note 134 at 5.

149. *See supra* note 138 and accompanying text.

150. 11 U.S.C. § 560.

151. H.R. REP. NO. 484, *supra* note 134 at 5.

152. *Id.* at 6.

153. *Id.* at 5–6.

154. 11 U.S.C. § 546(g). *See supra* notes 141 and 142 and accompanying text.

155. 11 U.S.C. § 901.

156. 11 U.S.C. §§ 109(b)(2), 109(d).

157. Congress has created a new federal entity, the Resolution Trust Corporation (RTC), to administer the insolvencies of thrift institutions that were insured by the now-abolished Federal Savings and Loan Insurance Corporation (FSLIC) and that (1) had already failed and been placed under the control of the FSLIC as of August 9, 1989, or (2) fail between August 9, 1989, and August 9, 1992. 12 U.S.C. § 1441a(b)(3)(A). The FSLIC, before its demise, provided deposit insurance to all federally chartered, and many state chartered, savings and loan associations, as well as many federal and state savings banks. The FDIC will succeed to the RTC's power to administer insolvencies involving these types of insured institutions that occur after September 30, 1993. 12 U.S.C. § 1821(c).

158. Generally, the appointment of a conservator for an insolvent bank contemplates the continued operation, and possible rehabilitation, of the bank and is, in theory, analogous to a reorganization proceeding in bankruptcy. The appointment of a receiver, on the other hand, contemplates the liquidation of the bank's assets and payment to creditors. In recent practice, the FDIC has not used the conservatorship device in administering bank insolvencies, opting instead to liquidate through a receivership, usually after arranging for a purchase of certain assets and assumption of certain liabilities by a solvency institution. Other assets and liabilities remain in the receivership estate. FIRREA further confuses matters by defining the term "receiver" to include a conservator. 12 U.S.C. § 1813(j). There are some provisions in FIRREA that clearly distinguish between the FDIC's powers as conservator as opposed to receiver, and, presumably, those distinctions will be given effect notwithstanding the definition of receiver.

159. 12 U.S.C. §§ 191, 203, 1821(c)(2)(A).

160. 12 U.S.C. § 1821(c)(3)(A), (c)(4), (c)(9), (c)(10).

161. This section of the chapter will discuss, in general terms, the options most recently used by the FDIC in administering insolvencies—straight liquidation and depositor payoff, or an assisted purchase and assumption transaction (P&A). For a more detailed discussion of these options, and various permutations of these forms of insolvency resolution, *see* Office of the Comptroller of the Currency, Examining Circular 246, *Accounting for Failed Bank Acquisitions,* at [Current] Fed. Banking L. Rep. (CCH) ¶ 70,351 (Aug. 1, 1989); Letter from Valerie J. Best, FDIC Counsel, 1991 FDIC Interp. Ltr. LEXIS 21 (Feb. 5, 1991). *See generally* Robert W. Norcross, Jr. *The Bank Insolvency Game: FDIC Superpowers, the* D'Oench *Doctrine, and Federal Common Law,* 103 BANKING L.J. 316, 318–24 (1986).

162. 12 U.S. C. §§ 1821(a), 1823(c), 1823(d).

163. 12 U.S.C. § 1821(e)(12)(A).

164. *See* 12 U.S.C. § 1821(n)(1). The bridge bank has, with some limitations, all corporate powers of a national bank. 12 U.S.C. § 1821(n)(4). The FDIC controls the operation of the bridge bank by virtue of its ability to appoint all directors. *See* 12 U.S.C. § 1821(n)(1)(D). *See also* 12 U.S.C. § 1821(n)(4)(k) (bridge bank may not transfer assets or liabilities without prior approval of FDIC).

165. The FDIC's ability to transfer assets and liabilities, including control rights, to a bridge bank and then out of the bridge bank as a P&A, appears virtually unfettered. *See* 12 U.S.C. §§ 1821(n)(1)(B), 1821(n)(3).

166. 12 U.S.C. § 1821(e)(8)(D)(i).

167. 12 U.S.C. § 1821(e)(8).

168. *Id.*

169. FDIC Statement of Policy on Qualified Financial Contracts (Dec. 12, 1989), at 6–7 (hereinafter QFC Statement). Copies of this statement of policy are available from the FDIC. *See* Notice of Availability, 55 Fed. Reg. 7027 (Feb. 28, 1990).

170. *Id.*; 12 U.S.C. § 1821(e)(9).

171. QFC Statement, *supra* note 169. In contrast to a proceeding under the Bankruptcy Code, no automatic stay applies in a bank insolvency proceeding.

172. *See generally* 12 U.S.C. §§ 1821(d)(3), (d)(5).

173. *See* Letter of John L. Douglas, FDIC General Counsel, to Frances Bermanzohn (Dec. 15, 1989), *reprinted in Counselling Creditors of Banks and Thrifts,* at 285 (PLI Course Handbook No. 561) (hereinafter Douglas Letter).

174. 12 U.S.C. § 1821(e)(1) (repudiation power).

175. 12 U.S.C. § 1821(e)(3)(C).

176. *See* Douglas Letter, *supra* note 173.

177. 12 U.S.C. § 1821(d)(13)(C).

178. 12 U.S.C. § 1821(d)(12).

179. 12 U.S.C. § 1821(d)(11), as enacted in Section 3001 of the Omnibus Budget Reconciliation Act of 1993, Pub. L. No. 103-66, 107 Stat. 336, 337 (enacted Aug. 10, 1993).

180. 12 U.S.C. § 194; Converse Rubber Co. v. Boston-Continental Nat'l Bank, 12 F. Supp. 887 (D. Mass. 1935).

181. These states are: Alaska, California, Colorado, Georgia, Hawaii, Idaho, Indiana, Iowa, Kansas, Louisiana, Missouri, Nebraska, New Mexico (only to the extent of $100 for each depositor), North Dakota, Oklahoma, Oregon, South Dakota, Tennessee ($10 per depositor), Texas, Utah, Virginia, and West Virginia.

182. *See supra* note 168 and accompanying text.

183. FIRREA protects, in a conservatorship situation, a contracting party's rights to exercise termination, liquidation, or acceleration clauses in QFCs where a default has

occurred under such QFC that is enforceable under applicable noninsolvency law. 12 U.S.C. § 1821(e)(8)(E). This provision, however, is explicitly made subject to paragraph 12 of Section 1821(e), which is the provision permitting the FDIC to enforce contracts notwithstanding ipso facto provisions. Accordingly, in a conservatorship, mere insolvency is not enough to permit a party to terminate or accelerate.

184. The "all-or-none" transfer rule, unlike the time limitations imposed upon the FDIC receiver, does provide a real benefit to QFC creditors. Absent the all-or-none rule, the FDIC could select for transfer those QFCs on which the counterparty owes money, while retaining in the receivership (and repudiating) those on which the bank owed money. The claims for repudiation may very well prove worthless, especially in light of depositor preference laws, if applicable. See *supra* notes 179 and 180 and accompanying text. The all-or-none rule permits a counterparty to calculate its "net" position on all QFCs (offsetting amounts owed against amounts due it) and rely on a calculation of net QFC exposure, regardless of the insolvency of its bank counterparty or the transfer of its QFCs out of that bank.

185. A federal statutory provision enacted in late 1991, after FIRREA and the QFC statement, arguably could be viewed to override or modify the application of the QFC statement on certain of the points discussed in the text. That provision, contained as Sections 401–407 of the Federal Deposit Insurance Corporation Act of 1991 (FDICIA), requires that "notwithstanding any other provision of law," obligations owed under "netting contracts" between "financial institutions" (which term includes insured banks) shall be netted "in accordance with, and subject to the conditions of, the terms of any applicable netting contract." It appears that the typical master swap agreement would be a "netting contract" subject to these provisions. Although the issue is not free from doubt, these provisions of FDICIA may override FIRREA's provisions concerning a swap counterparty's limited liability to liquidate and "close out" its positions under a master agreement. The FDIC, however, has not to date modified or recanted any of the provisions of its QFC statement in light of these provisions, and hence the effect of these provisions in a bank insolvency remains unclear.

186. 12 U.S.C. § 1821(e)(11).

187. *See* Batson, Douglas, Brown & Connolly, *The Management and Liquidation of Financial Institutions Under the Financial Institutions Reform, Recovery and Enforcement Act of 1989*, in *The Closing of a Bank or Thrift: The Law of FDIC/RTC Conservatorships and Receiverships*, at 3-15, 3-21 (presented at ABA Seminar, Wash. D.C. (June 6–7, 1991)); Robert W. Norcross, Jr., *A Comparison of Similar Provisions in Titles 11 and 12*, in RESOLUTION TRUST CORPORATION—BANKRUPTCIES, LIQUIDATIONS, AND SALES OF ASSETS, at 191, 200–01 (PLI Course Handbook No. 553 (1990)).

188. 12 U.S.C. § 1821(e)(8)(C)(i).

189. 12 U.S.C. § 1821(e)(8)(C)(ii).

190. 12 U.S.C. § 1823(e)(4).

191. 12 U.S.C. § 1821(d)(9).

192. 12 U.S.C. § 1823(e).

193. 315 U.S. 447 (1942).

194. *D'Oench*, 315 U.S. at 460. *See* Steven A. Weiss & Kenneth E. Kraus, D'Oench *Protection for Private Institutions Assisting the FDIC: A Necessary Component of the Thrift and Bank Bailout*, 108 BANKING L.J. 256, 262–64 (1991).

195. FDIC v. Merchants Nat'l Bank, 725 F.2d 634, 638 (11th Cir.), *cert. denied*, 469 U.S. 829 (1984); Beighley v. FDIC, 676 F. Supp. 130, 132 (N.D. Tex. 1987), *aff'd*, 868 F.2d 776 (5th Cir. 1989). This chapter does not address the myriad applications of *D'Oench* and

Section 13(e) by the FDIC to defeat defenses and counterclaims asserted by a bank's debtors in order to offset or defeat the FDIC's recovery on loans owed to the bank. These issues are addressed in more detail in Weiss & Kraus, *supra* note 192, at 262–69. The focus of this article is on risks to contract creditors of banks. These creditors, nonetheless, should be aware that *D'Oench* and, especially, Section 13(e) may be applied to defeat their claims against a receivership.

196. QFC Statement, *supra* note 169, at 3–5.

APPENDIX 8A

(Local Currency—Single Jurisdiction)

ISDA®

International Swap Dealers Association, Inc.

MASTER AGREEMENT

dated as of ....

.... and ....

have entered and/or anticipate entering into one or more transactions (each a "Transaction") that are or will be governed by this Master Agreement, which includes the schedule (the "Schedule"), and the documents and other confirming evidence (each a "Confirmation") exchanged between the parties confirming those Transactions.

Accordingly, the parties agree as follows:—

1. Interpretation

(a) ***Definitions***. The terms defined in Section 12 and in the Schedule will have the meanings therein specified for the purpose of this Master Agreement.

(b) ***Inconsistency***. In the event of any inconsistency between the provisions of the Schedule and the other provisions of this Master Agreement, the Schedule will prevail. In the event of any inconsistency between the provisions of any Confirmation and this Master Agreement (including the Schedule), such Confirmation will prevail for the purpose of the relevant Transaction.

(c) ***Single Agreement***. All Transactions are entered into in reliance on the fact that this Master Agreement and all Confirmations form a single agreement between the parties (collectively referred to as this "Agreement"), and the parties would not otherwise enter into any Transactions.

2. Obligations

(a) ***General Conditions***.

(i) Each party will make each payment or delivery specified in each Confirmation to be made by it, subject to the other provisions of this Agreement.

(ii) Payments under this Agreement will be made on the due date for value on that date in the place of the account specified in the relevant Confirmation or otherwise pursuant to this Agreement, in freely transferable funds and in the manner customary for payments in the required currency. Where settlement is by delivery (that is, other than by payment), such delivery will be made for receipt on the due date in the manner customary for the relevant obligation unless otherwise specified in the relevant Confirmation or elsewhere in this Agreement.

(iii) Each obligation of each party under Section 2(a)(i) is subject to (1) the condition precedent that no Event of Default or Potential Event of Default with respect to the other party has occurred and is continuing, (2) the condition precedent that no Early Termination Date in respect of the relevant Transaction has occurred or been effectively designated and (3) each other applicable condition precedent specified in this Agreement.

(b) ***Change of Account.*** Either party may change its account for receiving a payment or delivery by giving notice to the other party at least five Local Business Days prior to the scheduled date for the payment or delivery to which such change applies unless such other party gives timely notice of a reasonable objection to such change.

(c) ***Netting.*** If on any date amounts would otherwise be payable:—

(i) in the same currency; and

(ii) in respect of the same Transaction,

by each party to the other, then, on such date, each party's obligation to make payment of any such amount will be automatically satisfied and discharged and, if the aggregate amount that would otherwise have been payable by one party exceeds the aggregate amount that would otherwise have been payable by the other party, replaced by an obligation upon the party by whom the larger aggregate amount would have been payable to pay to the other party the excess of the larger aggregate amount over the smaller aggregate amount.

The parties may elect in respect of two or more Transactions that a net amount will be determined in respect of all amounts payable on the same date in the same currency in respect of such Transactions, regardless of whether such amounts are payable in respect of the same Transaction. The election may be made in the Schedule or a Confirmation by specifying that subparagraph (ii) above will not apply to the Transactions identified as being subject to the election, together with the starting date (in which case subparagraph (ii) above will not, or will cease to, apply to such Transactions from such date). This election may be made separately for different groups of Transactions and will apply separately to each pairing of branches or offices through which the parties make and receive payments or deliveries.

(d) ***Default Interest; Other Amounts.*** Prior to the occurrence or effective designation of an Early Termination Date in respect of the relevant Transaction, a party that defaults in the performance of any payment obligation will, to the extent permitted by law and subject to Section 6(c), be required to pay interest (before as well as after judgment) on the overdue amount to the other party on demand in the same currency as such overdue amount, for the period from (and including) the original due date for payment to (but excluding) the date of actual payment, at the Default Rate. Such interest will be calculated on the basis of daily compounding and the actual number of days elapsed. If, prior to the occurrence or effective designation of an Early Termination Date in respect of the relevant Transaction, a party defaults in the performance of any obligation required to be settled by delivery, it will compensate the other party on demand if and to the extent provided for in the relevant Confirmation or elsewhere in this Agreement.

3. Representations

Each party represents to the other party (which representations will be deemed to be repeated by each party on each date on which a Transaction is entered into) that:—

(a) ***Basic Representations.***

(i) ***Status.*** It is duly organised and validly existing under the laws of the jurisdiction of its organisation or incorporation and, if relevant under such laws, in good standing;

(ii) ***Powers.*** It has the power to execute this Agreement and any other documentation relating to this Agreement to which it is a party, to deliver this Agreement and any other documentation relating to this Agreement that it is required by this Agreement to deliver and to perform its obligations under this Agreement and any obligations it has under any Credit Support Document to which it is a party and has taken all necessary action to authorise such execution, delivery and performance;

(iii) ***No Violation or Conflict.*** Such execution, delivery and performance do not violate or conflict with any law applicable to it, any provision of its constitutional documents, any order or judgment of any court or other agency of government applicable to it or any of its assets or any contractual restriction binding on or affecting it or any of its assets;

(iv) ***Consents***. All governmental and other consents that are required to have been obtained by it with respect to this Agreement or any Credit Support Document to which it is a party have been obtained and are in full force and effect and all conditions of any such consents have been complied with; and

(v) ***Obligations Binding***. Its obligations under this Agreement and any Credit Support Document to which it is a party constitute its legal, valid and binding obligations, enforceable in accordance with their respective terms (subject to applicable bankruptcy, reorganisation, insolvency, moratorium or similar laws affecting creditors' rights generally and subject, as to enforceability, to equitable principles of general application (regardless of whether enforcement is sought in a proceeding in equity or at law)).

(b) ***Absence of Certain Events***. No Event of Default or Potential Event of Default or, to its knowledge, Termination Event with respect to it has occurred and is continuing and no such event or circumstance would occur as a result of its entering into or performing its obligations under this Agreement or any Credit Support Document to which it is a party.

(c) ***Absence of Litigation***. There is not pending or, to its knowledge, threatened against it or any of its Affiliates any action, suit or proceeding at law or in equity or before any court, tribunal, governmental body, agency or official or any arbitrator that is likely to affect the legality, validity or enforceability against it of this Agreement or any Credit Support Document to which it is a party or its ability to perform its obligations under this Agreement or such Credit Support Document.

(d) ***Accuracy of Specified Information***. All applicable information that is furnished in writing by or on behalf of it to the other party and is identified for the purpose of this Section 3(d) in the Schedule is, as of the date of the information, true, accurate and complete in every material respect.

4. Agreements

Each party agrees with the other that, so long as either party has or may have any obligation under this Agreement or under any Credit Support Document to which it is a party:—

(a) ***Furnish Specified Information***. It will deliver to the other party any forms, documents or certificates specified in the Schedule or any Confirmation by the date specified in the Schedule or such Confirmation or, if none is specified, as soon as reasonably practicable.

(b) ***Maintain Authorisations***. It will use all reasonable efforts to maintain in full force and effect all consents of any governmental or other authority that are required to be obtained by it with respect to this Agreement or any Credit Support Document to which it is a party and will use all reasonable efforts to obtain any that may become necessary in the future.

(c) ***Comply with Laws***. It will comply in all material respects with all applicable laws and orders to which it may be subject if failure so to comply would materially impair its ability to perform its obligations under this Agreement or any Credit Support Document to which it is a party.

5. Events of Default and Termination Events

(a) ***Events of Default***. The occurrence at any time with respect to a party or, if applicable, any Credit Support Provider of such party or any Specified Entity of such party of any of the following events constitutes an event of default (an "Event of Default") with respect to such party:—

(i) ***Failure to Pay or Deliver***. Failure by the party to make, when due, any payment under this Agreement or delivery under Section 2(a)(i) or 2(d) required to be made by it if such failure is not remedied on or before the third Local Business Day after notice of such failure is given to the party;

(ii) ***Breach of Agreement***. Failure by the party to comply with or perform any agreement or obligation (other than an obligation to make any payment under this Agreement or delivery under Section 2(a)(i) or 2(d) or to give notice of a Termination Event) to be complied with or performed by the party in accordance with this Agreement if such failure is not remedied on or before the thirtieth day after notice of such failure is given to the party;

(iii) ***Credit Support Default.***

(1) Failure by the party or any Credit Support Provider of such party to comply with or perform any agreement or obligation to be complied with or performed by it in accordance with any Credit Support Document if such failure is continuing after any applicable grace period has elapsed;

(2) the expiration or termination of such Credit Support Document or the failing or ceasing of such Credit Support Document to be in full force and effect for the purpose of this Agreement (in either case other than in accordance with its terms) prior to the satisfaction of all obligations of such party under each Transaction to which such Credit Support Document relates without the written consent of the other party; or

(3) the party or such Credit Support Provider disaffirms, disclaims, repudiates or rejects, in whole or in part, or challenges the validity of, such Credit Support Document;

(iv) ***Misrepresentation.*** A representation made or repeated or deemed to have been made or repeated by the party or any Credit Support Provider of such party in this Agreement or any Credit Support Document proves to have been incorrect or misleading in any material respect when made or repeated or deemed to have been made or repeated;

(v) ***Default under Specified Transaction.*** The party, any Credit Support Provider of such party or any applicable Specified Entity of such party (1) defaults under a Specified Transaction and, after giving effect to any applicable notice requirement or grace period, there occurs a liquidation of, an acceleration of obligations under, or an early termination of, that Specified Transaction, (2) defaults, after giving effect to any applicable notice requirement or grace period, in making any payment or delivery due on the last payment, delivery or exchange date of, or any payment on early termination of, a Specified Transaction (or such default continues for at least three Local Business Days if there is no applicable notice requirement or grace period) or (3) disaffirms, disclaims, repudiates or rejects, in whole or in part, a Specified Transaction (or such action is taken by any person or entity appointed or empowered to operate it or act on its behalf);

(vi) ***Cross Default.*** If "Cross Default" is specified in the Schedule as applying to the party, the occurrence or existence of (1) a default, event of default or other similar condition or event (however described) in respect of such party, any Credit Support Provider of such party or any applicable Specified Entity of such party under one or more agreements or instruments relating to Specified Indebtedness of any of them (individually or collectively) in an aggregate amount of not less than the applicable Threshold Amount (as specified in the Schedule) which has resulted in such Specified Indebtedness becoming, or becoming capable at such time of being declared, due and payable under such agreements or instruments, before it would otherwise have been due and payable or (2) a default by such party, such Credit Support Provider or such Specified Entity (individually or collectively) in making one or more payments on the due date thereof in an aggregate amount of not less than the applicable Threshold Amount under such agreements or instruments (after giving effect to any applicable notice requirement or grace period);

(vii) ***Bankruptcy.*** The party, any Credit Support Provider of such party or any applicable Specified Entity of such party:—

(1) is dissolved (other than pursuant to a consolidation, amalgamation or merger); (2) becomes insolvent or is unable to pay its debts or fails or admits in writing its inability generally to pay its debts as they become due; (3) makes a general assignment, arrangement or composition with or for the benefit of its creditors; (4) institutes or has instituted against it a proceeding seeking a judgment of insolvency or bankruptcy or any other relief under any bankruptcy or insolvency law or other similar law affecting creditors' rights, or a petition is presented for its

winding-up or liquidation, and, in the case of any such proceeding or petition instituted or presented against it, such proceeding or petition (A) results in a judgment of insolvency or bankruptcy or the entry of an order for relief or the making of an order for its winding-up or liquidation or (B) is not dismissed, discharged, stayed or restrained in each case within 30 days of the institution or presentation thereof; (5) has a resolution passed for its winding-up, official management or liquidation (other than pursuant to a consolidation, amalgamation or merger); (6) seeks or becomes subject to the appointment of an administrator, provisional liquidator, conservator, receiver, trustee, custodian or other similar official for it or for all or substantially all its assets; (7) has a secured party take possession of all or substantially all its assets or has a distress, execution, attachment, sequestration or other legal process levied, enforced or sued on or against all or substantially all its assets and such secured party maintains possession, or any such process is not dismissed, discharged, stayed or restrained, in each case within 30 days thereafter; (8) causes or is subject to any event with respect to it which, under the applicable laws of any jurisdiction, has an analogous effect to any of the events specified in clauses (1) to (7) (inclusive); or (9) takes any action in furtherance of, or indicating its consent to, approval of, or acquiescence in, any of the foregoing acts; or

(viii) ***Merger Without Assumption.*** The party or any Credit Support Provider of such party consolidates or amalgamates with, or merges with or into, or transfers all or substantially all its assets to, another entity and, at the time of such consolidation, amalgamation, merger or transfer:—

(1) the resulting, surviving or transferee entity fails to assume all the obligations of such party or such Credit Support Provider under this Agreement or any Credit Support Document to which it or its predecessor was a party by operation of law or pursuant to an agreement reasonably satisfactory to the other party to this Agreement; or

(2) the benefits of any Credit Support Document fail to extend (without the consent of the other party) to the performance by such resulting, surviving or transferee entity of its obligations under this Agreement.

(b) ***Termination Events.*** The occurrence at any time with respect to a party or, if applicable, any Credit Support Provider of such party or any Specified Entity of such party of any event specified below constitutes an Illegality if the event is specified in (i) below, and, if specified to be applicable, a Credit Event Upon Merger if the event is specified pursuant to (ii) below or an Additional Termination Event if the event is specified pursuant to (iii) below:—

(i) ***Illegality.*** Due to the adoption of, or any change in, any applicable law after the date on which a Transaction is entered into, or due to the promulgation of, or any change in, the interpretation by any court, tribunal or regulatory authority with competent jurisdiction of any applicable law after such date, it becomes unlawful (other than as a result of a breach by the party of Section 4(b)) for such party (which will be the Affected Party):—

(1) to perform any absolute or contingent obligation to make a payment or delivery or to receive a payment or delivery in respect of such Transaction or to comply with any other material provision of this Agreement relating to such Transaction; or

(2) to perform, or for any Credit Support Provider of such party to perform, any contingent or other obligation which the party (or such Credit Support Provider) has under any Credit Support Document relating to such Transaction;

(ii) ***Credit Event Upon Merger.*** If "Credit Event Upon Merger" is specified in the Schedule as applying to the party, such party ("X"), any Credit Support Provider of X or any applicable Specified Entity of X consolidates or amalgamates with, or merges with or into, or transfers all or substantially all its assets to, another entity and such action does not constitute an event described in Section 5(a)(viii) but the creditworthiness of the resulting, surviving or transferee entity is materially weaker than that of X, such Credit Support Provider or such Specified Entity, as the case may be, immediately prior to such action (and, in such event, X or its successor or transferee, as appropriate, will be the Affected Party); or

(iii) ***Additional Termination Event.*** If any "Additional Termination Event" is specified in the Schedule or any Confirmation as applying, the occurrence of such event (and, in such event, the Affected Party or Affected Parties shall be as specified for such Additional Termination Event in the Schedule or such Confirmation).

(c) ***Event of Default and Illegality.*** If an event or circumstance which would otherwise constitute or give rise to an Event of Default also constitutes an Illegality, it will be treated as an Illegality and will not constitute an Event of Default.

6. Early Termination

(a) ***Right to Terminate Following Event of Default.*** If at any time an Event of Default with respect to a party (the "Defaulting Party") has occurred and is then continuing, the other party (the "Non-defaulting Party") may, by not more than 20 days notice to the Defaulting Party specifying the relevant Event of Default, designate a day not earlier than the day such notice is effective as an Early Termination Date in respect of all outstanding Transactions. If, however, "Automatic Early Termination" is specified in the Schedule as applying to a party, then an Early Termination Date in respect of all outstanding Transactions will occur immediately upon the occurrence with respect to such party of an Event of Default specified in Section 5(a)(vii)(1), (3), (5), (6) or, to the extent analogous thereto, (8), and as of the time immediately preceding the institution of the relevant proceeding or the presentation of the relevant petition upon the occurrence with respect to such party of an Event of Default specified in Section 5(a)(vii)(4) or, to the extent analogous thereto, (8).

(b) ***Right to Terminate Following Termination Event.***

(i) ***Notice.*** If a Termination Event occurs, an Affected Party will, promptly upon becoming aware of it, notify the other party, specifying the nature of that Termination Event and each Affected Transaction and will also give such other information about that Termination Event as the other party may reasonably require.

(ii) ***Two Affected Parties.*** If an Illegality under Section 5(b)(i)(1) occurs and there are two Affected Parties, each party will use all reasonable efforts to reach agreement within 30 days after notice thereof is given under Section 6(b)(i) on action to avoid that Termination Event.

(iii) ***Right to Terminate.*** If:—

(1) an agreement under Section 6(b)(ii) has not been effected with respect to all Affected Transactions within 30 days after an Affected Party gives notice under Section 6(b)(i); or

(2) an Illegality other than that referred to in Section 6(b)(ii), a Credit Event Upon Merger or an Additional Termination Event occurs,

either party in the case of an Illegality, any Affected Party in the case of an Additional Termination Event if there is more than one Affected Party, or the party which is not the Affected Party in the case of a Credit Event Upon Merger or an Additional Termination Event if there is only one Affected Party may, by not more than 20 days notice to the other party and provided that the relevant Termination Event is then continuing, designate a day not earlier than the day such notice is effective as an Early Termination Date in respect of all Affected Transactions.

(c) ***Effect of Designation.***

(i) If notice designating an Early Termination Date is given under Section 6(a) or (b), the Early Termination Date will occur on the date so designated, whether or not the relevant Event of Default or Termination Event is then continuing.

(ii) Upon the occurrence or effective designation of an Early Termination Date, no further payments or deliveries under Section 2(a)(i) or 2(d) in respect of the Terminated Transactions will be required to be made, but without prejudice to the other provisions of this Agreement. The amount, if any, payable in respect of an Early Termination Date shall be determined pursuant to Section 6(e).

(d) ***Calculations.***

(i) ***Statement.*** On or as soon as reasonably practicable following the occurrence of an Early Termination Date, each party will make the calculations on its part, if any, contemplated by Section 6(e) and will provide to the other party a statement (1) showing, in reasonable detail, such calculations (including all relevant quotations and specifying any amount payable under Section 6(e)) and (2) giving details of the relevant account to which any amount payable to it is to be paid. In the absence of written confirmation from the source of a quotation obtained in determining a Market Quotation, the records of the party obtaining such quotation will be conclusive evidence of the existence and accuracy of such quotation.

(ii) ***Payment Date.*** An amount calculated as being due in respect of any Early Termination Date under Section 6(e) will be payable on the day that notice of the amount payable is effective (in the case of an Early Termination Date which is designated or occurs as a result of an Event of Default) and on the day which is two Local Business Days after the day on which notice of the amount payable is effective (in the case of an Early Termination Date which is designated as a result of a Termination Event). Such amount will be paid together with (to the extent permitted under applicable law) interest thereon (before as well as after judgment), from (and including) the relevant Early Termination Date to (but excluding) the date such amount is paid, at the Applicable Rate. Such interest will be calculated on the basis of daily compounding and the actual number of days elapsed.

(e) ***Payments on Early Termination.*** If an Early Termination Date occurs, the following provisions shall apply based on the parties' election in the Schedule of a payment measure, either "Market Quotation" or "Loss", and a payment method, either the "First Method" or the "Second Method". If the parties fail to designate a payment measure or payment method in the Schedule, it will be deemed that "Market Quotation" or the "Second Method", as the case may be, shall apply. The amount, if any, payable in respect of an Early Termination Date and determined pursuant to this Section will be subject to any Set-off.

(i) ***Events of Default.*** If the Early Termination Date results from an Event of Default:—

(1) *First Method and Market Quotation.* If the First Method and Market Quotation apply, the Defaulting Party will pay to the Non-defaulting Party the excess, if a positive number, of (A) the sum of the Settlement Amount (determined by the Non-defaulting Party) in respect of the Terminated Transactions and the Unpaid Amounts owing to the Non-defaulting Party over (B) the Unpaid Amounts owing to the Defaulting Party.

(2) *First Method and Loss.* If the First Method and Loss apply, the Defaulting Party will pay to the Non-defaulting Party, if a positive number, the Non-defaulting Party's Loss in respect of this Agreement.

(3) *Second Method and Market Quotation.* If the Second Method and Market Quotation apply, an amount will be payable equal to (A) the sum of the Settlement Amount (determined by the Non-defaulting Party) in respect of the Terminated Transactions and the Unpaid Amounts owing to the Non-defaulting Party less (B) the Unpaid Amounts owing to the Defaulting Party. If that amount is a positive number, the Defaulting Party will pay it to the Non-defaulting Party; if it is a negative number, the Non-defaulting Party will pay the absolute value of that amount to the Defaulting Party.

(4) *Second Method and Loss.* If the Second Method and Loss apply, an amount will be payable equal to the Non-defaulting Party's Loss in respect of this Agreement. If that amount is a positive number, the Defaulting Party will pay it to the Non-defaulting Party; if it is a negative

number, the Non-defaulting Party will pay the absolute value of that amount to the Defaulting Party.

(ii) ***Termination Events.*** If the Early Termination Date results from a Termination Event:—

(1) *One Affected Party.* If there is one Affected Party, the amount payable will be determined in accordance with Section 6(e)(i)(3), if Market Quotation applies, or Section 6(e)(i)(4), if Loss applies, except that, in either case, references to the Defaulting Party and to the Non-defaulting Party will be deemed to be references to the Affected Party and the party which is not the Affected Party, respectively, and, if Loss applies and fewer than all the Transactions are being terminated, Loss shall be calculated in respect of all Terminated Transactions.

(2) *Two Affected Parties.* If there are two Affected Parties:—

(A) if Market Quotation applies, each party will determine a Settlement Amount in respect of the Terminated Transactions, and an amount will be payable equal to (I) the sum of (a) one-half of the difference between the Settlement Amount of the party with the higher Settlement Amount ("X") and the Settlement Amount of the party with the lower Settlement Amount ("Y") and (b) the Unpaid Amounts owing to X less (II) the Unpaid Amounts owing to Y; and

(B) if Loss applies, each party will determine its Loss in respect of this Agreement (or, if fewer than all the Transactions are being terminated, in respect of all Terminated Transactions) and an amount will be payable equal to one-half of the difference between the Loss of the party with the higher Loss ("X") and the Loss of the party with the lower Loss ("Y").

If the amount payable is a positive number, Y will pay it to X; if it is a negative number, X will pay the absolute value of that amount to Y.

(iii) ***Adjustment for Bankruptcy.*** In circumstances where an Early Termination Date occurs because "Automatic Early Termination" applies in respect of a party, the amount determined under this Section 6(e) will be subject to such adjustments as are appropriate and permitted by law to reflect any payments or deliveries made by one party to the other under this Agreement (and retained by such other party) during the period from the relevant Early Termination Date to the date for payment determined under Section 6(d)(ii).

(iv) ***Pre-Estimate.*** The parties agree that if Market Quotation applies an amount recoverable under this Section 6(e) is a reasonable pre-estimate of loss and not a penalty. Such amount is payable for the loss of bargain and the loss of protection against future risks and except as otherwise provided in this Agreement neither party will be entitled to recover any additional damages as a consequence of such losses.

7. Transfer

Neither this Agreement nor any interest or obligation in or under this Agreement may be transferred (whether by way of security or otherwise) by either party without the prior written consent of the other party, except that:—

(a) a party may make such a transfer of this Agreement pursuant to a consolidation or amalgamation with, or merger with or into, or transfer of all or substantially all its assets to, another entity (but without prejudice to any other right or remedy under this Agreement); and

(b) a party may make such a transfer of all or any part of its interest in any amount payable to it from a Defaulting Party under Section 6(e).

Any purported transfer that is not in compliance with this Section will be void.

8. Miscellaneous

(a) ***Entire Agreement.*** This Agreement constitutes the entire agreement and understanding of the parties with respect to its subject matter and supersedes all oral communication and prior writings with respect thereto.

(b) ***Amendments.*** No amendment, modification or waiver in respect of this Agreement will be effective unless in writing (including a writing evidenced by a facsimile transmission) and executed by each of the parties or confirmed by an exchange of telexes or electronic messages on an electronic messaging system.

(c) ***Survival of Obligations.*** Without prejudice to Sections 2(a)(iii) and 6(c)(ii), the obligations of the parties under this Agreement will survive the termination of any Transaction.

(d) ***Remedies Cumulative.*** Except as provided in this Agreement, the rights, powers, remedies and privileges provided in this Agreement are cumulative and not exclusive of any rights, powers, remedies and privileges provided by law.

(e) ***Counterparts and Confirmations.***

(i) This Agreement (and each amendment, modification and waiver in respect of it) may be executed and delivered in counterparts (including by facsimile transmission), each of which will be deemed an original.

(ii) The parties intend that they are legally bound by the terms of each Transaction from the moment they agree to those terms (whether orally or otherwise). A Confirmation shall be entered into as soon as practicable and may be executed and delivered in counterparts (including by facsimile transmission) or be created by an exchange of telexes or by an exchange of electronic messages on an electronic messaging system, which in each case will be sufficient for all purposes to evidence a binding supplement to this Agreement. The parties will specify therein or through another effective means that any such counterpart, telex or electronic message constitutes a Confirmation.

(f) ***No Waiver of Rights.*** A failure or delay in exercising any right, power or privilege in respect of this Agreement will not be presumed to operate as a waiver, and a single or partial exercise of any right, power or privilege will not be presumed to preclude any subsequent or further exercise, of that right, power or privilege or the exercise of any other right, power or privilege.

(g) ***Headings.*** The headings used in this Agreement are for convenience of reference only and are not to affect the construction of or to be taken into consideration in interpreting this Agreement.

9. Expenses

A Defaulting Party will, on demand, indemnify and hold harmless the other party for and against all reasonable out-of-pocket expenses, including legal fees, incurred by such other party by reason of the enforcement and protection of its rights under this Agreement or any Credit Support Document to which the Defaulting Party is a party or by reason of the early termination of any Transaction, including, but not limited to, costs of collection.

10. Notices

(a) ***Effectiveness.*** Any notice or other communication in respect of this Agreement may be given in any manner set forth below (except that a notice or other communication under Section 5 or 6 may not be given by facsimile transmission or electronic messaging system) to the address or number or in accordance with the electronic messaging system details provided (see the Schedule) and will be deemed effective as indicated:—

(i) if in writing and delivered in person or by courier, on the date it is delivered;

(ii) if sent by telex, on the date the recipient's answerback is received;

(iii) if sent by facsimile transmission, on the date that transmission is received by a responsible employee of the recipient in legible form (it being agreed that the burden of proving receipt will be on the sender and will not be met by a transmission report generated by the sender's facsimile machine);

(iv) if sent by certified or registered mail (airmail, if overseas) or the equivalent (return receipt requested), on the date that mail is delivered or its delivery is attempted; or

(v) if sent by electronic messaging system, on the date that electronic message is received,

unless the date of that delivery (or attempted delivery) or that receipt, as applicable, is not a Local Business Day or that communication is delivered (or attempted) or received, as applicable, after the close of business on a Local Business Day, in which case that communication shall be deemed given and effective on the first following day that is a Local Business Day.

(b) ***Change of Addresses.*** Either party may by notice to the other change the address, telex or facsimile number or electronic messaging system details at which notices or other communications are to be given to it.

11. Governing Law and Jurisdiction

(a) ***Governing Law.*** This Agreement will be governed by and construed in accordance with the law specified in the Schedule.

(b) ***Jurisdiction.*** With respect to any suit, action or proceedings relating to this Agreement ("Proceedings"), each party irrevocably:—

(i) submits to the jurisdiction of the English courts, if this Agreement is expressed to be governed by English law, or to the non-exclusive jurisdiction of the courts of the State of New York and the United States District Court located in the Borough of Manhattan in New York City, if this Agreement is expressed to be governed by the laws of the State of New York; and

(ii) waives any objection which it may have at any time to the laying of venue of any Proceedings brought in any such court, waives any claim that such Proceedings have been brought in an inconvenient forum and further waives the right to object, with respect to such Proceedings, that such court does not have any jurisdiction over such party.

Nothing in this Agreement precludes either party from bringing Proceedings in any other jurisdiction (outside, if this Agreement is expressed to be governed by English law, the Contracting States, as defined in Section 1(3) of the Civil Jurisdiction and Judgments Act 1982 or any modification, extension or re-enactment thereof for the time being in force) nor will the bringing of Proceedings in any one or more jurisdictions preclude the bringing of Proceedings in any other jurisdiction.

(c) ***Waiver of Immunities.*** Each party irrevocably waives, to the fullest extent permitted by applicable law, with respect to itself and its revenues and assets (irrespective of their use or intended use), all immunity on the grounds of sovereignty or other similar grounds from (i) suit, (ii) jurisdiction of any court, (iii) relief by way of injunction, order for specific performance or for recovery of property, (iv) attachment of its assets (whether before or after judgment) and (v) execution or enforcement of any judgment to which it or its revenues or assets might otherwise be entitled in any Proceedings in the courts of any jurisdiction and irrevocably agrees, to the extent permitted by applicable law, that it will not claim any such immunity in any Proceedings.

12. Definitions

As used in this Agreement:—

"Additional Termination Event" has the meaning specified in Section 5(b).

"Affected Party" has the meaning specified in Section 5(b).

"***Affected Transactions***" means (a) with respect to any Termination Event consisting of an Illegality, all Transactions affected by the occurrence of such Termination Event and (b) with respect to any other Termination Event, all Transactions.

"***Affiliate***" means, subject to the Schedule, in relation to any person, any entity controlled, directly or indirectly, by the person, any entity that controls, directly or indirectly, the person or any entity directly or indirectly under common control with the person. For this purpose, "control" of any entity or person means ownership of a majority of the voting power of the entity or person.

"***Applicable Rate***" means:—

(a) in respect of obligations payable or deliverable (or which would have been but for Section 2(a)(iii)) by a Defaulting Party, the Default Rate;

(b) in respect of an obligation to pay an amount under Section 6(e) of either party from and after the date (determined in accordance with Section 6(d)(ii)) on which that amount is payable, the Default Rate;

(c) in respect of all other obligations payable or deliverable (or which would have been but for Section 2(a)(iii)) by a Non-defaulting Party, the Non-default Rate; and

(d) in all other cases, the Termination Rate.

"***consent***" includes a consent, approval, action, authorisation, exemption, notice, filing, registration or exchange control consent.

"***Credit Event Upon Merger***" has the meaning specified in Section 5(b).

"***Credit Support Document***" means any agreement or instrument that is specified as such in this Agreement.

"***Credit Support Provider***" has the meaning specified in the Schedule.

"***Default Rate***" means a rate per annum equal to the cost (without proof or evidence of any actual cost) to the relevant payee (as certified by it) if it were to fund or of funding the relevant amount plus 1% per annum.

"***Defaulting Party***" has the meaning specified in Section 6(a).

"***Early Termination Date***" means the date determined in accordance with Section 6(a) or 6(b)(iii).

"***Event of Default***" has the meaning specified in Section 5(a) and, if applicable, in the Schedule.

"***Illegality***" has the meaning specified in Section 5(b).

"***law***" includes any treaty, law, rule or regulation and "***lawful***" and "***unlawful***" will be construed accordingly.

"***Local Business Day***" means, subject to the Schedule, a day on which commercial banks are open for business (including dealings in foreign exchange and foreign currency deposits) (a) in relation to any obligation under Section 2(a)(i), in the place(s) specified in the relevant Confirmation or, if not so specified, as otherwise agreed by the parties in writing or determined pursuant to provisions contained, or incorporated by reference, in this Agreement, (b) in relation to any other payment, in the place where the relevant account is located, (c) in relation to any notice or other communication, including notice contemplated under Section 5(a)(i), in the city specified in the address for notice provided by the recipient and, in the case of a notice contemplated by Section 2(b), in the place where the relevant new account is to be located and (d) in relation to Section 5(a)(v)(2), in the relevant locations for performance with respect to such Specified Transaction.

"***Loss***" means, with respect to this Agreement or one or more Terminated Transactions, as the case may be, and a party, an amount that party reasonably determines in good faith to be its total losses and costs (or gain, in which case expressed as a negative number) in connection with this Agreement or that Terminated Transaction or group of Terminated Transactions, as the case may be, including any loss of bargain, cost of funding or, at the election of such party but without duplication, loss or cost incurred as a result of its terminating, liquidating, obtaining or reestablishing any hedge or related trading position (or any gain resulting from any of them). Loss includes losses and costs (or gains) in respect of any payment or delivery required to have been made (assuming satisfaction of each applicable condition precedent) on or before the relevant Early Termination Date and not made, except, so as to avoid duplication, if Section 6(e)(i)(1) or (3) or 6(e)(ii)(2)(A) applies. Loss does not include a party's legal fees and out-of-pocket expenses referred to under Section 9. A party will determine its Loss as of the relevant Early Termination Date, or, if that is not reasonably practicable, as of the earliest date thereafter as is reasonably practicable. A party may (but need not) determine its Loss by reference to quotations of relevant rates or prices from one or more leading dealers in the relevant markets.

"***Market Quotation***" means, with respect to one or more Terminated Transactions and a party making the determination, an amount determined on the basis of quotations from Reference Market-makers. Each quotation will be for an amount, if any, that would be paid to such party (expressed as a negative number) or by such party (expressed as a positive number) in consideration of an agreement between such party (taking into account any existing Credit Support Document with respect to the obligations of such party) and the quoting Reference Market-maker to enter into a transaction (the "Replacement Transaction") that would have the effect of preserving for such party the economic equivalent of any payment or delivery (whether the underlying obligation was absolute or contingent and assuming the satisfaction of each applicable condition precedent) by the parties under Section 2(a)(i) in respect of such Terminated Transaction or group of Terminated Transactions that would, but for the occurrence of the relevant Early Termination Date, have been required after that date. For this purpose, Unpaid Amounts in respect of the Terminated Transaction or group of Terminated Transactions are to be excluded but, without limitation, any payment or delivery that would, but for the relevant Early Termination Date, have been required (assuming satisfaction of each applicable condition precedent) after that Early Termination Date is to be included. The Replacement Transaction would be subject to such documentation as such party and the Reference Market-maker may, in good faith, agree. The party making the determination (or its agent) will request each Reference Market-maker to provide its quotation to the extent reasonably practicable as of the same day and time (without regard to different time zones) on or as soon as reasonably practicable after the relevant Early Termination Date. The day and time as of which those quotations are to be obtained will be selected in good faith by the party obliged to make a determination under Section 6(e), and, if each party is so obliged, after consultation with the other. If more than three quotations are provided, the Market Quotation will be the arithmetic mean of the quotations, without regard to the quotations having the highest and lowest values. If exactly three such quotations are provided, the Market Quotation will be the quotation remaining after disregarding the highest and lowest quotations. For this purpose, if more than one quotation has the same highest value or lowest value, then one of such quotations shall be disregarded. If fewer than three quotations are provided, it will be deemed that the Market Quotation in respect of such Terminated Transaction or group of Terminated Transactions cannot be determined.

"***Non-default Rate***" means a rate per annum equal to the cost (without proof or evidence of any actual cost) to the Non-defaulting Party (as certified by it) if it were to fund the relevant amount.

"***Non-defaulting Party***" has the meaning specified in Section 6(a).

"***Potential Event of Default***" means any event which, with the giving of notice or the lapse of time or both, would constitute an Event of Default.

"***Reference Market-makers***" means four leading dealers in the relevant market selected by the party determining a Market Quotation in good faith (a) from among dealers of the highest credit standing which satisfy all the criteria that such party applies generally at the time in deciding whether to offer or to make an extension of credit and (b) to the extent practicable, from among such dealers having an office in the same city.

"***Scheduled Payment Date***" means a date on which a payment or delivery is to be made under Section 2(a)(i) with respect to a Transaction.

"***Set-off***" means set-off, offset, combination of accounts, right of retention or withholding or similar right or requirement to which the payer of an amount under Section 6 is entitled or subject (whether arising under this Agreement, another contract, applicable law or otherwise) that is exercised by, or imposed on, such payer.

"***Settlement Amount***" means, with respect to a party and any Early Termination Date, the sum of:—

(a) the Market Quotations (whether positive or negative) for each Terminated Transaction or group of Terminated Transactions for which a Market Quotation is determined; and

(b) such party's Loss (whether positive or negative and without reference to any Unpaid Amounts) for each Terminated Transaction or group of Terminated Transactions for which a Market Quotation cannot be determined or would not (in the reasonable belief of the party making the determination) produce a commercially reasonable result.

"***Specified Entity***" has the meaning specified in the Schedule.

"***Specified Indebtedness***" means, subject to the Schedule, any obligation (whether present or future, contingent or otherwise, as principal or surety or otherwise) in respect of borrowed money.

"***Specified Transaction***" means, subject to the Schedule, (a) any transaction (including an agreement with respect thereto) now existing or hereafter entered into between one party to this Agreement (or any Credit Support Provider of such party or any applicable Specified Entity of such party) and the other party to this Agreement (or any Credit Support Provider of such other party or any applicable Specified Entity of such other party) which is a rate swap transaction, basis swap, forward rate transaction, commodity swap, commodity option, equity or equity index swap, equity or equity index option, bond option, interest rate option, foreign exchange transaction, cap transaction, floor transaction, collar transaction, currency swap transaction, cross-currency rate swap transaction, currency option or any other similar transaction (including any option with respect to any of these transactions), (b) any combination of these transactions and (c) any other transaction identified as a Specified Transaction in this Agreement or the relevant confirmation.

"***Terminated Transactions***" means with respect to any Early Termination Date (a) if resulting from a Termination Event, all Affected Transactions and (b) if resulting from an Event of Default, all Transactions (in either case) in effect immediately before the effectiveness of the notice designating that Early Termination Date (or, if "Automatic Early Termination" applies, immediately before that Early Termination Date).

"***Termination Event***" means an Illegality or, if specified to be applicable, a Credit Event Upon Merger or an Additional Termination Event.

"***Termination Rate***" means a rate per annum equal to the arithmetic mean of the cost (without proof or evidence of any actual cost) to each party (as certified by such party) if it were to fund or of funding such amounts.

"***Unpaid Amounts***" owing to any party means, with respect to an Early Termination Date, the aggregate of (a) in respect of all Terminated Transactions, the amounts that became payable (or that would have become payable but for Section 2(a)(iii)) to such party under Section 2(a)(i) on or prior to such Early Termination Date and which remain unpaid as at such Early Termination Date and (b) in respect of each Terminated Transaction, for each obligation under Section 2(a)(i) which was (or would have been but for Section 2(a)(iii)) required to be settled by delivery to such party on or prior to such Early Termination Date and which has not been so settled as at such Early Termination Date, an amount equal to the fair market value of that which was (or would have been) required to be delivered as of the originally scheduled date for delivery, in each case together with (to the extent permitted under applicable law) interest, in the currency of such amounts, from (and including) the date such amounts or obligations were or would have been required to have been paid or performed to (but excluding) such Early Termination Date, at the Applicable Rate. Such amounts of interest will be calculated on the basis of daily compounding and the actual number of days elapsed. The fair market value of any obligation referred to in clause (b) above shall be reasonably determined by the party obliged to make the determination under Section 6(e) or, if each party is so obliged, it shall be the average of the fair market values reasonably determined by both parties.

IN WITNESS WHEREOF the parties have executed this document on the respective dates specified below with effect from the date specified on the first page of this document.

....	....
(Name of Party)	(Name of Party)
By:	By: ....
Name:	Name:
Title:	Title:
Date:	Date:

(Local Currency—Single Jurisdiction)

ISDA®

International Swap Dealers Association, Inc.

U.S. MUNICIPAL COUNTERPARTY SCHEDULE
to the
Master Agreement

dated as of ....

between .... and ....
("Party A") ("Party B")

Part 1. **Termination Provisions.**

(a) ***"Specified Entity"*** means in relation to Party A for the purpose of:—

Section 5(a)(v) (Default under Specified Transaction), ...

Section 5(a)(vi) (Cross Default), ...

Section 5(a)(vii) (Bankruptcy), ...

Section 5(b)(ii) (Credit Event Upon Merger), ...

and in relation to Party B for the purpose of:—

Section 5(a)(v) (Default under Specified Transaction), ...

Section 5(a)(vi) (Cross Default), ...

Section 5(a)(vii) (Bankruptcy), ...

Section 5(b)(ii) (Credit Event Upon Merger), ...

(b) ***"Specified Transaction"*** will have the meaning specified in Section 12 of this Agreement unless another meaning is specified here ....

....

....

(c) The ***"Cross Default"*** provisions of Section 5(a)(vi) will/will not * apply to Party A
will/will not * apply to Party B

If such provisions apply:—

"Specified Indebtedness" will have the meaning specified in Section 12 of this Agreement unless another meaning is specified here ....

....

* Delete as applicable.

"Threshold Amount" means ....

....

(d) The *"Credit Event Upon Merger"* provisions of Section 5(b)(ii) will/will not * apply to Party A
will/will not * apply to Party B

(e) The *"Automatic Early Termination"* provision of Section 6(a) will/will not * apply to Party A
will/will not * apply to Party B

(f) *Payments on Early Termination.* For the purpose of Section 6(e) of this Agreement:—

(i) Market Quotation/Loss * will apply.

(ii) The First Method/The Second Method * will apply.

(g) *Additional Termination Event* will/will not apply*. The following shall constitute an Additional Termination Event:— ....

....

....

....

....

....

For the purpose of the foregoing Termination Event, the Affected Party or Affected Parties shall be:— ..

....

(h) *Events of Default.*

(i) *Bankruptcy.* Clause (6) of Section 5(a)(vii) of this Agreement is hereby amended to read in its entirety as follows:—

"(6)(A) seeks or becomes subject to the appointment of an administrator, provisional liquidator, conservator, receiver, trustee, custodian or other similar official for it or for all or substantially all its assets or (B) in the case of a Government Entity, any Credit Support Provider of such Government Entity or any applicable Specified Entity of such Government Entity, (I) there shall be appointed or designated with respect to it, an entity such as an organisation, board, commission, authority, agency or body to monitor, review, oversee, recommend or declare a financial emergency or similar state of financial distress with respect to it or (II) there shall be declared or introduced or proposed for consideration by it or by any legislative or regulatory body with competent jurisdiction over it, the existence of a state of financial emergency or similar state of financial distress in respect of it;".

(ii) *Merger Without Assumption.* Section 5(a)(viii) of this Agreement is hereby amended to read in its entirety as follows:—

"(viii) *Merger Without Assumption.* The party or any Credit Support Provider of such party consolidates or amalgamates with, or merges with or into, or transfers all or substantially all its assets to, another entity (or, without limiting the foregoing, if such party is a Government Entity, an entity such as an organisation, board, commission, authority, agency or body succeeds to the principal functions of, or powers and duties granted to, such party or any Credit Support Provider of such party) and, at the time of such consolidation, amalgamation, merger, transfer or succession:—

(1) the resulting, surviving, transferee or successor entity fails to assume all the obligations of such party or such Credit Support Provider under this Agreement or any Credit Support Document to

---

* Delete as applicable.

which it or its predecessor was a party by operation of law or pursuant to an agreement reasonably satisfactory to the other party to this Agreement; or

(2) the benefits of any Credit Support Document fail to extend (without the consent of the other party) to the performance by such resulting, surviving, transferee or successor entity of its obligations under this Agreement."

(i) ***Termination Events.*** Section 5(b)(ii) of this Agreement is hereby amended to read in its entirety as follows:—

"(ii) ***Credit Event Upon Merger.*** If "Credit Event Upon Merger" is specified in the Schedule as applying to the party, such party ("X"), any Credit Support Provider of X or any applicable Specified Entity of X consolidates or amalgamates with, or merges with or into, or transfers all or substantially all its assets to, another entity (or, without limiting the foregoing, if X is a Government Entity, an entity such as an organisation, board, commission, authority, agency or body succeeds to the principal functions of, or powers and duties granted to, X, any Credit Support Provider of X or any Specified Entity of X) and such action does not constitute an event described in Section 5(a)(viii) but the creditworthiness of the resulting, surviving, transferee or successor entity is materially weaker than that of X, such Credit Support Provider or such Specified Entity, as the case may be, immediately prior to such action (and, in such event, X or its successor or transferee, as appropriate, will be the Affected Party); or".

Part 2. **Agreement to Deliver Documents.**

For the purpose of Section 4(a) of this Agreement, each party agrees to deliver the following documents, as applicable:—

Party required to deliver document	**Form/Document/ Certificate**	**Date by which to be delivered**	**Covered by Section 3(d) Representation**
....	....	....	Yes/No*
....	....	....	Yes/No*
....	....	....	Yes/No*
....	....	....	Yes/No*
....	....	....	Yes/No*

Part 3. **Miscellaneous.**

(a) ***Addresses for Notices.*** For the purpose of Section 10(a) of this Agreement:—

Address for notices or communications to Party A:—

Address: ....

Attention: ....

Telex No.: .... Answerback: ....

Facsimile No.: .... Telephone No.: ....

Electronic Messaging System Details: ....

Address for notices or communications to Party B:—

Address: ....

Attention: ....

Telex No.: .... Answerback: ....

* Delete as applicable.

Facsimile No.: .... Telephone No.: ....

Electronic Messaging System Details: ....

(b) ***Calculation Agent.*** The Calculation Agent is ...., unless otherwise specified in a Confirmation in relation to the relevant Transaction.

(c) ***Credit Support Document.*** Details of any Credit Support Document:— ....

....

....

....

(d) ***Credit Support Provider.*** Credit Support Provider means in relation to Party A, ...

....

....

Credit Support Provider means in relation to Party B, ...

....

....

(e) ***Governing Law.*** This Agreement will be governed by and construed in accordance with the laws of the State of New York (without reference to choice of law doctrine).

(f) ***Netting of Payments.*** Subparagraph (ii) of Section 2(c) of this Agreement will not apply to the following Transactions or groups of Transactions (in each case starting from the date of this Agreement/in each case starting from ....*) ....

....

....

(g) ***"Affiliate"*** will have the meaning specified in Section 12 of this Agreement unless another meaning is specified here ....

....

(h) ***"Covered Indenture"*** means ....

....

(i) ***"Covered Indenture Incorporation Date"*** means ....

....

(j) ***"Government Entity"*** means Party A/Party B.*

* Delete as applicable.

Part 4 Other Provisions.

(a) ***Obligations.*** Section 2(a)(iii) of this Agreement is hereby amended to read in its entirety as follows:—

"(iii) Each obligation of each party under Section 2(a)(i) is subject to (1) the condition precedent that no Event of Default, Potential Event of Default or Incipient Illegality with respect to the other party has occurred and is continuing, (2) the condition precedent that no Early Termination Date in respect of the relevant Transaction has occurred or been effectively designated and (3) each other applicable condition precedent specified in this Agreement.

(b) ***Representations.***

(i) The introductory clause of Section 3 of this Agreement is hereby amended to read in its entirety as follows:—

"Each party represents to the other party (which representations will be deemed to be repeated by each party on each date on which a Transaction is entered into and, in the case of the representations in Section 3(a) and 3(e), at all times until the termination of this Agreement) that:—".

(ii) Section 3(a)(ii) of this Agreement is hereby amended to read in its entirety as follows:—

"(ii) ***Powers.*** It has the power to execute this Agreement and any other documentation relating to this Agreement to which it is a party, to deliver this Agreement and any other documentation relating to this Agreement that it is required by this Agreement to deliver and to perform its obligations under this Agreement and any obligations it has under any Credit Support Document to which it is a party and has taken all necessary action and made all necessary determinations and findings to authorise such execution, delivery and performance;".

(iii) Section 3(b) of this Agreement is hereby amended to read in its entirety as follows:—

"(b) ***Absence of Certain Events.*** No Event of Default or Potential Event of Default or, to its knowledge, Incipient Illegality (in the case of a Government Entity) or Termination Event with respect to it has occurred and is continuing and no such event or circumstance would occur as a result of its entering into or performing its obligations under this Agreement or any Credit Support Document to which it is a party."

(iv) Section 3 of this Agreement is hereby amended by adding the following subsection "(e)" thereto, which subsection shall only apply to the Government Entity:—

"(e) ***Non-Speculation.*** This Agreement has been, and each Transaction hereunder will be (and, if applicable, has been), entered into for purposes of managing its borrowings or investments and not for purposes of speculation."

(v) Section 3 of this Agreement is hereby amended by adding the following subsection "(f)" thereto:—

"(f) ***No Immunity.*** It is not entitled to claim immunity on the grounds of sovereignty or other similar grounds with respect to itself or its revenues or assets (irrespective of their use or intended use) from (i) suit, (ii) jurisdiction of any court, (iii) relief by way of injunction, order for specific performance or for recovery of property, (iv) attachment of its assets (whether before or after judgment) or (v) execution or enforcement of any judgment to which it or its revenues or assets might otherwise be made subject to in any Proceedings (as defined in Section 11(b)) in the courts of any jurisdiction and no such immunity (whether or not claimed) may be attributed to such party or its revenues or assets."

(c) ***Agreements.***

(i) The introductory clause of Section 4 of this Agreement is hereby amended to read in its entirety as follows:—

"Each party agrees with the other (or, in the case of Section 4(d) and (e), the Government Entity agrees with the other party) that, so long as either party has or may have any obligation under this Agreement or under any Credit Support Document to which it is a party:—".

(ii) Section 4 of this Agreement is hereby amended by adding the following subsections "(d)" and "(e)" thereto:—

"(d) ***Compliance with Covered Indenture.*** The Government Entity will observe, perform and fulfill each provision in the Covered Indenture applicable to such Government Entity in effect on the Covered Indenture Incorporation Date, as any of those provisions may be amended, supplemented or modified for purposes of this Agreement with the prior written consent of the other party hereto (the "Incorporated Provisions"), with the effect that such other party hereto will have the benefit of each of the Incorporated Provisions (including without limitation, covenants, right to consent to certain actions subject to consent under the Covered Indenture and delivery of financial statements and other notices and information). In the event the Covered Indenture ceases to be in effect prior to the termination of this Agreement, the Incorporated Provisions (other than those provisions requiring payments in respect of bonds, notes, warrants or other similar instruments issued under the Covered Indenture) will remain in full force and effect for purposes of this Agreement as though set forth herein until such date on which all of the obligations of the Government Entity under this Agreement and any obligations of the Government Entity or any Credit Support Provider of the Government Entity under a Credit Support Document have been fully satisfied. The Incorporated Provisions are hereby incorporated by reference and made a part of this Agreement to the same extent as if such provisions were set forth herein. For purposes of this Agreement, the Incorporated Provisions shall be construed as though (i) all references therein to any party making loans, extensions of credit or financial accommodations thereunder or commitments therefor (the "Financings") were to the other party hereto and (ii) to the extent that such Incorporated Provisions are conditioned on or relate to the existence of such Financings or the Government Entity having any obligations in connection therewith, all references to such Financings or obligations were to the obligations of the Government Entity under this Agreement. Any amendment, supplement, modification or waiver of any of the Incorporated Provisions without the prior written consent of the other party hereto shall have no force and effect with respect to this Agreement. Any amendment, supplement or modification for which such consent is obtained shall be part of the Incorporated Provisions for purposes of this Agreement. **

(e) ***Notice of Incipient Illegality.*** If an Incipient Illegality occurs, the Government Entity will, promptly upon becoming aware of it, notify the other party, specifying the nature of that Incipient Illegality and will also give such other information about that Incipient Illegality as the other party may reasonably require."

(d) ***Jurisdiction.*** Section 11(b) of this Agreement is hereby amended to read in its entirety as follows:—

"(b) ***Jurisdiction.*** With respect to any suit, action or proceedings relating to this Agreement ('Proceedings'), each party irrevocably:—

(i) submits, to the fullest extent permitted by applicable law, to the non-exclusive jurisdiction of each of the courts of the State of New York, the United States District Court located in the Borough of Manhattan in New York City, the courts of the state in which the Government Entity or the other party's principal executive offices are located and the United States District Court with jurisdiction over the location of the Government Entity or the other party's principal executive offices; and

** This provision may require modification or deletion depending on the circumstances.

(ii) waives, to the fullest extent permitted by applicable law, (1) any objection which it may have at any time to the laying of venue of any Proceedings brought in any such court, (2) any claim that such Proceedings have been brought in an inconvenient forum and (3) the right to object, with respect to such Proceedings, that such court does not have any jurisdiction over such party.

Nothing in this Agreement precludes either party from bringing Proceedings in any other jurisdiction nor will the bringing of Proceedings in any one or more jurisdictions preclude the bringing of Proceedings in any other jurisdiction."

(e) ***Definitions.*** Section 12 of this Agreement is hereby amended to add the following definitions in their appropriate alphabetical order:—

" ***'Covered Indenture'*** has the meaning specified in the Schedule."

" ***'Covered Indenture Incorporation Date'*** has the meaning specified in the Schedule."

" ***'Government Entity'*** has the meaning specified in the Schedule."

" ***'Incipient Illegality'*** means (a) the enactment by any legislative body with competent jurisdiction over a Government Entity of legislation which, if adopted as law, would render unlawful (i) the performance by such Government Entity of any absolute or contingent obligation to make a payment or delivery or to receive a payment or delivery in respect of a Transaction or the compliance by such Government Entity with any other material provision of this Agreement relating to such Transaction or (ii) the performance by a Government Entity or a Credit Support Provider of such Government Entity of any contingent or other obligation which the Government Entity (or such Credit Support Provider) has under any Credit Support Document relating to such Transaction, (b) any assertion in any proceeding, forum or action by a Government Entity, in respect of such Government Entity or in respect of any entity located or organised under the laws of the state in which such Government Entity is located to the effect that performance under this Agreement or similar agreements is unlawful or (c) the occurrence with respect to a Government Entity or any Credit Support Provider of such Government Entity of any event that constitutes an Illegality."

PRIMARY SOURCES

Current as of November 1993

Treas. Reg. Section 1.148-4(h)

(h) *Qualified hedging transactions*—(1) *In general.* Payments made or received by an issuer under a qualified hedge (as defined in paragraph (h)(2) of this section) relating to bonds of an issue are taken into account (as provided in paragraph (h)(3) of this section) to determine the yield on the issue. Except as provided in paragraph (h)(4) of this section, the issue is treated as a variable yield issue. These hedging rules apply solely for purposes of section 148.

(2) *Qualified hedge defined.* A *qualified hedge* is a contract that satisfies each of the following requirements:

(i) *Hedge*—(A) *In general.* The contract is a *hedge* entered into primarily to reduce the issuer's risk of interest rate changes with respect to a borrowing. For example, the contract may be an interest rate swap, an interest rate cap, a futures contract, a forward contract, or an option.

(B) *No significant investment element.* A contract is not a hedge under paragraph (h)(2)(i)(A) of this section if it contains a significant investment element (i.e., an expected return). For example, variable rate bonds held by the issuer do not meet the requirements of this paragraph (h)(2)(i). A contract may contain a significant investment element if the payments under the contract do not correspond closely in time and amount to the interest payments on the bonds being hedged. For example, an interest rate swap generally contains a significant investment element if it requires any payments other than periodic payments, within the meaning of section 446 and the regulations thereunder (*periodic payments*) (e.g., an up-front payment for an off-market swap) before its termination date. Similarly, an interest rate cap generally contains a significant investment element if the cap rate is less than the on-market swap rate on the date the cap is entered into. For this purpose, the on-market swap rate is the single fixed rate for which the rate or index that is the subject of the cap could be swapped in an on-market interest rate swap that requires only periodic payments and that has a term equal to the term of the cap.

(ii) *Parties.* The contract is entered into between the issuer or the political subdivision on behalf of which the issuer issues the bonds (collectively referred to in this paragraph (h) as the *issuer*) and a provider that is not a related party (the *hedge provider*).

(iii) *Hedged bonds.* The hedge covers all of one or more groups of substantially identical bonds in the issue (i.e., all of the bonds having the same interest rate, maturity, and terms). If the hedge does not cover all interest payments on all of the substantially identical bonds being hedged, it must cover, in whole or in part, the same specific identifiable interest payments on each of the substantially identical bonds. Thus, for example, a qualified hedge may include a hedge of all or a pro rata portion of each interest payment on the variable rate bonds in an issue for the first five years following their issuance. For purposes of this paragraph (h), unless the context clearly requires otherwise, *hedged bonds* means the specific bonds or portions thereof (i.e., the specific interest payments) covered by a hedge.

(iv) *Interest based.* Changes in the value of the contract are based primarily on interest rate changes. For example, an interest rate swap or a futures contract on

Treasury securities may qualify. A commodity swap or an option on a commodity futures contract, however, is not a qualified hedge.

(v) *Size.* The contract does not hedge an amount larger than the issuer's risk with respect to interest rate changes on the hedged bonds.

(vi) *Receipts.* The payments to the issuer under the contract correspond closely, in both time and amount, to the specific interest payments being hedged on the hedged bonds.

(vii) *Timing and duration.* Payments do not begin to accrue under the contract on the date earlier than the sale date of the hedged bonds and do not accrue longer than the hedged interest payments on the hedged bonds.

(viii) *Source of payments.* Payments to the hedge provider are reasonably expected to be made from the same source of funds that, absent the hedge, would be reasonably expected to be used to pay principal and interest on the hedged bonds.

(ix) *Identification.* The hedge is identified by the actual issuer on its books and records maintained for the hedged bonds on or before the later of the date on which the parties enter into the contract or the issue date of the hedged bonds. The identification specifies the hedge provider, the terms of the hedge, and the hedged bonds. The identification contains sufficient detail to establish that the requirements of this paragraph (h)(2) and, if applicable, paragraph (h)(4) of this section are satisfied. The existence of the hedge is noted on all forms filed with the Internal Revenue Service for the issue after the date on which the hedge is entered into.

(3) *Accounting for qualified hedges*—(i) *In general.* Except as otherwise provided in paragraph (h)(4) of this section, payments made or received by the issuer under a qualified hedge are treated as payments made or received, as appropriate, on the hedged bonds that are taken into account in determining the yield on those bonds. These payments are reasonably allocated to the hedged bonds in the period to which the payments relate, as determined under paragraph (h)(3)(iii) of this section. Payments made or received by the issuer include payments deemed made or received when a contract is terminated or deemed terminated under this paragraph (h)(3). Payments reasonably allocable to the reduction of risk of interest rate changes and to the hedge provider's overhead under this paragraph (h) are included as payments made or received under a qualified hedge.

(ii) *Exclusions from hedge.* Payments for services or other items under the contract that are not expressly treated as payments under the qualified hedge under paragraph (h)(3)(i) of this section are not payments with respect to a qualified hedge.

(iii) *Timing and allocation of payments.* The period to which a payment made by the issuer relates is determined under general Federal income tax principles, including, without limitation, section 446 and the regulations thereunder on notional principal contracts, and adjusted as necessary to reflect the end of a computation period and the start of a new computation period. Except as provided in paragraph (h)(3)(iv) of this section, a payment received by the issuer is taken into account in the period that the interest payment that the payment hedges is required to be made.

(iv) *Termination payments*—(A) *Termination defined.* A termination of a qualified hedge includes any sale, assignment, or other disposition of the hedge by the issuer, or the acquisition by the issuer of an offsetting hedge. A deemed termination occurs when the hedged bonds are redeemed.

(B) *General rule.* A payment made or received by an issuer to terminate a qualified hedge, including gain or loss realized or deemed realized, is treated as a payment made or received on the hedged bonds, as appropriate. The payment is reasonably allocated to the remaining periods originally covered by the terminated hedge in a manner that reflects the economic substance of the hedge.

(C) *Special rule for terminations when bonds are redeemed.* Except as otherwise provided in this paragraph (h)(3)(iv)(C) and in paragraph (h)(3)(iv)(D) of this section, when a qualified hedge is deemed terminated because the hedged bonds are redeemed, the fair market value of the contract on the redemption date is treated as a termination payment made or received on that date. When hedged bonds are redeemed, any payment received by the issuer on termination of a hedge, including a termination payment or a deemed termination payment, reduces, but cannot exceed, the interest payments made by the issuer on the hedged bonds in the computation period ending on the termination date. The excess, if any, is reasonably allocated over the bond years in the immediately preceding computation period or periods to the extent necessary to eliminate the excess.

(D) *Special rules for refundings.* To the extent that the hedged bonds are redeemed using the proceeds of a refunding issue, the termination payment is accounted for under paragraph (h)(3)(iv)(B) by treating it as a payment on the refunding issue, rather than the hedged bonds. In addition, to the extent that the refunding issue, rather than the hedged bonds, has been redeemed, paragraph (h)(3)(iv)(C) applies to the termination payment by treating it as a payment on the redeemed refunding issue.

(4) *Certain variable yield issues treated as fixed yield issues*—(i) *In general.* Except as otherwise provided in paragraph (h)(4)(ii)(C) of this section, if the issuer of a variable yield issue enters into an interest rate swap that is a qualified hedge, the hedged bonds are treated as fixed yield bonds if—

(A) *Start date.* The date on which payments begin to accrue on the swap is not later than 15 days after the issue date of the hedged bonds;

(B) *Maturity.* The term of the swap is equal to the term of the hedged bonds or the entire period during which the hedged bonds bear interest at variable interest rates.

(C) *No nonperiodic payments.* Payments to be made or received under the swap are reasonably expected to correspond closely, in time and amount, to payments on the hedged bonds (i.e., no nonperiodic payments). Swap payments made within 15 days of the related payments on the hedged bonds generally so correspond.

(D) *Notional principal amount.* The notional principal amount used to compute both fixed and variable payments on the swap equals the principal amount of all the variable yield bonds in the issue.

(E) *Payments and interest rate.* Under the swap, the issuer makes level payments based on a fixed interest rate and receives payments based on a variable interest rate that is substantially the same as the interest rate on the hedged bonds. These interest rates are treated as substantially the same if they are reasonably expected to be substantially the same throughout the term of the hedge. For example, an objective 30-day tax-exempt variable rate index or other objective index (e.g., LIBOR, J.J. Kenney Index, PSA Municipal swap index) may be adjusted to correspond to an issuer's individual 30-day interest rate.

(ii) *Accounting*—(A) *In general.* If a hedged bond is treated as a fixed yield bond under this paragraph (h)(4), the fixed-rate payments made by the issuer on the swap are substituted for the actual interest payments on the hedged bonds for purposes of computing yield on that bond. For this purpose, the fixed-rate payments are the amounts determined by multiplying the notional principal amount by the fixed rate (i.e., the amount determined before netting the fixed and variable amounts due under the swap).

(B) *Effect of termination generally.* Except as otherwise provided in paragraph (h)(4)(ii)(C) of this section, for purposes of §1.148–3, as of the termination date of a qualified hedge covered by this paragraph (h)(4), the issue of which the hedged bonds are a part is treated as if it were reissued on the termination date. The redemption price of the retired issue and the issue price of the new issue equal the aggregate values of all the bonds of the issue on the termination date. In computing the yield on the new issue, any termination payment is accounted for under paragraph (h)(3)(iv) of this section, applied by treating the termination payment as made or received on the deemed new issue under this paragraph (h)(4)(ii)(B).

(C) *Effect of early termination.* If the swap is terminated or deemed terminated within 5 years after the issue date of the issue of which the hedged bonds are a part, the general rules under this paragraph (h)(4) do not apply, and, for purposes of §1.148–3, the hedged bonds are treated as variable yield bonds from the issue date.

(5) *Authority of the Commissioner*—(i) *In general.* A contract is not a qualified hedge if the Commissioner determines, based on all the facts and circumstances, that treating the contract as a qualified hedge would provide a material potential for arbitrage, or a principal purpose for entering into the contract is that arbitrage potential. For example, a contract that requires a substantial nonperiodic payment may constitute, in whole or part, an embedded loan, investment-type property, or other investment.

(ii) *Other qualified hedges.* The Commissioner, by publication of a revenue ruling or revenue procedure, may specify contracts that do not otherwise meet the requirements of paragraph (h)(2) of this section as qualified hedges.

(iii) *Recomputation of yield.* If an issuer enters into a hedge that is not properly identified or otherwise fails to meet the requirements of this section, the Commissioner may recompute the yield on the issue taking the hedge into account if the failure to take the hedge into account distorts that yield or otherwise fails to clearly reflect the economic substance of the transaction.

Treas. Reg. Section 301.7701–2 Associations

(a) *Characteristics of corporations.* (1) The term "association" refers to an organization whose characteristics require it to be classified for purposes of taxation as a corporation rather than as another type of organization such as a partnership or a trust. There are a number of major characteristics ordinarily found in a pure corporation which, taken together, distinguish it from other organizations. These are: (i) Associates, (ii) an objective to carry on business and divided the gains therefrom, (iii) continuity of life, (iv) centralization of management, (v) liability for corporate debts limited to corporate property, and (vi) free transferability of interests. Whether a particular organization is to be classified as an association must be determined by taking into account the presence or absence of each of these corporate characteristics. The presence or absence of these characteristics will depend upon the facts in each individual case. In addition to the major characteristics set forth in this subparagraph other factors may be found in some cases which may be significant in classifying an organization as an association, a partnership, or a trust. An organization will be treated as an association if the corporate characteristics are such that the organization more nearly resembles a corporation than a partnership or trust. See Morrissey et al. v. Commissioner (1935) 296 U.S. 344.

(2) Since associates and an objective to carry on business for joint profit are essential characteristics of all organizations engaged in business for profit (other than the so-called one-man corporation and the sole proprietorship), the absence of either of these essential characteristics will cause an arrangement among co-owners of property for the development of such property for the separate profit of each not to be classified as an association. Some of the major characteristics of a corporation are common to trusts and corporations, and others are common to partnerships and corporations. Characteristics common to trusts and corporations are not material in attempting to distinguish between a trust and an association, and characteristics common to partnerships and corporations are not material in attempting to distinguish between an association and a partnership. For example, since centralization of management, continuity of life, free transferability of interests, and limited liability are generally common to trusts and corporations, the determination of whether a trust which has such characteristics is to be treated for tax purposes as a trust or as an association depends on whether there are associates and an objective to carry on business and divide the gains therefrom. On the other hand, since associates and an objective to carry on business and divide the gains therefrom are generally common to both corporations and partnerships, the determination of whether an organization which has such characteristics is to be treated for tax purposes as a partnership or as an association depends on whether there exists centralization of management, continuity of life, free transferability of interests, and limited liability.

(3) An unincorporated organization shall not be classified as an association unless such organization has more corporate characteristics than noncorporate characteristics. In determining whether an organization has more corporate characteristics than noncorporate characteristics, all characteristics common to both types of organizations shall not be considered. For example, if a limited partnership has

centralized management and free transferability of interests but lacks continuity of life and limited liability, and the limited partnership has no other characteristics which are significant in determining its classification, such limited partnership is not classified as an association. Although the limited partnership also has associates and an objective to carry on business and divide the gains therefrom, these characteristics are not considered because they are common to both corporations and partnerships.

(4) The rules of this section and §§ 301.7701–3 and 301.7701–4 are applicable only to taxable years beginning after December 31, 1960. However, for any taxable year beginning after December 31, 1960, but before October 1, 1961, any amendment of the agreement establishing the organization will, in the case of an organization in existence on November 17, 1960, be treated for purposes of determining the classification of the organization as being in effect as of the beginning of such taxable year (i) if the amendment of the agreement is made before October 1, 1961, and (ii) if the amendment results in the classification of the organization under the rules of this section and §§ 301.7701–1, 301.7701–3, and 301.7701–4 in the same manner as the organization was classified for tax purposes on November 17, 1960.

(5) All references in this section to the Uniform Limited Partnership Act shall be deemed to refer both to the original Uniform Limited Partnership Act (adopted in 1916) and to the revised Uniform Limited Partnership Act (adopted by the National Conference of Commissioners on Uniform State Laws in 1976).

(b) *Continuity of life.* (1) An organization has continuity of life if the death, insanity, bankruptcy, retirement, resignation, or expulsion of any member will not cause a dissolution of the organization. On the other hand, if the death, insanity, bankruptcy, retirement, resignation, or expulsion of any member will cause a dissolution of the organization, continuity of life does not exist. If the retirement, death, or insanity of a general partner of a limited partnership causes a dissolution of the partnership, unless the remaining general partners agree to continue the partnership or unless all remaining members agree to continue the partnership, continuity of life does not exist. See Glensder Textile Company (1942) 46 B.T.A. 176 (A., C.B. 1942–1, 8).

(2) For purposes of this paragraph, dissolution of an organization means an alteration of the identity of an organization by reason of a change in the relationship between its members as determined under local law. For example, since the resignation of a partner from a general partnership destroys the mutual agency which exists between such partner and his copartners and thereby alters the personal relation between the partners which constitutes the identity of the partnership itself, the resignation of a partner dissolves the partnership. A corporation, however, has a continuing identity which is detached from the relationship between its stockholders. The death, insanity, or bankruptcy of a shareholder or the sale of a shareholder's interest has no effect upon the identity of the corporation and, therefore, does not work a dissolution of the organization. An agreement by which an organization is established may provide that the business will be continued by the remaining members in the event of the death or withdrawal of any member, but such agreement does not establish continuity of life if under local law the death or withdrawal of any member causes a dissolution of the organization. Thus, there may be a dissolution of the organization and no continuity of life although the business is continued by the remaining members.

(3) An agreement establishing an organization may provide that the organization is to continue for a stated period or until the completion of a stated undertak-

ing or such agreement may provide for the termination of the organization at will or otherwise. In determining whether any member has the power of dissolution, it will be necessary to examine the agreement and to ascertain the effect of such agreement under local law. For example, if the agreement expressly provides that the organization can be terminated by the will of any member, it is clear that the organization lacks continuity of life. However, if the agreement provides that the organization is to continue for a stated period or until the completion of a stated transaction, the organization has continuity of life if the effect of the agreement is that no member has the power to dissolve the organization in contravention of the agreement. Nevertheless, if, notwithstanding such agreement, any member has the power under local law to dissolve the organization, the organization lacks continuity of life. Accordingly, a general partnership subject to a statute corresponding to the Uniform Partnership Act and a limited partnership subject to a statute corresponding to the Uniform Limited Partnership Act both lack continuity of life.

(c) *Centralization of management.* (1) An organization has centralized management if any person (or any group of persons which does not include all the members) has continuing exclusive authority to make the management decisions necessary to the conduct of the business for which the organization was formed. Thus, the persons who are vested with such management authority resemble in powers and functions the directors of a statutory corporation. The effective operation of a business organization composed of many members generally depends upon the centralization in the hands of a few of exclusive authority to make management decisions for the organization, and therefore, centralized management is more likely to be found in such an organization than in a smaller organization.

(2) The persons who have such authority may, or may not, be members of the organization and may hold office as a result of a selection by the members from time to time, or may be self-perpetuating in office. See Morrissey et al. v. Commissioner (1935) 296 U.S. 344. Centralized management can be accomplished by election to office, by proxy appointment, or by any other means which has the effect of concentrating in a management group continuing exclusive authority to make management decisions.

(3) Centralized management means a concentration of continuing exclusive authority to make independent business decisions on behalf of the organization which do not require ratification by members of such organization. Thus, there is not centralized management when the centralized authority is merely to perform ministerial acts as an agent at the direction of a principal.

(4) There is no centralization of continuing exclusive authority to make management decisions, unless the managers have sole authority to make such decisions. For example, in the case of a corporation or a trust, the concentration of management powers in a board of directors or trustees effectively prevents a stockholder or a trust beneficiary, simply because he is a stockholder or beneficiary, from binding the corporation or the trust by his acts. However, because of the mutual agency relationship between members of a general partnership subject to a statute corresponding to the Uniform Partnership Act, such a general partnership cannot achieve effective concentration of management powers and, therefore, centralized management. Usually, the act of any partner within the scope of the partnership business binds all the partners; and even if the partners agree among themselves that the powers of management shall be exclusively in a selected few, this agreement will be ineffective as against an outsider who had no notice of it. In addition, limited partnerships subject to a statute corresponding to the Uniform

Limited Partnership Act, generally do not have centralized management, but centralized management ordinarily does exist in such a limited partnership if substantially all the interests in the partnership are owned by the limited partners. Furthermore, if all or a specified group of the limited partners may remove a general partner, all the facts and circumstances must be taken into account in determining whether the partnership possesses centralized management. A substantially restricted right of the limited partners to remove the general partner (*e.g.*, in the event of the general partner's gross negligence, self-dealing, or embezzlement) will not itself cause the partnership to possess centralized management.

(d) *Limited liability.* (1) An organization has the corporate characteristic of limited liability if under local law there is no member who is personally liable for the debts of or claims against the organization. Personal liability means that a creditor of an organization may seek personal satisfaction from a member of the organization to the extent that the assets of such organization are insufficient to satisfy the creditor's claim. A member of the organization who is personally liable for the obligations of the organization may make an agreement under which another person, whether or not a member of the organization, assumes such liability or agrees to indemnify such member for any such liability. However, if under local law the member remains liable to such creditors notwithstanding such agreement, there exists personal liability with respect to such member. In the case of a general partnership subject to a statute corresponding to the Uniform Partnership Act, personal liability exists with respect to each general partner. Similarly, in the case of a limited partnership subject to a statute corresponding to the Uniform Limited Partnership Act, personal liability exists with respect to each general partner, except as provided in subparagraph (2) of this paragraph (d).

(2) in the case of an organization formed as a limited partnership, personal liability does not exist, for purposes of this paragraph, with respect to a general partner when he has no substantial assets (other than his interest in the partnership) which could be reached by a creditor of the organization and when he is merely a "dummy" acting as the agent of the limited partners. Notwithstanding the formation of the organization as a limited partnership, when the limited partners act as the principals of such general partner, personal liability will exist with respect to such limited partners. Also, if a corporation is a general partner, personal liability exists with respect to such general partner when the corporation has substantial assets (other than its interest in the partnership) which could be reached by a creditor of the limited partnership. A general partner may contribute his services, but no capital, to the organization, but if such general partner has substantial assets (other than his interest in the partnership), there exists personal liability. Furthermore, if the organization is engaged in financial transactions which involve large sums of money, and if the general partners have substantial assets (other than their interests in the partnership), there exists personal liability although the assets of such general partners would be insufficient to satisfy any substantial portion of the obligations of the organization. In addition, although the general partner has no substantial assets (other than his interest in the partnership), personal liability exists with respect to such general partner when he is not merely a "dummy" acting as the agent of the limited partners. If the limited partnership agreement provides that a general partner is not personally liable to creditors for the debts of the partnership (other than debts for which another general partner is personally liable), it shall be presumed that personal liability does not exist with respect to that partner unless it is established that the provision is ineffective under local law.

(e) *Free transferability of interests.* (1) An organization has the corporate characteristic of free transferability of interests if each of its members or those members owning substantially all of the interests in the organization have the power, without the consent of other members, to substitute for themselves in the same organization a person who is not a member of the organization. In order for this power of substitution to exist in the corporate sense, the member must be able, without the consent of other members, to confer upon his substitute all the attributes of his interest in the organization. Thus, the characteristic of free transferability of interests does not exist in a case in which each member can, without the consent of other members, assign only his right to share in profits but cannot so assign his rights to participate in the management of the organization. Furthermore, although the agreement provides for the transfer of a member's interest, there is no power of substitution and no free transferability of interest if under local law a transfer of a member's interest results in the dissolution of the old organization and the formation of a new organization.

(2) If each member of an organization can transfer his interest to a person who is not a member of the organization only after having offered such interest to the other members at its fair market value, it will be recognized that a modified form of free transferability of interests exists. In determining the classification of an organization, the presence of this modified corporate characteristic will be accorded less significance than if such characteristic were present in an unmodified form.

(f) *Cross reference.* See paragraph (b) of § 301.7701–3 for the application to limited partnerships of the rules relating to corporate characteristics.

(g) *Examples.* The application of the rules described in this section may be illustrated by the following examples:

Example 1. [Reserved]

Example 2. A group of seven doctors forms a clinic for the purpose of furnishing, for profit, medical and surgical services to the public. They each transfer assets to the clinic, and their agreement provides that except upon complete liquidation of the organization on the vote of three-fourths of its members, no member has any individual interest in its assets. Their agreement also provides that neither the death, insanity, bankruptcy, retirement, resignation, nor expulsion of a member shall cause the dissolution of the organization. However, under the applicable local law, a member who withdraws does have the power to dissolve the organization. While the agreement provides that the management of the clinic is to be vested exclusively in an executive committee of four members elected by all the members, this provision is ineffective as against outsiders who had no notice of it; and, therefore, the act of any member within the scope of the organization's business binds the organization insofar as such outsiders are concerned. While the agreement declares that each individual doctor alone is liable for acts of malpractice, members of the clinic are, nevertheless, personally liable for all debts of the clinic including claims based on malpractice. No member has the right, without the consent of all the other members, to transfer his interest to a doctor who is not a member of the clinic. The organization has associates and an objective to carry on business and divide the gains therefrom. However, it does not have the corporate characteristics of continuity of life, centralized management, limited liability, and free transferability of interests. The organization will be classified as a partnership for all purposes of the Internal Revenue Code.

Example 3. A group of 25 lawyers forms an organization for the purpose of furnishing, for profit, legal services to the public. Their agreement provides that the organization will dissolve upon the death, insanity, bankruptcy, retirement, or expulsion of a member. While their agreement provides that the management of the organization is to be vested exclusively in an executive committee of five members elected by all the members, this provision is ineffective as against outsiders who had no notice of it; and, therefore, the act of any member within the scope of the organization's business binds the organization insofar as such outsiders are concerned. Members of the organization are personally liable for all debts, or claims against, the organization. No member has the right, without the consent of all the other members, to transfer his interest to a lawyer who is not a member of the organization. The organization has associates and an objective to carry on business and divide the gains therefrom. However, the four corporate characteristics of limited liability, centralized management, free transferability of interests, and continuity of life are absent in this case. The organization will be classified as a partnership for all purposes of the Internal Revenue Code.

Example 4. A group of 25 persons forms an organization for the purpose of engaging in real estate investment activities. Each member has the power to dissolve the organization at any time. The management of the organization is vested exclusively in an executive committee of five members elected by all the members, and under the applicable local law, no one acting without the authority of this committee has the power to bind the organization by his acts. Under the applicable local law, each member is personally liable for the obligations of the organization. Every member has the right to transfer his interest to a person who is not a member of the organization, but he must first advise the organization of the proposed transfer and give it the opportunity on a vote of the majority to purchase the interest at its fair market value. The organization has associates and an objective to carry on business and divide the gains therefrom. While the organization does have the characteristics of centralized management and a modified form of free transferability of interests, it does not have the corporate characteristics of continuity of life and limited liability. Under the circumstances presented, the organization will be classified as a partnership for all purposes of the Internal Revenue Code.

Example 5. A group of 25 persons forms an organization for the purpose of engaging in real estate investment activities. Under their agreement, the organization is to have a life of 20 years, and under the applicable local law, no member has the power to dissolve the organization prior to the expiration of that period. The management of the organization is vested exclusively in an executive committee of five members elected by all the members, and under the applicable local law, no one acting without the authority of this committee has the power to bind the organization by his acts. Under the applicable local law, each member is personally liable for the obligations of the organization. Every member has the right to transfer his interest to a person who is not a member of the organization, but he must first advise the organization of the proposed transfer and give it the opportunity on a vote of the majority to purchase the interest at its fair market value. The organization has associates and an objective to carry on business and divide the gains therefrom. While the organization does not have the corporate characteristics of limited liability, it does have continuity of life, centralized management, and a modified form of free transferability of interests. The organization will be classified as an association for all purposes of the Internal Revenue Code.

Example 6. A group of 25 persons forms an organization for purposes of engaging in real estate investment activities. Each member has the power to dissolve the organization at any time. The management of the organization is vested exclusively in an executive committee of five members elected by all the members, and under the applicable local law, no one acting without the authority of this committee has the power to bind the organization by his acts. Under the applicable local law, the liability of each member for the obligations of the organization is limited to paid and subscribed capital. Every member has the right to transfer his interest to a person who is not a member of the organization, but he must first advise the organization of the proposed transfer and give it the opportunity on a vote of the majority to purchase the interest at its fair market value. The organization has associates and an objective to carry on business and divide the gains therefrom. While the organization does not have the characteristic of continuity of life, it does have limited liability, centralized management, and a modified form of free transferability of interests. The organization will be classified as an association for all purposes of the Internal Revenue Code.

Example 7. A group of 25 persons forms an organization for the purpose of investing in securities so as to educate the members in principles and techniques of investment practices and to share the income from such investments. While the agreement states that the organization will operate until terminated by a three-fourths vote of the total membership and will not terminate upon the withdrawal or death of any member, under the applicable local law, a member has the power to dissolve the organization at any time. The business of the organization is carried on by the members at regular monthly meetings and buy or sell action may be taken only when voted by a majority of the organization's membership present. Elected officers perform only ministerial functions such as presiding at meetings and carrying out the directions of the members. Members of the organization are personally liable for all debts of, or claims against, the organization. No member may transfer his membership. The organization has associates and an objective to carry on business and divide the gains therefrom. However, the organization does not have the corporate characteristics of limited liability, free transferability of interests, continuity of life, and centralized management. The organization will be treated as a partnership for all purposes of the Internal Revenue Code.

[32 FR 15241, Nov. 3, 1967, as amended by T.D. 7515, 42 FR 55612, Oct. 18, 1977; T.D. 7889, 48 FR 18805, Apr. 26, 1983]

Treas. Reg. Section 301.7701–4 Trusts

(a) *Ordinary trusts.* In general, the term "trust" as used in the Internal Revenue Code refers to an arrangement created either by a will or by an inter vivos declaration whereby trustees take title to property for the purpose of protecting or conserving it for the beneficiaries under the ordinary rules applied in chancery or probate courts. Usually the beneficiaries of such a trust do no more than accept the benefits thereof and are not the voluntary planners or creators of the trust arrangement. However, the beneficiaries of such a trust may be the persons who create it and it will be recognized as a trust under the Internal Revenue Code if it was created for the purpose of protecting or conserving the trust property for beneficiaries who stand in the same relation to the trust as they would if the trust had been created by others for them. Generally speaking, an arrangement will be treated as a trust under the Internal Revenue Code if it can be shown that the purpose of the arrangement is to vest in trustees responsibility for the protection and conservation of property for beneficiaries who cannot share in the discharge of this responsibility and, therefore, are not associates in a joint enterprise for the conduct of business for profit.

(b) *Business trusts.* There are other arrangements which are known as trusts because the legal title to property is conveyed to trustees for the benefit of beneficiaries, but which are not classified as trusts for purposes of the Internal Revenue Code because they are not simply arrangements to protect or conserve the property for the beneficiaries. These trusts, which are often known as business or commercial trusts, generally are created by the beneficiaries simply as a device to carry on a profit-making business which normally would have been carried on through business organizations that are classified as corporations or partnerships under the Internal Revenue Code. However, the fact that the corpus of the trust is not supplied by the beneficiaries is not sufficient reason in itself for classifying the arrangement as an ordinary trust rather than as an association or partnership. The fact that any organization is technically cast in the trust form, by conveying title to property to trustees for the benefit of persons designated as beneficiaries, will not change the real character of the organization if, applying the principles set forth in §§ 301.7701–2 and 301.7701–3, the organization more nearly resembles an association or a partnership than a trust.

(c) *Certain investment trusts*—(1) An "investment" trust will not be classified as a trust if there is a power under the trust agreement to vary the investment of the certificate holders. *See Commissioner v. North American Bond Trust,* 122 F. 2d 545 (2d Cir. 1941), *cert. denied,* 314 U.S. 701 (1942). An investment trust with a single class of ownership interests, representing undivided beneficial interests in the assets of the trust, will be classified as a trust if there is no power under the trust agreement to vary the investment of the certificate holders. An investment trust with multiple classes of ownership interests will ordinarily be classified as an association or a partnership under § 301.7701–2; however, an investment trust with multiple classes of ownership interests, in which there is no power under the trust agreement to vary the investment of the certificate holders, will be classified as a trust if the trust is formed to facilitate direct investment in the assets of the trust and the existence of multiple classes of ownership interests is incidental to that purpose.

(2) The provisions of paragraph (c)(1) of this section may be illustrated by the following examples:

Example 1. A corporation purchases a portfolio of residential mortgages and transfers the mortgages to a bank under a trust agreement. At the same time, the bank as trustee delivers to the corporation certificates evidencing rights to payments from the pooled mortgages; the corporation sells the certificates to the public. The trustee holds legal title to the mortgages in the pool for the benefit of the certificate holders but has no power to reinvest proceeds attributable to the mortgages in the pool or to vary investments in the pool in any other manner. There are two classes of certificates. Holders of class A certificates are entitled to all payments of mortgage principal, both scheduled and prepaid, until their certificates are retired; holders of class B certificates receive payments of principal only after all class A certificates have been retired. The different rights of the class A and class B certificates serve to shift to the holders of the class A certificates, in addition to the earlier scheduled payments of principal, the risk that mortgages in the pool will be prepaid so that the holders of the class B certificates will have "call protection" (freedom from premature termination of their interests on account of prepayments). The trust thus serves to create investment interests with respect to the mortgages held by the trust that differ significantly from direct investment in the mortgages. As a consequence, the existence of multiple classes of trust ownership is not incidental to any purpose of the trust to facilitate direct investment, and accordingly, the trust is classified as an association or a partnership under § 301.7701–2.

Example 2. Corporation M is the originator of a portfolio of residential mortgages and transfers the mortgages to a bank under a trust agreement. At the same time, the bank as trustee delivers to M certificates evidencing rights to payments from the pooled mortgages. The trustee holds legal title to the mortgages in the pool for the benefit of the certificate holders, but has no power to reinvest proceeds attributable to the mortgages in the pool or to vary investments in the pool in any other manner. There are two classes of certificates. Holders of class C certificates are entitled to receive 90 percent of the payments of principal and interest on the mortgages; class D certificate holders are entitled to receive the other ten percent. The two classes of certificates are identical except that, in the event of a default on the underlying mortgages, the payment rights of class D certificate holders are subordinated to the rights of class C certificate holders. M sells the class C certificates to investors and retains the class D certificates. The trust has multiple classes of ownership interests, given the greater security provided to holders of class C certificates. The interests of certificate holders, however, are substantially equivalent to undivided interests in the pool of mortgages, coupled with a limited recourse guarantee running from M to the holders of class C certificates. In such circumstances, the existence of multiple classes of ownership interests is incidental to the trust's purpose of facilitating direct investment in the assets of the trust. Accordingly, the trust is classified as a trust.

Example 3. A promoter forms a trust in which shareholders of a publicly traded corporation can deposit their stock. For each share of stock deposited with the trust, the participant receives two certificates that are initially attached, but may be separated and traded independently of each other. One certificate represents the right to dividends and the value of the underlying stock up to a specified amount; the other certificate represents the right to appreciation in the stock's value above the specified amount. The separate certificates represent two different classes of ownership interest in the trust, which effectively separate dividend rights on the stock held by the trust from a portion of the right to appreciation in the value of such stock. The multiple classes of ownership interests are designed to permit investors, by transferring one of the certificates and retaining the other, to fulfill their varying investment objectives of seeking primarily either dividend income or capital appreciation from the stock held by the trust. Given that the trust serves to create investment interests with respect to the stock held by the trust that differ significantly from direct investment in such stock, the trust is not formed to facilitate direct investment in the assets of the trust. Accordingly, the trust is classified as an association or a partnership under § 301.7701–2.

Example 4. Corporation N purchases a portfolio of bonds and transfers the bonds to a bank under a trust agreement. At the same time, the trustee delivers to N certificates evidencing interests in the bonds. These certificates are sold to public investors. Each certificate represents the right to receive a particular payment with respect to a specific bond. Under section 1286, stripped coupons and stripped bonds are treated as separate bonds for federal income tax purposes. Although the interest of each certificate holder is different from that of each other certificate holder, and the trust thus has multiple classes of ownership, the multiple classes simply provide each certificate holder with a direct interest in what is treated under section 1286 as a separate bond. Given the similarity of the interests acquired by the certificate holders to the interests that could be acquired by direct investment, the multiple classes of trust interests merely facilitate direct investment in the assets held by the trust. Accordingly, the trust is classified as a trust.

(d) *Liquidating trusts.* Certain organizations which are commonly known as liquidating trusts are treated as trusts for purposes of the Internal Revenue Code. An organization will be considered a liquidating trust if it is organized for the primary purpose of liquidating and distributing the assets transferred to it, and if its activities are all reasonably necessary to, and consistent with, the accomplishment of that purpose. A liquidating trust is treated as a trust for purposes of the Internal Revenue Code because it is formed with the objective of liquidating particular assets and not as an organization having as its purpose the carrying on of a profit-making business which normally would be conducted through business organizations classified as corporations or partnerships. However, if the liquidation is unreasonably prolonged or if the liquidation purpose becomes so obscured by business activities that the declared purpose of liquidation can be said to be lost or abandoned, the status of the organization will no longer be that of a liquidating trust. Bondholders' protective committees, voting trusts, and other agencies formed to protect the interests of security holders during insolvency, bankruptcy, or corporate reorganization proceedings are analogous to liquidating trusts but if subsequently utilized to further the control or profitable operation of a going business on a permanent continuing basis, they will lose their classification as trusts for purposes of the Internal Revenue Code.

[32 FR 15241, Nov. 3, 1967, as amended by T.D. 8080, 51 FR 9952, Mar. 24, 1986]

15 U.S.C. § 77c Classes of securities under this subchapter

(a) Except as hereinafter expressly provided, the provisions of this subchapter shall not apply to any of the following classes of securities:

(2) Any security issued or guaranteed by the United States or any territory thereof, or by the District of Columbia, or by any State of the United States, or by any political subdivision of a State or territory, or by any public instrumentality of one or more States or territories, or by any person controlled or supervised by and acting as an instrumentality of the Government of the United States pursuant to authority granted by the Congress of the United States; or any certificate of deposit for any of the foregoing; or any security issued or guaranteed by any bank; or any security issued by or representing an interest in or a direct obligation of a Federal Reserve bank; or any interest or participation in any common trust fund or similar fund maintained by a bank exclusively for the collective investment and reinvestment of assets contributed thereto by such bank in its capacity as trustee, executor, administrator, or guardian; or any security which is an industrial development bond (as defined in section 103(c)(2) of Title 26) the interest on which is excludable from gross income under section 103(a)(1) of Title 26 if, by reason of the application of paragraph (4) or (6) of section 103(c) of Title 26 (determined as if paragraphs (4)(A), (5), and (7) were not included in such section 103(c)), paragraph (1) of such section 103(c) does not apply to such security; or any interest or participation in a single trust fund, or in a collective trust fund maintained by a bank, or any security arising out of a contract issued by an insurance company, which interest, participation, or security is issued in connection with (A) a stock bonus, pension, or profit-sharing plan which meets the requirements for qualification under section 401 of Title 26, (B) an annuity plan which meets the requirements for the deduction of the employer's contributions under section 404(a)(2) of Title 26, or (C) a governmental plan as defined in section 414(d) of Title 26 which has been established by an employer for the exclusive benefit of its employees or their beneficiaries for the purpose of distributing to such employees or their beneficiaries the corpus and income of the funds accumulated under such plan, if under such plan it is impossible, prior to the satisfaction of all liabilities with respect to such employees and their beneficiaries, for any part of the corpus or income to be used for, or diverted to, purposes other than the exclusive benefit of such employees or their beneficiaries, other than any plan described in clause (A), (B), or (C) of this paragraph (i) the contributions under which are held in a single trust fund or in a separate account maintained by an insurance company for a single employer and under which an amount in excess of the employer's contribution is allocated to the purchase of securities (other than interests or participations in the trust or separate account itself) issued by the employer or any company directly or indirectly controlling, controlled by, or under common control with the employer, (ii) which covers employees some or all of whom are employees within the meaning of section 401(c)(1) of Title 26, or (iii) which is a plan funded by an annuity contract described in section 403(b) of Title 26. The Commission, by rules and regulations or order, shall exempt from the provisions of section 77e of this title any interest or participation issued in connection with a stock bonus, pension, profit-sharing, or annuity plan which covers employees

some or all of whom are employees within the meaning of section 401(c)(1) of Title 26, if and to the extent that the Commission determines this to be necessary or appropriate in the public interest and consistent with the protection of investors and the purposes fairly intended by the policy and provisions of this subchapter. For purposes of this paragraph, a security issued or guaranteed by a bank shall not include any interest or participation in any collective trust fund maintained by a bank; and the term "bank" means any national bank, or any banking institution organized under the laws of any State, territory, or the District of Columbia, the business of which is substantially confined to banking and is supervised by the State or territorial banking commission or similar official; except that in the case of a common trust fund or similar fund, or a collective trust fund, the term "bank" has the same meaning as in the Investment Company Act of 1940.

15 U.S.C. § 80a–3

(c) Notwithstanding subsection (a) of this section, none of the following persons is an investment company within the meaning of this subchapter:

(1) Any issuer whose outstanding securities (other than short-term paper) are beneficially owned by not more than one hundred persons and which is not making and does not presently propose to make a public offering of its securities. For purposes of this paragraph:

(A) Beneficial ownership by a company shall be deemed to be beneficial ownership by one person, except that, if the company owns 10 per centum or more of the outstanding voting securities of the issuer, the beneficial ownership shall be deemed to be that of the holders of such company's outstanding securities (other than short-term paper) unless, as of the date of the most recent acquisition by such company of securities of that issuer, the value of all securities owned by such company of all issuers which are or would, but for the exception set forth in this subparagraph, be excluded from the definition of investment company solely by this paragraph, does not exceed 10 per centum of the value of the company's total assets. Such issuer nonetheless is deemed to be an investment company for purposes of section 80a–12(d)(1) of this title.

(B) Beneficial ownership by any person who acquires securities or interests in securities of an issuer described in the first sentence of this paragraph shall be deemed to be beneficial ownership by the person from whom such transfer was made, pursuant to such rules and regulations as the Commission shall prescribe as necessary or appropriate in the public interest and consistent with the protection of investors and the purposes fairly intended by the policy and provisions of this subchapter, where the transfer was caused by legal separation, divorce, death, or other involuntary event.

15 U.S.C. § 80a–3(c)

(5) Any person who is not engaged in the business of issuing redeemable securities, face-amount certificates of the installment type or periodic payment plan certificates, and who is primarily engaged in one or more of the following businesses: (A) Purchasing or otherwise acquiring notes, drafts, acceptances, open accounts receivable, and other obligations representing part or all of the sales price of merchandise, insurance, and services; (B) making loans to manufacturers, wholesalers, and retailers of, and to prospective purchasers of, specified merchandise, insurance, and services; and (C) purchasing or otherwise acquiring mortgages and other liens on and interests in real estate.

15 U.S.C. § 80a–12 Functions and activities of investment companies

(d)(1)(A) It shall be unlawful for any registered investment company (the "acquiring company") and any company or companies controlled by such acquiring company to purchase or otherwise acquire any security issued by any other investment company (the "acquired company"), and for any investment company (the "acquiring company") and any company or companies controlled by such acquiring company to purchase or otherwise acquire any security issued by any registered investment company (the "acquired company"), if the acquiring company and any company or companies controlled by it immediately after such purchase or acquisition own in the aggregate—

(i) more than 3 per centum of the total outstanding voting stock of the acquired company;

(ii) securities issued by the acquired company having an aggregate value in excess of 5 per centum of the value of the total assets of the acquiring company; or

(iii) securities issued by the acquired company and all other investment companies (other than treasury stock of the acquiring company) having an aggregate value in excess of 10 per centum of the value of the total assets of the acquiring company.

(B) It shall be unlawful for any registered open-end investment company (the "acquired company"), any principal underwriter therefor, or any broker or dealer registered under the Securities Exchange Act of 1934, knowingly to sell or otherwise dispose of any security issued by the acquired company to any other investment company (the "acquiring company") or any company or companies controlled by the acquiring company, if immediately after such sale or disposition—

(i) more than 3 per centum of the total outstanding voting stock of the acquired company is owned by the acquiring company and any company or companies controlled by it; or

(ii) more than 10 per centum of the total outstanding voting stock of the acquired company is owned by the acquiring company and other investment companies and companies controlled by them.

(iii) securities issued by the acquired company and all other investment companies (other than treasury stock of the acquiring company) having an aggregate value in excess of 10 per centum of the value of the total assets of the acquiring company.

(C) It shall be unlawful for any investment company (the "acquiring company") and any company or companies controlled by the acquiring company to purchase or otherwise acquire any security issued by a registered closed-end investment company, if immediately after such purchase or acquisition the acquiring company, other investment companies having the same investment adviser, and companies controlled by such investment companies, own more than 10 per centum of the total outstanding voting stock of such closed-end company.

(D) The provisions of this paragraph (1) shall not apply to a security received as a dividend or as a result of an offer of exchange approved pursuant to section 80a–11 of this title or of a plan of reorganization of any company (other than a plan devised for the purpose of evading the foregoing provisions).

(E) The provisions of this paragraph (1) shall not apply to a security (or securities) purchased or acquired by an investment company if—

(i) the depositor of, or principal underwriter for, such investment company is a broker or dealer registered under the Securities Exchange Act of 1934, or a person controlled by such a broker or dealer;

(ii) such security is the only investment security held by such investment company (or such securities are the only investment securities held by such investment company, if such investment company is a registered unit investment trust that issues two or more classes or series of securities, each of which provides for the accumulation of shares of a different investment company); and

(iii) in the event such investment company is not a registered investment company, the purchase or acquisition is made pursuant to an arrangement with the issuer of, or principal underwriter for the issuer of, the security whereby such investment company is obligated—

(aa) either to seek instructions from its security holders with regard to the voting of all proxies with respect to such security and to vote such proxies only in accordance with such instructions, or to vote the shares held by it in the same proportion as the vote of all other holders of such security, and

(bb) to refrain from substituting such security unless the Commission shall have approved such substitution in the manner provided in section 80a–26 of this title.

(F) The provisions of this paragraph (1) shall not apply to securities purchased or otherwise acquired by a registered investment company if—

(i) immediately after such purchase or acquisition not more than 3 per centum of the total outstanding stock of such issuer is owned by such registered investment company and all affiliated persons of such registered investment company; and

(ii) such registered investment company has not offered or sold after January 1, 1971, and is not proposing to offer or sell any security issued by it through a principal underwriter or otherwise at a public offering price which includes a sales load of more than 1-1/2 per centum.

No issuer of any security purchased or acquired by a registered investment company pursuant to this subparagraph shall be obligated to redeem such security in an amount exceeding 1 per centum of such issuer's total outstanding securities during any period of less than thirty days. Such investment company shall exercise voting rights by proxy or otherwise with respect to any security purchased or acquired pursuant to this subparagraph in the manner prescribed by subparagraph (E) of this subsection.

(G) For the purposes of this paragraph (1), the value of an investment company's total assets shall be computed as of the time of a purchase or acquisition or as closely thereto as is reasonably possible.

(H) In any action brought to enforce the provisions of this paragraph (1), the Commission may join as a party the issuer of any security purchased or otherwise acquired in violation of this paragraph (1), and the court may issue any order with respect to such issuer as may be necessary or appropriate for the enforcement of the provisions of this paragraph (1).

17 C.F.R. § 230.144A Private resales of securities to institutions

PRELIMINARY NOTES

1. This section relates solely to the application of section 5 of the Act and not to antifraud or other provisions of the federal securities laws.

2. Attempted compliance with this section does not act as an exclusive election; any seller hereunder may also claim the availability of any other applicable exemption from the registration requirements of the Act.

3. In view of the objective of this section and the policies underlying the Act, this section is not available with respect to any transaction or series of transactions that, although in technical compliance with this section, is part of a plan or scheme to evade the registration provisions of the Act. In such cases, registration under the Act is required.

4. Nothing in this section obviates the need for any issuer or any other person to comply with the securities registration or broker-dealer registration requirements of the Securities Exchange Act of 1934 (the *Exchange Act*), whenever such requirements are applicable.

5. Nothing in this section obviates the need for any person to comply with any applicable state law relating to the offer or sale of securities.

6. Securities acquired in a transaction made pursuant to the provisions of this section are deemed to be *restricted securities* within the meaning of § 230.144(a)(3) of this chapter.

7. The fact that purchasers of securities from the issuer thereof may purchase such securities with a view to reselling such securities pursuant to this section will not affect the availability to such issuer of an exemption under section 4(2) of the Act, or Regulation D under the Act, from the registration requirements of the Act.

(a) *Definitions.* (1) For purposes of this section, *qualified institutional buyer* shall mean:

(i) Any of the following entities, acting for its own account or the accounts of other qualified institutional buyers, that in the aggregate owns and invests on a discretionary basis at least $100 million in securities of issuers that are not affiliated with the entity:

(A) Any *insurance company* as defined in section 2(13) of the Act;

(B) Any *investment company* registered under the Investment Company Act of 1940 (the *Investment Company Act*) or any *business development company* as defined in section 2(a)(48) of that Act;

(C) Any *Small Business Investment Company* licensed by the U.S. Small Business Administration under section 301(c) or (d) of the Small Business Investment Act of 1958;

(D) Any *plan* established and maintained by a state, its political subdivisions, or any agency or instrumentality of a state or its political subdivisions, for the benefit of its employees;

(E) Any *employee benefit plan* within the meaning of title I of the Employee Retirement Income Security Act of 1974;

(F) Any *business development company* as defined in section 202(a)(22) of the Investment Advisers Act of 1940;

(G) Any organization described in section 501(c)(3) of the Internal Revenue Code, corporation (other than a bank as defined in section 3(a)(2) of the Act or a savings and loan association or other institution referenced in section 3(a)(5)(A) of the Act or a foreign bank or savings and loan association or equivalent institution), partnership, or Massachusetts or similar business trust; and

(H) Any *investment adviser* registered under the Investment Advisers Act.

(ii) Any *dealer* registered pursuant to section 15 of the Exchange Act, acting for its own account or the accounts of other qualified institutional buyers, that in the aggregate owns and invests on a discretionary basis at least $10 million of securities of issuers that are not affiliated with the dealer, *Provided,* That securities constituting the whole or a part of an unsold allotment to or subscription by a dealer as a participant in a public offering shall not be deemed to be owned by such dealer;

(iii) Any *dealer* registered pursuant to section 15 of the Exchange Act acting in a riskless principal transaction on behalf of a qualified institutional buyer;

NOTE: A registered dealer may act as agent, on a non-discretionary basis, in a transaction with a qualified institutional buyer without itself having to be a qualified institutional buyer.

(iv) Any investment company registered under the Investment Company Act, acting for its own account or for the accounts of other qualified institutional buyers, that is part of a family of investment companies which own in the aggregate at least $100 million in securities of issuers, other than issuers that are affiliated with the investment company or are part of such family of investment companies. *Family of investment companies* means any two or more investment companies registered under the Investment Company Act, except for a unit investment trust whose assets consist solely of shares of one or more registered investment companies, that have the same investment adviser (or, in the case of unit investment trusts, the same depositor), Provided That, for purposes of this section:

(A) Each series of a series company (as defined in Rule 18f-2 under the Investment Company Act [17 CFR 270.18f-2]) shall be deemed to be a separate investment company; and

(B) Investment companies shall be deemed to have the same adviser (or depositor) if their advisers (or depositors) are majority-owned subsidiaries of the same parent, or if one investment company's adviser (or depositor) is a majority-owned subsidiary of the other investment company's adviser (or depositor);

(v) Any entity, all of the equity owners of which are qualified institutional buyers, acting for its own account or the accounts of other qualified institutional buyers; and

(vi) Any *bank* as defined in section 3(a)(2) of the Act, any savings and loan association or other institution as referenced in section 3(a)(5)(A) of the Act, or any foreign bank or savings and loan association or equivalent institution, acting for its own account or the accounts of other qualified institutional buyers, that in the aggregate owns and invests on a discretionary basis at least $100 million in securities of issuers that are not affiliated with it and that has an audited net worth of at least $25 million as demonstrated in its latest annual financial statements, as of a date not more than 16 months preceding the date of sale under the Rule in the case of a U.S. bank or savings and loan association, and not more than 18 months preceding such date of sale for a foreign bank or savings and loan association or equivalent institution.

(2) In determining the aggregate amount of securities owned and invested on a discretionary basis by an entity, the following instruments and interests shall be ex-

cluded: securities issued or guaranteed by the United States or by any person controlled or supervised by and acting as an instrumentality of the Government of the United States pursuant to authority granted by the Congress of the United States; bank deposit notes and certificates of deposit; loan participations; repurchase agreements; securities owned but subject to a repurchase agreement; and currency, interest rate and commodity swaps.

(3) The aggregate value of securities owned and invested on a discretionary basis by an entity shall be the cost of such securities, except where the entity reports its securities holdings in its financial statements on the basis of their market value, and no current information with respect to the cost of those securities has been published. In the latter event, the securities may be valued at market for purposes of this section.

(4) In determining the aggregate amount of securities owned by an entity and invested on a discretionary basis, securities owned by subsidiaries of the entity that are consolidated with the entity in its financial statements prepared in accordance with generally accepted accounting principles may be included if the investments of such subsidiaries are managed under the direction of the entity, except that, unless the entity is a reporting company under section 13 or 15(d) of the Exchange Act, securities owned by such subsidiaries may not be included if the entity itself is a majority-owned subsidiary that would be included in the consolidated financial statements of another enterprise.

(5) For purposes of this section, *riskless principal transaction* means a transaction in which a dealer buys a security from any person and makes a simultaneous offsetting sale of such security to a qualified institutional buyer, including another dealer acting as riskless principal for a qualified institutional buyer.

(6) For purposes of this section, *effective conversion premium* means the amount, expressed as a percentage of the security's conversion value, by which the price at issuance of a convertible security exceeds its conversion value.

(7) For purposes of this section, *effective exercise premium* means the amount, expressed as a percentage of the warrant's exercise value, by which the sum of the price at issuance and the exercise price of a warrant exceeds its exercise value.

(b) *Sales by persons other than issuers or dealers.* Any person, other than the issuer or a dealer, who offers or sells securities in compliance with the conditions set forth in paragraph (d) of this section shall be deemed not to be engaged in a distribution of such securities and therefore not to be an underwriter of such securities within the meaning of sections 2(11) and 4(1) of the Act.

(c) *Sales by Dealers.* Any dealer who offers or sells securities in compliance with the conditions set forth in paragraph (d) of this section shall be deemed not to be a participant in a distribution of such securities within the meaning of section 4(3)(C) of the Act and not to be an underwriter of such securities within the meaning of section 2(11) of the Act, and such securities shall be deemed not to have been offered to the public within the meaning of section 4(3)(A) of the Act.

(d) *Conditions to be met.* To qualify for exemption under this section, an offer or sale must meet the following conditions:

(1) The securities are offered or sold only to a qualified institutional buyer or to an offeree or purchaser that the seller and any person acting on behalf of the seller reasonably believe is a qualified institutional buyer. In determining whether a prospective purchaser is a qualified institutional buyer, the seller and any person acting on its behalf shall be entitled to rely upon the following non-exclusive methods of establishing the prospective purchaser's ownership and discretionary investments of securities:

(i) The prospective purchaser's most recent publicly available financial statements, *Provided* That such statements present the information as of a date within 16 months preceding the date of sale of securities under this section in the case of a U.S. purchaser and within 18 months preceding such date of sale for a foreign purchaser;

(ii) The most recent publicly available information appearing in documents filed by the prospective purchaser with the Commission or another United States federal, state, or local governmental agency or self-regulatory organization, or with a foreign governmental agency or self-regulatory organization, *Provided* That any such information is as of a date within 16 months preceding the date of sale of securities under this section in the case of a U.S. purchaser and within 18 months preceding such date of sale for a foreign purchaser;

(iii) The most recent publicly available information appearing in a recognized securities manual, *Provided* That such information is as of a date within 16 months preceding the date of sale of securities under this section in the case of a U.S. purchaser and within 18 months preceding such date of sale for a foreign purchaser; or

(iv) A certification by the chief financial officer, a person fulfilling an equivalent function, or other executive officer of the purchaser, specifying the amount of securities owned and invested on a discretionary basis by the purchaser as of a specific date on or since the close of the purchaser's most recent fiscal year, or, in the case of a purchaser that is a member of a family of investment companies, a certification by an executive officer of the investment adviser specifying the amount of securities owned by the family of investment companies as of a specific date on or since the close of the purchaser's most recent fiscal year;

(2) The seller and any person acting on its behalf takes reasonable steps to ensure that the purchaser is aware that the seller may rely on the exemption from the provisions of section 5 of the Act provided by this section;

(3) The securities offered or sold:

(i) Were not, when issued, of the same class as securities listed on a national securities exchange registered under section 6 of the Exchange Act or quoted in a U.S. automated interdealer quotation system; *Provided*, That securities that are convertible or exchangeable into securities so listed or quoted at the time of issuance and that had an effective conversion premium of less than 10 percent, shall be treated as securities of the class into which they are convertible or exchangeable; and that warrants that may be exercised for securities so listed or quoted at the time of issuance, for a period of less than 3 years from the date of issuance, or that had an effective exercise premium of less than 10 percent, shall be treated as securities of the class to be issued upon exercise; and *Provided further*, That the Commission may from time to time, taking into account then-existing market practices, designate additional securities and classes of securities that will not be deemed of the same class as securities listed on a national securities exchange or quoted in a U.S. automated inter-dealer quotation system; and

(ii) Are not securities of an open-end investment company, unit investment trust or face-amount certificate company that is or is required to be registered under section 8 of the Investment Company Act; and

(4)(i) In the case of securities of an issuer that is neither subject to section 13 or 15(d) of the Exchange Act, nor exempt from reporting pursuant to Rule 12g3–2(b) (§ 240.12g3–2(b) of this chapter) under the Exchange Act, nor a foreign government as defined in Rule 405 (§ 230.405 of this chapter) eligible to register securities under Schedule B of the Act, the holder and a prospective purchaser designated by the holder have the right to obtain from the issuer, upon request of the holder, and the prospective purchaser has received from the issuer, the seller, or a person acting on either of their behalf, at or prior to the time of sale, upon such prospective purchaser's request to the holder or the issuer, the following information (which shall be reasonably current in relation to the date of resale under this section): a very brief statement of the nature of the business of the issuer and the products and services it offers; and the issuer's most recent balance sheet and profit and loss and retained earnings statements, and similar financial for such part of the two preceding fiscal years as the issuer has been in operation (the financial statements should be audited to the extent reasonably available).

(ii) The requirement that the information be *reasonably current* will be presumed to be satisfied if:

(A) The balance sheet is as of a date less than 16 months before the date of resale, the statements of profit and loss and retained earnings are for the 12 months preceding the date of such balance sheet, and if such balance sheet is not as of a date less than 6 months before the date of resale, it shall be accompanied by additional statements of profit and loss and retained earnings for the period from the date of such balance sheet to a date less than 6 months before the date of resale; and

(B) The statement of the nature of the issuer's business and its products and services offered is as of a date within 12 months prior to the date of resale; or

(C) With regard to foreign private issuers, the required information meets the timing requirements of the issuer's home country or principal trading markets.

(e) Offers and sales of securities pursuant to this section shall be deemed not to affect the availability of any exemption or safe harbor relating to any previous or subsequent offer or sale of such securities by the issuer or any prior or subsequent holder thereof.

[55 FR 17945, Apr. 30, 1990]

17 C.F.R. § 270.2a–7 Money market funds

(a) *Definitions*—(1) *Amortized Cost Method* of valuation shall mean the method of calculating an investment company's net asset value whereby portfolio securities are valued at the fund's acquisition cost as adjusted for amortization of premium or accretion of discount rather than at their value based on current market factors.

(2) *Business day* means any day, other than Saturday, Sunday, or any customary business holiday.

(3) *Collateralized fully* in the case of a repurchase agreement shall mean that:

(i) The value of the securities collateralizing the repurchase agreement (reduced by the transaction costs (including loss of interest) that the money market fund reasonably could expect to incur if the seller defaults) is, and during the entire term of the repurchase agreement remains, at least equal to the resale price provided in the agreement; and

(ii) The money market fund or its custodian either has actual physical possession of the collateral or, in the case of a security registered on a book entry system, the book entry is maintained in the name of the money market fund or its custodian; and

(iii) The money market fund retains an unqualified right to possess and sell the collateral in the event of a default by the seller; and

(iv) The collateral consists entirely of Government securities or securities that, at the time the repurchase agreement is entered into, are rated in the highest rating category by the Requisite NRSROs.

(4) *Demand Feature* shall mean a Put that entitles the holder to receive the principal amount of the underlying security or securities and that may be exercised either:

(i) At any time on no more than 30 days' notice; or

(ii) At specified intervals not exceeding 397 calendar days and upon no more than 30 days' notice.

(5) *Eligible Security* shall mean:

(i) A security with a remaining maturity of 397 days or less that is rated (or that has been issued by an issuer that is rated with respect to a class of Short-term debt obligations, or any security within that class, that is comparable in priority and security with the security) by the Requisite NRSROs in one of the two highest rating categories for Short-term debt obligations (within which there may be subcategories or gradations indicating relative standing); or

(ii) A security:

(A) That at the time of issuance was a Long-term security but that has a remaining maturity of 397 calendar days or less, and

(B) Whose issuer has received from the Requisite NRSROs a rating, with respect to a class of Short-term debt obligations (or any security within that class) that is now comparable in priority and security with the security, in one of the two highest rating categories for Short-term debt obligations (within which there may be sub-categories or gradations indicating relative standing); or

(iii) An Unrated Security that is of comparable quality to a security meeting the requirements of paragraph (a)(5) (i) or (ii) of this section, as determined by the money market fund's board of directors: *Provided, however,* That:

(A) The board of directors may base its determination that a Standby Commitment is an Eligible Security upon a finding that the issuer of the commitment presents a minimal risk of default; and

(B) A security that at the time of issuance was a Long-term security but that has a remaining maturity of 397 calendar days or less and that is an Unrated Security is not an Eligible Security if the security has a Long-term rating from any NRSRO that is not within the NRSRO's two highest categories (within which there may be subcategories or gradations indicating relative standing).

(6) *First Tier Security* shall mean any Eligible Security that:

(i) Is rated (or that has been issued by an issuer that is rated with respect to a class of Short-term debt obligations, or any security within that class, that is comparable in priority and security with the security) by the Requisite NRSROs in the highest rating category for Short-term debt obligations (within which there may be sub-categories or gradations indicating relative standing); or

(ii) Is a security described in paragraph (a)(5)(ii) of this section whose issuer has received from the Requisite NRSROs a rating, with respect to a class of Short-term debt obligations (or any security within that class) that now is comparable in priority and security with the security, in the highest rating category for Short-term debt obligations (within which there may be sub-categories or gradations indicating relative standing); or

(iii) Is an Unrated Security that is of comparable quality to a security meeting the requirements of clauses (i) and (ii) of paragraph (a)(6) of this section, as determined by the fund's board of directors.

(7) *Floating Rate Instrument* shall mean a security the terms of which provide for the adjustment of its interest rate whenever a specified interest rate (such as a bank's designated prime lending rate) changes and which, at any time, can reasonably be expected to have a market value that approximates its par value.

(8) *Government security* shall mean any Government security as defined in section 2(a)(16) of the Act.

(9) *Long-term* shall mean having a remaining maturity greater than 366 days.

(10) *NRSRO* shall mean any nationally recognized statistical rating organization, as that term is used in paragraphs (c)(2)(vi) (E), (F) and (H) of rule 15c3–1 under the Securities Exchange Act of 1934 (17 CFR 240.15c3-1(c)(2)(vi) (E), (F) and (H)), that is not an affiliated person, as defined in section 2(a)(3)(c) of the Act (15 U.S.C. 80a–2(a)(3)(c)), of the issuer of, or any insurer, guarantor or provider of credit support for, the instrument.

(11) *Penny-Rounding Method* of pricing shall mean that method of computing an investment company's price per share for purposes of distribution, redemption and repurchase whereby the current net asset value per share is rounded to the nearest one percent.

(12) A *Put* shall mean a right to sell a specified underlying security or securities within a specified period of time and at a specified exercise price, that may be sold, transferred or assigned only with the underlying security or securities.

(13) *Requisite NRSROs* shall mean

(i) Any two NRSROs that have issued a rating with respect to a security or class of debt obligations of an issuer, or

(ii) If only one NRSRO has issued a rating with respect to such security or issuer at the time the fund purchases or rolls over the security, that NRSRO.

(14) *Second Tier Security* shall mean any Eligible Security that is not a First Tier Security.

(15) *Short-term* shall mean having a remaining maturity of 366 days or less.

(16) *Standby Commitment* shall mean a Put that entitles the holder to achieve same day settlement and to receive an exercise price equal to the amortized cost of the underlying security or securities plus accrued interest, if any, at the time of exercise.

(17) *Tax exempt fund* shall mean any money market fund that holds itself out as distributing income exempt from regular federal income tax.

(18) *Total Assets* shall mean, with respect to a money market fund using the Amortized Cost Method, the total amortized cost of its assets and, with respect to any other money market fund, the total market-based value of its assets.

(19) An *Unconditional Put* or an *Unconditional Demand Feature* shall mean a Put or a Demand Feature (including any guarantee, letter of credit or similar unconditional credit enhancement) that by its terms would be readily exercisable in the event of a default in the payment of principal or interest on the underlying security or securities.

(20) Any *Unrated Security* shall mean:

(i) A security with a remaining maturity of 397 days or less issued by an issuer that does not have a current Short-term rating assigned by any NRSRO:

(A) To the security, or

(B) To the issuer with respect to a class of Short-term debt obligations (or any security within that class) that is comparable in priority and security with the security; and

(ii) A security:

(A) That at the time of issuance was a Long-term security but that has a remaining maturity of 397 calendar days or less, and

(B) Whose issuer has not received from any NRSRO a rating with respect to a class of Short-term debt obligations (or any security within that class) that now is comparable in priority and security with the security; and

(iii) A security that is a rated security and is the subject of an external credit support agreement that was not in effect when the security (or the issuer) was assigned its rating.

A security is not an Unrated Security if any Short-term debt obligation ("reference security") that is issued by the same issuer and is comparable in priority and security with that security is rated by a NRSRO. The status of such security as an Eligible Security or First Tier Security shall be the same as that of the reference security.

(21) A *Variable Rate Instrument* shall mean a security the terms of which provide for the adjustment of its interest rate on set dates (such as the last day of a month or calendar quarter) and which, upon such adjustment, can reasonably be expected to have a market value that approximates its par value.

(b) *Holding Out.* It shall be an untrue statement of material fact within the meaning of section 34(b) of the Act (15 U.S.C. 80a–33(b)) for a registered investment company, in any registration statement, application, report, account, record, or other document filed or transmitted pursuant to the Act, including any advertisement, pamphlet, circular, form letter, or other sales literature addressed to or intended for distribution to prospective investors that is required to be filed with the Commission by section 24(b) of the Act (15 U.S.C. 80a–24(b)) to:

(1) Adopt the term "money market" as part of its name or title or the name or title of any redeemable security of which it is the issuer, or

(2) Hold itself out to investors as, or adopt a name which suggests that it is, a money market fund or the equivalent of a money market fund, unless such registered investment company meets the conditions of paragraphs (c)(2), (c)(3), and (c)(4) of this section. For purposes of this paragraph, a name which suggests that a registered investment company is a money market fund or the equivalent thereof shall include one which uses such terms as "cash," "liquid," "money," "ready assets" or similar terms.

(c) *Share Price Calculations.* The current price per share, for purposes of distribution, redemption and repurchase, of any redeemable security issued by any registered investment company ("money market fund"), notwithstanding the requirements of section 2(a)(41) of the Act (15 U.S.C. 80a–2(a)(41)) and of rule 2a–4 (17 CFR 270.2a–4) and rule 22c–1 (17 CFR 270.22c–1) thereunder, may be computed by use of the Amortized Cost Method or the Penny-Rounding Method: *Provided, however,* That:

(1) *Board Findings.* The board of directors of the money market fund shall determine, in good faith, that it is in the best interests of the fund and its shareholders to maintain a stable net asset value per share or stable price per share, by virtue of either the Amortized Cost Method or the Penny-Rounding Method, and that the money market fund will continue to use such method only so long as the board of directors believes that it fairly reflects the market-based net asset value per share.

(2) *Portfolio Maturity.* The money market fund shall maintain a dollar-weighted average portfolio maturity appropriate to its objective of maintaining a stable net asset value per share or price per share: *Provided, however,* That the money market fund will not:

(i) Except as provided in paragraph (c)(2)(ii) of this section, purchase any instrument with a remaining maturity of greater than 397 calendar days, or

(ii) In the case of a money market fund not using the Amortized Cost Method, purchase a Government security with a remaining maturity of greater than 762 calendar days; or

(iii) Maintain a dollar-weighted average portfolio maturity that exceeds ninety days.

(3) *Portfolio Quality.* The money market fund will limit its portfolio investments, including Puts and repurchase agreements, to those United States dollar-denominated instruments that its board of directors determines present minimal credit risks (which determination must be based on factors pertaining to credit quality in addition to the rating assigned to such instruments by a NRSRO) *and* which are at the time of acquisition Eligible Securities. In the case of an Unrated Security (including a demand instrument) other than a Government security, or a security that is an Eligible Security based on the rating of one NRSRO, unless the fund is a tax exempt fund, the acquisition of each such security by the money market fund must be approved or ratified by the money market fund's board of directors. For purposes of this section:

(i) A demand instrument that has an Unconditional Demand Feature may be determined to be an Eligible Security or a First Tier Security based solely on whether the Unconditional Demand Feature is an Eligible Security or First Tier Security, as the case may be; and

(ii) A demand instrument that does not have an Unconditional Demand Feature is not an Eligible Security or a First Tier Security unless it meets the requirements for being an Eligible Security or First Tier Security, as the case may be, and, in addition, the demand instrument or the Long-term debt securities of the issuer of the demand instrument have been rated by the Requisite NRSROs in one of the two highest rating categories for Long-term debt obligations (within which there may be sub-categories or gradations indicating relative standing), or, if unrated, are determined to be of comparable quality by the money market fund's board of directors.

(4)(i) *Portfolio Diversification: General.* Except for a Tax exempt fund, immediately after the acquisition of any security (other than a Government security):

(A) The money market fund shall not have invested more than five percent of its Total Assets in securities issued by the issuer of the security: *Provided, however,* That a fund may invest more than five percent of its Total Assets in the First Tier Securities of a single issuer for a period of up to three Business days after the purchase thereof (subject to section 5(b)(1) of the Act (15 U.S.C. 80a–5(b)(1)) if the money market fund is a diversified investment company): *Provided, further,* That the fund may not make more than one investment in accordance with the foregoing proviso at any time; and

(B) In the event that such security is a Second Tier Security, the money market fund shall not have invested more than

(1) The greater of one percent of its Total Assets or one million dollars in securities issued by that issuer which, when acquired by the fund (either initially or upon any subsequent roll over) where Second Tier Securities, and

(2) Five percent of its Total Assets in securities which, when acquired by the fund (either initially or upon any subsequent roll over) were Second Tier Securities. For purposes of making calculations under paragraph (c)(4)(i)(A) of this section, a repurchase agreement shall be deemed to be an acquisition of the underlying securities, provided that the obligation of the seller to repurchase the securities from the money market fund is Collateralized Fully.

(ii) *Portfolio Diversification: Puts.* Immediately after the acquisition of any Put, no more than five percent of the money market fund's Total Assets may be invested in securities issued by or subject to Puts from the same institution, *Provided, however,* That if the money market fund is a Tax exempt fund, the foregoing condition shall only be applicable with respect to 75 percent of its Total Assets.

(iii) *General.* For purposes of paragraph (c)(4) of this section:

(A) A Put will be considered to be from the party to whom the money market fund will look for payment of the exercise price;

(B) An Unconditional Put will be considered to be a guarantee of the underlying security or securities; and

(C) A guarantee of, or Unconditional Put with respect to, a security will not be deemed to be issued by the institution providing the guarantee or the Put, provided that the value of all securities held by the money market fund and issued or guaranteed by the issuer providing the guarantee or Put shall not exceed ten percent of the money market fund's Total Assets.

(5)(i) *Security Downgrades.* In the event that (A) a portfolio security of a money market fund ceases to be a First Tier Security (either because it no longer has the highest rating from the Requisite NRSROs or, in the case of an Unrated Security, the board of directors of the money market fund determines that it is no longer of comparable quality to a First Tier Security), or (B) the money market fund's investment adviser (or any person to whom the money market fund's board of directors has delegated portfolio management responsibilities) becomes aware that any Unrated Security or Second Tier Security held by the money market fund has, since the security was acquired by the fund, been given a rating by any NRSRO below the NRSRO's second highest rating category, the board of directors of the money market fund shall reassess promptly whether such security presents minimal credit risks and shall cause the money market fund to take such action as the board of directors determines is in the best interests of the money market fund and its shareholders; *Provided, however,* That the reassessment required by paragraph (c)(5)(i)(B) of this section is not required if, in accordance with the procedures adopted by the board of directors, the security is disposed of (or matures) within five Business days of the adviser becoming aware of the new rating and the board is subsequently notified of the adviser's actions.

(ii) *Defaults and Other Events.* In the event:

(A) Of a default with respect to a portfolio security (other than an immaterial default unrelated to the financial condition of the issuer); or

(B) A portfolio security of a money market fund ceases to be an Eligible Security; or

(C) It has been determined that a security no longer presents minimal credit risks;

absent a finding by the board of directors that disposal of the portfolio security would not be in the best interests of the money market fund (which determination may take into account, among other factors, market conditions that could affect the orderly disposition of the security), the money market fund shall dispose of such security as soon as practicable consistent with achieving an orderly disposition of the security, by sale, exercise of any Demand Feature or otherwise.

(iii) *Notice to the Commission.* In the event of a default with respect to one or more portfolio securities (other than an immaterial default unrelated to the financial condition of the issuer) which immediately before default accounted for 1/2 of 1 percent or more of a money market fund's Total Assets, the money market fund shall promptly notify the Commission of such fact and the actions the money market fund intends to take in response to such situation. Notification under this paragraph shall be made telephonically or by means of a facsimile transmission, followed by letter sent by first class mail, directed to the attention of the Director of the Division of the Investment Management.

(6) *Required Procedures: Amortized Cost Method.* In the case of a money market fund using the Amortized Cost Method:

(i) In supervising the money market fund's operations and delegating special responsibilities involving portfolio management to the money market fund's investment adviser, the money market fund's board of directors, as a particular responsibility within the overall duty of care owed to its shareholders, shall establish written procedures reasonably designed, taking into account current market conditions and the money market fund's investment objectives, to stabilize the money market fund's net asset value per share, as computed for the purpose of distribution, redemption and repurchase, at a single value.

(ii) Included within the procedures adopted by the board of directors shall be the following:

(A) Written procedures providing that the extent of deviation, if any, of the current net asset value per share calculated using available market quotations (or an appropriate substitute which reflects current market conditions) from the money market fund's amortized cost price per share, shall be calculated at such intervals as the board of directors determines appropriate and reasonable in light of current market conditions; periodic review by the board of directors of the amount of the deviation as well as the methods used to calculate the deviation; and maintenance of records of the determination of deviation and the board's review thereof; and

(B) In the event such deviation from the money market fund's amortized cost price per share exceeds 1/2 of 1 percent, a requirement that the board of directors shall promptly consider what action, if any, should be initiated by the board of directors; and

(C) Where the board of directors believes the extent of any deviation from the money market fund's amortized cost price per share may result in material dilution or other unfair results to investors or existing shareholders, it shall cause the fund to take such action as it deems appropriate to eliminate or reduce to the extent reasonably practicable such dilution or unfair results.

(7) *Required Procedures: Penny-Rounding Method.* In the case of a money market fund using the Penny-Rounding Method, in supervising the money market fund's operations and delegating special responsibilities involving portfolio management to the money market fund's investment adviser, the money market fund's board of directors undertakes, as a particular responsibility within the overall duty of care owed to its shareholders, to assure to the extent reasonably practicable, taking into account current market conditions affecting the money market fund's investment objectives, that the money market fund's price per share as computed for the purpose of distribution, redemption and repurchase, rounded to the nearest one percent, will not deviate from the single price established by the board of directors.

(8) *Record Keeping and Reporting.* The money market fund will record, maintain, and preserve permanently in an easily accessible place a written copy of the procedures (and any modifications thereto) described in paragraphs (c)(5), (c)(6), (c)(7) and (e) of this section, and the money market fund will record, maintain, and preserve for a period of not less than six years (the first two years in an easily accessible place) a written record of the board of directors' considerations and actions taken in connection with the discharge of its responsibilities, as set forth above, to be included in the minutes of the board of directors' meetings. The documents preserved pursuant to this condition shall be subject to inspection by the Commission in accordance with section 31(b) of the Act (15 U.S.C. 80a–30(b)) as if such documents were records required to be maintained pursuant to rules adopted under section 31(a) of the Act (15 U.S.C. 80a–30(a)). If any action was taken pursuant to paragraphs (c)(5)(ii) (with respect to defaulted securities) or (c)(6)(ii)(B) of this section, the money market fund will attach an exhibit to the Form N-SAR (17 CFR 274.101) filed for the period in which the action was taken describing with specificity the nature and circumstances of such action. The money market fund will report in an exhibit to such Form any securities it holds on the final day of the reporting period that are not Eligible Securities.

(d) *Maturity of Portfolio Instruments.* For the purposes of this rule, the maturity of a portfolio instrument shall be deemed to be the period remaining (calculated from the trade date or such other date on which the fund's interest in the instrument is subject to market action) until the date noted on the face of the instrument as the date on which the principal amount must be paid, or in the case of an instrument called for redemption, the date on which the redemption payment must be made, except that:

(1) An instrument that is issued or guaranteed by the United States government or any agency thereof which has a variable rate of interest readjusted no less frequently than every 762 days shall be deemed to have a maturity equal to the period remaining until the next readjustment of the interest rate.

(2) A Variable Rate Instrument, the principal amount of which is scheduled on the face of the instrument to be paid in 397 calendar days or less shall be deemed to have a maturity equal to the period remaining until the next readjustment of the interest rate.

(3) A Variable Rate Instrument that is subject to a Demand Feature shall be deemed to have a maturity equal to the longer of the period remaining until the next readjustment of the interest rate or the period remaining until the principal amount can be recovered through demand.

(4) A Floating Rate Instrument that is subject to a Demand Feature shall be deemed to have a maturity equal to the period remaining until the principal amount can be recovered through demand.

(5) A repurchase agreement shall be deemed to have a maturity equal to the period remaining until the date on which the repurchase of the underlying securities is scheduled to occur, or, where no date is specified, but the agreement is subject to a demand, the notice period applicable to a demand for the repurchase of the securities.

(6) A portfolio lending agreement shall be treated as having a maturity equal to the period remaining until the date on which the loaned securities are scheduled to be returned, or where no date is specified, but the agreement is subject to demand, the notice period applicable to a demand for the return of the loaned securities.

(e) *Delegation.* The money market fund's board of directors may delegate to the fund's investment adviser or officers the responsibility to make any determination required to be made by the board of directors under this section (other than the determinations required by the second sentence of paragraph (c)(3) (which may be delegated subject to ratification by the money market fund's board of directors) and paragraphs (c)(1), (c)(5)(i)(B), (c)(5)(ii), (c)(6)(i), (c)(6)(ii), and (c)(7) of this section) provided that the board:

(1) Establishes and periodically reviews written guidelines (including guidelines for determining whether instruments present minimal credit risks as required in paragraph (c)(3) of this section) and procedures under which the delegate makes such determinations; and

(2) Exercises adequate oversight (through periodic reviews of fund investments and the delegate's procedures in connection with investment decisions and prompt review of the adviser's actions in the event of the default of a security that requires notification of the Commission under paragraph (c)(5)(iii) of this section) to assure that the guidelines and procedures are being followed.

[56 FR 8124, Feb. 27, 1991, as amended at 56 FR 23106, May 20, 1991; 56 FR 26030, June 6, 1991]

17 C.F.R. PART 270—RULES AND REGULATIONS, INVESTMENT COMPANY ACT OF 1940

1. The authority citation for part 270 continues to read, in part, as follows:

Authority: 15 U.S.C. 80a–1 *et seq.*, sections 80a–37, 80a–39 unless otherwise noted;* * *

2. By adding § 270.3a–7 to read as follows:

17 C.F.R. § 270.3a–7 Issuers of Asset-Backed Securities

(a) Notwithstanding section 3(a) of the Act, any issuer who is engaged in the business of purchasing, or otherwise acquiring, and holding eligible assets (and in activities related or incidental thereto), and who does not issue redeemable securities will not be deemed to be an investment company; *Provided That:*

(1) The issuer issues fixed-income securities or other securities which entitle their holders to receive payments that depend primarily on the cash flow from eligible assets;

(2) Securities sold by the issuer or any underwriter thereof are fixed-income securities rated, at the time of initial sale, in one of the four highest categories assigned long-term debt or in an equivalent short-term category (within either of which there may be sub-categories or gradations indicating relative standing) by at least one nationally recognized statistical rating organization that is not an affiliated person of the issuer or of any person involved in the organization or operation of the issuer, except that:

(i) Any fixed-income securities may be sold to accredited investors as defined in paragraphs (1), (2), (3), and (7) of rule 501(a) under the Securities Act of 1933 (17 CFR 230.501(a)) and any entity in which all of the equity owners come within such paragraphs; and

(ii) Any securities may be sold to qualified institutional buyers as defined in rule 144A under the Securities Act (17 CFR 230.144A) and to persons (other than any rating organization rating the issuer's securities) involved in the organization or operation of the issuer or an affiliate, as defined in rule 405 under the Securities Act (17 CFR 230.405), of such a person;

Provided, That the issuer or any underwriter thereof effecting such sale exercises reasonable care to ensure that such securities are sold and will be resold to persons specified in paragraphs (a)(2) (i) and (ii) of this section;

(3) The issuer acquires additional eligible assets, or disposes of eligible assets, only if:

(i) The assets are acquired or disposed of in accordance with the terms and conditions set forth in the agreements, indentures, or other instruments pursuant to which the issuer's securities are issued;

(ii) The acquisition or disposition of the assets does not result in a downgrading in the rating of the issuer's outstanding fixed-income securities; and

(iii) The assets are not acquired or disposed of for the primary purpose of recognizing gains or decreasing losses resulting from market value changes; and

(4) If the issuer issues any securities other than securities exempted from the Securities Act by section 3(a)(3) thereof (15 U.S.C. 77c(a)(3)), the issuer:

(i) Appoints a trustee that meets the requirements of section 26(a)(1) of the Act and that is not affiliated, as that term is defined in rule 405 under the Securities Act (17 CFR 230.405), with the issuer or with any person involved in the organization or operation of the issuer, which does not offer or provide credit or credit enhancement to the issuer, and that executes an agreement or instrument concerning the issuer's securities containing provisions to the effect set forth in section 26(a)(3) of the Act;

(ii) Takes reasonable steps to cause the trustee to have a perfected security interest or ownership interest valid against third parties in those eligible assets that principally generate the cash flow needed to pay the fixed-income security holders, provided that such assets otherwise required to be held by the trustee may be released to the extent needed at the time for the operation of the issuer; and

(iii) Takes actions necessary for the cash flows derived from eligible assets for the benefit of the holders of fixed-income securities to be deposited periodically in a segregated account that is maintained or controlled by the trustee consistent with the rating of the outstanding fixed-income securities.

(b) For purposes of this section:

(1) *Eligible assets* means financial assets, either fixed or revolving, that by their terms convert into cash within a finite time period plus any rights or other assets designed to assure the servicing or timely distribution of proceeds to security holders.

(2) *Fixed-income securities* means any securities that entitle the holder to receive:

(i) A stated principal amount; or

(ii) Interest on a principal amount (which may be a notional principal amount) calculated by reference to a fixed rate or to a standard or formula which does not reference any change in the market value or fair value of eligible assets; or

(iii) Interest on a principal amount (which may be a notional principal amount) calculated by reference to auctions among holders and prospective holders, or through remarketing of the security; or

(iv) An amount equal to specified fixed or variable portions of the interest received on the assets held by the issuer; or

(v) Any combination of amounts described in paragraphs (b)(2) (i), (ii), (iii), and (iv) of this section; *Provided,* That substantially all of the payments to which the holders of such securities are entitled consist of the foregoing amounts.

By the Commission.

Dated: November 19, 1992.

Margaret H. McFarland,
Deputy Secretary.

[FR Doc. 92–28728 Filed 11–25–92; 8:45 am]

This letter was originally submitted on the letterhead of Brown & Wood, New York, N.Y.

Securities Act of 1933
Sections 3(a)(2) and 5

Investment Company Act of 1940
Section 3(a)

April 10, 1989

Office of Chief Counsel
Division of Corporation Finance

Office of Chief Counsel
Division of Investment Management

Securities and Exchange Commission
450 Fifth Street, N.W.
Judiciary Plaza
Washington, D.C. 20549

Re: *Merrill Lynch, Pierce, Fenner & Smith Incorporated*

Ladies and Gentlemen:

We are writing on behalf of Merrill Lynch, Pierce, Fenner & Smith Incorporated ("Merrill Lynch"), a registered broker-dealer and a municipal securities dealer, in connection with its Municipal Tax-exempt Investment Growth Receipts Program for Callable Bonds (the "Proposed Program").

We respectfully request that you confirm that:

(i) the Division of Corporation Finance will not recommend that the Securities and Exchange Commission (the "Commission") take any enforcement action under the Securities Act of 1933, as amended (the "Securities Act"), against Merrill Lynch or any other party involved in the Proposed Program, if the Proposed Program operates without registration of any security under the Securities Act; and

(ii) the Division of Investment Management will not recommend that the Commission take any enforcement action under the Investment Company Act of 1940, as amended (the "Investment Company Act"), if, in connection with the Proposed Program, the Custodian described below operates without registration of the Proposed Program as an investment company under the Investment Company Act.

The Existing Program

Since November 1986, Merrill Lynch has conducted Municipal Tax-exempt Investment Growth Receipt ("Municipal TIGR") Programs for Pre-Refunded Bonds and for Non-Callable Bonds (together, the "Existing Program") offering from time to time custodial receipts for components of stripped municipal bonds (the "Bonds"). The Existing Program is described generally in the enclosed Offering Circular, dated January 17, 1989, as supplemented, and has the features of a typical stripped-municipal program, including those features listed below.

In a letter dated January 19, 1989, from the Division of Market Regulation to the Municipal Securities Rulemaking Board (the "MSRB letter"), the staff of that Division addressed whether receipts sold pursuant to a stripped coupon municipal bond program were subject to the Board's Rules. In concluding that they were, the staff necessarily determined that the stripped coupon securities were "municipal securities" for purposes of Section 15B of the Securities Exchange Act of 1934, as amended (the "Exchange Act").

The conclusions of the MSRB letter were conditioned upon the program sponsor's obtaining an opinion of counsel as to the accuracy of representations in the offering circular that:

(a) owners of the stripped coupon securities will have all the rights and privileges of owners of the underlying municipal securities;

(b) each receipt holder, as a real party in interest, will have the right, upon default of the underlying municipal securities, to proceed directly and individually against the issuer of those securities; and

(c) the receipt holder will not be required to act in concert with other receipt holders or the custodian;

and were additionally conditioned upon the following factors:

(1) each receipt represents the entire interest in a discrete, identified interest payment or principal payment on the underlying municipal security;

(2) the custodian bank performs only clerical or ministerial services on behalf of the receipt holders;

(3) neither the custodian nor sponsor additionally will guarantee or otherwise enhance the creditworthiness of the underlying municipal security or the stripped coupon security;

(4) the custodian undertakes to notify receipt holders in the event of a default, and forward to receipt holders copies of all communications from the issuer of the underlying municipal security to the bondholders;

(5) an opinion of counsel is provided indicating that the underlying municipal securities will not be considered assets of either the sponsoring firm or custodian bank; and

(6) other factors are not present, such as remarketing agreements, that would require the investors in the stripped coupon securities to rely upon the sponsor to obtain the benefit of their investment.

Except for differences required by the economic substance of the Existing Program, its custodial arrangements are similar in all material respects to those that formed the basis for the no-action positions of the Division of Corporation Finance and the Division of Investment Management relating to custodial receipts for bonds insured in the secondary market. *Financial Security Assurance Inc.* (December 1, 1987); *Financial Guaranty Insurance Company* (November 18 and 29, 1988).*

---

*The response of the Division of Investment Management in the Financial Guaranty Insurance Company letter enumerates relevant factors similar to those expressed in the MSRB letter as follows:

(1) A custody receipt does not represent an undivided interest in all of the Securities held by the custodian but rather represents a direct interest in a Security;

(2) Each owner of a custody receipt would retain the absolute right to proceed directly against the issuer of the underlying security and would not be obligated to join the Custodian, Financial, or any other owner as a condition precedent to proceeding against any issuer;

While the MSRB letter expressed no view regarding whether the stripped coupon securities were "separate securities" for purposes of the Exchange Act, we submit that the conclusion that such securities constituted "municipal securities" under that Act necessarily determined that no separate security was created by virtue of the stripping and custody arrangements. Moreover, we believe that the analysis undertaken in the MSRB letter parallels the analysis required to determine whether a particular stripping and custody arrangement involves the creation of a separate security under the Securities Act or an investment company under the Investment Company Act.

The Existing Program complies with the nine conditions outlined in the MSRB letter. Accordingly, we are of the opinion that the holder of a Municipal TIGR has a direct ownership interest in the underlying Bond. Thus, there is no pooling of assets or other factor that could give rise to issuance of a separate security or creation of an investment company.

The Proposed Program

The Existing Program is limited to Bonds that are not redeemable prior to maturity (or to a redemption date fixed in an advance refunding). In addition, such Bonds have not included provisions for acceleration of maturity upon default. These limitations were imposed to avoid the risk of total loss faced, as the Existing Program is structured, by the owner of an interest component ("Coupon Municipal TIGR") upon redemption or acceleration of the related Bonds prior to the due date of the interest payment. Based upon its experience to date, Merrill Lynch believes that the demand for Municipal TIGRs is greater than can be satisfied by stripping Bonds that fit the Existing Program.

To facilitate the stripping of Bonds subject to call or acceleration, Merrill Lynch proposes to recharacterize the ownership rights evidenced by the Municipal TIGRs in accordance with economic reality, to recognize that each Bond component, at any given time, has an economic value equivalent to the present value (the face amount of the Municipal TIGR discounted to an earlier date at an appropriate interest rate) of the future payment represented by that Municipal TIGR.

The present value allocation approach provides for a fair allocation of proceeds among the outstanding component parts upon any acceleration, whether by reason of redemption or default. At any given time, the present value of all component parts (all future interest payments plus principal amount) of a fixed interest bearing instrument will equal the stated principal amount, if the discount rate used in determining present value is the stated interest rate. If so determined by Merrill Lynch at the initial sale of a series of Municipal TIGRs, different discount rates may be used to reflect the offering yields. (The price at which a Municipal TIGR is issued is itself the present value of its face amount discounted at the applicable market rate.) In either case, the basis of calculation will be objectively determined, provided to the Custodian at issuance, disclosed to investors, and applied consistently to ownership, voting rights, and distribution of prepayments. If the amount of a Bond prepayment does not equal the sum of the defined present values of the related Municipal TIGRs ("Present Values"), either because

(3) The Custodian would forward to each owner any notices it receives concerning the Securities, and could take action with respect to the Securities, e.g., voting, only upon instruction form the owner; and

(4) The Custodian performs only ministerial, rather than discretionary, functions that are necessary to solve certain secondary market Security identification problems and to provide economically the insurance benefits to the owners.

the stated rate was not used or because the prepayment is more (redemption at a premium) or less (default) than par, the prepayment will be applied proportionately to the Present Values.

The ownership rights and the mechanics of redemption, acceleration and voting, in the Proposed Program are as follows:

Municipal TIGRs. Each Municipal TIGR evidences a direct interest in one of the scheduled payments of interest (Coupon Municipal TIGRs) or principal (and redemption premium, if any, in the case of pre-refunded or other bonds scheduled to be redeemed on a certain date) (Principal Municipal TIGRs) on the underlying Bonds, such ownership interest to be valued at the Present Value of such payment in the event of early redemption or acceleration.

Coupon Municipal TIGRs. Each Coupon Municipal TIGR evidences ownership of one of the semiannual interest payments due on the underlying Bonds up to and including the date on which principal of the underlying Bonds is payable, such ownership interest to be valued at the Present Value of such interest payment in the event of early redemption or acceleration.

Principal Municipal TIGRs. Principal Municipal TIGRs evidence ownership of the principal and redemption premium, if any, payable at maturity or scheduled redemption on the underlying Bonds, such ownership interest to be valued at the Present Value thereof in the event of early redemption or acceleration.

Redemption of Bonds. Interest payments received by the Custodian upon redemption of Bonds prior to maturity of the related Municipal TIGRs shall be distributed to the holders of the related Coupon Municipal TIGRs maturing on or, if the redemption date is not a maturity date of Coupon Municipal TIGRs, next following the redemption date. Principal and redemption premium, if any, received on such redemption shall be distributed in redemption of the related Municipal TIGRs maturing after the redemption date, including Coupon Municipal TIGRs and Principal Municipal TIGRs, proportionately to the Present Values (net of interest accrued to such date) of such Municipal TIGRs at the redemption date.

Upon redemption of less than all the Bonds of a series, the Municipal TIGRs to be redeemed shall be selected in a manner deemed fair and appropriate by the Custodian.

Default on Bonds. If the Issuer of any Bond defaults on the payment of any interest or principal evidenced by a Municipal TIGR, the Custodian shall promptly give notice to holders of the related series of Municipal TIGRs. Such notice shall set forth (a) the identity of the issue of Bonds, (b) the date and nature of such default, (c) the face amount of the interest or principal, (d) the numbers of the Municipal TIGRs evidencing the defaulted interest or principal, and (e) any other information that the Custodian may deem appropriate. The Custodian will not be authorized to assert the rights and privileges of Municipal TIGR holders and will have no duty to do so. In the event the Custodian receives money or other property in connection with the payment of interest or principal after default, the Custodian shall promptly give notice, as provided in the Custody Agreement, to the holders of the affected series of Municipal TIGRs. Such notice shall state that, not later than 90 days after the receipt of such money or other property, the Custodian shall distribute such money or other property in accordance with the Custody Agreement and the characterization given such payments by the issuer of, or the Trustee for, the Bonds. Interest shall be allocated to Coupon Municipal TIGRs in order of maturity and pro rata within a maturity. Principal received upon acceleration of maturity of Bonds (i) on account of Bonds stated to mature on or before the date of acceleration shall be allocated to the related Principal Municipal TIGRs and (ii) on account of Bonds stated to mature thereafter shall be allocated to the related Municipal TIGRs maturing after the effective date of such acceleration, including Coupon Municipal TIGRs and Principal Municipal TIGRs, proportionately to their Present Values at such date; if acceleration has not been declared, or has been rescinded, the principal shall be allocated, pro rata, to Principal Municipal TIGRs that are due or overdue. In the event that no characterization is made or the characterization is not clear, the Custodian shall seek instructions from a court in which proceedings against the issuer are pending or bring an action in a court of competent jurisdiction in the State of New York seeking to have such court determine the relative rights of the holders of Municipal TIGRs to any such payments. The expenses of such action incurred by the Custodian shall be paid by the holders of Municipal TIGRs to the extent of the payments received by the Custodian.

Present Value. Should Bonds be redeemed or declared due and payable upon default prior to maturity (or, in the case of Bonds scheduled to be redeemed on a certain date, scheduled redemption) the principal and any redemption premium received by the Custodian shall be owned by the holders of, and allocated proportionately to the Present Values of, the related Municipal TIGRs maturing after the redemption or acceleration date, including Coupon Municipal TIGRs and Principal Municipal TIGRs; Present Values to be determined by the Custodian based on a schedule or formula either provided by Merrill Lynch at the initial delivery of the Municipal TIGRs or (if no such schedule or formula is so provided) computed by discounting the respective face amounts thereof from the respective stated maturities or redemption dates to the date of redemption or acceleration at the stated interest rate on the Bonds, compounded semiannually.

For voting purposes, Municipal TIGRs that have not reached stated maturity shall be weighted by such schedule, formula or computation; Municipal TIGRs that are due or overdue, and unpaid, if any, shall be weighted by their face amounts or the unpaid remainders thereof.

Voting Rights. In the event of any action requiring a vote of the holders of any Bonds, the Custodian shall deliver to the holders of Municipal TIGRs related to such Bonds its proxy for such vote, returnable to the Custodian, who shall vote solely in accordance with such proxies, weighted by Present Value. The Custodian shall not take any action as the nominal holder or owner of the Bonds, either alone or as part of a group of such holders or owners, without the affirmative direction of a majority in interest, based upon Present Value, of the holders of the Municipal TIGRs related thereto after notifying such holders of such action.

Analysis

In deciding whether the Proposed Program involves the creation of a separate security under the Securities Act or an investment company under the Investment Company Act, we have addressed the question whether the present value concept imposes duties upon the Custodian that are more than ministerial. In this regard, the MSRB letter requires compliance with the following factor:

(2) the custodian bank performs only clerical or ministerial services on behalf of the receipt holders;

and further states in note 7:

In this regard, we would emphasize that, as described above, the custodial arrangements generally are structured to ensure that the custodian's role is essentially passive and that in all material respects the receipt holder is the real party in interest and otherwise treated as the beneficial owner of an interest in the underlying municipal security.

We believe that application of prepayments on Bonds in proportion to the Present Value of the component parts thereof, consistent with the holders' ownership and voting rights, does not violate condition (2) as expanded upon in note 7.

Incidental to the initial offering of a series of Municipal TIGRs, Merrill Lynch may provide to the Custodian a schedule or formula for determining the Present Value of the various bond components represented by the Municipal TIGRs. If prepared, this schedule or formula will reflect the yields to maturity of the Municipal TIGRs based on market conditions at the offering. Alternatively, the Custodian may be directed to compute Present Value by discounting the face amounts of the Municipal TIGRs at the interest rate on the underlying Bonds. In either case, the Custodian's duties are (a) ministerial, (b) designed to facilitate the distribution of prepayments to the beneficial owners thereof and (c) consistent with the duties of other corporate trustees in similar circumstances. For example, zero coupon bonds are issued subject to redemption pursuant to an appreciation schedule that is economically equivalent to the redemption of Municipal TIGRs at their present values. *See, e.g.*, Official Statement dated October 20, 1988, covering $275,001,169.50 New York City Municipal Water Finance Authority Water and Sewer System Revenue Bonds, Fiscal 1989 Series A, page 4 and Appendix G (copy enclosed). The trustee for such bonds performs the same calculation upon redemption that the Municipal TIGR Custodian would perform in computing Present Value.

Conclusion

We believe that the above-cited no-action letters and the MSRB letter set forth the conditions to the exempt status of the Municipal TIGR program under the Securities Act and the Investment Company Act and that the Municipal TIGR program, including the Proposed Program, is in compliance with these conditions. We are, accordingly, of the opinion that the Municipal TIGR program, including the Proposed Program, neither gives rise to any security separate from the underlying exempt Bonds for purposes of the Securities Act nor creates an investment company within the meaning of the Investment Company Act. For the reasons stated above, we request that you confirm that, with reference specifically to the Proposed Program for callable bonds, (i) the Municipal TIGRs may be issued without registration under Section 5 of the Securities Act and (ii) the Custodian may operate without registration as an investment company under the Investment Company Act.

In view of the importance of the outcome of this request to our client in proceeding with the Proposed Program, we respectfully request a response to this letter as soon as practicable. If you have any questions concerning the Proposed Program or the issues raised in this letter, please do not hesitate to contact Thomas R. Smith, Jr. at (212) 839-5535 or Homer Schaaf at (212) 839-5566.

Very truly yours,

Enclosures

This letter was originally submitted on the letterhead of Brown & Wood, New York, N.Y.

July 13, 1989

Edward L. Pittman
Securities and Exchange Commission
Division of Market Regulation
450 5th Street, N.W.
Washington, D.C. 20549

Re: *Merrill Lynch Municipal TIGR Program*

Dear Ed:

This letter follows up our telephone conversation last Friday with respect to the no-action request of Merrill Lynch, Pierce, Fenner & Smith Incorporated dated April 10, 1989 with respect to the Municipal TIGR Program for Callable Bonds (the "Proposed Program"). A single series of Municipal TIGRs will consist of Coupon TIGRs and Principal TIGRs. Each Municipal TIGR will evidence ownership of a scheduled payment of interest (Coupon TIGRs) or principal (Principal TIGRs) on the underlying Bonds.

Prior to the date hereof the Municipal TIGR Program has not included Bonds containing provisions making such Bonds subject to prepayment either by redemption prior to maturity or by acceleration of maturity upon default because of the uncertainties as to how the prepayment might be allocated among the TIGR components. The owner of a Coupon TIGR faces the risk of total loss upon prepayment prior to the due date of the interest payment represented by such Coupon TIGR if such prepayment should be allocated in its entirety to the Principal TIGRs. To facilitate the stripping of Bonds subject to prepayment, the Proposed Program will characterize the ownership rights with respect to Municipal TIGRs to provide for the valuation of such Municipal TIGRs at any given time at their then present value ("Present Value").

Present Value is calculated by discounting the face amount of the Municipal TIGR from its payment date to an earlier date at an appropriate interest rate ("discount rate"). The Present Value characterization of the ownership rights is in accordance with economic reality and recognizes that each Bond component, at any given time, has an economic value equivalent to an appropriately determined Present Value. At any given time, the Present Value of all component parts (all future interest payments plus principal amount) of a fixed interest bearing instrument will equal the stated principal amount, if the discount rate used in determining Present Value is the stated interest rate.

Another way of looking at this is to recognize that each separate TIGR component is a zero coupon obligation. The value of a zero coupon obligation prior to maturity is not its face amount payable at maturity but rather its then Present Value, a fact which is well recognized in the market place. It is for this reason that zero coupon instruments subject to prepayments incorporate an appreciation schedule that provides for the prepayments to be made in an amount equal to the then Present Value thereof rather than the face amount.

To avoid the possibility of Coupon TIGR extinguishment upon prepayment, the Proposed Program will contain provisions that specifically incorporate the foregoing economic reality into the custody arrangements and provide for the proportionate allocation of proceeds received upon prepayment among the then outstanding Coupon TIGRs and Principal TIGRs based upon their respective Present Values at the time of prepayment. The Custodian will be provided with a schedule or formula for determining the Present Value of the various Bond components represented by the Municipal TIGR at any given time. Based upon this determination, a specific percentage of any prepayment can be allocated to each Bond component at any point in time. The custody arrangements will provide that the holder of each Bond component (represented by Coupon and Principal TIGRs) has a divided interest in any prepayment in an amount equal to the percentage of the prepayment allocated to such Bond component under the Present Value allocation formula.

You have asked us to consider whether this Present Value allocation method provides the various TIGR holders with undivided interests in the prepayment raising questions under a series of participation no-action letters to the effect that a separate security exists when the participation consists of an undivided interest in an underlying security or, more commonly, a pool of underlying securities. *Josephthal & Co.*, [1974–75 Transfer Binder] Fed. Sec. L. Rep. (CCH) ¶ 80,116 (available Nov. 24, 1974); *Underwood, Neuhaus & Co.*, [1974–75 Transfer Binder] Fed. Sec. L. Rep. (CCH) ¶ 80,156 (available Feb. 13, 1975); *The Security Bank, N.A.* (available July 16, 1979); *Bank of Oregon* (available December 20, 1979); *Buffalo Savings Bank* (available October 25, 1982); *NEA-New Hampshire Payroll Investment Plan* (available April 29, 1983); and *League Central Credit Union* (available August 21, 1987). In particular, you have asked if the Present Value allocation method provides the Coupon TIGR holders with an undivided interest in the principal payment on the underlying Bond.

It is respectfully submitted that the Present Value allocation method does not create undivided interests in the prepayment. In the first place, the prepayment amount should not be equated with the principal payment. If the prepayment represented only the principal component of the Bond, it would be in an amount equal to the principal payment's Present Value at the time of prepayment. The prepayment represents a payment with respect to the whole Bond (not only the principal amount but also each outstanding interest payment). The Present Value allocation method works because, as discussed above, the prepayment will approximate the total of the Present Values of each of these component parts of the underlying Bond. This enables the custodian (applying a mechanical formula) to divide and allocate the prepayment among the various component parts of the Bonds represented by the TIGRs. The custody arrangements will provide that the holder of each Bond component (represented by Coupon and Principal TIGRs) has a divided interest in any prepayment in an amount equal to the percentage of the prepayment allocated to such Bond component under the Present Value allocation formula. It is our opinion that this clearly distinguishes the Proposed Program from the participation no-action letters involving undivided interests in underlying securities.

Hopefully, this letter is responsive to the matters we discussed last Friday. Please do not hesitate to contact Thomas R. Smith, Jr. at (212) 839-5535 or Homer D. Schaaf at (212) 839-5566 as to any further questions.

Very truly yours,

cc: Catherine T. Dixon
Elizabeth T. Tsai

This letter was originally submitted on the letterhead of Brown & Wood, New York, N.Y.

July 19, 1989

Edward L. Pittman
Securities and Exchange Commission
Division of Market Regulation
450 5th Street, N.W.
Washington, D.C. 20549

Re: *Merrill Lynch Municipal TIGR Program*

Dear Ed:

In our telephone conversation on Friday, July 14, you asked us to consider Release No. 34–5633 (January 31, 1958) (the "Release") in the context of the Municipal TIGR Program (particularly paragraph (i) of such Release). The Release addressed the circumstances upon which offerings of mortgages under arrangements which provide for a variety of services to the investor might be deemed to constitute an "investment contract" and thus a "security" within the meaning of the federal securities laws. The Release listed services and attributes of the arrangements which in the opinion of the SEC may give rise to the creation of "investment contracts" with paragraph (i) therein referring to "providing for fractional interests in mortgages or deeds of trust."

It is submitted that the separate security analysis required for the Municipal TIGR program differs markedly from the investment contract analysis under consideration in the Release. Fractionalization is a factor in determining the circumstances which may give rise to the creation of an "investment contract" in the context of an offering of mortgages. On the other hand, the separate security analysis involves participations in underlying securities. Accordingly, fractionalization is endemic to all participation or custodial programs including the programs which were the subject of the letter dated January 19, 1989 from the Division of Market Regulation to the Municipal Securities Rulemaking Board (the "MSRB Letter") and *Financial Security Assurance, Inc.* (December 1, 1987). In conducting a separate security analysis, the question is not whether fractionalization exists in the participation arrangement, but whether the participation interest represents a divided interest in the underlying security or an undivided interest in something that cannot otherwise be divided (i.e., a pool of different securities, a pooling to enable investors to purchase a large denomination certificate of deposit which in smaller denominations would be subject to an interest rate limitation).

In a series of no-action letters, the staff of the Commission has agreed that the fractionalization inherent in participations or custody-type arrangements do not result in the issuance of a separate security when the beneficial owner of the fractional interest is deemed to have a direct distinct interest in the underlying security and the right to proceed individually and directly against the obligor of such security, the custodian's functions are purely administrative and involve no investment discretion and no investment purpose is involved in the custodial arrangement (i.e., the pooling did not present an opportunity for profit or investment risk that would not be present were such funds invested directly in the underlying security). *Financial Security Assurance Inc.* (dated December 1, 1987); *Financial Guaranty Insurance Company* (letters dated November 18 and 29, 1988). See also the following no-action letters which relate to primary participation programs in which the issuer of the underlying security is a party: *Best Products Co., Inc.* (available February 11, 1980) (master note arrangement); *Prudential-American Securities Inc.* (available January 26, 1975) (aggregation arrangement involving banker's acceptances); *Blyth Eastman Dillon & Company* (available May 21, 1975) (commercial paper safekeeping and hypothecation plan); *Bankers Trust Company* (available July 4, 1982) (sale of depository receipts for underlying banker's acceptances); *Kelling & Co., Inc.* (available October 22, 1984) (certificates of participation in municipal leases); *Lincoln Federal Savings and Loan Association* (available January 8, 1985) (pooling of customers' funds in money market deposit accounts); *E.F. Hutton & Company Inc.* (available March 28, 1985) (units of participation in FSLIC-insured certificates of deposit); *United Financial Banking Companies, Inc.* (available May 11, 1988) (master note commercial paper program).

We also discussed the Municipal TIGR program as a secondary market participation program and the relationship in such programs between beneficial holders of the fractional interests represented by the Municipal TIGRs and the issuer of the underlying municipal bonds (the "Issuer"). The Issuer is not a party to the custody arrangements in secondary market participation arrangements and it has no knowledge of the identity of the holders of the Municipal TIGRs. However, it does not follow from this that the Municipal TIGRs do not represent the Issuer's obligations. Under the bond registration system it is quite possible that the only holders known to an Issuer of bonds could be financial intermediaries holding for their members or customers through layers of nominee and sub-nominee accounts, and there may be no knowledge on the part of the Issuer as to the identity of the beneficial owners, much less any specific acknowledgment of its obligations to any particular beneficial owner. Frequently, the Issuer knows only a depository system selected by it such as The Depository Trust Company. The custodial arrangements pursuant to which the Municipal TIGRs are issued can be viewed as nothing more than a formal secondary market nominee arrangement.

If the Issuer should default on its obligation evidenced by a Municipal TIGR, the holder of the Municipal TIGR, as the real party in interest, is entitled to proceed directly against the Issuer and no one else. In such proceedings, the holder of the Municipal TIGR obviously must establish his beneficial ownership of the principal or interest payment evidenced by the Municipal TIGR (which would be valued at its present value upon acceleration) on the basis of traditional principles of principal and agency law.

If the Issuer makes full payment on its obligation to the record holder thereof, it has satisfied its obligation. If such payment is not transmitted properly by the financial intermediaries (including the Custodian) maintaining the nominee and sub-nominee accounts and does not reach the beneficial owner, such beneficial owner has a cause of action against the Custodian (or another financial intermediary between the Issuer and the beneficial owner) for wrongful conversion of his funds.[1] It is well established that the custodial or agency risk of wrongful conver-

---

[1]Under the formal custodial arrangements pursuant to which the Municipal TIGRs are issued, the Custodian acts as the functional equivalent of a registrar, transfer agent and dividend

sion does not create a separate security or interpose another obligor (or a joint obligor) with respect to the Bonds. If this were the case, all municipal obligations held in nominee or street name accounts would be subject to losing their exempt status under the federal securities laws and the banks and brokers holding securities on behalf of beneficial owners would be faced with staggering potential liabilities.

Most of the letters cited above involve the fractionalization of whole debt instruments. The MSRB Letter and the Municipal TIGR program involve stripping (the further fractionalization of component parts of the underlying Bonds) but the fundamental principals remain the same. In stripping, the custodian is able to identify and provide the beneficial holder with a direct distinct interest in the component part of the Bond and the right to proceed individually and directly against the obligor of such security. The same is true in connection with prepayments. In such case, applying the mechanical formula prescribed by the present value allocation method, the custodian is able to identify direct distinct interests in the prepayment based upon their respective present values which are allocable to the then outstanding component parts of the Bond represented by Municipal TIGRs. The holders of the Municipal TIGRs with respect to such component parts have the same rights to proceed against the portion of the prepayment allocated to them as would be the case upon the stated maturity of such component part.

Hopefully, this letter is responsive to the matters we discussed last Friday. Please do not hesitate to contact Thomas R. Smith, Jr. at (212) 839-5535 or Homer D. Schaaf at (212) 839-5566 as to any further questions.

Very truly yours,

cc: Catherine T. Dixon
Elizabeth T. Tsai

paying agent. The custodial arrangement is designed to provide an efficient mechanism pursuant to which payments on the component parts of the Bonds will be made through the financial intermediaries to the proper beneficial owner.

This letter was originally submitted on the letterhead of Brown & Wood, New York, N.Y.

August 1, 1989

Ms. Abigail Arms
Division of Corporation Finance
Securities and Exchange Commission
450 Fifth Street
Washington, D.C. 20549

Re: *Merrill Lynch Municipal TIGR*

Dear Ms. Arms:

This letter is in response to our telephone conversation of July 24, 1989 relating to the no-action request of Merrill Lynch, Pierce, Fenner & Smith Incorporated dated April 10, 1989 with respect to the Municipal TIGR Program for Callable Bonds (the "Proposed Program").[1] In such conversation, you asked us to consider whether the present value allocation method that would be set forth in the custody agreement for the Proposed Program results in "a recharacterization of payment rights" and "a redetermination of the obligor/obligee relationship." Pointing out that a prepayment extinguishes the right to receive future interest payments, you asked us to consider whether it is possible for the custody agreement to provide the holder of a Coupon TIGR with respect to such extinguished future interest payments any right against the issuer with respect to a prepayment (inquiring whether the only right of the holder of the Coupon TIGR in that instance would be against the custodian).

We do not believe that the present value allocation method results in a recharacterization of payment rights resulting from a prepayment because of the fact that a prepayment relates to all the then outstanding component parts of a bond and compensates the holder of a bond for forfeiture of his income payments over the remaining term of the bond as well as the payment of principal at maturity of such bond.[2] The holders of Coupon TIGRs and Principal TIGRs have a direct ownership interest in such component parts and, therefore, are entitled to be compensated for the value of such component parts. The present value allocation method allocates the prepayment to the various component parts based upon the present value of each component part. It does not recharacterize rights but rather identifies that portion of the prepayment which rightfully relates to the various component parts. The principal portion of the bond has been separated from the interest payments

---

[1]A single series of Municipal TIGRs will consist of Coupon TIGRs and Principal TIGRs. Each Municipal TIGR will evidence ownership of a scheduled payment of interest (Coupon TIGRs) or principal (Principal TIGRs) on the underlying Bonds.

[2]The rationale of the present value allocation method and the reasons why it provides for a fair allocation of the prepayment amongst the various component parts of the underlying bonds is discussed in our letter of July 13, 1989 to Edward L. Pittman, a copy of which is attached hereto as Exhibit A.

and if the prepayment were deemed to relate only to the principal amount, then the holders of the Principal TIGR would receive more than the present value thereof and would reap a windfall.[3] This recharacterization discussion raises the same issues discussed in the Pittman letter attached hereto as to whether the present value allocation method provides the various TIGR holders with undivided interests in the prepayment.

You have asked us to address thc question of whether the custody agreement can assign portions of the prepayment to the various component parts and convey rights to the Coupon TIGR holders against the issuer as to such portion of the prepayment. The custody agreement provides each TIGR holder with a direct discrete divided interest in a specific portion of the underlying bond and provides the TIGR holder with the right to proceed individually and directly against the obligor of such bond under the principles of law governing the assignment of claims. As discussed above, the present value allocation divides the prepayment into direct discrete divided interests related to the component parts based upon a mechanical formula. It is submitted that a proper assignment of these distinct interests in the prepayment can be made in the custody agreement to the holders of TIGRs representing the various component parts based upon the same assignment of claims legal theory relevant to the fundamental stripping issue addressed in our draft Municipal TIGR opinion on pp. 17–18 (a copy of which you have received).

The stripping and sale of the discrete interests in the underlying bond provided for in the custody agreement constitutes an assignment of claims as a matter of law. As discussed in our opinion, the general rule in this regard is that rights are assignable unless the assignment: (1) would materially change the duty of the obligor; (2) would materially increase the burden or risk imposed upon the obligor by the contract; (3) would materially impair the obligor's chance of obtaining return performance; (4) is forbidden by statute or is otherwise inoperative on grounds of public policy; or (5) is validly precluded by contract. Restatement (Second) of Contracts § 317(2). When the obligor's duty is solely to pay money on an otherwise fully executed contract, a change in the person to whom the payment is to be made is ordinarily not considered material. *Id.*, comment (d).

Under the bond registration system, neither the obligation of the issuer on the bonds nor the burden associated with fulfilling its obligation will be affected by the Municipal TIGR program. The issuer will be required to make all interest and principal payments and all prepayments solely to the registered owner (the Custodian or its direct or indirect nominee), regardless of how many beneficial owners exist. The Custodian will merely allocate such prepayment among the holders of the component parts of the bonds based on the value of such holders' interests calculated pursuant to the mechanical formula described herein. Accordingly, we believe that there is a valid assignment of the rights with respect to the discrete interests in the component parts of the underlying bond (including the discrete interests in any prepayment with respect to such component parts) inasmuch as there

[3]The present value (i.e., the value in today's dollars) of the Principal TIGRs which evidence an ownership interest in the principal amount of a $100,000 bond bearing interest at the rate of 10% and scheduled to mature on August 15, 1993 is approximately $62,092. The remaining $37,908 constitutes the aggregate present value of the interest payments scheduled to be paid on the bond to maturity which are owned by the holders of Coupon TIGRs. Therefore, payment today of $100,000 to the holders of such Principal TIGRs upon prepayment of the underlying bond would overcompensate such holders at the expense of holders of the Coupon TIGRs.

is no change in the performance due from the obligor. Of course, as discussed in the draft Municipal TIGR opinion on pp. 20–21, the holder of the Municipal TIGR obviously must establish beneficial ownership of the component part (valued at present value upon acceleration) evidenced by the Municipal TIGR on the basis of traditional principles of principal and agency law.

Hopefully, this letter is responsive to the matters we discussed last Monday. Please do not hesitate to contact Thomas R. Smith, Jr. at (212) 839-5535 or Homer D. Schaaf at (212) 839-5566 as to any further questions.

Very truly yours,

cc: Edward L. Pittman
Catherine T. Dixon
Elizabeth T. Tsai

This letter was originally submitted on the letterhead of Brown & Wood, New York, N.Y.

Securities Act of 1933
Sections 3(a) and 5

Investment Company Act of 1940
Section 3(a)

August 1, 1990

Office of Chief Counsel
Division of Corporation Finance

Office of Chief Counsel
Division of Investment Management

Securities and Exchange Commission
450 Fifth Street, N.W.
Judiciary Plaza
Washington, D.C. 20549

Re: *Merrill Lynch, Pierce, Fenner & Smith Incorporated*

Ladies and Gentlemen:

This letter further supplements our no-action request of April 10, 1989 (the "1989 Letter")[1] on behalf of Merrill Lynch, Pierce, Fenner & Smith Incorporated ("Merrill Lynch") in connection with its Municipal Tax-exempt Investment Growth Receipts ("Municipal TIGR's") program. A copy of the 1989 Letter is enclosed.

The 1989 Letter describes the existing Municipal TIGR's program (referred to therein as the "Existing Program") pursuant to which Merrill Lynch offers custodial receipts for components of stripped municipal bonds ("Bonds"). The Existing Program is limited to Bonds that are not redeemable prior to maturity (or to a redemption date fixed in an advance refunding) and do not contain provisions for acceleration of maturity upon default. These limitations were imposed to eliminate the possibility that an owner of a Municipal TIGR relating to an interest payment will incur a total loss of such payment upon redemption or acceleration of the underlying Bonds prior to the due date of the interest payment. The 1989 Letter sought a no-action response with respect to a proposed Municipal TIGR program (referred to therein on the "Proposed Program") which would facilitate the stripping of Bonds subject to call or acceleration by utilizing a present value allocation

[1]The 1989 Letter was also supplemented by letters of this firm to Edward L. Pittman dated July 13, 1989 and July 19, 1989 and to Abigail Arms dated August 1, 1989. In addition, a meeting with respect to the matter was held with members of the staff of the Commission on November 8, 1989.

method of allocating proceeds paid upon redemption or any acceleration of maturity among the holders of the Municipal TIGR's relating to of the then outstanding components of the Bonds.

Based upon our discussions, the requests and representations in the 1989 Letter are hereby modified as follows:

1. We request your advice solely with respect to the Existing Program. Our previous request relating to the Proposed Program, as defined in the 1989 Letter, including the present value allocation method; is withdrawn.
2. In the 1989 letter we indicated, among other things, that Merrill Lynch would obtain an opinion of counsel as to the accuracy of representations in the offering circular that:
   (a) owners of the stripped coupon securities will have all the rights and privileges of owners of the underlying municipal securities;
   (b) each receipt holder, as a real party in interest, will have the right, upon default of the underlying municipal securities, to proceed directly and individually against the issuer of those securities; and
   (c) the receipt holder will not be required to act in concert with other receipt holders or the custodian.

Such opinion will not be limited to the accuracy of representations to investors, but will specifically address, among other matters, the substance of these three items.

For the reasons set forth in the 1989 Letter, as herein modified, we are of the opinion that under the Existing Program the holder of a Municipal TIGR has a direct ownership interest in the underlying Bond and that the Existing Program neither results in the issuance of a security separate from the underlying Bonds for purposes of the Securities Act of 1933 nor creates an investment company within the meaning of the Investment Company Act of 1940. Accordingly we respectfully request that you confirm that:

(i) the Division of Corporation Finance will not recommend that the Securities and Exchange Commission take any enforcement action under the Securities Act of 1933, against Merrill Lynch or any other party involved in the Existing Program, if the Existing Program operates without registration of any security under the Securities Act of 1933; and

(ii) the Division of Investment Management will not recommend that the Securities and Exchange Commission take any enforcement action under the Investment Company Act of 1940, if, in connection with the Existing Program, the custodian issuing the custody receipts with respect to the Municipal TIGR program operates without registration of the Existing Program as an investment company under the Investment Company Act of 1940.

If you have any questions concerning the issues raised in this letter, please do not hesitate to contact Thomas R. Smith, Jr., at (212) 839-5535 or Homer Schaaf at (212) 839-5566.

Very truly yours,

Enclosures

Response of the Office of Chief Counsel Division of Corporation Finance

Re: Merrill Lynch, Pierce, Fenner & Smith Incorporated Incoming letters dated April 10, 1989, July 13, 1989, July 19, 1989, August 1, 1989 and August 1, 1990

Based on the facts presented, this Division concurs in your view that the custodial receipts evidencing separate rights to receive payment of the interest and principal portions of the described municipal securities under the Municipal Tax-Exempt Investment Growth Receipts Programs for Pre-Refunded Bonds and Non-Callable Bonds (together the "Existing Program") would be exempt from registration under section 3(a)(2) of the Securities Act of 1933 ("Securities Act"). Our position is based on your representations: (1) that the owners of the stripped coupon securities ("receipt holders") will have all the rights and privileges of owners of the underlying municipal securities; (2) that each receipt holder, as a real party in interest, will have the right, upon default of the underlying municipal securities, to proceed directly and individually against the issuer of those securities; (3) and that the receipt holder will not be required to act in concert with other receipt holders or the custodian.[1] Our position is further conditioned on the sponsor obtaining an opinion of counsel to this effect, as well as the following factors: (1) each receipt represents the entire interest in a discrete, identified interest payment or principal payment on the underlying municipal security; (2) the custodian bank performs only clerical or ministerial services on behalf of the receipt holders; (3) neither the custodian nor sponsor additionally will guarantee or otherwise enhance the creditworthiness of the underlying municipal security or the stripped coupon security; (4) the custodian undertakes to notify receipt holders in the event of a default, and to forward to receipt holders copies of all communications from the issuer of the underlying municipal security to the bondholders; (5) an opinion of counsel is provided indicating that the underlying municipal securities will not be considered assets of either the sponsoring firm or custodian bank; and (6) other factors are not present, such as remarketing agreements, that would require the investors in the stripped coupon securities to rely upon the sponsor to obtain the benefit of their investment.[2]

---

[1]You should note that this interpretive position does not apply where the issuer has officially disavowed any obligation to the receipt holders.

[2]In this regard, we would emphasize that, as described above, the custodial arrangements generally are structured to ensure that the custodian's role is essentially passive and that in all material respects the receipt holder is the real party in interest and otherwise treated as the beneficial owner of an interest in the underlying municipal security. Any material change in the nature of these custody arrangements could lead to a different result regarding our determination that the stripped coupon securities are appropriately treated as exempt from registration pursuant to section 3(a)(2) of the Securities Act. *See, e.g., Gary Plastic Packaging Corp.* v. *Merrill Lynch, Pierce, Fenner & Smith, Inc.*, 756 F.2d 230 (2nd Cir. 1985) and *SEC* v. *American Board of Trade*, 751 F.2d 529 (2nd Cir. 1984).

The Division of Market Regulation also has asked us to advise you that, based solely upon the representations contained in your letters, they concur in this position with respect to the application of section 3(a)(12)(A)(ii) of the Securities Exchange Act of 1934 ("Exchange Act") concerning municipal securities, as defined in section 3(a)(29) of the Exchange Act, to the Existing Program.[3]

The Division of Investment Management has asked us to inform you that the Existing Program would not create an investment company within the meaning of the Investment Company Act of 1940 if it is operated in accordance with your representations and the conditions set forth in the foregoing response of the Division of Corporation Finance, particularly that each receipt represents the entire interest in a discrete, identified interest payment or principal payment on the underlying municipal security.

Because these positions are based on the representations made to the Division in your letters, it should be noted that any different facts or conditions might require a different result.

Sincerely,

Abigail Arms
Deputy Chief Counsel

---

[3] The Division of Market Regulation expresses no view on whether securities issued pursuant to the Existing Program would be considered separate securities for other purposes of the Exchange Act, including for purposes of calculating mark-ups and determining compliance with Rule 15c2–12 under the Act. *See, also,* Letter from Richard G. Ketchum, Director, Division of Market Regulation, SEC, to Angela Desmond, General Counsel, Municipal Securities Rulemaking Board, (January 19, 1989) [1989 Transfer Binder] Fed. Sec. L. Rep. (CCH) ¶ 78,949 (concerning the application of the Municipal Securities Rulemaking Board's rules to stripped coupon securities).

This letter was originally submitted on the letterhead of Kephart, Fisher & Rogers, Columbus, Ohio

October 18, 1988

Securities and Exchange Commission
Division of Investment Management
450 Fifth Street, N.W.
Room 5130
Washington, D.C. 20549
Attention: Chief Counsel

Re: Meuse, Rinker, Chapman, Endres & Brooks

Ladies and Gentlemen:

On behalf of our client, Meuse, Rinker, Chapman, Endres & Brooks ("MRCEB"), we request the concurrence of Staff of the Division of Investment Management in our opinion that the certificates of beneficial ownership (the "Certificates") in the grantor trust described below (the "Trust") containing a pool of tax-exempt industrial development bonds (the "Bonds") do not constitute either "voting securities" within the meaning of Section 2(b)(42) of the Investment Company Act of 1940 (the "'40 Act") for purposes of Section 3(c)(1) of the '40 Act, or "voting stock" within the meaning of Section 12(d)(1) of the '40 Act.

I. *DESCRIPTION OF THE TRANSACTION*

A. *Introduction*

MRCEB proposes to act as the placement agent of the Certificates in a private placement to "accredited investors" within the meaning of the Securities Act of 1933 (the "'33 Act"). The placement would be structured as a sale not involving a public offering under Rule 506 of Regulation D or Section 4(2) of the '33 Act. (See *"Plan of Initial Sale," infra.*) The Certificates represent undivided beneficial ownership of the Bonds. (See *"The Certificates," infra.*) The Bonds are "industrial development bonds" within the meaning of Section 103 of the Internal Revenue Code of 1954, as amended. The proceeds of the Bonds, which were issued by various governmental issuers, were loaned to one or more borrowers (the "Borrower") for the acquisition of land or depreciable property to be used in the business of the Borrower. The Bonds will be acquired from their present holders via a tender offer by Bond Acquisition Corp. ("BAC"), a closely held special purpose corporation unrelated to any Borrower, which will deposit the Bonds into the Trust upon completion of the tender offer. The Trust, once established, will be a "grantor trust" within the meaning of Sections 671 *et seq.* of the Internal Revenue Code of 1986, as amended. (See *"The Trust," infra.*) The Certificates will be secured by a bank letter of credit, insurance policy, pledge of collateral or other credit enhancement device (the "Credit Facility") and will also be entitled to the benefit of options (the "Options") which will permit the holders of the Certificates (the "Holders") to tender the Certificates for purchase by BAC at 100% of the principal amount thereof periodically, such as every six months. (See *"The Credit Facility"* and *"The Options," infra.*) Additionally, BAC will have certain obligations to purchase the Bonds if they become taxable, upon a default in payment or upon expiration of the Credit Facility (the "Repurchase Obligations") and to pay the Trust any deficiency with respect to payments due on any Certificate (the "Deficiency Obligations"). The Options, Repurchase Obligations and Deficiency Obligations will each be secured by the Credit Facility.

In connection with its plans for placing the Certificates, MRCEB has identified certain entities as being potential purchasers. These prospective buyers include entities registered as investment companies under the '40 Act. MRCEB is concerned that if the Certificates are "voting securities" within the meaning of the '40 Act, no purchaser would be able to acquire more than 10 percent of the Certificates without jeopardizing the private placement exception to registration under Section 3(c)(1) of the '40 Act by reason of the attribution rules of Section 3(c)(1). Furthermore, if the Certificates constitute "voting stock" within the meaning of Section 12(d)(1) of the '40 Act, no registered investment company could acquire more than 3% of the Certificates. Each of these concerns, if valid, would necessitate greater expense and more difficulty in the placement of the Certificates and subsequent remarketings.

The remainder of this Section I describes the material features of the transaction. Section II of this letter sets forth our analysis of the relevant provisions of the '40 Act. Section III summarizes our opinion as to why the operative law and policy considerations in this case permit the conclusion that the Certificates should not be considered either voting securities or voting stock.

B. *The Trust*

The Trust will be a passive grantor trust established pursuant to a trust agreement (the "Trust Agreement") between BAC and a corporate trustee (the "Trustee"). The Trustee will not invest any trust assets other than certain amounts which could be paid to it from time to time by the Credit Facility to protect the Holders in the event any payment is deemed to be a preferential transfer under federal bankruptcy law. Such moneys would be invested only in short-term U.S. Government obligations pending resolution of the preferential transfer question. The Trustee will collect payments of principal of and interest on the Bonds as they are made by the present trustee of each issue of Bonds and forward appropriate amounts to the Holders.

The Trust Agreement will provide that no Holder will have any right to vote or in any manner otherwise control the management and operation of the Trust, or the obligations of the parties to the Trust Agreement. The Holders will have no power to remove the Trustee or vote on or otherwise approve any successor trustee.

In order for us to give an approving opinion that the Holders of the Certificates are the owners of the Bonds for federal income tax purposes, we must be satisfied that certain burdens and benefits of ownership belong to the Holders. A significant benefit which owners of property generally enjoy is the ability to dispose of their property. Therefore the Trust Agreement will contain a provision which will require the Trustee to sell any or all of the Bonds out of the Trust at a price of not less than par plus accrued interest upon the direction of the Holders of 70 percent of the outstanding principal amount of the Certificates. The proceeds of any such sale would be distributed to the Holders. No new obligations could be deposited into the Trust in replacement of any Bonds sold. If the direction to the

Trustee is that it sell all the Bonds, then such a direction would be equivalent to a decision to terminate and liquidate the Trust.

C. *The Certificates*

The Certificates will be issued by the Trust in exchange for the Bonds, which will be deposited in the Trust by BAC immediately following its purchase of the Bonds pursuant to the tender offer. The Bonds bear interest at a fixed rate, payable semi-annually. In all cases, nationally recognized bond counsel rendered an opinion on the date the Bonds were issued that interest on the Bonds is excludable from gross income for purposes of federal income taxation.

Principal payments and prepayments received on the Bonds will be passed through to the Holders. Such pass-through will be effected by mandatory redemptions of the required principal amount of Certificates, selected by lot by the Trustee.

The Certificates will be issued in denominations of $5,000 or any integral multiple thereof, with a minimum purchase by any investor of $500,000. The Holders of Certificates will be paid interest semi-annually at a variable rate (the "Pass-Through Rate") which will be established by MRCEB, as discussed below, based upon market rates, taking into account the time period between the exercise of the Options (the "Interest Adjustment Period"). For example, if the Interest Adjustment Period is semi-annual, the Holders of Certificates would be paid interest at a rate competitive with six-month tax-exempt obligations of comparable credit quality. The Pass-Through Rate for each interest Adjustment Period will be established approximately two weeks prior to the commencement of the Interest Adjustment Period to allow Holders time to exercise the Options if they are not satisfied with the new Pass-Through Rate.

The Pass-Through Rate can never exceed the weighted average interest rate on the Bonds. In the event extreme market conditions would, absent such limitation, cause the Pass-Through Rate to exceed the weighted average interest rate on the Bonds, MRCEB, as Remarketing Agent for the Certificates (the "Remarketing Agent"), will be permitted to remarket Certificates at a discount, with any such discount being paid by the Credit Facility or BAC. Additionally, if under such conditions the Certificates cannot be remarketed, BAC or the Credit Facility will be obligated to purchase such Certificates pursuant to the Options.

In establishing the Pass-Through Rate for each Interest Adjustment Period, the Remarketing Agent will be provided with an index (the "Interest Index") by an indexing agent (the "Indexing Agent"). The Indexing Agent will not be affiliated with any party to the transaction and will be a nationally recognized municipal securities evaluation service. The Remarketing Agent will establish the Pass-Through Rate for each Interest Adjustment Period based upon a percentage of the Interest Index within certain parameters (e.g. 85% to 125% of the Interest Index), taking into consideration current market transactions and the solicitation of bids from a specified number of institutional investors. Once established, the Pass-Through Rate will be fixed for the Interest Adjustment Period; provided that, because the Pass-Through Rate applicable to the Certificates cannot exceed the weighted average interest rate on the Bonds, if due to certain unforeseen circumstances the weighted average interest rate on the Bonds drops below the Pass-Through Rate then in effect, the Pass-Through Rate will drop to the new weighted average interest rate on the Bonds and the Holders will have a special Option to tender their Certificates.

D. *Credit, Liquidity and Administrative Fees*

Subject to certain maximum percentage limitations the rate differential (if any) between the weighted average interest rate on the Bonds and the Pass-Through Rate will be paid to BAC (the "Credit, Liquidity and Administrative Fees"), and out of such moneys, BAC will pay all ongoing expenses of the Trust, including the fees of the Trustee, Indexing Agent and the Remarketing Agent, fees for the Credit Facility and costs of servicing the Bonds. Any Credit, Liquidity and Administrative Fees in excess of the above-enumerated fees and expenses will be retained by BAC as compensation to it for the guarantees and liquidity it provides and for undertaking the interest rate risk inherent in this type of transaction. To the extent that there are no Credit, Liquidity and Administrative Fees available, BAC will nevertheless agree to pay all ongoing expenses of the Trust and fees for the Credit Facility. To the extent the difference between the weighted average interest rate on the Bonds and the Pass-Through Rate exceeds the maximum Credit, Liquidity and Administrative Fee, such moneys will remain in the Trust and be passed through to the Holders as additional interest.

The interest rate risk referred to in the preceding paragraph arises due to the fact that by providing the Options, BAC assumes the risk that short-term rates used in pricing the Certificates could equal or exceed the longer term rates on the Bonds. If such circumstances arise, BAC would be obligated to pay ongoing expenses of the Trust and the fees for the Credit Facility even though no Credit, Liquidity and Administrative Fees would be available, and could be forced to pay discounts to remarket Certificates or purchase Certificates which could not be remarketed.

E. *Plan of Initial Sale*

MRCEB proposes to act as placement agent for the Trust and solicit purchasers of the Certificates either in compliance with Rule 506 of Regulation D or in such other manner as will not involve a "public offering" within the meaning Section 3(c)(1) of the '40 Act and Section 4(2) of the '33 Act. No public offering of the Certificates would ever be made. A private placement memorandum will be prepared which will contain appropriate disclosure regarding the transaction, the participants and relevant documents.

The Certificates will be marketed on the basis of the ability of the Credit Facility to provide for payment of all principal of and pass-through interest with respect to the Certificates and payment of all obligations of BAC pursuant to the Options, the Repurchase Obligations and the Deficiency Obligations.

MRCEB anticipates that the primary market for the Certificates will be institutional and other accredited investors, including registered investment companies that invest funds in short-term tax-exempt obligations.

F. *The Options*

While the Holders will not be granted the right to surrender Certificates for redemption by the Trust, BAC will agree unconditionally to purchase Certificates at par on certain periodic dates pursuant to the Options. The agreement of BAC will run directly to the Holders and will be separate from, and will not be a part of, the obligations of the Trust and the Trustee. The obligation of BAC to make the payments required of it pursuant to the Options will be secured by the Credit Facility. The Remarketing Agent will remarket Certificates which are sold from time to time by the Holders pursuant to the exercise of the Options. Such remarketing will be done only by means of private placements to accredited investors.

MRCEB anticipates that, if the Pass-Through Rate for any Interest Adjustment Period is not competitive with comparably secured obligations in the market, Holders will tend to exercise the Options prior to the commencement of such Interest Adjustment Period. The method of determining the Pass-Through Rate will be designed to maintain competitive rates to minimize the likelihood that the Options will be exercised.

In connection with exercises of the Options, the Remarketing Agent will attempt to place tendered Certificates bearing the new Pass-Through Rate in the secondary market on the payment date on or immediately prior to which the Certificates shall have been tendered for purchase. In so doing, the Remarketing Agent may place those Certificates at such discounts from the principal amounts of the Certificates as are necessary in its judgment, giving due regard to prevailing financial market conditions. Any discount on resale will be paid by BAC or the Credit Facility to the Remarketing Agent, provided that no discount may exceed a specified percentage of the amount secured by the Credit Facility (e.g. 5%). The Holders selling the Certificates will receive 100% of the principal amount sold.

In the event that the Remarketing Agent is not successful in placing in the secondary market any Certificate delivered to the Remarketing Agent, the purchase price of such Certificate will be paid by BAC or the Credit Facility at 100% of the principal amount thereof.

Based upon MRCEB's experience with tax-exempt obligations bearing interest at rates determined by periodic market conditions, it is anticipated that as Remarketing Agent it will remarket the Certificates at or very close to 100% of the principal amount without the necessity for utilization of the obligation of BAC to purchase the Certificates.

II. *LAW AND ANALYSIS*

Because the Trust is formed for the purpose of acquiring and investing in securities, it will be considered to be an investment company unless an exception under Section 3(c) of the '40 Act is applicable. Section 3(c)(1) of the '40 Act excludes from the definition of investment company:

> Any issuer whose outstanding securities (other than short-term paper) are beneficially owned by not more than one hundred persons and which is not making and does not presently propose to make a public offering of its securities. For the purposes of this paragraph:
>
> (A) Beneficial ownership by a company shall be deemed to be beneficial ownership by one person, except that, if such company owns 10 per centum or more of the outstanding *voting securities* of the issuer, the beneficial ownership shall be deemed to be that of the holders of such company's outstanding securities (other than short-term paper, unless, as of the date of the most recent acquisition by such company of securities of that issuer, the value of all securities owned by such company of all issuers which are or would, but for the exception set forth in this subparagraph, be excluded from the definition of investment company solely by this paragraph, does not exceed 10 percentum of the value of the company's total assets. *Such issuer nonetheless is deemed to be an investment company for purposes of section 12(d)(1).* (Emphasis supplied.)

Section 12(d)(1) of the '40 Act imposes limitations on the ability of a registered investment company (the "acquiring company") to acquire another investment company (the "acquired company"). Specifically, Section 12(d)(1)(A) provides:

> It shall be unlawful for any registered investment company (the "acquiring company") and any company or companies controlled by such acquiring company to purchase or otherwise acquire any security issued by any other investment company (the "acquired company"), and for any investment company (the "acquiring company") and any company or companies controlled by such acquiring company to purchase or otherwise acquire any security issued by any registered investment company (the "acquired company"), if the acquiring company and any company or companies controlled by it immediately after such purchase or acquisition own in the aggregate—
>
> (i) more than 3 per centum of the total outstanding *voting stock* of the acquired company;
>
> (ii) securities issued by the acquired company having an aggregate value in excess of 5 per centum of the value of the total assets of the acquiring company; or
>
> (iii) securities issued by the acquired company and all other investment companies (other than Treasury stock of the acquiring company) having an aggregate value in excess of 10 per centum of the value of the total assets of the acquiring company. (Emphasis supplied.)

"Voting security" is defined by Section 2(a)(42) of the '40 Act as "any security presently entitling the owner or holder thereof to vote for the election of directors of a company." "Voting stock" is not defined in the '40 Act. Even though "voting stock" could be construed as applying to a narrower class of securities than "voting security" and arguably inapplicable to unincorporated organizations such as the Trust, we believe the more prudent interpretation of voting stock is to construe "voting stock" as equivalent to "voting security."

As was stated previously, MRCEB desires to place the Certificates with a small number of registered investment companies pursuant to Rule 506 of Regulation D or Section 4(2) of the '33 Act. If the Certificates are voting securities, two difficulties arise. First, under Section 3(c)(1), if a company owns 10 percent or more of the voting securities of the Trust, the beneficial ownership of such securities will be deemed to be in the hands of the holders of the securities of such company (*i.e.*, there may exist more than 100 beneficial owners of the Trust). This problem may be avoided via the "exception to the exception" contained in Section 3(c)(1)(A), but MRCEB is concerned that it may not be able to adequately protect against an inadvertent violation of Section 3(c)(1) since the applicability of the exception to the attribution rules is determined with reference to the holdings of the acquiring company.

The second issue arises as a result of the application of Section 12(d)(1). If the Certificates constitute voting stock, a registered investment company could own no more than 3 percent of the Certificates. If only investment companies desire to purchase Certificates, at least 34 would need to be found. Such a limit could cause the amount available for purchase to be too small to be attractive to many investment companies, and, in the opinion of MRCEB, could seriously impair its ability to place and subsequently remarket Certificates. (MRCEB's opinion is that the requirements of Section 12(d)(1)(A)(ii) and (iii), which apply to all securities, not just voting stock, will not present a problem since the total assets of the prospective purchasers are of such a size as to make compliance with those limits relatively easy.)

The issue to be resolved is: Whether Certificates in the Trust which convey no power to vote, manage or otherwise control the management or operation of the

Trust, but allow a specified percentage of Holders to cause the Trustee to sell any or all of the Bonds in the Trust, are voting securities or voting stock under the '40 Act. It is our opinion that such Certificates are not voting stock or voting securities.

The Certificates do not fall within the plain meaning of the definition. The Holders will have no power to vote for directors, since the Trust has none. Additionally, and more relevant, the Trustee, which is the participant most like a director, is not appointed by a vote of the Holders and cannot be removed by the Holders. Furthermore, if the Trustee resigns, the Holders have no right to vote for or appoint a successor.

We are aware that in Pierce, Lewis & Dolan (available April 21, 1972) and numerous subsequent no-action requests, the Staff has taken the position that ownership interests may be deemed to be the functional equivalent to voting securities if there exists a power to exercise a controlling influence because of economic interest. No such power would exist in the case of the Trust. As stated above, the Holders will have no power to vote for the removal of the Trustee or select a successor if the Trustee resigns. Further, the Trust, being a passive investment vehicle, will have no management-type considerations, *i.e.*, there are no ongoing management decisions because the pool of Bonds is fixed at the inception of the Trust and no additional bonds may be added. Although the Holders of 70 percent of the principal amount of the Certificates have the right to direct the sale of some or all of the Bonds, this does not constitute a power over day-to-day management of the "business" or assets of the Trust, such as are normally undertaken by directors of corporations.

We note that in a recent no-action letter request dealing with a limited partnership, Horsley Keogh Venture Fund (April 27, 1988), the Staff appeared to have no objection to a provision of the partnership agreement which required the consent of 66 percent of holders of the limited partnership interests before a liquidation could occur. Although the initial proposal to liquidate could originate only with the general partner in that instance, the response of the Staff clearly implies that a decision to liquidate some or all of the property held by a company is not the same type of control which should be within the ambit of the definition of voting security or voting stock.

We understand that the primary policy reasons for the existence of Sections 12(d)(1) and 3(c)(1) is to avoid the creation of a "fund of funds," and sham or multi-tiered investment companies to layer on fees and expenses and influence portfolio management. These concerns are not present in this case. First, as in Kohlberg Kravis Roberts & Co. (available September 9, 1985), MRCEB will require that no potential purchaser may become a Holder if such purchaser is itself relying on Section 3(c)(1) to avoid registration as an investment company under the '40 Act. Additionally, the risks presented by a "fund of funds" arrangement which Section 12(d)(1) seeks to avoid are not present in this case.

In Frank Russell Investment Company (available January 3, 1984) the request letter enumerated four potential abuses which Section 12(d)(1) is intended to address, namely (a) acquisition of voting control of the investment company (b) undue influence of portfolio management through the threat of redemptions, loss of advisory fees and disruption of investment management by requiring large cash balances to meet redemptions (c) complexity of the structure leading to difficulty for the uninitiated stockholder to determine the time value of his investment and (d) the layering of sale charges, advisory fees and administrative costs.

As discussed above, the Holders will have no right to appoint, remove or replace the Trustee or otherwise manage or control the operation of the Trust. While one Holder could acquire the requisite percentage to require a liquidation, any such sale of Bonds must be at least equal to par plus accrued interest. Since the Credit Facility will in effect guarantee the Repurchase Obligations of BAC, a Holder who would not have approved a liquidation will suffer no harm from a redemption. MRCEB believes that, since the prospective purchasers typically purchase securities maturing or callable at par within the short term, the risk of an "early redemption" (one which occurs prior to the scheduled termination date of the Trust) is thoroughly understood and accepted by such purchasers.

As to undue influence on advisors, there will exist no person responsible for "portfolio management" in the usual sense because the Trust, being a passive entity, will not be making or need to make any day-to-day decisions as to portfolio matters. Additionally, the use of the Credit Facility ensures against the need for large cash balances. The Holders will have the right to tender the Certificates for purchase pursuant to the Options, but such a mechanism does not entail a redemption requiring cash and, in any event, the cash needs for remarketing are guaranteed via the Credit Facility.

With respect to complexity, the Holders will receive reports with each payment describing the amounts representing principal and interest on the Bonds. Additionally, the source of the interest paid will be identified on a state by state basis. The offering material will identify each Bond by issuer, maturity date and interest rate, as well as describe the circumstances (if any) under which an early redemption of the Bonds can occur. This information, combined with the sophisticated financial understanding of prospective purchasers, greatly minimizes any risk of confusion for the Holders.

Similarly, the concern of the Commission as to layering of costs is not present with the Trust. Frank Russell Investment Company, *supra.* identifies this layering as potentially including (i) two layers of administrative expenses, (ii) a sales load on a sales load and (iii) advisory fees. No sales load or advisory fees will be charged by the Trust or by BAC. The administrative fees associated with the Trust (trustee charges for registrations and transfers etc.) will be the usual and customary fees for services of this type and will not be significantly different from those imposed by a bond trustee. The Credit, Liquidity and Administrative Fees will be in large part consideration to BAC for granting the liquidity Options and undertaking the Repurchase Obligations and Deficiency Obligations. Since such undertakings by BAC are crucial to the structure of the transaction, involve substantial costs assumed by BAC and present substantial risks to BAC, it is appropriate that these fees be paid to BAC. We note that the Staff has responded favorably to no-action requests in several previous transactions involving these types of fees. See McDonald & Company Securities, Inc. (available December 14, 1983); McDonald & Company Securities, Inc. (available March 25, 1985); and Meuse Rinker Chapman Endres & Brooks Incorporated (available July 17, 1985).

III. *CONCLUSION*

As discussed above, the Certificates contain no right to elect or appoint directors of the Trust. The Holders will have no right to remove the Trustee or vote for a successor in the event of a withdrawal or resignation of the Trustee. Notwithstanding the ability of the Holders of 70 percent of the principal amount of Certificates to instruct the Trustee to sell any or all of the Bonds, in the context of a passive investment trust containing a fixed portfolio of Bonds such right is not one which properly could be considered to cause the Certificates to be treated as the functional equivalent of a voting security or voting stock. Furthermore, the evils normally associated with a "fund of funds" which Section 12(d)(1) is designed to avoid are not present with respect to the Trust. No "voting control" of the Trust will reside with the Holders. No right of redemption exists which could result in any undue influence over portfolio management because there are literally no portfolio management activities associated with the Trust, Holders may dispose of their Certificates via the Options without forcing a redemption and any sale of Bonds from the Trust is guaranteed by the Credit Facility, obviating the need for large cash reserves. The information to be provided to Holders, combined with the relative financial sophistication of such Holders as accredited investors effectively obviates any confusion associated with the structure of the transaction. The fees associated with the Trust, including the Credit, Liquidity and Administrative Fees are either minimal and customary (e.g. Trustee's fee for transfer and re-registration of Certificates) or are reasonable charges for the costs and risks incurred and have previously received no objection from the Staff in its consideration of other pass-through securities.

On the basis of the foregoing, we respectfully request that the Staff of the Division of Investment Management concur in our opinion that the Certificates will not constitute either voting securities within the meaning of Section 2(b)(42) of the '40 Act for purposes of Section 3(c)(1), or voting stock for purposes of Section 12(d)(1) of the '40 Act.

MRCEB would like to proceed with this transaction as soon as possible. Your prompt consideration of this matter will be greatly appreciated. If for any reason you feel that that Staff will be unable to grant a favorable response, we request that we be given an opportunity to discuss with the Staff the reasons for such response prior to the issuance of a formal response. In the event you require additional facts, or wish to discuss this matter further, please do not hesitate to contact the undersigned by calling collect at (614) 469-8191, or in his absence, Roger E. Kephart at the same number.

Very truly yours,

KEPHART, FISHER & ROGERS

By ______________________________
William T. Conard, II

Response of the Office of Chief Counsel Division of Investment Management

Our Ref. No. 88-711-CC
MEUSE, RINKER, CHAPMAN,
ENDRES & BROOKS
File No. 132-3

In your letter dated October 18, 1988, you request that we concur with your opinion that the certificates of beneficial ownership (the "Certificates") in the grantor trust described in your letter (the "Trust") do not constitute either "voting securities" within the meaning of section 2(a)(42) of the Investment Company Act of 1940 (the "Act") for purposes of section 3(c)(1) of the Act, or "voting stock" within the meaning of section 12(d)(1) of the Act.[1]

We understand the facts to be as follows. Meuse, Rinker, Chapman, Endres & Brooks ("MRCEB") proposes to act as the placement agent of the Certificates in a private placement to "accredited investors" within the meaning of the Securities Act of 1933. The Certificates represent undivided beneficial ownership of a pool of tax-exempt industrial development bonds (the "Bonds"). The Certificates convey no power to vote, manage, or otherwise control the management or operation of the Trust, but do allow that the owners of 70% of the outstanding principal amount of the Certificates may cause the trustee to sell any or all of the Bonds in the Trust. The Certificates will be secured by a bank letter of credit, insurance policy, pledge of collateral, or other credit enhancement device (the "Credit Facility") and will also be entitled to the benefit of options which will permit the holders of the Certificates (the "Holders") to tender the Certificates for purchase at 100% of the principal amount thereof periodically.

We would not recommend enforcement action to the Commission under sections 3(c) and 12(d)(1) if MRCEB, in reliance upon your opinion as counsel, treats the Certificates as though they are not: 1) voting securities for purposes of determining the availability of the exception from the definition of an investment company provided by section 3(c)(1) of the Act, and 2) voting stock for purposes of section 12(d)(1). This position is based on the facts and representations set out in your letter and in telephone conversations with the staff, specifically that:

1) MRCEB will not allow a potential purchaser to become a Holder if such purchaser was formed solely for the purpose of purchasing Certificates;[2]

---

[1] "Voting Security" is defined by section 2(a)(42) of the Act as "any security presently entitling the owner or holder thereof to vote for the election of directors of a company." "Voting stock" is not a term defined by the Act.

[2] In our December 29, 1988, telephone conversation you confirmed this representation.

2) MRCEB will not allow a potential purchaser to become a Holder if such purchaser is itself relying on section 3(c)(1) to avoid registration as an investment company under the Act;[3] and
3) no sales load or advisory fees will be charged by the Trust or by Bond Acquisition Corp., the closely held special purpose corporation that will acquire the Bonds via a tender offer.[4]

Because this position is based on your facts and representations, you should note that any different facts or conditions might require a different conclusion. Moreover, this response expresses only the Division's position on enforcement action and does not purport to express any legal conclusions on the questions presented.

W. John McGuire
Attorney

---

[3]*See* Horsely Keogh Venture Fund (pub. avail. April 27, 1988), Kohlberg Kravis Roberts & Co. (Sept. 9, 1985), Cigna Corporation (pub. avail. Oct. 1, 1984).

[4]*See also* Frank Russell Investment Company (pub. avail. Jan. 3, 1984) (sale to Canadian pension plans in excess of the limitations of section 12(d)(1)), The Cheapside Dollar Fund Limited (pub. avail. Dec. 15, 1971) (the sale to British pension plans in excess of the limitations of section 12(d)(1)).

This letter was originally submitted on the letterhead of John Nuveen & Co. Inc., Chicago, Ill.

Investment Company Act
Section 2(a)(41)
Rule 2a–7

July 31, 1990

Thomas S. Harman
Chief Counsel
Division of Investment Management
Securities and Exchange Commission
450 Fifth Street, N.W.
Washington, D.C. 20549

RE: No-Action Request: Rule 2a–7 Under the Investment Company Act of 1940

Dear Mr. Harman:

Nuveen Advisory Corp. ("Advisory Corp.") and the various "money market" funds for which Advisory Corp. serves or may in the future serve as investment adviser (the "Funds")[1] hereby request that the staff (the "Staff") of the Division of Investment Management advise us that it will not recommend that the Securities and Exchange Commission (the "Commission") take enforcement action against Advisory Corp. or the Funds if the Funds in reliance on Rule 2a–7 under the Investment Company Act of 1940 (the "Act"), purchase long-term tax-exempt fixed rate instruments that, by virtue of certain demand features, have effectively been converted into short-term tax-exempt variable rate demand instruments ("Tender Option Bonds"), as described more fully below, and value such instruments at amortized cost.

Rule 2a–7

Rule 2a–7 under the Act generally provides that an investment company that wishes to utilize the amortized cost method of valuing its portfolio securities or the penny-rounding method of pricing its shares (a "money market" fund) may not purchase any instrument with a remaining maturity of greater than one year or maintain a dollar-weighted average portfolio maturity of more than 120 days.

[1]Advisory Corp. is registered as an investment adviser under the Investment Advisers Act of 1940 and currently serves as investment adviser to four "money market" Funds or portfolios registered under the Act: Nuveen Tax-Exempt Money Market Fund, Inc., Nuveen Tax-Free Reserves, Inc., Nuveen Tax-Free Money Market Fund, Inc. and the Money Market Portfolio of Nuveen California Tax-Free Fund, Inc. Each of the current Funds uses the amortized cost method of valuing its securities in conformance with Rule 2a–7. This request for no-action relates to such Funds as well as to registered "money market" Funds or Fund portfolios using the amortized cost method of valuation that may hereafter be advised by Advisory Corp.

However, under Rule 2a–7(b)(3), a "demand feature"[2] may be used to shorten the maturity of a "variable rate instrument"[3] in which case the instrument is deemed to have a maturity equal to the longer of (1) the period remaining until the next readjustment of the interest rate on such instrument or (2) the period remaining until the principal amount of the instrument can be recovered through demand.

Prior to the amendments to Rule 2a–7 promulgated in 1986 (the "1986 Amendments"), a demand feature could not be used to shorten the maturity of a variable rate or floating rate instrument unless the demand ran to the issuer of the instrument. The 1986 Amendments—in recognition of a "reissuance" problem under the Internal Revenue Code (described below)—removed this requirement, and Rule 2a–7 now permits money market funds to use demand features, including put options, running to third parties to shorten the maturities of variable rate or floating rate instruments under certain conditions and subject to certain limitations. *See* Investment Company Act Release No. 14983, [85–86 Transfer Binder] Fed. Sec. L. Rep. (CCH) para. 83,972 ("Release No. 14983").

The Funds desire to purchase fixed rate bonds subject to third party puts that satisfy the requirements of a "demand feature" as described below, but that also include a mechanism that provides for the periodic adjustment of tender fees such that the net interest rate to the bondholder after payment of the tender fee can reasonably be expected to cause the bond-put combination to have a market value that approximates the par value of the bond. Such "synthetic" variable rate instruments are widely accepted in the marketplace as equivalent to more traditional variable rate instruments. The specific question raised in this letter is whether a money market fund may, under Rule 2a–7, purchase such instruments. For the reasons set forth below, we believe that instruments of this type may be characterized as "variable rate instruments" subject to a "demand feature" for purposes of Rule 2a–7, and therefore may be purchased by the Funds.

Description of Tender Option Bonds

A Tender Option Bond is a tax-exempt bond having a relatively long maturity (typically 5 to 25 years) and bearing interest at a fixed rate generally substantially higher than prevailing short-term tax-exempt rates, that has been coupled with the agreement of a third party, such as a bank, broker-dealer or other financial institution[4], pursuant to which such institution grants bondholders the option, at periodic intervals (usually every six months, but in no event less than every twelve months), to tender (put) their bonds to the institution and receive the face

---

[2]Rule 2a–7(c)(5) defines a "demand feature" as a put that entitles the holder to receive the principal amount of the underlying security or securities and that may be exercised either (1) at any time on no more than 30 days' notice or (2) at specified intervals not exceeding one year and upon no more than 30 days' notice.

[3]Rule 2a–7(c)(7) defines a "variable rate instrument" as one whose terms provide for the adjustment of its interest rate on set dates and which, upon such adjustment, can reasonably be expected to have a market value that approximates its par value.

[4]Such a third party option agreement may constitute a "security" within the meaning of Section 2(1) of the Securities Act of 1933, as amended ("1933 Act"). Such an option agreement, if issued by a bank, would generally be exempt from registration under the 1933 Act pursuant to Section 3(a)(2) thereunder. We understand that broker-dealers or other non-bank financial institutions either register their option agreements under the 1933 Act or issue such option agreements without registration pursuant to a line of no-action letters relating to put facilities that are marketed only in connection with the related underlying bonds.

value thereof.[5] Holders of Tender Option Bonds are assessed periodic variable "tender fees" by the institution (which fees are paid on behalf of bondholders by the bond trustee from bondholder interest payments), compensating the grantor of the tender option for the liquidity and price stability it provides to the bondholder.[6] Such fees are established for each tender period at a rate equal to the difference between the bonds' fixed coupon rate and the rate, as determined by a remarketing or similar agent at or near the commencement of such period, that would cause the bonds, coupled with the tender option, to trade at par on the date of such determination.[7] Thus, after payment of tender fees to the institution, the bondholder effectively holds demand paper that bears interest at the prevailing short-term tax-exempt rate.[8]

---

[5]Such an agreement is typically entered into between the financial institution and the bond trustee for the benefit of the bondholders. In order to avoid "reissuance" concerns (described below), the municipal obligor is not a party to the agreement. Such an agreement also typically involves a remarketing agent, whose function is to create a secondary market in the bonds. However, in the event the remarketing agent is unable to remarket bonds tendered to it by a bondholder, the bonds may then be tendered by the bondholder to the financial institution at their face value.

[6]Bondholders may elect to relinquish the rights conferred under the tender agreement, in which case they would not be assessed the tender fee; as discussed in note 9, *infra*, the Funds would not relinquish any tender option or purchase bonds with respect to which the tender option had been relinquished. Typically, the tender option agreement will provide that, after a certain date, a bondholder may no longer relinquish his tender rights. If a bondholder fails to relinquish his rights on or prior to that date, any party (including the original holder) who holds the bond after that date is entitled to the rights conferred by, but is also required to pay the variable tender fees provided for under, the agreement.

[7]For example, assume a Tender Option Bond where the underlying fixed rate bond has a stated annual interest rate of 9% payable semi-annually on June 1 and December 1. Typically, a remarketing agent would determine, within the 30-day period prior to June 1 (or December 1, as the case may be), a rate for the succeeding six-month period that would enable the underlying bonds, coupled with the tender option and after the tender fee, to trade at par (say 6%). After the remarketing agent makes such determination, the bondholder is given a period of time, typically a week, to tender his bonds to the remarketing agent for remarketing. If the remarketing agent is unable to remarket, at par, the bonds that have been tendered to it, the bonds may be tendered to (i.e., put to) the institution at par prior to the commencement of the new period. If on the other hand, the bondholder elects to retain the bonds, the bondholder would receive interest at 6% per annum for the period commencing on June 1 (or December 1, as the case may be), with the remaining 3% per annum being paid by the bond trustee on behalf of the bondholder as a tender fee to the institution that provides the tender option.

[8]In the event the remarketing agent were to determine that, for a given period, the interest rate that would cause the bonds to trade at par should equal or exceed the coupon interest rate on the bonds, no tender fee would be due to the institution for the interest payment period in question (although the tender option agreement would remain in force), and the bonds would pay the full fixed coupon rate for that period. The situation in which the prevailing short-term tax-exempt rate exceeds the fixed coupon rate on the bonds, so that even the elimination of the tender fee would not be sufficient to enable the bonds to trade at par, is comparable to the situation in which the prevailing short-term tax-exempt rate exceeds the maximum "cap" rate that is frequently applicable to traditional variable or floating rate tax-exempt instruments. The mere existence of a maximum "cap" rate, in and of itself, does not disqualify an instrument from being considered a variable rate instrument for purposes of Rule 2a–7. In Investment Company Act Release No. 14607, [84–85 Transfer Binder] Fed. Sec. L. Rep. (CCH) para. 83,795 ("Release No. 14607") at p. 87,548, n.10;

Tender Option Bonds have been developed to meet the demand for short-term tax-exempt variable rate demand paper and at the same time to respond to "reissuance" concerns under the Internal Revenue Code (the "Code"). As the Commission acknowledged in Investment Company Act Release No. 14607, "reissuance" concerns have prompted municipal obligors to devise new strategies for issuing variable rate demand obligations. Id. at p. 87,548. The Commission noted in that release that when the holder of a municipal security exercises an issuer demand feature and the security is put back to the issuer or to a direct agent of the issuer, a subsequent remarketing of the security may constitute a reissuance of the security under the Code. Id. When this occurs, a municipal obligor may be forced to requalify the security as tax-exempt prior to remarketing it. Id. Recent changes to the Code, however, have made it increasingly difficult for a pre-existing municipal issue to be requalified as tax-exempt. Id. at n. 11.

In response to the "reissuance" problem, issuers of municipal securities have structured demand features that do not run to the issuer or its agent, but run instead to a separate entity that possesses sufficient credit to honor the demands. The securities that are put to the separate entity are then remarketed without ever having entered into the possession of the issuer or a direct agent of the issuer. By so structuring the demand feature, the issuer is able to treat the remarketing of the securities as nothing more than a secondary market transaction and not a reissuance of the securities. *Id.* Tender Option Bonds represent a variation on this strategy in that they are designed to respond to the demand for variable rate demand paper without running afoul of the restrictions of the Code.

Discussion

In light of the Commission's willingness, as evidenced by the 1986 Amendments, to accommodate the various strategies that have arisen in response to the demand by money market funds for tax-free short-term instruments in the face of reissuance concerns, and because the periodic adjustment of tender fees serves as a mechanism for adjusting the interest rate on the Tender Option Bonds such that they are in fact functionally equivalent to traditional variable rate paper—the proof of which is that Tender Option Bonds are perceived and purchased by sophisticated investors as variable rate paper—we believe that Tender Option Bonds should be treated as "variable rate instruments" subject to a "demand feature" for purposes of Rule 2a–7.

First, the tender option feature applicable to Tender Option Bonds qualifies as a "demand feature" for purposes of Rule 2a–7(c)(5) in that, except in limited circumstances,[9] (1) it grants the holder of the Tender Option Bonds the right to

---

p. 87,551, n. 31., the Commission noted that interest rate readjustments on short-term variable rate paper are frequently limited by caps which define the maximum upper and lower rates. The purchase by a money market fund of paper subject to such caps is acceptable, therefore, as long as, at the time of purchase, the fund reasonably expects that prevailing short-term rates will not exceed the maximum cap rate at the time of the next interest rate readjustment. The fixed coupon rate on the bonds underlying Tender Option Bonds is the functional equivalent of an interest rate cap applicable to traditional variable rate paper. The Staff implicitly acknowledged this principle in *Shearson Lehman/American Express, Inc.*, discussed *infra*.

[9]Those exceptions are: first, under certain circumstances, a bondholder may affirmatively "relinquish" its right to tender all or a portion of the bonds held by it, and thereby avoid having to pay tender fees with respect to such bonds. The Funds would not purchase any long-term bonds with respect to which the tender option feature has been relinquished and would not themselves relinquish the tender option. Second, the tender option feature is likely to be structured as a "con-

sell the underlying bonds within a specified period of time not exceeding one year and upon no more than 30 days' notice and receive the principal amount thereof, and (2) it may be sold, transferred or assigned only with the underlying bonds.

Next, Tender Option Bonds differ from traditional variable rate tax-exempt demand instruments only in that, in the case of Tender Option Bonds, the underlying security is an instrument with a fixed rate of interest that is converted to what is effectively a variable rate of interest by the variable tender fee arrangement, while in the case of traditional variable rate demand paper, the security by its terms provides for a variable rate of interest. Because the underlying bonds and the tender arrangement are inseparable in the hands of a Fund (*see* n. 9, *supra*), Tender Option Bonds are for all purposes virtually identical to variable rate paper: the interest rate to the bondholder varies with the short-term interest rates at every tender fee reset date, and the holder can demand and receive payment of the principal amount of the bonds on any tender date. Accordingly, Tender Option Bonds should be deemed to be "variable rate instruments" within the meaning of Rule 2a–7.

The Staff has raised no objection to the use of variable tender fees as a mechanism for adjusting interest rates for purposes of Rule 2a–7 in at least one prior no-action letter. *See Shearson Lehman/American Express, Inc.* (pub. avail. March 25, 1985) ("*Shearson*"). In that letter, a trust issued certificates of participation ("Certificates") against a fixed pool of industrial development bonds, housing bonds and certain other tax-exempt obligations bearing interest at either a fixed percentage of a prime rate (subject to fixed minimum and maximum rates) or at fixed rates. In order to provide investors, including money-market funds, with desired liquidity, the financial institution that sponsored the trust offered a liquidity put to the initial holder of each Certificate, exercisable at any time upon seven days' notice at a price equal to the unpaid principal amount of the Certificate, plus accrued interest. Each liquidity put had a term of one week, but was extended automatically each week unless expressly cancelled by the Certificateholder. During the term the liquidity

---

ditional" put that would terminate in the event of a default in payment of principal or interest on the underlying bonds. Rule 2a–7, however, clearly contemplates that a conditional put may qualify as a demand feature for purposes of the rule, so long as the bonds are rated, or determined to be, high quality both as short-term and long-term instruments. *See*, Rule 2a–7(a)(2)(iv). The Funds would purchase only Tender Option Bonds that satisfy these criteria. Third, the institution that provides the tender option may have the right, upon notice, to terminate its obligations under the option at or after a specified future date. As described in the text under "Request for No-Action," however, the Funds would tender or otherwise dispose of any Tender Option Bonds prior to such date. Finally, the institution may also be given a right to terminate its obligations under a put option agreement in the event of a non-financial default on the underlying bonds, a very substantial downgrading in the rating of underlying bonds (i.e., to a rating lower than investment grade) or a determination that interest on the underlying bonds is no longer tax-exempt. A "non-financial default" is a breach of a material contractual covenant by the issuer of the underlying bonds, generally one that has not been cured within a specified number of days (often 30) after receipt of notice of such breach. Examples of such covenants would include the requirement to maintain a certain amount in a debt service reserve account, limitations as to the use of the proceeds of the bond offering, and restrictions on the issuance of senior indebtedness. As described in the text under "Request for No-Action," in no event would a Fund purchase Tender Option Bonds whose tender features are terminable under such circumstances, unless the Fund reasonably believed after careful analysis at the time of purchase and each time it is subsequently determined not to exercise a tender option that the circumstances that could give rise to such a termination would not occur prior to the time of the next tender opportunity.

put was in effect, the rate of interest passed through and payable on the Certificate was a rate set weekly by a third party and intended to result in a market value for the Certificate roughly equal to the unpaid principal amount of the Certificate, plus accrued interest. Such pass-through rate was less than the rate of interest on the underlying municipal obligations that would otherwise be passed through to a Certificateholder. The difference in such rates was designed to compensate the institution for providing liquidity to Certificateholders. Thus, the arrangement described in *Shearson* is virtually indistinguishable from the Tender Option Bonds described herein.[10]

Request for No-Action

Based on the foregoing, we respectfully request that the Staff advise us that it will not recommend any enforcement action in the event the Funds were to purchase Tender Option Bonds, provided the following conditions are met:

1) The Funds would not purchase any such Bonds unless the demand features applicable thereto are exercisable by the Funds within one year of the date of such purchase upon no more than 30 days' notice and are thereafter exercisable by the Funds no less frequently than annually upon no more than 30 days' notice.
2) The Funds would not purchase any such Bonds unless, at the time of such purchase, Advisory Corp. reasonably expects, (a) based upon its assessment of current and historical interest rate trends, that prevailing short-term tax-exempt rates will not exceed the stated interest rate on the underlying bonds at the time of the next tender fee adjustment, and (b) that the circumstances which might entitle the grantor of a tender option to terminate such tender option would not occur so as to permit termination prior to the time of the next tender opportunity.
3) At the time of each tender opportunity, the Funds would exercise the tender option with respect to such Bonds unless Advisory Corp. reasonably expects, (a) based upon its assessment of current and historical interest rate trends, that short-term tax-exempt rates will not exceed the stated interest rate on the underlying bonds at the time of the next tender fee adjustment, and (b) that the circumstances which might entitle the grantor of a tender option to terminate such tender option would not occur so as to permit termination prior to the time of the next tender opportunity.
4) The Fund would exercise the tender feature with respect to such Bonds, or otherwise dispose of such Bonds, prior to the time the tender option is scheduled to expire pursuant to the terms of the agreement under which the tender option is granted; and

[10]The only significant difference between the arrangement described in *Shearson* and that described herein is that in *Shearson*, which was decided before the 1986 Amendments, it was important for counsel to demonstrate that the put feature ran to the issuer of the Certificates. Shortly after the issuance of the *Shearson* letter, the Staff stated that it was presently considering the broader policy implications of the positions taken by it in *Shearson*. The Staff thus cautioned that the *Shearson* letter should not be relied on as a Staff interpretive or enforcement position. It appears to us, however, that the positions the Staff had under reconsideration did not include the issue of whether Certificates in question constituted "variable rate instruments," but rather such issues as whether, on the facts under consideration in *Shearson*, the put should be deemed to run to the is-

suer or to a third party.

5) The Funds would otherwise comply with the provisions of Rule 2a–7 in connection with the purchase of such Bonds, including, without limitation, the requisite determination by a Fund's Board of Directors that the Tender Option Bonds in question meet the "high quality" standards described in Rule 2a–7(a)(2)(iv).

Please feel free to call the undersigned (312/917-7946) or Gifford R. Zimmerman, Assistant General Counsel (312/917-7945), if you have any questions or need additional information regarding this request. If the Staff is unable to concur with the conclusions set forth herein, we would appreciate the opportunity to discuss these matters with the Staff prior to the issuance of its response.

Very truly yours,

NUVEEN ADVISORY CORP.

James J. Wesolowski
Vice President and Secretary

JJW:ar
16591

Response of the Office of Chief Counsel Division of Investment Management

Our Ref. No. 90–411–CC
Nuveen Advisory Corp.
File No. 801–12353

Your letter dated July 31, 1990, requests our assurance that we would not recommend that the Commission take any enforcement action against Nuveen Advisory Corp. ("Advisory Corp.") and the money market funds (the "Funds") for which Advisory Corp. serves or may in the future serve as investment adviser,[1] if the Funds, in reliance on Rule 2a–7 under the 1940 Act,[2] purchase certain "synthetic" variable rate instruments ("Tender Option Bonds") as described in your letter, and value such instruments at amortized cost.

You state that a Tender Option Bond is a tax-exempt bond having a relatively long maturity (typically 5 to 25 years) and bearing interest at a fixed rate generally substantially higher than prevailing short-term tax-exempt rates, that has been coupled with the agreement of a third party financial institution,[3] pursuant to which the institution grants bondholders the option, at periodic intervals (usually every six months, but in no event less than every twelve months), to tender (put) their

---

[1] You state that Advisory Corp. currently serves as investment adviser to four money market funds or portfolios registered under the Investment Company Act of 1940 ("1940 Act"): Nuveen Tax-Exempt Money Market Fund, Inc., Nuveen Tax-Free Reserves, Inc., Nuveen Tax-Free Money Market Fund, Inc., and the Money Market Portfolio of Nuveen California Tax-Free Fund, Inc. Each of these funds or portfolios uses the amortized cost method of valuing its securities in conformance with Rule 2a–7 under the 1940 Act. You state that your request for no-action relates to such funds as well as to registered money market funds or fund portfolios using the amortized cost method of valuation that may hereafter be advised by Advisory Corp.

[2] Rule 2a–7 generally provides that an investment company that wishes to use the amortized cost method of valuing its portfolio securities or the penny-rounding method of pricing its shares (a money market fund) may not purchase any instrument with a remaining maturity of greater than one year or maintain a dollar-weighted average portfolio maturity of more than 120 days. However, under Rule 2a–7(b)(3), a "demand feature" may be used to shorten the maturity of a variable rate instrument," in which case the instrument is deemed to have a maturity equal to the longer of (1) the period remaining until the next readjustment of the interest rate on such instrument or (2) the period remaining until the principal amount of the instrument can be recovered through demand.

Rule 2a–7(c)(5) defines a "demand feature" as a put that entitles the holder to receive the principal amount of the underlying security or securities and that may be exercised either (1) at any time on no more than 30 days' notice or (2) at specified intervals not exceeding one year and upon no more than 30 days' notice.

Rule 2a–7(c)(7) defines a "variable rate instrument" as one whose terms provide for the adjustment of its interest rate on set dates and which, upon such adjustment, can reasonably be expected to have a market value that approximates its par value.

[3] We express no opinion on the status of third party option agreements under the Securities Act of 1933.

bonds to the institution and receive the face value thereof. Holders of Tender Option Bonds are assessed periodic, variable "tender fees" by the institution (which fees are paid on behalf of bondholders by the bond trustee from bondholder interest payments). Such fees are established for each tender period at a rate equal to the difference between the bonds' fixed coupon rate and the rate, as determined by a remarketing or similar agent at or near the commencement of such period, that would cause the bonds, coupled with the tender option, to trade at par on the date of such determination. You represent, therefore, that, after payment of tender fees to the institution, the bondholder effectively holds demand paper that bears interest at the prevailing short-term tax-exempt rate.

On the basis of the facts and representations in your letter, we would not recommend that the Commission take any enforcement action against Advisory Corp. or the Funds under Rule 2a–7 if the Funds purchase Tender Option Bonds and value such instruments at amortized cost *provided*:

1. The Funds would not purchase any such Tender Option Bonds unless the demand features applicable thereto are exercisable by the Funds within one year of the date of such purchase upon no more than 30 days' notice and are thereafter exercisable by the Funds no less frequently than annually upon no more than 30 days' notice;
2. The Funds would not purchase any such Tender Option Bonds unless, at the time of such purchase, Advisory Corp. reasonably expects, (a) based upon its assessment of current and historical interest rate trends, that prevailing short-term tax-exempt rates will not exceed the stated interest rate on the underlying bonds at the time of the next tender fee adjustment, and (b) that the circumstances which might entitle the grantor of a tender option to terminate the tender option[4] would not occur prior to the time of the next tender opportunity;
3. At the time of each tender opportunity, the Funds would exercise the tender option with respect to such Tender Option Bonds unless Advisory Corp. reasonably expects, (a) based upon its assessment of current and historical interest rate trends, that short-term tax-exempt rates will not exceed the stated interest rate on the underlying bonds at the time of the next tender fee adjustment, and (b) that the circumstances which might entitle the grantor of a tender option to terminate the tender option would not occur prior to the time of the next tender opportunity;
4. The Funds would exercise the tender feature with respect to such Tender Option Bonds, or otherwise dispose of such Tender Option Bonds, prior to

[4] In note 9 of your letter, you state, among other things, that the institution that provides the tender option may be given a right to terminate its obligations under a put option agreement in the event of a non-financial default on the underlying bonds, a very substantial downgrading in the rating of underlying bonds (*i.e.*, to a rating lower than investment grade), or a determination that interest on the underlying bonds is no longer tax-exempt. As more fully described in your letter, a "non-financial default" generally is a breach of a material contractual covenant by the issuer of the underlying bonds that has not been cured within a specified number of days after receipt of notice of such breach. You represent that in no event would a Fund purchase Tender Option Bonds whose tender features are terminable under such circumstances, unless the Fund reasonably believes, after careful analysis at the time of purchase and each time it is subsequently determined not to exercise a tender option, that the circumstances that could give rise to such a termination would not occur prior to the time of the next tender opportunity.

the time the tender option is scheduled to expire pursuant to the terms of the agreement under which the tender option is granted;

5. The Funds would otherwise comply with the provisions of Rule 2a–7 in connection with the purchase of such Tender Option Bonds, including, without limitation, the requisite determination by a Fund's Board of Directors that the Tender Option Bonds in question meet the "high quality" standards described in Rule 2a–7(a)(2)(iv); and
6. In the event of a default of the security underlying a Tender Option Bond, or the termination of the tender option agreement, the Funds would lock to the maturity date of the underlying security for purposes of compliance with Rule 2a–7, for example, in calculating the Fund's dollar-weighted average portfolio maturity.

Because this position is based on the particular facts and representations in your letter, you should note that any different facts or circumstances may require a different conclusion. Further, our response represents our position on enforcement action only and does not purport to express any legal or interpretive position on the questions presented.

L. Hope Lewis
Attorney

This letter was originally submitted on the letterhead of the Securities and Exchange Commission, Washington, D.C.

For RELEASE Tuesday, November 6, 1962

SECURITIES ACT OF 1933
Release No. 4552

NON-PUBLIC OFFERING EXEMPTION

The Commission today announced the issuance of a statement regarding the availability of the exemption from the registration requirements of Section 5 of the Securities Act of 1933 afforded by the second clause of Section 4(1) of the Act for "transactions by an issuer not involving any public offering," the so-called "private offering exemption." Traditionally, the second clause of Section 4(1) has been regarded as providing an exemption from registration for bank loans, private placements of securities with institutions, and the promotion of a business venture by a few closely related persons. However, an increasing tendency to rely upon the exemption for offerings of speculative issues to unrelated and uninformed persons prompts this statement to point out the limitations on its availability.

Whether a transaction is one not involving any public offering is essentially a question of fact and necessitates a consideration of all surrounding circumstances, including such factors as the relationship between the offerees and the issuer, the nature, scope, size, type and manner of the offering.

The Supreme Court in *S.E.C.* v. *Ralston Purina Co.*, 346 U.S. 119, 124, 125 (1953), noted that the exemption must be interpreted in the light of the statutory purpose to "protect investors by promoting full disclosure of information thought necessary to informed investment decisions" and held that "the applicability of Section 4(1) should turn on whether the particular class of persons affected need the protection of the Act." The Court stated that the number of offerees is not conclusive as to the availability of the exemption, since the statute seems to apply to an offering "whether to few or many."[1] However, the Court indicated that "nothing prevents the Commission, in enforcing the statute, from using some kind of numerical test in deciding when to investigate particular exemption claims." It should be emphasized, therefore, that the number of persons to whom the offering is extended is relevant only to the question whether they have the requisite association with and knowledge of the issuer which make the exemption available.

Consideration must be given not only to the identity of the actual purchasers but also to the offerees. Negotiations or conversations with or general solicitations of an unrestricted and unrelated group of prospective purchasers for the purpose of ascertaining who would be willing to accept an offer of securities is inconsistent with a claim that the transaction does not involve a public offering even though ultimately there may only be a few knowledgeable purchasers.[2]

---

[1]See, also, *Gilligan, Will & Co.* v. *S.E.C.*, 267 F. 2d 461, 467 (C.A. 2, 1959), *cert. denied*, 361 U.S. 896 (1960).

[2]Reference is made to the so-called "investment clubs" which have been organized under claim of an exemption from the registration provisions of the Securities Act of 1933 as well as the

A question frequently arises in the context of an offering to an issuer's employees. Limitation of an offering to certain employees designated as key employees may not be a sufficient showing to qualify for the exemption. As the Supreme Court stated in the *Ralston Purina* case: "The exemption as we construe it, does not deprive corporate employees, as a class, of the safeguards of the Act. We agree that some employee offerings may come within Section 4(1), e.g., one made to executive personnel who because of their position have access to the same kind of information that the Act would make available in the form of a registration statement. Absent such a showing of special circumstances, employees are just as much members of the investing 'public' as any of their neighbors in the community." The Court's concept is that the exemption is necessarily narrow. The exemption does not become available simply because offerees are voluntarily *furnished* information about the issuer. Such a construction would give each issuer the choice of registering or making its own voluntary disclosures without regard to the standards and sanctions of the Act.

The sale of stock to promoters who take the initiative in founding or organizing the business would come within the exemption. On the other hand, the transaction tends to become public when the promoters begin to bring in a diverse group of uninformed friends, neighbors and associates.

The size of the offering may also raise questions as to the probability that the offering will be completed within the strict confines of the exemption. An offering of millions of dollars to non-institutional and non-affiliated investors or one divided, or convertible, into many units would suggest that a public offering may be involved.

When the services of an investment banker, or other facility through which public distributions are normally effected, are used to place the securities, special care must be taken to avoid a public offering. If the investment banker places the securities with discretionary accounts and other customers without regard to the ability of such customers to meet the tests implicit in the *Ralston Purina* case, the exemption may be lost. Public advertising of the offerings would, of course, be incompatible with a claim of a private offering. Similarly, the use of the facilities of a securities exchange to place the securities necessarily involves an offering to the public.

An important factor to be considered is whether the securities offered have come to rest in the hands of the initial informed group or whether the purchasers are merely conduits for a wider distribution. Persons who act in this capacity, whether or not engaged in the securities business, are deemed to be "underwriters" within the meaning of Section 2(11) of the Act. If the purchasers do in fact acquire the securities with a view to public distribution, the seller assumes the risk of possible violation of the registration requirements of the Act and consequent civil liabilities.[3] This has led to the practice whereby the issuer secures from the initial

---

Investment Company Act of 1940. It should not be assumed that so long as the investment club, which is an investment company within the meaning of the latter Act, does not *obtain* more than 100 members, a public offering of its securities, namely the memberships, will not be involved. An investment company may be exempt from the provisions of the Investment Company Act if its securities are owned by not more than 100 persons *and* it is not making and does not presently propose to make a public offering of its securities. (Section 3(c)(1)). Both elements must be considered in determining whether the exemption is available.

[3]See Release No. 33-4445.

purchasers representations that they have acquired the securities for investment. Sometimes a legend to this effect is placed on the stock certificates and stop-transfer instructions issued to the transfer agent. However, a statement by the initial purchaser, at the time of his acquisition, that the securities are taken for investment and not for distribution is necessarily self-serving and not conclusive as to his actual intent. Mere acceptance at face value of such assurances will not provide a basis for reliance on the exemption when inquiry would suggest to a reasonable person that these assurances are formal rather than real. The additional precautions of placing a legend on the security and issuing stop-transfer orders have proved in many cases to be an effective means of preventing illegal distributions. Nevertheless, these are only precautions and are not to be regarded as a basis for exemption from registration. The nature of the purchaser's past investment and trading practices or the character and scope of his business may be inconsistent with the purchase of large blocks of securities for investment. In particular, purchases by persons engaged in the business of buying and selling securities require careful scrutiny for the purpose of determining whether such person may be acting as an underwriter for the issuer.

The view is occasionally expressed that, solely by reason of continued holding of a security for the six-month capital-gain period specified in the income-tax laws, or for a year from the date of purchase, the security may be sold without registration. There is no statutory basis for such assumption. Of course, the longer the period of retention, the more persuasive would be the argument that the resale is not at variance with an original investment intent, but the length of time between acquisition and resale is merely one evidentiary fact to be considered. The weight to be accorded this evidentiary fact must, of necessity, vary with the circumstances of each case. Further, a limitation upon resale for a stated period of time or under certain circumstances would tend to raise a question as to original intent even though such limitation might otherwise recommend itself as a policing device. There is no legal justification for the assumption that holding a security in an "investment account" rather than a "trading account," holding for a deferred sale, for a market rise, for sale if the market does not rise, or for a statutory escrow period, without more, establishes a valid basis for an exemption from registration under the Securities Act.[4]

An unforeseen change of circumstances since the date of purchase may be a basis for an opinion that the proposed resale is not inconsistent with an investment representation. However, such claim must be considered in the light of all of the relevant facts. Thus, an advance or decline in market price or a change in the issuer's operating results are normal investment risks and do not usually provide an acceptable basis for such claim of changed circumstances. Possible inability of the purchaser to pay off loans incurred in connection with the purchase of the stock would ordinarily not be deemed an unforeseeable change of circumstances. Further, in the case of securities pledged for a loan, the pledgee should not assume that he is free to distribute without registration. The Congressional mandate of disclosure to investors is not to be avoided to permit a public distribution of unregistered securities because the pledgee took the securities from a purchaser, subsequently delinquent.[5]

---

[4]See Release No. 33–3825 re The Crowell-Collier Publishing Company.

[5]*S.E.C.* v. *Guild Films Company, Inc. et al.*, 279 F. 2d 485 (C.A. 2, 1960), *cert. denied sub nom.*, *Santa Monica Bank* v. *S.E.C.*, 364 U.S. 819 (1960).

The view is sometimes expressed that investment companies and other institutional investors are not subject to any restrictions regarding disposition of securities stated to be taken for investment and that any securities so acquired may be sold by them whenever the investment decision to sell is made, no matter how brief the holding period. Institutional investors are, however, subject to the same restrictions on sale of securities acquired from an issuer or a person in a control relationship with an issuer insofar as compliance with the registration requirements of the Securities Act is concerned.

Integration of Offerings

A determination whether an offering is public or private would also include a consideration of the question whether it should be regarded as a part of a larger offering made or to be made. The following factors are relevant to such question of integration: whether (1) the different offerings are part of a single plan of financing, (2) the offerings involve issuance of the same class of security, (3) the offerings are made at or about the same time, (4) the same type of consideration is to be received, (5) the offerings are made for the same general purpose.

What may appear to be a separate offering to a properly limited group will not be so considered if it is one of a related series of offerings. A person may not separate parts of a series of related transactions, the sum total of which is really one offering, and claim that a particular part is a non-public transaction. Thus, in the case of offerings of fractional undivided interests in separate oil or gas properties where the promoters must constantly find new participants for each new venture, it would appear to be appropriate to consider the entire series of offerings to determine the scope of this solicitation.

As has been emphasized in other releases discussing exemptions from the registration and prospectus requirements of the Securities Act, the terms of an exemption are to be strictly construed against the claimant who also has the burden of proving its availability.[6] Moreover, persons receiving advice from the staff of the Commission that no action will be recommended if they proceed without registration in reliance upon the exemption should do so only with full realization that the tests so applied may not be proof against claims by purchasers of the security that registration should have been effected. Finally, Sections 12(2) and 17 of the Act, which provide civil liabilities and criminal sanctions for fraud in the sale of a security, are applicable to the transactions notwithstanding the availability of an exemption from registration.

---

[6] *S.E.C.* v. *Sunbeam Gold Mining Co.*, 95 F. 2d 699, 701 (C.A. 9, 1938); *Gilligan, Will & Co.* v. *S.E.C.*, 267 F. 2d 461, 466 (C.A. 2, 1959); *S.E.C.* v. *Ralston Purina Co.*, 346 U.S. 119, 126 (1953); *S.E.C.* v. *Culpepper et al*, 270 F. 2d 241, 246 (C.A. 2, 1959).

a Hazell v Hammersmith and Fulham London Borough Council and others

HOUSE OF LORDS

LORD KEITH OF KINKEL, LORD BRANDON OF OAKBROOK, LORD TEMPLEMAN, LORD b GRIFFITHS AND LORD ACKNER

10, 11, 15–18, 22, 23, 25, 29 OCTOBER, 5, 6, 8, 12 NOVEMBER 1990, 24 JANUARY 1991

Local authority – Statutory powers – Implied power – Implied power used for improper purpose – Interest rate swap transactions – Local authority incorporated by charter c *entering into financial transactions involving speculation on interest rate movements – Auditor claiming that local authority having no power to enter into transactions – Auditor seeking declaration that local authority's capital market activity ultra vires – Whether local authority having capacity to enter into swap transactions – Whether capacity conferred by statute – Whether local authority having capacity to enter into swap transactions for limited purpose of interest rate risk management – Whether swap* d *transactions tainted with improper purpose of speculative trading – London Government Act 1963, s 1(2) – Local Government Act 1972, s 111(1) – Local Government Finance Act 1982, s 19.*

In 1983 the local authority, a London borough which had been incorporated by royal charter pursuant to s 1(2)[a] of the London Government Act 1963, established e a capital market fund for the purpose of conducting transactions involving interest rate movements. Between 1987 and 1988 the local authority's activity in the capital markets increased dramatically both in the volume and range of transactions, which by then included interest rate swaps, swap options, caps, floors and collars, forward rate agreements and gilt and cash options. In the majority of f transactions the local authority would benefit if interest rates fell, but would incur substantial losses if interest rates rose. In July 1988 the district auditor challenged the legality of the local authority's interest rate swap transactions on the ground that they amounted to speculative trading for profit, since the authority had made no attempt to match its actual debts and investments with any of the transactions, all of which had been entered into without any detailed analysis of the interest g that was due to be paid or received, or of the interest rate risks involved or of the steps which might be taken to mitigate or secure protection against losses. Thereafter the local authority ended all further participation in swap transactions and pursued an interim strategy of containment designed to limit the extent of its exposure to losses which had resulted from a rise in interest rates, while gradually extricating itself from the market. In February 1989 the local authority h terminated its capital market activities, apart from seven transactions which were consequent on other parties exercising options. The auditor later applied pursuant to s 19[b] of the Local Government Finance Act 1982 for a declaration that the items appearing in the local authority's capital market fund account for the fiscal years 1987 and 1988 were contrary to law and for an order for rectification of the accounts. A number of banks involved in the local authority's capital market j activities were granted leave to be joined as respondents to the auditor's application in order to protect their commercial interests. The Divisional Court granted the declaration sought by the auditor and ordered the 1987 and 1988 accounts to be

---

a Section 1(2) is set out at p 564 *h* to p 565 *a*, post

b Section 19, so far as material, is set out at p 566 *e* to *g*, post

rectified, holding inter alia (i) that the local authority could not rely on its status as an incorporated municipal corporation to give it the capacity of a natural person *a*
to enter into contracts and its capacity to contract was therefore limited to the powers conferred on it by statute and (ii) that, although a local authority had an implied power under s 111(1)[c] of the Local Government Act 1972 to do anything which facilitated the discharge of any of its functions, the swap transactions entered into by the local authority did not fall within the ambit of s 111(1). The banks appealed. The Court of Appeal allowed the appeal in part, holding that the *b*
swap transactions entered into by the local authority prior to 25 July 1988 were unlawful because they were tainted with the improper purpose of speculative trading but those entered into during the interim strategy period from 25 July 1988 to February 1989 were lawful because they had been carried out for the lawful purpose of mitigating or averting potential loss to the ratepayers. The *c*
auditor and the local authority appealed to the House of Lords.

Held – The appeals would be allowed for the following reasons—

(1) A local authority had no power to enter into interest rate swap transactions, which by their nature involved speculation in future interest trends, with the object of making a profit in order to increase the available resources of the local authority, because they were inconsistent with the borrowing powers of a local *d*
authority as defined and controlled by the provisions of Pt 1 of Sch 13 to the 1972 Act and were not saved by s 111(1) of the Act since they did not 'facilitate' and were not 'conducive or incidental to' the discharge by a local authority of its borrowing functions as limited by the Act. Furthermore, since such transactions were unlawful, the fact that those entered into after July 1988 were intended to *e*
eliminate or reduce the risks inherent in the earlier swap transactions did not render them lawful (see p 548 *a b d h*, p 550 *b*, p 552 *g*, p 553 *a c*, p 554 *f* to *j*, p 555 *f*, p 556 *b* to *d*, p 558 *b* to *e g* to p 559 *a*, p 561 *b e g h*, p 562 *d e g h*, p 567 *d j* to p 568 *c*, p 569 *c* to *e g* to *j* and p 570 *a*, post).

(2) Although the local authority had been incorporated by royal charter and was a legal entity with all the powers of a natural person the charter did not confer *f*
on the borough or the council any greater power than the statutory power exercisable by any other local authority, since the grant of incorporation had been made by virtue of the royal prerogative and in pursuance of the 1963 Act, the combined effect of which was to create a statutory corporation. It followed that the council had no power to carry out the swap transactions either in its own name or in the name of the borough (see p 548 *a b*, p 564 *g*, p 565 *f* to p 566 *a c d*, *g*
p 567 *d* and p 570 *a*, post).

Decision of the Court of Appeal [1990] 3 All ER 33 reversed.

Notes

For a local authority's power to incur expenditure in general, see 28 *Halsbury's Laws* (4th edn) paras 1245, 1247, and for cases on the subject, see 33 *Digest* *h*
(Reissue) 31–34, *96–104*.

For the London Government Act 1963, s 1, see 26 *Halsbury's Statutes* (4th edn) 414.

For the Local Government Act 1972, s 111, Sch 13, see 25 *Halsbury's Statutes* (4th edn) (1990 reissue) 272, 445.

For the Local Government Finance Act 1982, s 19, see ibid 697. *j*

As from 1 April 1990 Pt I of Sch 13 to the 1972 Act was repealed by s 194(2) of and Pt I of Sch 12 to the Local Government and Housing Act 1989, which Act makes further provision about the finance of local authorities.

---

c Section 111(1), so far as material, is set out at p 553 *j* to p 554 *a*, post

Cases referred to in opinions

A-G v Great Eastern Rly Co (1880) 5 App Cas 473, HL.

A-G v Mersey Rly Co [1907] AC 415, HL.

Bonanza Creek Gold Mining Co Ltd v R [1916] 1 AC 566, [1916–17] All ER Rep 999, PC.

Cotman v Brougham [1918] AC 514, [1918–19] All ER Rep 265, HL.

Holsworthy UDC v Holsworthy RDC [1907] 2 Ch 62.

Norwich Provident Insurance Society, Re, Bath's case (1878) 8 Ch D 334.

Riche v Ashbury Railway Carriage and Iron Co Ltd (1874) LR 9 Exch 224, Ex Ch; *rvsd* (1875) LR 7 HL 653.

Rutter v Chapman (1841) 8 M & W 1, 151 ER 925.

Small v Smith (1884) 10 App Cas 119, HL.

Sutton's Hospital Case (1612) 10 Co Rep 1a, [1558–1774] All ER Rep 11, 77 ER 937, Ex Ch.

Wenlock (Baroness) v River Dee Co (1883) 36 Ch D 675, CA; *affd* (1885) 10 App Cas 354, HL.

Conjoined appeals

The applicant, Anthony John Hazell (the auditor), and the first respondent to the application, Hammersmith and Fulham London Borough Council, appealed with leave of the Court of Appeal against the decision of that court (Sir Stephen Brown P, Nicholls and Bingham LJJ) ([1990] 3 All ER 33, [1990] 2 QB 697) on 22 February 1990 allowing in part the appeals of the second, third, fourth and sixth respondents to the appeal and application, Midland Bank plc, Security Pacific National NA, Chemical Bank and Mitsubishi International Finance plc (the banks), and the fifth respondent to the appeal and application, Barclays Bank plc (Barclays), against the order of the Divisional Court (Woolf LJ and French J) ([1990] 3 All ER 33, [1990] 2 QB 697) dated 1 November 1989 whereby the Divisional Court granted the auditor a declaration that items appearing in the capital markets fund account of the council for the financial years beginning 1 April 1987 and 1 April 1988 were contrary to law on the ground, inter alia, that the itemised interest rate swap transactions constituted purely speculative trading and, as such, did not fall within the scope of a local authority's subsidiary powers under s 111(1) of the Local Government Act 1972, and ordered rectification of the accounts for those years. The Court of Appeal ordered that the declaration of the Divisional Court should stand save in so far as it related to transactions entered into on or after 25 July 1988 and that there should be no order for rectification and further ordered that questions relating to the enforceability of the transactions reflected in the accounts should not be decided in the proceedings then before the court. The banks did not challenge the declaration granted by the Court of Appeal in respect of transactions entered into prior to 25 July 1988. The facts are set out in the opinion of Lord Templeman.

Michael Barnes QC and *John Howell* (instructed by *A A Child*) for the auditor.

Peter Scott QC, *Catherine Newman* and *Nigel Giffin* (instructed by *Herbert Smith*) for the council.

Gordon Pollock QC, *Elizabeth Gloster QC* and *Rhodri Davies* (instructed by *Clifford Chance*) for the banks.

Jonathan Sumption QC and *Catharine Otton-Goulder* (instructed by *Linklaters & Paines*) for Barclays.

Their Lordships took time for consideration.

24 January 1990. The following opinions were delivered.

LORD KEITH OF KINKEL. My Lords, I have had the advantage of considering in draft the speech to be delivered by my noble and learned friend Lord Templeman. I agree with it, and for the reasons he gives would allow the appeal and restore the orders of the Divisional Court.

LORD BRANDON OF OAKBROOK. My Lords, I have had the advantage of reading in draft the speech prepared by my noble and learned friend Lord Templeman. I agree with it and for the reasons which he gives I would allow the appeal and make the orders proposed by him.

LORD TEMPLEMAN. My Lords, by the Local Government Act 1972 England was divided into local government areas consisting of counties, districts, London boroughs and parishes. The local authority charged with the administration of local government in a local government area consists of an elected council which 'shall have all such functions as are vested in them by this Act or otherwise': see ss 2(1) and (2) and 14(1) of and para 1(2) of Sch 2 to the 1972 Act. A local authority, although democractically elected and representative of the area, is not a sovereign body and can only do such things as are expressly or impliedly authorised by Parliament. The functions of a principal council, defined by s 270 of the 1972 Act as a county, district or London borough council, extend under many statutes to public health, housing, planning and highways and other environmental matters and to education, housing and social and welfare services, including the care and protection of children, the sick and the elderly. The expenditure incurred by a local authority in the discharge of its functions is funded partly by grants from Parliament, derived from the taxpayer, partly by rates and community charges derived from local residents and partly by income lawfully generated by the council in the due performance of some of its functions, for example rents from council houses. Authorised expenditure by a local authority may be short term or long term. The authority will require revenue to pay its employees periodically and revenue to finance the capital cost of a housing or property development which may cost millions of pounds and produce revenue for a century. The receipt of revenue never coincides with expenditure because grants and rates are received at intervals which do not coincide with outgoings. Moreover the burden of long-term expenditure is in fairness spread over future generations of taxpayers and ratepayers and not imposed entirely on those who pay when the expenditure is incurred. Accordingly Parliament has conferred on a local authority controlled power to borrow short term and long term.

The borrowing powers of a local authority are defined and controlled by the provisions of Pt I of Sch 13 to the 1972 Act, to which I must hereafter refer in detail. Those provisions limit the purpose and method of borrowing by a local authority and dictate internal accounting for repayment. A local authority which is lawfully borrowing may choose to borrow at a fixed or variable rate of interest. The advantages of a fixed interest rate are certainty and protection against increases in current interest rates from time to time. The disadvantage of a fixed interest is that no benefit can be derived from a fall in interest rates.

In exercise of their borrowing powers, the appellant Hammersmith and Fulham London Borough Council (the council) borrowed sums which on 31 March 1989 amounted to £390m, largely representing borrowings incurred to undertake capital projects over many years. Each borrowing had its own terms of repayment. The interest rate differed from one loan to another; some loans were at fixed rates of interest and some at variable rates of interest. The council when taking up a loan must have considered that its resources would be adequate to meet its obligations under the terms of the loan. No doubt has been cast on the legality of any of the council's borrowings. Each outstanding loan remains payable with interest according to its terms, which cannot be altered without the consent of the lender.

From December 1983 onwards and principally between April 1987 and 23 February 1989 the council entered into numerous interest swap contracts. The council was in each contract anticipating a rise or fall in interest rates generally and if its anticipation was fulfilled would derive from the contract a profit which could then be employed, but was not bound to be employed, by the council in meeting the interest burden of its borrowings. The question is whether the council possessed power to enter into any swap contract.

To determine this question it is necessary to consider the statutory powers of local authorities and the nature and effect of the swap transactions which have been carried out by the council. These transactions are alleged by the appellant district auditor (the auditor) to have been unlawful. Some of the transactions were carried out with the respondent banks (the banks). A decision that all the transactions were unlawful could have serious financial repercussions on the banks and other parties to unlawful transactions. The banks have therefore joined in these proceedings. The banks concede that the swap transactions carried out by the council between April 1987 and July 1988 were unlawful but contend that some of the transactions carried out after July 1988 were or may on investigation prove to have been lawful. All the transactions were held by the Divisional Court (Woolf LJ and French J) ([1990] 3 All ER 33, [1990] 2 QB 697) to be unlawful. The Court of Appeal (Sir Stephen Brown P, Nicholls and Bingham LJJ) ([1990] 3 All ER 33, [1990] QB 697) held that some of the transactions may have been incidental to the statutory functions of the council and therefore lawful.

The auditor appeals to this House against the decision of the Court of Appeal that some of the transactions entered into by the council could and may have been lawful. The council feel obliged to support the auditor and to argue that all the swap transactions entered into by the council were unlawful.

The evidence discloses that about 1981 there appeared in the world of international finance a new swap market comprising interest rate swaps, currency swaps and, recently, asset swaps. An illuminating article entitled 'Recent developments in the swap market' by Miss G M S Hammond in the *Bank of England Quarterly Bulletin* of February 1987 explains that the swap market assists traders to solve financial problems arising out of variations in interest rates and currency exchange rates, different taxation regimes and rates of inflation and different creditworthiness. In the simplest case a bank which found it easy to raise fixed finance would swap its interest obligations with a company which could only borrow at variable rates but for good commercial reasons needed the certainty and security of fixed rates. In a more complicated case an American company creditworthy in the United States might build a ship in Italy for an English subsidiary claiming capital allowances and would require short-term and long-term borrowings and payments in Italian and British currency. A European trader creditworthy in his country might need to expend and borrow dollars. Through the intermediation of a bank the American company and the European trader could by swap transactions ensure that fluctuations in interest rates and exchange rates did not have disastrous consequences. The swap market enables a borrower to raise funds in the market to which the borrower has best access but to make interest and principal payments in its preferred form of currency. The

swap market has provided a valuable method of carrying on international trade
and finance. Swaps may involve speculation or may eliminate speculation. In *a*
most cases the advantage sought by a user of the swap market is the elimination
of speculation and uncertainty.

The transactions in the swap market which are now impugned were not carried
out in order to enable the council to borrow or to enable the council to choose to
borrow at a fixed rate rather than at a variable rate or vice versa. The transactions
were undertaken in the hope that the burden of interest payable in respect of *b*
borrowings by the council would be mitigated by profits from swap contracts
whereby the council successfully forecast movements in interest rates. If the
council swapped from a fixed interest to a variable interest the council gained if,
after the swap, interest rates went down. The council lost if, after the swap,
interest rates rose. Similarly, if the council swapped from variable interest to fixed
interest the council gained if, after the swap, interest rates went up and lost if *c*
interests rates went down.

Swaps employed by the council and said by the banks to be available to all local
authorities are lucidly and comprehensively described in the judgment of the
Divisional Court and in particular in Appendix A to that judgment (see [1990] 3
All ER 33 at 63, [1990] 2 QB 697 at 739–740). The simplest form is a swap *d*
contract described as—

> 'an agreement between two parties by which each agrees to pay the other
> on a specified date or dates an amount calculated by reference to the interest
> which would have accrued over a given period on the same notional principal
> sum assuming different rates of interest are payable in each case. For example, *e*
> one rate may be fixed at 10% and the other rate may be equivalent to the six-
> month London Inter-Bank Offered Rate (LIBOR). If the LIBOR rate over the
> period of the swap is higher than 10% then the party agreeing to receive
> "interest" in accordance with LIBOR will receive more than the party entitled
> to receive the 10%. Normally neither party will in fact pay the sums which
> it has agreed to pay over the period of the swap but instead will make a *f*
> settlement on a "net payment basis" under which the party owing the greater
> amount on any day simply pays the difference between the two amounts due
> to the other.'

LIBOR is the interest rate at which major banks offer to lend funds to other
major banks in the London Inter-Bank Market. It may correspond to the rate of *g*
interest being offered on Eurodollar deposits. Eurodollars are United States dollars
held outside the United States.

LIBOR has been used in these proceedings to demonstrate the operation and
effect of swap transactions. LIBOR is not the only basis for swaps. The fixed rate
agreed for a short-term swap transaction may differ from the rate agreed for a
long-term swap. In a swap transaction the winning party to a contract relies on *h*
the financial ability and integrity of the loser. All these complications have led to
a swap industry which includes brokers advising clients and banks acting as
intermediaries or guaranteeing performance by their clients of their swap
operations. These complications do not affect the principle involved in these
proceedings but emphasise that swap transactions are not free of cost and
emphasise the degree of speculation inherent in a swap transaction which is *j*
undertaken solely for the purpose of obtaining a profit by forecasting future
interest trends.

If a local authority borrowed £10m in 1986 for five years at 10% per annum
and LIBOR in 1987 was 12%, the local authority would be unlikely to contemplate

a swap. But if in 1987 LIBOR was 10% and the local authority believed that LIBOR would fall to 8% the local authority might be minded to enter into a swap. In that event the local authority would agree to pay a bank LIBOR every year and the bank would agree to pay interest at 10% on a notional sum of £10m until 1991. If in 1988 LIBOR fell to 8%, the bank would pay the local authority £200,000 being the difference between the LIBOR of 8% and the fixed rate of 10% on £10m. The local authority must still pay interest at 10% on the sum of £10m actually borrowed in 1986 but the gain of £200,000 from the bank would be available to meet the interest payment. If in 1988 LIBOR instead of falling to 8% rose from 10% to 12%, the local authority would pay the bank £200,000 and would also be bound to discharge the interest at 10% due on the sum borrowed in 1986. The success of the swap 'replacing' the fixed rate of 10% by LIBOR would depend on LIBOR falling below 10% and on average remaining below 10% until 1991.

If a local authority correctly forecast a fall in interest rates, the authority could protect itself against a subsequent rise. If, in the example given, the local authority borrowed £10m in 1986 for five years at 10% and in 1987 thought that interest rates would fall, the local authority could enter into a swap transaction to pay LIBOR and receive 10%. If in 1988 LIBOR fell to 8% the local authority could enter into another swap to pay 8% and receive LIBOR. The effect of the two swaps would be to guarantee 2% to the local authority and this gain could be used to help pay the 10% on the actual borrowing. If in 1988 or thereafter the local authority thought that interest rates were likely to fall below 8% the local authority could enter into another swap which if successful would provide a further gain indirectly reducing the burden of interest payments and that gain could again be consolidated. A swap transaction is successful if a rise or fall in interest rates is correctly forecast; once the forecast has been proved to be accurate the local authority can consolidate the gain thus made by a reverse swap. But if after any swap transaction entered into in anticipation of a fall in interest rates there is a rise in LIBOR of if after any transaction anticipating a rise in interest rates there is a fall in LIBOR the local authority will suffer a loss which will be payable in addition to the net interest payable under the terms of the original borrowing. For a local authority the swap market provides the opportunity of reducing indirectly the burden of interest on its borrowings at the risk of increasing that burden. The only evidence presented by a local authority (other than the council) was the evidence of the treasurer of Westminster City Council. He deposed that Westminster City Council entered into approximately 12 swap transactions between 1983 and 1989; on investigation by the auditor it appeared to him that only nine transactions had been entered into. The treasurer of Westminster City Council does not vouchsafe any details. He says:

> 'By way of example the council might enter into a swap contract under which a 11 per cent. per annum fixed rate of interest is swapped for, say, a variable interest rate of 10 per cent. This gives an immediate benefit to the council of a one per cent. difference in interest rate. Were market rates of interest to rise above 11 per cent. I would enter into another reverse swap contract to return to a position of paying the fixed rate of 11 per cent. again.'

The treasurer does not explain why a bank would be willing to accept a variable rate of 10% while agreeing to pay a fixed rate of 11%. Nor does he explain why a bank would be willing to accept a fixed rate of 11% after market rates of interest had risen above 11%. As I understand it, the treasurer begins by exploiting the favourable rate of interest obtainable by a local authority on its borrowing from public sources. The fact remains that a swap transaction depends for its success on interest rates rising or falling in conformity with the expectation of the local authority at the date of the swap.

From investigations made by the auditor it appears that 77 local authorities out of 450 principal local authorities entered into about 400 swap transactions, nearly all between 1987 and 1989. Only ten local authorities (other than the council) entered into more than ten swaps and only 18 (other than the council) entered into more than five. By 31 March 1989 the council had entered into 592 swap transactions and 297 of these were still outstanding. The total notional principal sum involved in all the transactions entered into by the council amounted in the aggregate to £6,052m. The transactions outstanding on 31 March 1989 involved notional principal sums amounting in the aggregate to £2,996m. These figures distort the position because some swap transactions were a hedge against others. But there is no doubt that the volume of swap business undertaken by the council was immense. The council's actual borrowing on that date amounted to £390m, its estimated expenditure for the year ending 31 March 1989 was £85·7m and its quoted budget for that year was £44·6m. The auditor swore an affidavit on 30 May 1989 in which, after exhibiting a summary of calculations, he said:

> '... this indicates that at current interest levels and using the five year swap rate on 9 February 1989 (11 per cent.) as the basis for the calculation for swaps, swap options, caps and floors (including collars) the result would be a loss of £74·4m. If interest rates fall, the council will still lose £12·8m. if the fall is by one per cent. If interest rates rose by one per cent., the council will lose £185·7m. If six month LIBOR on 9 February 1989 (13 per cent.) is used as the basis of the calculation for swaps, swap options, caps and floors (including collars) the result would be a loss of £292·7m. If interest rates fall, the council will still lose £193·5m. if the fall is by one per cent. If interest rates rise by one per cent. the council will lose £406·3m.'

A local authority might wish to undertake swap transactions for three different reasons. First, a local authority which believed that interest rates were falling and that all swaps were lawful, could enter into swap agreements to pay LIBOR and receive a fixed rate of 10%. If the swap transaction was affected by reference to a notional principal sum of £100m and LIBOR fell to 9%, the local authority would make a profit of £1m. If LIBOR rose to 11% the local authority would lose £1m. This general speculation is admitted to be unlawful. The banks admit that the swap transactions by the council between April 1987 and July 1988 were unlawful because in that period the council were simply speculating. Secondly, a local authority which believed that interest rates were falling and that swaps designed to reduce the burden of interest payments on a particular borrowing were lawful, could enter into a swap for that purpose. Thus, if the local authority had borrowed £10m at a fixed rate of 10% and believed that interest rates were falling, the local authority could enter into a swap agreement to pay LIBOR and receive 10%. If LIBOR fell to 9% the local authority would make a profit of £100,000. If LIBOR rose to 11% the local authority would lose £100,000. This swap agreement is referred to as a 'parallel contract' because the notional principal sum involved does not exceed a principal sum borrowed and because the effect of the contract and any subsequent swap transaction entered into for the same purpose is said to convert indirectly a fixed interest obligation into a variable interest obligation or vice versa. The swap agreement in these circumstances is said to be a 'parallel contract' and to 'replace' the interest payable under the actual borrowing. The banks contend that the local authority may lawfully enter into parallel contracts and the council may have done so. But a parallel contract does not in fact replace the interest under the original borrowing and the swap transaction is a speculation no different in quality though different in magnitude from a swap contract which is not entered into by reference to any existing borrowing.

Thirdly, a local authority might seek to increase the proportion which its variable interest rate obligations bore to its fixed interest obligations. If 90% of the local authority's borrowings were at fixed rates of interest and 10% at variable rates, the local authority might by swapped contracts agree to pay fixed interest and receive LIBOR and thus increase the proportion of its variable interest obligations. This process is known as 'reprofiling'. The banks contend that a local authority may lawfully enter into swaps for the purpose of reprofiling and the council may have done so. But if there is any difference between reprofiling and general speculation the notional sums must be limited to notional sums corresponding to some existing interest obligations. Basically therefore 'reprofiling' is only an extension of 'replacing'.

Swap transactions include swap contracts, swap options, caps and floors, gilt options and cash options and forward rate agreements, all of which are explained in Appendix A to the judgment of the Divisional Court ([1990] 3 All ER 33 at 63–64, [1990] 2 QB 697 at 739–741). All these transactions are said by the banks, with some hesitation so far as cash options are concerned, to be lawful if undertaken by a local authority provided the transactions are 'replacement' or 'reprofiling' exercises intended to provide profits to be employed in the reduction of interest on particular borrowings and are limited to profits and losses on amounts which do not exceed the principal sums borrowed. The most material distinction between swap contracts and other types of swap transactions is that swap contracts do not usually require the payment of a premium whereas swap options and other types of swap transactions usually provide for a premium to be paid. The rate of interest which will attract payment when an option is exercised is negotiated in the light of the size and date of the payment of the premium. Swap transactions which involve premiums and options exercisable at future dates may increase the element of speculation and distort the local authority's pattern of borrowing. A local authority should, so far as possible, spread the burden of capital borrowing evenly over present and future taxpayers and ratepayers. A premium which is received by a local authority in 1990 reduces the cost of the borrowing in 1990 but increases the annual cost if and when the option is exercised. A premium which is paid by a local authority in 1990 increases the immediate cost of the borrowing in 1990 in the hope that the cost will be reduced when the option becomes exercisable.

The banks concede that local authorities have no express power to enter into any swap transaction. The banks contend that local authorities have an implied power to enter into 'replacement' and 'reprofiling' swap contracts. The council may have entered into some lawful 'replacement' or 'reprofiling' swap contracts. In addition the banks contend that the council was entilted to enter into swap transactions after July 1988 in order to mitigate the effect of unlawful swap transactions previously undertaken.

These arguments of the banks are based on s 111(1) of the 1972 Act, which, so far as material, provides:

> 'Without prejudice to any powers exercisable apart from this section but subject to the provisions of this Act . . . a local authority shall have power to do anything (whether or not involving expenditure, borrowing or lending of

> money or the acquisition or disposal of any property or rights) which is calculated to facilitate, or is conducive or incidental to, the discharge of any *a* of their functions.'

The banks contend that swap transactions which are intended to 'replace' or 'reprofile' existing interest obligations are within the words of s 111 'calculated to facilitate' or are 'conducive to' or are 'incidental to' the discharge by the local authority of its admitted function of borrowing or an alleged function of debt *b* management.

Counsel for the auditor submitted that a local authority's power to borrow is not a 'function' within the meaning of s 111 and that the local authority can do nothing which only facilitates or is conducive to or incidental to the power of borrowing.

In *A-G v Great Eastern Rly Co* (1880) 5 App Cas 473 at 481 Lord Blackburn said: *c*

> '. . . where there is an Act of Parliament creating a corporation for a particular purpose, and giving it powers for that particular purpose, what it does not expressly or impliedly authorize is to be taken to be prohibited . . .'

In the same case Lord Selborne LC said (at 478) that the doctrine of ultra vires— *d*

> 'ought to be reasonably, and not unreasonably, understood and applied, and that whatever may fairly be regarded as incidental to, or consequential upon, those things which the Legislature has authorized, ought not (unless expressly prohibited) to be held, by judicial construction, to be *ultrà vires*.'

In the same vein Lord Blackburn said (at 481): *e*

> '. . . those things which are incident to, and may reasonably and properly be done under the main purpose, though they may not be literally within it, would not be prohibited.'

Section 111 embodies these principles.

I agree with the Court of Appeal that in s 111 the word 'functions' embraces *f* 'all the duties and powers of a local authority: the sum total of the activities Parliament has entrusted to it' (see [1990] 3 All ER 33 at 83, [1990] 2 QB 697 at 785). Those activities are its functions. Accordingly, a local authority can do anything which is calculated to facilitate or is conducive or incidental to the local authority's function of borrowing.

So the question is whether a swap transaction is 'calculated to facilitate, or is *g* conducive or incidental to' the discharge of the local authority's function of borrowing.

Swap transactions could be said to 'facilitate' borrowing if the prospect of being able to reduce the burden of interest by swaps encouraged the local authority to enter into a borrowing which it would otherwise decide against. But this approach *h* is impermissible. A local authority when considering expenditure must carefully consider the amount required to be borrowed and the resources available for payment of interest and capital. A local authority which borrowed in reliance on future successful swap operations would be failing in its duty to act prudently in the interests of the ratepayers.

Similarly, swap operations cannot be said to be 'conducive to' borrowing *j* because local authorities should not be encouraged to borrow by the prospect of swap transactions. It was submitted that swap transactions are 'incidental to' borrowing. The first difficulty is that a swap transaction is a separate collateral contract which may be undertaken long after a borrowing has been effected. The local authority hopes that by a successful forecast of future interest trends it will

provide itself with an income which can be employed in paying the interest on a
a borrowing. Assuming that this objection is not fatal, it is then necessary to
consider what kinds of operations have been held to have been incidental to the
discharge of the functions of a statutory corporation.

In *Small v Smith* (1884) 10 App Cas 119 a building society which had power to enter into a second mortgage was held not to have an incidental power to guarantee payment of a prior mortgage. The Earl of Selborne LC said (at 133):

b

> 'But the argument really is that because the rules permit this kind of
> security to be taken, that is to say, give very large and general powers as to
> securities, which do not exclude the taking of a security on which there is a
> prior mortgage, therefore there is a potential necessity for entering into a
> transaction of this kind to protect that security, and therefore there is a
> c reasonable implication that there is power to do it. But I wholly deny that
> there is any potential necessity at all . . . there is no more potential necessity
> for doing this in order to meet a temporary inconvenience than there is for
> doing anything else in the world which in the opinion of the directors might
> tend to obviate that inconvenicence.'

d The same reasoning could be applied to the argument that a local authority
needs power to swap because it has power to borrow.

In *Baroness Wenlock v River Dee Co* (1885) 10 App Cas 354 a statutory river company possessed express power to borrow £50,000 secured by bond or mortgage. Any implied power to borrow was negatived by the express power to borrow not more than £50,000. Lord Watson said (at 362):

e

> 'The qualification attached by the legislature to the borrowing powers sanctioned by the Act of 1851 [14 & 15 Vict c lxxxvii (River Dee Co)], was, in my opinion, fatal to the continued existence of any implied power which the company had under their previous statutes.'

As will be seen, Pt I of Sch 13 to the 1972 Act imposes restrictions on the
f borrowing powers of local authorities.

In *A-G v Mersey Rly Co* [1907] AC 415 a railway company was held not entitled to run a number of omnibuses which it claimed were incidental to the railway enterprise itself. Lord Loreburn LC said (at 415):

> 'The rule of law has been laid down in this House to the effect that it must
> g be shewn that the business can fairly be regarded as incidental to or
> consequential upon the use of the statutory powers; and it is a question in
> each case whether it is so or whether it is not so.'

Lord Macnaghten said (at 417):

h

> 'The question is this: Is the business of omnibus proprietors as the
> defendants were carrying it on when the action was brought reasonably
> incidental to their business as authorized by their special Act? The principle
> to be applied is perfectly clear. The difficulty is all in the application.
> Hundreds of cases may be suggested where the thing done comes very near
> j the line and may fairly be open to a difference of opinion . . . Here, I think,
> the respondents [defendants] have transgressed the line. It may be that in
> doing what they wish to do they cannot help it. But that, in my opinion, is
> no justification for their action. If they wish to extend their undertaking
> beyond the limits authorized by their charter, the proper course is to apply
> to Parliament for further powers. In my opinion a matter of this sort is much

> better left to Parliament. There everybody who has a right to be heard will be listened to, and there the interests of the public will be protected.' a

The same considerations apply in the present case.

Several other authorities were cited to illustrate incidental powers but each case turned on its own facts.

The authorities deal with widely different statutory functions but establish the general proposition that, when a power is claimed to be incidental, the provisions b of the statute which confer and limit functions must be considered and construed. The question is not whether swap transactions are incidental to borrowing but whether swap transactions are incidental to a local authority's borrowing function having regard to the provisions and limitations of the 1972 Act regulating that function.

The authorities also show that a power is not incidental merely because it is c convenient or desirable or profitable. A swap transaction undertaken by a local authority involves speculation in future interest trends with the object of making a profit in order to increase the available resources of the local authorities. There are many trading and currency and commercial swap transactions which eliminate or reduce speculation. Individual trading corporations and others may speculate as much as they please or consider prudent. But a local authority is not a trading d or currency or commercial operator with no limit on the method or extent of its borrowing or with powers to speculate. The local authority is a public authority dealing with public moneys, exercising powers limited by Sch 13.

Section 172 of the 1972 Act directs that Pt I of Sch 13 'shall have effect with respect to the powers of local authorities to borrow and lend money and with e respect to their funds'. Part I of Sch 13, so far as material, provides:

> '1. Without prejudice to section 111 above—(*a*) a principal council may borrow money for the purpose of lending money to another authority ... (*b*) a local authority ... may borrow money for any other purpose or class of purpose approved for the purposes of this sub-paragraph by the Secretary of State and in accordance with any conditions subject to which the approval is f given ...'

The Secretary of State from time to time issues block borrowing approval and may give a specific approval. The block borrowing approval defines the purposes for which money may be borrowed, the period during which borrowings must be repaid and limits the aggregate amount which an authority can borrow. For g example, money may be borrowed for a maximum period of 60 years for land purchase and house building, for 40 years for other building and landscaping works and for 20 years for some furniture and other equipment. The maximum periods relate roughly to the expected life of the asset for which the money is to be borrowed.

h Paragraph 2(1) provides that 'Where a local authority are authorised by or under this Act or any other enactment to borrow money, they may raise the money' by mortgage, by the issue of stock, by the issue of debentures or annuity certificates, by the issue of bonds, by the issue of bills and '(*f*) by an agreement entered into with the Public Works Loan Commissioners under section 2 of the Public Works Loans Act 1965', or by any other means approved by the Secretary j of State with the consent of the Treasury.

Borrowings from the Public Works Loan Commissioners (the PWLB) account for some 80% or more of local authority borrowings. The PWLB offer loans to local authorities at fixed or variable rates both of which are below the market rate because of the power of the government to negotiate its own borrowings. If a local authority borrows at a variable rate from the PWLB the local authority may elect thereafter on one occasion by the terms of the loan to change from a variable rate to a fixed rate without penalty. If, therefore, a local authority is compelled to borrow at a time when interest rates are thought to be abnormally high, the authority can borrow from the PWLB at a variable rate and then convert into a fixed rate when interest rates have fallen.

By para 4(1) 'The Secretary of State may by regulations made with the consent of the Treasury' prescribe the form of any mortgage deed, regulate the issue of stocks and bonds including the terms on which they may be issued, and regulate the manner of transfer dealing with and redeeming any mortgage deed, stocks or bonds.

Thus the Secretary of State retains complete control over local authority borrowings.

By para 5(1) 'A local authority may borrow by the issue of bills, payable within twelve months from the date of issue', inter alia, such sums as may be required for the purpose of defraying expenses pending the receipt of revenues; but the amount so borrowed is limited to a specified proportion of the authority's estimated gross income derived from rates.

It might have been thought that a similar power was incidental to the local authority's function of borrowing but any incidental power is negatived by this express provision:

> '7.—(1) Where expenditure incurred by a local authority for any purpose is defrayed by borrowing, the local authority shall . . . debit the account from which that expenditure would otherwise fall to be defrayed with a sum equivalent to an instalment of principal and interest combined such that if paid annually it would secure the payment of interest at the due rate on the outstanding principal together with the repayment of the principal not later than the end of the fixed period [of the loan].'

If a local authority borrowed at a fixed rate and entered into a swap contract to 'replace' the fixed rate by a variable rate, para 7 does not enable any variation to be made in the required annual debit and does not take into account profits made or losses suffered as a result of the swap.

Paragraph 8 provides:

> 'A local authority who borrow money . . . may during the fixed period borrow further sums, without the approval of the Secretary of State under that sub-paragraph, for the purpose of repaying the money so borrowed.'

Paragraph 8 thus confers an express power on the local authority truly to replace a loan. This power could be exercised, for example, if a fixed loan of 15% could be replaced by a fixed loan of 10% after rates had fallen. Such a true replacement would not involve the local authority making gains or suffering losses associated with swap transactions.

Paragraph 10 provides:

> '(1) A local authority may, without the approval of the Secretary of State . . . borrow by way of temporary loan or overdraft from a bank or otherwise any sums which they may temporarily require—(*a*) for the purpose of defraying expenses . . . pending the recepit of revenues . . .'

Here again what might have been thought to be an incidental power is made the subject of express enactment.

Paragraph 20 provides:

> 'A person lending money to a local authority shall not be bound to inquire whether the borrowing of the money is legal or regular or whether the *a* money raised was properly applied and shall not be prejudiced by an illegality or irregularity, or by the misapplication of non-application of any of that money.'

The banks concede that this paragraph cannot be construed so as to afford protection to persons who enter into swap transactions with local authorities. *b*

When a local authority considers whether to expend money and if so whether to borrow and on what terms, the local authority must have regard to the provisions of Sch 13, the method of borrowing and terms of repayment, the prevailing interest rates and the possibility that interest rates may rise or fall during the period of the loan. If the local authority finds that after it has borrowed there has been a violent change in interest rates which affects a particular *c* borrowing, the local authority is not without remedial action. It can convert a loan taken out with the PWLB from variable rate of interest into a fixed rate of interest. It can pay off an expensive loan and take out a new loan. It is said that the cost of paying off an old loan and taking out a new loan would be greater than the cost of entering into swap transactions. But this fact alone cannot render swap transactions legal. *d*

Schedule 13 establishes a comprehensive code which defines and limits the powers of a local authority with regard to its borrowing. The schedule is in my view inconsistent with any incidental power to enter into swap transactions.

There is a further difficulty. If swap transactions are incidental to the function of borrowing, it would appear that swap transactions can only be entered into by *e* the local authority and not by a committee or officer. Section 101(6), before its amendment by s 45(5) of the Local Government and Housing Act 1989, provided:

> 'A local authority's functions with respect to levying, or issuing a precept for, a rate or borrowing money shall be discharged only by the authority.'

The Court of Appeal found that s 111 applied but that s 101(6) did not. The *f* court managed to reach this conclusion by accepting the argument that swap transactions are not so much incidental to the function of borrowing as incidental to the function of debt management, defined as a duty to take reasonable care to manage its borrowing prudently in the best interests of the ratepayers. Before this House, counsel for the banks repeated the submission that swap transactions, if not incidental to borrowing, were nevertheless incidental to debt management. *g*

Debt management is not a function. Debt management is a phrase which has been coined in this case to describe the activities of a person who enters the swap market for the purpose of making profits which can be employed in the payment of interest on borrowings. The expression 'debt management' could be employed to describe the duty of a local authority to consider from time to time whether it should change a variable PWLB loan into a fixed interest loan, whether it should *h* redeem one loan and take out another, whether when a new borrowing is contemplated the borrowing should be at a variable or fixed rate taking into account all the other borrowings of the local authority. Debt management is a phrase which describes prudent and lawful activities on the part of the local authority. If swap transactions were lawful a local authority would be under a *j* duty to consider entering into swap transactions as part of its duty of debt management. But if a swap transaction is not lawful then it cannot be lawful for a local authority to carry out a swap transaction under the guise of debt management.

The Divisional Court came to the conclusion that it would be inconsistent with the structure of the 1972 Act as a whole, to which the provisions of s 111(1) are expressly made subject, to regard swap transactions as falling within that subsection (see [1990] 3 All ER 33 at 51, [1990] 2 QB 697 at 725). I agree.

For the banks it was argued that swap transactions are akin to insurance which enables provision to be made for possible risks. By insurance, an assured sacrifices a premium which, when aggregated with premiums from other assured, will form a pool from which the insurer will indemnify the unfortunate victim (if any) who suffers from the risk insured against. A swap contract based on a notional principal sum of £1m under which the local authority promises to pay the bank £10,000 if LIBOR rises by 1% and the bank promises to pay the local authority £10,000 if LIBOR falls by 1% is more akin to gambling than insurance.

The Court of Appeal was impressed by the argument that if swap transactions were unlawful a local authority could not take advantage of reductions in interest rates. But the success of swaps depends on a successful forecast of future interest rates. The power of a local authority to choose between long-term and short-term borrowings and to choose between variable and fixed interest rates and the power of a local authority to borrow from the PWLB on favourable terms and to change from variable to fixed rates of interest and the power of the local authority to replace a borrowing with another borrowing provide opportunity for the local authority to consider whether the overall rate of interest paid by the local authority is reasonable and is protected against volatility of interest rates. The greater the volatility of interest rates, the greater the risk of loss to a local authority as a result of swap transactions. Despite the urgings of counsel for the banks to the contrary, it seem to me there are substantial risks. There is no evidence that local authorities which have abstained from the swap market have forfeited substantial profits. These are all matters for Parliament to consider and the banks are not debarred from impressing upon Parliament the advantages to local authorities of a power to enter into swap transactions.

In the case of a building society Parliament has conferred express power to enter into swap transactions but that power was only conferred after the building societies had been given wide powers of entering into commercial transactions. The powers to enter into swap transactions were at first limited and when extended Parliament continued to insist that the power should be subject to the approval of the members of the society who will suffer if the power is ineptly exercised.

The Building Societies Act 1986 conferred power on a building society to provide, inter alia, banking, investment and insurance services. Section 23 authorised a building society to effect contracts of a description to be prescribed by the Building Societies Commission with the consent of the Treasury for the purpose of reducing the risk of loss arising from changes in interest rates, currency rates or other forms of prescribed risk which affects its business. Section 23(5) directed that this power to hedge should only be exercisable if adopted by the society. The Building Societies (Prescribed Contracts) Order 1986, SI 1986/2098, made by the commission pursuant to the 1986 Act authorised a building society to enter into sterling interest rate swaps and capital and interest currency swaps but by art 3:

> '... (2) A society may only effect a prescribed contract where it has borrowed or intends to borrow a principal sum and the prescribed contract relates to a principal sum equal to it or less than it.
>
> (3) No prescribed contract may be effected by a society save where another participant is a bank authorised ... to hold funds of societies ...'

Thus in 1986 Parliament conferred on building societies, which by the 1986 Act were given wide functions, a power to enter into swap transactions which were limited to parallel contracts, could only be effected with leading banks, and only after the members of the society had approved the exercise of the power to hedge. In 1988 (by the Building Societies (Prescribed Contracts) Order 1988, SI 1988/1344) Parliament extended the hedging power so as to apply to all the forms of swap transactions which are specified in Appendix A to the judgment of the Divisional Court in these proceedings (see [1990] 3 All ER 33 at 63, [1990] 2 QB 697 at 739–740). Parliament, however, retained the requirement of approval by members of the society of the exercise of the power to hedge. It is for Parliament and not the courts to decide whether there should be conferred on local authorities unlimited power to hedge or a power limited for the protection of taxpayers and ratepayers. Parliament might decide that it was unnecessary or unwise to confer power on local authorities to enter the swap market at all.

Counsel for the banks contended that the application of the ultra vires doctrine in the present circumstances is so harsh that, if swap transactions entered into by local authorities are unlawful, the swap market and the banks and other parties to swap transactions will be involved in great difficulties, the creditworthiness of local authorities would be impaired and there would be an increase in taxation. The major problem concerns the activities of the council, which indulged in speculation on a vast and admittedly unlawful scale. It may not follow that, as between the council and the banks, payments made by the council before or after the period of the interim strategy can be recovered by the council. Nor does it follow that payments received by the council before or after the period of interim strategy cannot be recovered by the banks. The consequences of any ultra vires transaction may depend on the facts of each case. The banks have expressly reserved the right to argue in any proceedings arising out of a swap transaction that the banks are not tainted by illegality and that, for a variety of reasons which cannot now be canvassed, payments made pursuant to swap transactions can be retained by the banks or recovered from the council. The creditworthiness of local authorities has nothing to do with swap transactions. Paragraph 20 of Sch 13 to the 1972 Act is a complete protection for any person who lends money to a local authority. The object of the doctrine of ultra vires is the protection of the public. In *Cotman v Brougham* [1918] AC 514 at 520, [1918–19] All ER Rep 265 at 268 Lord Parker of Waddington referring to a company whose functions were defined by its memorandum of association said:

> 'The question whether or not a transaction is ultra vires is a question of law between the company and a third party. The truth is that the statement of a company's objects in its memorandum is intended to serve a double purpose. In the first place it gives protection to subscribers, who learn from it the purposes to which their money can be applied. In the second place it gives protection to persons who deal with the company, and who can infer from it the extent of the company's powers . . . Even a power to borrow money could not always be safely inferred, much less such a power as that of underwriting shares in another company.'

In the same case Lord Wrenbury said that the memorandum of association—

> 'must delimit and identify the objects in such plain and unambiguous manner as the reader can identify the field of industry within which the corporate activities are to be confined. The purpose, I apprehend, is twofold. The first is that the intending corporator who contemplates the investment of his capital should know within what field it is to be put at risk. The second

is that anyone who shall deal with the company shall know without reasonable doubt whether the contractual relation into which he contemplates entering with the company is one relating to a matter within its corporate objects.'

(See [1918] AC 514 at 522, [1918–19] All ER Rep 265 at 269.)

In the result, I am of the opinion that a local authority has no power to enter into a swap transaction. The banks nevertheless argued that swap transactions entered into by the council after July 1988 were lawful because they were intended to eliminate or reduce the risks inherent in earlier swap transactions. At the end of July 1988 the council was advised by the auditor that swap transactions which were not parallel contracts were of doubtful validity. For the purpose of this appeal, I assume, without deciding, that the council thereupon adopted a policy, now described as 'the interim strategy' of refraining from entering into swap transactions save for the purpose of reducing the potential loss which might be suffered as a result of earlier swap transactions. The interim strategy came to an end on 23 February 1989 when the council determined to take no further action with regard to existing or future swap transactions until the law had been clarified.

The interim strategy took the form of fresh swap transactions designed to hedge the risks of earlier transactions. In addition, some swaps were terminated by cash payments, some swap contracts may have been assigned, thus putting an end to the obligations of the council thereunder, and financial obligations under existing swap contracts were honoured. Since I have concluded that a local authority has no power to enter into swap transactions, it must follow that a swap transaction entered into pursuant to the interim strategy was also unlawful.

Any power to carry out the interim strategy activities must be derived from s 111 of the 1972 Act; a function must be identified to which the interim strategy activities were incidental. Miss Gloster QC on behalf of the banks submitted that the interim strategy activities were incidental to the duty of the council to take such reasonable steps as were very desirable or necessary to preserve and protect the ratepayers' funds from the adverse consequences of a previous act of the local authority, in circumstances where there were doubts at the time that the protective steps were taken as to whether the previous act was ultra vires or an abuse of power. In the alternative, Miss Gloster submitted that the interim strategy was carried out in discharge of or was incidental to the duty of the council to make arrangements for the proper administration of its financial affairs. My Lords, a local authority owes a duty to its ratepayers to preserve ratepayers' funds and to arrange for proper administration. But the reasonable steps and arrangements carried out by the council for the purpose of discharging its duties must be lawful. No authority was cited which suggested that in certain circumstances an ultra vires transaction could be remedied by another ultra vires transaction, possibly with different parties.

A large number of authorities were cited by way, it was said, of analogy. The first batch of authorities established the right of a corporation to compromise an ultra vires claim; but in each case the compromise did not involve the corporation in performing any unlawful act.

In *Re Norwich Provident Insurance Society, Bath's Case* (1878) 8 Ch D 334 at 340 Jessel MR said that a corporation has under the general law the same right to compromise claims brought against it as individual persons have:

'It would be a startling proposition that, whereas an individual may always avoid having to resort to litigation by compromising a claim against him, a

> corporation can never avoid it, but must either fight out the claim or make arrangements sanctioned by the order of a Court of Justice; yet such would be the result of holding that a corporation has no such general power.'

In my opinion it would be a startling proposition that an individual or a corporation may always avoid having resort to litigation by agreeing, by way of compromise, to carry out an unlawful. act.

The position was made abundantly clear by Warrington J in *Holsworthy UDC v Holsworthy RDC* [1907] 2 Ch 62. He decided that a compromise agreement entered into bona fide by two councils was not rendered invalid by the fact that one of the claims included in the compromise subsequently proved to be unfounded in law. Warrington J said (at 73):

> '... a compromise, if entered into bona fide, and *if it does not involve the doing of an act by one of the parties which is itself ultra vires*, may be made by and may be binding on a corporation just as on any individual ...' (I have emphasised the important words.)

In this House, Miss Gloster also cited, by way of analogy, the well-recognised authorities which established the jurisdiction of a court of equity to sanction a breach of trust by trustees. Such sanction may be granted retrospectively after the unauthorised transaction has been carried into effect. But, while a court has jurisdiction to sanction any transaction which the settlor could have authorised and which all beneficiaries being sui juris could sanction, the court has no jurisdiction to extend the powers conferred on a corporation by Parliament or to approve an unlawful transaction by a corporation. The Court of Appeal in the instant case summarised the authorities cited by Miss Gloster by way of analogy and observed ([1990] 3 All ER 33 at 90, [1990] 2 QB 697 at 794):

> '... it is sometimes necessary to accept that "what's done is done" and, even if it should not have been done, the law should lean in favour of such solution as enables the situation to be so far as possible rectified with minimum loss and inconvenience to all involved.'

The Court of Appeal therefore held that the interim strategy transactions were lawful. I do not believe that the Court of Appeal would have reached the same conclusion if it had not, erroneously in my opinion, already held that a swap transaction which is a parallel contract was within the power of a local authority. No authority is needed for the proposition that the law should lean in favour of such *lawful* solution as enables the situation to be so far as possible rectified with minimum loss and inconvenience to all involved. No authority satisfies me that the law should lean in favour of such *unlawful* solution as enables the situation to be so far as possible rectified with minimum loss and inconvenience to all involved.

Accordingly, swap transactions undertaken during the period of the interim strategy are no different from swap transactions entered into at any earlier period.

Finally, the banks deployed an argument described by the Court of Appeal as 'a somewhat arcane point' (see [1990] 3 All ER 33 at 72, [1990] 2 QB 697 at 769–770). The argument proceeds on the basis that, though the incorporated Hammersmith and Fulham borough can only act by the unincorporated Hammersmith and Fulham borough council and though the powers of the council are limited by the 1972 Act, the borough acting by the council has all the powers of a natural person and is not confined by the 1972 Act. Therefore any swap transaction entered into by the borough was lawful. It is conceded that neither the borough nor the council could lawfully devote moneys held as part of the general rate fund in order to comply with swap transaction obligations because the general rate fund may only be expended by the council and solely for purposes authorised by the 1972 Act and other statutes. But it is contended that there might be some property perhaps generously donated to the borough which was in some way not held by the borough acting by the council for the benefit of the ratepayers or which, although held for the benefit of the taxpayers, was not subject to the same inhibitions as the general rate fund and other property held for the benefit of the ratepayers. This argument strikes me as being not so much arcane as absurd.

The arguments starts with the year 1612 and the report of *Sutton's Hospital Case* 10 Co Rep 1, [1558–1774] All ER Rep 11. That report, although largely incomprehensible in 1990, has been accepted as 'express authority' that at common law it is an incident to a corporation to use its common seal for the purpose of binding itself to anything to which a natural person could bind himself and to deal with its property as a natural person might deal with his own: see *Riche v Ashbury Railway Carriage and Iron Co Ltd* (1874) LR 9 Exch 224 at 263. The doctrine applies only to a corporation created by an exercise of the royal prerogative. A corporation created by or under a statute has no power except the powers granted expressly or by implication by that statute. As will appear, the corporation in the present case was a hybrid, created by royal charter issued pursuant to a statute. *Sutton's Hospital Case* did not deal with this situation.

There is a long history of the incorporation of municipalities. The Municipal Corporations Act 1835 and the Municipal Corporations (General) Act 1837 regulated boroughs already incorporated by royal charter and provided that upon the petition of the inhabitant householders the Crown might create a new municipal borough, incorporate the inhabitants and extend to that municipal borough and the inhabitants the provisions of the Municipal Corporations Acts. In *Rutter v Chapman* (1841) 8 M & W 1 at 74, 151 ER 925 at 955 per Patteson J it was decided that the effect of the 1837 Act was—

> 'not in derogation or abridgment of the power of the Crown to grant charters of incorporation at common law, which it may still do without any petition; but it is to enable the Crown, in case of any such petition, to extend to any new corporation, when created, the powers of the Municipal Corporations Act, some of which, as for instance the taxing of the inhabitants by a borough rate, may not have been grantable by the Crown at common law. The act does not profess to enable the Crown to grant charters, but only, if it shall think fit to grant them upon petition, to extend to the grantees, by those charters, certain powers and privileges.'

In *Bonanza Creek Gold Mining Co Ltd v R* [1916] 1 AC 566, [1916–17] All ER Rep 999 the Privy Council considered the effect of a royal charter granted pursuant to statute. The British North America Act 1867, by ss 12 and 65, transferred to the Lieutenant Governor of Ontario the prerogative power of incorporation in relation to the province. Section 92 of the 1867 Act conferred exclusive power upon the provincial legislature to make laws in relation to the incorporation of companies with provincial objects. The Ontario Companies Act (1897) passed pursuant to s 92 authorised the incorporation of companies by the Lieutenant Governor. Viscount Haldane, delivering the advice of the Board, said ([1916] 1 AC 566 at 577–578, [1916–17] All ER Rep 999 at 1003–1004):

> '... that it is wrong, in answering the question what powers the corporation possesses when incorporated exclusively by statute, to start by assuming that the Legislature meant to create a company with a capacity resembling that of

> a natural person, such as a corporation created by charter would have at common law . . .'

It must not be assumed—

> 'that the Legislature has had a common law corporation in view, whereas the wording may not warrant the inference that it has done more than concern itself with its own creature. Such a creature, where its entire existence is derived from the statute, will have the incidents which the common law would attach if, but only if, the statute has by its language gone on to attach them . . . The question is simply one of interpretation of the words used. For the statute may be so framed that executive power to incorporate by charter, independently of the statute itself, which some authority, such as a Lieutenant-Governor, possessed before it came into operation, has been left intact. Or the statute may be in such a form that a new power to incorporate by charter has been created, directed to be exercised with a view to the attainment of, for example, merely territorial objects, but not directed in terms which confine the legal personality which the charter creates to existence for the purpose of these objects and within territorial limits. The language may be such as to show an intention to confer on the corporation the general capacity which the common law ordinarily attaches to corporations created by charter.'

In my opinion, where a statute authorises the grant of a royal charter, then, the extent of the powers exercisable by a corporation created by a charter granted pursuant to the statute will depend on the true construction and intent of the statute.

Under the London Government Act 1939, consolidating earlier legislation, the administrative county of London included 28 metropolitan boroughs. By s 17:

> '(1) For every metropolitan borough there shall be a metropolitan borough council consisting of the mayor, aldermen and councillors, and the council shall have all such functions as are vested in it by this Act or otherwise.
>
> (2) A borough council shall be a body corporate . . . and shall have perpetual succession and a common seal with power to hold land for the purposes of its constitution without licence in mortmain.'

A London metropolitan borough council being created by statute could only exercise the powers conferred by statute. Neither the council nor the borough, so far as it existed apart from the council, had the powers of a natural person.

By s 1(1) of the London Government Act 1963 the metropolitan boroughs of the county of London were enlarged, reorganised and converted into London boroughs forming part of the administrative area of the Greater London Council. Section 1 of the 1963 Act continued as follows:

> '(2) If in the case of any London borough, on representations in that behalf made to the Privy Council by the Minister, Her Majesty by the advice of her Privy Council thinks fit to grant a charter of incorporation of the inhabitants of that borough, Her Majesty may by that charter—(*a*) make provision with respect to the name of the borough; and (*b*) subject to the provisions of this Act, make any provision such as may be made by virtue of section 131 of the Local Government Act 1933 by a charter granted under Part VI of that Act; and any charter which purports to be granted in pursuance of the Royal prerogative and this subsection shall be deemed to be valid and within the

powers of this Act and Her Majesty's prerogative and the validity thereof shall not be questioned in any legal proceedings whatever.

(3) In the case of any London borough whose inhabitants are not incorporated by such a charter as is referred to in the last foregoing subsection, provision for their incorporation shall be made by the Minister by order (hereafter in this Act referred to as an "incorporation order") which may include any such provision as is mentioned in paragraph (*a*) or (*b*) of that subsection . . .

(6) The Municipal Corporations Act 1882 shall apply to every London borough and . . . the expression "borough" when used in relation to local government . . . shall . . . include a London borough; and the council of a London borough shall be a local authority . . .'

The 1963 Act did not confer and showed no intention of conferring on London boroughs or their councils any power exceeding the statutory power formerly exercised by metropolitan borough councils. Under the 1963 Act every London borough was bound to be incorporated, either by the Crown under s 1(2) or by the minister under s 1(3). Nevertheless the banks argue that it is possible that some swap transactions were entered into by the council and that other swap transactions were entered into by the borough acting by the council. Swap transactions entered into by the council would be unlawful for the reasons I have already indicated but, say the banks, swap transactions entered into by the borough acting by the council would be lawful because the borough, which was in 1964 incorporated by the Crown, possessed all the powers of a natural person. If the argument for the banks is correct, the 1963 Act had the effect of dividing London boroughs into two classes. The first class incorporated by the Crown upon the representations of the minister would have all the powers of a natural person. The second class, incorporated by the minister, would have only the powers conferred by statute. Yet both classes of London boroughs would fulfil exactly the same functions by exactly the same machinery. Councils of both classes whether or not acting on behalf of the borough would be constrained by the limitations on their powers imposed by statute. In my opinion the 1963 Act intended and provided that every London borough should be constrained by statute. This does not mean that Parliament intended or provided for any restraint on the royal prerogative. The Crown retained the right, in theory at any rate, to incorporate a London borough otherwise than on the representation of the minister and in sole exercise of the prerogative. But if the Crown elected to incorporate a London borough pursuant to the 1963 Act then in my opinion the combined effect of the statute and the charter was to create a statutory corporation.

A royal charter dated 10 March 1964 referred to the 1963 Act and recited that representations for incorporation had been made by the minister in accordance with the Act. The grant of incorporation was expressed to have been made 'by virtue of our Prerogative Royal and in pursuance of the London Government Act 1963 and of all other powers and authorities enabling us in this behalf'. The charter ordered and declared as follows:

'1. The London Borough comprised of the areas of the existing Metropolitan Boroughs of Fulham and Hammersmith (hereinafter referred to as "the Borough") shall be named the "London Borough of Hammersmith".

2. The inhabitants of the Borough shall be and are hereby incorporated by the name of "The Mayor, Aldermen and Burgesses of the London Borough of Hammersmith" with perpetual succession and a Common Seal . . .'

In my opinion that charter made pursuant to the 1963 Act did not confer on the borough or the council any greater power than the statutory power exercisable *a* by any other London borough. On 1 September 1979 the name of the borough was changed to the 'London Borough of Hammersmith and Fulham'.

There is a further obstacle to the argument of the banks. By para 1(2) of Sch 2 to the 1972 Act:

> 'For every London borough there shall be a council consisting of the mayor *b* and councillors and the council shall exercise all such functions as are vested in the municipal corporation of the borough or in the council of the borough by this Act or otherwise.'

The council is constrained by statute and cannot enter into swap transactions. In my opinion the council cannot ignore its statutory constraints and lawfully exercise in the name of the borough a power which upon the true construction of *c* the statutory powers of the council was not open to the council. For example, the council is restrained by para 3 of Sch 13 to the 1972 Act from borrowing in a foreign currency without the consent of the Treasury. The council could not lawfully without the consent of the Treasury borrow in a foreign currency in the name of the borough. So in the present case the council has no power to carry out *d* swap transactions either in its own name or in the name of the borough.

In the final result the council had no power to enter into the swap transactions which are recorded in the capital markets fund account kept by the council. By s 19 of the Local Government Finance Act 1982:

> '(1) Where it appears to the auditor carrying out the audit of any accounts *e* under this Part of this Act that any item of account is contrary to law he may apply to the court for a declaration that the item is contrary to law except where it is sanctioned by the Secretary of State.'

The auditor is responsible for auditing the accounts of the council. The section continues: *f*

> '(2) On an application under this section the court may make or refuse to make the declaration asked for, and where the court makes that declaration, then . . . it may also . . . (*c*) order rectification of the accounts . . .
>
> (5) On an application or appeal under this section relating to the accounts of a body, the court may make such order as the court thinks fit for the payment by that body of expenses incurred in connection with the application *g* or appeal by the auditor or the person to whom the application or appeal relates or by whom the appeal is brought, as the case may be . . .'

In the present case the Divisional Court on 1 November 1989 made certain orders and declarations. In particular:

> *h* '. . . IT IS ORDERED AND DECLARED that the items of account appearing within the Capital Markets Fund Account of the Council of the London Borough of Hammersmith and Fulham for the financial years beginning on the 1st April 1987 and 1st April 1988 are contrary to law.
>
> IT IS FURTHER ORDERED that the accounts of the said Council for the financial years beginning on 1st April 1987 and 1st April 1988 be rectified with liberty *j* to the parties to apply if what is required to rectify the said accounts is not agreed.'

These orders were varied by the Court of Appeal but in my opinion should now be restored in their original form.

The Divisional Court made certain orders with regard to costs and expenses. *a* These orders were not varied by the Court of Appeal and should stand.

The Court of Appeal ordered that one-half of the costs of the banks incurred in the appeal should be paid by the auditor. This order should be discharged.

The auditor, having succeeded in this House against the banks, is entitled to an order for his costs of the appeal to the Court of Appeal and the appeal to this House to be taxed and paid by the banks. The council must bear its own costs of *b* the appeal to the Court of the Appeal and the appeal to this House.

The auditor seeks under s 19(5) of the 1982 Act an order against the council for his expenses (so far as they exceed taxes costs) incurred in the appeal to the Court of Appeal and in the appeal to this House. These expenses if not paid by the council will form part of the general expenses of the audit and supervision of *c* public authorities borne by the taxpayer. Since the council was not responsible for the appeal to the Court of Appeal or the appeal to this House and since the appeal dealt with questions of general importance, no order for the council to pay the expenses of the auditor should be made.

LORD GRIFFITHS. My Lords, for the reasons given in the speech of my noble *d* and learned friend Lord Templeman, I would allow this appeal and restore the orders of the Divisional Court.

LORD ACKNER. My Lords,

The legality of interest swaps by local authorities

e The determination of the issue—are interest swap transactions capable of being within the powers of local authorities?—depends, in my judgment, on the answer to a single question—are interest swap transactions incidental to the borrowing powers conferred upon local authorities by statute?

So expressed, it emphasises that which I consider so important, namely that the word 'incidental' must be construed in its context and not in isolation.

f The question is so formulated by reason of the provisions of s 111(1) and (3) of the Local Government Act 1972, which provides:

> '(1) . . . subject to the provisions of this Act . . . a local authority shall have power to do any thing (whether or not involving the . . . borrowing . . . of money . . .) which is . . . incidental to the discharge of any of their functions.
>
> *g* (3) A local authority shall not by virtue of this section raise money . . . by means of . . . borrowing . . . except in accordance with the enactments relating to those matters . . .'

Since s 111 is expressly made 'subject to the provisions of this Act', regard must be had to the other provisions of the Act and in particular to s 172, which *h* provides:

> 'Part I of Schedule 13 to this Act shall have effect with respect to the powers of local authorities to borrow and lend money and with respect to their funds . . .'

I accept that 'functions' in s 111(1) covers the powers and duties of the local *j* authority under the various provisions of the Act. The function with which your Lordships are concerned is the power to borrow. Schedule 13 to the Act contains extremely detailed provisions dealing with the powers of the local authority to borrow money. The schedule provides a high degree of limitation and control of those powers. Part I of the schedule in effect contains a detailed code as to the powers of local authorities to borrow and lend money. Paragraph 8 is of particular significance since it provides:

> 'A local authority who borrow money under paragraph 1(*b*) above may during the fixed period borrow further sums, without the approval of the Secretary of State under that sub-paragraph, for the purpose of repaying the money so borrowed.'

It would thus appear that 'debt or interest management' has been narrowly confined. Given this *express* limited power then I would expect to find that any additional such power would also need to be given in express terms in the statute. No such power is to be found.

The purpose and function of swap transactions is not to facilitate, to help or to make more easy the discharge by the local authority of its function of borrowing. The original underlying debt or debts continue in existence and are all unaffected by the swap transactions. In many cases the swap transactions are entered into long after the underlying borrowing and probably were not even in contemplation when such borrowing took place. The function and purpose of the swap transactions is to alleviate the consequences of borrowing by the local authority purchasing what has been conveniently called 'a stream of income' or 'a cash flow' which will enable it to reduce the net cost of its borrowing. In the words of Mr Sumption QC, appearing for Barclays Bank, interest swap transactions are 'a risk mitigating activity'. They are designed not to meet any specific loss but to seek to ensure that the local authority pays as little interest on its loans as can be achieved. In this respect they are indistinguishable from any other transaction which involves the hope of gain, which gain is intended to reduce a risk attendant on an underlying transaction. Although the phrase 'debt management' may be a convenient one, swap transactions in fact leave the debt wholly unmanaged.

Even in the most limited form of 'hedging' the swap transaction involves the local authority incurring the following risks: (1) that the movement of interest rates will be contrary to what is anticipated, with the result that the local authority will have wasted the transaction costs, that is the money paid to its brokers for arranging the swap; (2) the credit risk that the opposite party to the transaction may default.

The 'parallel' swap doctrine propounded by the Court of Appeal, which is not espoused by Mr Sumption, if it were to provide an appropriate limitation on what would otherwise be very extensive powers, needs careful definition, which is not to be found in the Court of Appeal's judgment. There are frequent references in the judgment to the need for 'a linkage' with a particular debt or a particular borrowing. How close this linkage must be is nowhere stated.

I have found the position of building societies helpful. The Building Societies Act 1986 conferred on building societies a power, which did not previously exist, to enter into a limited category of swap transactions. Subsequently, in the Building Societies (Prescribed Contracts) Order 1988, SI 1988/1344, Parliament radically extended this power. It was clearly Parliament's policy to proceed gradually with this new market so as to ensure adequate public protection. Parliament's concern to protect ratepayers from excessive borrowing or lending by local authorities is clearly demonstrated by the restrictions imposed by Sch 13. To leave ratepayers unprotected from unlimited resort to the swap market would clearly run counter to this policy. This litigation demonstrates forcibly the considerable risks involved in these transactions, and how serious wrong decisions can be. Whether or not local authorities should be empowered to use this market raises important questions of policy. Parliament may or may not be satisfied that there is sufficient need to justify the risks involved even in limited hedging operations. The evidence before your Lordships was that 80% to 90% of local authority borrowing was achieved through the Public Works Loan Board at advantageous fixed interest rates. To 'hedge' such borrowing with variable rate interest swaps would be to move from certainty to uncertainty. Whether or not power should be given to local authorities to engage in interest swaps and if so the nature of those swaps involves a balancing operation—balancing the advantages against the risks in the light of the overall need for such activity. This is essentially a matter that should be left to Parliament, which, as with building societies, may wish to proceed, if at all, by stages.

I therefore conclude that swap transactions are essentially speculative methods of raising money in the hope of reducing the burden of interest payable on money already borrowed. They are a separate and distinct activity, a form of diversification. In view of the circumscribed power of borrowing conferrred by the statute (see in particular Pt I of Sch 13 to the Act) interest swap activities cannot be treated as incidental to the function of borrowing conferred upon authorities by the Act.

Interim strategy

It is common ground that the power to carry out the interest swap activities involved in the interim strategy must be derived from the statute. Thus once again your Lordships are brought back to s 111. Once more an underlying function must be identified, to which the interim strategy activities were incidental. However on this occasion the underlying function cannot be the original borrowing. The interim strategy activities were clearly incidental to the initial ultra vires activities of unlawful interest swapping, since the purpose and function of the interim strategy activities was to mitigate the damage done by, or the risks outstanding arising from, the unlawful interest swaps. Where then is the lawful underlying function to be found?

Miss Gloster QC, who appeared on behalf of the banks other than Barclays Bank, in her able argument suggested that this function arose: (a) under s 111 of the Local Government Act 1972 and was comprised in the duties of a local authority to hold and preserve ratepayers' funds. Even were I to assume, and I am not persuaded that it would be right to do so, that the obligation of a local authority to exercise proper care with regard to these activities is a function within the meaning of s 111, that obligation can only be discharged by lawful means; (b) under s 151 by reason of the local authority's duty to 'make arrangements for the proper administration of their financial affairs'. Section 151 is however concerned with administrative matters and once again I am not persuaded it provides any 'function' within the meaning of s 111. However, were it to do so, then in discharging its obligations and duties under this section the local authority is only entitled to have resort to lawful, as opposed to unlawful, activities.

Miss Gloster accepted that all the interim strategy activities took place in the swap market. Indeed, this was a part of the strategy, since otherwise it might have been disclosed that there was considerable doubt about the legal validity of the earlier transactions. Although there were clearly different categories of swap activities involved, as a matter of principle they could not be differentiated for the purpose of deciding the lawfulness of the transactions. I therefore conclude that the only underlying activity to which the interim swap activities were incidental was the original ultra vires interest swaps. Accordingly, they suffered likewise from the same stigma of being unlawful.

For the above reasons and for those set out so much more fully by my noble and learned friend Lord Templeman, I too would allow these appeals and make *a* the identical consequential orders.

Appeals allowed.

Mary Rose Plummer Barrister. *b*

Calif. Gov't Code § 5922 Bonds and investments; contracts to place on interest rate, currency, cash-flow, or other basis; foreign currency; proceeds

Notwithstanding any other provision of law, all of the following apply:

(a) In connection with, or incidental to, the issuance or carrying of bonds, or acquisition or carrying of any investment or program of investment, any state or local government may enter into any contracts which the state or local government determines to be necessary or appropriate to place the obligation or investment of the state or local government, as represented by the bonds, investment or program of investment and the contract or contracts, in whole or in part, on the interest rate, currency, cash-flow, or other basis desired by the state or local government, including, without limitation, contracts commonly known as interest rate swap agreements, currency swap agreements, forward payment conversion agreements, futures, or contracts providing for payments based on levels of, or changes in, interest rates, currency exchange rates, stock or other indices, or contracts to exchange cash flows or a series of payments, or contracts, including, without limitation, interest rate floors or caps, options, puts or calls to hedge payment, currency, rate, spread, or similar exposure. These contracts or arrangements may also be entered into by state or local governments in connection with, or incidental to, entering into or maintaining any agreement which secures bonds, including bonds issued by private entities. These contracts and arrangements shall be entered into with the parties, selected by the means, and contain the payment, security, default, remedy, and other terms and conditions, determined by the state or local government, after giving due consideration for the creditworthiness of the counterparties, where applicable, including any rating by a nationally recognized rating agency or any other criteria as may be appropriate.

No local government shall enter into any of the contracts or arrangements pursuant to this subdivision, unless its governing body first determines that the contract or arrangement or program of contracts is designed to reduce the amount or duration of payment, currency, rate, spread, or similar risk or result in a lower cost of borrowing when used in combination with the issuance of bonds or enhance the relationship between risk and return with respect to the investment or program of investment in connection with, or incident to, the contract or arrangement which is to be entered into.

(b) Bonds issued by a state or local government may be payable in accordance with their terms, in whole or in part, in currency other than lawful money of the United States of America, provided that the state or local government enter into a currency swap or similar agreement for payments in lawful money of the United States of America, which covers the entire amount of the debt service payment obligation of the state or local government with respect to the bonds payable in other currency, and provided further that if the term of that agreement is less than the term of the bonds, the state or local government shall covenant to enter into additional agreements as may be necessary to cover the entire amount of the debt service payment obligation. An issuer shall include in its written notice to the California Debt Advisory Commission pursuant to subdivision (g) of Section 8855 a statement of its intent to issue bonds payable in a currency other than lawful money of the United States of America.

(c) In connection with, or incidental to, the issuance or carrying of bonds, or entering into any of the contracts or arrangements referred to in subdivision (a), the state or local government may enter into credit enhancement or liquidity agreements, with payment, interest rate, currency, security, default, remedy, and other terms and conditions as the state or local government determines.

(d) Proceeds of bonds and any moneys set aside and pledged to secure payment of the bonds or any of the contracts entered into pursuant to this section, may be invested in securities or obligations described in the ordinance, resolution, indenture, agreement, or other instrument providing for the issuance of the bonds or the contract and may be pledged to and used to service any of the contracts or agreements entered into pursuant to this section.

(Added by Stats.1987, c. 846, § 1.)

11 U.S.C. § 362 Automatic stay

(a) Except as provided in subsection (b) of this section, a petition filed under section 301, 302, or 303 of this title, or an application filed under section 5(a)(3) of the Securities Investor Protection Act of 1970 (15 U.S.C. 78eee(a)(3)), operates as a stay, applicable to all entities, of—

(1) the commencement or continuation, including the issuance or employment of process, of a judicial, administrative, or other action or proceeding against the debtor that was or could have been commenced before the commencement of the case under this title, or to recover a claim against the debtor that arose before the commencement of the case under this title;
(2) the enforcement, against the debtor or against property of the estate, of a judgment obtained before the commencement of the case under this title;
(3) any act to obtain possession of property of the estate or of property from the estate or to exercise control over property of the estate;
(4) any act to create, perfect, or enforce any lien against property of the estate;
(5) any act to create, perfect, or enforce against property of the debtor any lien to the extent that such lien secures a claim that arose before the commencement of the case under this title;
(6) any act to collect, assess, or recover a claim against the debtor that arose before the commencement of the case under this title;
(7) the setoff of any debt owing to the debtor that arose before the commencement of the case under this title against any claim against the debtor; and
(8) the commencement or continuation of a proceeding before the United States Tax Court concerning the debtor.

(b) The filing of a petition under section 301, 302, or 303 of this title, or of an application under section 5(a)(3) of the Securities Investor Protection Act of 1970 (15 U.S.C. 78eee(a)(3)), does not operate as a stay—

(1) under subsection (a) of this section, of the commencement or continuation of a criminal action or proceeding against the debtor;
(2) under subsection (a) of this section, of the collection of alimony, maintenance, or support from property that is not property of the estate;
(3) under subsection (a) of this section, of any act to perfect an interest in property to the extent that the trustee's rights and powers are subject to such perfection under section 546(b) of this title or to the extent that such act is accomplished within the period provided under section 547(3)(2)(A) of this title;
(4) under subsection (a)(1) of this section, of the commencement or continuation of an action or proceeding by a governmental unit to enforce such governmental unit's police or regulatory power;

(5) under subsection (a)(2) of this section, of the enforcement of a judgment, other than a money judgment, obtained in an action or proceeding by a governmental unit to enforce such governmental unit's police or regulatory power;

(6) under subsection (a) of this section, of the setoff by a commodity broker, forward contract merchant, stockbroker, financial institutions, or securities clearing agency of any mutual debt and claim under or in connection with commodity contracts, as defined in section 761(4) of this title, forward contracts, or securities contracts, as defined in section 741(7) of this title, that constitutes the setoff of a claim against the debtor for a margin payment, as defined in section 101(34), 741(5), or 761(15) of this title, or settlement payment, as defined in section 101(35) or 741(8) of this title, arising out of commodity contracts, forward contracts, or securities contracts against cash, securities, or other property held by or due from such commodity broker, forward contract merchant, stockbroker, financial institutions, or securities clearing agency to margin, guarantee, secure, or settle commodity contracts, forward contracts, or securities contracts;

(7) under subsection (a) of this section, of the setoff by a repo participant, of any mutual debt and claim under or in connection with repurchase agreements that constitutes the setoff of a claim against the debtor for a margin payment, as defined in section 741(5) or 761(15) of this title, or settlement payment, as defined in section 741(8) of this title, arising out of repurchase agreements against cash, securities, or other property held by or due from such repo participant to margin, guarantee, secure or settle repurchase agreements;

(8) under subsection (a) of this section, of the commencement of any action by the Secretary of Housing and Urban Development to foreclose a mortgage or deed of trust in any case in which the mortgage or deed of trust held by the Secretary is insured or was formerly insured under the National Housing Act and covers property, or combinations of property, consisting of five or more living units;

(9) under subsection (a) of this section, of the issuance to the debtor by a governmental unit of a notice of tax deficiency;

(10) under subsection (a) of this section, of any act by a lessor to the debtor under a lease of nonresidential real property that has terminated by the expiration of the stated term of the lease before the commencement of or during a case under this title to obtain possession of such property; or[1]

(11) under subsection (a) of this section, of the presentment of a negotiable instrument and the giving of notice of and protesting dishonor of such an instrument;

(12) under subsection (a) of this section, after the date which is 90 days after the filing of such petition, of the commencement or continuation, and conclusion to the entry of final judgment, of an action which involves a debtor subject to reorganization pursuant to chapter 11 of this title and which was brought by the Secretary of Transportation under the Ship Mortgage Act, 1920 (46 App.U.S.C. 911 et seq.) (including distribution of any proceeds of sale) to foreclose a preferred ship or fleet mortgage, or a security interest in or relating to a vessel or vessel under construc-

tion, held by the Secretary of Transportation under section 207 or title XI of the Merchant Marine Act, 1936 (46 App.U.S.C. 1117 and 1271 et seq., respectively), or under applicable State law;

(13) under subsection (a) of this section, after the date which is 90 days after the filing of such petition, of the commencement or continuation, and conclu-sion to the entry of final judgment, of an action which involves a debtor subject to reorganization pursuant to chapter 11 of this title and which was brought by the Secretary of Commerce under the Ship Mortgage Act, 1920 (46 App.U.S.C.911 et seq.) (including distribution of any proceeds of sale) to foreclose a preferred ship or fleet mortgage in a vessel or a mortgage, deed of trust, or other security interest in a fishing facility held by the Secretary of Commerce under section 207 or title XI of the Merchant Marine Act, 1936 (46 App.U.S.C. 1117 and 1271 et seq., respectively); or[1]

(14)[2] under subsection (a) of this section, of the setoff by a swap participant, of any mutual debt and claim under or in connection with any swap agreement that constitutes the setoff of a claim against the debtor for any payment due from the debtor under or in connection with any swap agreement against any payment due to the debtor from the swap participant under or in connection with any swap agreement or against cash, securities, or other property of the debtor held by or due from such swap participant to guarantee, secure or settle any swap agreement.[3]

(14)[2] under subsection (a) of this section, of any action by an accrediting agency regarding the accreditation status of the debtor as an educational institution;

(15) under subsection (a) of this section, of any action by a State licensing body regarding the licensure of the debtor as an educational institution; or

(16) under subsection (a) of this section, of any action by a guaranty agency, as defined in section 435(j) of the Higher Education Act of 1965 (20 U.S.C. 1001 et seq.) or the Secretary of Education regarding the eligibility of the debtor to participate in programs authorized under such Act.

The provisions of paragraphs (12) and (13) of this subsection shall apply with respect to any such petition filed on or before December 31, 1989.

(c) Except as provided in subsections (d), (e), and (f) of this section—
  (1) the stay of an act against property of the estate under subsection (a) of this section continues until such property is no longer property of the estate; and
  (2) the stay of any other act under subsection (a) of this section continues until the earliest of—
    (A) the time the case is closed;
    (B) the time the case is dismissed; or
    (C) if the case is a case under chapter 7 of this title concerning an individual or a case under chapter 9, 11, 12, or 13 of this title, the time a discharge is granted or denied.

(d) On request of a party in interest and after notice and a hearing, the court shall grant relief from the stay provided under subsection (a) of this section, such as by terminating, annulling, modifying, or conditioning such stay—

(1) for cause, including the lack of adequate protection of an interest in property of such party in interest; or
(2) with respect to a stay of an act against property under subsection (a) of this section, if—
 (A) the debtor does not have an equity in such property; and
 (B) such property is not necessary to an effective reorganization.

(e) Thirty days after a request under subsection (d) of this section for relief from the stay of any act against property of the estate under subsection (a) of this section, such stay is terminated with respect to the party in interest making such request, unless the court, after notice and a hearing, orders such stay continued in effect pending the conclusion of, or as a result of, a final hearing and determination under subsection (d) of this section. A hearing under this subsection may be a preliminary hearing, or may be consolidated with the final hearing under subsection (d) of this section. The court shall order such stay continued in effect pending the conclusion of the final hearing under subsection (d) of this section if there is a reasonable likelihood that the party opposing relief from such stay will prevail at the conclusion of such final hearing. If the hearing under this subsection is a preliminary hearing, then such final hearing shall be commenced not later than thirty days after the conclusion of such preliminary hearing.

(f) Upon request of a party in interest, the court, with or without a hearing, shall grant such relief from the stay provided under subsection (a) of this section as is necessary to prevent irreparable damage to the interest of an entity in property, if such interest will suffer such damage before there is an opportunity for notice and a hearing under subsection (d) or (e) of this section.

(g) In any hearing under subsection (d) or (e) of this section concerning relief from the stay of any act under subsection (a) of this section—
(1) the party requesting such relief has the burden of proof on the issue of the debtor's equity in property; and
(2) the party opposing such relief has the burden of proof on all other issues.

(h) An individual injured by any willful violation of a stay provided by this section shall recover actual damages, including costs and attorneys' fees, and, in appropriate circumstances, may recover punitive damages.

(Pub.L. 95–598, Nov. 6, 1978, 92 Stat. 2570; Pub.L. 97–222, § 3, July 27, 1982, 96 Stat. 235; Pub.L. 98–353, Title III, §§ 304, 363(b), 392, 441, July 10, 1984, 98 Stat. 352, 363, 365, 371; Pub.L. 99–509, Title V, § 5001(a), Oct. 21, 1986, 100 Stat. 1911; Pub.L. 99–554, Title II, §§ 257(j), 283(d), Oct. 27, 1986, 100 Stat. 3115, 3116; Pub.L. 101–311, Title I, § 102, Title II, § 202, June 25, 1990, 104 Stat. 267, 269; Pub.L. 101–508, Title III, § 3007(a)(1), Nov. 5, 1990, 104 Stat. 1388–28.)

Notes

1. So in original. The word "or" probably should not appear.
2. So in original. Two pars. (14) have been enacted.
3. So in original. The period probably should be a semicolon.

11 U.S.C. § 365 Executory contracts and unexpired leases

(a) Except as provided in sections 765 and 766 of this title and in subsections (b), (c), and (d) of this section, the trustee, subject to the court's approval, may assume or reject any executory contract or unexpired lease of the debtor.

(b) (1) If there has been a default in an executory contract or unexpired lease of the debtor, the trustee may not assume such contract or lease unless, at the time of assumption of such contract or lease, the trustee—

(A) cures, or provides adequate assurance that the trustee will promptly cure, such default;

(B) compensates, or provides adequate assurance that the trustee will promptly compensate, a party other than the debtor to such contract or lease, for any actual pecuniary loss to such party resulting from such default; and

(C) provides adequate assurance of future performance under such contract or lease.

(2) Paragraph (1) of this subsection does not apply to a default that is a breach of a provision relating to—

(A) the insolvency or financial condition of the debtor at any time before the closing of the case;

(B) the commencement of a case under this title; or

(C) the appointment of or taking possession by a trustee in a case under this title or a custodian before such commencement.

(3) For the purposes of paragraph (1) of this subsection and paragraph (2)(B) of subsection (f), adequate assurance of future performance of a lease of real property in a shopping center includes adequate assurance—

(A) of the source of rent and other consideration due under such lease, and in the case of an assignment, that the financial condition and operating performance of the proposed assignee and its guarantors, if any, shall be similar to the financial condition and operating performance of the debtor and its guarantors, if any, as of the time the debtor became the lessee under the lease;

(B) that any percentage rent due under such lease will not decline substantially;

(C) that assumption or assignment of such lease is subject to all the provisions thereof, including (but not limited to) provisions such as a radius, location, use, or exclusivity provision, and will not breach any such provision contained in any other lease, financing agreement, or master agreement relating to such shopping center; and

(D) that assumption or assignment of such lease will not disrupt any tenant mix or balance in such shopping center.

(4) Notwithstanding any other provision of this section, if there has been a default in an unexpired lease of the debtor, other than a default of a kind specified in paragraph (2) of this subsection, the trustee may not require a lessor to provide services or supplies incidental to such lease before assumption of such lease unless the lessor is compensated under the terms of such lease for any services and supplies provided under such lease before assumption of such lease.

(c) The trustee may not assume or assign any executory contract or unexpired lease of the debtor, whether or not such contract or lease prohibits or restricts assignment of rights or delegation of duties, if—

(1)(A) applicable law excuses a party, other than the debtor, to such contract or lease from accepting performance from or rendering performance to an entity other than the debtor or the debtor in possession, whether or not such contract or lease prohibits or restricts assignment of rights or delegation of duties; and

(B) such party does not consent to such assumption or assignment; or

(2) such contract is a contract to make a loan, or extend other debt financing or financial accommodations, to or for the benefit of the debtor, or to issue a security of the debtor;

(3) such lease is of nonresidential real property and has been terminated under applicable nonbankruptcy law prior to the order for relief; or

(4) such lease is of nonresidential real property under which the debtor is the lessee of an aircraft terminal or aircraft gate at an airport at which the debtor is the lessee under one or more additional nonresidential leases of an aircraft terminal or aircraft gate and the trustee, in connection with such assumption or assignment, does not assume all such leases or does not assume and assign all of such leases to the same person, except that the trustee may assume or assign less than all of such leases with the airport operator's written consent.

(d) (1) In a case under chapter 7 of this title, if the trustee does not assume or reject an executory contract or unexpired lease of residential real property or of personal property of the debtor within 60 days after the order for relief, or within such additional time as the court, for cause, within such 60-day period, fixes, then such contract or lease is deemed rejected.

(2) In a case under chapter 9, 11, 12, or 13 of this title, the trustee may assume or reject an executory contract or unexpired lease of residential real property or of personal property of the debtor at any time before the confirmation of a plan but the court, on the request of any party to such contract or lease, may order the trustee to determine within a specified period of time whether to assume or reject such contract or lease.

(3) The trustee shall timely perform all the obligations of the debtor, except those specified in section 365(b)(2), arising from and after the order for relief under any unexpired lease of nonresidential real property, until such lease is assumed or rejected, notwithstanding section 503(b)(1) of this title. The court may extend, for cause, the time for performance of any such obligation that arises within 60 days after the date of the order for relief, but the time for performance shall not be extended beyond such 60-day period. This subsection shall not be

deemed to affect the trustee's obligations under the provisions of subsection (b) or (f) of this section. Acceptance of any such performance does not constitute waiver or relinquishment of the lessor's rights under such lease or under this title.

(4) Notwithstanding paragraphs (1) and (2), in a case under any chapter of this title, if the trustee does not assume or reject an unexpired lease of nonresidential real property under which the debtor is the lessee within 60 days after the date of the order for relief, or within such additional time as the court, for cause, within such 60-day period, fixes, then such lease is deemed rejected, and the trustee shall immediately surrender such nonresidential real property to the lessor.

(5) Notwithstanding paragraphs (1) and (4) of this subsection, in a case under any chapter of this title, if the trustee does not assume or reject an unexpired lease of nonresidential real property under which the debtor is an affected air carrier that is the lessee of an aircraft terminal or aircraft gate before the occurrence of a termination event, then (unless the court orders the trustee to assume such unexpired leases within 5 days after the termination event), at the option of the airport operator, such lease is deemed rejected 5 days after the occurrence of a termination event and the trustee shall immediately surrender possession of the premises to the airport operator; except that the lease shall not be deemed to be rejected unless the airport operator first waives the right to damages related to the rejection. In the event that the lease is deemed to be rejected under this paragraph, the airport operator shall provide the affected air carrier adequate opportunity after the surrender of the premises to remove the fixtures and equipment installed by the affected air carrier.

(6) For the purpose of paragraph (5) of this subsection and paragraph (f)(1) of this section, the occurrence of a termination event means, with respect to a debtor which is an affected air carrier that is the lessee of an aircraft terminal or aircraft gate—

(A) the entry under section 301 or 302 of this title of an order for relief under chapter 7 of this title;

(B) the conversion of a case under any chapter of this title to a case under chapter 7 of this title; or

(C) the granting of relief from the stay provided under section 362(a) of this title with respect to aircraft, aircraft engines, propellers, appliances, or spare parts, as defined in section 101 of the Federal Aviation Act of 1958 (49 App.U.S.C. 1301), except for property of the debtor found by the court not to be necessary to an effective reorganization.

(7) Any order entered by the court pursuant to paragraph (4) extending the period within which the trustee of an affected air carrier must assume or reject an unexpired lease of nonresidential real property shall be without prejudice to—

(A) the right of the trustee to seek further extensions within such additional time period granted by the court pursuant to paragraph (4); and

(B) the right of any lessor or any other party in interest to request, at any time, a shortening or termination of the period within which the trustee must assume or reject an unexpired lease of nonresidential real property.

(8) The burden of proof for establishing cause for an extension by an affected air carrier under paragraph (4) or the maintenance of a previously granted extension under paragraph (7)(A) and (B) shall at all times remain with the trustee.

(9) For purposes of determining cause under paragraph (7) with respect to an unexpired lease of nonresidential real property between the debtor that is an affected air carrier and an airport operator under which such debtor is the lessee of an airport terminal or an airport gate, the court shall consider, among other relevant factors, whether substantial harm will result to the airport operator or airline passengers as a result of the extension or the maintenance of a previously granted extension. In making the determination of substantial harm, the court shall consider, among other relevant factors, the level of actual use of the terminals or gates which are the subject of the lease, the public interest in actual use of such terminals or gates, the existence of competing demands for the use of such terminals or gates, the effect of the court's extension or termination of the period of time to assume or reject the lease on such debtor's ability to successfully reorganize under chapter 11 of this title, and whether the trustee of the affected air carrier is capable of continuing to comply with its obligations under section 365(d)(3) of this title.

(e) (1) Notwithstanding a provision in an executory contract or unexpired lease, or in applicable law, an executory contract or unexpired lease of the debtor may not be terminated or modified, and any right or obligation under such contract or lease may not be terminated or modified, at any time after the commencement of the case solely because of a provision in such contract or lease that is conditioned on—

(A) the insolvency or financial condition of the debtor at any time before the closing of the case;

(B) the commencement of a case under this title; or

(C) the appointment of or taking possession by a trustee in a case under this title or a custodian before such commencement.

(2) Paragraph (1) of this subsection does not apply to an executory contract or unexpired lease of the debtor, whether or not such contract or lease prohibits or restricts assignment of rights or delegation of duties, if—

(A) (i) applicable law excuses a party, other than the debtor, to such contract or lease from accepting performance from or rendering performance to the trustee or to an assignee of such contract or lease, whether or not such contract or lease prohibits or restricts assignment of rights or delegation of duties; and

(ii) such party does not consent to such assumption or assignment; or

(B) such contract is a contract to make a loan, or extend other debt financing or financial accommodations, to or for the benefit of the debtor, or to issue a security of the debtor.

(f) (1) Except as provided in subsection (c) of this section, notwithstanding a provision in an executory contract or unexpired lease of the debtor, or in applicable law, that prohibits, restricts, or conditions the assignment of such contract or lease, the trustee may assign such contract or lease under paragraph (2) of this subsection; except that the trustee may not assign an unexpired lease of nonresidential real property under which the debtor is an affected air carrier that is the lessee of an aircraft terminal or aircraft gate if there has occurred a termination event.

(2) The trustee may assign an executory contract or unexpired lease of the debtor only if—

(A) the trustee assumes such contract or lease in accordance with the provisions of this section; and

(B) adequate assurance of future performance by the assignee of such contract or lease is provided, whether or not there has been a default in such contract or lease.

(3) Notwithstanding a provision in an executory contract or unexpired lease of the debtor, or in applicable law that terminates or modifies, or permits a party other than the debtor to terminate or modify, such contract or lease or a right or obligation under such contract or lease on account of an assignment of such contract or lease, such contract, lease, right, or obligation may not be terminated or modified under such provision because of the assumption or assignment of such contract or lease by the trustee.

(g) Except as provided in subsections (h)(2) and (i)(2) of this section, the rejection of an executory contract or unexpired lease of the debtor constitutes a breach of such contract or lease—

(1) if such contract or lease has not been assumed under this section or under a plan confirmed under chapter 9, 11, 12, or 13 of this title, immediately before the date of the filing of the petition; or

(2) if such contract or lease has been assumed under this section or under a plan confirmed under chapter 9, 11, 12, or 13 of this title—

(A) if before such rejection the case has not been converted under section 1112, 1307, or 1208 of this title, at the time of such rejection; or

(B) if before such rejection the case has been converted under section 1112, 1307, or 1208 of this title—

(i) immediately before the date of such conversion, if such contract or lease was assumed before such conversion; or

(ii) at the time of such rejection, if such contract or lease was assumed after such conversion.

(h) (1) If the trustee rejects an unexpired lease of real property of the debtor under which the debtor is the lessor, or a timeshare interest under a timeshare plan under which the debtor is the timeshare interest seller, the lessee or timeshare interest purchaser under such lease or timeshare plan may treat such lease or timeshare plan as terminated by such rejection, where the disaffirmance by the trustee amounts to such a breach as would entitle the lessee or timeshare interest purchaser to treat such lease or timeshare plan as terminated by virtue of its own terms, applicable nonbankruptcy law, or other agreements the lessee or timeshare interest purchaser has made with other parties; or, in the alternative, the lessee or timeshare interest purchaser may remain in possession of the leasehold or timeshare interest under any lease or timeshare plan the term of which has commenced for the balance of such term and for any renewal or extension of such term that is enforceable by such lessee or timeshare interest purchaser under applicable nonbankruptcy law.

(2) If such lessee or timeshare interest purchaser remains in possession as provided in paragraph (1) of this subsection, such lessee or timeshare interest purchaser may offset against the rent reserved under such lease or moneys due for such timeshare interest for the balance of the term after the date of the rejection of such lease or timeshare interest, and any such renewal or extension thereof, any damages occurring after such date caused by the nonperformance of any obligation of the debtor under such lease or timeshare plan after such date, but such lessee or timeshare interest purchaser does not have any rights against the estate on account of any damages arising after such date from such rejection, other than such offset.

(i) (1) If the trustee rejects an executory contract of the debtor for the sale of real property or for the sale of a timeshare interest under a timeshare plan, under which the purchaser is in possession, such purchaser may treat such contract as terminated, or, in the alternative, may remain in possession of such real property or timeshare interest.

(2) If such purchaser remains in possession—

(A) such purchaser shall continue to make all payments due under such contract, but may,[1] offset against such payments any damages occurring after the date of the rejection of such contract caused by the nonperformance of any obligation of the debtor after such date, but such purchaser does not have any rights against the estate on account of any damages arising after such date from such rejection, other than such offset; and

(B) the trustee shall deliver title to such purchaser in accordance with the provisions of such contract, but is relieved of all other obligations to perform under such contract.

(j) A purchaser that treats an executory contract as terminated under subsection (i) of this section, or a party whose executory contract to purchase real property from the debtor is rejected and under which such party is not in possession, has a lien on the interest of the debtor in such property for the recovery of any portion of the purchase price that such purchaser or party has paid.

(k) Assignment by the trustee to an entity of a contract or lease assumed under this section relieves the trustee and the estate from any liability for any breach of such contract or lease occurring after such assignment.

(l) If an unexpired lease under which the debtor is the lessee is assigned pursuant to this section, the lessor of the property may require a deposit or other security for the performance of the debtor's obligations under the lease substantially the same as would have been required by the landlord upon the initial leasing to a similar tenant.

(m) For purposes of this section 365 and sections 541(b)(2) and 362(b)(10), leases of real property shall include any rental agreement to use real property.

(n) (1) If the trustee rejects an executory contract under which the debtor is a licensor of a right to intellectual property, the licensee under such contract may elect—

(A) to treat such contract as terminated by such rejection if such rejection by the trustee amounts to such a breach as would entitle the licensee to treat such contract as terminated by virtue of its own terms, applicable nonbankruptcy law, or an agreement made by the licensee with another entity; or

(B) to retain its rights (including a right to to[1] enforce any exclusivity provision of such contract, but excluding any other right under applicable nonbankruptcy law to specific performance of such contract) under such contract and under any agreement supplementary to such contract, to such intellectual property (including any embodiment of such intellectual property to the extent protected by applicable nonbankruptcy law), as such rights existed immediately before the case commenced, for—
   (i) the duration of such contract; and
   (ii) any period for which such contract may be extended by the licensee as of right under applicable nonbankruptcy law.

(2) If the licensee elects to retain its rights, as described in paragraph (1)(B) of this subsection, under such contract—
   (A) the trustee shall allow the licensee to exercise such rights;
   (B) the licensee shall make all royalty payments due under such contract for the duration of such contract and for any period described in paragraph (1)(B) of this subsection for which the licensee extends such contract; and
   (C) the licensee shall be deemed to waive—
      (i) any right of setoff it may have with respect to such contract under this title or applicable nonbankruptcy law; and
      (ii) any claim allowable under section 503(b) of this title arising from the performance of such contract.

(3) If the licensee elects to retain its rights, as described in paragraph (1)(B) of this subsection, then on the written request of the licensee the trustee shall—
   (A) to the extent provided in such contract, or any agreement supplementary to such contract, provide to the licensee any intellectual property (including such embodiment) held by the trustee; and
   (B) not interfere with the rights of the licensee as provided in such contract, or any agreement supplementary to such contract, to such intellectual property (including such embodiment) including any right to obtain such intellectual property (or such embodiment) from another entity.

(4) Unless and until the trustee rejects such contract, on the written request of the licensee the trustee shall—
   (A) to the extent provided in such contract or any agreement supplementary to such contract—
      (i) perform such contract; or
      (ii) provide to the licensee such intellectual property (including any embodiment of such intellectual property to the extent protected by applicable nonbankruptcy law) held by the trustee; and
   (B) not interfere with the rights of the licensee as provided in such contract, or any agreement supplementary to such contract, to such intellectual property (including such embodiment), including any right to obtain such intellectual property (or such embodiment) from another entity.

(o) In the case under chapter 11 of this title, the trustee shall be deemed to have assumed (consistent with the debtor's other obligations under section 507), and shall immediately cure any deficit under, any commitment by the debtor to the Federal Deposit Insurance Corporation, the Resolution Trust

Corporation, the Director of the Office of Thrift Supervision, the Comptroller of the Currency, or the Board of Governors of the Federal Reserve System, or its predecessors or successors, to maintain the capital of an insured depository institution, and any claim for a subsequent breach of the obligations thereunder shall be entitled to priority under section 507. This subsection shall not extend any commitment that would otherwise be terminated by any act of such an agency.

(p) In this section, "affected air carrier" means an air carrier, as defined in section 101(3) of the Federal Aviation Act of 1958, that holds 65 percent or more in number of the aircraft gates at an airport—

(1) which is a Large Air Traffic Hub as defined by the Federal Aviation Administration in Report FAA-AP 92–1, February 1992; and

(2) all of whose remaining aircraft gates are leased or under contract on the date of enactment of this subsection.

(Pub.L. 95–598, Nov. 6, 1978, 92 Stat. 2574; Pub.L. 98–353, Title III, §§ 362, 402–404, July 10, 1984, 98 Stat. 361, 367; Pub.L. 99–554, Title II, §§ 257(j), (m), 283(e), Oct. 27, 1986, 100 Stat. 3115, 3117; Pub.L. 100–506, § 1(b), Oct. 18, 1988, 102 Stat. 2538; Pub.L. 101–647, Title XXV, § 2522(c), Nov. 29, 1990, 104 Stat. 4866; Pub.L. 102–365, § 19(b)–(e), Sept. 3, 1992, 106 Stat. 982–984.)

Note

1. So in original.

11 U.S.C. § 544 Trustee as lien creditor and as successor to certain creditors and purchasers

(a) The trustee shall have, as of the commencement of the case, and without regard to any knowledge of the trustee or of any creditor, the rights and powers of, or may avoid any transfer of property of the debtor or any obligation incurred by the debtor that is voidable by—
  (1) a creditor that extends credit to the debtor at the time of the commencement of the case, and that obtains, at such time and with respect to such credit, a judicial lien on all property on which a creditor on a simple contract could have obtained such a judicial lien, whether or not such a creditor exists;
  (2) a creditor that extends credit to the debtor at the time of the commencement of the case, and obtains, at such time and with respect to such credit, an execution against the debtor that is returned unsatisfied at such time, whether or not such a creditor exists; or
  (3) a bona fide purchaser of real property, other than fixtures, from the debtor, against whom applicable law permits such transfer to be perfected, that obtains the status of a bona fide purchaser and has perfected such transfer at the time of the commencement of the case, whether or not such a purchaser exists.

11 U.S.C. § 546 Limitations on avoiding powers

(a) An action or proceeding under section 544, 545, 547, 548, or 553 of this title may not be commenced after the earlier of—
   (1) two years after the appointment of a trustee under section 702, 1104, 1163, 1302, or 1202 of this title; or
   (2) the time the case is closed or dismissed.

(b) The rights and powers of a trustee under sections 544, 545, and 549 of this title are subject to any generally applicable law that permits perfection of an interest in property to be effective against an entity that acquires rights in such property before the date of such perfection. If such law requires seizure of such property or commencement of an action to accomplish such perfection, and such property has not been seized or such action has not been commenced before the date of the filing of the petition, such interest in such property shall be perfected by notice within the time fixed by such law for such seizure or commencement.

(c) Except as provided in subsection (d) of this section, the rights and powers of a trustee under sections 544(a), 545, 547, and 549 of this title are subject to any statutory or common-law right of a seller of goods that has sold goods to the debtor, in the ordinary course of such seller's business, to reclaim such goods if the debtor has received such goods while insolvent, but—
   (1) such a seller may not reclaim any such goods unless such seller demands in writing reclamation of such goods before ten days after receipt of such goods by the debtor; and
   (2) the court may deny reclamation to a seller with such a right of reclamation that has made such a demand only if the court—
      (A) grants the claim of such a seller priority as a claim of a kind specified in section 503(b) of this title; or
      (B) secures such claim by a lien.

(d) In the case of a seller who is a producer of grain sold to a grain storage facility, owned or operated by the debtor, in the ordinary course of such seller's business (as such terms are defined in section 557 of this title) or in the case of a United States fisherman who has caught fish sold to a fish processing facility owned or operated by the debtor in the ordinary course of such fisherman's business, the rights and powers of the trustee under sections 544(a), 545, 547, and 549 of this title are subject to any statutory or common law right of such producer or fisherman to reclaim such grain or fish if the debtor has received such grain or fish while insolvent, but—
   (1) such producer or fisherman may not reclaim any grain or fish unless such producer or fisherman demands, in writing, reclamation of such grain or fish before ten days after receipt thereof by the debtor; and
   (2) the court may deny reclamation to such a producer or fisherman with the right of reclamation that has made such a demand only if the court secures such claim by a lien.

(e) Notwithstanding sections 544, 545, 547, 548(a)(2), and 548(b) of this title, the trustee may not avoid a transfer that is a margin payment, as defined in section 101(34), 741(5), or 761(15) of this title, or settlement payment, as defined in section 101(35) or 741(8) of this title, made by or to a commodity broker, forward contract merchant, stockbroker, financial institution, or securities clearing agency, that is made before the commencement of the case, except under section 548(a)(1) of this title.

(f) Notwithstanding sections 544, 545, 547, 548(a)(2), and 548(b) of this title, the trustee may not avoid a transfer that is a margin payment, as defined in section 741(5) or 761(15) of this title, or settlement payment, as defined in section 741(8) of this title, made by or to a repo participant, in connection with a repurchase agreement and that is made before the commencement of the case, except under section 548(a)(1) of this title.

(g) Notwithstanding sections 544, 545, 547, 548(a)(2) and 548(b) of this title, the trustee may not avoid a transfer under a swap agreement, made by or to a swap participant, in connection with a swap agreement and that is made before the commencement of the case, except under section 548(a)(1) of this title.

(Pub.L. 95–598, Nov. 6, 1978, 92 Stat. 2597; Pub.L. 97–222, § 4, July 27, 1982, 96 Stat. 236; Pub.L. 98–353, Title III, §§ 351, 393, 461, July 10, 1984, 98 Stat. 358, 365, 377; Pub.L. 99–554, Title II, §§ 257(d), 283(*l*), Oct. 27, 1986, 100 Stat. 3114, 3117; Pub.L. 101–311, Title I, § 103, Title II, § 203, June 25, 1990, 104 Stat. 268, 269.)

11 U.S.C. § 547 Preferences

(b) Except as provided in subsection (c) of this section, the trustee may avoid any transfer of an interest of the debtor in property—
  (1) to or for the benefit of a creditor;
  (2) for or on account of an antecedent debt owed by the debtor before such transfer was made;
  (3) made while the debtor was insolvent;
  (4) made—
    (A) on or within 90 days before the date of the filing of the petition; or
    (B) between ninety days and one year before the date of the filing of the petition, if such creditor at the time of such transfer was an insider; and
  (5) that enables such creditor to receive more than such creditor would receive if—
    (A) the case were a case under chapter 7 of this title;
    (B) the transfer had not been made; and
    (C) such creditor received payment of such debt to the extent provided by the provisions of this title.

11 U.S.C. § 548 Fraudulent transfers and obligations

(a) The trustee may avoid any transfer of an interest of the debtor in property, or any obligation incurred by the debtor, that was made or incurred on or within one year before the date of the filing of the petition, if the debtor voluntarily or involuntarily—

(1) made such transfer or incurred such obligation with actual intent to hinder, delay, or defraud any entity to which the debtor was or became, on or after the date that such transfer was made or such obligation was incurred, indebted; or

(2) (A) received less than a reasonably equivalent value in exchange for such transfer or obligation; and

(B) (i) was insolvent on the date that such transfer was made or such obligation was incurred, or became insolvent as a result of such transfer or obligation;

(ii) was engaged in business or a transaction, or was about to engage in business or a transaction, for which any property remaining with the debtor was an unreasonably small capital; or

(iii) intended to incur, or believed that the debtor would incur, debts that would be beyond the debtor's ability to pay as such debts matured.

(b) The trustee of a partnership debtor may avoid any transfer of an interest of the debtor in property, or any obligation incurred by the debtor, that was made or incurred on or within one year before the date of the filing of the petition, to a general partner in the debtor, if the debtor was insolvent on the date such transfer was made or such obligation was incurred, or became insolvent as a result of such transfer or obligation.

(c) Except to the extent that a transfer or obligation voidable under this section is voidable under section 544, 545, or 547 of this title, a transferee or obligee of such a transfer or obligation that takes for value and in good faith has a lien on or may retain any interest transferred or may enforce any obligation incurred, as the case may be, to the extent that such transferee or obligee gave value to the debtor in exchange for such transfer or obligation.

(d) (1) For the purposes of this section, a transfer is made when such transfer is so perfected that a bona fide purchaser from the debtor against whom applicable law permits such transfer to be perfected cannot acquire an interest in the property transferred that is superior to the interest in such property of the transferee, but if such transfer is not so perfected before the commencement of the case, such transfer is made immediately before the date of the filing of the petition.

(2) In this section—

(A) "value" means property, or satisfaction or securing of a present or antecedent debt of the debtor, but does not include an unperformed promise to furnish support to the debtor or to a relative of the debtor;

(B) a commodity broker, forward contract merchant, stockbroker, financial institution, or securities clearing agency that receives a margin payment, as defined in section 101(34), 741(5) or 761(15) of this title, or settlement payment, as defined in section 101(35) or 741(8) of this title, takes for value to the extent of such payment;

(C) a repo participant that receives a margin payment, as defined in section 741(5) or 761(15) of this title, or settlement payment, as defined in section 741(8) of this title, in connection with a repurchase agreement, takes for value to the extent of such payment; and

(D) a swap participant that receives a transfer in connection with a swap agreement takes for value to the extent of such transfer.

(Pub.L. 95–598, Nov. 6, 1978, 92 Stat. 2600; Pub.L. 97–222, § 5, July 27, 1982, 96 Stat. 236; Pub.L. 98–353, Title III, §§ 394, 463, July 10, 1984, 98 Stat. 365, 378; Pub.L. 99–554, Title II, § 283(n), Oct. 27, 1986, 100 Stat. 3117; Pub.L. 101–311, Title I, § 104, Title II, § 204, June 25, 1990, 104 Stat. 268, 269.)

11 U.S.C. § 553 Setoff

(a) Except as otherwise provided in this section and in sections 362 and 363 of this title, this title does not affect any right of a creditor to offset a mutual debt owing by such creditor to the debtor that arose before the commencement of the case under this title against a claim of such creditor against the debtor that arose before the commencement of the case, except to the extent that—
 (1) the claim of such creditor against the debtor is disallowed other than under section 502(b)(3) of this title;
 (2) such claim was transferred, by an entity other than the debtor, to such creditor—
  (A) after the commencement of the case; or
  (B) (i) after 90 days before the date of the filing of the petition; and
   (ii) while the debtor was insolvent; or
 (3) the debt owed to the debtor by such creditor was incurred by such creditor—
  (A) after 90 days before the date of the filing of the petition;
  (B) while the debtor was insolvent; and
  (C) for the purpose of obtaining a right of setoff against the debtor.

(b) (1) Except with respect to a setoff of a kind described in section 362(b)(6), 362(b)(7), 362(b)(14),,[1] 365(h)(2), or 365(i)(2) of this title, if a creditor offsets a mutual debt owing to the debtor against a claim against the debtor on or within 90 days before the date of the filing of the petition, then the trustee may recover from such creditor the amount so offset to the extent that any insufficiency on the date of such setoff is less than the insufficiency on the later of—
  (A) 90 days before the date of the filing of the petition; and
  (B) the first date during the 90 days immediately preceding the date of the filing of the petition on which there is an insufficiency.
 (2) In this subsection, "insufficiency" means amount, if any, by which a claim against the debtor exceeds a mutual debt owing to the debtor by the holder of such claim.

(c) For the purposes of this section, the debtor is presumed to have been insolvent on and during the 90 days immediately preceding the date of the filing of the petition.

(Pub.L. 95–598, Nov. 6, 1978, 92 Stat. 2602; Pub.L. 98–353, Title III, §§ 395, 467, July 10, 1984, 98 Stat. 365, 380; Pub.L. 101–311, Title I, § 105, June 25, 1990, 104 Stat. 268.)

1. So in original.

11 U.S.C. § 560 Contractual right to terminate a swap agreement

The exercise of any contractual right of any swap participant to cause the termination of a swap agreement because of a condition of the kind specified in section 365(e)(1) of this title or to offset or net out any termination values or payment amounts arising under or in connection with any swap agreement shall not be stayed, avoided, or otherwise limited by operation of any provision of this title or by order of a court or administrative agency in any proceeding under this title. As used in this section, the term "contractual right" includes a right, whether or not evidenced in writing, arising under common law, under law merchant, or by reason of normal business practice.

(Added Pub.L. 101–311, Title I, § 106(a), June 25, 1990, 104 Stat. 268.)

FDIC STATEMENT OF POLICY ON QUALIFIED FINANCIAL CONTRACTS

This statement of policy of the Board of the Directors of the Federal Deposit Insurance Corporation ("FDIC") addresses two issues regarding the treatment by the FDIC of qualified financial contracts ("QFCs"), as such term is defined in section 11(e)(8)(D)(i) of the Federal Deposit Insurance Act ("FDI Act"), 12 U.S.C. 1821 *et seq.* as amended by the Financial Institutions Reform, Recovery, and Enforcement Act of 1989 ("FIRREA"). In making this statement of policy, the Board of Directors recognizes the uniqueness of QFCs in the financial markets. Such contracts and transactions allow for appropriate liquidity and hedging operations in financial institutions. Generally transactions are conducted in a highly regulated industry providing further safeguards. In providing this policy statement it is the intent of the Board to provide guidance to the financial markets with regard to the treatment of these contracts in the event the FDIC is appointed receiver or conservator of a financial institution. With the exception of federal fund ("fed funds") transactions which likewise occupy a unique position in the depository institution industry, the Board does not intend to provide in this policy statement any indication or guidance of the treatment by a receiver or conservator of any other type of contract other than those specifically so defined as qualified financial contracts in the FDI Act or as may be subsequently defined by the Board pursuant to the FDI Act. For purposes of the requirements set out in sections 11(d)(9), 11(n)(4)(I) and 13(e) it is intended that this policy statement apply not only to QFCs but to fed funds transactions as well. It is specifically understood and intended by the Board that this policy statement may be relied upon by counterparties to these types of transactions. It is the Board's intention that this policy statement be effective unless revoked or otherwise withdrawn upon 45 days notice provided in the *Federal Register* and such notice or withdrawal shall operate prospectively only. Nothing in this policy statement is intended to apply to transactions between a bank or thrift and a counterparty which is an affiliate of the bank or thrift. This policy statement is intended to provide a "safe harbor" for bona fide transactions conducted by depository institutions and nonaffiliated counterparties.

I. *Written Agreement Requirements*

Any QFC (including any ancillary agreements, such as a master agreement or security arrangements) that complies with the following criteria will be deemed to satisfy the requirements set forth in sections 11(d)(9), 11(n)(4)(I) and 13(e) of the FDI Act:

1. The QFC is evidenced by a writing (including a confirmation) that either is sent by the depository institution to the counterparty or by the counterparty to the depository institution. In either case, the writing must be sent reasonably contemporaneously with the parties' agreement to enter into the specific QFC transaction. The writing need not be signed unless otherwise required by applicable non-insolvency law;

2. The depository institution, by corporate action, was authorized under applicable non-insolvency law to enter into the QFC. A depository institution will be deemed to have taken such corporate action if the counterparty has relied in good faith either on a resolution (or extract thereof) provided by the institution's corporate secretary or assistant secretary or on a written representation (whether in a master agreement or otherwise) from an officer of the level of vice president or higher, as to the depository institution's authority; and
3. The writing (or a copy thereof) evidencing the QFC and the evidence of authority must be maintained by the depository institution in its official books and records. However, the counterparty may, by appropriate evidence (including the production of copies maintained by the counterparty) establish the existence of the writing and the evidence of authority.

The Board of Directors intends that the FDIC apply the above criteria and the FDI Act requirements in a manner generally consistent with reasonable business trading practices in the QFC markets, in view of Congress's recognition in FIRREA of the important role QFCs play in providing liquidity and portfolio and risk management to depository institutions. Without limiting the criteria set forth above, it is anticipated that the FDIC will look to the totality of the circumstances surrounding such transactions including the counterparty's good faith attempt to comply with all reasonable trading practices and requirements, any non-insolvency law requirements and the requirements stated herein. Further, the Board does not consider the amendments made by FIRREA to the FDI Act requirements to be applicable to QFCs entered into prior to August 9, 1989, although compliance with the foregoing criteria with respect to such pre-FIRREA QFCs would be considered compliance with any pre-FIRREA requirements.

II. *Section 11(e)(10) of the FDI Act*

The FDIC as receiver for a depository institution will act in accordance with the following procedures in applying sections 11(e)(8)(A) and 11(e)(10) of the FDI Act. These procedures are consistent with certain provisions of section 212 of FIRREA that had been contained in the bills passed by the House and Senate but were inadvertently omitted in the final statute. Moreover, the final statute as written contains inconsistencies which may not be harmonized except by the inclusion of these inadvertently omitted provisions:

1. In applying section 11(e)(10) of the FDI Act, the receiver shall use its best efforts to notify a party to a QFC whether it has effected a transfer of asset or liabilities in accordance with section 11(e)(9)(A) of the FDI Act prior to *12 noon* local time on the business day following appointment of the receiver.
2. The provisions of section 11(e)(8)(A) of the FDI Act shall not apply if a party to a QFC is notified by the receiver of the failed depository institution by the *close of business* (New York time) on the business day following its appointment that the receiver has transferred to a single insured depository institution (other than one in default): (a) all QFCs between the failed depository institution and such party and its affiliates; (b) all claims of the party and its affiliates under such QFCs against the failed depository insti-

tution (other than claims subordinated by any such QFC to the claims of general unsecured creditors); (c) all claims of the failed depository institution against the party and its affiliates under such QFCs; and (d) all property securing claims under such QFCs.

3. Neither a bridge bank nor an institution organized by the FDIC and immediately placed into conservatorship or placed into conservatorship at the time of a purchase and assumption transaction with the receiver of a failed institution for which FDIC has been appointed receiver shall be considered a depository institution in default for purposes of paragraph 2.
4. For purposes of section 11(e)(10) of the FDI Act, the receiver shall be deemed to have notified a party if it has taken steps reasonably calculated to provide notice to such party. In providing guidance in both of these areas relating to qualified financial contracts and with regard to sections 11(d)(9), 11(n)(4)(I) and (13)(e) requirements which apply to fed funds transactions, it is the intention of the Board of Directors to provide appropriate guidance to the financial markets. It is intended by the Board of Directors that this policy statement ultimately becomes the basis for regulations which should be adopted in due course. However, given the importance of these unique types of transactions and contracts it is the desire of the Board of Directors to provide this guidance in the most expeditious form possible. Further, the Board notes that on this day the Resolution Trust Corporation adopted these same policies with regard to the same transactions.

By order of the Board of Directors this 12th day of December 1989.

TABLE OF CASES

In re Affiliated Food Stores, Inc. Group Ben. Trust, 134 B.R. 215 (Bankr. N.D. Tex. 1991)
American Nat'l Bank of Austin v. United States, 421 F.2d 442 (5th Cir. 1970), *rev'g* 296 F. Supp. 512 (W.D. Tex. 1968)
American Nat'l Bank of Austin v. U.S., 573 F.2d 1201 (Ct. Cl. 1978)
In re Ameriswiss Assocs., 148 B.R. 349 (Bankr. S.D. Fla. 1992)
In re Arehart, 52 B.R. 308 (Bankr. M.D. Fla. 1985)
In re Armstead and Margaret Wayson Trust, 29 B.R. 58 (Bankr. D. Md. 1982)
In re Augie/Restivo Baking Co., Ltd., 860 F.2d 515 (2d Cir. 1988)
In re Baker & Getty Fin. Servs., Inc., 78 B.R. 139 (Bankr. N.D. Ohio 1987)
In re Ball Mountain Dam Hydroelectric Project, 154 Vt. 189, 576 A.2d 124 (1990)
Bank of Cal. v. Commissioner, 30 B.T.A. 556 (1934), *aff'd,* 80 F.2d 389 (9th Cir. 1935)
Beighley v. FDIC, 676 F. Supp. 130 (N.D. Tex. 1987), *aff'd,* 868 F.2d 776 (5th Cir. 1989)
In re Bevill, Bresler & Schuman Asset Management Corp., 67 B.R. 557 (D.N.J. 1986)
In re BKC Realty Trust, 125 B.R. 65 (Bankr. D.N.H. 1991)
Brooklyn Trust Co. v. Commissioner, 80 F.2d 865 (2d Cir.), *cert. denied,* 298 U.S. 659 (1936)
In re Cahill, 15 B.R. 639 (Bankr. E.D. Pa. 1981)
In re Captran Creditors Trust, 53 B.R. 741 (Bankr. M.D. Fla. 1985)
Chemical Bank N.Y. Trust Co. v. Kheel, 369 F.2d 845 (2d Cir. 1966)
In re Citizens Bank & Trust Co. of Park Ridge, 8 B.R. 812 (Bankr. N.D. Ill. 1981)
Citizens Nat'l Bank of Waco v. United States, 551 F.2d 832 (Ct. Cl. 1977)
City and County of Denver v. State, 788 P.2d 764 (Colo. 1990)
Clemente Global Growth Fund v. Pickens, 705 F. Supp. 958 (S.D.N.Y. 1989)
Commissioner v. Buckley, 128 F.2d 124 (9th Cir. 1942)
Commissioner v. Chase Nat'l Bank of City of N.Y., 122 F.2d 540 (2d Cir. 1941)
Commissioner v. City Nat'l Bank & Trust Co., 142 F.2d 771 (10th Cir.), *cert. denied,* 323 U.S. 764 (1944)
Commissioner v. North Am. Bond Trust, 122 F.2d 545 (2d Cir. 1941), *cert. denied,* 314 U.S. 701 (1942)
In re Constitutional Trust No. 2-562, 114 B.R. 627 (Bankr. D. Minn. 1990)
In re Continental Vending Mach. Corp., 517 F.2d 997 (2d Cir. 1975)
In re Contractor's Equip. Supply Co., 861 F.2d 241 (9th Cir. 1988)
Converse Rubber Co. v. Boston-Continental Nat'l Bank, 12 F. Supp. 887 (D. Mass 1935)
In re Currie, 57 B.R. 224 (Bankr. M.D. La. 1986)
In re Margaret E. DeHoff Trust I, 114 B.R. 189 (Bankr. W.D. Mo. 1990)
Deputy v. du Pont, 308 U.S. 488 (1940)

D'Oench, Duhme & Co. v. FDIC, 315 U.S. 447 (1942)
In re Dolton Lodge Trust No. 35188, 22 B.R. 918 (Bankr. N.D. Ill. 1982)
In re Donut Queen, 41 B.R. 706 (Bankr. E.D.N.Y. 1984)
In re Dreske Greenway Trust, 14 B.R. 618 (Bankr. E.D. Wis. 1981)
In re Drexel Burnham Lambert Group, Inc., 138 B.R. 723 (Bankr. S.D.N.Y. 1992)
Eastgroup Properties v. Southern Motel Ass'n, Ltd., 935 F.2d 245 (11th Cir 1991)
In re Evergreen Valley Resort, Inc., 23 B.R. 659 (Bankr. D. Me. 1982)
In re Ralph Faber Trust, 113 B.R. 599 (Bankr. D.N.D. 1990)
Fall River Elec. Light Co. v. Commissioner, 23 B.T.A. 168 (1931)
FDIC v. Merchants Nat'l Bank, 725 F.2d 634, *cert. denied*, 469 U.S. 829 (1984)
Federal Nat'l Mortgage Ass'n v. Commissioner, 100 T.C. No. 36 (June 17, 1993)
In re Federated Dept. Stores, Inc., 1990 Bankr. LEXIS 2453 (Bankr. S.D. Ohio Nov. 21, 1990)
First Am. Nat'l Bank of Nashville v. United States, 467 F.2d 1098 (6th Cir. 1972), *aff'g* 327 F. Supp. 675 (M.D. Tenn. 1971)
In re First City Mortgage Co., 69 B.R. 765 (Bankr. N.D. Tex. 1987)
First Nat'l Bank in Wichita v. Commissioner, 19 B.T.A. 744 (1930), *aff'd*, 57 F.2d 7 (10th Cir. 1932)
Fish v. East, 114 F.2d 177 (10th Cir. 1940)
In re Flora Mir Candy Corp., 432 F.2d 1060 (2d Cir. 1970)
In re Gladstone Glen, 628 F.2d 1015 (7th Cir. 1980)
Gold Coast Leasing Co. v. California Carrots, Inc., 93 Cal. App. 3d 274, 155 Cal. Rptr. 511 (1979)
In re Golden Plan of Cal., Inc., 829 F.2d 705 (9th Cir. 1986)
Goldstein v. Madison Nat'l Bank, 89 B.R. 274 (D.D.C. 1988)
In re Gonic Realty Trust, 50 B.R. 710 (Bankr. D.N.H. 1985)
Hamilton Depositors Corp. v. Nicholas, 111 F.2d 385 (10th Cir. 1940)
In re Betty L. Hays Trust, 65 B.R. 665 (Bankr. D. Neb. 1986)
Hazell v. Hammersmith and Fulman London Borough Council and others, [1991] 1 All E.R. 545 (H.L. 1991)
In re Hemex Liquidation Trust, 129 B.R. 91 (Bankr. W.D. La. 1991)
In re Heritage N. Dunlap Trust, 120 B.R. 252 (Bankr. D. Mass. 1990)
Holywell Corp. v. Bank of N.Y., 59 B.R. 340 (S.D. Fla. 1986)
In re Hurricane Elkhorn Coal Corp. II, 19 B.R. 609 (Bankr. W.D. Ky. 1982)
In re Johnson, 82 B.R. 618 (Bankr. S.D. Fla. 1988)
In re Joseph Kanner Hat Co., Inc., 482 F.2d 937 (2d Cir. 1973)
In re L & V Realty Trust, 61 B.R. 423 (Bankr. D. Mass. 1986)
In re Langley, 30 B.R. 595 (Bankr. N.D. Ind. 1983)
In re Lease-A-Fleet, Inc., 141 B.R. 869 (Bankr. E.D. Pa. 1992)
In re Lemons & Assocs., Inc., 67 B.R. 198 (Bankr. D. Nev. 1986)
Livingston Parish Police Jury v. Lee, 598 So.2d 1086 (La. Ct. App. 1991)
In re Lombard-Wall Inc., No. 82-B-11556 (Bankr. S.D.N.Y. Sept. 14, 1982)
In re Luth, 28 B.R. 564 (Bankr. D. Idaho 1983)
Lyon v. Ty-Wood Corp., 212 Pa. Super. 69, 239 A.2d 819 (1968)
In re Major Funding Corp., 82 B.R. 443 (Bankr. S.D. Tex. 1987)
Major's Furniture Mart, Inc. v. Castle Credit Corp., 602 F.2d 538 (3d Cir. 1979)
In re Medallion Realty Trust, 103 B.R. 8 (Bankr. D. Mass. 1989), *aff'd*, 120 B.R. 245 (D. Mass. 1990)
Mid-Atlantic Supply, Inc. v. Three Rivers Aluminum Co., 790 F.2d 1121 (4th Cir. 1986)

In re Milani Family Irrevocable Trust, 62 B.R. 6 (Bankr. S.D. Fla. 1986)
In re Mohan Kutty Trust, 134 B.R. 987 (Bankr. M.D. Fla. 1991)
Morrissey v. Commissioner, 296 U.S. 344 (1935)
In re Mosby, 61 B.R. 636 (E.D. Mo. 1985), *aff'd per curiam,* 791 F.2d 628 (8th Cir. 1986)
In re Munford, Inc., 115 B.R. 390 (Bankr. N.D. Ga. 1990)
In re North Shore Nat'l Bank of Chicago Land Trust No. 362, 17 B.R. 867 (Bankr. N.D. Ill. 1982)
Octagon Gas Systems, Inc. v. Rimmer, No. 92-6065 (10th Cir. May 27, 1993)
Old Colony R.R. Co. v. Commissioner, 284 U.S. 552 (1932)
In re Old Second Nat'l Bank of Aurora, 7 B.R. 37 (Bankr. N.D. Ill. 1980)
In re Ophir Trust, 112 B.R. 956 (Bankr. E.D. Wis. 1990)
In re O.P.M. Leasing Servs., Inc., 30 B.R. 642 (Bankr. S.D.N.Y. 1983)
Osborne v. State, 439 N.E.2d 677 (Ind. Ct. App. 1982)
In re Parade Realty, Inc., Employees Retirement Pension Trust, 134 B.R. 7 (Bankr. D. Haw. 1991)
Patrick Media Group, Inc. v. Ad-Ex, Inc., 608 N.E.2d 427 (Ill. App. Ct. 1992)
Pennsylvania Co. for Insurances v. United States, 146 F.2d 392 (3d Cir. 1944)
Pennsylvania Co. for Insurances v. United States, 138 F.2d 869 (3d Cir. 1943), *cert. denied,* 321 U.S. 788 (1944)
People v. Service Inst., Inc., 101 Misc. 2d 549, 421 N.Y.S.2d 325 (N.Y. Sup. Ct. 1979)
Petron Trading Co. v. Hydrocarbon Trading & Transp. Co., 663 F. Supp. 1153 (E.D. Pa. 1986)
In re St. Augustine Trust, 109 B.R. 494 (Bankr. M.D. Fla. 1990)
In re SCR Trust, 20 B.R. 17 (Bankr. M.D. La. 1982)
SEC v. Ralston Purina Co., 346 United States 119, 125 (1953)
In re Vivian A. Skaife Irrevocable Trust Agreement No. 1, 90 B.R. 325 (Bankr. E.D. Tenn. 1988)
In re Snider Bros., Inc., 18 B.R. 230 (Bankr. D. Mass. 1982)
In re S.O.A.W. Enters., Inc., 32 B.R. 279 (Bankr. W.D. Tex. 1983)
Southern Rock, Inc. v. B&B Auto Supply, 711 F.2d 683 (5th Cir. 1983)
In re Steury, 94 B.R. 553 (Bankr. N.D. Ind. 1988)
In re Tarnow, 749 F.2d 464 (7th Cir. 1984)
Third Nat'l Bank in Nashville v. United States, 71-1 U.S.T.C. para. 9248 (M.D. Tenn. 1971), *aff'd,* 454 F.2d 689 (6th Cir. 1972)
Ticonderoga Farms, Inc. v. County of Loudoun, 242 Va. 170, 409 S.E.2d 446 (1991)
In re Treasure Island Land Trust, 2 B.R. 332 (Bankr. M.D. Fla. 1980)
In re Tru Block Concrete Prods., Inc., 27 B.R. 486 (Bankr. S.D. Cal. 1983)
Union Planters Nat'l Bank of Memphis v. United States, 426 F.2d 115 (6th Cir. 1970), *rev'g* 295 F. Supp. 1151 (W.D. Tenn. 1968)
In re Universal Clearing House Co., 60 B.R. 985 (D. Utah 1986)
In re Vecco Constr. Indus., Inc., 4 B.R. 407 (Bankr. E.D. Va. 1980)
In re Village Green Realty Trust, 113 B.R. 105 (Bankr. D. Mass. 1990)
In re Visiting Home Serv., Inc., 643 F.2d 1356 (9th Cir. 1981)
In re Walker, 79 B.R. 59 (Bankr. M.D. Fla. 1987)
In re Jay M. Weisman Irrevocable Children's Trust of 1981, 62 B.R. 286 (Bankr. M.D. Fla. 1986)
In re Westchester County Civil Serv. Employees Ass'n, Inc., Benefit Fund, 111 B.R. 451 (Bankr. S.D.N.Y. 1990)
In re Woodson Co., 813 F.2d 266 (9th Cir. 1987)
In re Woodsville Realty Trust, 120 B.R. 2 (Bankr. D.N.H. 1990)

GLOSSARY

The product names and definitions set forth herein are for general informational purposes only. Moreover, the identification of a specific product as an "embedded swap bond" or a "tender option certificate," for example, is intended merely to assist readers in their general understanding of the products in the market. The particular features of the products, of course, will differ. Readers should always review the specific terms of any transaction and should not rely on this glossary for evaluating any product or investment. Moreover, the products and their features change continually, and readers should consider developments that have occurred since this book was published.

ACES:* The proprietary name for The First Boston Corporation's primary tender option bonds.

Auction Rate Bonds: Floating-rate tax-exempt bonds whose rate is periodically reset pursuant to a so-called dutch auction procedure. In connection with each interest rate reset date, the auction agent receives instructions from current bondholders regarding whether they would like to hold or sell all or a portion of the bonds. In addition, they can instruct the auction agent to sell the bonds unless the interest rate is reset to a specified rate.

BEARS:* The proprietary name of Bear Stearns & Co.'s primary tender option bonds.

Bifurcation: The tax characterization of certain contingent debt instruments as consisting of a debt instrument comprising the noncontingent payments and a separate property right. Proposed original issue discount regulations issued in 1991 require bifurcation where interest rate payments are based upon certain contingent payment formulas.

Bits and Pieces:* The proprietary name of Lehman Brothers' bonds structured to resemble components of a bond, such as interest rate and principal strips. An investor can select specific "bits and pieces" to construct an aggregate security that meets its specifications.

Bulls and Bears:* The proprietary name of Lehman Brothers' embedded swap and cap bonds. Generically, the names refer to bonds that provide for increasing interest rate in a bull market and bonds that provide for increasing interest rate in a bear market.

Cap RITES:* The proprietary name of Merrill Lynch & Co., Inc.'s embedded cap bonds.

CREDOS:* (Citicorp Reset Detachable Option Securities) The proprietary name of Citibank, N.A.'s combined stepped coupon and detachable call bond.

*This is a service mark of the respective bank or investment bank listed in the accompanying text. It is included here with their permission.

Custodial Receipts: Secondary market products that represent an indirect interest in a tax-exempt bond (or a pool of tax-exempt bonds) that is held by a custodian.

DAYS:* The proprietary name of J.P. Morgan Securities' embedded cap bonds.

Deconstruction: The classification of a financial product as comprised of two or more separate products for tax purposes. Existing examples of deconstruction include the bifurcation rule for certain contingent payment bonds (under the original issue discount rules) and the embedded loan rule applicable to notional principal contracts with significant nonperiodic payments (such as premiums or upfront fees).

Deferred Fixed Rate Bonds:* The proprietary name of Merrill Lynch & Co., Inc.'s embedded Treasury short position in a municipal bond for up to one year.

Derivative Rate Bonds: Tax-exempt bonds whose interest rate is periodically reset and based on formulas linked to interest rate indices such as Kenny or the PSA Municipal Swap Index.

Embedded Cap Bonds: Tax-exempt bonds bearing an interest rate that is equal to a fixed rate plus a supplemental component economically resembling an interest rate cap (i.e., if a specified variable rate exceeds an agreed base rate, additional amounts are paid). The issuer will also enter into an interest rate cap agreement based on a notional principal amount equal to the principal amount of the bonds.

Embedded Loan: A portion of a notional principal contract that is recharacterized as a loan for tax purposes, deemed to exist if certain nonperiodic payments, such as up-front premiums, made with respect to a notional principal contract are "significant." The existence of such payments will cause certain derivative products to be treated for tax purposes as being comprised of two distinct assets: an "at market" notional principal contract and an embedded loan.

Embedded Swap Bonds: Tax-exempt bonds with respect to which the issuer has entered into a swap agreement based on a notional principal amount equal to the principal amount of the bonds.

FLOAT/RITES:* The proprietary name of Merrill Lynch & Co., Inc.'s auction rate and inverse floater bonds.

Forward Swaps, Caps, and Floors: The parties agree today to enter into a swap, cap, or floor on which payment obligations begin on a given date in the future.

Indexed Caps:* The proprietary name of Goldman, Sachs & Co.'s embedded cap bonds.

Indexed INFLOS:* The proprietary name of Goldman, Sachs & Co.'s embedded swap bonds.

Indexed Rate Bonds: Tax-exempt bonds whose interest rate is periodically reset and based on a formula that incorporates an index, such as [Bond Rate + (Base Rate minus Kenny)].

Indexed STARS:* The proprietary name of Bear, Stearns & Co.'s positively floating embedded swap bonds.

Indexed STRIPES:* The proprietary name of Bear, Stearns & Co.'s inverse floating embedded swap bonds.

INFLOS:* The proprietary name of Goldman, Sachs & Co.'s inverse floater bonds.

---

*This is a service mark of the respective bank or investment bank listed in the accompanying text. It is included here with their permission.

Integration: Taking into account the impact of a swap or cap in the computation of bond yield or investment yield for purposes of determining whether a bond issuer has earned impermissible arbitrage or is subject to arbitrage rebate on the investment of bond proceeds.

Interest Rate Caps, Floors, and Collars: In an interest rate cap, the "buyer" pays a single fixed amount and the "seller" makes periodic payments based on the excess of a given floating rate over a given annual rate. In an interest rate floor, the "buyer" pays a single fixed amount while the "seller" makes periodic payments based on the excess of a given annual rate over a given floating rate. In a collar, a cap and floor are combined, such that one party makes floating-rate payments on the cap and the other makes floating-rate payments on the floor.

Inverse Floaters: Tax-exempt bonds bearing an interest rate that moves inversely to market rates. Typically, the interest rate on an inverse floater is expressed as an above-market (as of the date the bond is issued) fixed rate of interest, reduced by an amount determined by reference to a market-based or bond-specific floating interest rate.

Longs:* The proprietary name of Donaldson, Lufkin & Jenrette's inverse floater bonds.

Multiple Component Securities:* The proprietary name of Merrill Lynch & Co., Inc.'s bonds structured to resemble components of a bond, such as interest rate and principal strips. An investor can select specific components to construct an aggregate security that meets its specifications.

Notional Principal Contract: A tax term for a financial instrument (such as an interest rate swap, cap, or floor) that provides for the payment of amounts by one party to another at specified intervals calculated by reference to a specified index upon a hypothetical "notional" principal amount in exchange for specified consideration or a promise to pay similar amounts.

PARS:* The proprietary name of Goldman, Sachs & Co.'s auction rate bonds.

PEIRS:* The proprietary name of J.P. Morgan Securities' secondary market tender option bonds.

P-FLOATS:* The proprietary name of Merrill Lynch & Co., Inc.'s puttable, synthetic floating-rate tender bonds under the partnership structure.

Primary Products: Tax-exempt bonds that provide for the payment of interest under various complex formulas. Primary products include products that enable investors to obtain yields above current market rates (such as inverse floating-rate bonds) and products that provide a means of obtaining higher yields if and when interest rates rise. The interest paid under these formulas may resemble a fixed rate of interest based upon the principal amount invested plus an additional return that an investor could receive through other means, such as entering into interest rate swap, cap, or floor contracts (such as an embedded swap or cap bond). Some current primary products include RIBS/SAVRS, Indexed INFLOS, Indexed Caps Bonds, Cap RITES, and Short RITES.

RAYS:* The proprietary name of J.P. Morgan Securities' inversely floating embedded swap bonds.

REDs:* The proprietary name of The First Boston Corporation's refund escrow deposits. This product is essentially a forward contract to acquire a tax-exempt bond

---

*This is a service mark of the respective bank or investment bank listed in the accompanying text. It is included here with their permission.

at a specified interest rate and a specified price on a future date. The amounts necessary to fund the future acquisition are deposited in an escrow until they are used to acquire the bonds.

Reverse Short-RITES:* The proprietary name of Merrill Lynch & Co., Inc.'s synthetic floating-rate bond with an embedded fixed-payor swap.

RIBS:* The proprietary name of Lehman Brothers' inverse floater bonds.

RITES:* The proprietary name of Merrill Lynch & Co., Inc.'s inverse floating-rate bonds.

SAVRS:* The proprietary name of Lehman Brothers' auction rate bonds.

Secondary Products: Financial products that result in an indirect ownership interest in a tax-exempt bond (or bonds). Prominent secondary products include tender option bonds/synthetic floating-rate securities; custodial receipts; swap-based products; stripped bonds; interests in partnership structures; and interests in tax-exempt asset pools.

Shorts: The proprietary name of Donaldson, Lufkin & Jenrette's auction rate bonds.

Short-RITES:* The proprietary name of Merrill Lynch & Co., Inc.'s indexed inverse floating-rate bonds.

SMARTs:* The proprietary name of Citibank, N.A.'s forward bond or swap contracts. The forward contract enables issuers to obtain the approximate economic effects of an advance refunding.

STARS:* The proprietary name of Bear, Stearns & Co.'s auction rate bonds.

STRIPES:* The proprietary name of Bear, Stearns & Co.'s inverse floating-rate bonds.

Stripped Tax-Exempt Bonds: Represent particular payments or portions of payments on an underlying tax-exempt bond. A stripped tax-exempt bond is typically created by depositing a tax-exempt bond with a custodian and issuing custodial receipts evidencing the various stripped interests in the underlying bond.

Surfs:* (Step-up Recovery Floating Rate bonds) The proprietary name of a type of Lehman Brothers' embedded cap bond that can be used to hedge against a flattening yield curve and against interest rate risks.

Swap Options ("Swaptions"): For a fee, one party has the right, on a given date or dates, to require the other to enter into a swap. The holder of a call swaption has the right to enter into a swap where it receives fixed payments and makes floating payments. The holder of a put swaption, in contrast, has the right to enter into a swap where it receives floating payments and makes fixed payments.

Synthetic Floating-Rate Bonds: Synthetic variable-rate tax-exempt securities that are created when a sponsor or seller "attaches" to an already existing long-term tax-exempt bond a mechanism such as a tender fee arrangement or a swap arrangement that provides for the ability of the holder of the security to tender the security at par on a regular basis in exchange for fees or other payments that, in the aggregate, are equal to the difference between the interest rate on the long-term tax-exempt bond and a comparable short-term market interest rate on the bond.

*This is a service mark of the respective bank or investment bank listed in the accompanying text. It is included here with their permission.

Tax-Exempt Bond: A bond issued directly by a state or local governmental unit or an entity that qualifies as an "on behalf of issuer" for federal income tax purposes.

Tax-Exempt EAGLE Trusts:* The proprietary name of Citibank, N.A.'s secondary market synthetic floating-rate bonds.

TEIRS:* The proprietary name of J.P. Morgan Securities' secondary market inverse floating-rate securities.

TEMIC: (Tax-Exempt Municipal Investment Conduit) The acronym is used in model legislation released in 1993 to identify a proposed special form of entity for tax purposes that would be available for qualifying secondary market tax-exempt derivative products. The proposal, if enacted, would provide increased certainty regarding the tax treatment for secondary market tax-exempt derivative products in much the same way that the real estate mortgage investment conduit (REMIC) rules enacted in 1986 (Sections 860A-860G of the Internal Revenue Code) provided increased certainty regarding the tax treatment of collateralized mortgage obligations in the secondary mortgage market.

Tender Option Bonds: The name given by various sponsors to secondary market synthetic floating-rate bonds issued under their programs.

TMARS:* The proprietary name of J.P. Morgan Securities' auction rate bonds.

TMIRS:* The proprietary name of J.P. Morgan Securities' inverse floating-rate bonds.

TXCs:* The proprietary name of The First Boston Corporation's bonds structured to resemble components of a bond, such as interest rate and principal strips. An investor can select specific components to construct an aggregate security that meets its specifications.

TXRs:* The proprietary name of The First Boston Corporation's stripped municipal bonds.

YES:* (Yield Enhancement Security bonds) The proprietary name of a type of Lehman Brothers' embedded cap bond that can be used to hedge against a flattening yield curve.

ZEBRAs:* (Zero Basis Risk Adjustable Swaps) The proprietary name of Citibank, N.A.'s swap structure used in connection with an embedded swap bond where the floating rate is based on the actual floating rate paid by the issuer on the related bonds. Hence, there is "zero basis risk" to the issuer.

---

*This is a service mark of the respective bank or investment bank listed in the accompanying text. It is included here with their permission.